AMERICA'S POLYPHONIC PAST

Second Edition

Edited by Eve Kornfeld

San Diego State University

PEARSON
Custom
Publishing

PEARSON
Longman

Cover Art: *One from Many,* by Robin MacDonald-Foley.

Printed in the United States of America

10 9 8 7 6 5 4 3

ISBN 0-536-38803-2

2007300031

MT/MR

Please visit our web site at *www.pearsoncustom.com*

PEARSON CUSTOM PUBLISHING
75 Arlington Street, Suite 300, Boston, MA 02116
A Pearson Education Company

Contents

America's Polyphonic Past

Introduction

Polyphonic music features many voices, each with its own distinct and independent melodic line. Unlike music based upon a single melody and accompanying harmony, polyphony gives each voice an interesting melody to develop. In polyphony, no one voice takes the lead, forcing the others to follow meekly behind it. At different moments in the music, different voices may stand out most, but none is ever entirely subservient to another. Tracing the relationships of the voices and melodic lines in polyphonic music can be quite complicated, as these relationships may change with each performance. Polyphony thus challenges its listener to interpret the music and to participate in the creation of its meaning. It is an active, creative process.

Early American history can be viewed in much the same way. Traditional histories of early America tended to feature the voices of only the rich and powerful, and heard others only as serving or reacting to them—as a single melody and accompanying harmony. But the historical research of the past quarter century reveals a more interesting and complex pattern, in which "outsiders" to the dominant culture developed ideas, values, and beliefs of their own and sustained them over time. Their alternative visions formed distinct, independent melodic lines. Taken together, the many voices of early America created America's polyphonic past.

This volume offers an introduction to America's polyphonic past. Readers will encounter familiar names and voices (including the Puritan leader John Winthrop, Thomas Paine, Thomas Jefferson, and other Founding Fathers) and will recognize the traditional narrative of American harmony, liberty, and equality that they present. But readers will also find less familiar names and voices here, presenting distinct and competing narratives. The Puritans' famous vision of America as a religious City upon a Hill, for example, is countered not only by Anne Hutchinson and other religious dissenters and challengers of male privilege over the centuries, but also by the very different notion of freedom and success held by the planters of the early Chesapeake. Those southern planters' voices were strong and enduring in American history, but so were the opposing voices of the servants and slaves the planters held in bondage. Their more expansive definition of liberty and equality also carries down through the centuries, echoing in the protests of urban workers in Revolutionary America and of reformers and abolitionists in the nineteenth century.

In these pages, one may trace various narrative or melodic lines as they develop over time and space: from Puritan leaders to Founding Fathers; from the early Chesapeake planters to the Antifederalists; from Anne Hutchinson to the convicted "witches" of Salem to the evangelical

1

Baptists of Revolutionary Virginia to Quaker Elizabeth Drinker of Philadelphia; or from America's first indentured servants and slaves to the urban artisans and laborers of Revolutionary America to Frederick Douglass, Henry David Thoreau, and Harriet Beecher Stowe. Comprehending the relationships among these many voices and narratives or melodies is a challenging task, but ultimately a fascinating and creative one, to which the reader must bring multiple perspectives and experiences. We can no longer listen for just one voice or one narrative line. Quiet contemplation and conversation with others engaged in the process of interpretation are both necessary, as our own cultural diversity can help us to see America's historical diversity. Only then can we begin to understand and appreciate America's polyphonic past.

Eve Kornfeld
Professor of History
San Diego State University

1

Selection from "Description of New-England" (1624)

Captain John Smith

from "Description of New-England" (1624)

Captain John Smith

———•—————•—————•———

Therefore I conclude, if the heart and entrails of those regions were sought, if their land were cultured, planted, and manured [worked] by men of industry, judgment, and experience; what hope is there, or what need they doubt, having the advantages of the sea, but it might equalize any of these famous kingdoms in all commodities, pleasures, and conditions: seeing even the very hedges do naturally afford us such plenty, as no ship need return away empty, and only use but the season of the sea, fish will return an honest gain, besides all other advantages; her treasures having yet never been opened, nor her originals wasted, consumed, nor abused. . . .

All sorts of cattle may here be bred and fed in the isles or peninsulas securely for nothing. In the interim, till they increase (if need be) observing the seasons, I durst undertake to have corn enough from the savages for three hundred men, for a few trifles; and if they should be untowards [unwilling], as it is most certain they will, thirty or forty good men will be sufficient to bring them all in subjection, and make this provision, if they understand what to do: two hundred whereof may eight or nine months in the year be employed in helping the fishermen, till the rest provide other necessaries, fit to furnish us with other commodities. . . .

Who can desire more content that hath small means, or but only his merit to advance his fortunes, than to tread and plant that ground he hath purchased by the hazard of his life; if he have but the taste of virtue and magnanimity, what to such a mind can be more pleasant than planting and building a foundation for his posterity, got from the rude earth by God's blessing and his own industry without prejudice to any; if he have any grain of faith or zeal in religion, what can he do less hurtful to any, or more agreeable to God, than to seek to convert those poor savages to know Christ and humanity, whose labors with discretion will triply requite thy charge and pain; what so truly suits with honor and honesty, as the discovering things unknown, erecting towns, peopling countries, informing the ignorant, reforming things unjust, teaching virtue and gain to our native mother country [and providing] a kingdom to attend her, find employment for those that are idle, because they know not what to do; so far from wronging any, as to cause posterity to remember thee; and remembering thee, ever honor that remembrance with praise. . . .

2

"The First American Boom: Virginia 1618 to 1630"

Edmund S. Morgan

The First American Boom: Virginia 1618 to 1630

Edmund S. Morgan*

American historians have always taken delight in the success that followed the introduction of private enterprise in England's first American colonies. Ralph Hamor recorded the spectacular change that came over Virginia with Gov. Thomas Dale's assignment of private gardens to settlers in 1614: "When our people were fedde out of the common store and laboured jointly in the manuring of the ground, and planting corne, glad was that man that could slippe from his labour, nay the most honest of them in a generall businesse, would not take so much faithfull and true paines, in a weeke, as now he will doe in a day, neither cared they for the increase, presuming that howsoever their harvest prospered, the generall store must maintain them, by which meanes we reaped not so much corne from the labours of 30 men, as three men have done for themselves."[1] To which A. L. Rowse adds the comment that comes naturally to all of us: "Well, of course."[2]

Governor Dale's assignment of private gardens in 1614 amounted to only three acres a man, and he gave no one title to the land. But by 1617 a substantial number of colonists had fulfilled their obligations to the Virginia Company and worked entirely for themselves. In the following year the "old planters," those who had come to Virginia before 1616, paying their own way, acquired a hundred acres of land in fee simple. Later settlers paying their own way were to get fifty acres apiece and another fifty for every other person whose way they paid. The Company reached for a new source of profit from the labours of tenants who would be transported to Virginia at Company expense. In seven years, while they lived and worked on Company lands, they would pay rent on a half-and-half, sharecropping basis. And further to encourage immigration and financial investment the Company authorized groups or individual members of the Company to set up "particular plantations" of their own and man them either with servants or with tenants who, like the Company tenants, would work for themselves but give part of their proceeds for a term of years to the men who paid their passage. With the introduction of these new measures in 1618, private enterprise triumphed over the semi-military work gangs that had kept Virginia going, but barely going, in its first years.[3]

In the six years that followed the triumph of private enterprise, Virginia killed off between three and four thousand Englishmen. An estimated thirty-five hundred to four thousand immigrants increased the population of the colony from about one thousand in 1618 to probably no more than fifteen hundred in 1624.[4] In that year the Virginia Company—itself a

9

private enterprise—was dissolved in disgrace. The royal officials who then took over the government of the colony did not revert to any communal system of work for the colonists. Private enterprise was there to stay. Nevertheless, the failure of the Virginia Company and the staggering death rate suggest that our "Well, of course" to the first success of private enterprise in the colony is perhaps a little hasty. We need not and should not conclude that allowing men to work for themselves was responsible for the disasters that struck Virginia in the years after 1618. Still, it may be worth inquiring into the way that the incentives of private enterprise operated in the colony during those years, and how those incentives affected the fate of the Company and the later history of the colony.

Modern scholarship has placed the blame for the failure of the Virginia Company on the shoulders of Sir Edwin Sandys, who poured men into Virginia faster than the colony could absorb and support them.[5] Without the capital to equip them properly, Sandys concentrated on getting men across the ocean, not only tenants for the Company's lands but artisans of various kinds to set up production of iron, glass, silk, and ships. Moreover, he encouraged dozens of private investors to establish particular plantations. Ship captains crowded men aboard and dumped them in the colony by hundreds, half dead and without provisions. Most of them died soon after, from malnutrition or from disease aggravated by malnutrition. When the king found out what was happening, he dissolved the Company.

There were of course other well-known reasons for Virginia's troubles, particularly the quarreling among different factions within the Company, the king's desire to maximize his revenues from customs duties on Virginia tobacco, and the Indian massacre of 1622, which alone accounted for 347 deaths. But there can be no doubt that the big mistake was the transportation to Virginia of such masses of unprepared and unprovisioned settlers, for whom the colonists already there had neither food nor housing. Admitting this much, we may nevertheless press the question why a colony that had been in existence for eleven years in 1618 was unable to provide a welcome for so many helping hands. And since the answer commonly given has centered in the lack of food supplies, it will be appropriate to begin by examining what people who lived at the time said about the scarcity of provisions, considering their statements from the harvest of one year to the harvest of the next.

1619–1620. When George Yeardley arrived as governor in April 1619 to inaugurate the Company's new program, he took over a colony in which the supplies of cattle and corn had been depleted. Yeardly reported that he would devote himself in the coming year to getting a good crop of corn.[6] During that summer, in spite of an epidemic that weakened and killed large numbers, the colony reaped unprecedented harvests, and by the end of September the settlers enjoyed, according to John Pory (no friend of Yeardley), "a marvelous plenty, suche as hath not bene seen since our first coming into the lande."[7] In January 1620 John Rolfe too reported the abundance of corn, and of fish brought from Newfoundland and sturgeon caught in Virginia.[8] According to these leaders of the settlement, Virginians were apparently well fed in the winter of 1619–1620.

1620–1621. I have found no surviving reports about the amount of corn grown in the summer of 1620, but in November Sir Edwin Sandys informed the Company that the settlers no longer wanted English meal sent them. Instead they preferred beads for trade with the Indians.[9] It is evident from other sources too that the colonists were getting corn from the Indians. In December, long after harvest time, George Thorpe observed that "this countrey meandes [i.e., mends, improves] in plentie of victuall everie daie," and he probably meant in supplies obtained from the Indians.[10] By May 1621 Capt. Thomas Nuce, a newcomer, observed that the men sent under his charge lived "very barely for the most part: havinge no other foode but bread and water and such manner of meate as they make of the Mayze: which I would to God I Could say they had in any reasonable plenty." They would have been distressed, he said, if one of their ships had not brought in corn from Chesapeake Bay, where the colony now had "good and free trade" (with the Indians).[11] The winter of 1620–1621 was apparently not a plentiful one, but there was no talk of starvation. In June George Thorpe reported that people were blessed with good health and good hope of a plentiful harvest of all kinds.[12]

1621–1622. Again there is no specific report of the harvest. On December 15, 1621, Peter Arondelle, another newcomer, complained of his family's lean diet of one and one-half pints of musty meal a day per man.[13] But the governor and Council reported in January that in the nine ships which had arrived during the autumn, none of the passengers died on the way and all continued in health.[14] A ship from Ireland in November came "soe well furnished with all sortes of provisione, aswell as with Cattle, as wee could wishe all men would follow theire example."[15] If Arondelle's complaint represents a general scarcity in the colony it was not serious enough to lower his enthusiasm for Virginia, because just two weeks later he was writing home about the abundance of cattle and hogs both wild and domestic and observing that "any laborious honest man may in a shorte time become ritche in this Country."[16] The winter of 1621–1622 produced no other surviving complaints of scarcity. There was even some boasting that new immigrants no longer need fear danger from "wars, or famine, or want of convenient lodging and looking to."[17]

Then, on March 22, the Indians struck, killing not only settlers but also much needed cattle. The outlying plantations had to be abandoned. Planting operations had to be curtailed, for corn furnished shelter to lurking Indians.[18] There was no choice but to seek relief from the Indians themselves, not those who had participated in the massacre, but those to the north or south. Various captains were commissioned to get corn from them, by trade if they could, by force if they could not. There was not even a remote possibility that the harvest might be sufficient.

1622–1623. The corn obtained from the Indians and from the settlers' meager crops fell far short of the need, and most Virginians went hungry, as the prices of whatever provisions there were skyrocketed.[19] On July 2, 1623, Delphebus Canne, recently arrived in Virginia from England, regretted not having brought more meal, oatmeal, and peas for sale to the settlers, because "now the land is destitute of food." But he noted that the weather had been good and that people anticipated a large harvest of both corn and tobacco. Moreover, ships were expected daily from Canada and Newfoundland, with enough fish for the whole ensuing year.[20]

1623–1624. Whether the corn crop and the awaited cargoes from the north fulfilled expectations is not clear. In January the governor and Council reported that "the scarsitie this foreruninge yeere hath been greate, and who could expect less, after such a massacre, yett none to our knowledg hath Perished through wante, many seasoned men goinge through theire labours, beside harde marches, which endured the same Comone scarsitie."[21] By April enough provisions had been obtained from the Indians so that the crisis was over.[22]

The reports all reflect some scarcity of food between 1618 and 1624. But only during the year following the massacre was the scarcity acute, and in the winter and spring after the bumper harvest of 1619 there seems to have been no scarcity at all. Yet it is precisely from this winter and spring that we have the most explicit complaints from Virginia about people arriving without adequate provisions. On November 4, 1619, when a hundred Company tenants arrived "lusty and well" on the *Bona Nova*, the governor and Council calculated that the 544 bushels of meal sent with them would last only five and one-half months at two pounds a man per day. Fifty men were therefore parcelled out for a year to private planters.[23] Yet two or three months earlier, when a Dutch ship put in at the colony, the governor and cape merchant, in a famous transaction, bartered Virginia provisions for twenty-odd Negroes, who certainly came ashore unsupplied with anything.[24] It is not recorded that the Negroes were put to work for the Company. The following June, after some four hundred more settlers arrived, Governor Yeardley wrote plaintively to the Company, urging them to send subsequent ships with more provisions, adding that "yf such nombers of people come upon me unexpected, and that at an unhealthfull season and to late to sett Corne I cannott then be able to feed them owt of others labors." In the future, he begged them, they should send men before Christmas (by November 4 perhaps?) with six months' provisions (instead of five and one-half?).[25]

Yeardley's complaints, his purchase of the Negroes, and his disposal of the men from the *Bona Nova* at a time when the colony was reporting an unprecedented abundance, suggest that the problem was not altogether one of whether supplies existed. It was a question of who had them and of who could pay for them. In a year of plenty the governor and Council were unable or unwilling to make use of fifty men without supplies when other Virginians *were* able and willing to do so. The great shortage of supplies, to which we attribute the failure of the Sandys program, was not an absolute shortage in which all Virginians shared and suffered alike. It was a shortage that severely afflicted the Company and its dependents, but it furnished large opportunities for private entrepreneurs, and larger ones for Company officials who knew how to turn public distress to private profit.

Throughout the period when too many men were arriving with too few supplies, the established settlers were so eager for more workers that they paid premium wages for them, even when they had to feed as well as pay them. In 1621 the governor and Council set maximum wage rates at three shillings a day for ordinary laborers and four shillings for most skilled craftsmen (joiners got five). If the workman was furnished with food for the day, the rate was only a shilling a day less.[26] These figures amount to three or four times the maximum wages of day labor established by county justices in England, where a man who was fed by his employer generally received about half the wage of one who furnished his own food.[27] Food was comparatively less valuable in Virginia than in England.

Daily wage earners were only one part of Virginia's labor force. An increasing number of workers were servants bound for a period of years. These came at a lower rate, and these were what the planters wanted. It had been common in England for farmers to hire servants by the year, and employers in many trades were required by law to hire their labor by the year.[28] But servants who wanted to go to Virginia were willing to pledge several years' work, usually four to seven years, in return for transportation and maintenance. If a Virginia planter could import a man from England, the cost of his passage to the colony was about six pounds; his provisions and clothes for the voyage and to start him out in the New World might run another four to six pounds.[29] At this rate the cost per year for a servant in Virginia was not much more, and might be less, than in England; for in England too masters had to provide food and shelter and sometimes clothing for their bound servants, and a year's pay for an agricultural worker ran from thirty to fifty shillings in the first decades of the seventeenth century.[30]

Although the planter or entrepreneur who brought a servant to the New World ran the risk of losing his investment through death, Virginia planters evidently shared Edwin Sandys's belief that the rewards outweighed the risks. Despite the fact that bound servants had to be fed, clothed, and housed, Virginians could not get enough of them. Everybody wanted servants. Even tenants who had been unable to pay their own passage to the colony wanted servants. Richard Berkeley and John Smyth of Nibley received from the tenants at their particular plantation a request for two servants apiece "for their owne pryvate benefit and imploymentes."[31] Indeed, as John Pory put it, "our principall wealth . . . consisteth in servants."[32] And after the Virginia Company had been dissolved, former Governor Yeardley, now representing the interests of the colonists, urged the royal commission in charge of the colony "to advance the Plantacion for the future by sending great number of people."[33]

From what little can be discovered about the value of a man's labor in the soil of Virginia between 1618 and 1624, it is not hard to see why the demand for servants was so high, even in the face of a food scarcity. At the time when Sandys took over the Company and began pouring men into the colony, Virginia had just begun to ship tobacco in quantity to the English market. The prices it brought were considerably lower than those for Spanish tobacco, but high enough to excite the cupidity of every settler. In the colony in 1619 the best grade sold for export at three shillings a pound.[34] In 1623 what reached England was worth no more than half that, and in bartering within the colony it was said to have passed at less than a shilling a pound.[35] In a lawsuit recorded in 1624, it was reckoned at two shillings a pound and in 1625 at three shillings again.[36] The boom lasted until 1629 or 1630 when the price tumbled to a penny a pound.[37] Though it recovered somewhat in ensuing years, it never again reached the dizzy heights of the 1620s. During that decade the profits from tobacco growing were enough to keep everybody scrambling for servants in order to grow as many plants as possible.

The amount of tobacco one man could produce in a year by his own labor varied from place to place, from year to year, and from man to man. In 1619 John Rolfe, who introduced tobacco cultivation in Virginia, estimated that a man could tend four acres of corn and one thousand plants of tobacco.[38] Four years later William Capps, an "old planter," said that a man could tend two thousand plants and that this would make five hundred "weight" (presumably five hundred pounds) of tobacco. He also maintained that in 1623 three of his boys, whom he calculated as equal to a man and a half, had produced 3,000 weight of tobacco and 110 barrels (550 bushels) of corn.[39] Richard Brewster, working with three men, was said to have grown 2,800 weight of tobacco and 100 bushels of corn.[40] In 1626 William Spencer testified in court that in 1620 he had overseen the labor of six or seven men who had produced three or four thousand weight.[41] The figures differ, perhaps because some of the authors were boasting, because some men worked harder than others, and because tobacco harvests varied sharply from year to year for reasons beyond human control.[42] But by any calculation the returns from labor invested in growing tobacco were high. John Pory, after the exceptionally good harvest of 1619, said that one man had cleared £200 sterling by his own labor and another with six servants had cleared £1,000 sterling. These, he admitted, were "rare examples, yet possible to be done by others."[43]

Because of the chances for such profits, Jamestown in the last years of the Virginia Company, while a charnel house, was also the first American boom town. There was no gold or silver. A man could not make a fortune by himself. But if he could stay alive and somehow get control of a few servants and keep them alive, he could make more in a year than he was likely to make in several in England. And if he could get a large number of servants, he might indeed make a fortune.

In a boom town not everyone strikes it rich; and even those who come in from the hills with a pocketful of gold generally give it up in a hurry—for drink, for women, even for food and clothing at bonanza prices. Life is cheap, but nothing else is. Those who have what gold will buy get the gold a good deal easier and faster than the miners who dig it. And the pleasures and comforts of normal human relationships, the things that gold will not buy, are not to be had at all. Men have come there not to settle down, but to make their pile and move on. But the easy-come, easy-go miner generally carries away as little as he carries in.

So it was in Virginia, where tobacco took the place of gold. Virginia's counterpart of the easy-come, easy-go miner was the small planter who squandered his small crop on the liquor and luxuries that show up in boom towns. "Our Cowe-keeper here of James Citty," wrote John Pory in 1618, "on Sundayes goes acowterd all in freshe flaming silkes and a wife of one that in England had professed the black arte not of a scholler but of a collier of Croydon, weares her rough bever hatt with a faire perle hattband, and a silken suite therto correspon-dent."[44] The first legislative assembly in Virginia in 1619 felt obliged to pass acts against excess in apparel and also against drunkenness.[45] For it was drink more than clothes that the planters craved. The thirst of Virginians became notorious in England, and the ships that sailed up the James River were heavily freighted with sack and strong waters, even if they neglected to bring more solid fare.[46]

Virginians needed drink, if for nothing else, to solace them for losing the comforts of a settled life. Few were able, like the collier from Croydon, to enjoy the company of a wife. Women were scarcer than corn or liquor in Virginia and fetched a higher price. Seeking to overcome the shortage, the Company dispatched shiploads of maids (for whom prospective husbands were expected to pay), but the numbers were not large enough to alter the atmo-sphere of transience that pervaded the boom town.[47] The lonely men who pressed aboard every ship in the James River to drown their cares in drink looked on Virginia "not as a place of Habitacion but onely of a short sojourninge."[48] They would marry and settle down later somewhere else.

The whole appearance of the settlements, a mere collection of ramshackle hovels, argued that this was only a stopping place. It was a time when Englishmen of all classes were putting up larger and more substantial buildings throughout their own country;[49] and an Englishman's idea of a house was something solid, preferably of brick or stone. If it had to be made of wood, the walls at least should be plastered. Visitors to Virginia rightly judged the intentions of the settlers from the way they were content to live: "Their houses stands scattered one from another, and are onlie made of wood, few or none of them beeing framed houses but punches [posts] sett into the Ground And covered with Boardes so as a firebrand is sufficient to con-sume them all."[50] In fact, it did not even take a firebrand. Virginia "houses" could be kept stand-ing only with difficulty. At Charles City, where the settlers had considered themselves fortunate to be released earlier than others from the Company's service, they went on building "such houses as before and in them lived with continual repairs, and buildinge new where the old failed."[51] There was no point in putting up more than a temporary shelter if you did not intend to stay; and as late as 1626 the governing council admitted that what people looked for in Virginia was only "a present Cropp, and theire hastie retourne."[52]

The present crop stood in the way of everything else. Although the government required everyone to plant a certain amount of corn, men would risk both prosecution and hunger in order to put their time into tobacco. Even self-preservation came second. After the massacre, when the government adopted a policy of continuous attack against the Indians, it was difficult to get men to leave their crops in order to carry on the war for a few days. When the governor commanded them to go, they would "Crye out of the loss of Tyme," and when a campaign lasted as long as two weeks, they would demand "that they might have leave to retourne, lest it should prove theire utter undoinge."[53] When William Capps, who had had some experience in Indian fighting, volunteered to lead an expedition of forty men, he found that even the governing council was unwilling to spare them. Capps, whose speech comes through vividly in his letters, had his own explanation of the reasons for the Council's refusal: "take away one of my men," he pictures them saying to themselves, "there's 2000 Plantes gone, thates 500 waight of Tobacco, yea and what shall this man doe, runne after the Indians? soft, I have perhaps 10, perhaps 15, perhaps 20 men and am able to secure my owne Planta-tion; how will they doe that are fewer? let them first be Crusht alitle, and then perhaps they will themselves make up the Nomber for their owne safetie. Theis I doubt are the Cogita-cions of some of our worthier men."[54]

As in other boom towns, a large share of the winnings was carried away by those who sup-plied the flaming silks and strong waters, by men who had even less intention of settling down than the planters. The ships that anchored in Virginia's great rivers every summer were, as one settler observed, moving taverns,[55] whose masters, usually private traders, got the greater part of the tobacco that should have been enriching the colonists and the shareholders of the Company. Since the Company had never been able to satisfy the needs of the colonists, it was helpless to prevent them from trading with outsiders, and by 1620 it gave up trying.[56] Thereafter, the most it could do was to invest its dwindling funds in the subcorporations, known as "magazines," through which still hopeful members tried to recoup some of their losses.

A magazine was supposed to turn a profit by exchanging supplies for tobacco or other commodities or from the promise of tobacco when the next crop was in. But somehow the promises were not kept. The floating taverns got the tobacco before it could reach the "cape merchant," as the man in charge of a magazine was known, and all magazines seem to have ended with a loss to the investors in England.[57] There were sometimes as many as seventeen sail of ships to be seen at one time in the James River, and the Virginians swarmed aboard them to drink and carouse and squander their tobacco. Anything that smelled of alcohol would sell, and the governor and Council complained bitterly of the "rates which unconscionable marchantes and maryners doe impose upon our necessities . . . especyally of rotten Wynes which destroy our bodies and empty our purses."[58] One trader even "boasted that the only sale of fower buttes of wyne would be Sufficyent to clere the whole Vioage."[59]

The private traders from abroad were not the only ones who seized the commercial opportunities of the boom. Complaints reached England against Virginians who got to the ships first and engrossed the commodities most in demand, to resell at monopoly prices.[60] And after the massacre, when corn was at its scarcest, those who had boats and could get a commission from the governor were able to bring back hundreds of bushels from the Chesapeake region, some of it bought, some of it stolen, some of it taken by force from the Indians there. At the price of corn then prevailing in Jamestown, these voyages to the Chesapeake must have been highly profitable, and there were charges that the chief men of the colony were only too willing to prolong the scarcity by discouraging or forbidding the planting of corn. As long as the shortage lasted, "they onely haveinge the means in these extremities to Trade for Corne with the Natives doe hereby engrosse all into their hands and soe sell itt abroad att their owne prizes. . . ."[61] In the winter of 1622–1623 English meal was selling at thirty shillings the bushel and Indian corn at ten to fifteen shillings. By April even Indian corn was at twenty to thirty shillings "and non to bee had but with great men."[62] If thirty shillings a bushel in Virginia meant, as the officers of the colony claimed, only ten pounds of tobacco and therefore only ten or fifteen shillings,[63] nevertheless a man who accumulated a thousand bushels of corn on a short trip to the Chesapeake region would be able to trade it for ten thousand pounds of tobacco, worth from five hundred to a thousand pounds sterling.

Although Sir Edwin Sandys had been bent on profit for the Company's investors, profiteering, whether by residents or transients, had been no part of his plans for Virginia. He had hoped to offer a refuge for the underpaid English laborer and at the same time build a community without want and without oppression. Ironically, Virginia suffered both want and oppression, as Sandys's concentration on getting men across the water unwittingly played into the hands of local profiteers who engrossed not only goods but men. Virginia differed from later American boom towns in that success depended not on acquiring the right piece of land but on acquiring men. Land that would grow tobacco was everywhere, so abundant that people frequently did not bother at first to secure patents for the amounts they were entitled to.[64] Instead, men rushed to stake out claims to men, stole them, lured them, fought over them—and bought and sold them, bidding up the prices to four, five, and six times the initial cost.[65] The Company's program obligingly poured men into Virginia for the scramble.

Since the number of older, seasoned servants was limited not only by the high death rate but also by completion of their terms of servitude, it was mainly the newcomers under the Sandys program whose labor enriched the aggressive and enterprising traders and planters.

At first sight it might seem that the death rate among the new arrivals (even higher than among men who had survived their first year in the country) was so great as to nullify any advantages to those who sought to exploit them. But the records show that enough of them survived to make up almost the whole labor force and also the vast majority of the population of Virginia by 1625. The muster of inhabitants taken in January and February of that year gives the date of arrival in the colony for 740 of the 1,210 living persons listed.[66] Of the 740, only 110 had come to Virginia before 1618.[67] The muster list also reveals that among the fifteen planters who held ten or more servants or "men" in 1625, only two servants out of 199 whose arrival dates are known had come before 1618.[68]

The bondage of the men sent under the Sandys program was of several kinds. The time and produce of the ordinary bound servant belonged completely to his master. Tenants might live and work independently on the land of the Company or of some other master, but they had to surrender half of what they earned. There were also "apprentices," often known as "*Duty* boys" from the name of the ship (the *Duty*) on which some of them were transported. They were bound to serve for seven years under any planters who would pay ten pounds apiece for them. After their seven years' service, they were to be tenants bound for another seven years. If, however, a *Duty* boy committed a crime at any time during the first seven years, his term as a servant was to begin again for another seven years.[69] Sandys doubtless envisaged the transportation of these children, taken from the streets of London and sent without their own consent, as a favor both to them and to those they served: he would rescue the boys from vice and idleness and at the same time reward the servant-starved planters, who were to make Virginia prosper.

The role of the *Duty* boys reveals, in fact, the main thrust of Sandys's plans for Virginia. Sandys was a champion of the rights of Englishmen against the impositions of the Stuart monarchy. In Virginia he would enable men to live without the heavy burdens of taxation that the expenses of government imposed on Englishmen, with or without their consent. But his way of doing it was to enlist, with or without consent, the surplus labor of England. Send men and boys to Virginia, and let them work there, both for the planters and for the officers of government. Eventually they would have their freedom and a more prosperous life than they could have looked forward to in England. Meanwhile they would enrich everybody else and make possible a government without heavy taxes, whose officers "should not need to prey upon the people."[70]

For the support of each office of government Sandys persuaded the Company to allot a tract of land and a quota of tenants to work it for the incumbent. When a man left an office, he was supposed to turn over both the land and its tenants to his successor. The amounts were generous. The governor got three thousand acres and one hundred tenants, the treasurer and the marshall fifteen hundred acres and fifty tenants apiece, the vice admiral three hundred acres and twelve tenants.[71] Whenever a new office was created or when the Company wished to reward someone for especially meritorious service, the way to do it was to give him land and tenants.[72] When the secretary was found to be taking high fees for issuing land grants, he was forbidden to charge for his services and given land and tenants instead.[73]

The result of this beneficence was to lay open every surviving tenant sent by the Company to exploitation by any officer who claimed him as part of his quota of tenants. And if an officer did not commandeer him, someone else would. Whether a man came as a servant, as an apprentice, as a tenant, or on his own, he was vulnerable. If death disposed of the master who could rightly claim his labor, an heir, real or fraudulent, would quickly lay hold of him. Or if, having paid his own transportation, he arrived in Virginia with no master but also with no provisions, he was easy prey for anyone who could feed and shelter him. Even if he came sufficiently supplied to set himself up independently, a bad harvest, insurmountable debts, or Indian depredations might force him into the service of a bigger operator. This was particularly true after the massacre, when it was reported that ordinary men who had made a start on their own were obliged, for fear of the Indians, "to forsake their houses (which were very farre scattered) and to joyne themselves to some great mans plantation."[74]

Some planters were not above ransoming captives from the Indians in order to claim their labor. Jane Dickenson and her husband Ralph were tenants of Nicholas Hide when Ralph was killed in the massacre of 1622 and Jane was carried into captivity. After some time Dr. John Pott, the physician who had been sent to Virginia at Company expense, ransomed Jane for two pounds of glass beads. Ten months after her deliverance she complained to the governor and Council that she was held in a servitude that "differeth not from her slavery with the Indians," Dr. Pott alleging that she was "linked to his servitude with a towefold Chaine the one for her late husbands obligation [to Hide] and thother for her ransome, of both which shee hopeth that in Conscience shee ought to be discharged, of the first by her widdowhood, of the second by the law of nations, Considering shee hath already served teen months, tow much for two pound of beades."[75] Other complaints reached London that "divers old Planters and others did allure and beguile divers younge persons and others (ignorant and unskillfull in such matters) to serve them upon intollerable and unchristianlike conditions upon promises of such rewardes and recompence, as they were no wayes able to performe nor ever meant."[76]

Among the worst offenders were the Company's own officials in the colony. In Sandys's shipments of men bound to the Company they had perceived an opportunity for exploiting not only the tenants but the Company itself. The fact that the men arrived without adequate provisions furnished an excuse for treating tenants as servants.[77] Instead of being seated on Company lands where they could build houses of their own (as the Company's instructions required), the tenants were hired out to private planters, like the fifty men who arrived "lusty and well" on the *Bona Nova*.[78] Although the officers reported that they hired out the sickly rather than the able-bodied, the Company got word that it was the other way round: the strongest men, who might have benefited the Company most, were put to work on private plantations. And "where it is pretended this placinge them with old planters is for theire health, they are so unmercifully used that it is the greatest cause of our Tenntes discontent. . . ."[79] Thus while Company men labored unhappily on the lands of private planters, Company land went uncleared, unfenced, and unplanted. It would be difficult to believe that the Company officials perceived no personal advantage in this situation.

The hiring out of some tenants should have meant more food for those who remained in the Company's care. Apparently, however, the hired men's share of provisions was converted to private uses;[80] and the men who continued as Company tenants were deprived even of the supplies intended for them. Whatever the Company sent, the officers appropriated, and gave the tenants only Indian corn and water,[81] a diet not calculated to speed the recovery of men weakened by a long voyage. But malnutrition and the diseases consequent upon it were not the only reasons for the low productivity of the Company men. According to one dissatified London investor, the reason the Company tenants accomplished so little was because "the officers Tenantes were cheifely reguarded and the generall Companies Tenantes the more neglected,"[82] by which he probably meant that the officers made it their business to get a day's work out of their own assigned tenants but not out of the rest. Moreover, John Pory reported to the Company in 1624, the officers were seating the men assigned to their offices "on their private Lands, not upon that [that] belongeth to their office," so that the crop produced on these private lands of the officers "alwaies exceeds yours"; and since the land set aside for officers lay "unmanured [i.e., uncultivated] to any purpose," it would yield little profit to the succeeding officers. The existing ones, Pory added, used the Company's tenants "to row them up and downe, whereby both you and they lose more then halfe."[83]

It is only fair to add that what the Company wanted for Virginia probably could not have been achieved by even the most faithful and assiduous of officers. The Company wanted a stable, diversified society, where men would make reasonable profits and live ordinary, reasonable lives. It was Virginia's misfortune in the last years of the Company to offer opportunities for profit that were much more than reasonable.

The men who seized the opportunities and captured the labor of Virginia's perishing immigrants are not difficult to identify. In January and February 1625 a muster of the inhabitants indicated the names and numbers of every man's "men" or servants, including both tenants and genuine servants.[84] The fifteen who had ten or more may be taken as the winners in the servant sweepstakes:

Ralph Hamor	10
John Pott	12
Edward Bennett	12
William Epps	13
William Peirce	13
Roger Smith	14
William Barry	15
Francis Wyatt	17
Edward Blaney	17
William Tucker	17
Daniel Gookin	20
Samuel Mathews	23
George Sandys	37
George Yeardley	39
Abraham Peirsey	39

Some of these men may have won fair and square; about several of them we know very little.[85] But the careers of the others make it a question whether we should call them labor barons or robber barons. It would be tedious to pile up the evidence about each of them, but a few simple facts may be suggestive.

The frontrunner, Abraham Peirsey, with 39 servants, had been "a verie poore man" when he came to Virginia in 1616 as the cape merchant in charge of the Company's magazine. Although he sold goods at two or three times the prices set by the investors, the magazine under his direction showed a loss, and in 1626 he had not yet paid the investors for the goods sold. But when he died two years later, he "left the best Estate that was ever yett knowen in Virginia."[86] Edward Blaney succeeded Peirsey as cape merchant in 1620. At his death in 1626 he too had not paid for the goods he sold, but he had acquired seventeen servants. He had also succeeded in embezzling a fair amount by marrying a widow and successfully claiming an estate left by a man with the same surname as his wife's first husband, a trick played by a number of quick-witted Virginians at the death of a stranger who happened to bear the same surname.[87] George Sandys, treasurer of the colony, having failed to receive the full quota of tenants assigned to his office, simply appropriated sixteen Company tenants as his servants. Although for some time before his departure for England in 1625 he refused to execute his office (the commission having expired), he continued to hold the tenants in bondage. One of them, listed in the muster as a freeman, wrote to a friend, "he maketh us serve him whether wee will or noe and how to helpe yt we doe not knowe for hee beareth all the sway."[88]

William Tucker, who may originally have been a ship captain, probably came to Virginia between 1617 and 1619.[89] Some time before 1622 he was entrusted by John Ferrar and associates with £900 worth of goods to sell in Virginia, for which, like other Virginia factors, he failed to deliver either cash or accounts.[90] He was one of the men commissioned to trade with the Indians for corn in 1622–1623 and was also empowered to negotiate peace with the Pamunkeys of the Potomac River area. His methods of dealing may be judged by his success in poisoning two hundred Pamunkeys with wine brought for that purpose, which he gave them to drink in celebration of the peace treaty he pretended to conclude with them.[91] By 1632 the House of Burgesses was finding his attitude toward his fellow Virginians unsatisfactory and objected to the Privy Council about merchants "who have by needlesse and unprofitable Commodities . . . ingaged the inhabitants in debts of Tobacco, to the value almost of theire ensuinge croppe . . . amonge whome we have good cause to complayne of Captayne *Tucker*, who hath farr exceeded all other marchaunts in the prizes of theire goods. . . ."[92]

Ralph Hamor, though he wrote one of the most effective pamphlets in praise of Virginia, got off to a slow start or else lost heavily in the massacre. In 1623, when other men were already getting rich, George Sandys observed that "Captain Hamor is miserablie poore and necessitie will inforce him to shiftes."[93] The shifts to which he resorted included trading with the Indians and selling English goods at prices that brought accusations of extortion.[94] By 1625, with ten men growing tobacco for him, he was far from poor.

Dr. John Pott seems to have been more assiduous in pursuit of cattle and servants than of his duties as physician. In 1623 George Sandys dismissed him as a mere cipher,[95] but by 1628 he was acting governor. According to his successor, Gov. John Harvey, he took advantage of the position to advance his private interest "by foule and coveteous ways," in particular "by cutting out the markes of other mens neate cattell and markinge them for himselfe with his owne handes, whereby he hath gotten into a greate stock of cattell." Harvey pardoned him because of the colony's need for his services as a physician and because Harvey found his delinquencies to have been in imitation of "the example of a former governor who passed unquestioned for many notable oppressions."[96]

The former governor to whom Harvey referred was probably George Yeardley, who had found Virginia a rewarding environment from the beginning. According to John Pory, when Yeardley arrived there in 1610, he carried with him nothing more valuable than a sword.[97] But when he visited London in 1617, after his first term as governor of Virginia, he was able "out of his meer gettings here" to spend "very near three thousand poundes." Before returning to the colony he got himself knighted, and Londoners observed that "he flaunts it up and down the streets in extraordinary bravery, with fourteen or fifteen fair liveries after him."[98]

Yeardley, when appointed governor in 1618, was assigned three thousand acres of land and one hundred tenants plus thirty more in 1620 to make up for deaths among the first group.[99] When Yeardley gave up the governorship in 1621, he turned over only forty-six tenants. The governor's Council, which now included Yeardley, wrote to the Company in London that "as for the rest of the Tenantes Sir George yardley denieth to make them good, And sayeth that havinge made noe strong Agrement with you at any tyme he holdeth nott him selfe tyed unto yt, And therfore should take it for a matter of great Injustice to bee Compelled therunto."[100] Yeardley, whom William Capps characterized as a "right worthie Statesman, for his own profit,"[101] did not give up his tenants, and the records contain accusations against him of detaining servants belonging to other planters and of keeping as a servant a young man whose relatives had paid his way.[102] He remained nevertheless a member of the Council and was again serving as governor when he died in 1627. He was one of those commissioned to trade for corn after the massacre of 1622 and was accused by one settler of discouraging the planting of corn, the word being "that Sir G. Yardlie should provide them Corne if they would provide Tobacco."[103] He did, in fact, provide the corn, one thousand bushels in January 1623 alone.[104] At his death Yeardley's estate was apparently valued at only about

£10,000.[105] But it is not unlikely that he had already transferred much of what he owned to his wife and children in order to circumvent the litigation that a substantial will often produced.[106]

It seems evident that while the Virginia Company was failing in London a number of its officers in the colony were succeeding. In order to do so they not only rendered less than faithful service to their employers; they also reduced other Virginians to a condition which, while short of slavery, was also some distance from the freedom that Englishmen liked to consider as their birthright. The Company in 1618 had inaugurated a popularly elected representative assembly, but the effective power for at least ten or fifteen years longer remained in the governor and his Council.[107] By no coincidence, the Council consisted almost entirely of the men holding large numbers of servants. Between 1619 and 1627 Hamor, Pott, Smyth, Sandys, Tucker, Mathews, and Yeardley sat on it, while Wyatt and Yeardley took turns in the governor's chair. These men, with a more than average interest in controlling the labor force, were thus enabled to maintain their personal ascendancy not only over their servants but over all lesser men. Whether operating under the Company or, after 1625, under the king, they met every challenge to their authority with a rigor not exceeded by what we know of the earlier absolute government of John Smith or Thomas Dale.

In May 1624, when they discovered that Richard Barnes had uttered "base and detracting" speeches against the governor, they ordered that he "be disarmed, and have his armes broken and his tongue bored through with a awl. shall pass through a guard of 40 men and shalbe butted by every one of them, and att the head of the troope kicked downe and footed out of the fort: that he shalbe banished out of *James Cittye* and the Iland, that he shall not be capable of any priviledge of freedome of the countrey, and that (before he goe out of the Iland) he shall put in suretyes of £200 bond for the good behaviour."[108] When John Heny was reprimanded by Captain Tucker for going aboard a ship contrary to the governor's command, Heny made the mistake of saying, after Tucker had left, that Tucker "would be the death of him as he was of *Robert leyster.*" For these words, reported to the Council, Heny got sixty stripes and had to beg forgiveness of Tucker, pay him one hundred pounds of tobacco, and be imprisoned until he could give bond for good behavior.[109]

Heny's offense came at a time when the Council had also heard of murmurs against their execution of Richard Cornish, a ship master, for sodomy. There is no record of the execution, but some of the testimony in the case was recorded, and there can be no doubt that the execution took place.[110] Afterwards, on a voyage to Canada, one Edward Nevell met up with Cornish's brother, and upon the latter's inquiry as to how the execution came about, Nevell replied, "he was put to death through a scurvie boys meanes, and no other came against him." For this statement, made aboard ship off Canada where the governing council of Virginia could scarcely claim jurisdiction, Nevell upon his return to Virginia was required to "stand one the pillory with a paper one his head shewinge the cause of his offence inthe markett place, and to loose both his Ears and to serve the Colony for A yeere, And forever to be incapable to be A ffreeman of the Countrey."[111] A month later Thomas Hatch was heard to say in a private house in James City "that in his consyence he thought the said Cornishe was put to death wrongfully." Hatch had the misfortune to be a *Duty* boy, and his seven-year period of service was nearly up. The court therefore ordered that "*Thomas Hatch* for his offence shalbe whipt from the forte to the gallows and from thence be whipt back againe, and be sett uppon the Pillory and there to loose one of his eares, And that his service to Sir *George Yeardley* for seaven yeers Shalbegain [again] from the present dye."[112]

The councillors not only guarded their authority jealously, and perhaps unconstitutionally, but not infrequently they wielded it on their own behalf, participating in decisions that favored their interests. Sandys sat at a meeting in which Luke Eden was seeking payment of twenty bushels of corn due him from Sandys. Whether Eden got the corn is not recorded, but he did get himself fined two hundred pounds of tobacco and laid neck and heels "for his lewd behavior and unreverent speche" toward Sandys in the council chamber.[113] Wyatt participated in a judgment that awarded him a Negro servant "notwithstandinge, any sale by Capt. *Jonnes* to Capt. *Bass*, or any other chaleng by the ships company" (Captain Jones had brought a privateer into the James for provisions and apparently considered the servant part of the ship's booty).[114] Abraham Peirsey sat at a meeting that had Richard Crocker put in the pillory with his ears nailed for saying that Peirsey and Hamor were not fit to sit on the Council because "they deale uppon nothing but extortion."[115] Yeardley sat at a meeting that ordered the execution of a man for killing a calf of Yeardley's and at another meeting that awarded him as tenants all the *Duty* boys who had finished their terms as servants.[116] He also participated in sentencing John Radish to lie neck and heels because Radish "Caryed over Sir *George Yardley* his servants to his house at unsesonable tyme of the night and there gave them Entertainment and made them drunke."[117]

It was apparently not without reason that ordinary men grumbled at the government. In the words of William Tyler, "nether the Governor nor Counsell could or would doe any poore men right, but that they would shew favor to great men and wronge the poore."[118]

It may be contended that severe discipline was necessary in a colony consisting predominantly of lusty young men who had just shaken loose the fetters of home and country. And it must be acknowledged that the men entrusted with government did protect some of the rights of servants. When a master failed to teach an indentured apprentice his trade or when he sought to hold a servant beyond the term of his indenture, the Council might interfere. Dr. Pott was ordered by a meeting at which he was himself present either to teach his apprentice the art of an apothecary (which he was neglecting to do) or else pay him wages.[119]

Nevertheless serious differences made servitude in Virginia more onerous than servitude in England. The ordinary term of service that a man agreed to work in Virginia was not a year but several years; and the wages to which he was entitled had been paid in advance in the form of transportation across the ocean. Almost all servants were therefore in a condition resembling that of the least privileged type of English servant, the parish apprentice, a child who (to relieve the community of supporting him) was bound to service by court order until he was twenty-one or twenty-four, with no obligation on his appointed master's part to teach him a trade or to pay him. In Virginia a master had little reason to treat his servant well in order to obtain a renewal of his services at the expiration of his term, and a servant had little reason to work hard in order to assure being rehired, because men would not bind themselves out for a second long term when they could make more by working for themselves. There was accordingly the more reason for a master to assert his authority in order to get what he considered a full quota of work from his servants. Not surprisingly it was reported in England that Virginians "abuse their servantes there with intollerable oppression and hard usage."[120]

The records are not sufficiently complete to show how extensive the abuse of servants may have been, but there is some evidence that the Council in Virginia (until 1634 the only court) supported masters in severities that would not have been allowed in England. The most extreme example is the case of John and Alice Proctor and their servants Elizabeth Abbott and Elias Hinton, both of whom died after a series of beatings inflicted by the Proctors and by other servants acting under orders from the Proctors. Thomas Gates testified that he counted five hundred lashes inflicted on the girl at one time and warned Proctor that he might as well kill her and be done with it. Alice Bennett, who examined her, "fownd she had been sore beaten and her body full of sores and holes very dangerously raunckled and putrified both above her wast and upon her hips and thighes." Other witnesses testified that Proctor beat Hinton with a rake. Yet there is no indication that the Proctors were punished.[121] By contrast we find English courts undertaking the work of correcting unruly servants themselves (as the statutes required) and even on occasion forbidding masters to do it.[122] In Virginia, servants who found themselves in the hands of brutal masters like the Proctors had no way out. Some ran away to the Indians and went native, or escaped to the Dutch settlements or to New England. But any Virginian who harbored another man's servant was liable to prosecution, and the records speak often of runaways apprehended and returned to their masters. Even the compassionate witnesses who testified against the Proctors indicated that when the maid came to them for shelter they had instead returned her to her master and mistress in her half-dead condition, with entreaties that *they* pardon *her*!

But whether physically abused or not, Englishmen found servitude in Virginia more degrading than servitude in England. In England the hiring of workers was dignified by law and customs that gave a servant some control over his own life. He had to give his master three months' notice if he intended to leave at the end of his term, and in order to move from one place to another, he had to have a testimonial that his term of service was finished. But by the same token, a master could not turn away a servant before his term was up and had to give him three months' advance notice that his contract would not be renewed.[123] Once a year, in the petty sessions held by the constables, servants could renew their contracts or make new ones, with the constables recording the transaction. These sessions, usually held in a churchyard, came to be known as hiring fairs and constituted a kind of open labor market where workmen sold their annual services.[124] But in Virginia it was the masters who sold the workmen, and there was no annual hiring fair. Masters bought and sold servants at any time for any period of years covered by their transportatin contracts; and during that period a servant might find himself sold without his consent from one master to another. In 1633 a Dutch sea captain found the planters gambling at cards with their servants as stakes.[125] Virginians dealt in servants the way Englishmen dealt in land or chattels.

This development was a simple outgrowth of the extreme demand for labor in combination with the long terms of service that were exacted for transportation to Virginia. In England itself, after labor became more valuable, the demand produced a certain amount of buying and selling of industrial apprentices. When a man had more apprentices than he needed, he might with the permission of his guild sell an apprentice to another master of the guild.[126] But industrial apprentices were a special case, and the idea of a large-scale market in men, or at least in English men, was shocking to Englishmen. "My Master Atkins," wrote Thomas Best from Virginia in 1623, "hath sold me for a £150 sterling like a damnd slave."[127] This "buying and selling men and boies" had already become a scandal by 1619, when John Rolfe noted that it "was held in *England* a thing most intolerable."[128] Capt. John Smith denounced the "pride, covetousnesse, extortion, and oppression" of men who sold "even men, women and children for who will give most." It would be better, he said, that these profiteers be "made such merchandize themselves, then suffered any longer to use that trade."[129] And in 1625 Thomas Weston refused to carry servants in his ship from Canada to Virginia because "servants were sold heere upp and downe like horses, and therfore he held it not lawfull to carie any."[130]

Other shipmasters were not so scrupulous, and the dissolution of the Virginia Company brought no end to the market in men or to their importation. So much did the planters count on continued importations that the Council during the 1620s awarded as yet unarrived, unknown, and unnamed servants to the victors in lawsuits.[131] A servant, by going to Virginia, became for a number of years a thing, a commodity with a price. Although the government might protect him against continuation in this status beyond the time agreed upon, it was not likely to shorten his term or give him his freedom, even if his master's crimes against him were serious enough to warrant the death penalty. The servant who was the victim of Richard Cornish's homosexual attack did not win his freedom by his master's execution. Even though no other man had a legal claim to his service, the court decreed that he must choose another master, who in return was to compensate the government for the costs of prosecuting Cornish.[132] A servant in Virginia, as long as his term had not expired, was a machine to make tobacco for somebody else.

"Like a damnd slave," said Thomas Best. To buy and sell servants for a brief period of years was not the same as buying and selling men for life and their unborn children with them. But it was a step in that direction. We can perhaps see, then, in boom-time Virginia not only the fleeting ugliness of private enterprise operating temporarily without check, not only greed magnified by opportunity, producing fortunes for a few and misery for many. We may also see Virginians beginning to move toward a system of labor that treated men as things.

Notes

*Mr. Morgan is a member of the Department of History, Yale University.

[1] Ralph Hamor, *A True Discourse of the Present State of Virginia* (Richmond, 1957 [orig. publ. London, 1615]), 17.

[2] *Ibid.*, xvi.

[3] The classic account of the new program is Wesley F. Craven, *Dissolution of the Virginia Company: The Failure of a Colonial Experiment* (New York, 1932), 47–80.

[4] A list of "the Living and Dead in Virginia," Feb. 16, 1623/4, gives 1,292 persons living. A muster of all the inhabitants made in Jan. and Feb. 1624/5 gives 1,210 persons. The two lists are in the Colonial Office Group, Class 1, Piece 3, Public Record Office. Hereafter cited as C. O. 1/3. Both are printed in John Camden Hotten, *The Original Lists of Persons of Quality . . . and Others Who Went from Great Britain to the American Plantations, 1600–1700* (London, 1874), 169–195, 201–265. The muster is also printed in Annie L. Jester and Martha W. Hiden, *Adventurers of Purse and Person, 1607–1625* (Princeton, 1956), 5–69. I suggest 1,500 as a maximum figure, because it seems likely that the persons taking these lists missed a number of people. There are records of the Council meeting as a court to try cases on Jan. 17, 24, and 30, and Feb. 8, 1624/5, the time when the census was being taken. H. R. McIlwaine, ed., *Minutes of the Council and General Court of Colonial Virginia* (Richmond, 1924), 43–47. Hereafter cited as *Minutes of Council.* The minutes mention the names of 66 persons in such a way as to indicate that they were alive and in Virginia. Of these 66, only 55 can be found in the muster, even when allowance is made for variations in spelling and possible misreadings of the manuscript. Of the remaining 11, 7 can be accounted for as sailors or shipmasters, though 2 of these (William Cowse and Gilbert Peppett) remained in Virginia. But four persons not listed in the muster (Francis Bolton, Edward Grundon or Grindon, William English, and Christopher Barker) were clearly resident in Virginia at the time of the muster and continued to figure both in the *Minutes of Council* and in other documents of the period.

A comparison of the names in the 1625 list, which gives the date of arrival in the colony for 740 persons, with the names on the 1624 list shows that of 697 living persons listed as arriving before 1624, more than 150 are missing from the 1624 list. This figure does not include women, whose names might have changed during the year's interval, and it makes allowance for the vagaries of 17th-century spelling, assuming for example that George Bailife is George Bayley, William Cooksey is William Coxe, and Pharow Phlinton is Farrar Flinton. Although a few of the persons missing from the 1624 list may have been absent from the colony when the 1625 list was made, it seems likely that the 1624 list is short by at least 20%, and the 1625 list by perhaps 10%. On the number of immigrants and the death rate see Craven, *Dissolution of Virginia Company*, 300–302. The figures may reflect some return migration to England.

[5] Again the authoritative account is Craven, *Dissolution of Virginia Company.* I wish to emphasize that the present article is not intended as a challenge to Craven. It is intended rather as an exploration of developments within the colony that accompanied and aggravated the difficulties resulting from the Sandys program.

[6] Susan M. Kingsbury, ed., *The Records of the Virginia Company of London* (Washington, 1906–1935), III, 118–122. Hereafter cited as *Virginia Company Records*.

[7] *Ibid.*, 220; I, 310.

[8] *Ibid.*, III, 241–248.

[9] *Ibid.*, I, 423.

[10] *Ibid.*, III, 417.

[11] *Ibid.*, 455–456.

[12] *Ibid.*, 462.

[13] *Ibid.*, 534–535.

[14] *Ibid.*, 582.

[15] *Ibid.*, 587.

[16] *Ibid.*, 589.

[17] Alexander Brown, *The First Republic in America* (Boston, 1898), 464–465.

[18] Edward D. Neill, *Virginia Carolorum* (Albany, 1886), 53; *Virginia Company Records*, III, 613–614; IV, 186, 234.

[19] *Virginia Company Records*, IV, 41–42, 58–62, 89, 231–235. See also Philip A. Bruce, *Economic History of Virginia in the Seventeenth Century* (New York, 1895), II, 6–8.

[20] Delphebus Canne to John Delbridge, July 2, 1623, *Virginia Magazine of History and Biography*, VI (1898–1899), 373–374.

[21] *Virginia Company Records*, IV, 452.

[22] *Ibid.*, 475. The harvest in the summer of 1624 was plentiful. Gov. Sir Francis Wyatt and Council of Virginia to earl of Southampton and Council and Company of Virginia, Dec. 2, 1624, in W. Noel Sainsbury *et al.*, eds., *Calendar of State Papers, Colonial Series, America and West Indies, 1574–1660* (London, 1860), no. 30 (C. O. 1/3, 102).

[23] *Virginia Company Records*, III, 226, 246; John Smith, *Travels and Works*, ed. Edward Arber (Edinburgh, 1910), II, 542.

[24] *Virginia Company Records*, III, 243. It is perhaps no coincidence that in 1625 Yeardley (governor in 1619) and Abraham Peirsey (cape merchant in 1619) held 15 of the 23 Negroes then in the colony.

[25] *Ibid.*, 299.

[26] Francis Wyatt, Wyatt Manuscripts, *William and Mary Quarterly*, 2d Ser., VII (1927), 246; *Virginia Company Records*, III, 590. See also the similar rates set in tobacoo in Bermuda in 1623 and 1627, J. H. Lefroy, *Memorials of the Discovery and Early Settlement of the Bermudas or Somers Islands 1515–1685* (London, 1877–1879), I, 305.

[27] J. E. T. Rogers, *A History of Agriculture and Prices in England* (Oxford, 1866–1900), VI, 632–633, 692–695; S. A. H. Burne, ed., *The Staffordshire Quarter Sessions Rolls* (Kendal, 1931–), V, 259–261, 324–326.

[28] 25 Edw. III, c. 2; 3 Edw. VI, c. 22; 5 Eliz. I, c. 4.

[29] *Virginia Company Records*, III, 499–500; Neill, *Virginia Carolorum*, 109–111; George Reade to Robert Reade, Apr. 24, 1640, *Va. Mag. Hist. Biog.*, XIII (1905–1906), 387; Bruce, *Economic History*, I, 629; William Bullock, *Virginia Impartially Examined . . .* (London, 1649), 49.

[30] See references in note 27 and Calendar of Essex Quarter Sessions (typescript in Essex Records Office, microfilm in University of Wisconsin Library and Yale University Library), XVII, 116.

[31] *Virginia Company Records*, III, 399. At least two Company tenants, Francis Fowler and Thomas Dunthorne, held servants in 1626. See *Minutes of Council*, 96, 108, 136, 137.

[32] *Virginia Company Records*, III, 221. It follows that the rising demand ran up the price of servants in Virginia to an amount well above the mere cost of transportation and maintenance.

[33] C. O. 1/3, 227–228; Sir George Yeardley, Propositions touching Virginia, 1625, *Wm. and Mary Qtly.*, 2d Ser., VIII (1928), 162.

[34] *Virginia Company Records*, III, 162. The figure 3d. given here is an obvious misprint for 35.

[35] *Ibid.*, IV, 264; H. R. McIlwaine, ed., *Journals of the House of Burgesses of Virginia 1619–1658/59* (Richmond, 1915), 24. Hereafter cited as *Journals of Burgesses*.

[36] *Minutes of Council*, 33, 43.

[37] Evidence about the exact time of the collapse is scanty, but see Gov. John Harvey to the Privy Council, May 29, 1630, *Va. Mag. Hist. Biog.*, VII (1899–1900), 382; C. O. 1/8, 17–18; C. O. 1/9, 248–249; C. O. 1/10, 14–17.

[38] Smith, *Works*, II, 541.

[39] *Virginia Company Records*, II, 524; IV, 38.

[40] *Ibid.*, II, 524.

[41] *Minutes of Council*, 99; *Virginia Company Records*, I, 256, 268.

[42] If we may judge from the English customs records of tobacco imported from Virginia, Bermuda, and Maryland, a good year often produced twice the amount of a poor year and sometimes almost three times the amount. See figures in Neville Williams, "England's Tobacco Trade in the Reign of Charles I," *Va. Mag. Hist. Biog.*, LXV (1957), 403–449; Stanley Gray and V. J. Wyckoff, "The International Tobacco Trade in the Seventeenth Century," *Southern Economic Journal*, VII (1940), 16–25; Importations of Tobacco, September 29, 1614, to September 29, 1621, "Lord Sackville's Papers respecting Virginia," *American Historical Review*, XXVII (1921–1922), 526; and Elizabeth B. Schumpeter, *English Overseas Trade Statistics 1697–1808* (Oxford, 1960), 52–55.

[43] *Virginia Company Records*, III, 221. By the 1640s it was expected that one man's crop might amount to 1,500 or 2,000 pounds, which at 1619 prices would have brought from £225 to £300 per man. Bullock, *Virginia Examined*, 63; Samuel Hartlib, *The Reformed Virginia Silk-worm, . . .* (London, 1655), in Peter Force, ed., *Tracts and Other Papers Relating Principally to the Origin, Settlement, and Progress of the Colonies in North America, From the Discovery of the Country to the Year 1776* (Washington, 1836–1846), III, no. 13, 36; [?], *A Perfect Description of Virginia . . .* (London, 1649), in *ibid.*, II, no. 8, 4.

[44] *Virginia Company Records*, III, 221.

[45] *Ibid.*, 165.

[46] *Ibid.*, 658, 666; IV, 11, 14, 23, 271–273; Wyatt, A Proclamation Against Drunkennes, Wyatt MSS, *Wm. and Mary Qtly.*, 2d Ser., VII (1927), 247.

[47] *Virginia Company Records*, I, 256, 269, 566; III, 493; IV, 231. By 1624 the total female population by count, including children, was 244 out of 1,292. In 1625 it was 282 out of 1,220. There are 58 living persons of indeterminable sex in the 1624 list and 10 in the 1625 list. Most of these are children, but some are persons with names like Francis. See note 4.

[48] *Ibid.*, I, 566.

[49] W. G. Hoskins, "The Rebuilding of Rural England, 1570–1640," *Past and Present*, No. 4 (Nov., 1953), 44–59.

[50] *Virginia Company Records*, IV, 259.

[51] *Journals of Burgesses*, 33. Planters who had built houses at Kecoughtan on land later claimed by the Company were paid from 70 to 100 pounds of tobacco for them in 1625. At the maximum valuation of 3s. a pound this would make the best house worth £15 (*Minutes of Council*, 41). In spite of the high wages of carpenters in Virginia, this was probably no more than half what an English husbandman's house might be worth. As late as 1642, Gov. Berkeley was ordered by the

Privy Council to require everyone with 500 acres to build a brick house "and also not to suffer men to build slight cottages as heretofore hath been there used. And to remove from place to place, only to plant Tobacco." Charles I to Sir William Berkeley, Instructions to Berkeley, 1642, *Va. Mag. Hist. Biog.*, II (1894–1895), 284, 287.

[52] *Virginia Company Records*, IV, 572.

[53] *Ibid.*, 451.

[54] *Ibid.*, 38.

[55] Smith, *Works*, I, 103–104.

[56] *Virginia Company Records*, I, 303; III, 362.

[57] *Ibid.*, II, 52, 218–219; III, 502–505; IV, 14, 23.

[58] *Ibid.*, IV, 453.

[59] *Ibid.*, cf. III, 528, 658–659; IV, 11.

[60] *Ibid.*, III, 504, 703–704; IV, 261.

[61] *Ibid.*, II, 375; IV, 186, 234.

[62] *Ibid.*, IV, 89, 231, 234.

[63] *Journals of Burgesses*, 24.

[64] This is evident from any comparison of the dates of patents with the dates of transportation of persons for which headrights were claimed. When Abraham Peirsey made his will in Mar. 1626/7, he had not yet taken up land for the servants he had transported since 1620. Neill, *Virginia Carolorum*, 404.

[65] Smith, *Works*, II, 618; *Virginia Company Records*, IV, 235.

[66] See note 4. A convenient breakdown of the information in the muster about numbers of cattle and supplies listed for each household is in "The Virginia Census, 1624–25," *Va. Mag. Hist. Biog.*, VII (1899–1900), 364–367, but this does not analyze dates of arrival or ages and some of the figures are incorrect. The muster was evidently taken by various people who did not all put down the same kinds of information. The dates of arrival are complete for some plantations; others show no dates at all; and still others show dates for some names but not for others. It seems safe to assume that the 740 are roughly typical of the remaining 470, who include, however, a number of children born in the colony.

[67] The rest had come as follows:

1618: 59
1619: 78
1620: 124
1621: 114
1622: 95
1623: 117
1624: 43

[68] I have not counted the few children of servants, but I have included the few wives, and I have assumed that "men," presumably tenants, were under the control of the person under whose name they are listed.

[69] *Virginia Company Records*, I, 270–271, 293, 304–307, 411–412, 424, 520; III, 259; *Minutes of Council*, 117.

[70] *Virginia Company Records*, IV, 523.

[71] *Ibid.*, I, 256, 268, 454, 549.

[72] *Ibid.*, 431; III, 277–280, 313.

[73] *Ibid.*, I, 332–333; II, 94–95, 109.

[74] [?] to Rev. Joseph Mead, Apr. 4, 1623, *Va. Mag. Hist. Biog.*, LXXI (1963), 410.

[75] *Virginia Company Records*, IV, 473.

[76] *Ibid.*, II, 113; see also, II, 442.

[77] The officers also cited the lack of housing. But the Company had repeatedly ordered the construction of guest houses to quarter newcomers until they could build houses of their own. The officers in the colony regularly found excuses to evade the orders. *Ibid.*, III, 489, 493, 532.

[78] *Ibid.*, 479, 489. The same hiring out of tenants by those to whom they were entrusted apparently also occurred in Bermuda. Lefroy, *Memorials*, I, 165.

[79] *Virginia Company Records*, III, 489.

[80] *Ibid.*

[81] *Ibid.*, IV, 175.

[82] *Ibid.*, I, 456–457.

[83] Smith, *Works*, II, 571. See also *Virginia Company Records*, III, 479.

[84] See notes 4 and 68. The number of persons employing 10 or more servants in Virginia, with a living population of a little over 1,200 in 1625, was almost as large as in the English county of Gloucestershire in 1608, where the total population was probably more than 50,000 (men aged 20 to 60 amounted to 19,402). See A. J. and R. H. Tawney, "An Occupational Census of the Seventeenth Century," *Economic History Review*, V (1934–1935), 25–64.

[85] Wyatt, who served as governor 1621–1626, and Peirce seem to have made their way without eliciting complaints. Bennett, a Puritan merchant of London and Amsterdam, came to Virginia only after the dissolution of the Company and did not remain. His estate was built up through the efforts of his brother Robert, who sold provisions at prices that drew protests (John B. Boddie, *Seventeenth Century Isle of Wight County, Virginia* [Chicago, 1938], 34–53; *Virginia Company Records*, IV, 453). Gookin too was in Virginia only briefly, though his sons and overseers seem to have done very well for him (Frederick W. Gookin, *Daniel Gookin* [Chicago, 1912], 38–48). Barry and Smith were agents of the Company, and most of the men listed under their names were probably Company tenants and not appropriated to private profit (*Virginia Company Records*, I, 433; *Minutes of Council*, 78, 90). Samuel Mathews was to play a prominent role in the colony in the 1630s and 1640s. He married Peirsey's widow and by 1638 boasted the best estate in the country (Massachusetts Historical Society, *Collections*, 4th Ser., IX [1871], 136n; W. G. Stanard, ed., "Abstracts of Virginia Land Patents," *Va. Mag. Hist. Biog.*, I [1893–1894], 187–188; W. N. Sainsbury, ed., "Virginia in 1638–39," *ibid.*, XI [1903–1904], 170–182). Epps, described both as "a mad ranting fellow" and as "a proper yong man," killed another man in a drunken brawl in 1619 and was charged with adultery in 1627. He became a leading figure on the eastern shore, but by 1633 he had moved to St. Christopher (Felix Hull, ed., "The Tufton Manuscripts and the Virginia Connection," *ibid.*, LXV [1957], 313–327; *Virginia Company Records*, III, 121, 242; *Minutes of Council*, 48, 50, 91, 140, 148; Susie M. Ames, ed., *County Court Records of Accomack-Northampton, Virginia, 1632–1640* [Washington, 1954], 9, 21, 67, 116, 163–164).

[86] Stanard, ed., "Abstracts," *Va. Mag. Hist. Biog.*, I (1893–1894), 187; Sainsbury, ed., "Virginia in 1638–39," *ibid.*, XI (1903–1904), 175–182; C. O. 1/8, 15–18; *Minutes of Council*, 118; *Virginia Company Records*, I, 333; II, 219. But the estate was appraised at only 60,000 pounds of tobacco, worth at the time a shilling a pound. Success in boom-time Virginia did not necessarily result in lasting wealth.

[87] *Virginia Company Records*, III, 449, 503–504, 526; IV, 106–107, 111, 263–265; *Minutes of Council*, 93, 121. Blaney evidently married the widow of William Powell. The widow brought with her an estate of which her husband had taken possession on the basis of his name after the owner, Capt. Nathaniel Powell, died in the massacre of 1622. Capt. Nathaniel Powell was

actually no relation to William Powell, and Nathaniel Powell's surviving brother, Thomas Powell, was trying to recover the estate from Blaney at the time of the latter's death (Petition of Thomas Powell, July 21, 1626, *Va. Mag. Hist. Biog.*, XVI [1907–1908], 30–31; C. O. 1/4, 36).

[88] Lefroy, *Memorials*, I, 264; Gov. Francis West and Council to Privy Council, Mar. 4, 1628, *Va. Mag. Hist. Biog.*, VII (1899–1900), 259; C. O. 1/4, 111. See in general Richard B. Davis, *George Sandys, Poet-Adventurer* (New York, 1955).

[89] He invested in the Company in 1617, and in 1619 he represented Kecoughtan in the House of Burgesses, *Virginia Company Records*, III, 58, 154, 535.

[90] *Ibid.*, II, 104.

[91] *Ibid.*, IV, 221–222; Wyatt, Wyatt MSS, *Wm. and Mary Qtly.*, 2d Ser., VII (1927), 206–207.

[92] *Journals of Burgesses*, 55–56. See also Gov. Harvey's complaints against him, Harvey to the Lords Commissioners, May 27, 1632, *Va. Mag. Hist. Biog.*, VIII (1900–1901), 149–150. Tucker was not slow to perceive the danger of Dutch competition to his high profits. He did his best to secure from the government in England a prohibition of Dutch trading in Virginia ([William Tucker], Reasons Against Permitting Dutch Trade to Virginia, Aug., 1633, in *ibid.*, 154; C. O. 1/6, 135, 207–212).

[93] *Virginia Company Records*, IV, 110–111.

[94] Wyatt, Wyatt MSS, *Wm. and Mary Qtly.*, 2d Ser., VII (1927), 204–205, 212, 254; *Minutes of Council*, 48, 132, 135.

[95] *Virginia Company Records*, IV, 110.

[96] Harvey to Lord Dorchester, May 29, to the Privy Council, with enclosures, May 29, 1630, Privy Council to Harvey, with enclosure, Sept. 30, 1630, *Va. Mag. Hist. Biog.*, VII (1899–1900), 378, 381, 382–385. The quotation is on p. 381. See also William W. Hening, ed., *The Statutes at Large; being a Collection of All the Laws of Virginia . . .* (Richmond, 1809–1823), I, 145–146; C. O. 1/6, 36–43; Charles I to Harvey, July 25, Dorchester to Harvey, July 27, 1631, Report of Virginia Commissioners on Dr. Pott's Case, Aug. 20, Memorial in Behalf of Dr. Pott, Aug., 1631, *Va. Mag. Hist. Biog.*, VIII (1900–1901), 33–35; Mass. Hist. Soc., *Collections*, 4th Ser., IX (1871), 143n–144n.

[97] *Virginia Company Records*, III, 221.

[98] *New-England Historical and Genealogical Register*, XXXVIII (1884), 70.

[99] *Virginia Company Records*, I, 268, 332; III, 471.

[100] *Ibid.*, III, 584.

[101] *Ibid.*, IV, 37. Capps's opinion was shared by the earl of Dorset, who blamed the ruin of Southampton Hundred to Yeardley's "being a man wholy adicted to his private." Dorset to Gov. John Harvey, Aug. 1629, Sackville Manuscripts, Library of Congress microfilm (British Manuscripts Project, K334).

[102] *Virginia Company Records*, II, 113, 119; IV, 510–514.

[103] *Ibid.*, IV, 186.

[104] *Ibid.*, 9–10.

[105] *Tyler's Quarterly Historical and Genealogical Magazine*, II (1921), 121.

[106] His sons Francis and Argall later cut a large figure in Norfolk and Northampton Counties.

[107] Even the assembly showed itself to be a meeting of masters when the first session, in 1619, adopted measures to secure every man's right to his servants. As protection against servants fraudulently claiming freedom it ordered the establishment of a registry of all servants in the colony and of all that should come in the future, with the dates of expiration of their terms. It also decreed that if a servant, before leaving England, contracted to serve one master in Virginia and then contracted to serve another (who perhaps made a more attractive offer), he should serve two full terms, one with each master (*Virginia Company Records*, III, 167, 171, 174).

108 *Minutes of Council*, 14.

109 *Ibid.*, 85.

110 See references to case in *ibid.*, 34, 42, 47, 81, 83, 85.

111 *Ibid.*, 85.

112 *Ibid.*, 93.

113 *Ibid.*, 57.

114 *Ibid.*, 66–68, 73.

115 *Ibid.*, 135–136.

116 *Ibid.*, 4–5, 154.

117 *Ibid.*, 58

118 *Ibid.*, 19.

119 *Ibid.*, 117.

120 *Virginia Company Records*, II, 442.

121 *Minutes of Council*, 22–24.

122 W. L. Sachse, ed., *Minutes of the Norwich Court of Mayoralty 1630–1631* (Norfolk Record Society, *Publications*, XV [London, 1942]), 90.

123 5 Eliz. I, c. 4, paragraphs 4, 7.

124 Margaret G. Davies, *The Enforcement of English Apprenticeship: A Study in Applied Mercantilism 1563–1642* (Cambridge, Mass., 1956), 191, 196–197, 233. There are records of some of these petty sessions in the typescript calendar of Essex Quarter Sessions. A good contemporary description is in Henry Best, *Rural Economy in Yorkshire in 1641 . . .*, ed. Charles Best Robinson (Surtees Society, *Publications*, XXXIII [Durham, 1857]), 134–136.

125 New-Hork Historical Society, *Collections*, 2d Ser., III (1857), 36.

126 O. Jocelyn Dunlop and Richard D. Denman, *English Apprenticeship & Child Labour; a History* (London, 1912), 57–58, 127–129.

127 *Virginia Company Records*, IV, 235. If the figure is correct and Atkins bore the initial expense of transportation and support, he must have made a profit of several hundred per cent on the transaction. The original letter does not survive. The quotation is from a contemporary transcript in the Manchester Papers, Nos. 338, 339, Public Record Office, in which it is likely that the scribe erred.

128 Smith, *Works*, II, 542.

129 *Ibid.*, 618.

130 *Minutes of Council*, 82.

131 *Ibid.*, 63, 134, 155, 160, 170, 181.

132 *Ibid.*, 47.

3

Selection from Bound Labor: The Indentured Servant

Bound Labor:
The Indentured Servant

The Hazards of Servitude

7. An Assault on Charity Dallen, 1649

Lower Norfolk County Order Book, 1646–1651, fol. 120.

The deposition of Joseph Mulders Aged 23 yeares or thereabouts Sworne and examined Sayeth

That Deborah Fernehaugh, the Mistress of this deponent, did beate her mayd Sarvant in the quartering house before the dresser more Liken a dogge then a Christian, and that at a Certaine time, I felt her head, which was beaten as soft as a sponge, in one place, and that as there shee was a weeding, shee complayned and sayd, her backe bone as shee thought was broken with beating, and that I did see the mayds arme naked which was full of blacke and blew bruises and pinches, and her necke Likewise and that afterwards, I tould my Mistress of it and said, that two or three blowes, could not make her in such a Case, and after this my speeches shee Chidge [i.e., chided] the said mayd, for shewing her body to the men, and very often afterwards she the said mayd would have showen mee, how shee had beene beaten, but I refused to have seene it, saying it concernes me not, I will doe my worke and if my Mistress abuse you; you may complaine, and about 8 dayes since, being about the time shee last went to Complaine, I knew of her goeing, but would not tell my mistress of it, although shee asked mee, and sayd I could not chuse but know of it, and further hee sayeth not

swɔrne the 31th July 1649   The Marke of
Thomas Bridge Clerk of Court   Joseph X Mulders

Michaell Mikaye aged 22 yeares of there abouts, sworne and examined, sayeth verbatim as the above mentioned deponent sayeth and deposeth and further sayeth not

sworne the 31th July *1649*   The Marke of
Thomas Bridge Clerk of Court   Michael X Mikay

Upon the depositions of Joseph Mulders and Michaell Mikaye of the misusage of Charetie dallen, by her Mistress Deborah Fernehaugh, and by many other often Complaints, by other sufficient testimonies, and although the said Deborah hath had advertisement thereof from the Court yet persisteth in the very Ill usadge of her said sarvant, as appeareth to the board, It is therefore ordered that the said Charetie Dallen shall no longer remaine in the house or service with her said Mistress, but is to bee and Continue at the house of Mr. Thomas Lambard [Lambert], untill such time as the said Deborah Fernehaugh shall sell or otherwise dispose of her said servant, for her best advantage of her the said Deborah.

8. James Revel Describes the Servant's Plight, ca. 1680

> James Revel, "The Poor Unhappy Transported Felon's Sorrowful Account of His Fourteen Years Transportation at Virginia in America," ed. John Melville Jennings, *Virginia Magazine of History and Biography*, LVI (1948), 189–194.

PART I

My loving Countrymen pray lend an Ear,
    To this Relation which I bring you here,
My sufferings at large I will unfold,
Which tho' 'tis strange, 'tis true as e'er was told,
    Of honest parents I did come (tho' poor,)
Who besides me had never Children more;
Near Temple Bar was born their darling son,
And for some years in virtue's path did run.
    My parents in me took great delight,
And brought me up-at School to read and write,
And cast accompts likewise, as it appears,
Until that I was aged thirteen years.
    Then to a Tin-man I was Prentice bound,
My master and mistress good I found,
They lik'd me well, my business I did mind,
From me my parents comfort hop'd to find.
    My master near unto Moorfields did dwell,
Where into wicked company I fell;
To wickedness I quickly was inclin'd
Thus soon is tainted any youthful mind.
    I from my master then did run away,
And rov'd about the streets both night and day:
Did with a gang of rogues a thieving go,
Which filled my parents heart with grief and woe.
    At length my master got me home again,
And used me well, in hopes I might reclaim, . . .
I promis'd fair, but yet could not refrain,
    But to my vile companions went again: . . .
One night was taken up one of our gang,
Who five impeach'd and three of these were hang'd.
    I was one of the five was try'd and cast,
Yet transportation I did get at last; . . .
    In vain I griev'd, in vain my parents weep,

For I was quickly sent on board the Ship:
With melting kisses and a heavy heart,
I from my dearest parents then did part.

PART II

In a few Days we left the river quite,
  And in short time of land we lost the sight,
The Captain and the sailors us'd us well,
But kept us under lest we should rebel.
  We were in number much about threescore,
A wicked lowsey crew as e'er went o'er;
Oaths and Tobacco with us plenty were,
For most did smoak, and all did curse and swear.
  Five of our number in our passage died,
Which were thrown into the Ocean wide:
And after sailing seven Weeks and more,
We at Virginia all were put on shore.
  Where, to refresh us, we were wash'd and cleaned
That to our buyers we might the better seem;
Our things were gave to each they did belong,
And they that had clean linnen put it on.
  Our faces shav'd, comb'd out our wigs and hair,
That we in decent order might appear,
Against the planters did come down to view,
How well they lik'd this fresh transported crew.
The Women s[e]parated from us stand,
As well as we, by them for to be view'd;
And in short time some men up to us came,
Some ask'd our trades, and others ask'd our names.
  Some view'd our limbs; and other's turn'd us round
Examening like Horses, if we're sound,
What trade are you, my Lad, says one to me,
A Tin-man, Sir, that will not do, says he[.]
  Some felt our hands and view'd our legs and feet,
And made us walk, to see we were compleat;
Some view'd our teeth, to see if they were good,
Or fit to chew our hard and homely Food.
  If any like our look, our limbs, our trade,
The Captain then a good advantage made:
For they a difference made it did appear.
'Twixt those for seven and for fourteen year.
  Another difference there is alow'd,
They who have money have most favour show'd;
For if no cloaths nor money they have got,
Hard is their fate, and hard will be their lot.
  At length a grim old Man unto me came,
He ask'd my trade, and likewise ask'd my Name:
I told him I a Tin-man was by trade,
And not quite eighteen years of age I said.
  Likewise the cause I told that brought me there,

That I for fourteen years transported were,
And when he this from me did understand,
He bought me of the Captain out of hand,

PART III

Down to the harbour I was took again,
    On board of a sloop, and loaded with a chain;
Which I was forc'd to wear both night and day,
For fear I from the Sloop should get away.
    My master was a man but of ill fame,
Who first of all a Transport thither came,
In Reppahannock county we did dwell,
Up Reppahannock river known full well,
    And when the Sloop with loading home was sent
An hundred mile we up the river went
The weather cold and very hard my fare,
My lodging on the deck both hard and bare,
    At last to my new master's house I came,
At the town of Wicocc[o]moco call'd by name,
Where my Europian clothes were took from me,
Which never after I again could see.
    A canvas shirt and trowsers then they gave,
With a hop-sack frock in which I was to slave:
No shoes nor stockings had I for to wear,
Nor hat, nor cap, both head and feet were bare.
    Thus dress'd into the Field I nex[t] must go,
Amongst tobacco plants all day to hoe,
At day break in the morn our work began,
And so held to the setting of the Sun.
    My fellow slaves were just five Transports more,
With eighteen Negroes, which is twenty four:
Besides four transport women in the house,
To wait upon his daughter and his Spouse,
    We and the Negroes both alike did fare,
Of work and food we had an equal share;
But in a piece of ground we call our own,
The food we eat first by ourselves were sown,
    No other time to us they would allow,
But on a Sunday we the same must do:
Six days we slave for our master's good,
The seventh day is to produce our food.
    Sometimes when that a hard days work we've done,
Away unto the mill we must be gone;
Till twelve or one o'clock a grinding corn,
And must be up by daylight in the morn.
    And if you run in debt with any one,
It must be paid before from thence you come;
For in publick places they'll put up your name,
That every one their just demands may claim,
    And if we offer for to run away,

For every hour we must serve a day;
For every day a Week, They're so severe,
For every week a month, for every month a year
But if they murder, rob or steal when there,
Then straightway hang'd, the Laws are so severe;
For by the Rigour of that very law
They're much kept under and to stand in awe.

PART IV

At length, it pleased God I sick did fall
But I no favour could receive at all,
For I was Forced to work while I could stand,
Or hold the hoe within my feeble hands.

    Much hardships then in deed I did endure,
No dog was ever nursed so I'm sure,
More pity the poor Negroe slaves bestowed
Than my inhuman brutal master showed.

    Oft on my knees the Lord I did implore,
To let me see my native land once more;
For through God's grace my life I would amend
And be a comfort to my dearest friends.

    Helpless and sick and being left alone,
I by myself did use to make my moan;
And think upon my former wicked ways,
How they had brought me to this wretched case.

    The Lord above who saw my Grief and smart,
Heard my complaint and knew my contrite heart,
His gracious Mercy did to me afford,
My health again was unto me restor'd.

    It pleas'd the Lord to grant me so much Grace,
That tho' I was in such a barbarous place,
I serv'd the Lord with fervency and zeal,
By which I did much inward comfort feel.

    Thus twelve long tedious years did pass away,
And but two more by law I had to stay:
When Death did for my cruel Master call,
But that was no relief to us at all.

    The Widow would not the Plantation hold,
So we and that were both for to be sold,
A lawyer rich who at James-Town did dwell,
Came down to view it and lik'd it very well.

    He bought the Negroes who for life were slaves,
But no transported Fellons would he have,
So we were put like Sheep into a fold,
There unto the best bidder to be sold,

PART V

A Gentleman who seemed something grave,
Unto me said, how long are you to slave;
Not two years quite, I unto him reply'd,

That is but very short indeed he cry'd.
    He ask'd my Name, my trade, and whence I came
And what vile Fate had brought me to that shame?
I told him all at which he shook his head,
I hope you have seen your folly now, he said,
    I told him yes and truly did repent,
But that which made me most of all relent
That I should to my parents prove so vile,
I being their darling and their only child.
    He said no more but from me short did turn,
While from my Eyes the tears did trinkling run,
To see him to my overseer go,
But what he said to him I do not know.
    He straightway came to me again,
And said no longer here you must remain,
For I have bought you of that Man said he,
Therefore prepare yourself to come with me.
    I with him went with heart oppressed with woe,
Not knowing him, or where I was to go;
But was surprised very much to find
He used me so tenderly and kind.
    He said he would not use me as a slave,
But as a servant if I well behav'd;
And if I pleased him when my time expir'd,
He'd send me home again if I required.
    My kind new master did at James Town dwell;
By trade a Cooper, and liv'd very well:
I was his servant on him to attend.
Thus God, unlook'd for raised me up a friend.

PART VI

Thus did I live in plenty and at ease,
    Having none but my master for to please,
And if at any time he did ride out,
I with him rode the country round about.
    And in my heart I often cry'd to see,
So many transport fellons there to be;
Some who in England had lived fine and brave,
Were like old Horses forced to drudge and slave.
    At length my fourteen years expired quite,
Which fill'd my very soul with fine delight;
To think I shoud no longer there remain,
But to old England once return again.
    My master for me did express much love,
And as good as his promise to me prov'd:
He got me ship'd and I came home again
With joy and comfort tho' I went asham'd,
    My Father and my Mother wel I found,
Who to see me, with Joy did much abound:
My Mother over me did weep for Joy,

My Father cry'd once more to see my Boy;
     Whom I thought dead, but does alive remain,
And is returned to me once again;
I hope God has so wrought upon your mind,
No more wickedness you'll be inclined,
     I told them all the dangers I went thro'
Likewise my sickness and my hardships too;
     Which fill'd their tender hearts with sad surprise,
While tears ran trinkling from their aged eyes.
     I begg'd them from all grief to refrain,
Since God had brought me to them home again,
The Lord unto me so much grace will give,
For to work for you both While I live,
     My country men take warning e'er too late,
Lest you should share my hard unhappy fate;
Altho' but little crimes you here have done,
Consider seven or fourteen years to come,
     Forc'd from your friends and country for to go,
Among the Negroes to work at the hoe;
In distant countries void of all relief,
Sold for a slave because you prov'd a thief.
     Now young men with speed your lives amend,
Take my advice as one that is your friend:
For tho' so slight you make of it while here,
Hard is your lot when once the[y] get you there.

9. *Edward Whittell Commits Suicide, 1664*

Accomack County Order Book, 1663–1666, fol. 67.

Jurymen Summoned to view the Corps of Edward Whittell Servant to John Reney of the County of Accomack, who was found hanged in a tobacco house on the plantation [where] the said Reney now lives upon the 8th of Aprill *1664* The Jury whose names are hereunto Subscribed haveing viewed the Corpes and place where the said Whittell had hanged himself, and examined two Evidences doe finde that the said Whittell for want of Grace was guilty of his owne death

[jurors' names omitted]

John Crook aged 25 yeares Sworne and examined Saith that your deponent comeing to the house of John Reney the said Reney missing one of his Servants makeing enquirey after him the said Servant was found hanged on a barr in a tobacco house, the deponent supposing that there was life Remaining in him cut the said Servant downe, Supposing therby to preserve him and further your deponent Saith not.
Sworne before me the 8th April 1664.   John Crooke
Hugh Yeo

Thomas Middleton aged 21 years or their about Sworne and examined saith your deponent goeing forth to worke the 8th of this instant Aprill in the morninge with the rest of your deponent's fellow servants one Edward Whittell being one of them the said Whittell complayning that hee was not very well, went as your deponent thought into the house, your deponents master coming and mising the said Whittell asked your deponent where hee was, whereupon your deponent makeing search where the said Whittell was gon found him hanged in the tobacco house and further saith not.

Sworne before me the 8th Aprill *1664*   the marke of
Hugh Yeo   Thomas X Middleton

Problems Created by the Use of Servant Labor

10. A Runaway, 1680

Middlesex County Order Book, 1680–1694, 362.

Adam Ballentine Servant to mr. Robert Price Comes in Court and vollentaryly Acknowledges to Serve his said Master two yeares and a halfe In Recompense of his often runing away after his first time by Indenture is over.

11. A Bastard Child, 1656

Charles City County Order Book, 1655–1665, 53.

Whereas Ann Parke servant to Elizabeth Hatcher widdow is Complained of and proved to have Comitted Fornication and borne a Child in the time of her service: It is therefore ordered that the said Ann shall double the time of service due to be performed by her to her mistress or her assigns, from the time of her departure, according to act in that Case made and provided.

12. A Frivolous Lawsuit, 1681

Accomack County Order Book, 1678–1682/83, 260.

Whereas William Wallworth and Benedict Talbot Servants to Capt. Hilary Stringer brought an information to this Court on behalf of his Majesty against theire Master Capt. Hilary Stringer wherein they accused their Said Master for occasioning the death of a Servant woman named Ellinor Tanner late Servant to Capt. Hillary Stringer and alledging the Neighborhood to be well knowing of the truth thereof the Court takeing the same into due examination and haveing maturely weighed and considered all things alleadged by the said Servants against theire said Master and allsoe a former examination of the Court of Northampton taken thereupon as allso all other evidences presented and likewise all the Neighborhoods testimonys that know anything relating thereto It appeares to the Court a most false and most malitious accusation by the said servants combination contrived thereby hopeing to acquitt themselves of the notorious wrong they had done their said Master the Court doe adjudge the said information so brought by the said Servants on behalf of his Majesty against their said Master to be notoriously false and Scandallous and order that the Said Servants make Satisfaction by Service after theire time by Indenture or Custome be expired for all charges whatsoever accrewed by reason of their Said Causless information and complaint against their Said Master and that the Said Capt. Stringer to pay the present charge thereof:

13. Theft of Master's Goods, 1684

Accomack County Deeds, Wills, and Inventories, 1676–1690, fols. 389–390.

A Declaration or Confession of [Roger] Court Crotosse one of Col. John Wests Servants of some misdemeanors Comitted or done by him or other Servants belonging to the said Col. West.

1st. Saith that about a year since he went from mary branch to his masters mill [with] John Fisher a Servant to his master alsoe (being miller) to fetch some meale the miller not being within[,] this declarant Saith he went into the mill and there lookinge for meale found in a Caske amongst Some woole and yarne a turkey warme and the feathers pluckt of[f] and the neck twisted about which Turkey this declarant drest and with a negro of his masters Eat it, And about two nights after this declarant goeing from mary branch to Chequonessex with one Sandy Coloured Turkey and one black turkey under his armes John Fisher then had this declarant to say nothing but come to the mill at night and he should eate parte of them which this declarant did and eate parte of one of them but did not See the other

2nd. That at the last Springe the aforesaid John Fisher perswaded this declarant and Thomas Hartly (another of Col. Wests Servants) to kill a Lamb and lent us his knife to kill it which accordingly we did and carried into the Swamp and [word illegible] drest it some of it wee then Eat and next morning he went with us and he Eat what he would and Said it was well done

3rd. That about August last the said John Fisher perswaded this declarant and a negro Tony to carry a Sheep from Chequonessex to mary branch and there kill it but if it were not fatt then lett it loose amongst the Sheep there att mary branch And there take one of the best of those Sheep and kill it accordingly wee carry away a Sheep upon the horse Tyger from Chequonessex and killed it att mary branch house but did not Exchange it as he ordered: The next day John Fisher came and Eat Some of it and Carryed some of it with him.

4th. That about the last of August last this declarant and the aforesaid John Fisher and the aforesaid Thomas Hartley (by Fishers perswasions) killed a Sow att Chequonessex house and by the said John Fishers order fleade [i.e., flayed] her and tyed up her gutts in the skin and Stones with them and threw them into the pond afterwards wee tooke a Pott and the Sowe and carryed them into the Swamp and there drest halfe of it and the rest wee Eat at the Indian towne.

5th. That about the seaventh day of october last this declarant beinge att breakfast att Chequonessex house heard mr Francis Chambers bid the aforesaid John Fisher Catch two piggs and bring them in afterwards this declarant beinge at plow the said Fisher bad[e] him goe along with him to help him and take his gun with him which he accordingly did And shott one pigg and would have carried that into the house but the said John Fisher would not but had him goe kill another for one would not doe but this declarant could not[.] there upon the said Fisher said he would roast that and gott a Spitt for the purpose and asked this declar- ant if he Could gett fire who answered he could not thereupon the said Fisher Stopt the touchhole of the Gunn and gott fire and there roasted it and Eat it[.] In the time the pigg was roasting old mr Johnson Came to the fire but the said Fisher seeing him come ran away with the spit and kept out of sight untill the old man went away

6th. That abought a fortnight or three weeks since this declarant and the aforesaid John Fisher Thomas Hartley and Jack A negro at two severall times killed four piggs one of them being marked with my masters marke carryed them away and Eate them.

[7th.] That on Tuesday last was a fortnight att night to this declarant and the said Thomas Hardey sitting by the fire in the middle roome the said John Fisher came to us and bad[e] us goe along with him (which we did) then he went out with us to the henhouse and said Jonny Negro had hid a bag of potatoes there and that he would steale them whereupon he put downe a board by the doore and then unlockt the doore And tooke the Potatoes presently after the same night this declarant and Thomas Hartley went to the henhouse againe and tooke a Turkey and a hen and carryed them into the shoomakers shop loft and there pluckt them and boyled them in the shop

8th. That about a week since my master Calling this declarant the said Fisher and Hartley to question for our misdemeanors Afterwards the said Fisher said to us that if he was brought to any damage he would begone and if he could gett there he would send his master a very Loveing Letter that his sheep his hoggs and turkeys were very fat *etc.*

9[th.] That what is above written and declared is very true And that this Declarant can depose to the same when Called Dated this 6th day of November anno Domini *1684*

10[th.] also this declarant farther saith that there was another sheep killed by him and John Fisher which he did not remember when he was examined before Col. [Daniel] Jenifer.

The marke of
Roger X Court Crotosse

14. *A Servant Assaults His Mistress, 1679*

Accomack County Order Book, 1678–1682/83, 88–89.

The Examination of Elizabeth Bowen Widdow—
saith—That on Sunday evening being the eighteenth day of May 1679 Thomas Jones her servant did come into her Roome and with a naked Rapier in his hand did tell her he would kill her and said shee had sent Will Waight to her Mothers and that shee had got a master for them, but hee would bee her Master and allso said that he would not kill her if shee would let him lye with her all night and bade her goe to bed and she answered she would not and Runn in with his Rapier and bent it, then he said he woald cutt her throat but she getting [to] the dore did run out of dores and he after her and ketched [her] in the yard and as she was standing did endeavour to cutt her throat with a knife but could not and then he threw her down and did there allso indeavour to cutt her throat but she prevented it by defending her throat with her hands and bending the knife hee took her [petti]coats and threw [them] over her head and gave her two or three blows in the face with his fist and bade her get her gun and did in this act with the Knife scurrify her throat and brest and cut her right hand with six or seven cutts very much and that she with bending the Rapier and knife cut her hands and fingers very much

Elizabeth Bowen

Whereas Elizabeth Bowin Widdow did by her examination upon oath in open Court declare that Thomas Jones her servant in a most barbarous and villanous nature sett upon and most desparately attempted to murder the said Bowin with a naked Rapier and Knife to cut her throat which had been perpatrated and committed had it not bee[n] Providentially and strongly prevented by the said Bowins resistance recieving severall wounds in her endeavours to prevent the sam[e] which was allso confessed by the said Jones: The Court takeing the same into their serious Considerations do order as a just reward for his said horrid offense and crime that the sherriff Forthwith take him into Custody and that he forthwith receive thirty nine lashes on the bare back well laid on: and to have his haire cutt off and an Iron Coller forthwith put about his neck dureing the Courts pleasure and after the time for which he was to serve his said mistris is expired to serve his said mistris or assignes one whole yeare according to Act for laying violent hands on his said mistriss and allso two yeares for his wounding her as aforesaid and after due punishment inflicted accordingly The Court do further order that the sherriff deliver the said Jones to the said Elizabeth Bowin or order (it being by her request) and the said Bownig [*sic*] to Pay Court Charges the said Jones makeing satisfaction for the same after his time of service is expired—

15. A Servant's Plot to Revolt, 1687

Middlesex County Order Book, 1680–1694, 309–310.

Upon Examination of John Nickson a man Servant belonging to Ralph Wormeley Esq. who was Comitted to this Common Goall for having with diverse other ill disposed Servants and others entered into a Disigne and Conspiracy to procure Gunnes powder and Shott and other Armes and to Assemble themselves together with Designe to Runnaway and with Force and Armes as aforesaid to withstand and Oppose all persons that should endeavour to Suppress them; And the same tending to the great disturbance of his Majesties Peace and the Terrour of his Leige People It is therefore ordered that the said John Nickson bee returned into the said Goall there to bee kept in safe Custody until the next Court held for this County And that in the meane time Strict inquiry bee made after all the Rest of the said Conspirators in order to their Apprehention And being proceeded against with the said Nickson According to Law, and that all person that Can give any Evidence against the said Nickson And his said Accomplishes [i.e., accomplices] bee Supened or bound over to appeare to give their Evidence on behalfe of our Sovereign Lord the King.

4

Selections from The Puritan Dilemma: The Story of John Winthrop

Edmund S. Morgan

Reprinted from *The Puritan Dilemma, The Story of John Winthrop*, Second Edition, by Edmund S. Morgan. Copyright © 1999, 2003 by Edmund S. Morgan. Published by Longman, Inc., a Pearson Education Company, New York, New York 10036.

I
The Taming of the Heart

Edmund S. Morgan

⸻ • ⸻

When Henry VIII turned his back on the Pope, dissolved the monasteries, and confiscated their property, many Englishmen rejoiced. Their country could now join in the Protestant Reformation and gain a purer church. Adam Winthrop, a London cloth merchant with ready cash, was pleased for a simpler reason: he was able to buy part of the confiscated monastery at Bury St. Edmunds, in Suffolk. He paid the King £408, 11s. 3d. for the manor of Groton and thus transformed himself into a country gentleman. That was in 1544.

Forty-four years later, in the year when English sailors defeated the Spanish Armada, and with it the last serious effort by a Catholic power to recapture England for the Pope, John Winthrop was born, grandson to Adam. John's father, also called Adam, came into possession of Groton Manor a few years after John's birth and brought his family to live there on the old monastic estate.

Groton was a good place to grow up in—gently rolling country, checkered with dark wood lots and bright fields of wheat, rye, peas, barley, hops, with here and there a shallow pond, stocked with fat carp, which were harvested regularly like any other crop. The heart of the place was a huge half-timbered barn whose steep thatched roof covered the stalls of cart horses, milk cattle, and a few fine saddle horses for the lord of the manor and his lady. And there was a great house, where John, the only son of the family, knew he would one day sit in his father's place and preside over the modest entourage of servants and tenants who lived in this small world.

Though small, it was not an isolated world. A constant procession of uncles and aunts and cousins marched through it, bearing strange tales of strange places. One had gone to Spain with the Earl of Essex to attack the Catholic king, but had been himself converted to Catholicism by a Jesuit priest. Another shuttled back and forth between Groton and Ireland, setting the ladies' tongues wagging wherever he went, and finally getting himself excommunicated, apparently because he failed to obtain a proper divorce from one wife before marrying another. The Winthrop tribe was a large one, and sooner or later, good or bad, they all showed up at Groton.

John's father, the second Adam Winthrop of Groton, was one of the good ones. He had been trained in the law, but after coming into possession of the manor he devoted himself entirely to the difficult business of making it a success. For nearly half a century prices had been rising all over England and Europe, with disastrous results for gentlemen like himself, who lived on the rents received from tenants. Rents were often fixed by law, so that they could not be raised to match the rise in prices, nor could the tenants be evicted. Such was the case with some of the lands at Groton; on the rest the lord of the manor could grow crops for his own use or for sale. Adam saw where the main chance lay and made the most of the untenanted lands. Groton was near enough to London to profit by the rising metropolitan demand for foodstuffs; and by the time John was five years old, Adam was collecting £62 a year from the sale of crops, a little more than he obtained from all his rents. In addition to Groton Manor, he held land as a tenant on three or four manors nearby, and he was constantly buying more. Adam was a country gentleman, but he was also a good businessman, and the Winthrop family fortunes rose steadily under his guidance. It would be up to John to keep them rising. From Adam he learned how.

What else John learned from his father or his mother would be hard to say. The few surviving letters of his mother's suggest that she was a pious woman, and he may have received a religious bent from her. However, with a Roman Catholic and an excommunicated bigamist familiar and welcome guests at the manor, the Winthrops cannot have been a narrow-minded family.

When John was seven, Adam was paying John Chaplyn, vicar of a nearby church, for "scholinge." The boy was evidently being prepared for college. It had already become fashionable for gentlemen and even noblemen to send their sons to the universities, and Suffolk men went to Cambridge. Adam himself had gone there, in fact had married as his first wife the sister of John Still, then master of Trinity College. Probably through this connection he gained the office of auditor at Trinity and St. John's, and every year in late November or early December mounted his horse and rode away to Cambridge to audit the accounts and renew old friendships. In 1602 on one of his regular trips he got his son admitted, and the following March John, now fifteen, went off to college.

Here the great Thomas Nevile, master of Trinity, was pulling down old buildings and throwing up new ones to produce the magnificent court with its great fountain in the center. At the same time he was making the college foremost in the university for scholarship. The students responded to his efforts not merely in their studies, but in ways that students esteem more highly than scholarship: they had "provision of stones layd up; and also of some bucketts to be provided to fetch water from her conduyt, to poure downne upon St. John's men." They also had a reputation for demonstrating their prowess in another manner: "Oh the greivous sinnes of T Colledg," sighed one pious student a few years before Winthrop entered, for the boys "had a woman which was from chamber to chamber on the night tyme."

How all this struck John Winthrop is hard to say. He later remembered that his "lusts were so masterly as no good could fasten upon mee," but this was a conventional way for men of his time to speak of their youth. He was certainly homesick: "I fell into a lingring feaver, which took away the comfort of my life. For being there neglected, and despised, I went up and down mourning with myself." Since it was not customary for sons of gentlemen to stay at college long enough for a degree anyhow, John was back at Groton within two years, ready to do his part in advancing the family fortunes.

Opportunity came quickly. About the time of his return Mr. John Forth of Great Stambridge in the neighboring county of Essex paid a visit to Adam Winthrop, and the two of them talked about a possible match between John and Forth's daughter Mary. It was proper for parents to arrange these things. The children might be consulted, but marriages involved the transfer of large amounts of property belonging to the parents. When a boy and girl were married, the father of each of them was expected to endow the couple with capital in land, goods, or money, and every father wished to make a good bargain, to get as much as possible out of the other father. Adam's bargain with Forth evidently was a favorable one and included large quantities of land. When John returned from Cambridge, he and his father rode to Great Stambridge, and on March 28, 1605, the couple were contracted, a ceremony corresponding to our engagement. Within three weeks they were married, John having then attained the age of seventeen. Ten months later he was a father.

It was a solemn young man who brought his youth to a close by so early a marriage. Somewhere, at Groton or Cambridge or Great Stambridge—it is impossible to say where—John Winthrop had caught a fever more lingering than the one that took away his comforts in college. He had caught the fever of Puritanism.

Superficially Puritanism was only a belief that the Church of England should be purged of its hierarchy and of the traditions and ceremonies inherited from Rome. But those who had caught the fever knew that Puritanism demanded more of the individual than it did of the church. Once it took possession of a man, it was seldom shaken off and would shape—some people would say warp—his whole life. Puritanism was a power not to be denied. It did great things for England and for America, but only by creating in the men and women it affected a tension which was at best painful and at worst unbearable. Puritanism required that a man devote his life to seeking salvation but told him he was helpless to do anything but evil. Puritanism required that he rest his whole hope in Christ but taught him that Christ would utterly reject him unless before he was born God had foreordained his salvation. Puritanism required that man refrain from sin but told him he would sin anyhow. Puritanism required that he reform the world in the image of God's holy kingdom but taught him that the evil of the world was incurable and inevitable. Puritanism required that he work to the best of his ability at whatever task was set before him and partake of the good things that God had filled the world with, but told him he must enjoy his work and his pleasures only, as it were, absent-mindedly, with his attention fixed on God.

These paradoxical, not to say contradictory, requirements affected different people in different ways. Some lived in an agony of uncertainty, wondering each day whether God had singled them out for eternal glory or eternal torment. Some enjoyed a holy certainty and went their indomitable ways with never a look backward. Some spent their lives demonstrating to themselves and everyone else how holy they were. All labored hard, and some by so doing amassed great wealth or won fame among their fellow men—but never dared enjoy it.

Puritanism meant many things. But to young John Winthrop it principally meant the problem of living in this world without taking his mind off God. It would have been easier to withdraw from the world, as the monks and hermits did, to devote oneself wholly to God, but that was not permitted. Puritans must live in the world, not leave it. For a time Winthrop thought he would study divinity and enter the ministry. In that profession he might at least have been freed from the distractions of ordinary business in order to concentrate his attention on God. But his friends dissuaded him, and anyway it was not so much his business as his pleasures that laid snares for him. He was a countryman of simple tastes who liked good food, good drink, and good company. He liked his wife. He liked to stroll by the river with a fowling piece and have a go at the birds. He liked to smoke a pipe. He liked to tinker with gadgets. He liked all the things that God had given him, and he knew it was right to like them, because they were God-given. But how was one to keep from liking them too much? How love the world with moderation and God without?

After his marriage he tried one way after another to keep his exuberant worldly spirit within bounds and gradually denied himself many of the things that he liked most. He resolved, as he noted in a sporadic record he kept of his religious experiences, to give up his tinkering "and to content my selfe with such things as were lefte by our forefathers." He resolved to give up shooting, after a prolonged and revealing argument with himself. For one thing, he said, it was against the law, and "thoughe the lawe cannot binde from the use of the creatures, yet it may limitt the manner of taking them." It took too much time. It was too strenuous ("it toyles a mans bodye overmuch"). It was dangerous. It was expensive (if you were caught, the fine was more than a man ought to pay for such a sport). Finally he came to the most telling point: "lastly for mine owne part I have ever binne crossed in usinge it, for when I have gone about it not without some woundes of conscience, and have taken much paynes and hazarded my healthe, I have gotten sometimes a verye little but most commonly nothinge at all towards my cost and laboure." In other words, he was a poor shot!

To Winthrop there was nothing incongruous or hypocritical about this reasoning. Shooting was not a legitimate recreation for a Puritan unless he got a satisfaction from it proportionate to the time and effort it cost. No Puritan objected to recreation as such; indeed it was necessary for a man to indulge in frivolous pleasures from time to time, in order that he might return to his work refreshed. But to serve the purpose, recreation had to be fun and not exhaust a man physically or bore him or frustrate him. It was no fun for Winthrop to return weary from a shoot with nothing in his bag to hand his wife for dinner.

Dinner itself was another problem. He found that he liked his food too well and after a heavy meal was more ready to continue with other pleasures of the flesh than to go back to the tedious business of casting accounts and collecting rents. Whenever he indulged himself excessively in this or any other way he regretted it afterwards and compensated by an overzealous abstemiousness, so that for a time his life vibrated dizzily between indulgence and restraint: "When I had some tyme abstained from suche worldly delights as my heart most desired, I grewe very melancholick and uncomfortable, for I had been more careful to refraine from an outward conversation in the world, than to keepe the love of the world out of my heart, or to uphold my conversation in heaven; which caused that my comfort in God failinge, and I not daringe to meddle with any earthly delights, I grewe into a great dullnesse and discontent: which beinge at last perceived, I examined my heart, and findinge it needfull to recreate my minde with some outward recreation, I yielded unto it, and by a moderate exercise herein was much refreshed." But here grew the mischief: "I perceivinge that God and mine owne conscience did alowe me so to doe in my need, I afterwards tooke occasion, from the benefite of Christian libertie, to pretend need of recreation when there was none, and so by degrees I ensnared my heart so farre in worldly delights, as I cooled the graces of the spirit by them."

And so the cycle would begin again. It was no good to put temptations away; that was to live out of the world. Once when he had gone to London on a business trip, which freed him to enjoy God undistracted by the cares and pleasures that surrounded him at home—London itself apparently held no temptations for him—he found that he felt only a spiritual deadness, "without any great sence either of guilt or peace." From this experience he drew the appropriate Puritan conclusion, "that he which would have suer peace and joye in Christianitye, must not ayme at a condition retyred from the world and free from temptations, but to knowe that the life which is most exercised with tryalls and temptations is the sweetest, and will prove the safeste. For such tryalls as fall within compasse of our callinges, it is better to arme and withstande them than to avoide and shunne them."

This was what he had been telling himself all along and continued to tell himself again and again: "O Lord, crucifie the world unto me, that though I cannot avoyd to live among the baites and snares of it, yet it may be so truely dead unto me and I unto it, as I may no otherwise love, use, or delight in any the most pleasant, profitable, etc, earthly comforts of this life, than I doe the ayre which I continually drawe in, or the earthe which I ever tread upon, or the skye which I ever behould."

As the years went by and he kept repeating these injunctions to himself, Winthrop gradually reduced the extent of his oscillation between abstinence and excess. It took time, time to cool the blood, time to grow in the spiritual strength that alone could hold him to a steady course of godliness in a world of temptations. But in the end, before he was forty, he was successful in containing the tension. How successful was evident in his married life.

Marriage he knew to be a good thing, but like everything else it had to be prevented from becoming too good. A man must love his wife, and she must love him. Love was a duty and hopefully a pleasure too, but it must be kept within bounds. It must never exceed or overpower or in any way diminish love for God. The possibility of rivalry between these two kinds of love was no mere figure of speech, for the Puritan's religion was no desiccated moralism. The Puritan loved his God with all the sensual abandon he denied himself in dealing with the world. John Winthrop, who was generally considered a grave and sober man by his contemporaries, found the most suitable images for his religion in the Song of Solomon, and in a letter to a friend might suddenly turn to address God in an embarrassingly sexual apostrophe: "Drawe us with the sweetnesse of thine odours, that we may runne after thee, allure us, and speak kindly to thy servantes, that thou maist possess us as thine owne, in the kindnesse of youth and the love of marriage . . . let us heare that sweet voyce of thine, my love my dove, my undefiled: spread thy skirt over us and cover our deformitye, make us sicke with thy love: let us sleep in thine armes, and awake in thy kingdome."

Some religions, recognizing the difficulty of reconciling this kind of heavenly passion with the love of a wife or mistress, have advocated celibacy. For the Puritan no such solution was open. He must know and enjoy both kinds of love at once.

John Winthrop's first wife was an earthly woman who listened patiently to his religious counsels and behaved herself as befitted the wife of a gentleman, but never caught the fire of Puritanism that burned in her husband. She bore him six children in ten years and died in 1615. Within six months he consoled himself by marrying Thomasine Clopton, a godly young woman of an old and respected Suffolk family. On the first anniversary of their wedding she too died, and after waiting a little over a year, at the age of thirty John married again, this time Margaret Tyndal, the daughter of Sir John Tyndal of Much Maplestead in Essex. As usual, John seems to have received a substantial dowry, but from Margaret's later letters it is evident that he received much more than that.

Margaret was a very womanly woman, one of the most appealing in American history. "A very gracious woman," her husband once called her, and the adjective was as fitting in the modern sense as in the religious one that he intended. Her letters, written in a neat and labored script, are full of tenderness, as for example when her husband was in London and afflicted with a sore hand: "I will not looke for any longe letters this terme because I pitty your poore hande if I had it heare I would make more of it than ever I did, and bynde it up very softly for feare of hurting it." Or again, "It is now late and bed time and I must bid thee good night before I am wilinge for I could finde in my hart to sit and talke with thee all night." But she is as much a Puritan as her husband and never forgets that he is only a man and that her highest love must be reserved for God, who is pleased "to exercise us with one affliction after another in love, lest wee should forget our selves and love this world to much." She can even write, with no intention of irony, that a solemn letter of her husband's "did make a very good supply in stead of a sarmon."

John's letters during his occasional absences from Groton often had a good deal of the sermon about them, but they were never lacking in homely warmth. "It is now bedd tyme," he closes one, "but I must lye alone, therefore I make lesse haste." Every letter takes up the theme of their love and how it must lose itself in a higher love, but the tension has been contained, and he can slip easily from reflections on eternity to "I feared thou shouldst take could and therefore I have sent thee another garment." In Margaret Tyndal he had found a woman he could love without losing himself in mere earthly passion.

At thirty Winthrop had become familiar with himself. He knew what temptations were likely to conquer him, and he had discovered how to meet them. Above all else he had learned to stick to business. If he worked hard at whatever task lay before him, he could take his pleasures in stride. Of course work itself could be a snare. It was easy to become engrossed in it for its own sake or for the sake of the worldly rewards it brought. A man who labored merely for gain, with no thought for God, was no better than a libertine. But he who worked because God willed it, multiplying his talents like a good and faithful servant, could throw himself into his job almost as a way of worship, without fear of losing balance. That he might amass a fortune in the process was an incidental benefit, not to be treated as a goal, but not to be rejected if it came. Though Winthrop was a notably conscientious worker, he apparently had no difficulty in maintaining the right attitude to his work. It never obscured his view of God as the pleasures of the flesh so often did.

Winthrop's principal work during the early years of his first marriage was doubtless the management of his estate. For three years he and his bride lived on at Groton, where, under Adam's watchful eye, he could collect rents and fines from tenants and supervise the farming without exposing his estate to the dangers of youth and inexperience. From Groton the couple moved to Mary's home in Great Stambridge, where the dowry lands were located. In both places, along with advice in managing his own lands, he probably received the opportunity to participate in running the larger parental estates.

During these same years he began the study of law. Perhaps the ordinary affairs of a country gentleman left him with more free time than a conscientious Puritan gentleman could legitimately claim for recreation; or perhaps he made time for study, because a knowledge of the law would better enable him to perform the work in life which God had set him. As future lord of Groton Manor he would need to know something of the law or else hire someone who did, for at regular intervals, probably every three weeks, he would have to hold a manorial court at which his tenants might sue each other in a wide variety of small actions. The lord of the manor did not have to preside himself. Adam Winthrop occasionally held courts for neighboring lords, and when John was twenty-one, on a visit home from Stambridge, Adam let him hold his first court at Groton, presumably to give him a little experience in a job that would occupy him extensively in the future.

Holding manorial court was good training not only for a future lord of the manor, but for any gentleman who might someday wish to practice law. That John Winthrop may have been thinking of this possibility is suggested by the fact that in 1613 he was admitted to Gray's Inn, one of the Inns of Court in London, where young gentlemen studied law. How long he stayed there is not evident, but by 1617 he was back in Suffolk as one of the county's justices of the peace, a post reserved for persons of importance—and importance meant property.

By the criterion of property John Winthrop was becoming a man of importance. Sometime before 1618 his father turned over the lordship of Groton Manor to him. This, combined with the properties acquired through his different wives, must have left him better off than his father had been. Adam, at any rate, seems never to have held the office of justice. Though John did not hold it continuously, it gave him a larger acquaintance with the law than he could have gained in the manorial court, for the quarter sessions of the justices of the peace tried almost every kind of criminal case except those involving treason. Moreover, as a justice, John gained something that might prove more valuable to his career than a knowledge of the law—a familiarity with the other big men of the county.

From his point of view this was not all gain. Though he kept himself strictly to business, working at his job with the devotion that he knew God demanded of him, he found that the other justices took a somewhat lighter view of their duties and of the world in general. For a man who was doing his best to keep his earthly passions in check, it was a trying experience to come up against some of these confident squires. "Methought," he wrote later, "I hearde all men tellinge me I was a foole, to sett so light by honour, credite, welthe, jollitie etc: which I sawe so many wise men so much affecte and joye in, and to tye my comforte to a conversation in heaven, which was no where to be seene, no way regarded, which would bring my selfe and all my gifts into contempt." He comforted himself with the fact that the servants of God always meet with contempt in this world, and fortified himself as he trotted to or from the sessions by saying prayers and singing psalms.

In spite of his meticulous attention to duty, in spite of his want of humor and his psalm-singing, it is unlikely that many of his new associates laughed at him. He was not the only Puritan gentleman in Suffolk. Sir Nathaniel Barnardiston, as big a man as you could find out-side the ranks of the nobility, with an estate said to be worth £4000 a year, was a Puritan too. His grandfather had been educated under Calvin at Geneva, during the exile of the Protes-tants in the days of Queen Mary, and he himself was as ardent a believer as Winthrop. Mov-ing into the circle occupied by the leading men of the country, Winthrop found others who shared his views, men with their eyes on heaven but their hands in the everyday business of their callings. Through these men of consequence Winthrop felt his own world expand. His father had once studied law in London, but had then retired to the fastness of Groton Manor. For Adam, Groton was world enough. John was moving along another path, toward a larger world.

As he moved, the problem of living in the world assumed new dimensions. He had learned to discipline himself, to use the good things of the earth without being used by them. But as he moved out from Groton Manor into a position of prominence in the county, as he joined in executing the laws of the land, he could not fail to see that living in the world demanded more than a taming of the heart. The world itself required discipline. Though a Puritan must live in it, he need not, must not, take it as he found it. The world, within limits, was plastic, and Winthrop was beginning to feel that he should lend a hand in shaping it.

III
A Shelter and a Hiding Place

Edmund S. Morgan

———•——•——•———

The idea of going to the New World was not novel. For more than a century Englishmen and other Old World travelers had drifted back and forth across the Atlantic, coasting the shores of North America, looking for a way through to the Pacific, looking for gold, catching fish, and trading with the strange people they encountered. The people had little to trade except for the furs of American animals, but what they got in return was more than the cloth and kettles and trinkets offered to them. The Europeans unwittingly brought with them a host of diseases—tuberculosis, diphtheria, smallpox—against which the native inhabitants had none of the biological immunities that the winnowing of centuries had conferred on the popula- tion of the Old World. As a result, by the time Winthrop and his friends thought of settling across the seas, massive epidemics had wiped out most of the men and women who might have stood in their way. By 1629 a few English settlers and fishermen had already moved in, planting themselves here and there along the American coast and on the islands that stood off it, learning to live from the land, with the assistance of the surviving natives (who neverthe- less continued to die both silently and violently from the contact).

The King of England had no hesitation in laying claim to the whole continent, or of authorizing his subjects to people it for him. They had settled Virginia in 1607; and although the colonists had perished at first almost as rapidly as they came, two or three thousand of them were well established now. Others had colonized Bermuda and Barbados. In New En- gland a group of Separatists had been living at Plymouth since 1620; and in 1623 a contin- gent of fishermen and farmers put down at Cape Ann, backed by a company of merchants calling themselves the Dorchester Adventurers. Though the merchants gave up by 1627 and most of the settlers returned to England, a few hung on in a village they named Salem.

In the circles where Winthrop moved, among the Puritan gentry of the eastern coun- ties, there had been interest in colonization even before Charles I's final dissolution of Parlia- ment in 1629. Noblemen with Puritan leanings had already invested in such ventures and showed a continuing interest that can scarcely be attributed to any financial returns they obtained. The founding of colonies was a notoriously unprofitable activity, and though the hope of striking it rich still led otherwise sane businessmen to invest modestly in colonies, there was probably a thought in the minds of many Puritans who squandered their money this way that a colony in the New World, if managed properly, might prove a port in the storm that was obviously brewing. Some wanted to acquire an island in the West Indies; others favored New England.

Actually a group of gentlemen and noblemen known as the Council for New England had already received a royal grant to the whole of New England in 1620. They had not yet made a serious colonizing effort, but they were willing to allow settlements on their land; and in 1628 they granted a charter to a group of Puritan merchants organized as the New England Company. The charter authorized the company to settle and govern the area from three miles south of the Charles River to three miles north of the Merrimack. This tract included the settlement at Salem, and the company immediately sent over Captain John Endecott, a veteran of the Dutch wars and a good Puritan, to take charge there. With him they sent a shipload of servants whom he was to employ in collecting the commodities supposed to abound in the country— sarsaparilla and sassafras (valued at the time as medicines), furs, and silk grass.

John Winthrop was not a member of the New England Company, and he was not optimistic about the prospects of colonial life. His second son, Henry, had gone to Barbados to make his fortune in 1627 and returned two years later with expensive habits and no fortune. But Barbados was not a Puritan settlement. When his oldest son, John, Jr., proposed to join Endecott's group, Winthrop received the idea favorably, if not enthusiastically. "I know not wheare you should goe with such religious company and under such hope of blessinge," he told his son, but urged him not to commit himself permanently to living in the New World. John thought it over, decided to try the Mediterranean instead, and went off on a fourteen-month tour of Constantinople, Leghorn, and Venice. Before he returned, the New England Company had been transformed into the Massachusetts Bay Company, and John Winthrop himself was deeply interested in it. There had evidently been some doubt about the validity of the charter from the Council for New England, and before investing heavily in the region, the members of the New England Company wished to make their title to it more secure. In March 1629, just a week before Charles dissolved his last Parliament, they managed—how is not clear—to obtain a royal charter confirming the grant and changing the name of the company to the Governor and Company of the Massachusetts Bay in New England.

Winthrop was at Groton when the royal charter was granted but took the road shortly afterwards to attend the Easter term of court. At London he found gentlemen putting their heads together over a bottle to whisper things that one no longer dared to speak aloud. Parliament was at an end; Arminian prelates were riding high; the Tower was loaded with Puritan patriots. Everywhere, for those who could see through the glitter of Charles's self-assurance, the clouds of God's wrath seemed to be gathering. Members of the Massachusetts Bay Company were looking toward their colony with quickened interest. Winthrop doubtless talked with some of them. Possibly he already had emigration in mind when he wrote home to Margaret on May 15, 1629, "If the Lord seeth it wilbe good for us, he will provide a shelter and a hidinge place for us and ours."

A fortnight later he was able to snatch a brief holiday at Groton before the Trinity term of court began on June 5. As he and Margaret sat together in the long June evenings there was much to talk about: not only the alarming degeneration of the country but the even more spectacular degeneration of their son Henry, who had been painting the town red ever since his return from Barbados. On a visit to Uncle Fones in London he had turned the household into a veritable inn for his riotous companions and on top of that had wooed and won his cousin Bess, Fones's daughter, without so much as a by-your-leave from her father. Fones told Winthrop, "They both pretend to have proceeded so far that there is no recalling of it." They had been hastily married and shipped off to Groton for a honeymoon. But both John and Margaret feared that Henry had not yet settled down, and it would be easy for a father to think that the boy might behave in a more godly fashion if he lived in a more godly community. At any rate, Winthrop thought more and more of New England, and Margaret, being the woman she was, doubtless assured him that she would follow wherever he led.

Winthrop returned to his duties in London to find that his brother-in-law, Emmanuel Downing, was leaning strongly in the same direction, and he wrote at once to Margaret, "I am still more confirmed in that course which I propounded to thee." Two weeks later he sent her news "that wilbe more wellcome to thee, than a greate deale of other. My Office is gone, and my chamber, and I shalbe a saver in them both: so as I hope, we shall now enjoye each other againe as we desire." Possibly Winthrop resigned the office voluntarily in preparation for emigration. But whether he left England or not, his work in London was hardly worth continuing. The expense of travel and lodgings ate up most of the extra earnings, and since the doors to preferment were now closing against Puritans, the job was unlikely to be a springboard to a higher and more effective public office, which might have compensated for the pain of being so often separated from Margaret.

Though he had not yet made a firm decision to leave England, he had certainly begun to lean in that direction. As he himself later phrased it, "when God intendes a man to a worke he setts a Byas on his heart so as tho' he be tumbled this way and that yet his Bias still drawes him to that side, and there he restes at last." Winthrop's bias was now drawing him toward New England. To be sure that God had set it in him, he analyzed the problem of emigration as though it were a legal case, himself the client, and amassed evidence from as many sources as he could reach: from the directors of the Massachusetts Bay Company to satisfy himself of their motives and of the likelihood of success; from the Puritan clergymen he knew, for their opinion of its acceptability to God; from his friends, because they knew him and his situation and would not hesitate to speak plainly if they detected self-deception in his decisions. The sum of all the evidence he incorporated into a remarkable series of documents, designed to convince himself and others of the desirability of moving to New England. They were circulated among important Puritans and were a powerful persuasive to Winthrop's contemporaries.

Winthrop had no desire to become a martyr. His arguments were those of a man accustomed to success and intending to have more of it. Several arguments demonstrated that England offered fewer opportunities for worldly success than America. "This land growes wearye of her Inhabitants," he wrote, referring to the depression which had put so many people, especially in Suffolk, out of work. People were too extravagant: a man was hard pressed to "keep sayle with his equalls," and all arts and trades were "carried in that deceiptfull and unrighteous course, as it is allmost impossible for a good and upright man to maintaine his charge and live comfortably in any of them," even an attorney in the Court of Wards. Indeed, in no trade could one expect a suitable recompense for time and labor, "except falshood he admitted to equall the balance." At the same time land was so hard to come by that men would spend as much for an acre or two as would buy many hundreds in America.

But wait. The King might lay claim to the continent, but what about the people already living there? Winthrop had heard of the epidemics that had wiped out so many, though he could scarcely have known how many, and he saw in their destruction the hand of God making way for the godly. Those who remained alive would have no need for the vast tracts of land around them. There would be, he argued, "more than enough for them and us," especially as he had heard that "they inclose no ground, neither have they cattell to maintayne it." So "why may not christians have liberty to go and dwell amongst them in their waste lands and woods (leaving them such places as they have manured for their corne) as lawfully as Abraham did among the Sodomites?" The translation of Indians into Sodomites was more than a figure of speech, for Europeans had already formed an enduring image of native Americans as savages under the thrall of Satan. Christians moving in among them would help save their souls and improve their lives, even while the Christians made the most of their own God-given talents in exploiting the opportunities of the New World.

Those opportunities probably figured more largely in Winthrop's religious consciousness than any missionary impulse. Just as he considered hunting with a gun a bad form of recreation because he got so little profit from it, so the move to New England would be wrong unless there was a good chance that the colony could be an economic success. A man's duty to God was to work at his calling and improve his talents like a good and faithful servant. If he could do it better in New England than in old, that was good reason for moving. God was the overwhelming reality, indeed the only reality. Success and failure were relevant only as indications, and not always reliable ones, of His satisfaction or displeasure with a man's efforts to serve Him as he passed through life.

In framing his arguments Winthrop relied heavily on the opinions and advice of the Puritan ministers he most respected. The most compelling argument on his list was the judgment which they thought God would shortly bring upon England. "All other Churches of Europe are brought to desolation," he wrote, "and it cannot be, but the like Judgment is comminge upon us: And who knows, but that God hath provided this place, to be a refuge for manye, whom he meanes to save out of the general destruction." He recorded the objection raised by some of his friends, that "we have feared a Judgment a longe tyme, but yet we are safe, soe it were better to staye till it come," to which he added the grim rejoinder: "It is like that this consideration made the Churches beyonde the seas (as the Palatinate, Rochell etc.) to sitt still at home, and not look out for shelter while they might have found it." The fact that so many of the ministers approved of the New England enterprise he felt to be a reliable sign of its acceptability to God, for surely God would not "seduce his people by his owne prophetts" to follow a course contrary to His will.

The Puritan clergy were also concerned about the infection of the younger generation by the contagious wickedness that surrounded them in England. "The fountains of learninge and religion are so corrupted," wrote Winthrop, "that most Children even the best wittes and of fayrest hopes, are perverted corrupted and utterly overthrowne by the multitude of evil examples and the licentious government of those seminaryes." Nowhere in the numerous drafts of Winthrop's arguments was a denial or an objection raised to this reason for emigration. Winthrop was apparently not the only Puritan father with a wayward son.

America offered many advantages over England; it was folly to sit still and wait the harvest of wrath that other men had sown. But one other thought kept recurring to Winthrop, a gnawing doubt not easily downed: would it not be deserting the world and one's fellow sinners to flee into a brave new land? Though one professed affection for all the saints and all the true churches of England, was it not in fact an act of separation to put three thousand miles of water between oneself and them? Though there might be opportunities to serve the Lord in New England, was it not a duty, especially for a man of some prominence, a justice of the peace, say, to stay in England and keep on striving to bring righteousness there?

This was the question that troubled Winthrop most, and he posed it plainly: "It wilbe a great wronge to our owne Churche and Countrye to take awaye the good people, and we shall laye it the more open to the Judgment feared." Other Puritans felt the objection strongly too, and applied it closely to Winthrop, who was becoming a more important man to the Puritan cause than he may himself have realized. Robert Ryece, a well-known Suffolk antiquary and one of the many friends whom Winthrop consulted, told him bluntly, "The church and common welthe heere at home, hath more neede of your best abyllitie in these dangerous tymes, than any remote plantation."

In his first attempt, Winthrop was unable to answer this objection to his own complete satisfaction. He minimized the number of people involved: those who went would be few, as nothing by comparison with those left behind. Many served no public function in England. Besides, the church of Christ ought to be considered universal, without respect to countries, and it would be a good thing to convert the Indians. These were weak arguments, as he must have known, for he drew up another list, designed to prove "that persons of good use here (yea in publike service) may be transplanted for the furtherance of this plantation in New England."

Though Winthrop's own capacities for public service had hitherto been demonstrated only in local and minor offices, though he had never sat in Parliament, those who knew him evidently recognized that he had extraordinary talents. The members of the Massachusetts Bay Company in particular set their hearts on persuading him to join them, and the new list probably embodied the arguments they advanced to convince him that his services would be more acceptable to God in Massachusetts than in England. The line of reasoning this time was persuasive. The work of planting a godly colony in New England was acknowledged by all to be lawful and honorable. To ensure success, men of ability must engage in it. Probably few would feel inclined to do so, and therefore those with an inclination should also feel an obligation to go. In any case it was better to raise a new church where one did not exist than to labor to better part of an old one. Moreover, a lesser public office might lawfully be deserted for a larger one in another place. Finally, it might be a greater service to the churches of England to preserve a remnant pure in the wilderness than to strive in vain for purity at home. In better times the remnant could expand and extend itself back to the mother country. "It was a good service to the Churche of the Jewes that Joseph and Marye forsooke them, that their mesiah might be preserved for them against tymes of better service." As Winthrop struggled to get over his most difficult moral hurdle, these last two arguments gave him confidence.

His friends in the Bay Company could press the argument of lesser and greater public offices by assuring him that in New England important men would be few, and he would certainly have a leading hand in public affairs, whereas in England his role was minor and likely to become more so in consequence of his dwindling estate. Three of his sons had come of age, and he had launched them with gifts of land that left his own holdings shrunk to half their former size. He would thus no longer be so important a man in the county and would therefore not be appointed to the public offices he could otherwise expect, "and so if he should refuse this opportunitye, that talent, which God hathe bestowed upon him for publike service, were like to be buried." In the margin he phrased it more pungently: "When a man is to wade throughe a deepe water, there is required tallnesse, as well as Courage, and if he findes it past his depth, and God open a gapp another waye, he may take it." Winthrop knew that in England he was not tall enough to do anything effective for the cause of God against the towering ungodliness of King Charles, but in New England Charles would cast a small shadow indeed, and Winthrop would be the giant.

Winthrop did not aim at power for the sake of power, but he longed to use his talents in the cause of God. Massachusetts, his friends in the Bay Company assured him, was the place to do so. The colony was to be a refuge for truth, a religious rather than a commercial enterprise. To attract godly settlers was the main concern, and Winthrop could not deny the argument that, if men who were "knowne to be godly and live in wealthe and prosperity heere, shall forsake all this" to participate in the emigration, their presence would go far to convince the right kind of people that the enterprise was what it purported to be. Winthrop did not doubt the sincerity of his friends in the Bay Company, but they were, after all, only members of the company and could not with authority speak for the whole. The other members might be too shrewd to gainsay the godly motive, which was "such a bewtifull pretexte" that it furnished the answer to all objections. This was the comment of Robert Ryece, who was suspicious of the whole business. "The pipe goeth sweete," he warned Winthrop, "tyll the Byrde be in the nett, many bewtifull hopes are sett before your eyes to allewer you to danger."

What guarantee could there be that the suspicions of Ryece were unwarranted? What if godly settlers failed to be attracted? Or if, after they got to America, the weakling relative or favorite of some influential company official were sent to misrule them and perhaps wreck the whole venture? And if the new colony proved financially unsuccessful, what was to prevent the Massachusetts Bay Company from pulling out and leaving the settlers holding the bag? These were disturbing questions; but a complete and daring answer was already in preparation.

IV
The Way to a New England

Edmund S. Morgan

Winthrop was in close communication with the leaders of the Massachusetts Bay Company throughout the weeks when he was trying to make up his mind. On July 28, 1629, he and several other prominent Puritans who were interested in emigrating assembled in Lincolnshire to talk it over. They met at Tattershall, the home of Isaac Johnson and his wife the Lady Arbella. Johnson was a member of the company, himself planning to emigrate, and one of those most intimately concerned with trying to enlist Winthrop in the enterprise. He had summoned the meeting to discuss a plan for the government of the colony, a plan so extraordinary that it swept away Winthrop's last doubts.

The Massachusetts Bay Company was a trading corporation with powers of ownership and government over a specified area. There were other such corporations in England with powers over other areas. All held their meetings at London or Plymouth or whatever other English city had been assigned in their charters, and sent governors to carry out their orders in their respective domains across the seas. When the Massachusetts Bay Company obtained its charter, the King and his advisers undoubtedly assumed that it would hold its meetings in London, and so presumably did the members of the company. But through oversight, design, or indifference, no place of meeting was prescribed. It was now proposed to take advantage of the omission by moving the place of meeting to the colony itself. In this way the governor of the company could become himself the governor of the colony, and the general court of the company could become the legislative assembly of the colony.

This daring proposal would effectively remove the colony from control by the Crown. The governmental powers of the company were extensive, greater in many ways than those which the King exercised in England. But as long as the company held its meetings in England, the King and his ministers could easily keep the members under surveillance. If they got too far out of line, as the Virginia Company of London had, they might forfeit their charter, and the King might take over the government of the colony. But if the company moved lock, stock, and barrel to the New World, who would ever know what they were up to?

The advantages of such a move to the Puritans who composed the majority of the membership were obvious. If the company moved to New England, it could become in effect a self-governing commonwealth, with the charter a blank check justifying everything it did. It would thus be able to enforce the laws of God and win divine favor. It could create in New England the kind of society that God demanded of all His servants but that none had yet given Him. The colony would not be a mere commercial enterprise, nor would it be simply a hiding place from the wrath of God. It would be instead the citadel of God's chosen people, a spearhead of world Protestantism.

To be part of such a holy enterprise would justify a man in casting off larger responsibilities than those of a justice of the peace. And it was made clear to Winthrop that his part in the venture would be a crucial one. For two weeks he remained in Lincolnshire, while Johnson and others impressed upon him the extraordinary opportunity and the urgency of his participation. In the end he was forced to admit (speaking in the third person), "It is come to that Issue as (in all probabilitye) the wellfare of the Plantation dependes upon his goeinge, for divers of the Cheife undertakers (upon whom the reste depende) will not goe without him." He could hesitate no longer. On August 26 he rode to Cambridge, where he with eleven other leading Puritans signed an agreement to be ready by the following March to embark for New England, provided that "before the last of September next the whole governement together with the Patent for the said plantacion bee first by an order of Court legally transferred and established to remayne with us and others which shall inhabite upon the said plantacion."

Matthew Cradock, the governor of the company, had meanwhile officially informed the members of the proposal, and on August 29 they met to consider it. Seven of those who had participated in the Cambridge agreement were on hand to press for acceptance. Some members, who had no intention of going to the colony themselves, were reluctant to let their controlling reins slip free, but enough were moved by the arguments of the Cambridge group so that when the question was finally put, "it appeared by the generall consent of the Company, that the government and pattent should bee setled in New England."

Winthrop was thus committed to his decision. The recognition that he must live in the world had led him to the paradoxical conclusion that he should withdraw from the only part of the world he had ever known. Having learned to use the good things that God gave man, he had reached out to strike down the evils that God forbade, and in so doing found that he must save not merely Groton or Suffolk County but England herself. And now he had determined to reach still farther: England, for the moment, could not be saved in England, and perhaps could not be saved at all. The only hope was to cross the water and establish a government of Christ in exile.

The next six months were hectic ones. Before sailing he must put all his affairs in order, transform into the unstable currency of the day the lands which he and his father and grandfather had so painfully acquired, prepare to leave, perhaps forever, the manor where every corner, every tree, every hollow in the ground was as familiar as his own hand. He had learned his Puritan lessons well, and he never set down what it cost him in heartache to put this good part of the world behind him. He did not attempt to conceal, however, what it meant to leave Margaret, even for a short time.

For a while he thought of taking her with him on the first voyage, but when she and Henry's wife both became pregnant, it seemed best that they wait out their time in England. Samuel, Margaret's two-year-old, would stay with them. So would Forth, who was about to be married, and John, Jr., whom Winthrop deputed to conclude the family business and keep the colonists supplied during the first year. John, Jr., had inherited his father's strength of character, and Winthrop was happy to have him at his back. He knew too that John would take good care of Margaret. She was disheartened by the prospect of their separation. As he hurried about his preparations for departure, he dashed off brief letters to cheer her and calm her anxiety about his own safety. "My dear wife," he would write, "be of good courage, it shall go well with thee and us . . . therefore rayse up thy thoughts, and be merrye in the Lorde."

Winthrop had little time for his family in these last months. While winding up his personal affairs he suddenly found the direction of the whole New England enterprise thrust upon him. He had anticipated that he would have a leading role in New England, and when the company decided to transfer the government and charter to New England, he knew that some member who was going there would be elected governor. But he seems not to have expected that he would be the man, even though he was by now a member of the company and therefore eligible for the office. On October 20, 1629, the General Court of the Massachusetts Bay Company (the title of the meeting of members), after nominating four candidates for governor, Winthrop, John Humfrey, Isaac Johnson, and Sir Richard Saltonstall, picked Winthrop by "a generall vote and full consent." "So it is," he wrote his wife, "that [it] hath pleased the Lorde to call me to a further trust in this business of the plantation, than either I expected or finde my selfe fitt for." This at least assured him that he had been right in thinking he would find a more active employment of his talents in the New England venture than at home, but it also meant a great deal of unexpected work to be done before sailing. He must now take charge of the arrangements for the whole expedition: ships, provisions, and passengers.

Of the three, the last was the most difficult task. Winthrop had already started to drum up settlers before he became governor. As soon as he returned from Tattershall with his own mind made up, he set to work on the local prospects. He also committed to paper the arguments and answers to objections which had for weeks been piling up in his own mind. These passed from hand to hand in prominent Puritan circles, where the main campaign was conducted. There were, however, many non-Puritans who were eager to join the godly expedition for economic reasons. It was Winthrop's privilege to reject unsuitable applicants, but it was also his responsibility to see the colony supplied with men trained in all the trades necessary to its success. However desirable it was to have none but godly settlers, if the passenger list lacked a necessary sawyer, cooper, surgeon, or whatever, he must supply one somehow. Much of his time went to sifting letters of recommendation, searching out suitable men with suitable trades, and arranging sponsors to pay the passage of those who could not pay their own. It was generally possible to find someone who would pay the fare of the skilled but poor, and give them bed and board for a specified number of years in return for their services. Settlers who could afford it carried a number of these servants with them, and some of the most essential craftsmen were doubtless transported at the company's expense. Winthrop himself brought at least four entire families and probably more as part of his own household.

While putting together and equipping and financing his expedition, Winthrop had to deal with a problem created by the transformation of a trading company into a holy experiment. The Massachusetts Bay Company had attracted many stockholders who did not wish to adventure their lives along with their money in the New World. The problem was to furnish these less ardent souls with some return on their investment. An agreement was finally worked out whereby the remaining resources of the company would be managed for seven years by "undertakers"—five in England, five in Massachusetts—the profits to be distributed at the end of the period. Long before the seven years were up, it became apparent that there would be no profits. Nevertheless, though the Massachusetts Bay Company, like most colonizing companies, did not prove a sound business investment, probably most of the men who footed the bill did not count the money as wholly lost.

Winthrop's difficulties as governor, even while still in England, were not entirely financial and managerial. As preparations went forward, people all over England talked about the venture. A thousand men and women were selling their possessions and saying good-bye to their friends. Since most of them were Puritans, it was easy to infer that they were Separatists, come-outers who had decided at last to repudiate and defy both England and her churches. Winthrop and his friends were very sensitive to the charge. They were painfully aware that to all appearances they were walking out of a difficult situation. They were sure that they were acting in the best interests of those who remained behind, that the pure church they intended to establish in New England would someday, somehow, rescue its English parent from the mire of corruption. But the fact that their action looked like desertion worried them far more than the dangers they would face in a wilderness. It gave them a half-recognized sense of guilt that cropped out occasionally in unexpected ways. Thomas Shepard, who became one of New England's most eminent ministers and a pillar of strength to Winthrop during a subsequent crisis, later confessed he was all but overcome when his first attempt to leave England was thwarted by stormy seas: "The Lord made me feare my affliction came in part for running too far in a way of separation from the mixt Assemblies in England: tho I blesse God I have ever beleeved that there are true churches in many parishes in England where the Lord sets up able men and ministers of his gospell; and I have abhorred to refuse to heare any able minister in England." Another minister, George Phillips, who lived near Groton and accompanied Winthrop to New England, was so obsessed with the need for avoiding separatism, so determined to avow his participation in the world with all its sins, that he declared not only the churches of England but also those of Rome to be true churches.

Such feelings did not prevent Phillips from leaving his own church for a purer one in the New World. But they made him and many other leaders of New England highly sensitive to any suggestion of schism from the Church of England. The founders were so dazzled by the godly purpose and unique opportunity of their mission in the wilderness that they could not acknowledge their departure from England as in fact a separation. They felt bound to protest too often and too loudly that it was no such thing. Before they left, John Cotton, the brilliant young minister of Boston in Lincolnshire, came down to Southampton and preached them a sermon reassuring them that they had a clear call from God for the work they had undertaken. But in order to reaffirm to their countrymen that they were not religious snobs, bent on demonstrating superior holiness, they published a statement avowing their great affection for the Church of England. They were not, they insisted, Separatists. They were not "of those that dreame of perfection in this world." They did not disavow their membership in the Church of England. "We desire," they told their countrymen, "you would be pleased to take notice of the principals, and body of our company, as those who esteeme it our honour, to call the Church of England, from whence wee rise, our deare Mother, and cannot part from our native Country, where she specially resideth, without much sadnes of heart, and many teares in our eyes, ever acknowledging that such hope and part as wee have obtained in the common salvation, we have received in her bosome, and suckt it from her breasts." It was an eloquent statement, a little too eloquent, but all the more deeply felt because of the facts that seemed to belie it.

Winthrop and his friends issued their statement from aboard the *Arbella*, the flagship of the expedition, on April 7, 1630, and the next day the ship was under way. Across the receding water his thoughts reached confidently back to Margaret. They had made an agreement to think of each other every Monday and Friday between five and six o'clock and so hold communion together. As soon as possible she would join him. "Oh how it refresheth my heart," he wrote to her, "to thinke that I shall yet againe see thy sweet face in the lande of the livinge, that lovely countenance that I have so much delighted in, and beheld with so great contente!"

And in the other direction, still more insistent, lay the vision of a new England.

VI
A Special Commission

Edmund S. Morgan

To please God the Puritans demanded of themselves a standard of behavior not far different from that required by most modern codes of morality. They did not think it necessary to be either prudes or prohibitionists. They did not dress in drab clothes or live in drab houses or speak in drab words. The people who appear in the pages of Winthrop's journal, the good men and women who showered him with venison and partridges and fat hogs to celebrate Margaret's arrival, the boys and girls who skipped rope on the decks of the *Arbella*, the men who built ships and caught fish and planted corn were all human enough.

Nevertheless, the Puritans did make strong demands on human nature, for they were engaged in a mission that required great exertion. They had undertaken to establish a society where the will of God would be observed in every detail, a kingdom of God on earth. While still aboard the *Arbella*, Winthrop had explained to his fellow emigrants their solemn commitment to this task. Every nation, they all knew, existed by virtue of a covenant with God in which it promised to obey His commands. They had left England because England was failing in its promise. In high hope that God was guiding them and would find their efforts acceptable, they had proposed to form a new society. Now God had demonstrated His approval. He had made way for them by a "special overruling providence." By staying His wrath so long and allowing them to depart in peace, by delivering them safe across the water, He had sealed a covenant with them and given them a special responsibility to carry out the good intentions that had brought them into the wilderness. Theirs was a special commission. And "when God gives a special Commission," Winthrop warned them, "He lookes to have it stricktly observed in every Article."

All must therefore work together to attain the end of their coming. They must not allow any selfish private motives to interfere with their plan, for though every society must make its covenant with God, they had been singled out, like Israel of old, to serve as a model for others. They would be a city set on a hill: "the eies of all people are uppon us; soe that if wee shall deal falsely with our god in this worke wee have undertaken and soe cause him to withdrawe his present help from us, wee shall be made a story and a by-word through the world, wee shall open the mouthes of enemies to speake evill of the wayes of god and all professours for Gods sake; wee shall shame the faces of many of gods worthy servants, and cause theire

64

prayers to be turned into Cursses upon us till wee be consumed out of the good land whither wee are goeing."

Winthrop was determined that Massachusetts should not deal falsely with God. Before arriving in New England, he and the other leaders of the exodus had thought long and hard about the articles of God's special commission, and they were confident that they knew what was required of them. They knew, in the most elementary terms, that they must punish every sin committed in Massachusetts. And punish they did, with the eager cooperation of the whole community, who knew that sin unpunished might expose them all to the wrath of God. Families became little cells of righteousness where the mother and father disciplined not only their children but also their servants and any boarders they might take in. In order that no one should escape this wholesome control, it was forbidden for anyone to live alone: unmarried men and maids were required to place themselves in some family if their own had been left behind. Parents were obliged to take care that all their children and apprentices learned to read, so that everyone would be able to see for himself in the Bible what opportunities for salvation God offered to man and what sins He forbade. The churches were thronged every Sunday with willing and unwilling worshipers—everyone was required to attend—and church members guarded each other's morals by censuring or excommunicating those who strayed from the straight path.

With virtually the whole population for a police force Winthrop found it no problem to punish sin. It was sometimes difficult, however, to determine exactly what was sinful and what was not. The grosser forms of sin were easily identified. Among the emigrants were men—and women too—who stole and fought and made love without a marriage contract and cursed their betters with primeval eloquence. In these cheerful practitioners sin wore obvious labels. But some cases were not so clear. The line between sin and mere temptation or between sin and simple human pleasure was often a thin one. Yet Winthrop knew that that line must be firmly drawn, for it would be as wrong to forbid what God allowed as it would be to allow what He forbade.

How easy it was to err and how earnestly the Puritans sought to avoid error may be seen in their treatment of the problem of alcohol. The Puritans did not make the simple mistake of condemning all use of alcohol. Liquor was one of the good things that God had furnished His people for their comfort, nourishment, and recreation. Drunkenness, however, was wrong, and the Puritans punished it without hesitation. But the path from drink to drunkenness was so short and easy that they found it hard to decide whether any barriers should be placed along it. Since the path seemed to be even shorter for Indians than for Englishmen, the authorities at one time forbade the sale of all liquors to them but later relented on the ground that it was "not fit to deprive the Indians of any lawfull comfort which God aloweth to all men by the use of wine." For themselves the closest the Puritans came to a self-denying ordinance was a law forbidding people to drink toasts to one another. In passing it they hoped to prevent drunkenness, quarreling, bloodshed, uncleanness, misuse of precious time—and the waste of wine and beer.

Here, in spite of the appeal to frugality, they went beyond the terms of God's commission, for they were forbidding a temptation rather than a sin. Winthrop's friend and adviser Thomas Shepard, the respected minister of the church at Cambridge, pointed out the defection. The law, said Shepard in a letter to Winthrop, was all wrong. By treating a temptation as a sin, it would provoke God, for this was making "more sins than (as yet is seene) God himselfe hath made."

In general Winthrop avoided such errors of judgment himself. But many men who had not learned the lesson he had were determined to set up more sins than God did, because they did not know the limits of man's ability and of God's commands. These well-meaning zealots failed to recognize that God's kingdom on earth must still be a kingdom of flesh and blood, and their misdirected zeal soon indicated to Winthrop that he faced a far more difficult problem to control the good than to punish the wicked.

The authorities in England, of course, had a way of handling the problem of fanatics: bore their tongues, cut off their ears, brand them, imprison them, silence them. Though all these methods were ultimately used in Massachusetts, they did not commend themselves to anyone with Winthrop's political sense. The result of their use in England was not the suppression but the multiplication of fanatics, who swarmed out of the country to Holland and to New England. (They did not leave as fast as they multiplied, however, and in ten years' time rose up to overwhelm their oppressors.)

In Massachusetts Winthrop had no intention of making the mistakes that King Charles and Bishop Laud were making in England. He welcomed all Puritans who fled from the mother country. Every ship that arrived in Boston carried its cargo of them, simple men and women for the most part, who had come with much the same purpose in mind that he had, people who had learned not to aim higher than God demanded, and not lower, either. But among them was a liberal proportion of those who did aim too high.

Some were Separatists, men who had renounced the Church of England and proposed to live and worship in unblemished purity in the New World. Theirs was the position that Winthrop and his friends had expressly disavowed in the statement issued aboard the *Arbella* before departure. Others, while not separatist in name (because they failed to repudiate the Anglican Church), were nevertheless separatist by nature. They too looked for perfection in this world and had come to New England to be right while the rest of the world went wrong.

This separatist impulse was probably present to some degree in most settlers. The men who came to New England had shown, by so doing, that they were unwilling to tolerate evils that other men found tolerable. They had burned their bridges; they had lost whatever they had to lose through intransigence, and they were in consequence all the more ready to insist on their opinions, all the more reluctant to compromise. Some of them had stood before Bishop Laud and defied him. Would they hesitate to defy John Winthrop or anyone else who ventured to disagree with them?

To construct a commonwealth of such persons, a commonwealth "wherin the least known evils are not to bee tollerated," was a delicate task. Their constant demand for purity threatened in several ways the success of Winthrop's mission to the wilderness. Not only did they seek to read into the commission articles which God, in Winthrop's view at least, had not put there, but when their extravagant demands were not met, they threatened to disrupt the colony. The Separatist was always ready to disagree with his neighbors and, when they failed to meet his standards, to withdraw into a lofty and querulous independence, accompanied by all whom he could persuade to join him. In a population so heavily burdened with principles as that of Massachusetts, the danger of such withdrawals was constant. And if the process once began, there was no telling where it would stop. Separatism might splinter the colony into a hundred earnest little Utopias, each feeding on its own special type of holiness and each breeding new types, multiplying, like earthworms, by division. Separatists could disintegrate the colony and dissolve its special commission.

Separatism posed another, external danger when it reached the point of repudiating the churches of England. Winthrop and most of his colleagues thought that such a repudiation would be wrong in itself, a failure of charity, an arrogation of too exclusive a righteousness. But it would also be a danger to the execution of the colony's special commission, because it might excite the anger of the English Government. If the King and his bishops heard that Massachusetts disavowed the Church of England, they might revoke the charter and put an end to the whole experiment.

This was a danger not easily met. It was impossible to censor every letter sent home, and jubilant Puritans frequently wrote back in gloating terms about the purity of their churches by comparison with the corruption of England. "You that are under lee I hope forgett us not that are yett in the storme," an English friend wrote apprehensively to Winthrop, but too many New Englanders remembered their friends in England only to vaunt it over them. Occasionally individuals would return to the mother country to settle unfinished business, and these first innocents abroad proved quite as insufferable in their claims of superior holiness as later generations in their claims of superior plumbing. As a result the colony was in continual danger of interference from England.

The history of Massachusetts during Winthrop's lifetime is very largely the history of his efforts to meet the various dangers presented by separatism. No one could have been better equipped for the task, for Winthrop was obliged to do for Massachusetts precisely what he had already done for himself. He had learned not to avoid but to face temptations, not to spurn the good things that God had given him; even so he must restrain the overzealous from setting for the community a standard of godliness that would deny the humanity of human beings. He had learned not to expect perfection in this world, and to march in company with other sinners, for sin, though it must be punished, could not be stamped out. Even so he must temper the zeal of the Separatists and prevent them from splitting the community or leading it in search of impossible goals.

His success in suppressing the separatist impulse within himself was good reason for supposing that he might suppress it in Massachusetts. But he could not have foreseen how much more powerful a force separatism would prove in New England than it had in old.

In England the focal point of Puritan irritation had always been the church, and in Massachusetts the most important requirement of the colony's special commission, everyone agreed, was the establishment of churches organized precisely as God commanded. English Puritans had considered this crucial matter for three generations but had never been able to agree on what precisely God did command. They all knew there must be an end to bishops and archbishops, an end to the idolatrous ritual and trappings that exalted the clergy instead of God in the divine service, but they disagreed about two important matters.

One group, known as Presbyterians, insisted that the bishops be replaced by another organization, with churches and clergy arranged in a pyramidal structure: groups of churches would be formed into presbyteries, presbyteries into synods, and these collective bodies would exercise a supervisory control over their members. The other Puritans, who ultimately took the name of Congregationalists, had a simpler plan: destroy the bishops and then let each individual church, each congregation, be sufficient to itself. There was, they said, no church larger than a congregation.

The second point on which Presbyterians and Congregationalists differed was the composition of the church. The Presbyterians wished to continue the practice of admitting to membership and to the sacraments everyone who did not forefeit the privilege by some scandalously sinful behavior. The Congregationalists, on the other hand, insisted that membership be confined to persons who could prove, beyond a reasonable doubt, that they had been singled out by God for salvation. It was possible to tell who was a saint, they thought, even in this world, and while everyone must be made to attend church, only the saints should be admitted to membership.

The Congregationalists thus wished to make more sweeping changes than the Presbyterians. Some of them were so impatient with the Church of England that they did not wait for the opportunity to change it but simply withdrew and formed their own churches. These were the Separatists already noticed. Restriction of membership and local independence made it possible to begin a Congregational church anywhere that a handful of saints could be gathered for the purpose. Indeed, one of the men who first expounded the system called it "reformation without tarrying for any," a phrase which adequately states the aim of separatists in all ages.

In the mass migration of the 1630's many Separatists came and doubtless many Presbyterians, but the leaders and probably the majority of immigrants were Congregationalists who had declined to repudiate the English churches. Because they had refused to separate, they had had no previous practical experience in the operation of congregationalism and, with a very few exceptions, knew it only from books. Winthrop, for example, had been the patron of the church at Groton, with power to appoint the minister there. It is possible that he allowed the congregation to make the choice, according to Congregational precept, and it is likely that the Groton church was very lax about conforming to the prescribed rituals of the Church of England, but there could have been no exclusion of the unregenerate from membership. Consequently, neither Winthrop nor any of the other Puritans, who came from similar situations, could have appreciated in advance what forces would be released and what problems created by the wholesale practice of Congregationalism.

The first church within the boundaries of Massachusetts Bay to be founded in the congregational manner was "gathered" (the term usually employed) on July 20, 1629, at Salem by the settlers sent out under Endecott. As the great wave of men and women arrived the following year, they followed the instructions in their books and gathered churches as rapidly as they dug themselves in. By 1635 a dozen churches were scattered round the bay from Hingham to Newbury.

At its beginning a church contained only a handful of members. Usually it was thought proper to start with at least seven, though at Charlestown there were only four. The first members chose a minister and began the process of sifting the population of their town, or "plantation," to find the saints. In England a reputation for godliness and the willingness to join in a church forbidden by law had probably been sufficient evidence of sainthood. But in Massachusetts, with no bishop on hand to threaten the proceedings, churches became more choosy. Candidates were now obliged to describe their inward spiritual experiences, how they reached the moment of conversion, and how their subsequent lives had exhibited its effects. If they passed this examination, they were allowed to subscribe the church covenant, by which they agreed to join with the other members in worship and holy living. Having done so, they then participated in the judgment of future candidates. Generally a unanimous consent was required for every admission.

For ten years the human flood swept into Massachusetts, pushing up the rivers, swarming over the champion lands, some twenty thousand souls, and every soul was checked off as saved or damned. The effect on those who failed to make the grade is difficult to calculate. Some were doubtless conscientious Puritans who simply never felt the moving of grace in their souls and did not want admission without it. Others may have been hardened sinners who scorned admission on any terms, men who could wield a hammer and a spade and a tankard and curse the godly with a free heart. Whoever they were they made surprisingly few complaints about exclusion from the privileges of church membership.

The effect on the saints, however, was profound. They were required continually to pass judgment of the most dreadful kind on their fellow men. They must search not only their own souls for signs of grace, but also the souls of their neighbors. As they gathered together in their pure churches, placing the mark of holiness on their own foreheads and of damnation on most of their neighbors, the experience could not fail to induce that intellectual arrogance which is the breeder of separatism. Though in England they had denounced the evils of separation, the very act of forming a Congregational church necessitated an assumption of superior purity and thereby encouraged a separatist frame of mind. Never in

American history did a community produce separatists more attractive or more dangerous than those of early Massachusetts.

What made them dangerous was that the Congregationalism which propagated them also blocked the most obvious means of controlling them. Both in the Church of England and in the Presbyterian system a central organization could police the orthodoxy of individual churches. Congregationalism allowed no central organization: every church was independent. Thus while one distinctive feature of Congregationalism, regenerate membership, encouraged separatism, another feature, congregational autonomy, destroyed the most effective method of control. The people of Massachusetts had in fact undertaken an almost impossible task: they had accepted a commission which required them to follow a specific body of religious principles; but among those principles was one which encouraged the development of schism and another which denied them the means of preventing it.

The Puritans tried always to rest their religious principles, like their social, political, legal, and moral ones, on the Bible, the infallible guidebook for establishing a kingdom of God on earth. But the Bible, while it spoke with unquestioned authority, said different things to different people. To some it seemed to prescribe Presbyterianism, to others Congregationalism, and to different Congregationalists it said different things about baptism or sanctification or communion. The Congregationalists who founded New England were pretty well agreed on what it said about most matters, but among so many earnest students of the Bible, there was always one to discover a new and heretical meaning in a familiar passage and to demand that everyone else accept it. More often than not the innovator was a minister who used his pulpit to persuade his congregation, and the separatist impulse would soon be threatening to split that congregation away from the rest of the colony. With congregational independence recognized as a fundamental principle, what was to prevent it?

Fortunately, reason could heal differences as well as create them, and the Puritans were extraordinarily reasonable men. The zeal with which they studied the Bible sprang from supreme confidence in the ability of reason to find the truth there. Not knowledge but ignorance, they believed, was the mother of heresy. Therefore they listened with respect to everyone who could give reasons for an opinion, and if they thought the reasons faulty, they used every possible argument to show why. The paper relics of their contests have survived: the arguments and the answers to arguments and the replies to the answers and the answers to the replies to the answers, all loaded with scriptural citations. It was a tedious process, but usually it worked, because these people feared to err and took each other seriously.

Because they were so reasonable they were also able to do much by informal methods. The clergy were all learned men, skilled in marshaling arguments, and enjoyed therefore a social and intellectual prestige that enabled them to exert a powerful influence among their people—so powerful that New England Congregationalism came to be known as a speaking aristocracy in the face of a silent democracy. Though they were excluded from authority beyond their respective congregations, the handicaps of congregational independence were minimized when the ministers of a particular locality began meeting together in "consociations" to thrash out disagreements. If the ministers could agree, the congregations would be likely to. When an especially difficult problem arose, it was possible to call a synod, not of course the Presbyterian type of synod with authority to establish its findings, but a Congregational synod, which was simply a full meeting of the colony's ministers, whose findings had no more authority than the report of a committee of experts called in for consultation. No individual or church was obliged to abide by the report, but most pious men and women would hesitate to back their own views above the collective wisdom of the clergy.

Much could be done by such indirect methods to keep individuals and churches from flying off on separatist tangents. But in the end there had to be some tribunal, some court of last resort, to deal with the man or woman or church that had gone too far in separatism to listen to argument. Since each congregation could rightfully claim an absolute independence of the others, such a tribunal could not lie with the churches or with their clergy. But what was forbidden to the church was not necessarily forbidden to the state. The state was charged with the colony's commission. The state was responsible for suppressing heresy as well as drunkenness and theft and murder. In the hands of the state's government, then, lay the final, supreme responsibility. And John Winthrop came to Massachusetts as the head of that government. He had scarcely arrived when he began a series of moves to make of it a simple but effective instrument for controlling separatism and maintaining a colony united in the execution of God's commission.

IX
Separatism Unleashed

Edmund S. Morgan

As long as Winthrop held the reins of government he held them lightly. Though he never hesitated to strike down sin, he was keenly aware that Massachusetts was endangered more by separatist zeal than by worldly wickedness. He knew too that the time to check separatism was early, before it became blind to every obstacle. Argument, admonition, and patience were the most effective weapons against it. Winthrop used them to such advantage that for four years, while the settlers established themselves and their churches, Massachusetts was troubled by no deep rifts between man and man.

After the freemen turned Winthrop out of the governor's chair, they filled it for the three succeeding years with men of a less flexible nature. Thomas Dudley, John Haynes, and Henry Vane were all of a kind, easily intoxicated with their own righteousness. Of John Haynes, who succeeded Dudley as governor in 1635, it is enough to say that he had joined the attack on Winthrop's leniency. Henry Vane, a more complex character, was a mere boy of twenty-three when elected to the governorship in 1636, less than a year after his arrival in Massachusetts. His father was comptroller of the King's household, and he himself had an illustrious career in England ahead of him. At this time he was full of the magnetism, the enthusiasm, and the dedication of youth. Though he had a generosity of nature that was wholly lacking in Dudley, he had the same uncompromising devotion to principle, a devotion that would bring him one day to the scaffold. He was a good man, but a dangerous one to govern a colony already overloaded with zeal.

Though Winthrop's moderation had brought the colony successfully through the crucial first years, separatism still posed a threat to its mission if not to its survival. If the rigidity of his successors should prevail, there would be great danger of crippling schisms and secessions. The Great Migration was filling Massachusetts with men and women who were not afraid to take sides and not afraid to stand up against government. Among them, as it happened, was a man named Roger Williams, a charming, sweet-tempered, winning man, courageous, selfless, God-intoxicated—and stubborn—the very soul of separatism.

Williams had been in on the Massachusetts Bay project as early as Winthrop. During the meeting at Tattershall in 1629, when Winthrop talked the whole thing out with Isaac Johnson and the others, Williams had appeared and had probably taken part in the discussions. He was a young man, fresh from Cambridge, where he had studied divinity. In 1629 he was chaplain to Sir William Masham of High Laver in Essex. Sir William was one of Winthrop's clients in the Court of Wards, and Winthrop had doubtless heard good things of Williams from him.

Williams did not depart with Winthrop and the others in the spring of 1630 but arrived the following February, in the midst of that first dreadful winter. The ship which brought him was the *Lyon*, which Winthrop had sent back for provisions the previous fall. Winthrop noted her cargo approvingly, not only the supply of lemon juice which put an end to scurvy, but also the "godly minister." He arrived at an opportune time, for the Reverend John Wilson, teacher of the Boston church, was returning to England on the *Lyon* to fetch his wife. The congregation invited Williams to officiate during his absence, and here the first premonition of trouble appeared: he refused the offer. Williams had left England with none of the reluctance that troubled Winthrop and his friends, for Williams was an avowed Separatist: he felt no attachment whatever to the Church of England. In fact, since the churches of England were contaminated by the admission of unregenerate persons to communion, he could not regard them as churches at all. He had befouled himself by attending them in England; now that he was clear of them he cheerfully renounced them and repented his former weakness.

The Boston church, of course, did not admit unregenerate members. It was a true congregational church, open only to those who could prove themselves holy. But this was not enough for Williams. He could not bring himself to soil his new purity by joining in worship with people who, though pure themselves, failed to renounce the impurities of England. "I durst not," he later explained, "officiate to an unseparated people, as upon examination and conference I found them to be." Unless the members of the church would "make a public declaration of their repentance for having communion with the churches of England, while they lived there," he could not accept their offer.

Here was a Separatist indeed, who would separate not only from erroneous churches but also from everyone who would not denounce erroneous churches as confidently as he did. It is not clear whether the Boston church was tempted to accept his demands, but Winthrop assuredly was not. He liked Williams, as most people did, but this sweeping repudiation of the world went against his most deeply felt convictions. He prepared a little argument to demonstrate the necessity of reforming corruption "without an absolute separation." In it he rebuked all Separatists for their self-righteous denunciation of English church members as whores and drunkards. Although most Englishmen might be ignorant and misguided, he admitted, "yet whores and drunkards they are not: weake Christians they are indeed, and the weaker for want of that tender Care, that should be had of them: 1: by those that are sett over them to feede them: and next for that spirituall pride, that Sathan rooted into the hearts of their brethren, who when they are Converted, doe not, nor will not strengthen them, but doe Censure them, to be none of Gods people, nor any visible Christians."

Thus Winthrop reproached his young friend. Though Williams's opinions horrified him, it was characteristic of Winthrop to meet them with arguments and not merely with authority. There is no record that he made use of his position as governor to prevent the Boston church from accepting Williams's terms, but he may have hinted that he would do so if necessary, for before leaving Boston (within a few weeks), Williams expressed the dangerous opinion that civil magistrates had no authority in any religious matter, that they could not even require people to keep the Sabbath.

When Williams found that the Boston church was not pure enough for him, he made his way to Salem, where once again his charm and earnestness found an immediate response. In spite of his extreme views he never antagonized people by sanctimoniousness. He had a sweetness of spirit that clothed his harshest opinions with a mantle of holiness. He was a palpable saint, and in a society that set so high a value on sainthood, he could not fail to find men and women to follow wherever he might lead. At Salem John Endecott, whose heart was not easily won, capitulated at once. The church made Williams the same offer that the Boston church had.

Winthrop, hearing of what had happened, was alarmed, and after conferring with the assistants wrote sharply to Endecott, "marvelling" that the Salem church would choose a teacher who held such dangerous views. Williams's charms had not yet secured a strong enough hold on Salem to withstand the disapproval of the man who had pulled the colony through the starving months just finished, and who held, besides, the authority which God gave to righteous rulers. The offer was withdrawn, and Williams departed for the Plymouth colony, where Separatists were more welcome.

At Plymouth Williams was satisfied for a time. Though he worked hard at the hoe for his bread, as he later recalled, he found the church properly separated from the English churches and was content to join it and to assist the pastor by occasional preaching. William Bradford, the judicious governor of the colony, found him "a man godly and zealous, having many precious parts, but very unsettled in judgmente." Bradford was writing after the event, and his own judgment may have been unsettled by later developments, but it seems apparent that Williams's meticulous separatism proved too much even for Plymouth. In 1633, Bradford noted he "begane to fall into some strang opinions, and from opinion to practise; which caused some controversie betweene the church and him, and in the end some discontente on his parte, by occasion wherof he left them some thing abruptly."

The cause of Williams's discontent, by his own account, was the fact that the Plymouth church had not proved as separatist as he first supposed it to be. When members of the church returned on visits to England, they attended Church of England services there, and were not cast out of the Plymouth church for doing so. In this way the Plymouth church was communicating with the churches of England and by implication acknowledging them to be true churches. Williams, by remaining a member, shared in this acknowledgment; therefore he must leave them.

According to Cotton Mather, who wrote two generations later and is not to be taken at face value, Williams was the cause of another controversy at Plymouth. He was troubled, it seems, by the application of the title "Goodman" to unregenerate persons. This term was customarily attached to the names of yeomen, who were not entitled to be called "Master" (the designation of a gentleman) but were a step above common laborers, who bore no title to their names at all. Williams contended that "Goodman" should be reserved for regenerate persons who were truly "good." This was another of those problems that zealous Puritans could become absurdly concerned about, and when Winthrop visited the colony, they put the question to him. He was able to argue away their concern, and so "put a stop to the little, idle, whimsical conceits, then beginning to grow obstreperous." Although Mather's bias is evident, the position attributed to Williams was characteristic of the man: he could follow a belief to its conclusion with a passionate literalness that bordered on the ridiculous.

When he left Plymouth, in 1633, Williams carried his zeal once more to Salem, where his memory was still green. Winthrop had remained his friend, as a letter written by Williams from Plymouth attested, but one may doubt that Winthrop was as happy as the people of Salem were to see the young man back in Massachusetts Bay. At Salem they welcomed him to church membership and cautiously made him an unofficial assistant to the pastor. By not electing him to any church office they probably thought to avoid more trouble with the government. Although the Salem church made no formal renunciation of the English churches, Williams found the members sufficiently sympathetic to his views and almost at once began to lure them along the paths of perfectionism.

While at Plymouth, Williams had raised the question whether the colonists had any right to the land they occupied. Winthrop, hearing of this, now inquired of him about it, and Williams replied with a copy of an argument he had prepared on the subject. In order to appreciate the shock which this document must have given the magistrates of Massachusetts, one must remember that the English Civil War had not begun and that the Massachusetts Bay Company had gained its control over the colony by virtue of a patent from the King. Roger Williams declared that the King's authority to grant such control rested on "a solemn public lie." He also charged the King with blasphemy for referring to Europe as Christendom and applied to the King certain uncomplimentary passages from the Book of Revelation.

The magistrates were horrified by this lese majesty and ordered Williams to appear at the next General Court to be censured. Winthrop, as shocked as the others, took steps at once to see that the confrontation between Williams and the court should not become the occasion for mutual recriminations. He wrote to Endecott, acquainting him with the summons and describing the charges which would be laid against Williams. At the same time he outlined arguments that Endecott could use in bringing Williams to reconsider and retract his offensive views: the King's claim to Massachusetts was founded on no lie, "for his people were the first, that discovered these parts: but admitt he had been mistaken: was it ever knowne, that a true Christian did give his naturall Prince the lye? was he not the Lords annointed?" This and many other arguments Winthrop adduced, some based on Scripture, some based on common sense, and some on nonsense. "If we had no right to this lande," he concluded, "yet our God hathe right to it, and if he be pleased to give it us (taking it from a people who had so longe usurped upon him, and abused his creatures) who shall controll him or his termes?"

Williams was at least sufficiently chastened to appear penitently at the court, "and gave satisfaction," Winthrop records, "of his intention and loyalty. So it was left, and nothing done in it." This was Winthrop's way of dealing with Separatists, and hitherto it had worked. Perhaps even in the talented hands of Winthrop it could not have gone on working with so irrepressible a man as Williams. Perhaps the coming showdown was inevitable. But when it came, Massachusetts was in the hands of men far less able than Winthrop and fortunate indeed to have Winthrop's precedents to follow.

In November 1634, six months after the election of Dudley, the General Court heard that Williams was publicly teaching again that the King's patent was invalid before God and that the churches of England were anti-Christian. Once again the court gave orders for his appearance. Meanwhile, Williams went on arguing with all and sundry to the effect that Massachusetts ought to send the patent back to the King, with a request that he modify it by omitting all clauses relating to donation of land. Unless this were done, the sin of accepting the land from this public liar could not be expiated except by dissolving the colony and returning all the settlers to England, where they could make public acknowledgment of the evil they had done by coming to New England on such false pretenses.

Both alternatives were ridiculous. To insult the King by telling him to rewrite the patent and leave out the lies was as fantastic as to pull up stakes and go home in order to call him a liar at closer range. When the General Court met again in March 1635, Dudley was ready to deal with this madman, but John Cotton, in the name of the other ministers, presented a request that they be given a chance to persuade him privately of his errors. It was a reasonable request, for under Winthrop's rule they had often been consulted before the government took action on religious questions. Dudley, however, replied "that wee were deceived in him [Williams], if we thought he would condescend to learne of any of us: And what will you doe," he asked, "when you have run your course, and found all your labour lost?" Perhaps Dudley could have persuaded the Court of Assistants to let him handle Williams, but owing to his own machinations, the power of government no longer rested in the assistants alone but in the General Court of assistants and deputies. The deputies approved of the precedent set by Winthrop and, in spite of Dudley's opposition, decided to give the ministers a chance to reclaim their brother. The ministers' arguments and perhaps other "Councells from Flesh and Bloud" (as Williams later called them) induced him to abandon his attack on the charter and not to send a letter he had been preparing for the King advising His Majesty that he had been guilty of a lie.

This was the last time Williams troubled the colony about the patent, but at the next meeting of the assistants in April 1635, he was summoned again on another score. About a year before, the magistrates had ordered that all inhabitants who were not freemen should take a resident's oath to support the colony and its government against all enemies. Roger Williams saw in this measure another source of contamination for the godly and proceeded again to sound the alarm. The difficulty lay in the fact that an oath was considered an act of worship. If a magistrate (presumably regenerate) should tender an oath to a nonfreeman (presumably unregenerate), he would "thereby have communion with a wicked man in the worship of God, and cause him to take the name of God in vain." Here was Williams's separatism cropping out in still another form. He persuaded Endecott and many others to adopt his view, and though Endecott was quickly argued out of his error, so many people were convinced the government was violating rather than upholding the word of God that the court felt obliged temporarily to drop the oath and with it the charges against Williams.

Williams's separatism now began to spin faster, and he threw off a succession of strange opinions: that a regenerate man ought not to pray in company with an unregenerate one, not even with his wife or children, and that he ought not to give thanks after the sacrament or after meals. He also resumed the dangerous contention which he had first voiced when leaving Boston in 1631, that the civil government had no authority in religious matters, that it could not punish breaches of the first table (the first four of the Ten Commandments) except insofar as such breaches caused a disturbance of civil peace.

Somehow, too, he had been able to set the people of Salem spinning with him. Indeed they were all but bewitched with his heedless holiness, and when their minister, Samuel Skelton, died, they cast off caution and in the spring of 1635 chose Williams in his place—knowing well that the government would quickly move against them.

At the next General Court in July Williams was summoned again, to answer for his growing list of erroneous opinions; and the other ministers were asked to be there too and advise the court what to do with him. As the court met, he was at the height of his furious and indefatigable righteousness and fortified by the fact that as minister of the Salem church he could now claim the acknowledged principle of congregational independence in his defense. Any attempt by other ministers to remove him from office would infringe upon the independence of the Salem church. And any attempt by the government to remove him would be met by a defiant congregation. The ministers consulted and unanimously declared their opinion that any minister who obstinately maintained such opinions as Williams avowed, "whereby a church might run into heresy, apostasy, or tyranny," should be removed, "and that the other churches ought to request the magistrates so to do." The churches might be powerless by the principle of congregational independence, but the civil government was not and prepared at once to carry out the advice of the clergy.

Salem was petitioning the General Court at this time for land in Marblehead Neck; and the General Court, ready to fight with foul means as well as fair, refused the petition unless the Salem church dismissed Williams. The outraged church immediately sent off letters to the other churches urging the members to reprimand the magistrates and the deputies alike for this "heinous sin" (which indeed it was).

In this moment of crisis the future of Williams, of Salem, and of the colony hung precariously in balance. To crush the rebellion of an entire church would have proved a difficult, if not a bloody, if not an impossible, business. To crush it in the face of any widespread sympathy would certainly have split the colony, and had the Salem appeal reached the other churches, the members might have found much in it to win their sympathy.

At this juncture the ministers evidently felt as the General Court did, that any means were justified to keep the colony and its holy commission intact. It was the ministers who received the letters addressed by Salem to the other churches, and they simply refrained from communicating them to their members. But it was Williams himself who broke the deadlock and unwittingly pulled the colony out of danger by a final extravagant gesture, a gesture which proved too much for his Salem admirers. The churches of Massachusetts, he said, had given up the principle of congregational independence and had called in the government to help suppress it. They were no longer pure churches. His congregation must therefore renounce the other churches of Massachusetts. Unless they did so, he would be obliged himself to withdraw from the Salem church.

It was unfortunate for Williams that during this crisis he was confined to his bed by an illness and so forced to resort to letters. When he could support his arguments with his winning personality, they were much more compelling than they could be in writing. Reduced to ink and paper, they were apt to appear tedious, far-fetched, sanctimonious. But even his magnetic personal charm might have been insufficient to bring the people of Salem to the step he now demanded of them. The men and women who read his letter were acutely aware that the rest of the colony was against them, that the authority of government was against them, that the wisdom of other godly ministers was against them. His letter asked them in effect to renounce all the rest of the world, for if there were no true churches in the rest of Massachusetts, where else could there be any?

Winthrop says the whole Salem church was "grieved" with Williams's request. The supreme assurance of a Roger Williams is rare at any time, and in Salem a majority were unwilling to go as far as he asked. Probably some made their decision with one eye on the land of Marblehead Neck. But it is not necessary to assume such weakness for their actions. It is more likely that the majority simply could not bring themselves to declare that everyone outside Salem was wrong.

The final confrontation between Williams and the General Court came early in October 1635 at a full meeting, with all the ministers of the colony invited to attend. The charges preferred against him were of two kinds: his new and dangerous opinions, in particular his denial of the magistrates' authority in religious matters, and his seditious letters, one in the name of the Salem church attacking the General Court, and the second to the Salem church urging their separation from the other churches of the colony.

Williams made no attempt to deny the charges. He was as adamant as Luther at the Diet of Worms, and though offered a month's respite in which to prepare his defense, he waived the offer and justified every opinion. Even Thomas Hooker, the most eloquent spokesman of New England orthodoxy, could not move him. The court therefore ordered him to leave the colony within six weeks.

Returning to Salem (the court was held in Boston), Williams found his church unwilling to support him. His hard core of devoted followers did not constitute a majority. Rather than remain connected with a church which recognized the other churches of Massachusetts, he resigned his office and his membership. Perhaps because he seemed thus to have drawn his own fangs, the General Court extended the date for his departure until the following spring, on condition that he not "go about to draw others to his opinions."

It was a foolish requirement. The court should have known that Williams's charm drew people like a magnet and that he was not the kind of man to be silent simply because his opinions had displeased the government. Before the winter was far gone, the magistrates heard that "he had drawn above twenty persons to his opinion, and they were intended to erect a plantation about the Narragansett Bay, from whence the infection would easily spread into these churches, (the people being, many of them, much taken with the apprehension of his godliness)." The court decided to forestall this move by shipping him back to England. But before they could lay hands on him he was gone, off for Narragansett Bay in a bitter January.

Winthrop recorded the event in his journal without comment. He held Williams's views in the utmost abhorrence, and must have concurred in the sentence of banishment. By the time the sentence was delivered there was no alternative. The people of Massachusetts could scarcely have carried out their commission and allowed Williams to remain.

That Winthrop disapproved, either openly or privately, the move to ship Williams back to England was not suggested by his journal, but it was plainly implied by Williams himself in a letter written many years later. In 1670, when Winthrop was long in his grave, Williams wrote to a friend, "When I was unkindly and unchristianly, as I believe, driven from my house and land and wife and children, (in the midst of a New England winter, now about thirty-five years past,) at Salem, that ever honored Governor, Mr. Winthrop, privately wrote to me to steer my course to Narragansett Bay and Indians, for many high and heavenly and public ends, encouraging me, from the freeness of the place from any English claims or patents. I took his prudent motion as a hint and voice from God, and waving all other thoughts and motions, I steered my course from Salem (though in winter snow, which I feel yet) unto these parts . . ." Winthrop, unlike the other magistrates of Massachusetts, retained Williams's affection and respect. Indeed, during the first five years of his exile Williams's letters to Winthrop expressed an admiration bordering on adulation.

One of the first of these, written from Providence on October 24, 1636, answered a set of queries evidently sent by Winthrop. Now that the damage was done, Winthrop had asked his friend to cast up accounts: What had he gained by his "new-found practices"? Did he find his spirit as even as it was seven years before, when he and Winthrop first met? Was he not himself grieved to have grieved so many? Did he really think the rest of New England utterly forsaken of God? Could he not have remained in the New England churches without endangering his soul? What, after all, was he aiming at?

Williams's answers were like the man, humble and loving and respectful, but at the same time defiant, with a holy intransigence. They breathed throughout the spirit of separatism. He did indeed think that the Lord had forsaken New England for failing to separate her churches wholly from the filthiness of English corruption. And to Winthrop he offered the very advice that Winthrop could least willingly listen to. Where Winthrop had urged him to pause and consider whether everyone was wrong but him, he replied with an invitation to join him in splendid isolation: "Abstract yourselfe," he urged, "with a holy violence from the Dung heape of this Earth." Williams would not learn the lesson which Winthrop had taught himself so painfully before he left England, that there was no escape from the dung heap of this earth; and that those who sought one or thought they had found it acted with an unholy, not a holy, violence.

Winthrop watched the subsequent development of Williams's views along a course he might have predicted. Within a year or two Williams decided that the church must not include children simply on the basis of their parents' membership and abandoned the practice of infant baptism in the congregation he had gathered among the handful of the faithful who followed him to Providence. He had himself and all the other members rebaptized, but shortly began to question whether there could be a proper church at all until God raised up some new apostolic power. Finally he reached the position where he could not conscientiously have communion with anyone but his wife.

This was the limit of his separatism. He did not reach the ultimate absurdity of finding no one but himself fit to communicate with. Indeed, from this point forward his separatism, having reached the pinnacle of isolation, broke through to a new realm of freedom, unknown and undesired by other Puritans. While still in Massachusetts he had denied that the state had anything to do with religion, thus making of it an association for purely temporal, worldly purposes. And he had espoused a congregational independence so complete that when put into practice, it necessitated a hitherto unheard-of religious freedom. It must have been painful for a man who set so high a value on purity in religion to stand sponsor at Narragansett for religious opinions that he abhorred. Williams ended the pain by deciding that no church could attain purity in this world. He had effectively demonstrated the proposition to himself as he withdrew successively from the Church of England, from the churches of Massachusetts, and finally from everyone but his wife. What he saw at last was what Winthrop had tried to point out to him, that he was seeking an unattainable goal, that there was no escape from the dung heap of this earth.

Williams's reaction to this discovery was characteristic: since he could not escape the dung heap, he would embrace it. And so, Winthrop says, "having, a little before, refused communion with all, save his own wife, now he would preach to and pray with all comers."

To Winthrop this liberalism was as ridiculous as the former separatism. Williams's views on civil government had degraded the holy purpose of the state; now he degraded the still holier purpose of the church, welcoming the mixed multitude which he had formerly complained of so bitterly in the churches of England. Many of his followers were as disgusted with his about-face as Winthrop was. It would take another fifty years before a Solomon Stoddard could demonstrate to New England that since perfect purity could not be found in the visible church, the purest course was not to seek it. To Winthrop and to other New England Puritans of the 1630's such was the counsel not of wisdom but of despair and defeat, the very thing to be expected from a man like Williams, who leaped always from one extreme to another.

Winthrop was undoubtedly pained that Massachusetts had been unable to harness the zeal of so godly a man as Williams to the cause the colony was striving for. But he could take pride in the fact that the colony had not been split apart or lured into such an irresponsible pursuit of individual holiness as Williams advocated. The great majority of the population, even the great majority of the Salem church, kept their eyes on the goal that Winthrop had set them.

It was not a goal that any man could reach by himself, but a common goal which all must seek together, with church and state working side by side. It was a goal of godliness, and it needed godly men to reach it, but not those, like Williams, who pulled too hard and left the rest behind. If such wild ones could not be tamed, it was best to cut them loose, lest they overturn the whole enterprise. Williams had proved impossible to tame. Perhaps if Winthrop, with all his conciliatory skill, had been governor, it might have been done, and Massachusetts would have been the gainer. Since it was not done, the colony was better off without so great a dissenter.

X
Seventeenth-Century Nihilism

Edmund S. Morgan

On September 18, 1634, two hundred passengers disembarked at Boston's bustling, cluttered landing place and picked their way through the dirty streets. The squalor of the place was enough to make them quail, but they reminded themselves that it was holy ground, where they might worship God without bishops or kings or Romanizing ritual. Among the arrivals who strengthened their resolution with this thought were William Hutchinson and his wife Anne.

Winthrop described Hutchinson as "a man of a very mild temper and weak parts, and wholly guided by his wife." But a man with a wife like Anne Hutchinson could scarcely not have been guided by her. All we know about Anne Hutchinson was written by other hands than hers, for the most part by writers whose main purpose was to discredit her. Yet the force of her intelligence and character penetrate the libels and leave us angry with the writers and not with their intended victim.

Winthrop, who was one of the libelers, tells us at the outset that she was "a woman of a ready wit and bold spirit." This was an absurd understatement. Though Winthrop, in common with his century, believed that women's minds could not stand the strain of profound theological speculation, Anne Hutchinson excelled him not only in nimbleness of wit but in the ability to extend a theological proposition into all its ramifications. And like so many of the men and women of this time—like Roger Williams, for example—she was ready to trust her mind and to follow in whatever path it might lead her. In 1634 the path had led to Boston.

She was not, by intention at least, a Separatist; she had once been tempted in that direction but did not succumb. She had nevertheless determined that she must not attend a church where the minister failed to teach the doctrines of divine grace in their undiluted purity. Until 1633 she had listened to the sermons of the Reverend John Cotton at Boston in Lincolnshire and had known them for true preaching. She had also admired her brother-in-law, the Reverend John Wheelwright. But when Cotton and Wheelwright were silenced by the bishops, "there was none in England," she said, "that I durst heare." After Cotton departed for New England, she persuaded her husband to follow him.

In singling out John Cotton as her spiritual leader, Mrs. Hutchinson showed, by Puritan standards, excellent taste. Cotton had already won a reputation in England before he left, and the Boston church chose him as teacher shortly after his arrival in New England in September 1633. Here his fame rose steadily. Indeed, his wisdom was so revered that Hugh Peter, who was later to be honored as Cromwell's chaplain, urged that Cotton be commissioned to "go through the Bible, and raise marginal notes upon all the knotty places of the scriptures." Nathaniel Ward, the testy pastor of Ipswich, held himself unworthy to wipe John Cotton's slippers. And Roger Williams observed that many people in Massachusetts "could hardly believe that God would suffer Mr. Cotton to err."

Winthrop himself was one of Cotton's admirers and frequently took occasion to record the minister's opinions with approval. He valued most in Cotton what Mrs. Hutchinson did—the man's evangelical preaching of God's free grace. All New England Puritans believed in this doctrine, which they usually described in terms of a covenant between God and man whereby God drew the soul to salvation. Strictly speaking, there was nothing a man could do to lay hold of this "covenant of grace." If God predestined him to salvation, God would endow him with faith and fulfill the covenant. But the doctrine could be applied in a variety of ways, and the New England ministers had been suggesting the need to "prepare" oneself so as to facilitate the operation of God's saving grace when and if it should come.

Under the spell of this suggestion it was easy to develop notions of the kind that good Puritans always denounced as "Arminian"—whenever they could recognize them. Though preachers always took care to state that human efforts counted for nothing in the scale of eternity, it was easy to draw the opposite (Arminian) conclusion from their insistence on "preparation," easy to slip into Arminian ways of thinking without realizing it. The history of New England theology for a century and a half after the founding is the history of this steady tendency toward Arminianism, punctuated by periodic reassertions of the Calvinist dogma of divine omnipotence and human helplessness.

John Cotton was the first of a long line of preachers—among whom the most eminent was Jonathan Edwards—to make this reassertion. He did not make it in the unequivocal terms that Edwards did, and perhaps for that reason he did not end as Edwards did by being expelled from his church. Instead he pulled his congregation back from their Arminian wanderings and won their gratitude. Winthrop counted himself as one of those whom Cotton had rescued. He noted in January 1637, that "the Doctrine of free justification lately taught here took me in as drowsy a condition, as I had been in (to my remembrance) these twenty yeares, and brought mee as low (in my owne apprehension) as if the whole work had been to begin anew. But when the voice of peace came I knew it to bee the same that I had been acquainted with before . . ." Probably most members of the Boston church reacted to Cotton's preaching as Winthrop did. It woke them from their Arminian napping and sharpened their sense of God's free grace, but it did not make them feel in the end that their previous religious experiences had been false.

But the evangelical preaching of divine omnipotence and human helplessness has always produced extravagant results, for these doctrines may too easily be translated into a denial of any connection whatever between this world and the next. Puritanism allowed only a tenuous connection at best; it allowed a man to look at his life here as evidence of his prospects in eternity, but it gave him no opportunity to affect his eternal condition. When John Cotton warned his listeners away from the specious comfort of preparation and reemphasized the covenant of grace as something in which God acted alone and unassisted, a bold mind might believe that life in this world offered no evidence at all of eternal prospects. And Mrs. Hutchinson was nothing if not bold.

After her arrival in Boston her admission to the church was delayed for a time because one of her fellow passengers had been disturbed by some unorthodox opinions she had expressed on shipboard. But John Cotton evidently recognized her theological talents and her zeal, and within two years she was admitted and won the admiration of a large part of the congregation. It was not uncommon at this time for small groups to hold weekly meetings for religious discussions, in which the sermon of the previous Sunday furnished the starting point. Mrs. Hutchinson, who had gained a wide acquaintance in Boston by serving as a midwife, soon found herself the center of one of these meetings, held in her home. She would explain, to the best of her ability, what her beloved Mr. Cotton had said on Sunday and would then go on to expand some of his doctrines.

In these weekly meetings she carried the principles of divine omnipotence and human helplessness in a dangerous direction, toward the heresy known to theologians as Antinomianism. Since man was utterly helpless, she reasoned, when God acted to save him He placed the Holy Ghost directly within him, so that the man's life was thereafter directed by the Holy Ghost, and the man himself, in a sense, ceased to be. At the same time she concluded that human actions were no clue to the question of whether or not this transformation had taken place. The fact that a man behaved in a "sanctified" manner, breaking none of the laws of God, was no evidence that he was saved. In Puritan terminology this meant that "sanctification" was no evidence of "justification," that men's lives in this world offered no evidence of their prospects in the next. The orthodox Puritans never claimed that the correspondence was perfect: hypocrisy together with the thousand imperfections of human vision could deceive the most skillful examiner. But it was usually possible to recognize sanctification, and that sanctification resulted from justification was not to be doubted at all. Mrs. Hutchinson doubted and denied it. She was, it seemed, an Antinomian.

Winthrop first became alarmed by her teachings in October 1636, a few months after the departure of Roger Williams. He noted her errors and began a list of the awful conclusions that must ensue from them, but stopped and left a large blank in his journal, overcome perhaps by the train of horrors he saw before him. Before they were through with Mrs. Hutchinson the guardians of New England orthodoxy enumerated nearly a hundred dangerous propositions that could be deduced from her views. It is not possible to tell which propositions she actually endorsed and which were simply attributed to her, but the list is a formidable one, and strikes at the heart of the Puritan experiment.

Mrs. Hutchinson's first principle, "that the person of the Holy Ghost dwells in a justified person," was dangerously close to a belief in immediate personal revelation. It threatened the fundamental conviction on which the Puritans built their state, their churches, and their daily lives, namely that God's will could be discovered only through the Bible. In combination with the belief that sanctification offered no evidence of justification, it undermined the whole basis for moral endeavor which Puritan theologians had constructed since the time of Calvin. What reason for a man to exert himself for the right if he may "stand still and waite for Christ to doe all for him"? What reason for a church of saints, if "no Minister can teach one that is anoynted by the Spirit of Christ, more than hee knowes already unless it be in some circumstances"? What reason for a state ruled by the laws of God, if "the Will of God in the Word, or directions thereof, are not the rule whereunto Christians are bound to conforme themselves"?

These views were not necessarily separatist. Rather they were a seventeenth-century version of nihilism. But to make matters worse, Mrs. Hutchinson and her friends developed a new and especially invidious form of separatism, too. Though she denied that sanctification could be evidence of justification, she did maintain that any justified person could discern, presumably at the direction of the Holy Ghost within him, whether or not another person was justified. On the basis of this almighty insight Mrs. Hutchinson and her followers confidently pronounced any person they encountered as "under a covenant of grace" (really saved) or "under a covenant of works" (deluded and damned because relying on good works instead of divine grace), so that "it began to be as common here," Winthrop says, "to distinguish between men, by being under a covenant of grace or a covenant of works, as in other countries between Protestants and Papists." The wholesale destructiveness that might result from Mrs. Hutchinson's self-assurance became apparent when she hinted to her admirers that all the ministers in Massachusetts, with the exception of her two old favorites, John Cotton and John Wheelwright, were under a covenant of works and therefore unfit to preach the gospel.

Winthrop saw trouble ahead when he first took notice of Anne Hutchinson's views in October 1636. The weekly meetings at her house were steadily swelling, and the people who attended them walked the streets of Boston wearing the expression of devotees. Those rapt faces, Winthrop knew, carried a threat to the colony's commission. But there was no law against religious gatherings, and Mrs. Hutchinson was careful to state her heresies in equivocal language. It would be difficult to prove anything against her.

By the end of October 1636, her followers felt strong enough to seek an official spokesman for their doctrines in the Boston church. Because Mrs. Hutchinson was a woman, no one would think of proposing her for a church office, but her brother-in-law would do as well. John Wheelwright had arrived in June, with a reputation as an able preacher and with the additional recommendation of having been silenced by the bishops in England. Mrs. Hutchinson, of course, endorsed him, and he endorsed her. At a church meeting on October 30 it was moved that he be made a teacher, though the congregation possessed two other ministers—John Cotton as teacher and John Wilson as pastor. Winthrop grasped the chance to act and immediately opposed the election of a third minister, particularly one "whose spirit they knew not, and one who seemed to dissent in judgment."

As a member of the church, Winthrop had the right to a voice in its affairs, but no more than any other member, and he was up against a growing majority of the Boston church, which included the largest single concentration of freemen in the colony. He was also up against the popular young governor, Henry Vane, who was on his feet at once to say that Wheelwright's doctrines were no different from those of Cotton. Cotton himself neither admitted nor denied the similarity, but obviously was in sympathy with the majority.

More was at stake here than the welfare of the Boston church, and Winthrop, calling on his own reserve of popularity, was able to persuade the meeting not to elect Wheelwright. But the victory cost him many friends, even though he protested that he meant no personal slight to Wheelwright, and "did love that brother's person, and did honor the gifts and graces of God in him." In the weeks that followed, Wheelwright took himself off to the scattered settlement at Mount Wollaston, leaving behind a congregation that grew ever more resentful of Winthrop and his ally, the pastor John Wilson. Wilson, as pastor, had played second fiddle ever since John Cotton had arrived, but Mrs. Hutchinson's infectious contempt reduced his influence in the congregation to the vanishing point. He and Winthrop were left almost alone to console each other.

Winthrop as usual was sure that people would see things his way if they would only listen to reason, and as usual he set down in black and white the reason he hoped they would listen to. Fortunately, before presenting this document to his opponents he sent a copy to his friend Thomas Shepard, the pastor at Cambridge, who saw at once that Winthrop was no theologian. Though Winthrop knew better than his opponents the necessity of living in this world, he was no match for them in speculating about the next. His arguments, if one may judge from Shepard's criticisms (Winthrop's text is lost), were studded with expressions that smacked of Arminianism; "and so," Shepard warned him, "while you are about to convince them of errours, they will proclayme your selfe to hold foorth worse." Winthrop, who was no Arminian, probably destroyed his composition, and Boston remained deluded and defiant.

Though Winthrop could make no headway within his church, the rest of the colony was beginning to take alarm. The members of the Boston faction, like most religious fanatics, were not content to march quietly along their shortcut to Heaven. They hoped to entice the rest of the colony along it and thought the best way was to visit other congregations and heckle the ministers. This method did not prove as effective as Mrs. Hutchinson's winning words. The General Court began to take notice of the problem, and Governor Henry Vane found his popularity ebbing outside Boston as rapidly as Winthrop's had inside. In a petulant fit of tears Vane offered to resign, and the General Court obligingly agreed to let him. This so alarmed his Boston adherents, who enjoyed having a champion in the governor's chair, that they coaxed him hard to stay, and he finally allowed himself to be persuaded.

By the beginning of 1637 the colony was divided into two hostile camps, the one centering in Boston, the other spread out around it, each constantly sniping at the other. In January the General Court ordered a fast, so that the people might mourn their dissensions. But empty bellies seldom beget brotherly love, and when John Wheelwright showed up at the afternoon lecture by Cotton, he rose up at its conclusion to launch a momentous sermon of his own against those enemies of the Lord who thought that sanctification was an evidence of justification. These holy-seeming men, he said, must be put aside. They were under a covenant of works, and "the more holy they are, the greater enemies they are to Christ." True believers must hew them down: "we must lay loade upon them, we must kille them with the worde of the Lorde."

Wheelwright was speaking figuratively and not actually proposing a bloodbath, but he made it plain that he thought most of the existing ministers and probably most of the magistrates, too, could be dispensed with. Someone took down his words, and at the next meeting of the General Court, in spite of the protests of Vane and a few others, he was convicted of sedition. The sentence was deferred till the following session, which the court appointed to be in Cambridge, away from the immediate source of trouble.

This meeting, held the following May, was the regular time for election of officers. When it assembled, a petition from Boston was presented against the conviction of Wheelwright. Governor Vane wanted to deal with the petition before proceeding to election, but Winthrop and the other magistrates insisted on having the election first. When the votes were cast, it was found that Vane had not only failed of reelection but had been left out of the government altogether. The freemen had finally decided to recall the man who was best qualified to restore the peace. Winthrop was back in the governor's chair with Dudley once again as deputy governor. "There was great danger of a tumult that day," Winthrop noted, "and some laid hands on others," but seeing themselves outnumbered, the Bostonians finally decided that this was not the time to hew down the unholy holy and departed for home.

Winthrop now had the authority to crush the opposition, and it was certainly his inclination to bring the whole unhappy business to as speedy an end as possible. But to suppress or banish so large a segment of the population would be to effect the very separation he wished to avoid. His principal weapon must still be persuasion. Instead of dealing with Wheelwright at once, he again deferred sentence and arranged for a general day of humiliation and for a synod of ministers to be held in the late summer to discuss the points at issue and provide the court with a well-defined statement by which to judge the current heresies. Wheelwright was told that the court was still convinced of his guilt, "but if, upon the conference among the churches, the Lord should discover any further light to them than as yet they had seen, they should gladly embrace it." Nor did Winthrop deal with the opposition for their riotous behavior and insolent speeches on election day. Though there had been ample provocation for an indictment, the court hoped that by refraining from this and by deferring Wheelwright's sentence, "their moderation and desire of reconciliation might appear to all."

The ministers from the beginning had tried to win Cotton away from his heretical admirers, but he held firmly to the top of the fence. He did not endorse Mrs. Hutchinson's consignment of the other ministers to perdition, but he refused to believe that she and Wheelwright held the heresies imputed to them. At the same time he himself disapproved the current doctrine of preparation and maintained that more rigorous views had helped to effectuate a marked awakening of the spirit in Boston.

During the summer months Winthrop's dignity and patience were repeatedly taxed by the sulking saints of that town. Until shamed into it, Boston made no move to provide him with the sergeant halberdiers who customarily accompanied the governor to the first day of General Court and to Sunday meeting. Rather than press the point, he used his own servants and politely declined when at last the town left-handedly offered men but not sergeants. His comings and goings from Boston were also pointedly ignored, in marked contrast to the honor accorded him by other towns, which sent a guard to escort him into and out of their territory. And Henry Vane, until his departure for England on August 3, conducted himself with unabashed schoolboy discourtesy, refusing the invitation to sit in the magistrates' seats at the Boston church, though he had sat there ever since his arrival in the colony, refusing to attend a dinner party at Winthrop's home and instead carrying off the intended guest of honor, a visiting English nobleman, to dine on Noddle's Island with Samuel Maverick.

Although Winthrop set much store by his official dignity, he did not allow himself to be goaded into further recriminations. Once more he put his pen to work, and this time Thomas Shepard found little to criticize beyond the fact that he was too charitable to his opponents. But the charity was calculated. If he could not win over the leaders of the opposition, he might at least draw away their less extravagant followers.

At the same time he did not propose to allow them to increase their numbers by bringing over like-minded friends from England, where the Reverend Roger Brierly of Grindleton Chapel had recently been achieving notoriety by preaching doctrines similar to those of Mrs. Hutchinson. Winthrop feared that the Grindletonians, as Brierly's followers were called, would shortly be gravitating to Massachusetts, and he accordingly sponsored an order of court forbidding anyone to entertain strangers for more than three weeks without permission of the magistrates. This arbitrary restriction of immigration was denounced by Henry Vane as unchristian. Winthrop defended it but enforced it with his usual flexibility by granting the immigrant friends and relatives of Mrs. Hutchinson and Wheelwright four months in which to decide upon a location for settlement outside the colony.

On August 30 the ministers convened in a synod—all those of Massachusetts, including Wheelwright and Cotton, together with a delegation from Connecticut. For twenty-four days they defined to each other the dreadful doctrines that were polluting the air above Boston, and reached a remarkable unanimity. Even John Cotton, faced with a solid phalanx of his colleagues, squeezed his views into line. Wheelwright alone remained aloof. Close to a hundred heretical propositions were meticulously described and condemned, though the synod tactfully declined to attribute them to specific persons. The unanimous opinion of this body of experts must have given pause to many who had flirted with the new ideas, but a hard core of devotees in Boston continued a noisy defiance.

Winthrop could see no further avenue of persuasion and in November decided that it was time for action. Wheelwright was summoned again before the General Court and upon his refusal to give up teaching his heresies was banished. But Winthrop knew that Wheelwright was not the main source of the trouble. When the court had finished with him, they sent for his sister-in-law.

What followed was the least attractive episode in Winthrop's career. Anne Hutchinson was his intellectual superior in everything except political judgment, in everything except the sense of what was possible in this world. In nearly every exchange of words she defeated him, and the other members of the General Court with him. The record of her trial, if it is proper to dignify the procedure with that name, is one of the few documents in which her words have been recorded, and it reveals a proud, brilliant woman put down by men who had judged her in advance. The purpose of the trial was doubtless to make her conviction seem to follow due process of law, but it might have been better for the reputation of her judges if they had simply banished her unheard.

Mrs. Hutchinson confronted them at Cambridge, where magistrates and deputies crowded into the narrow benches of the meetinghouse, the only building of suitable size in the town. The ministers too were on hand, but only as witnesses, for this was a civil court, in which they had no authority. There was no jury, and no apparent procedure. The magistrates (and even some of the deputies) flung questions at the defendant, and exploded in blustering anger when the answers did not suit them. Even Winthrop was unable to maintain his usual poise in the face of Mrs. Hutchinson's clever answers to his loaded questions.

The court was somewhat handicapped, because Mrs. Hutchinson throughout the preceding months had played her hand so cleverly that only minor charges could be framed against her. The court was preparing to deal with all Wheelwright's supporters who had signed the petition in his favor. They would be disfranchised, disarmed, and in some cases banished. But Mrs. Hutchinson had signed nothing and so could be charged only with "countenancing and encouraging" those who did. To this was added the even weaker charge that she held in her home meetings of men and women which were not tolerable or comely in the sight of God or fitting for her sex. Following these was a last and more serious indictment, that she had traduced the faithful ministers of the colony.

The ground of the first charge was that in entertaining seditious persons she broke the Fifth Commandment: she dishonored the governors, who were the fathers of the commonwealth. This was not really a far-fetched interpretation, for the Puritans always justified subordination and subjection to the state on the basis of the Fifth Commandment. But Mrs. Hutchinson's "entertainment" of seditious persons could be considered seditious only by the most tenuous reasoning, and her nimble wit quickly devised a dilemma for the court. "Put the case, Sir," she said to Winthrop, "that I do fear the Lord and my parents, may not I entertain them that fear the Lord because my parents will not give me leave?"

Winthrop was unable to find his way around this logical impasse and took refuge in blind dogmatism: "We do not mean to discourse with those of your sex but only this; you do adhere unto them and do endeavor to set forward this faction and so you do dishonour us."

The court next called upon her to justify the weekly meetings at her house. In answer she quoted two passages of Scripture: Titus II, 3–5, which indicated that the elder women should instruct the younger, and Acts XVIII, 26, wherein Aquila and Priscilla "tooke upon them to instruct Apollo, more perfectly, yet he was a man of good parts, but they being better instructed might teach him."

There followed this interchange:

COURT: See how your argument stands, Priscilla with her husband, tooke Apollo home to instruct him privately, therefore Mistris Hutchinson without her husband may teach sixty or eighty.

MRS. H: I call them not. but if they come to me, I may instruct them.

COURT: Yet you shew us not a rule.

MRS. H: I have given you two places of Scripture.

COURT: But neither of them will sute your practise.

To this assertion Mrs. Hutchinson returned her most withering sarcasm: "Must I shew my name written therein?"

Mrs. Hutchinson was having the best of the argument, but the members of the court were only antagonized by her wit. As they saw it, she was usurping the position of a minister without the authority that a minister possessed from his election by a congregation. Her meetings were a fountain of dissension and separatism for which the community was liable to punishment by the Lord. On this note the court closed the argument: "We see no rule of God for this, we see not that any should have authority to set up any other exercises besides what authority hath already set up and so what hurt comes of this you will be guilty of and we for suffering you."

The greater part of the audience doubtless breathed a silent "Amen," and the trial moved forward to the final accusation, that she had insulted the ministers. The basis of this charge was a conference held the preceding December between the ministers and Mrs. Hutchinson. In spite of the fact that the conference had been private, and they had encouraged her to speak freely, they did not hesitate now to testify that she had designated them all, with the exception of Cotton and Wheelwright, as laboring under a covenant of works. One minister after another was called forward, and when the court adjourned for the day, the evidence against her on this charge looked overwhelming.

That night she went over some notes taken at the December conference by her most determined opponent, John Wilson. Finding some discrepancy between his notes and the testimony offered in court, she demanded the next morning that the ministers be required to give their evidence under oath. This created a considerable stir, because if the ministers swore to their testimony and it was proved to be wrong, they would be guilty not merely of perjury but of blasphemy, of taking the name of the Lord in vain. After much hemming and hawing by the other ministers John Cotton was called upon for the first time to give his version of the conference. With the tact which had enabled him to retain the favor of both sides he soothed the injured pride of his fellow ministers and then brought his speech to a dramatic close by declaring, "I must say that I did not find her saying they were under a covenant of works, nor that she said they did preach a covenant of works." And though pressed by the other ministers, he stood his ground.

With this testimony the case against Mrs. Hutchinson was about to collapse. The first two specifications against her had been too weakly sustained to warrant more than a serious admonition, and now the revered Mr. Cotton had knocked out the props from under the only remaining charge. The triumph was too much. Hitherto Mrs. Hutchinson had been on guard and had dexterously parried every thrust against her. Had she been content to hold her tongue at this point, her judges might have felt obliged to dismiss her with a censure. But instead she now proceeded to justify herself by a torrent of divine revelations.

Winthrop tried to stop her, but the floodgates were opened—perhaps by hysteria. Suddenly he must have seen where this outpouring might lead and was silent. The minutes raced by as she described how one thing after another had been revealed to her through scriptural passages thrust into her mind by God. To the Puritans this was an acceptable form of revelation. But then, still to the accompaniment of Biblical citations, she came to the revelation that she would come into New England and there be persecuted, but need fear no more than Daniel in the lions' den. "And see!" she cried, "this scripture fulfilled this day in mine eyes, therefore take heed what yee goe about to doe unto me . . . for I know that for this you goe about to do to me, God will ruine you and your posterity, and this whole State."

Here was the naked challenge. Winthrop and his colleagues believed that the Lord would punish Massachusetts if they *did not* punish Mrs. Hutchinson. Obviously either she or they were deluded, and they asked her "How shee did know that it was God that did reveale these things to her, and not Satan." With a final scriptural flourish to justify what she was about to do and with confidence in the Lord's deliverance, Mrs. Hutchinson at last threw off the confining authority of the Bible and swept arrogantly on.

Mrs. H: How did Abraham know that it was God that bid him offer his son, being a breach of the sixth commandment?
Court: By an immediate voice.
Mrs. H: So to me by an immediate revelation.
Court: How! an immediate revelation?
Mrs. H: By the voice of his own spirit to my soul.

Here it was at last, an acknowledgment of the heresy so long suspected. The Lord had indeed disclosed who was deluded, but He had left it to the court to strike her down! Winthrop recorded that "the Court and all the rest of the Assembly (except those of her owne party) did observe a speciall providence of God, that . . . her owne mouth should deliver her into the power of the Court, as guilty of that which all suspected her for, but were not furnished with proofe sufficient to proceed against her. . . ." It required only the briefest deliberation for the court to agree that Mrs. Hutchinson's words were sufficient cause for banishment, and when she said, "I desire to know wherefore I am banished," Winthrop gave the shabby final word: "Say no more, the court knows wherefore and is satisfied."

The sentencing of Anne Hutchinson was followed by the disfranchising and disarming of her closest adherents, who might at any moment receive an immediate revelation directing them to kill her judges. Religious enthusiasm was known to produce such results. Fortunately, the number of unwavering Hutchinson disciples was small. Her heretical declaration at the trial had driven off many in disillusionment. Though badly shaken, the Boston church for a time kept dogged faith that the declaration had been the result of unfair pressure and chicanery by the court. But when they sought to satisfy their doubts at a church meeting, Mrs. Hutchinson offered some testimony so obviously contrary to her own previous statements that they could only reluctantly conclude to abandon her. In March 1637, they voted to excommunicate her, and at the end of the month, her banishment having been deferred four months because of the winter and her pregnancy, she departed for Rhode Island, followed by the few faithful.

Winthrop's victory at the trial had been an unsavory triumph of arbitrary power, but happily it represented more than the mere crushing of a helpless woman. When she left, Massachusetts lost a brilliant mind, but God's commission was secured. Even the Boston church recovered from the troubles and was restored to unity. Only a little over a year later Winthrop looked back and congratulated himself on not having withdrawn from the church when every hand was turned against him. "By this time," he writes, "there appeared a great change in the church of Boston; for whereas, the year before, they were all (save five or six) so affected to Mr. Wheelright and Mrs. Hutchinson, and those new opinions, as they slighted the present governour and the pastor, looking at them as men under a covenant of works, and as their greatest enemies; but they bearing all patiently, and not withdrawing themselves, (as they were strongly solicited to have done,) but carrying themselves lovingly and helpfully upon all occasions, the Lord brought about the hearts of all the people to love and esteem them more than ever before, and all breaches were made up, and the church was saved from ruin beyond all expectation; which could hardly have been, (in human reason,) if those two had not been guided by the Lord to that moderation."

Thus the final lesson of the Hutchinson affair was the same lesson that Winthrop had been learning all his life, the importance of not separating.

5

Selection from The Examination of Mrs. Anne Hutchinson

The Examination of Mrs. Anne Hutchinson

November 1637
The Examination of Mrs. Anne
Hutchinson at the court at Newtown

Mr. Winthrop, governor. Mrs. Hutchinson, you are called here as one of those that have troubled the peace of the commonwealth and the churches here; you are known to be a woman that hath had a great share in the promoting and divulging of those opinions that are causes of this trouble . . . you have maintained a meeting and an assembly in your house that hath been condemned by the general assembly as a thing not tolerable nor comely in the sight of God nor fitting for your sex, and notwithstanding that was cried down you have continued the same. Therefore we have thought good to send for you to understand how things are, that if you be in an erroneous way we may reduce you that so you may become a profitable member here among us, otherwise if you be obstinate in your course that then the court may take such course that you may trouble us no further. Therefore I would intreat you to express whether you do not hold and assent in practice to those opinions and factions that have been handled in court already, that is to say, whether you do not justify Mr. Wheelwright's sermon and the petition.

Mrs. Hutchinson. I am called here to answer before you but I hear no things laid to my charge.

Gov. I have told you some already and more I can tell you.

Mrs. H. Name one Sir.

Gov. Have I not named some already?

Mrs. H. What have I said or done?

Gov. Why for your doings, this you did harbor and countenance those that are parties in this faction that you have heard of.

Mrs. H. That's matter of conscience, Sir.

Gov. Your conscience you must keep or it must be kept for you.

Gov. Let us state the case and then we may know what to do. That which is laid to Mrs. Hutchinson's charge is this, that she hath traduced the magistrates and ministers of this jurisdiction, that she hath said the ministers preached a covenant of works and Mr. Cotton a covenant of grace, and that they were not able ministers of the gospel, and she excuses it that she made it a private conference and with a promise of secrecy, &c. Now this is charged upon her, and they therefore sent for her seeing she made it her table talk, and then she said the fear of man was a snare and therefore she would not be affeared of them.

Mrs. H. This that yourself hath spoken, I desire that they may take their oaths upon.

Gov. That that we should put the reverend elders unto is this, that they would deliver upon oath that which they can remember themselves.

Mr. Shepard. I know no reason of the oath but the importunity of this gentlewoman.

Mr. Eliot. } We desire to see light why we should take an oath.
Mr. Shepard. }

Mr. Stoughton. Why it is an end of all strife and I think you ought to swear and put an end to the matter.

Mr. Peters. Our oath is not to satisfy Mrs. Hutchinson but the court.

Dep. Gov. Let her witnesses be called.

Gov. Who be they?

Mrs. H. Mr. Leveret and our teacher and Mr. Coggeshall.

Gov. Mr. Coggeshall was not present.

Mr. Coggeshall. Yes but I was, only I desired to be silent till I should be called.

Gov. Will you Mr. Coggeshall say that she did not say so?

Mr. Coggeshall. Yes I dare say that she did not say all that which they lay against her.

Mr. Peters. How dare you look into the court to say such a word?

Mr. Coggeshall. Mr. Peters takes upon him to forbid me. I shall be silent.

Mr. Stoughton. Ey, but she intended this that they say.

Gov. Well, Mr. Leveret, what were the words? I pray speak.

Mr. Leveret. To my best remembrance when the elders did send for her, Mr. Peters did with much vehemency and intreaty urge her to tell what difference there was between Mr. Cotton and them, and upon his urging of her she said, *The fear of man is a snare, but they that trust upon the Lord shall be safe.* And being asked wherein the difference was, she answered that they did not preach a covenant of grace so clearly as Mr. Cotton did, and she gave this reason of it because that as the apostles were for a time without the spirit so until they had received the witness of the spirit they could not preach a covenant of grace so clearly.[1]

Gov. Don't you remember that she said they were not able ministers of the new testament?

Mrs. H. Mr. Weld and I had an hour's discourse at the window and then I spake that, if I spake it.

Mr. Cotton. I did not think I should be called to bear witness in this cause and therefore did not labor to call to remembrance what was done; but the greatest passage that took impression upon me was to this purpose. The elders spake that they had heard that she had spoken some condemning words of their ministry, and among other things they did first pray her to answer wherein she thought their ministry did differ from mine, how the comparison sprang I am ignorant, but sorry I was that any comparison should be between me and my brethren and uncomfortable it was, she told them to this purpose that they did not hold forth a covenant of grace as I did, but wherein did we differ? why she said that they did not hold forth the seal of the spirit as he doth. Where is the difference there? say they. Why, saith she speaking to one or other of them, I know not to whom, you preach of the seal of the spirit upon a work and he upon free grace without a work or without respect to a work, he preaches the seal of the spirit upon free grace and you upon a work. I told her I was very sorry that she put comparisons between my ministry and theirs, for she had said more than I could myself, and rather I had that she had put us in fellowship with them and not have made that discrepancy . . . I must say that I did not find her saying they were under a covenant of works, nor that she said they did preach a covenant of works.

Gov. You say you do not remember, but can you say she did not speak so——

Mr. Cotton. I do remember that she looked at them as the apostles before the ascension.

Mr. Peters. I humbly desire to remember[2] our reverend teacher. May it please you to remember how this came in. Whether do you not remember that she said we were not sealed with the spirit of grace, therefore could not preach a covenant of grace, and she said further you may do it in your judgment but not in experience, but she spake plump that we were not sealed.

Mr. Cotton. You do put me in remembrance that it was asked her why cannot we preach a covenant of grace? Why, saith she, because you can preach no more than you know, or to that purpose, she spake. Now that she said you could not preach a covenant of grace I do not remember such a thing. I remember well that she said you were not sealed with the seal of the spirit.

Mr. Nowell. The witnesses do not answer that which you require.

Gov. I do not see that we need their testimony any further. Mr. Cotton hath expressed what he remembered, and what took impression upon him, and so I think the other elders also did remember that which took impression upon them.

Dep. Gov. They affirm that Mrs. Hutchinson did say they were not able ministers of the new testament.

Mr. Cotton. I do not remember it.

Mrs. H. If you please to give me leave I shall give you the ground of what I know to be true. Being much troubled to see the falseness of the constitution of the church of England, I had like to have turned Separatist; whereupon I kept a day of solemn humiliation and pondering of the thing; this scripture was brought unto me—he that denies Jesus Christ to be come in the flesh is antichrist[3]—This I considered of and in considering found that the papists did not deny him to be come in the flesh, nor we did not deny him—who then was antichrist? Was the Turk antichrist only? The Lord knows that I could not open scripture; he must by his prophetical office open it unto me. So after that being unsatisfied in the thing, the Lord was pleased to bring this scripture out of the Hebrews.[4] He that denies the testament denies the testator, and in this did open unto me and give me to see that those which did not teach the new covenant had the spirit of antichrist, and upon this he did discover the ministry unto me and ever since. I bless the Lord, he hath let me see which was the clear ministry and which the wrong. Since that time I confess I have been more choice and he hath let me to distinguish between the voice of my beloved and the voice of Moses, the voice of John Baptist and the voice of antichrist, for all those voices are spoken of in scripture. Now if you do condemn me for speaking what in my conscience I know to be truth I must commit myself unto the Lord.

Mr. Nowell. How do you know that that was the spirit?

Mrs. H. How did Abraham know that it was God that bid him offer his son, being a breach of the sixth commandment?

Dep. Gov. By an immediate voice.

Mrs. H. So to me by an immediate revelation.

Dep. Gov. How! an immediate revelation.

Mrs. H. By the voice of his own spirit to my soul. I will give you another scripture, Jeremiah 46:27–28—out of which the Lord showed me what he would do for me and the rest of his servants.[5]—But after he was pleased to reveal himself to me I did presently like Abraham run to Hagar. And after that he did let me see the atheism of my own heart for which I begged of the Lord that it might not remain in my heart, and being thus, he did shew me this (a twelvemonth after) which I told you of before. Ever since that time I have been confident of what he hath revealed unto me . . . When our teacher came to New England it was a great trouble unto me, my brother Wheelwright being put by also. I was then much troubled concerning the ministry under which I lived, and then that place in the 30th of Isaiah[6] was brought to my mind. *Though the Lord give thee bread of adversity and water of affliction yet shall not thy teachers be removed into corners any more, but thine eyes shall see thy teachers.* The Lord giving me this promise and they being gone there was none then left that I was able to hear, and I could not be at rest but I must come hither. Yet that place of Isaiah did much follow me, though the Lord give thee the bread of adversity and water of affliction. This place lying I say upon me then this place in Daniel[7] was brought unto me and did shew me that though I should meet with affliction yet I am the same God that delivered Daniel out of the lion's den, I will also deliver thee.—Therefore I desire you to look to it, for you see this scripture fulfilled this day and therefore I desire you that as you tender the Lord and the church and commonwealth to consider and look what you do. You have power over my body but the Lord Jesus hath power over my body and soul, and assure yourselves thus much, you do as much as in you lies to put the Lord Jesus Christ from you, and if you go on in this course you begin you will bring a curse upon you and your posterity, and the mouth of the Lord hath spoken it.

Dep. Gov. What is the scripture she brings?

Mr. Stoughton. Behold I turn away from you.

Dep. Gov. I desire Mr. Cotton to tell us whether you do approve of Mrs. Hutchinson's revelations as she hath laid them down.

Mr. Cotton. I know not whether I do understand her, but this I say, if she doth expect a deliverance in a way of providence—then I cannot deny it.

Dep. Gov. No Sir we did not speak of that.

Mr. Cotton. If it be by way of miracle then I would suspect it.

Dep. Gov. Do you believe that her revelations are true?

Mr. Cotton. That she may have some special providence of God to help her is a thing that I cannot bear witness against.

Dep. Gov. Good Sir I do ask whether this revelation be of God or no?

Mr. Cotton. I should desire to know whether the sentence of the court will bring her to any calamity, and then I would know of her whether she expects to be delivered from that calamity by a miracle or a providence of God.

Mrs. H. By a providence of God I say I expect to be delivered from some calamity that shall come to me.

Gov. The case is altered and will not stand with us now, but I see a marvellous providence of God to bring things to this pass that they are. We have been hearkening about the trial of this thing and now the mercy of God by a providence hath answered our desires and made her to lay open her self and the ground of all these disturbances to be by revelations . . . The ground work of her revelations is the immediate revelation of the spirit and not by the ministry of the word. And that is the means by which she hath very much abused the country that they shall look for revelations and are not bound to the ministry of the word, but God will teach them by immediate revelations and this hath been the ground of all these tumults and troubles. And I would that those were all cut off from us that trouble us, for this is the thing that hath been the root of all the mischief.

Court. We all consent with you.

Mr. Endicot. I speak in reference to Mr. Cotton. I am tender of you Sir and there lies much upon you in this particular, for the answer of Mr. Cotton doth not free him from that way which his last answer did bring upon him, therefore I beseech you that you'd be pleased to speak a word to that which Mrs. Hutchinson hath spoken of her revelations as you have heard the manner of it. Whether do you witness for her or against her.

Mr. Cotton. This is that I said Sir, and my answer is plain: that if she doth look for deliverance from the hand of God by his providence, and the revelation be in a word or according to a word, that I cannot deny.

Mr. Endicot. You give me satisfaction.

Dep. Gov. No, no, he gives me none at all.

Mr. Cotton. But if it be in a way of miracle or a revelation without the word that I do not assent to, but look at it as a delusion, and I think so doth she too as I understand her.

Dep. Gov. Sir, you weary me and do not satisfy me.

Mr. Cotton. I pray Sir give me leave to express my self. In that sense that she speaks I dare not bear witness against it.

Dep. Gov. These disturbances that have come among the Germans have been all grounded upon revelations[8], and so they that have vented them have stirred up their hearers to take up arms against their prince and to cut the throats one of another, and these have been the fruits of them, and whether the devil may inspire the same into their hearts here I know not, for I am fully persuaded that Mrs. Hutchinson is deluded by the devil, because the spirit of God speaks truth in all his servants.

Gov. I am persuaded that the revelation she brings forth is delusion.

All the court but some two or three ministers cry out, we all believe it—we all believe it. *Mr. Endicot.* I suppose all the world may see where the foundation of all these troubles among us lies.

Mr. Eliot. I say there is an expectation of things promised, but to have a particular revelation of things that shall fall out, there is no such thing in the scripture.

Gov. We will not limit the word of God.

Mr. Collicut. It is a great burden to us that we differ from Mr. Cotton and that he should justify these revelations. I would intreat him to answer concerning that about the destruction of England.

Gov. Mr. Cotton is not called to answer to any thing but we are to deal with the party here standing before us.

Gov. Seeing the court hath thus declared itself and hearing what hath been laid to the charge of Mrs. Hutchinson and especially what she by the providence of God hath declared freely without being asked, if therefore it be the mind of the court, looking at her as the principal cause of all our trouble, that they would now consider what is to be done to her.—

Mr. Coddington. I do think that you are going to censure therefore I desire to speak a word.

Gov. I pray you speak.

Mr. Coddington. There is one thing objected against the meetings. What if she designed to edify her own family in her own meetings may none else be present?

Gov. If you have nothing else to say but that, it is pity Mr. Coddington that you should interrupt us in proceeding to censure.

Mr. Coddington. I would say more Sir, another thing you lay to her charge is her speech to the elders. Now I do not see any clear witness against her, and you know it is a rule of the court that no man may be a judge and an accuser too. I do not speak to disparage our elders and their callings, but I do not see any thing that they accuse her of witnessed against her, and therefore I do not see how she should be censured for that. And for the other thing which hath fallen from her occasionally by the spirit of God, you know the spirit of God witnesses with our spirits, and there is no truth in scripture but God bears witness to it by his spirit, therefore I would entreat you to consider whether those things you have alleged against her deserve such censure as you are about to pass . . .

Notes

¹ Acts 1:8.

² Remind.

³ I John 2:18.

⁴ Hebrews 9:16.

⁵ "I will not make a full end of thee, but correct thee in measure; yet will I not leave thee wholly unpunished."

⁶ Isaiah 30:20.

⁷ Daniel 6:4–5.

⁸ Dudley is referring to the notorious John of Leyden, who led a violent Anabaptist revolt at Munster in 1535, after which Anabaptism became synonymous with fanaticism in the minds of many Protestants.

6

"Salem Possessed: The Social Origins of Witchcraft"

Paul Boyer and Stephen Nissenbaum

Salem Possessed: The Social Origins of Witchcraft

Paul Boyer and Stephen Nissenbaum

———•———•———•———

Historians have had difficulty justifying their continual fascination with Salem witchcraft. The undeniable tragedy of this painful episode seemed appropriate to literary and dramatic treatment, such as Nathaniel Hawthorne provided in The House of the Seven Gables *or Arthur Miller in* The Crucible. *But what, if anything, did it tell us about underlying social tensions in colonial New England? Did Salem's agony change anything? Many have been tempted to see the trials as a watershed between a bigoted, clergy-ridden seventeenth century and a more tolerant and enlightened eighteenth, but this reassuring argument has never survived close scrutiny.*

Paul Boyer and Stephen Nissenbaum have dramatically shifted the terms of the debate. They have applied to Salem Village the techniques of community study that were already transforming the social history of early New England. They argue that a deeply disturbing rift between commercial and expansive Salem Town (where the trials took place) and rural Salem Village (where the hysteria and accusations of witchcraft arose) best explains the pattern of accused and accusers, respectively.

This selection is a composite put together by the authors, principally from their book on Salem witchcraft, but also from some of their editorial summaries in their published compilation of Salem witchcraft papers. In pondering this stimulating essay, readers might ask themselves two questions. First, even if the Boyer-Nissenbaum pattern is a necessary *component in the tragedy of 1692, is it a* sufficient *explanation for what happened? Can it account for the gender structure of the event? Why were women both the major accusers and accused? Second, which was more novel in 1692—the commercial expansion of Salem Town, which had been a seaport since its founding, or the appearance on its hinderland of a village largely cut off from the Atlantic economy? Can we see here the beginnings of a cleavage that would dominate Revolutionary America a century later, the division of American society into commercial-cosmopolitan and agrarian-localist segments? If so, which one most requires historical explanation? Which departed more conspicuously from the personal experiences of the first generation of settlers?*

Except for a brief moment, the inhabitants of Salem Village were "ordinary" people living out their lives in an obscure seventeenth-century farming village. Had it not been for the extraordinary events of 1692, they would most probably have been overlooked by "serious" historians. But it is precisely *because* they were so unexceptional that their lives (and, for that matter, the trauma which overwhelmed them in 1692) are invested with real historical significance. When "Salem witchcraft," like some exotic cut flower, is plucked from the soil which nurtured it—or, to change the image, when the roles assigned to the actors of 1692 are shaped by a script not of their own making—then this terrible event cannot rise above the level of gripping melodrama. It is only as we come to sense how deeply the witchcraft outbreak was rooted in the prosaic, everyday lives of obscure and inarticulate men and women, and how profoundly those lives were being shaped by powerful forces of historical change, that the melodrama begins to take on the harsher contours of tragedy.

It began in obscurity, with cautious experiments in fortune telling. Books on the subject had "stolen" into the land; and all over New England, late in 1691, young people were being "led away with little sorceries." Fearful of the future, they began to cast spells and to practice "conjuration with sieves and keys, and peas, and nails, and horseshoes."[1]

In Essex County, Massachusetts, it was mainly young girls who met in small informal gatherings to discuss the future. One such circle centered in the household of the Rev. Samuel Parris of Salem Village, a Massachusetts farming community situated a few miles inland from the town of Salem proper. As these girls—Parris' nine-year-old daughter Betty, his niece Abigail Williams, and two of their friends—pursued their little experiments in fortune telling, matters imperceptibly began to get out of hand. The girls became frightened and upset, and soon their fears found bizarre and unsettling physical expression. As Boston merchant Robert Calef skeptically reconstructed these events in his 1700 history of Salem witchcraft, the girls began "getting into holes, and creeping under chairs and stools, and to use sundry odd postures and antic gestures, uttering foolish, ridiculous speeches, which neither they themselves nor any others could make sense of. . . ."[2]

Those who actually witnessed the symptoms found them less amusing than did Calef. Samuel Parris himself first turned for advice to the Village physician, who offered a chilling diagnosis: the girls were not ill from natural causes but were in the grip of the "Evil Hand"—malevolent witchcraft. What had already been a whispered suspicion was now out in the open. One Village matron proposed the application of an old procedure to determine whether the strange behavior of the girls really had a supernatural source: baking a "witch cake," compounded of rye meal mixed with urine from the afflicted girls, and feeding it to a dog. (If they were bewitched, so the folk wisdom went, the unlucky canine would display physical manifestations similar to their own.) The cook in the Parris household, a West Indian slave named Tituba, was recruited to undertake the unusual baking project.

By this time, more than a month had elapsed since the girls' strange behavior began, and still no legal action had been taken. By this time, too, the afflictions were beginning to spread ("plague-like," as Parris later put it) beyond the minister's house; soon they would come to affect about seven or eight other girls as well, ranging in age from twelve to nineteen, and including three from the household of Thomas Putnam, Jr. At last the troubled Village resorted to the law. On February 29, 1692, warrants went out for the arrest of three Village women whom the girls, under the pressure of intense adult questioning, had finally named as their tormenters: Sarah Good, Sarah Osborne, and Tituba herself.

Patterns of Accusation

The first three women to be accused can be seen as "deviants" or "outcasts" in their community— the kinds of people who anthropologists have suggested are particularly susceptible to such accusations. Tituba was a West Indian slave; Sarah Good was a pauper who went around the Village begging aggressively for food and lodging; "Gammer" Osborne, while somewhat better off, was a bedridden old woman.

In March, however, a new pattern began to emerge. Two of the three witches accused in that month—the third was little Dorcas Good—were church members (a sign of real respectability in the seventeenth century) and the wives of prosperous freeholders. This pattern continued and even intensified for the duration of the outbreak: the twenty-two persons accused in April included the wealthiest shipowner in Salem (Phillip English) and a minister of the gospel who was a Harvard graduate with a considerable estate in England (George Burroughs). By mid-May warrants had been issued against two of the seven selectmen of Salem Town; and by the end of the summer some of the most prominent people in Massachusetts and their close kin had been accused if not officially charged. As the attorney who prepared the cases against the accused wrote at the end of May, "The afflicted spare no person of what quality so ever."[3]

True, except for Burroughs, none of these persons of quality was ever brought to trial, much less executed. Some escaped from jail or house arrest, others were simply never arraigned. Nevertheless, the overall direction of the accusations remains clear: up the social ladder, fitfully but perceptibly, to its very top. Whatever else they may have been, the Salem witch trials cannot be written off as a communal effort to purge the poor, the deviant, or the outcast.

Just as the accusations thrust steadily upward through the social strata of provincial society, so, too, they pressed outward across geographic boundaries. Beginning within Salem Village itself, the accusations moved steadily into an increasingly wide orbit. The first twelve witches were either residents of the Village or persons who lived just beyond its borders. But of all the indictments which followed this initial dozen, only fifteen were directed against people in the immediate vicinity of Salem Village. The other victims came from virtually every town in Essex County, including the five which surrounded the Village. (In the town of Andover alone, there were more arrests than in Salem Village itself.)[4]

While almost all these arrests were made on the basis of testimony given by the ten or so afflicted girls of Salem Village (although in some cases they merely confirmed the validity of others' accusations), it is clear that the girls themselves did not actually know most of the people they named. Accusers and accused were in many if not most cases personally unacquainted. Whatever was troubling the girls and those who encouraged them, it was something deeper than the kind of chronic, petty squabbles between near neighbors which seem to have been at the root of earlier and far less severe witchcraft episodes in New England.

But if the outbreak's geographic pattern tends to belie certain traditional explanations, it raises other, more intriguing, interpretive possibilities. As Map 1 shows, there were fourteen accused witches who lived within the bounds of Salem Village. Twelve of these fourteen lived in the eastern section of the Village.

There were thirty-two adult Villagers who testified against these accused witches.[5] Only two of these lived in that eastern section. The other thirty lived on the western side. In other words, the alleged witches and those who accused them resided on opposite sides of the Village.

There were twenty-nine Villagers who publicly showed their skepticism about the trials or came to the defense of one or more of the accused witches. Twenty-four of these lived in the eastern part of the Village—the same side on which the witches lived—and only two of them in the west. Those who defended the witches were generally their neighbors, often their immediate neighbors. Those who accused them were not.

A Divided Community

The outbreak of 1692 did not suddenly flare up in a historical void, nor, for that matter, was it an isolated upheaval in an otherwise harmonious Puritan community. Even before 1692 Salem Village had hardly been a haven of tranquility. For years its 600-odd residents had been divided into two bitterly antagonistic factions. The source of their troubles lay in the very circumstances under which the Village had first come into existence. Originally the settlement (which is now the city of Danvers, and not to be confused with Salem proper) had simply been a part of the town of Salem, and when it was granted a limited and partial legal existence as "Salem Village" in 1672, it still remained in many ways a mere appendage of its larger and more prosperous neighbor. Some people in the Village were quite content with this satellite status, but others resented it and pressed for complete independence. The latter group, led by a numerous and powerful local family named Putnam, focused its efforts on an attempt to establish a separate church—the central pillar of any Puritan town. In 1672, to be sure, a meetinghouse for religious worship had been built in Salem Village, and in the intervening years several ministers had come and gone, but a full-scale Puritan church, with the power to baptize believers, conduct communion services, and discipline its members, had never been established.

At last in 1689, however, the independence-minded group in Salem Village managed to get its way, and a church was formed under the ministry of Samuel Parris, a thirty-six-year-old former merchant. But this victory was purchased at a heavy price, for the new minister, and the church he headed, represented only a single group in the community—a group led by the Putnams. (Fully half of the original twenty-six church members bore the Putnam name!)

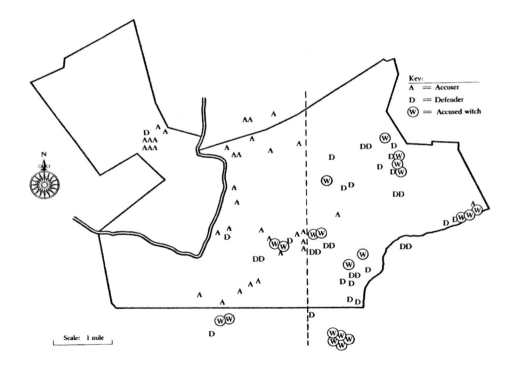

Map 1   *The Geography of Witchcraft: Salem Village, 1692*

Sources: Residential map of Salem Village in 1692 included as a frontispiece to volume one of Charles W. Upham, *Salem Witchcraft*, 22 vols. (Boston, 1867); W. Elliot Woodward, *Records of Salem Witchcraft Copied from the Original Documents*, 2 vols. (Roxbury, Mass., Privately printed, 1864; reissued in one volume, New York, Da Capo Press, 1969).

Note: The non-Village accused witches shown on this map are those whose places of residence lay on the fringes of the Village boundaries. The following persons are not included on the map or in the accompanying discussion: the "afflicted girls" (see note 5); Sarah and Dorcas Good, who had no fixed residence; Mary DeRich, whose residence we have been unable to locate; and the five Villagers who were both accusers and defenders in 1692.

The formation of the church, in short, did not serve to unify Salem Village, but only to intensify its inner divisions.

Factional tension was increased still more by the contractual terms under which Parris agreed to take over the Village pulpit: he exacted a maximum of economic concessions from the community—including the highly irregular procedure of securing full personal title to the Village parsonage and its surrounding land! These terms, coupled with Parris' intense and rigid personality, served to exacerbate local tensions—and to focus them clearly on Parris himself. Those Villagers who had all along opposed establishment of the church, and who now refused to join it—a group that included some of the community's wealthiest residents—determined to drive Parris out of his position. They refused to worship in the Village meetinghouse, pointedly attending elsewhere, and withheld payment of their local taxes (which went for the minister's salary and firewood). But their most deadly stroke came at the annual Village election in October 1691 when they swept out of office the existing five-man Village Committee (the local equivalent of a board of selectmen), dominated by Parris' friends, and elected a new Committee made up, to a man, of his known opponents.

The new anti-Parris Committee went quickly to work: it refused even to assess taxes for the payment of Parris' 1692 salary, and it challenged the legality of his "fraudulent" acquisition of the ministry-house and lands in 1689. Parris, now wholly dependent on the voluntary contributions of his supporters for money to purchase the necessities of life—and even for firewood to heat his house—was in desperately serious trouble at the beginning of 1692, and his Putnam supporters knew it.

Thus we begin to see the significance of the fact that of the first four "afflicted girls" in Salem Village, two lived in the household of Samuel Parris himself, and a third, Ann Putnam, was the twelve-year-old daughter of Parris' most dogged supporter, Thomas Putnam Jr. (In the coming weeks, the Thomas Putnam household would produce two more afflicted girls: Mercy Lewis, a servant girl, and Mary Walcott, a young relative.)

While these girls themselves may well have been unacquainted with the details of factional politics in the Village, they could hardly have remained untouched by the bitterness and resentment that pervaded their own households. It may be no accident that their physical torments set in after they had attempted, with scary results, to predict the future—a future that loomed as highly uncertain not only for the girls themselves but for the adults they knew best.

As the torments of the girls worsened in February 1692, it must have been difficult for Samuel Parris to distinguish between the political problems that threatened his professional survival and the bodily agonies that seemed to threaten the physical survival of his daughter and her friends. He was ready to lash out at the source of his troubles—wherever that might lie. In a sermon he delivered on February 14, Parris lamented "the present low condition of the church in the midst of its enemies," but added a prophecy that was as desperate as it was ominous: "Oh! Shortly the case will be far otherwise."[6]

Although the Rev. Samuel Parris served as the immediate focus of factional conflict in Salem Village, it is clear that he was not the ultimate source of that factionalism. Fortunately for us, the Villagers in their appeals to outside authorities produced several sets of petitions and counter-petitions, many of them complete with signatures, which allow us to analyze the nature of the struggle by reconstructing the membership of the two competing groups. By far the most useful of these petitions, for such a purpose, are the two addressed to Increase Mather and other elders of the Massachusetts churches in the spring of 1695, a month after an ecclesiastical council met at Salem Village in an effort to resolve the bitter differences in the church.[7] The eighty-four Salem Villagers, male and female, who signed the anti-Parris petition and the 105 who put their names to the pro-Parris petition represent a high percentage of the adult residents of the Village. (Our own "census" of Salem Village in 1692 suggests a population of about 215 persons over the age of twenty-one.)[8] As this strikingly full breakdown of the two factions is analyzed, certain patterns and correlations emerge which provide at least a beginning point for understanding the dynamics of Village factionalism in these years.

The Two Factions: A Profile

To begin with, there is a clear connection between membership in the Salem Village church and support for Samuel Parris. Of the sixty-two people who belonged to the Village church in May 1695 (not counting Parris himself and his wife), forty-two signed the pro-Parris petition and only eight the anti-Parris document. (Six of these eight were three of the "dissenting brethren" and their wives.) More striking still is the fact that of the twenty-five original members—those admitted when the church was formed on November 19, 1689—only one, Joshua Rea, Senior, opposed Parris in 1695.[9] Those who made the decision to cast their lot with the Salem Village church remained to the end overwhelmingly loyal to its minister.

But of the Villagers who retained their membership in other churches while worshiping with the Salem Village congregation, a far smaller percentage supported Parris. Of the eighteen such persons whose names appear on the petitions, only ten endorsed Parris, while eight opposed him.[10] Not church membership per se, but affiliation with the Salem Village church, is the decisive indicator of support for Parris.

In December 1695 Salem Village imposed a tax for the support of the ministry. Assessments on individual property owners were apportioned on the basis of their landholdings and other wealth, in accordance with a scale set by the General Court.[11] Of the eighty-nine adult Village males who signed one of the two petitions of 1695, all but three appear on the tax rolls of that year. Thus it is possible to analyze with a high degree of precision the comparative economic standing of the two factions.

As Table 1 shows, of the twelve most prosperous men among the petition signers (those taxed more than twenty shillings), only four supported Parris, while eight opposed him. (If we exclude the members of the Putnam family, whose unique situation requires separate treatment, the contrast is even more striking: only one non-Putnam in this most wealthy category supported Parris, while seven opposed him.) At the other end of the scale, thirty-one of the poorer men of the Village (those taxed at under ten shillings) backed Parris, with only fifteen in opposition. In other words, the richest men in the Village opposed Parris by a margin of better than two-to-one, while the poorest supported him in almost precisely the same proportion.[12]

Breaking the data down in another way, the average tax of the pro-Parris householders was just under eleven shillings, in contrast to an average of more than fifteen shillings for the opponents of Parris.[13] The fifty-one pro-Parris householders paid a total of £28 in the 1695 taxation, scarcely higher than the £26/15 paid by the considerably smaller number of householders (thirty-five) in the anti-Parris ranks. As these figures so vividly suggest, the opponents of Parris, while numerically a minority, owned virtually as much Village property as did his supporters.

We have reported the striking pattern which emerges when the places of residence of accused, accusers, and defenders in the witchcraft outbreak are plotted. As Map 2 shows, a similar geographic pattern distinguishes the pro-Parris from the anti-Parris faction.[14] The petitioners who lived nearest Salem Town (or, in a few cases, just over the Village line in the Town) opposed Parris by a ratio of six-to-one. Those whose houses were in the northwestern half of the Village, most remote from the Town, *supported* Parris by a ratio of better than four to one. (In the central section of the Village the two factions divided much more evenly, with the pro-Parris group somewhat in the preponderance.)

	Number of householders in each tax bracket		Percentage of householders in each tax bracket	
AMOUNT OF 1695-96 TAX	PRO-PARRIS (AVERAGE TAX: 10.9 SHILLINGS)	ANTI-PARRIS (AVERAGE TAX: 15.3 SHILLINGS)	PRO-PARRIS	ANTI-PARRIS
Under 10 shillings	31	15	61	43
10–20 shillings	16	12	31	34
Over 20 shillings	4	8	8	23
Total	51	35	100	100

table 1   Factionalism and Wealth in Salem Village, 1695

Sources: Tax list, Village Records, Dec. 13, 1695; pro-Parris and anti-Parris petitions as transcribed by Samuel Parris in the Village Church Records preceding the entry for June 2, 1695.

Commercial Town, Agricultural Village: The Seeds of Discord

But simply to describe the distinguishing characteristics of the two factions is no more than a first step. The next, and more difficult one, is to try to make some sense of these factions, particularly in the context of the protracted political struggles of the period. Our point of departure must be a central fact of Salem Village life: the immediate presence, directly to the south and east, of Salem Town. From almost any point of view, whether geographic or institutional, Salem Town dominated the horizon of the farmers of Salem Village (See Map 3).

What mattered was not simply the fact of the Town's power; it was also the quality of that power. By the 1690's Salem Town was a far cry from the community it had been, half a century earlier, when the first farmers had left it for the hinterland settlement which would become Salem Village. Prosperous from the start, the Town in the years after 1660 entered its great era of economic, and specifically mercantile, expansion. Well before the end of the century, that expansion had led (as one recent study puts it) to "a distinctly urban pattern of life" in Salem Town. The Town's growing commercial importance was officially recognized in 1683 when the General Court designated Boston and Salem as the colony's two "ports of entry" through which all imports and exports had to pass. Increasingly, Salem was gaining access to a broader trading orbit of which London was the center. Such evidence as the close correspondence during these years between grain prices in Salem and in London indicates that the "Atlantic Market" was becoming a reality—and the merchants of Salem Town were immersed in it, exporting cod and mackerel, furs, horses, grain, beef, pork, masts, and naval stores to the other American colonies, the West Indies, the Canaries, Newfoundland, and England, and importing tobacco, sugar, cloth, rum, and a host of other products. In the 1690's twenty-six Salem men owned twenty-one merchant vessels averaging nearly fifty tons each and comprising 12 percent of the total tonnage in Massachusetts. While this left Salem far behind dominant Boston, it did make her—as the 1683 legislation had recognized—the only other really significant mercantile center in the colony.[15]

One consequence of these developments was a sharp rise in the Town's relative wealth. In the first thirty years of its settlement—the period before 1660—the average size of individual Salem Town estates recorded in probate court had actually been lower than the average for the rest of Essex County; in contrast, during the period 1661–81, the estates of Salem Town dwellers averaged almost one-third higher than those from the rest of the county.

But Salem's rising prosperity and cosmopolitan connections did not benefit equally all segments of the Town population. Quite the contrary: in the 1661–81 period (again on the

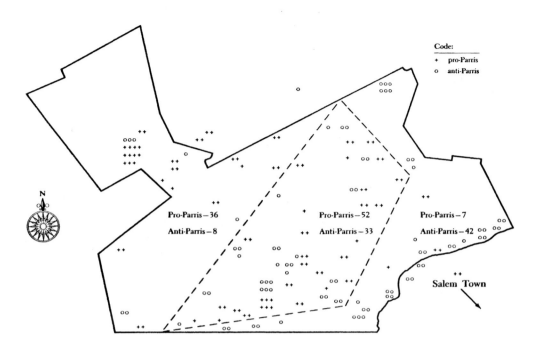

Map 2   *The Geography of Factionalism: Residential pattern of the Signers of the Pro-Parris and Anti-Parris Petitions of 1695*

Sources: The residential map of Salem Village included as a frontispiece in volume I of Charles W. Upham, *Salem Witchcraft*, 2 vols. (Boston, 1867); the pro-Parris and anti-Parris petitions, with signatures, as transcribed by Samuel Parris in the Salem Village Church Records preceding the entry for June 2, 1695.

Note: The figures indicate the number of pro-Parris and anti-Parris petitions signers who lived in that section. Included in the totals are eleven signers (six pro-Parris, five anti-Parris) who lived just beyond the Village bounds. Omitted are eleven other signers (one anti-Parris, ten pro-Parris) whose places of residence are unknown.

evidence of probated wills), the richest 10 percent of Salem's population controlled 62 percent of its wealth—almost three times as much as it had controlled a generation earlier.[16] What had happened, in fact, was that the prosperity of the Town had polarized the distribution of its wealth and propelled into a position of clear dominance a single group of men: the merchants.

The rise of the merchant class was reflected in Salem Town politics. In the years before 1665, twice as many farmers as merchants had been elected Town selectmen; in the 1665–1700 period, the merchants among the selectmen outnumbered the farmers by six to one.[17] Only those few farmers with close merchant ties and affinities continued to exercise any sustained political influence in the Town.

For the farmers of Salem Village, who represented about one-fifth of the Town's total population in this period,[18] these developments were looming realities which simultaneously enlarged the figurative dimensions of the Town in their eyes and diminished the stature of their own community. The percentage of Essex County wealth represented by farm assets and equipment in the seventeenth century shrank steadily and dramatically through the 1680's (the last decade for which data have been compiled). In the 1650's, on the basis of probated estates, farm wealth averaged 40 percent of the total; thirty years later it was hovering at about 9 percent. Although it may be going too far to claim, as has one recent student of Essex County economic history, that agriculture was a "declining industry" in these years,

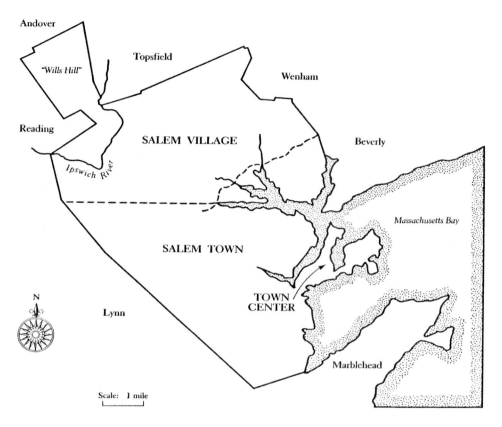

Map 3 *Salem: Town and Village*

it seems clear that it was no more than holding its own while the Town's commercial development shot ahead.[19]

Nor were these changes experienced merely as data buried in statistical tables; they were the vivid and tangible substance of everyday reality. In Salem no less than in Boston, the rise of an internationally oriented merchant class, connected by ties of marriage and mutual interest, spawned a style of life and a sensibility decidedly alien to the pre-capitalist patterns of village existence. The differences were becoming apparent even in the Town's physical appearance; while Salem in these years did not yet possess the breathtakingly beautiful mansions which the architect Samuel McIntire would design for its commercial aristocrats a century later, the trend was already clear. Even a Londoner who visited Salem Town in 1686, for example, was struck by the "many fine houses" he saw there.[20] If this was how the Town impressed an English cosmopolite, how must it have struck the farmers of Salem Village?

Even before the establishment of Salem Village in 1672, many of the residents of the area had recognized that it was more than geography that separated them from the Town of Salem. As early as 1667, in their petition to the General Court asking relief from the burden of attending military watch in Salem, the thirty-one signatories did not stop with the obvious point that they lived five to ten miles from Salem center; they went on to compare the "compact town" to their own "scattered" settlement, always vulnerable to Indian attack because its houses were so widely separated "one from another, some a mile, some further," so that even "six or eight watches will not serve us." They proceeded to inquire sarcastically "whether Salem Town hath not more cause to send us help to watch among ourselves than we have to go to them?"[21] But no help came forth from this direction. Lacking it, yet legally powerless to strike out on their own, many Salem Village residents even as early as the 1660's came to feel both exploited and neglected by the Town. Envy mingled with resentment in those Villagers who had constant cause to remember the dynamic and vaguely hostile urban presence on their southeasterly border.

The Development of Village Factionalism

But the looming presence of Salem Town was not perceived as hostile by everyone in the Village. If the changes in the Town had affected all the Villagers in the same way, or to the same degree, the Village's affairs in the final quarter of the seventeenth century would surely have taken quite a different turn. But as it actually happened, not every Villager had reason to feel alienated from the Town. Indeed, the economic and social transformations of the Town in these years affected different Villagers in quite different ways. The very developments which threatened many of them gave others reason to take heart. It was this fact, above all, that produced the factional lines which from the beginning divided the Village.

From the 1670's on, proximity to the Town, and even a direct involvement in its economic life, repeatedly emerged as a determining factor in the divisions which plagued the Village. These divisions pitted people who continued to identify with Salem Town against others for whom the Village, and what they saw as its distinctive interests, were paramount.

From this perspective, the geographic and economic profile of the two factions begins to take on meaning. For even though the Village's relationship to the Town was the crucial factor in the early history of the Village, that relationship was never simply a matter of Town versus Village. Within each, significant divisions were to be found. In the Town the dominant merchant group was challenged dramatically on a number of occasions. Similarly, as the demarcation lines of the two Village factions so clearly suggest, the Salem Villagers were by no means of one accord in their feelings toward the Town. To certain Salem Villagers, the urbanization and commercial growth of the Town seemed a promising and exciting development. The chance of a boundary line may have placed them in Salem Village, but their interests lay with the Town.

For they recognized that Salem Town required food, and that the Village was the nearest food-producing region. Furthermore, the Town's developing export trade was based in part on products which Salem Village could supply. While we do not know, because we lack the necessary commercial records, precisely how much Salem Village grain and beef went to fill the bellies of slaves and planters in Barbados, or how much Village timber helped build houses in Newfoundland or ships-of-the-line in England, we can be fairly certain that to some degree involvement in this larger market, or the possibility of such involvement, was a factor in the Village economy.

But Salem Village agriculture in these years was being pursued under certain adverse conditions: not only was productivity limited by primitive equipment, but the size of farms was shrinking as lands were divided among maturing sons of the third generation. Under these circumstances, relatively slight differences became crucial in determining which Village farmers would be able to cross the subsistence threshold and begin to profit by the Village's proximity to a populous trading center. In at least two important respects—quality of land and access to market—those farmers on the eastern (or Town) side of the Village had a significant advantage. Modern topographical maps show what any Salem Village farmer knew from first-hand experience: the best lands in the Village were the broad, flat meadows of the eastern part, nearest the coast, while the western part was increasingly broken up by sharp little hills and marshy depressions. The eastern side of the Village, too, was significantly closer to the network of roads and waterways which gave access to Salem Town and her markets. (The additional two or three miles may seem negligible today, but for the farmer who had to convey his goods by ox cart over rutted, muddy, and often flooded paths before reaching the better-maintained Ipswich Road, they certainly loomed large.) In both these respects, then, the farmers on this side of the Village had a crucial edge in supplying the needs of Salem Town and, to a limited degree, the broader Atlantic market of which it was a part. And Village geography, as we shall now see, had other effects as well.

The Ipswich Road: An Anti-Parris Paradigm

The eastern section of Salem Village, because of its location, boasted an unusually high concentration of what little non-agricultural economic activity was to be found in the community during the 1690's. One way to make this point is to examine with some care those Villagers who lived on or near the Ipswich Road, which formed the boundary between Salem Town and Salem Village, and which was the major northward route from Boston. Just south of the Village this thoroughfare was joined by an important spur road connecting it (and the Village itself) with the center of Salem Town. Even more important, the Ipswich Road—crossing, near their farthest point of navigability, no fewer than three rivers which flowed on into Salem harbor—was the site of several wharves and landing places from which goods and products could move by water between Village and Town. (See Map 4.)

More than any other inhabitants of the community, the Villagers who lived along the Ipswich Road were exposed to the Town and its concerns. Like a modern interstate highway, the road passed *by* the Village, not into it. With all kinds of travelers daily passing near their doors on the way to or from Salem Town, or Boston itself, town and province news were inevitably the common currency of conversation. The Village center, by contrast, well to the west, must have represented a considerably weaker pole of attraction.

It is not surprising that a number of the men living on or very near the Ipswich Road were engaged in occupations which brought them into regular contact with a wide range of individuals: occupations such as potter, physician, carpenter, innkeeper, sawmill operator, shoemaker, miller, sawyer (that is, wood finisher), and "dishturner." Particularly important, in terms of the Townward orientation of this part of Salem Village, were the four taverns which stood along a shot stretch of the Ipswich Road as it passed rough Salem Village. Three of these actually lay within the Village: the licensed taverns of Joshua Rea, Jr. and Walter Phillips, and the unlicensed—but well known and well patronized—tavern of Edward and Bridget Bishop. The other, operated by John Proctor, stood about a mile south of the Village boundary.[22]

The Ipswich Road, the part of the Village most intimately linked to Salem Town, boasted a particularly dense concentration of anti-Parris sentiment. Of the twenty-one Village householders who lived along this road or within one-quarter mile of it, only two signed the pro-Parris petition in 1695, while thirteen aligned themselves with Parris's opponents.[23] (From another angle, fully one-third of the householders in the anti-Parris faction lived along or near the Ipswich Road.)

The small entrepreneurs of the Ipswich Road were not the wealthiest or most prominent members of the anti-Parris group, but they shared to a particularly intense degree the feeling that their livelihood was linked to Salem Town more closely than to Salem Village. While the interests of the anti-Parris faction were far from identical to those of the merchants in the Town, they viewed the Town not as a threat, but as a center with which they might hope to establish a profitable commercial relationship. Conversely, they felt little sympathy—and ultimately much enmity—toward those who were working to widen the political gap between Town and Village. If the members of the pro-Parris faction had succeeded in breaking away from Salem entirely and establishing an independent town under their control, they could have acted in various ways to the disadvantage of the more commercially

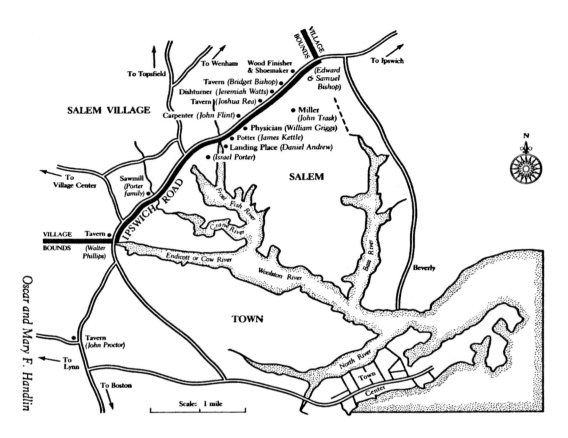

Map 4 *The Ipswich Road, 1692*

(Adapted from the frontispiece map of Salem Village in Charles W. Upham, *Salem Witchcraft*, (Boston, 1867). For the sources on the occupations of the Ipswich Road men, see n. 22.)

oriented Villagers, including the imposition of fees on the transport of products beyond the town boundaries. As early as 1666, when the separatist move was just getting underway, the Townsmen reported that even some inhabitants of the Farms were prepared to oppose any change which would force them to "forsake Salem."[24]

The Village Church: A Pro-Parris Paradigm

But, for the Salem Villager who would later join the pro-Parris faction, there was every reason to "forsake Salem." Remote from the Town, and cut off even from convenient access to it, he increasingly came to see his interests neglected by those in power there. Consistently, then, he opposed those in the Village who represented, or seemed to represent, the intrusive thrust of Salem Town and what it stood for, and just as consistently he worked to build up the Village as a strong and independent entity distinct from the Town. For him, the church which the Village lacked before 1689 promised more than religious solace; it loomed also as a potential counterweight, spiritual and political, to the unfamiliar developments which were gaining such force so near at hand.

Once the church did become a reality, it provided an institutional locus for all those Villagers who felt threatened by such developments. Predictably, these were not the richest men in the Village. Although our general impression of colonial New England communities is that those prosperous inhabitants at the top of the tax rolls tend to figure prominently on the church rolls as well, this was not the case in Salem Village. Of the thirteen Village householders taxed at more than one pound in December 1695, only three joined the Village church during Samuel Parris's tenure. (These three—John, Nathaniel, and Jonathan Putnam—were all members of the family which will receive separate consideration in the next chapter.) The Village church, in fact, was less of an institution through which the wealthiest members of the community gave expression to their special status than a bulwark against precisely these people—and against the insidious infection with which they seemed to be tainted.

But neither is this to say that the church was dominated by the *poorest* Villagers. Of the sixty-two Villagers taxed in 1695–96 at under ten shillings, only seven, or about 11 percent, were members of the Village church. (See Table 2.) It was, rather, the broad middle economic group in the Village—the taxpayers in the 10–20 shilling range on our tables—who made up the bulk of the church membership. Fifteen such men (more than 50 percent of those in this tax bracket) joined the Village church under Parris's ministry. These were the men who had a sufficiently large stake in the status quo to feel menaced by whatever might threaten it, yet not enough to be able to take real advantage of the commercial opportunities that were opening up. It was this group, politically conscious, literate, and defensive, that provided, along with several wealthy members of the Putnam family, the active core of Samuel Parris's support.

But there remains another crucial component in this support: the twenty-nine male *non-church* members who signed the pro-Parris petition, and who in fact with their wives made possible the forging of a pro-Parris majority in the Village. As Table 3 shows, these were primarily poor Villagers: twenty-one of the twenty-nine were taxed at under ten shillings in 1695, and two were not taxed at all. Some of them landless, some with only the most meager acreage, these were not, in the nature of things, men who have left us many clues as to the reason for their political allegiance. But, whatever their motives for remaining outside the church, we may speculate that they nevertheless perceived this institution as a friendly and sheltering buffer against the world beyond the fragile boundary lines of Salem Village.

The pro-Parris faction thus emerges as a coalition whose shared fears united it in support of Parris: a core group of Villagers of middling wealth who were also church members, supplemented by another group, approximately twice as large, of poorer Villagers who were not church members but who identified with the Village church and its minister. The church members provided the institutional structure and the political impetus, the others supplied the votes and the signatures.

Since the pro-Parris faction also played a leading role in the witchcraft prosecutions, it has typically been portrayed as a powerful and domineering clique. From the evidence, however, this group emerges as by far the more vulnerable of the two: less wealthy than its opposition, owning less land, quite literally hedged in by more flourishing anti-Parris neighbors and less able to benefit from the commercial developments centered in Salem Town.

If the Ipswich Road helped shape and define the anti-Parris faction, it also provided an objective focus for the amorphous fears of the pro-Parris group, for whom it would have seemed not so much the line which separated the Village from the Town, but the very channel through which the Town penetrated the Village. The road stood as a perpetual affront to those who felt the integrity of the Village to be menaced from just this quarter. Its residents, with their more commercial outlook and occupations, had in many cases already succumbed to the lure which menaced the Village as a whole.

The unusual concentration of taverns along the Ipswich Road dramatized the threat with particular vividness. The Puritans, of course, did not frown on alcohol as such, especially when it was consumed in the domestic circle; indeed, beer and wine were standard accompaniments to seventeenth-century New England fare. But they did fear, profoundly, the threat to social

table 2 Wealth and Salem Village Church Membership

Tax Bracket, 1695–96

TAXPAYERS	UNDER 10 SHILLINGS	10–20 SHILLINGS	OVER 20 SHILLINGS
Church members	7	15	3
Non-church members	55	14	10
Total	62	29	13

Sources: Tax list, Village Records, Dec. 13, 1695; membership information in the Church Records.

stability embodied in taverns and inns. As gathering places for wayfarers and strangers, they offered the individual at least partial and temporary escape from the overlapping restraints of family, church, and town. The obvious hesitation with which the courts licensed taverns, the close oversight the authorities exercised, and the haste with which licenses were revoked at any hint of disorderliness—all bear witness to the reality of this concern.[25]

A revealing glimpse into the social circumstances surrounding the establishment of one of these taverns emerges from John Proctor's request to the Salem selectmen in 1666 for a license to operate a tavern in his house on the Ipswich Road near the Salem Village line. His residence, he said, was "in the common roadway, which occasioneth several travelers to call in for some refreshment as they pass along." Since the free entertaining of these wayfarers was proving to be expensive, Proctor added: "I do therefore earnestly request you that you would be pleased to grant me liberty to set up a house of entertainment to sell beer, cider [and] liquors."[26] The court granted Proctor's petition, with the stipulation that he sell exclusively to strangers. Thus, from the Salem Village perspective, the Proctor house became a rendezvous point for outsiders—and *only* for outsiders.

For the pro-Parris Salem Villagers, with their particular anxieties, this generalized concern over taverns must have been especially intense. Given such a background, it is not surprising to find that three of the four Ipswich Road tavern keepers figured prominently in the climactic Village events of the 1690's—and two of these three as victims of those events. Joshua Rea, Jr., publicly expressed his opposition to the witchcraft trials in 1692 by signing a petition seeking to save Rebecca Nurse from the gallows. In 1695 Rea's name appears on the anti-Parris petition.[27] Two of the other tavern keepers, Bridget Bishop and John Proctor, were unable to take a stand for or against Parris in 1695: they had been hanged three years before for committing witchcraft.

table 3 Wealth and Salem Village Church Membership in the Pro-Parris Faction

TAXPAYERS	Tax bracket, 1695–96			*Average assessment*
	UNDER 10 SHILLINGS	10–20 SHILLINGS	OVER 20 SHILLINGS	
Pro-Parris church members (n = 21)	7	11	3	14.4 shillings
Pro-Parris non-church members (n = 27)	21	4	2	7.8 shillings

Sources: Tax list, Village Records, Dec. 13, 1695; pro-Parris petition as transcribed by Samuel Parris in the Village Church Records preceding the entry for June 2, 1695; membership information in the Church Records, *passim*.

Village Factionalism: A Wider Perspective

But still we have not penetrated to the heart of the matter. How could such a dispute have escalated to so bitter and deadly a level? Why were the two sides so long unable to find any political means to resolving the impasse?

To understand the intensity of the dispute, we must recognize the fact—self-evident to the men and women of Salem Village—that what was going on was not simply a personal quarrel, an economic dispute, or even a struggle or power, but a mortal conflict involving the very nature of the community itself. The fundamental issue was not who was to control the Village, but what its essential character was to be. To the Puritans of seventeenth-century New England, no social or political issue was without its moral dimension as well. For a community was more than simply a collection of individuals who happened to live and work together; it was itself an organism with a reality and an existence distinct from that of its component parts.

John Winthrop, the first governor of colonial Massachusetts, fully articulated this theme as early as 1630 in his lecture aboard the ship *Arabella*, as the first large contingent of Puritan settlers was sailing toward New England. "[W]e must be knit together in this work as one man," he declared; "We must delight in each other, . . . rejoice together, mourn together, labor and suffer together, always having before our eyes our commission and community in the work, our community as members of the same body."[28] Since each community was almost literally a "body," the individuals who composed it could neither logically nor practically regard themselves as autonomous creatures with their own "particular" interests. For a person to pursue such a self-determined course was as destructive and, ultimately, as absurd as for one part of the human body to pursue *its* own good: for a hand to refuse to release to the mouth the food it held in its grasp, for example, or for the mouth to refuse to pass along that food to the stomach. "Self-interest" was like that. If left uncontrolled, it could result only in the failure of the community and of every person within it.

Thus, Winthrop's insistence that the men and women aboard the *Arabella* were "members of the same body" was no casual figure of speech or sentimental paean to a vague commonality of feeling. It was, for Winthrop, a statement of certain very specific social and economic policies—policies which he enunciated again and again in his lecture: "We must be willing to abridge ourselves of our superfluities, for the supply of others' necessities"; "The care of the public must oversway all private respects"; "We must not look only on our own things, but also on the things of our brethren."[29] And Winthrop's scheme contained an enforcement procedure as well: the constant scrutiny and regulation of all facets of individual behavior in order to nip in the bud deviations that threatened the interests of the community as a whole.

The important thing is not whether very many people actually behaved in this fashion (almost certainly most of them did not), but rather the fact that when they did not act in this way—when they pursued their self-interest at the expense of the greater good of the whole—they felt that they were not behaving properly.

By the end of the seventeenth century, this sense that there was a dangerous conflict between private will and public good had become seriously eroded in many quarters by two generations of population growth, geographic dispersal, and economic opportunity: the emergence of pre-industrial capitalism.

But in the 1690's, it was still possible for the farmers of the pro-Parris faction to believe that the outcome of this struggle remained very much in question. Thus, for them, Salem Town was not suspect just because of its vaguely hostile political climate, or because it was following a different line of economic development, but because the total thrust of that commercial development represented a looming *moral* threat with implications of the most fundamental sort.

As we have seen, Salem Village itself in the late seventeenth century was neither a haven of pastoral tranquility nor an embodiment of John Winthrop's public-mindedness. And yet, coupled with the inescapable realities of social turbulence and diminished opportunity was the sense that if any place *could* offer shelter against sweeping social change and provide a setting where the Puritan social vision might yet be realized, it would likely be an agricultural, essentially noncommercial settlement such as Salem Village. The very nature of farm life, with its settled routines and seasonal rhythms, offered at least the illusion of social stability and continuity—and perhaps, in comparison to what was happening in Salem Town, it was more than illusion.

Many people in Salem Village sensed that this social order was being profoundly shaken by a superhuman force which had lured all too many into active complicity with it. We have chosen to construe this force as emergent mercantile capitalism. Salem Village called it witchcraft.

The Lure of Madame Bubble

It is tempting simply to label the pro-Parris faction as "Puritans," their opponents as "capitalists," and let it go at that. But we know from experience that human beings rarely fit quite so neatly into such categorical boxes. And as the work of several generations of scholars has made clear, the relationship between Puritanism and capitalism is itself deeply ambiguous. In any case, the pro-Parris Villagers were certainly no more a group of Winthrop's self-denying communitarians than their opponents were the materialistic individualists we commonly associate with nineteenth-century entrepreneurship. The similarities between our two little microcosmic groups would probably, to most modem eyes, have seemed far more noticeable than the subtle differences of emphasis and priority which set them apart.

And, still further, at a time when one world view was imperceptibly yielding to another, each faction must have shared enough of the other's outlook to feel its power and be drawn to it. The anti-Parris men must at times have sensed with a pang what they were giving up in turning toward the burgeoning Town and away from the Village. And the pro-Parris Villagers, for their part, must have felt deeply the lure of the forces which were transforming the Town: the very forces they feared and despised. This, too, helps us understand the intensity of the conflict. For the Villagers were not only at war with each other; they were also at war with themselves.

It was not only the accused witches who were tempted into complicity with the forces of change. We have stressed the conflicting emotions most Salem Villagers must have felt as they witnessed the transformation of Salem Town into a major commercial center, and as they saw an altered social and economic order beginning to take shape. The witchcraft testimony itself makes plain that even those who felt most uneasy about those developments were also deeply attracted by them. For one of Satan's most insidious guises in Salem Village during 1692 was that of thriving freeholder and prosperous merchant, and the afflicted girls of the Village acknowledged the persuasiveness of his blandishments by the very desperation with which they rebuffed him.

Often, to be sure, the strength of Satan's position in this bargaining lay solely in the threat of physical harm if the person he was recruiting refused to accept the contract he had to offer—usually, indeed, a literal contract, the parody of a church covenant. The Salem merchant Phillip English, for example, appeared spectrally to Susannah Sheldon, "and told me if I would touch his book, he would not bite me, but if I refused, then he did [*sic*] bite me."[30] The historian John Demos has recently emphasized the frequent references to such overtly aggressive behavior in the witchcraft testimony—the biting, choking, and pinching. But, as Demos also notes, there are other instances in which the aggression takes the more subtle form of wheedling through glittering promises of material gain and economic betterment.[31] The confessions which detailed these promises are at times poignant in their specificity: "new clothes," a "piece of money," "a pair of French fall shoes." Early in April, 1692, Satan appeared spectrally to Mercy Lewis, who worked in the household of Thomas Putnam, and offered her "gold and many fine things" if she would write in his book. A few weeks later Satan revisited young Mercy, this time in the form of Samuel Parris's unhappy predecessor in the Village pulpit, George Burroughs: "Mr. Burroughs carried me up to an exceeding high mountain and showed me all the kingdoms of the earth, and told me that he would give them all to me if I would write in his book." Parris's own servant girl, Abigail Williams, reported that she was "tempted by the offer of fine things." And his daughter Elizabeth Parris was promised by Satan that he would let her "go to a Golden City" if she would accept his rule.[32]

If "Satan," indeed, represented, at one level of consciousness, the forces of social change, it is appropriate that the afflicted girls should have found him simultaneously frightening and alluring; for that is also how they, and many of their elders, felt about the world they knew. This doubleness pervades the testimony of 1692 just as it pervades so much of the history of Salem Village. And it is precisely this doubleness which drove the witchcraft outbreak to its point of maximum psychological complexity.

For while the accusations thrust outward to draw in wealthy merchants and other ostentatious representatives of the new order—attempting thereby to affirm the externality of the menace—they simultaneously spiraled back toward the accusers themselves, until finally the distinction between accuser and accused, between afflicter and afflicted, threatened to vanish. Margaret Jacobs, an accuser of George Burroughs as well as of her own grandfather, George Jacobs, Sr., abjectly confessed to her own wickedness of heart after the two men had been executed. Deliverance Hobbs, a middle-aged woman who had for a time been afflicted, was herself on the examination stand by late April, accused of witchcraft: "Is it not a solemn thing, that last Lord's Day you were tormented, and now you are become a tormenter, so that you have changed sides? How comes this to pass?" When the tables were similarly turned upon Mary Warren, one of the principal afflicted girls, her examiner reiterated the same question: "You were a little while ago an afflicted person. Now you are an afflicter. How comes this to pass?"[33] One young woman charged with witchcraft, Sarah Cole of Lynn, was accused by the girls of the very act in which they themselves had engaged: fortune-telling.[34] Yet Sarah Cole was arrested as a witch, while Ann Putnam and Abigail Williams were called innocent victims of her witchcraft.

Indeed, if Samuel Parris himself had not been so skilled in the pulpit, it is not difficult to imagine that he, rather than George Burroughs, might have been the man finally pinpointed as the wizard masterminding the betrayal of the Village. Certainly Parris's behavior, far more than that of Burroughs, closely fit the pattern which Parris himself had described as clear proof of demonic possession. Burroughs may, in fact, have been a kind of surrogate for Parris: a substitute whose trial and execution helped Parris preserve both his ease of conscience and his continued immunity to accusation.[35]

How many other Salem Villagers had their own "George Burroughs"—a person they accused in an effort to expunge from their minds the suspicion that the real "guilt" was their own? A recent historian of sixteenth and seventeenth century witchcraft in Essex County, England, Alan Macfarlane, has concluded that some such process may have been what triggered many of the accusations there. Macfarlane notes how frequently the accused witch was a person whose neighbors had earlier denied him or her some requested favor or service, and he suggests that it was the accusers' sense of guilt over their own failures of neighborliness which underlay the accusations. He further hypothesizes that such outbreaks tended to occur (given a prevailing belief in witchcraft) when the evolution from a communal to an individualistic ethic reached a critical stage in a given locality. (Developments in the weaving industry had brought such a change early to this region of England.) Before the critical stage was reached, the peasant ethic of mutual interdependence remained strong: after it had been passed, erstwhile neighbors found themselves "far enough apart, so to speak, to be able to hate each other without repercussions on the mystical plane."[36]

For Salem Village (to apply Macfarlane's formula), the critical stage came in the 1690's, and the Villagers lashed out with accusations not only against those who seemed in one way or another to represent the new order, but also against those who reminded them how far they, themselves, had already been seduced from their traditional moorings. In justifying their refusal to help the desperately poor Sarah Good, for instance, the people with whom she had sought shelter offered a variety of explanations. Samuel Abbey turned her out of his house in the winter of 1690 "for quietness' sake"; Sarah Gadge "was afraid she had been with them that had the smallpox"; Henry Herrick drove her from his place "lest she should lie in the barn, and by smoking of her pipe should fire the barn."[37] In their very profusion, such excuses reveal the guilt which these farmers—themselves not so very much more certain of their livelihood than Sarah Good—must have experienced at their failure to respond to the homeless woman's plight.

Ultimately, then, Salem witchcraft, by reducing real human beings to a single set of threatening impulses and temptations which they seemed to embody, was a kind of allegory-in-reverse. Self-purgation through allegorical projection: this was hardly a style of thinking alien to the late-seventeenth-century Puritan mind. Take, for instance, John Bunyan's classic account of one man's journey toward holiness, *The Pilgrim's Progress*. As Bunyan's Pilgrim (his name is "Christian") makes his precarious way from the City of Destruction to the Celestial City, he is beset by a whole bevy of inner temptations which take human form: "Mr. Worldly Wiseman," "Mr. Money-Love," and the like. (It is intriguing that many of these characters—but not Christian himself—are of high social station, as their honorific titles suggest.)

One of Bunyan's allegorical characters, as it turns out, is a witch: her name is "Madame Bubble," and Christian meets her in a mysterious, foggy region called the Enchanted Ground. She, too, is of high social station—a "gentlewoman," Bunyan insists. Her clothes are "very pleasant," she loves "banqueting and feasting," and she always speaks "smoothly" with "a smile at the end of a sentence." Madame Bubble is constantly fingering the gold in her "great purse" and is most at ease with those who are "cunning to get money." She is, in short, an especially seductive personification of the interwoven appeal of wealth, sensual pleasure, and worldly sophistication. Madame Bubble promises to make "great and happy" anyone who will follow her, and Christian—rough-hewn, earnest, and sturdy though he may be—is powerfully tempted to do so. Only his companion Great Heart is able to fortify him against her blandishments. Not only will Madame Bubble lead a man to eternal damnation, Great Heart warns the Pilgrim, but she will accomplish this by wreaking havoc with his social and psychological equilibrium on this earth:

> 'Twas she that set Absolom against his father, and Jereboam against his master. 'Twas she that persuaded Judas to sell his Lord . . . ; none can tell of the mischief that she doth. She makes variance betwixt rulers and subjects, betwixt parents and children, 'twixt neighbour and neighbour, 'twixt a man and his wife, 'twixt a man and himself, 'twixt the flesh and the heart.[38]

Underscoring the characterization with which Bunyan had introduced Madame Bubble, Great Heart sums up in a word the perpetrator of all these disorders: "This woman is a witch."[39]

Madame Bubble appears in the second part of *The Pilgrim's Progress*, published just eight years before the Salem witchcraft outbreak. In creating this character (and giving her a name which would soon be applied to any alluring but unsound speculative venture, such as the "South-Sea Bubble" of 1720), John Bunyan offered a vivid and somber warning against the commercial attractions which were enticing a great many Puritans—in Salem Village no less than in Restoration England—as the seventeenth century drew to a close.

As the witchcraft outbreak gained momentum in 1692, the accusers were thus compelled to face the possibility that they were themselves being transformed by the forces of change that were buffeting Salem Village. Conversely, some of the accused would not confess to deeds they knew they had not committed, and for their honesty, they died. The ironies are staggering. In this act of collective expiation aimed at affirming a social order based on stability and reciprocal loyalty, the only participants to suffer death were those who insisted on remaining faithful to the essential requirement for stable social relationships: simple honesty. And the event which might have brought a kind of peace to Salem Village brought instead a period of conflict so bitter that even the generation of struggle that had led up to 1692 paled by comparison. The pin that was to have pricked Madame Bubble had somehow turned into a flailing, bloody sword.

Notes

[1] Cotton Mather. *The Life of His Excellency, Sir William Phips, General and Governor in Chief of the Province of the Massachusetts Bay, New England,* (Boston, 1697; reissued, New York, Covici-Friede, 1929), pp. 130–131.

[2] Robert Calef, *More Wonders of the Invisible World: Or, The Wonders of the Invisible World Display'd in Five Parts* (London, 1700), excerpted in George Lincoln Burr, ed., *Narratives of the Witchcraft Cases, 1648–1706* (New York: Charles Scribner's Sons, 1914; reissued, New York: Barnes and Noble, 1968), p. 342.

[3] Thomas Newton to "Worthy Sir," May 31, 1692, 135 Mass. Arch., p. 25.

[4] Our data is drawn from W. Elliot Woodward, *Records of Salem Witchcraft* and the WPA volumes at the Essex Institute. The arrest warrant usually gives the place of residence.

[5] This figure does not include the eight "afflicted girls" who were living in the Village or its immediate environs: Sarah Churchill; Elizabeth Hubbard; Mercy Lewis; Elizabeth Parris; Ann Putnam, Jr.; Mary Warren; Mary Walcott; and Abigail Williams. (A ninth, Sarah Bibber, was from Wenham, and the residences of two remaining, Elizabeth Booth and Susanna Sheldon, have not been positively identified.) We have excluded these eight—even though their inclusion would not substantially alter the geographic pattern which emerges—because, as we have earlier explained, we think it a mistake to treat the girls themselves as decisive shapers of the witchcraft outbreak as it evolved. There is an important additional reason as well: six of the eight were not living in their parents' households in 1692.

[6] Samuel Parris, sermon of February 14, 1692, in his manuscript volume of sermons preached in Salem Village, 1689–1695 (Connecticut Historical Society, Hartford), p. 144.

[7] Parris entered verbatim transcripts of these petitions, with signatures, in the Church Records, preceding the entry for June 2, 1695.

[8] Abbey Miller and Richard Henderson, "Census of Salem Village in January 1692," in Paul Boyer and Stephen Nissenbaum, eds., *Salem-Village Witchcraft: A Documentary Record of Local Conflict in Colonial New England* (Belmont, Calif., Wadsworth Publishing Co., 1972), pp. 383–393. Since some of the petition signers were under the age of twenty-one, the ratio of petition-signers (189) to the total over-21 Village population (*ca.* 215) was not quite so overwhelming as it might at first seem, but it was nevertheless strikingly high.

[9] The names of members were entered by Samuel Parris in the Church Records at the time they joined.

[10] These eighteen represent those who are identified by Parris as church members in his breakdown of the signers of the petitions, but who do not appear in the Church Records as members of the Salem Village church.

[11] Village Records, Jan. 18, 1695. Developed land was taxed at one penny per acre, unimproved land at one-half penny per acre—*ibid.*, Nov. 11, 1672 and March 6, 1685.

[12] Only sixteen known adult Village males failed to sign either petition. With one exception—Daniel Rea, who may have been out of the Village at the time—all sixteen were taxed in 1696 at under ten shillings, and six of them at three shillings, the rate normally assessed on propertyless individuals—Tax List, Village Records, Dec. 13, 1695.

[13] If each of these figures is reduced by three shillings (the amount of the "head tax" imposed on all adult males regardless of their landholdings), so that the figure represents Village landholdings alone, then the contrast between the average tax of the two groups becomes even starker: an average of seven shillings for the pro-Parris group, twelve for the anti-Parris group. The divergence in the relative economic standing of the two groups is confirmed on the Salem Town tax rolls as well. In the returns of the *Town* constables submitted in connection with a provincial tax levied by the General Court in October 1695, forty-six pro-Parris Villagers are assessed an average of 18.2 shillings, while the average for thirty-four anti-Parris Villagers is 23.3 shillings. See *Tax and Valuation Lists of Massachusetts Towns before 1776*, microfilm edition compiled by Ruth Crandall (Harvard University Library) reel 8: "Salem, 1689–1773." The tax from which the above statistics are derived is titled "1695. Rate Made by Virtue of an Act of Adjournment Made the 16th Day of October in the Sixth Year of Their Majesties' Reign, Entitled 'An Act for Payment of the Province Debt.'"

[14] Residential information from "Map of Salem Village, 1692," in Charles W. Upham, *Salem Witchcraft*, 2 vols. (Boston, 1867), I, following p. xvii.

[15] James Duncan Phillips, *Salem in the Seventeenth Century* (Boston, Houghton Mifflin, 1933), pp. 280–281; Donald Warner Koch, "Income Distribution and Political Structure in Seventeenth Century Salem, Mass.," 105 *EIHC* (1969), 51 ("distinctly urban pattern of life" quote); William I. Davisson, "Essex County Price Trends: Money and Markets in Seventeenth Century Massachusetts," *Essex Institute Historical Collections*, 103 (1967), 183–185 (hereafter *EIHC*); Bernard and Lotte Bailyn, *Massachusetts Shipping: 1697–1714, A Statistical Study* (Cambridge, Mass., Harvard University Press, 1959), Table II, p. 79.

[16] Koch, "Income Distribution and Political Structure," pp. 53, 59, 61.

[17] Marcia N. Gold, "Sectaries in Puritan Society: A Study of Seventeenth Century Salem Quakers," M.S. thesis, University of Wisconsin, 1969. Appendix I (List of selectmen with occupational and other data), pp. 104–108.

[18] Comparative population data from Miller and Henderson, "Census of Salem Village in January 1692," and, for Salem as a whole: William I. Davisson, "Essex County Wealth Trends: Wealth and Economic Growth in Seventeenth Century Massachusetts," 103 *EIHC* (1967), p. 294. The 4:1 population ratio of Town and Village is confirmed in the Town's 1695 tax rolls. Of the 429 adult males assessed to pay the Provincial tax that year, a total of 92 (21.4 percent) were Villagers. *Tax and Valuation Lists of Massachusetts Towns before 1776* (microfilm), "Salem, 1689–1773."

[19] Davisson, "Essex County Wealth Trends," pp. 325–326. Davisson's statistics also show a decade-by-decade decline in the average actual cash value of agricultural assets and equipment in estates probated from mid-century down to the late 1680's: from just over £81 in the 1650's to about £31 in the 1670's to £17 for the early years of the 1680's, where his study ends. Though Davisson sees this as further evidence that agriculture was "declining," it could also reflect the greater availability, and consequent lower valuations, of such equipment. Considerable agricultural activity was certainly still being pursued within the bounds of Salem Town proper in these years, particularly in the "Northfields" section lying between the Wooleston and the North Rivers and in the area, south of Salem Village, which later became the Town of Peabody. In speaking of the way Salem Villagers perceived "Salem Town," however, we are thinking of the bustling mercantile center which increasingly dominated the Town and imparted to it its distinctive flavor.

[20] Extract from *The Life and Errors of John Dunton, Late Citizen of London, Written by Himself in Solitude*, Massachusetts Historical Society, *Collections*, second series, 2 (1814), 117.

[21] Sidney Perley, *History of Salem* (Salem, 1924–28), II, 436–438.

[22] On the Ipswich Road taverns: Perley, *History of Salem*, III, 84 (Rea, Phillips), 266 (Bishop); *Records and Files of the Quarterly Courts of Essex County, Massachusetts* (Salem, 1912–75), VIII, 231 for Proctor (hereafter, *EQC*). On the other Ipswich Road occupations: Sidney Perley, "Rial Side: Part of Salem in 1700," 55 *EIHC* (1919), pp. 66 (James Kettle, potter), 67 (John Flint, carpenter), 69 (Jeremiah Watts, dishturner), and 63 (William Griggs, physician); Robert Calef, *More Wonders of the Invisible World* in George Lincoln Burr, ed., *Narratives of the Witchcraft Cases* (New York, Charles Scribner's Sons, 1914; reissued New York, Barnes and Noble, 1968), p. 370 (Samuel Bishop, shoemaker); 5 *EQC*, 385 (John Trask, miller); W. Elliot Woodward, *Records of Salem Witchcraft Copied from the Original Documents*, 2 vols. (Roxbury, Mass., Privately printed 1864; reissued in one volume, New York, Da Capo Press, 1969), I, 136 (Edward Bishop, sawyer, i.e., wood finisher). The only other Salem Village tavern was the one lying in the heart of the Village, next to the meetinghouse and operated by the firmly pro-Parris Nathaniel Ingersoll. It may be noteworthy that Ingersoll's license was not renewed in 1691, and instead one was granted to Walter Phillips, on the Ipswich Road—Perley, *History of Salem*, III, 84. Ingersoll's residence continued to function as a hostelry, however, and in 1692 the initial examinations of some accused witches were held here.

[23] There may have been three pro-Parris signers. Of the three men named "Edward Bishop" in the Village in these years, two lived along the Ipswich Road, and one did not. We have been unable to ascertain whether or not the one Edward Bishop who was pro-Parris (probably a step-grandson of Bridget Bishop's who married a Putnam) was one of the Ipswich Road Bishops.

[24] J. W. Hanson, *History of the Town of Danvers* (Danvers, 1848), p. 36. As an example of the kind of steps a town might take to impede the commercial activities of its residents, note the following action of the Town of Andover on January 1, 1675: "[N]o man shall have liberty after the first of January, 1675, to sell, or transport any cedar out of the town, either in shingles or otherwise, but shall forfeit twenty shillings for every thousand of shingles, or quantity of cedar proportionable, unless the town shall upon some extraordinary occasion grant liberty to the contrary"—6 *EQC*, 323. For a similar, though less stringent, action by Salem Town in 1669, see Salem Town Records, 41 *EIHC* (1905), 301–302.

[25] The Essex County court records, published and unpublished, are full of such cases.

[26] 3 *EQC*, 377.

[27] Upham, *Salem Witchcraft*, II, 272.

[28] John Winthrop, "A Modell of Christian Charity," *Winthrop Papers*, 5 vols. (Boston, Massachusetts Historical Society, 1929–1944), II, 294.

[29] *Ibid.*, 293–294.

[30] Woodward, *Records of Salem Witchcraft*, I, 169.

[31] John Demos, "Underlying Themes in the Witchcraft of Seventeenth Century New England," 75 *American Historical Review* (1970), 1311–1326, esp. 1320–1322.

[32] WPA, II (Examinations of Stephen Johnson—"French fall shoes") and Richard Carrier ("new clothes"); Woodward, *Records of Salem Witchcraft*, I, 277 (Susannah Sheldon—"a piece of money"); *ibid.*, I, 264 and II, 118 (Mercy Lewis); *ibid.*, I, 106 (Abigail Williams); Deodat Lawson, *A Brief and True Narrative of Some Remarkable Passages Relating to Sundry Persons Afflicted by Witchcraft, at Salem Village Which Happened From the Nineteenth of March, to the Fifth of April, 1692* (Boston, 1692), in Burr, *Narratives*, p. 160 (Elizabeth Parris). See also examination of Abigail Hobbs, April 19, 1692, WPA, II.

[33] Margaret Jacobs to George Jacobs, Jr., in Calef, *More Wonders of the Invisible World*, in Burr, *Narratives*, pp. 365–366; Woodward, *Records of Salem Witchcraft*, II, 188 (Deliverance Hobbs' examination); I, 120 (Mary Warren's examination).

[34] Examination of Sarah Cole, WPA, I.

[35] Indeed, the anti-Parris tract "handed about" the Village, apparently somewhat clandestinely, in the period just after the witchcraft episode, actually did accuse Parris of having sought information from the devil through the intermediary of Abigail Williams. It concluded with a reminder that King Saul had been put to death for heeding the Witch of Endor.

[36] Alan Macfarlane, *Witchcraft in Tudor and Stuart England* (New York, Harper and Row, 1970), pp. 158–164, 192–206, quoted passage on p. 202.

[37] Examination of Sarah Good, in Woodward, *Records of Salem Witchcraft*, I, 18–19 testimony of Samuel Abbey and wife and of Henry Herrick and Sarah Gadge, *ibid.*, I, 24–26, 29.

[38] John Bunyan, *The Pilgrim's Progress From This World to That Which Is to Come* (Part II, London, 1684), ed. James Blanton Wharey; second ed. edited by Roger Sharrock (Oxford, Oxford University Press, 1960), pp. 300, 301, 302–303.

[39] *Ibid.*, p. 301.

7

"Examination of Susanna Martin" (1692) *and* "Petition of Mary Easty" (1692)

I. Examination of Susanna Martin
II. Petition of Mary Easty

Examination of Susanna Martin (1692)

Susanna Martin

—◆—•—◆—

Before they came to trial, those charged with witchcraft were customarily interrogated by representatives of the court, who then drew up a deposition to be entered as evidence against them. The records of such interrogations preserve with great immediacy the heat of confrontation, as the court, by pitting accusers against accused, sought to extract what it wanted most: confession. In confession lay not only the defendant's best chance of acquittal (none who confessed were executed), but also the prospect for a communal sense of victory over Satan, who, it was believed, had ordered his minions to dissemble, deceive, and deny their fellowship with him. In the bristling defiance of one such defendant, Susanna Martin, we encounter not only a brave woman, but also the general dilemma in which New England found itself: innocent people were being tempted to admit crimes which they had not committed. To save their lives they were being asked to make a mockery of repentance, which had always been an act of absolute centrality in the Puritan concept of covenant obligation. "He that hides his sins shall not prosper," Robert Keayne had said in faithful articulation of the orthodox attitude toward confession, "but he that confesseth and forsaketh them shall find mercy." Susanna Martin was faced with a choice between mercy and self-respect. At both of her examinations, she chose the latter. A few weeks later she was hanged.

The text is from William E. Woodward, Records of Salem Witchcraft *(Roxbury, Mass., 1864), I, 196–200.*

The Examination of Susanna Martin, 2 May 1692.

As soon as she came in many had fits.

"Do you know this woman?"

Abigail Williams saith, "It is Goody Martin; she hath hurt me often." Others by fits were hindered from speaking. Elizabeth Hubbard said she hath not been hurt by her. John Indian said he hath not seen her. Mercy Lewis pointed to her and fell into a little fit. Ann Putnam threw her glove in a fit at her. The examinant laughed.

"What, do you laugh at it?"

"Well I may at such folly."

"Is this folly? The hurt of these persons?"

"I never hurt man, woman, or child."

Mercy Lewis cried out, "She hath hurt me a great many times and pulls me down."

Then Martin laughed again.

Mary Walcott saith, "This woman hath hurt me a great many times." Susan Sheldon also accused her of afflicting her.

"What do you say to this?"

"I have no hand in witchcraft."

"What did you do? Did not you give your consent?"

"No, never in my life."

"What ails this people?"

"I do not know."

"But what do you think?"

"I do not desire to spend my judgment upon it."

"Do not you think they are bewitched?"

"No, I do not think they are."

"Tell me your thoughts about them?"

"Why, my thoughts are my own when they are in; but when they are out they are another's."

"You said 'their master'—who do you think is their master?"

"If they be dealing in the black art you may know as well as I."

"Well, what have you done towards this?"

"Nothing."

"Why, it is you or your appearance."

"I cannot help it."

"That may be your master."

"I desire to lead myself according to the word of God."

"Is this according to God's word?"

"If I were such a person I would tell you the truth."

"How comes your appearance just now to hurt these?"

"How do I know?"

"Are not you willing to tell the truth?"

"I cannot tell: he that appeared in Samuel [the] shape [of] a glorified saint can appear in anyone's shape."[1]

"Do you believe these do not say true?"

"They may lie for aught I know."

"May not you lie?"

"I dare not tell a lie if it would save my life."

"Then you will speak the truth."

"I have spoke nothing else. I would do them any good."

"I do not think you have such affections for them whom just now you insinuated had the devil for their master."

Elizabeth Hubbard was afflicted and then the marshall who was by her said she [Martin] pinched her hand.

Several of the afflicted cried out they saw her upon the beam.

"Pray God discover you, if you be guilty."

"Amen, amen. A false tongue will never make a guilty person."

"You have been a long time coming to the court today; you can come fast enough in the night," said Mercy Lewis.

"No, sweetheart," said the examinant, and then Mercy Lewis and all or many of the rest were afflicted.

John Indian fell into a violent fit and said, "It was that woman, she bites, she bites," and then she was biting her lips.

"Have you not compassion for these afflicted?"

"No, I have none."

Some cried out there was the black man with her, and Goody Vibber, who had not accused her before, confirmed it.

Abigail Williams upon trial could not come near her, nor Goody Vibber, nor Mary Walcott. John Indian cried he would kill her if he came near her, but he was flung down in his approach to her.

"What is the reason these cannot come near you?"

"I cannot tell: it may be the devil bears me more malice than another."

"Do not you see how God evidently discovers you?"

"No. Not a bit for that."

"All the congregation think so."

"Let them think what they will."

"What is the reason these cannot come near you?"

"I do not know but they can if they will, or else if you please I will come to them."

"What is the black man whispering to you?"

"There was none whispered to me."

Petition of Mary Easty (1692)

Mary Easty

<hr>

Another of the nineteen persons convicted of the crime of witchcraft, Mary Easty, offered a petition to Governor Phips a few weeks before her hanging in the summer of 1692. Easty's moving plea is not a request for clemency for herself, but an appeal on behalf of others under indictment and those who might be accused in the future. Her brief statement is remarkable not only for its enormous dignity, but for the way in which it refuses to relinquish belief in New England's capacity to be just. Even as she proclaims her innocence and prepares for her death, Easty commits herself not to revenge but to helping the Puritan authorities see the truth. Hers is an expression of submission without servility. It is a statement of one person's faith that New England can still be saved from itself.

The text of Mary Easty's petition is from Woodward, Records of Salem Witchcraft, *II, 44–46.*

Petition of Mary Easty (20th May, 1692)

The humble petition of Mary Easty unto his Excellencies Sir William Phips, and to the Honored Judge and bench now sitting in judicature in Salem, and the Reverend Ministers, humbly sheweth:

That whereas your poor and humble petitioner, being condemned to die, do humbly beg of you to take it in your judicious and pious considerations that your poor and humble petitioner, knowing my own innocencie—blessed be the Lord for it—and seeing plainly the wiles and subtility of my accusers, by myself cannot but judge charitably of others that are going the way of myself, if the Lord steps not mightily in. I was confined a whole month upon the same account that I am condemned now for, and then cleared by the afflicted persons, as some of your Honors know. And in two days time I was cried out upon by them and have been confined and now am condemned to die. The Lord above knows my innocencie then and likewise does now, as at the great day will be known to men and angels. I petition to your Honors not for my own life, for I know I must die and my appointed time is set, but (the Lord knows it is) that if it be possible, no more innocent blood may be shed, which undoubtedly cannot be avoided in the way and course you go in. I question not but your Honors does to the utmost of your power in the discovery and selecting of witchcraft and witches, and would not be guilty of innocent blood for the world; but by my innocencie I know you are in the wrong way. The Lord in his infinite mercy direct you in this great work, if it be his blessed will that no more innocent blood be shed. I would humbly beg of you that your Honors would be pleased to examine these afflicted persons strictly and keep them apart some time, and likewise to try some of these confessing witches, I being confident there is several of them has belied themselves and others, as will appear if not in this world I am sure in the world to come, whither I am now a-going. And I question not but you'll see an alteration of these things they say myself and others, having made a league with the devil, we cannot confess. I know and the Lord knows, as will shortly appear, they belie me and so I question not but they do others. The Lord above, who is the searcher of all hearts, knows that as I shall answer it at the tribunal seat that I know not the least thing of witchcraft—therefore I cannot, I dare not, belie my own Soul. I beg your Honors not to deny this my humble petition from a poor dying innocent person, and I question not but that the Lord will give a blessing to your endeavors.

To his Excellency Sir William Phips, Governor, and to the Honored Judge and magistrates now sitting in judicature in Salem.

Note

[1] A reference to the visitation by the shade of Samuel to Saul (I Samuel 28:14–15).

8

"Slavery and Freedom: The American Paradox"

Edmund S. Morgan

Reprinted with permission from *Journal of American History*; © 1972 Organization of American Historians.

Slavery and Freedom: The American Paradox

Edmund S. Morgan

American historians interested in tracing the rise of liberty, democracy, and the common man have been challenged in the past two decades by other historians, interested in tracing the history of oppression, exploitation, and racism. The challenge has been salutary, because it has made us examine more directly than historians have hitherto been willing to do, the role of slavery in our early history. Colonial historians, in particular, when writing about the origin and development of American institutions have found it possible until recently to deal with slavery as an exception to everything they had to say. I am speaking about myself but also about most of my generation. We owe a debt of gratitude to those who have insisted that slavery was something more than an exception, that one fifth of the American population at the time of the Revolution is too many people to be treated as an exception.[1]

We shall not have met the challenge simply by studying the history of that one fifth, fruitful as such studies may be, urgent as they may be. Nor shall we have met the challenge if we merely execute the familiar maneuver of turning our old interpretations on their heads. The temptation is already apparent to argue that slavery and oppression were the dominant features of American history and that efforts to advance liberty and equality were the exception, indeed no more than a device to divert the masses while their chains were being fastened. To dismiss the rise of liberty and equality in American history as a mere sham is not only to ignore hard facts, it is also to evade the problem presented by those facts. The rise of liberty and equality in this country was accompanied by the rise of slavery. That two such contradictory developments were taking place simultaneously over a long period of our history, from the seventeenth century to the nineteenth, is the central paradox of American history.

The challenge, for a colonial historian at least, is to explain how a people could have developed the dedication to human liberty and dignity exhibited by the leaders of the American Revolution and at the same time have developed and maintained a system of labor that denied human liberty and dignity every hour of the day.

The paradox is evident at many levels if we care to see it. Think, for a moment, of the traditional American insistence on freedom of the seas. "Free ships make free goods" was the

This paper was delivered as the presidential address of the Organization of American Historians at Washington, D.C., April 6, 1972. Edmund S. Morgan is professor of history in Yale University.

cardinal doctrine of American foreign policy in the Revolutionary era. But the goods for which the United States demanded freedom were produced in very large measure by slave labor. The irony is more than semantic. American reliance on slave labor must be viewed in the context of the American struggle for a separate and equal station among the nations of the earth. At the time the colonists announced their claim to that station they had neither the arms nor the ships to make the claim good. They desperately needed the assistance of other countries, especially France, and their single most valuable product with which to purchase assistance was tobacco, produced mainly by slave labor. So largely did that crop figure in American foreign relations that one historian has referred to the activities of France in supporting the Americans as "King Tobacco Diplomacy," a reminder that the position of the United States in the world depended not only in 1776 but during the span of a long lifetime thereafter on slave labor.[2] To a very large degree it may be said that Americans bought their independence with slave labor.

The paradox is sharpened if we think of the state where most of the tobacco came from. Virginia at the time of the first United States census in 1790 had 40 percent of the slaves in the entire United States. And Virginia produced the most eloquent spokesmen for freedom and equality in the entire United States: George Washington, James Madison, and above all, Thomas Jefferson. They were all slaveholders and remained so throughout their lives. In recent years we have been shown in painful detail the contrast between Jefferson's pronouncements in favor of republican liberty and his complicity in denying the benefits of that liberty to blacks.[3] It has been tempting to dismiss Jefferson and the whole Virginia dynasty as hypocrites. But to do so is to deprive the term "hypocrisy" of useful meaning. If hypocrisy means, as I think it does, deliberately to affirm a principle without believing it, then hypocrisy requires a rare clarity of mind combined with an unscrupulous intention to deceive. To attribute such an intention, even to attribute such clarity of mind in the matter, to Jefferson, Madison, or Washington is once again to evade the challenge. What we need to explain is how such men could have arrived at beliefs and actions so full of contradiction.

Put the challenge another way: how did England, a country priding itself on the liberty of its citizens, produce colonies where most of the inhabitants enjoyed still greater liberty, greater opportunities, greater control over their own lives than most men in the mother country, while the remainder, one fifth of the total, were deprived of virtually all liberty, all opportunities, all control over their own lives? We may admit that the Englishmen who colonized America and their revolutionary descendants were racists, that consciously or unconsciously they believed liberties and rights should be confined to persons of a light complexion. When we have said as much, even when we have probed the depths of racial prejudice, we will not have fully accounted for the paradox. Racism was surely an essential element in it, but I should like to suggest another element, that I believe to have influenced the development of both slavery and freedom as we have known them in the United States.

Let us begin with Jefferson, this slaveholding spokesman of freedom. Could there have been anything in the kind of freedom he cherished that would have made him acquiesce, however reluctantly, in the slavery of so many Americans? The answer, I think, is yes. The freedom that Jefferson spoke for was not a gift to be conferred by governments, which he mistrusted at best. It was a freedom that sprang from the independence of the individual. The man who depended on another for his living could never be truly free. We may seek a clue to Jefferson's enigmatic posture toward slavery in his attitude toward those who enjoyed a seeming freedom without the independence needed to sustain it. For such persons Jefferson harbored a profound distrust, which found expression in two phobias that crop up from time to time in his writings.

The first was a passionate aversion to debt. Although the entire colonial economy of Virginia depended on the willingness of planters to go into debt and of British merchants to extend credit, although Jefferson himself was a debtor all his adult life—or perhaps because he was a debtor—he hated debt and hated anything that made him a debtor. He hated it because it limited his freedom of action. He could not, for example, have freed his slaves so long as he was in debt. Or so at least he told himself. But it was the impediment not simply to their freedom but to his own that bothered him. "I am miserable," he wrote, "till I shall owe not a shilling. . . ."[4]

The fact that he had so much company in his misery only added to it. His Declaration of Independence for the United States was mocked by the hold that British merchants retained over American debtors, including himself.[5] His hostility to Alexander Hamilton was rooted in his recognition that Hamilton's pro-British foreign policy would tighten the hold of British creditors, while his domestic policy would place the government in the debt of a class of native American creditors, whose power might become equally pernicious.

Though Jefferson's concern with the perniciousness of debt was almost obsessive, it was nevertheless altogether in keeping with the ideas of republican liberty that he shared with his countrymen. The trouble with debt was that by undermining the independence of the debtor it threatened republican liberty. Whenever debt brought a man under another's power, he lost more than his own freedom of action. He also weakened the capacity of his country to survive as a republic. It was an axiom of current political thought that republican government required a body of free, independent, property-owning citizens.[6] A nation of men, each of whom owned enough property to support his family, could be a republic. It would follow that a nation of debtors, who had lost their property or mortgaged it to creditors, was ripe for tyranny. Jefferson accordingly favored every means of keeping men out of debt and keeping property widely distributed. He insisted on the abolition of primogeniture and entail; he declared that the earth belonged to the living and should not be kept from them by the debts or credits of the dead; he would have given fifty acres of land to every American who did not have it—all because he believed the citizens of a republic must be free from the control of other men and that they could be free only if they were economically free by virtue of owning land on which to support themselves.[7]

If Jefferson felt so passionately about the bondage of the debtor, it is not surprising that he should also have sensed a danger to the republic from another class of men who, like debtors, were nominally free but whose independence was illusory. Jefferson's second phobia was his distrust of the landless urban workman who labored in manufactures. In Jefferson's view, he was a free man in name only. Jefferson's hostility to artificers is well known and is generally attributed to his romantic preference for the rural life. But both his distrust for artificers and his idealization of small landholders as "the most precious part of a state" rested on his concern for individual independence as the basis of freedom. Farmers made the best citizens because they were "the most vigorous, the most independant, the most virtuous. . . ." Artificers, on the other hand, were dependent on "the casualties and caprice of customers." If work was scarce, they had no land to fall back on for a living. In their dependence lay the danger. "Dependance," Jefferson argued, "begets subservience and venality, suffocates the germ of virtue, and prepares fit tools for the designs of ambition." Because artificers could lay claim to freedom without the independence to go with it, they were "the instruments by which the liberties of a country are generally overturned."[8]

In Jefferson's distrust of artificers we begin to get a glimpse of the limits—and limits not dictated by racism—that defined the republican vision of the eighteenth century. For Jefferson was by no means unique among republicans in his distrust of the landless laborer. Such a distrust was a necessary corollary of the widespread eighteenth-century insistence on the independent, property-holding individual as the only bulwark of liberty, an insistence originating in James Harrington's republican political philosophy and a guiding principle of American colonial politics, whether in the aristocratic South Carolina assembly or in the democratic New England town.[9] Americans both before and after 1776 learned their republican lessons from the seventeenth- and eighteenth-century British commonwealthmen; and the commonwealthmen were uninhibited in their contempt for the masses who did not have the propertied independence required of proper republicans.

John Locke, the classic explicator of the right of revolution for the protection of liberty, did not think about extending that right to the landless poor. Instead, he concocted a scheme of compulsory labor for them and their children. The children were to begin at the age of three in public institutions, called working schools because the only subject taught would be work (spinning and knitting). They would be paid in bread and water and grow up "inured to work." Meanwhile the mothers, thus relieved of the care of their offspring, could go to work beside their fathers and husbands. If they could not find regular employment, then they too could be sent to the working school.[10]

It requires some refinement of mind to discern precisely how this version of women's liberation from child care differed from outright slavery. And many of Locke's intellectual successors, while denouncing slavery in the abstract, openly preferred slavery to freedom for the lower ranks of laborers. Adam Ferguson, whose works were widely read in America, attributed the overthrow of the Roman republic, in part at least, to the emancipation of slaves, who "increased, by their numbers and their vices, the weight of that dreg, which, in great and prosperous cities, ever sinks, by the tendency of vice and misconduct to the lowest condition."[11]

That people in the lowest condition, the dregs of society, generally arrived at that position through their own vice and misconduct, whether in ancient Rome or modern Britain, was an unexamined article of faith among eighteenth-century republicans. And the vice that was thought to afflict the lower ranks most severely was idleness. The eighteenth-century's preferred cure for idleness lay in the religious and ethical doctrines which R. H. Tawney described as the New Medicine for Poverty, the doctrines in which Max Weber discerned the origins of the spirit of capitalism. But in every society a stubborn mass of men and women refused the medicine. For such persons the commonwealthmen did not hesitate to prescribe slavery. Thus Francis Hutcheson, who could argue eloquently against the enslavement of Africans, also argued that perpetual slavery should be "the ordinary punishment of such idle vagrants as, after proper admonitions and tryals of temporary servitude, cannot be engaged to support themselves and their families by any useful labours."[12] James Burgh, whose *Political Disquisitions* earned the praises of many American revolutionists, proposed a set of press gangs "to seize all idle and disorderly persons, who have been three times complained of before a magistrate, and to set them to work during a certain time, for the benefit of great trading, or manufacturing companies, &c."[13]

The most comprehensive proposal came from Andrew Fletcher of Saltoun. Jefferson hailed in Fletcher a patriot whose political principles were those "in vigour at the epoch of the American emigration [from England]. Our ancestors brought them here, and they needed little strengthening to make us what we are. . . ."[14] Fletcher, like other commonwealthmen, was a champion of liberty, but he was also a champion of slavery. He attacked the Christian church not only for having promoted the abolition of slavery in ancient times but also for having perpetuated the idleness of the freedmen thus turned loose on society. The church by setting up hospitals and almshouses had enabled men through the succeeding centuries to live without work. As a result, Fletcher argued, his native Scotland was burdened with 200,000 idle rogues, who roamed the country, drinking, cursing, fighting, robbing, and murdering. For a remedy he proposed that they all be made slaves to men of property. To the argument that their masters might abuse them, he answered in words which might have come a century and a half later from a George Fitzhugh: that this would be against the master's own interest, "That the most brutal man will not use his beast ill only out of a humour;

and that if such Inconveniences do sometimes fall out, it proceeds, for the most part, from the perverseness of the Servant."[15]

In spite of Jefferson's tribute to Fletcher, there is no reason to suppose that he endorsed Fletcher's proposal. But he did share Fletcher's distrust of men who were free in name while their empty bellies made them thieves, threatening the property of honest men, or else made them slaves in fact to anyone who would feed them. Jefferson's own solution for the kind of situation described by Fletcher was given in a famous letter to Madison, prompted by the spectacle Jefferson encountered in France in the 1780s, where a handful of noblemen had engrossed huge tracts of land on which to hunt game, while hordes of the poor went without work and without bread. Jefferson's proposal, characteristically phrased in terms of natural right, was for the poor to appropriate the uncultivated lands of the nobility. And he drew for the United States his usual lesson of the need to keep land widely distributed among the people.[16]

Madison's answer, which is less well known than Jefferson's letter, raised the question whether it was possible to eliminate the idle poor in any country as fully populated as France. Spread the land among them in good republican fashion and there would still be, Madison thought, "a great surplus of inhabitants, a greater by far than will be employed in cloathing both themselves and those who feed them. . . ." In spite of those occupied in trades and as mariners, soldiers, and so on, there would remain a mass of men without work. "A certain degree of misery," Madison concluded, "seems inseparable from a high degree of populousness."[17] He did not, however, go on to propose, as Fletcher had done, that the miserable and idle poor be reduced to slavery.

The situation contemplated by Madison and confronted by Fletcher was not irrelevant to those who were planning the future of the American republic. In a country where population grew by geometric progression, it was not too early to think about a time when there might be vast numbers of landless poor, when there might be those mobs in great cities that Jefferson feared as sores on the body politic. In the United States as Jefferson and Madison knew it, the urban labor force as yet posed no threat, because it was small; and the agricultural labor force was, for the most part, already enslaved. In Revolutionary America, among men who spent their lives working for other men rather than working for themselves, slaves probably constituted a majority.[18] In Virginia they constituted a large majority.[19] If Jefferson and Madison, not to mention Washington, were unhappy about that fact and yet did nothing to alter it, they may have been restrained, in part at least, by thoughts of the role that might be played in the United States by a large mass of free laborers.

When Jefferson contemplated the abolition of slavery, he found it inconceivable that the freed slaves should be allowed to remain in the country.[20] In this attitude he was probably moved by his or his countrymen's racial prejudice. But he may also have had in mind the possibility that when slaves ceased to be slaves, they would become instead a half million idle poor, who would create the same problems for the United States that the idle poor of Europe did for their states. The slave, accustomed to compulsory labor, would not work to support himself when the compulsion was removed. This was a commonplace among Virginia planters before the creation of the republic and long after. "If you free the slaves," wrote Landon Carter, two days after the Declaration of Independence, "you must send them out of the country or they must steal for their support."[21]

Jefferson's plan for freeing his own slaves (never carried out) included an interim educational period in which they would have been half-taught, half-compelled to support themselves on rented land; for without guidance and preparation for self support, he believed, slaves could not be expected to become fit members of a republican society.[22] And St. George Tucker, who drafted detailed plans for freeing Virginia's slaves, worried about "the possibility of their becoming idle, dissipated, and finally a numerous banditti, instead of turning their attention to industry and labour." He therefore included in his plans a provision for compelling the labor of the freedmen on an annual basis. "For we must not lose sight of this important consideration," he said, "that these people must be *bound* to labour, if they do not *voluntarily* engage therein. . . . In absolving them from the yoke of slavery, we must not forget the interests of society. Those interests require the exertions of every individual in some mode or other; and those who have not wherewith to support themselves honestly without corporal labour, whatever be their complexion, ought to be compelled to labour."[23]

It is plain that Tucker, the would-be emancipator, distrusted the idle poor regardless of color. And it seems probable that the Revolutionary champions of liberty who acquiesced in the continued slavery of black labor did so not only because of racial prejudice but also because they shared with Tucker a distrust of the poor that was inherent in eighteenth-century conceptions of republican liberty. Their historical guidebooks had made them fear to enlarge the free labor force.

That fear, I believe, had a second point of origin in the experience of the American colonists, and especially of Virginians, during the preceding century and a half. If we turn now to the previous history of Virginia's labor force, we may find, I think, some further clues to the distrust of free labor among Revolutionary republicans and to the paradoxical rise of slavery and freedom together in colonial America.

The story properly begins in England with the burst of population growth there that sent the number of Englishmen from perhaps three million in 1500 to four-and-one-half million by 1650.[24] The increase did not occur in response to any corresponding growth in the capacity of the island's economy to support its people. And the result was precisely that misery which Madison pointed out to Jefferson as the consequence of "a high degree of populousness." Sixteenth-century England knew the same kind of unemployment and poverty that Jefferson witnessed in eighteenth-century France and Fletcher in seventeenth-century Scotland. Alarming numbers of idle and hungry men drifted about the country looking for work or plunder. The government did what it could to make men of means hire them, but it also adopted increasingly severe measures against their wandering, their thieving, their roistering, and indeed their very existence. Whom the workhouses and prisons could not swallow the gallows would have to, or perhaps the army. When England had military expeditions to conduct abroad, every parish packed off its most unwanted inhabitants to the almost certain death that awaited them from the diseases of the camp.[25]

As the mass of idle rogues and beggars grew and increasingly threatened the peace of England, the efforts to cope with them increasingly threatened the liberties of Englishmen. Englishmen prided themselves on a "gentle government,"[26] a government that had been releasing its subjects from old forms of bondage and endowing them with new liberties, making the "rights of Englishmen" a phrase to conjure with. But there was nothing gentle about the government's treatment of the poor; and as more Englishmen became poor, other Englishmen had less to be proud of. Thoughtful men could see an obvious solution: get the surplus Englishmen out of England. Send them to the New World, where there were limitless opportunities for work. There they would redeem themselves, enrich the mother country, and spread English liberty abroad.

The great publicist for this program was Richard Hakluyt. His *Principall Navigations, Voiages and Discoveries of the English nation*[27] was not merely the narrative of voyages by Englishmen around the globe, but a powerful suggestion that the world ought to be English or at least ought to be ruled by Englishmen. Hakluyt's was a dream of empire, but of benevolent empire, in which England would confer the blessings of her own free government on the less fortunate peoples of the world. It is doubtless true that Englishmen, along with other Europeans, were already imbued with prejudice against men of darker complexions than their own. And it is also true that the principal beneficiaries of Hakluyt's empire would be Englishmen. But Hakluyt's dream cannot be dismissed as mere hypocrisy any more than Jefferson's affirmation of human equality can be so dismissed. Hakluyt's compassion for the poor and oppressed was not confined to the English poor, and in Francis Drake's exploits in the Caribbean Hakluyt saw, not a thinly disguised form of piracy, but a model for English liberation of men of all colors who labored under the tyranny of the Spaniard.

Drake had gone ashore at Panama in 1572 and made friends with an extraordinary band of runaway Negro slaves. "Cimarrons" they were called, and they lived a free and hardy life in the wilderness, periodically raiding the Spanish settlements to carry off more of their people. They discovered in Drake a man who hated the Spanish as much as they did and who had the arms and men to mount a stronger attack than they could manage by themselves. Drake wanted Spanish gold, and the Cimarrons wanted Spanish iron for tools. They both wanted Spanish deaths. The alliance was a natural one and apparently untroubled by racial prejudice. Together the English and the cimarrons robbed the mule train carrying the annual supply of Peruvian treasure across the isthmus. And before Drake sailed for England with his loot, he arranged for future meetings.[28] When Hakluyt heard of this alliance, he concocted his first colonizing proposal, a scheme for seizing the Straits of Magellan and transporting Cimarrons there, along with surplus Englishmen. The straits would be a strategic strong point for England's world empire, since they controlled the route from Atlantic to Pacific. Despite the severe climate of the place, the Cimarrons and their English friends would all live warmly together, clad in English woolens, "well lodged and by our nation made free from the tyrannous Spanyard, and quietly and courteously governed by our nation."[29]

The scheme for a colony in the Straits of Magellan never worked out, but Hakluyt's vision endured, of liberated natives and surplus Englishmen, courteously governed in English colonies around the world. Sir Walter Raleigh caught the vision. He dreamt of wresting the treasure of the Incas from the Spaniard by allying with the Indians of Guiana and sending Englishmen to live with them, lead them in rebellion against Spain, and govern them in the English manner.[30] Raleigh also dreamt of a similar colony in the country he named Virginia. Hakluyt helped him plan it.[31] And Drake stood ready to supply Negroes and Indians, liberated from Spanish tyranny in the Caribbean, to help the enterprise.[32]

Virginia from the beginning was conceived not only as a haven for England's suffering poor, but as a spearhead of English liberty in an oppressed world. That was the dream; but when it began to materialize at Roanoke Island in 1585, something went wrong. Drake did his part by liberating Spanish Caribbean slaves, and carrying to Roanoke those who wished to join him.[33] But the English settlers whom Raleigh sent there proved unworthy of the role assigned them. By the time Drake arrived they had shown themselves less than courteous to the Indians on whose assistance they depended. The first group of settlers murdered the chief who befriended them, and then gave up and ran for home aboard Drake's returning ships. The second group simply disappeared, presumably killed by the Indians.[34]

What was lost in this famous lost colony was more than the band of colonists who have never been traced. What was also lost and never quite recovered in subsequent ventures was the dream of Englishman and Indian living side by side in peace and liberty. When the English finally planted a permanent colony at Jamestown they came as conquerors, and their government was far from gentle. The Indians willing to endure it were too few in numbers and too broken in spirit to play a significant part in the settlement.

Without their help, Virginia offered a bleak alternative to the workhouse or the gallows for the first English poor who were transported there. During the first two decades of the colony's existence, most of the arriving immigrants found precious little English liberty in Virginia.[35] But by the 1630s the colony seemed to be working out, at least in part, as its first planners had hoped. Impoverished Englishmen were arriving every year in large numbers, engaged to serve the existing planters for a term of years, with the prospect of setting up their own households a few years later. The settlers were spreading up Virginia's great rivers, carving out plantations, living comfortably from their corn fields and from the cattle they ranged in the forests, and at the same time earning perhaps ten or twelve pounds a year per man from the tobacco they planted. A representative legislative assembly secured the traditional liberties of Englishmen and enabled a larger proportion of the population to participate in their own government than had ever been the case in England. The colony even began to look a little like the cosmopolitan haven of liberty that Hakluyt had first envisaged. Men of all countries appeared there: French, Spanish, Dutch, Turkish, Portuguese, and African.[36] Virginia took them in and began to make Englishmen out of them.

It seems clear that most of the Africans, perhaps all of them, came as slaves, a status that had become obsolete in England, while it was becoming the expected condition of Africans outside Africa and of a good many inside.[37] It is equally clear that a substantial number of Virginia's Negroes were free or became free. And all of them, whether servant, slave, or free, enjoyed most of the same rights and duties as other Virginians. There is no evidence during the period before 1660 that they were subjected to a more severe discipline than other servants. They could sue and be sued in court. They did penance in the parish church for having illegitimate children. They earned money of their own, bought and sold and raised cattle of their own. Sometimes they bought their own freedom. In other cases, masters bequeathed them not only freedom but land, cattle, and houses.[38] Northampton, the only county for which full records exist, had at least ten free Negro households by 1668.[39]

As Negroes took their place in the community, they learned English ways, including even the truculence toward authority that has always been associated with the rights of Englishmen. Tony Longo, a free Negro of Northampton, when served a warrant to appear as a witness in court, responded with a scatological opinion of warrants, called the man who served it an idle rascal, and told him to go about his business. The man offered to go with him at any time before a justice of the peace so that his evidence could be recorded. He would go with him at night, tomorrow, the next day, next week, any time. But Longo was busy getting in his corn. He dismissed all pleas with a "Well, well, Ile goe when my Corne is in," and refused to receive the warrant.[40]

The judges understandably found this to be contempt of court; but it was the kind of contempt that free Englishmen often showed to authority, and it was combined with a devotion to work that English moralists were doing their best to inculcate more widely in England. As England had absorbed people of every nationality over the centuries and turned them into Englishmen, Virginia's Englishmen were absorbing their own share of foreigners, including Negroes, and seemed to be successfully moulding a New World community on the English model.

But a closer look will show that the situation was not quite so promising as at first it seems. It is well known that Virginia in its first fifteen or twenty years killed off most of the men who went there. It is less well known that it continued to do so. If my estimate of the volume of immigration is anywhere near correct, Virginia must have been a death trap for at least another fifteen years and probably for twenty or twenty-five. In 1625 the population stood at 1,300 or 1,400; in 1640 it was about 8,000.[41] In the fifteen years between those dates at least 15,000 persons must have come to the colony.[42] If so, 15,000 immigrants increased the population by less than 7,000. There is no evidence of a large return migration. It seems probable that the death rate throughout this period was comparable only to that found in Europe during the peak years of a plague. Virginia, in other words, was absorbing England's surplus laborers mainly by killing them. The success of those who survived and rose from servant to planter must be attributed partly to the fact that so few did survive.

After 1640, when the diseases responsible for the high death rate began to decline and the population began a quick rise, it became increasingly difficult for an indigent immigrant to pull himself up in the world. The population probably passed 25,000 by 1662,[43] hardly what Madison would have called a high degree of populousness. Yet the rapid rise brought serious trouble for Virginia. It brought the engrossment of tidewater land in thousands and tens of thousands of acres by speculators, who recognized that the demand would rise.[44] It brought a huge expansion of tobacco production, which helped to depress the price of tobacco and the earnings of the men who planted it.[45] It brought efforts by planters to prolong the terms of servants, since they were now living longer and therefore had a longer expectancy of usefulness.[46]

It would, in fact, be difficult to assess all the consequences of the increased longevity; but for our purposes one development was crucial, and that was the appearance in Virginia of a growing number of freemen who had served their terms but who were now unable to afford land of their own except on the frontiers or in the interior. In years when tobacco prices were especially low or crops especially poor, men who had been just scraping by were obliged to go back to work for their larger neighbors simply in order to stay alive. By 1676 it was estimated that one fourth of Virginia's freemen were without land of their own.[47] And in the same year Francis Moryson, a member of the governor's council, explained the term "freedmen" as used in Virginia to mean "persons without house and land," implying that this was now the normal condition of servants who had attained freedom.[48]

Some of them resigned themselves to working for wages; others preferred a meager living on dangerous frontier land or a hand-to-mouth existence, roaming from one county to another, renting a bit of land here, squatting on some there, dodging the tax collector, drinking, quarreling, stealing hogs, and enticing servants to run away with them.

The presence of this growing class of poverty-stricken Virginians was not a little frightening to the planters who had made it to the top or who had arrived in the colony already at the top, with ample supplies of servants and capital. They were caught in a dilemma. They wanted the immigrants who kept pouring in every year. Indeed they needed them and prized them the more as they lived longer. But as more and more turned free each year, Virginia seemed to have inherited the problem that she was helping England to solve. Virginia, complained Nicholas Spencer, secretary of the colony, was "a sinke to drayen England of her filth and scum."[49]

The men who worried the uppercrust looked even more dangerous in Virginia than they had in England. They were, to begin with, young, because it was young persons that the planters wanted for work in the fields; and the young have always seemed impatient of control by their elders and superiors, if not downright rebellious. They were also predominantly single men. Because the planters did not think women, or at least English women, fit for work in the fields, men outnumbered women among immigrants by three or four to one throughout the century.[50] Consequently most of the freedmen had no wife or family to tame their wilder impulses and serve as hostages to the respectable world.

Finally, what made these wild young men particularly dangerous was that they were armed and had to be armed. Life in Virginia required guns. The plantations were exposed to attack from Indians by land and from privateers and petty-thieving pirates by sea.[51] Whenever England was at war with the French or the Dutch, the settlers had to be ready to defend themselves. In 1667 the Dutch in a single raid captured twenty merchant ships in the James River, together with the English warship that was supposed to be defending them; and in 1673 they captured eleven more. On these occasions Governor William Berkeley gathered the planters in arms and at least prevented the enemy from making a landing. But while he stood off the Dutch he worried about the ragged crew at his back. Of the able-bodied men in the colony he estimated that "at least one third are Single freedmen (whose Labour will hardly maintain them) or men much in debt, both which wee may reasonably expect upon any Small advantage the Enemy may gaine upon us, wold revolt to them in hopes of bettering their Condicion by Shareing the Plunder of the Country with them."[52]

Berkeley's fears were justified. Three years later, sparked not by a Dutch invasion but by an Indian attack, rebellion swept Virginia. It began almost as Berkeley had predicted, when a group of volunteer Indian fighters turned from a fruitless expedition against the Indians to attack their rulers. Bacon's Rebellion was the largest popular rising in the colonies before the American Revolution. Sooner or later nearly everyone in Virginia got in on it, but it began in the frontier counties of Henrico and New Kent, among men whom the governor and his friends consistently characterized as rabble.[53] As it spread eastward, it turned out that there were rabble everywhere, and Berkeley understandably raised his estimate of their numbers. "How miserable that man is," he exclaimed, "that Governes a People wher six parts of seavan at least are Poore Endebted Discontented and Armed."[54]

Virginia's poor had reason to be envious and angry against the men who owned the land and imported the servants and ran the government. But the rebellion produced no real program of reform, no ideology, not even any revolutionary slogans. It was a search for plunder, not for principles. And when the rebels had redistributed whatever wealth they could lay their hands on, the rebellion subsided almost as quickly as it had begun.

It had been a shattering experience, however, for Virginia's first families. They had seen each other fall in with the rebels in order to save their skins or their possessions or even to share in the plunder. When it was over, they eyed one another distrustfully, on the lookout for any new Bacons in their midst, who might be tempted to lead the still restive rabble on more plundering expeditions. When William Byrd and Laurence Smith proposed to solve the problems of defense against the Indians by establishing semi-independent buffer settlements on the upper reaches of the rivers, in each of which they would engage to keep fifty men in arms, the assembly at first reacted favorably. But it quickly occurred to the governor and council that this would in fact mean gathering a crowd of Virginia's wild bachelors and furnishing them with an abundant supply of arms and ammunition. Byrd had himself led such a crowd in at least one plundering foray during the rebellion. To put him or anyone else in charge of a large and permanent gang of armed men was to invite them to descend again on the people whom they were supposed to be protecting.[55]

The nervousness of those who had property worth plundering continued throughout the century, spurred in 1682 by the tobacco-cutting riots in which men roved about destroying crops in the fields, in the desperate hope of producing a shortage that would raise the price of the leaf.[56] And periodically in nearby Maryland and North Carolina, where the same conditions existed as in Virginia, there were tumults that threatened to spread to Virginia.[57]

As Virginia thus acquired a social problem analagous to England's own, the colony began to deal with it as England had done, by restricting the liberties of those who did not have the proper badge of freedom, namely the property that government was supposed to protect. One way was to extend the terms of service for servants entering the colony without indentures. Formerly they had served until twenty-one; now the age was advanced to twenty-four.[58] There had always been laws requiring them to serve extra time for running away; now the laws added corporal punishment and, in order to make habitual offenders more readily recognizable, specified that their hair be cropped.[59] New laws restricted the movement of servants on the highways and also increased the amount of extra time to be served for running away. In addition to serving two days for every day's absence, the captured runaway was now frequently required to compensate by labor for the loss to the crop that he had failed to tend and for the cost of his apprehension, including rewards paid for his capture.[60] A three week's holiday might result in a years extra service.[61] If a servant struck his master, he was to serve another year.[62] For killing a hog he had to serve the owner a year and the informer another year. Since the owner of the hog, and the owner of the servant, and the informer were frequently the same man, and since a hog was worth at best less than one tenth the hire of a servant for a year, the law was very profitable to masters. One Lancaster master was awarded six years extra service from a servant who killed three of his hogs, worth about thirty shillings.[63]

The effect of these measures was to keep servants for as long as possible from gaining their freedom, especially the kind of servants who were most likely to cause trouble. At the same time the engrossment of land was driving many back to servitude after a brief taste of freedom. Freedmen who engaged to work for wages by so doing became servants again, subject to most of the same restrictions as other servants.

Nevertheless, in spite of all the legal and economic pressures to keep men in service, the ranks of the freedmen grew, and so did poverty and discontent. To prevent the wild bachelors from gaining an influence in the government, the assembly in 1670 limited voting to land-holders and householders.[64] But to disfranchise the growing mass of single freemen was not to deprive them of the weapons they had wielded so effectively under Nathaniel Bacon. It is questionable how far Virginia could safely have continued along this course, meeting discontent with repression and manning her plantations with annual importations of servants who would later add to the unruly ranks of the free. To be sure, the men at the bottom might have had both land and liberty, as the settlers of some other colonies did, if Virginia's frontier had been safe from Indians, or if the men at the top had been willing to forego some of their profits and to give up some of the lands they had engrossed. The English government itself made efforts to break up the great holdings that had helped to create the problem.[65] But it is unlikely that the policy makers in Whitehall would have contended long against the successful.

In any case they did not have to. There was another solution, which allowed Virginia's magnates to keep their lands, yet arrested the discontent and the repression of other Englishmen, a solution which strengthened the rights of Englishmen and nourished that attachment to liberty which came to fruition in the Revolutionary generation of Virginia statesmen. But the solution put an end to the process of turning Africans into Englishmen. The rights of Englishmen were preserved by destroying the rights of Africans.

I do not mean to argue that Virginians deliberately turned to African Negro slavery as a means of preserving and extending the rights of Englishmen. Winthrop Jordan has suggested that slavery came to Virginia as an unthinking decision.[66] We might go further and say that it came without a decision. It came automatically as Virginians bought the cheapest labor they could get. Once Virginia's heavy mortality ceased, an investment in slave labor was much more profitable than an investment in free labor; and the planters bought slaves as rapidly as traders made them available. In the last years of the seventeenth century they brought them in such numbers that slaves probably already constituted a majority or nearly a majority of the labor force by 1700.[67] The demand was so great that traders for a time found a better market in Virginia than in Jamaica or Barbados.[68] But the social benefits of an enslaved labor force, even if not consciously sought or recognized at the time by the men who bought the slaves, were larger than the economic benefits. The increase in the importation of slaves was matched by a decrease in the importation of indentured servants and consequently a decrease in the dangerous number of new freedmen who annually emerged seeking a place in society that they would be unable to achieve.[69]

If Africans had been unavailable, it would probably have proved impossible to devise a way to keep a continuing supply of English immigrants in their place. There was a limit beyond which the abridgment of English liberties would have resulted not merely in rebellion but in protests from England and in the cutting off of the supply of further servants. At the time of Bacon's Rebellion the English commission of investigation had shown more sympathy with the rebels than with the well-to-do planters who had engrossed Virginia's lands. To have attempted the enslavement of English-born laborers would have caused more disorder than it cured. But to keep as slaves black men who arrived in that condition *was* possible and apparently regarded as plain common sense.

The attitude of English officials was well expressed by the attorney who reviewed for the Privy Council the slave codes established in Barbados in 1679. He found the laws of Barbados to be well designed for the good of his majesty's subjects there, for, he said, "although Negros in that Island are punishable in a different and more severe manner than other Subjects are for Offences of the like nature; yet I humbly conceive that the Laws there concerning Negros are reasonable Laws, for by reason of their numbers they become dangerous, and being a brutish sort of People and reckoned as goods and chattels in that Island, it is of necessity or at least convenient to have Laws for the Government of them different from the Laws of England, to prevent the great mischief that otherwise may happen to the Planters and Inhabitants in that Island."[70] In Virginia too it seemed convenient and reasonable to have different laws for black and white. As the number of slaves increased, the assembly passed laws that carried forward with much greater severity the trend already under way in the colony's labor laws. But the new severity was reserved for people without white skin. The laws specifically exonerated the master who accidentally beat his slave to death, but they placed new limitations on his punishment of "Christian white servants."[71]

Virginians worried about the risk of having in their midst a body of men who had every reason to hate them.[72] The fear of a slave insurrection hung over them for nearly two centuries. But the danger from slaves actually proved to be less than that which the colony had faced from its restive and armed freedmen. Slaves had none of the rising expectations that so often produce human discontent. No one had told them that they had rights. They had been nurtured in heathen societies where they had lost their freedom; their children would be nurtured in a Christian society and never know freedom.

Moreover, slaves were less troubled by the sexual imbalance that helped to make Virginia's free laborers so restless. In an enslaved labor force women could be required to make tobacco just as the men did; and they also made children, who in a few years would be an asset to their master. From the beginning, therefore, traders imported women in a much higher ratio to men than was the case among English servants,[73] and the level of discontent was correspondingly reduced. Virginians did not doubt that discontent would remain, but it could be repressed by methods that would not have been considered reasonable, convenient, or even safe, if applied to Englishmen. Slaves could be deprived of opportunities for association and rebellion. They could be kept unarmed and unorganized. They could be subjected to savage punishments by their owners without fear of legal reprisals. And since their color disclosed their probable status, the rest of society could keep close watch on them. It is scarcely surprising that no slave insurrection in American history approached Bacon's Rebellion in its extent or in its success.

Nor is it surprising that Virginia's freedmen never again posed a threat to society. Though in later years slavery was condemned because it was thought to compete with free labor, in the beginning it reduced by so much the number of freedmen who would otherwise have competed with each other. When the annual increment of freedmen fell off, the number that remained could more easily find an independent place in society, especially as the danger of Indian attack diminished and made settlement safer at the heads of the rivers or on the Carolina frontier. There might still remain a number of irredeemable, idle, and unruly freedmen, particularly among the convicts whom England exported to the colonies. But the numbers were small enough, so that they could be dealt with by the old expedient of drafting them for military expeditions.[74] The way was thus made easier for the remaining freedmen to acquire property, maybe acquire a slave or two of their own, and join with their superiors in the enjoyment of those English liberties that differentiated them from their black laborers.

A free society divided between large landholders and small was much less riven by antagonisms than one divided between landholders and landless, masterless men. With the freedman's expectations, sobriety, and status restored, he was no longer a man to be feared. That fact, together with the presence of a growing mass of alien slaves, tended to draw the white settlers closer together and to reduce the importance of the class difference between yeoman farmer and large plantation owner.[75]

The seventeenth century has sometimes been thought of as the day of the yeoman farmer in Virginia; but in many ways a stronger case can be made for the eighteenth century as the time when the yeoman farmer came into his own, because slavery relieved the small man of the pressures that had been reducing him to continued servitude. Such an interpretation conforms to the political development of the colony. During the seventeenth century the royally appointed governor's council, composed of the largest property-owners in the colony, had been the most powerful governing body. But as the tide of slavery rose between 1680 and 1720 Virginia moved toward a government in which the yeoman farmer had a larger share. In spite of the rise of Virginia's great families on the black tide, the power of the council declined; and the elective House of Burgesses became the dominant organ of government. Its members nurtured a closer relationship with their yeoman constituency than had earlier been the case.[76] And in its chambers Virginians developed the ideas they so fervently asserted in the Revolution: ideas about taxation, representation, and the rights of Englishmen, and ideas about the prerogatives and powers and sacred calling of the independent, property-holding yeoman farmer—commonwealth ideas.

In the eighteenth century, because they were no longer threatened by a dangerous free laboring class, Virginians could afford these ideas, whereas in Berkeley's time they could not. Berkeley himself was obsessed with the experience of the English civil wars and the danger of rebellion. He despised and feared the New Englanders for their association with the Puritans who had made England, however briefly, a commonwealth.[77] He was proud that Virginia, unlike New England, had no free schools and no printing press, because books and schools bred heresy and sedition.[78] He must have taken satisfaction in the fact that when his people did rebel against him under Bacon, they generated no republican ideas, no philosophy of rebellion or of human rights. Yet a century later, without benefit of rebellions, Virginians had learned republican lessons, had introduced schools and printing presses, and were as ready as New Englanders to recite the aphorisms of the commonwealthmen.

It was slavery, I suggest, more than any other single factor, that had made the difference, slavery that enabled Virginia to nourish representative government in a plantation society, slavery that transformed the Virginia of Governor Berkeley to the Virginia of Jefferson, slavery that made the Virginians dare to speak a political language that magnified the rights of freemen, and slavery, therefore, that brought Virginians into the same commonwealth political tradition with New Englanders. The very institution that was to divide North and South after the Revolution may have made possible their union in a republican government.

Thus began the American paradox of slavery and freedom, intertwined and interdependent, the rights of Englishmen supported on the wrongs of Africans. The American Revolution only made the contradictions more glaring, as the slaveholding colonists proclaimed to a candid world the rights not simply of Englishmen but of all men. To explain the origin of the contradictions, if the explanation I have suggested is valid, does not eliminate them or make them less ugly. But it may enable us to understand a little better the strength of the ties that bound freedom to slavery, even in so noble a mind as Jefferson's. And it may perhaps make us wonder about the ties that bind more devious tyrannies to our own freedoms and give us still today our own American paradox.

Notes

[1] Particularly Staughton Lynd, *Class Conflict, Slavery, and the United States Constitution: Ten Essays* (Indianapolis, 1967).

[2] Curtis P. Nettels, *The Emergence of a National Economy 1775–1815* (New York, 1962), 19. See also Merrill Jensen, "The American Revolution and American Agriculture," *Agricultural History*, XLIII (Jan. 1969), 107–24.

[3] William Cohen, "Thomas Jefferson and the Problem of Slavery," *Journal of American History*, LVI (Dec. 1969), 503–26; D. B. Davis, *Was Thomas Jefferson An Authentic Enemy of Slavery?* (Oxford, 1970); Winthrop D. Jordan, *White over Black: American Attitudes Toward the Negro, 1550–1812* (Chapel Hill, 1968), 429–81.

[4] Julian P. Boyd, ed., *The Papers of Thomas Jefferson* (18 vols., Princeton, 1950–), X, 615. For other expressions of Thomas Jefferson's aversion to debt and distrust of credit, both private and public, see *ibid.*, II, 275–76, VIII, 398–99, 632–33, IX, 217–18, 472–73, X, 304–05, XI, 472, 633, 636, 640, XII, 385–86.

[5] Jefferson's career as ambassador to France was occupied very largely by unsuccessful efforts to break the hold of British creditors on American commerce.

[6] See Caroline Robbins, *The Eighteenth-Century Commonwealthman: Studies in the Transmission, Development and Circumstance of English Liberal Thought from the Restoration of Charles II until the War with the Thirteen Colonies* (Cambridge, Mass., 1959); J. G. A. Pocock, "Machiavelli, Harrington, and English Political Ideologies in the Eighteenth Century," *William and Mary Quarterly*, XXII (Oct. 1965), 549–83.

[7] Boyd, ed., *Papers of Thomas Jefferson*, I, 344, 352, 362, 560, VIII, 681–82.

[8] *Ibid.*, VIII, 426, 682; Thomas Jefferson, *Notes on the State of Virginia*, William Peden, ed. (Chapel Hill, 1955), 165. Jefferson seems to have overlooked the dependence of Virginia's farmers on the casualties and caprice of the tobacco market.

[9] See Robbins, *The Eighteenth-Century Commonwealthmen*; Pocock, "Machiavelli, Harrington, and English Political Ideologies," 549–83; Michael Zuckerman, "The Social Context of Democracy in Massachusetts," *William and Mary Quarterly*, XXV (Oct. 1968), 523–44; Robert M. Weir, "'The Harmony We Were Famous For': An Interpretation of Pre-Revolutionary South Carolina Politics," *ibid.*, XXVI (Oct. 1969), 473–501.

[10] C. B. Macpherson, *The Political Theory of Possessive Individualism* (Oxford, 1962), 221–24; H. R. Fox Bourne, *The Life of John Locke* (2 vols., London, 1876), II, 377–90.

[11] Adam Ferguson, *The History of the Progress and Termination of the Roman Republic* (5 vols., Edinburgh, 1799), I, 384. See also Adam Ferguson, *An Essay on the History of Civil Society* (London, 1768), 309–11.

[12] Francis Hutcheson, *A System of Moral Philosophy* (2 vols., London, 1755), II, 202; David B. Davis, *The Problem of Slavery in Western Culture* (Ithaca, 1966), 374–78. I am indebted to David B. Davis for several valuable suggestions.

[13] James Burgh, *Political Disquisitions: Or, An ENQUIRY into public Errors, Defects, and Abuses . . .* (3 vols., London, 1774–1775), III, 220–21. See the proposal of Bishop George Berkeley that "sturdy beggars should . . . be seized and made slaves to the public for a certain term of years." Quoted in R. H. Tawney, *Religion and the Rise of Capitalism: A Historical Essay* (New York, 1926), 270.

[14] E. Millicent Sowerby, ed., *Catalogue of the Library of Thomas Jefferson* (5 vols., Washington, 1952–1959), I, 192.

[15] Andrew Fletcher, *Two Discourses Concerning the Affairs of Scotland; Written in the Year 1698* (Edinburgh, 1698). See second discourse (separately paged), 1–33, especially 16.

[16] Boyd, ed., *Papers of Thomas Jefferson*, VIII, 681–83.

[17] *Ibid.*, IX, 659–60.

[18] Jackson Turner Main, *The Social Structure of Revolutionary America* (Princeton, 1965), 271.

[19] In 1755, Virginia had 43,329 white tithables and 60,078 black. Tithables included white men over sixteen years of age and black men and women over sixteen. In the census of 1790, Virginia had 292,717 slaves and 110,936 white males over sixteen, out of a total population of 747,680. Evarts B. Greene and Virginia D. Harrington, *American Population before the Federal Census of 1790* (New York, 1932), 150–55.

[20] Jefferson, *Notes on the State of Virginia*, 138.

[21] Jack P. Greene, ed., *The Diary of Colonel Landon Carter of Sabine Hall, 1752–1778* (2 vols., Charlottesville, 1965), II, 1055.

[22] Boyd, ed., *Papers of Thomas Jefferson*, XIV, 492–93.

[23] St. George Tucker, *A Dissertation on Slavery with a Proposal for the Gradual Abolition of It, in the State of Virginia* (Philadelphia, 1796). See also Jordan, *White over Black*, 555–60.

[24] Joan Thrisk, ed., *The Agrarian History of England and Wales*, Vol. IV: *1500–1640* (Cambridge, England, 1967), 531.

[25] See Edmund S. Morgan, "The Labor Problem at Jamestown, 1607–18," *American Historical Review*, 76 (June 1971), 595–611, especially 600–06.

[26] This is Richard Hakluyt's phrase. See E. G. R. Taylor, ed., *The Original Writings & Correspondence of the Two Richard Hakluyts* (2 vols., London, 1935), I, 142.

[27] Richard Hakluyt, *The Principall Navigations, Voiages and Discoveries of the English nation . . .* (London, 1589).

[28] The whole story of this extraordinary episode is to be found in I. A. Wright, ed., *Documents Concerning English Voyages to the Spanish Main 1569–1580* (London, 1932).

[29] Taylor, ed., *Original Writings & Correspondence*, I, 139–46.

[30] Walter Raleigh, *The Discoverie of the large and bewtiful Empire of Guiana*, V. T. Harlow, ed. (London, 1928), 138–49; V. T. Harlow, ed., *Ralegh's Last Voyage: Being an account drawn out of contemporary letters and relations . . .* (London, 1932), 44–45.

[31] Taylor, ed., *Original Writings & Correspondence*, II, 211–377, especially 318.

[32] Irene A. Wright, trans. and ed., *Further English Voyages to Spanish America, 1583–1594: Documents from the Archives of the Indies at Seville . . .* (London, 1951), lviii, lxiii, lxiv, 37, 52, 54, 55, 159, 172, 173, 181, 188–89, 204–06.

[33] The Spanish reported that "Although their masters were willing to ransom them the English would not give them up except when the slaves themselves desired to go." *Ibid.*, 159. On Walter Raleigh's later expedition to Guiana, the Spanish noted that the English told the natives "that they did not desire to make them slaves, but only to be their friends; promising to bring them great quantities of hatchets and knives, and especially if they drove the Spaniards out of their territories." Harlow, ed., *Ralegh's Last Voyage*, 179.

[34] David Beers Quinn, ed., *The Roanoke Voyages 1584–1590* (2 vols., London, 1955).

[35] Morgan, "The Labor Problem at Jamestown, 1607–18," pp. 595–611; Edmund S. Morgan, "The First American Boom: Virginia 1618 to 1630," *William and Mary Quarterly*, XXVIII (April 1971), 169–98.

[36] There are no reliable records of immigration, but the presence of persons of these nationalities is evident from county court records, where all but the Dutch are commonly identified by name, such as "James the Scotchman," or "Cursory the Turk." The Dutch seem to have anglicized their names at once and are difficult to identify except where the records disclose their naturalization. The two counties for which the most complete records survive for the 1640s and 1650s are Accomack-Northampton and Lower Norfolk. Microfilms are in the Virginia State Library, Richmond.

[37] Because the surviving records are so fragmentary, there has been a great deal of controversy about the status of the first Negroes in Virginia. What the records do make clear is that not all were slaves and that not all were free. See Jordan, *White over Black*, 71–82.

[38] For examples, see Northampton County Court Records, Deeds, Wills, etc., Book III, f. 83, Book V, ff. 38, 54, 60, 102, 117–19; York County Court Records, Deeds, Orders, Wills, etc., no. 1, ff. 232–34; Surry County Court Records, Deeds, Wills, etc., no. 1, f. 349; Henrico County Court Records, Deeds and Wills 1677–1692, f. 139.

[39] This fact has been arrived at by comparing the names of householders on the annual list of tithables with casual identifications of persons as Negroes in the court records. The names of householders so identified for 1668, the peak year during the period for which the lists survive (1662–1677) were: Bastian Cane, Bashaw Ferdinando, John Francisco, Susan Grace, William Harman, Philip Mongum, Francis Pane, Manuel Rodriggus, Thomas Rodriggus, and King Tony. The total number of households in the county in 1668 was 172; total number of tithables 435; total number of tithable free Negroes 17; total number of tithable unfree Negroes 42. Thus nearly 29 percent of tithable Negroes and probably of all Negroes were free; and about 13.5 percent of all tithables were Negroes.

[40] Northampton Deeds, Wills, etc., Book V, 54–60 (Nov. 1, 1654).

[41] The figure for 1625 derives from the census for that year, which gives 1,210 persons, but probably missed about 10 percent of the population. Morgan, "The First American Boom," 170n–71n. The figure for 1640 is derived from legislation limiting tobacco production per person in 1639–1640. The legislation is summarized in a manuscript belonging to Jefferson, printed in William Waller Hening, *The Statutes at Large; Being a Collection of All the Laws of Virginia, from the First Session of the Legislature, in the Year 1619* (13 vols., New York, 1823), I, 224–25, 228. The full text is in "Acts of the General Assembly. Jan. 6, 1639–40," *William and Mary Quarterly*, IV (Jan. 1924), 17–35, and "Acts of the General Assembly, Jan. 6, 1639–40," *ibid.* (July 1924), 159–62. The assembly calculated that a levy of four pounds of tobacco per tithable would yield 18,584 pounds, implying 4,646 tithables (men over sixteen). It also calculated that a limitation of planting to 170 pounds per poll would yield 1,300,000, implying 7,647 polls. Evidently the latter figure is for the whole population, as is evident also from Hening, *Statutes*, I, 228.

[42] In the year 1635, the only year for which such records exist, 2,010 persons embarked for Virginia from London alone. See John Camden Hotten, ed., *The Original Lists of Persons of Quality . . .* (London, 1874), 35–145. For other years casual estimates survive. In February 1627/8 Francis West said that 1,000 had been "lately receaved." Colonial Office Group, Class 1, Piece 4, folio 109 (Public Record Office, London). Hereafter cited CO 1/4, f. 109. In February 1633/4 Governor John Harvey said that "this yeares newcomers" had arrived "this yeare." Yong to Sir Tobie Matthew, July 13, 1634, "Aspinwall Papers," *Massachusetts Historical Society Collections*, IX (1871), 110. In May 1635, Samuel Mathews said that 2,000 had arrived "this yeare." Mathews to ? , May 25, 1635, "The Mutiny in Virginia, 1635," *Virginia Magazine of History and Biography*, I (April 1894), 417. And in March 1636, John West said that 1,606 persons had arrived "this yeare." West to Commissioners for Plantations, March 28, 1636, "Virginia in 1636," *ibid.*, IX (July 1901), 37.

[43] The official count of tithables for 1662 was 11,838. Clarendon Papers, 82 (Bodleian Library, Oxford). The ratio of tithables to total population by this time was probably about one to two. (In 1625 it was 1 to 1.5; in 1699 it was 1 to 2.7.) Since the official count was almost certainly below the actuality, a total population of roughly 25,000 seems probable. All population figures for seventeenth-century Virginia should be treated as rough estimates.

[44] Evidence of the engrossment of lands after 1660 will be found in CO 1/39, f. 196; CO 1/40, f. 23; CO 1/48, f. 48; CO 5/1309, numbers 5, 9, and 23; Sloane Papers, 1008, ff. 334–35 (British Museum, London). A recent count of headrights in patents issued for land in Virginia shows 82,000 headrights claimed in the years from 1635 to 1700. Of these nearly 47,000 or 57 percent

(equivalent to 2,350,000 acres) were claimed in the twenty-five years after 1650. W. F. Craven, *White, Red, and Black: The Seventeenth-Century Virginian* (Charlottesville, 1971), 14–16.

[45] No continuous set of figures for Virginia's tobacco exports in the seventeenth century can now be obtained. The available figures for English imports of American tobacco (which was mostly Virginian) are in United States Bureau of the Census, *Historical Statistics of the United States, Colonial Times to 1957* (Washington, D.C., 1960), series Z 238–240, p. 766. They show for 1672 a total of 17,559,000 pounds. In 1631 the figure had been 272,300 pounds. Tobacco crops varied heavily from year to year. Prices are almost as difficult to obtain now as volume. Those for 1667–1675 are estimated from London prices current in Warren Billings, "Virginia's Deploured Condition, 1660–1676: The Coming of Bacon's Rebellion" (doctoral dissertation, Northern Illinois University, 1969), 155–59.

[46] See below.

[47] Thomas Ludwell and Robert Smith to the king, June 18, 1676, vol. LXXVII, f. 128, Coventry Papers Longleat House, American Council of Learned Societies British Mss. project, reel 63 (Library of Congress).

[48] *Ibid.*, 204–05.

[49] Nicholas Spencer to Lord Culpeper, Aug. 6, 1676, *ibid.*, 170. See also CO 1/49, f. 107.

[50] The figures are derived from a sampling of the names of persons for whom headrights were claimed in land patents. Patent Books I–IX (Virginia State Library, Richmond). Wyndham B. Blanton found 17,350 women and 75,884 men in "a prolonged search of the patent books and other records of the times. . . ," a ratio of 1 woman to 4.4 men. Wyndham B. Blanton, "Epidemics, Real and Imaginary, and other Factors Influencing Seventeenth Century Virginia's Population," *Bulletin of the History of Medicine*, XXXI (Sept.–Oct. 1957), 462. See also Craven, *White, Red, and Black*, 26–27.

[51] Pirates were particularly troublesome in the 1680s and 1690s. See CO 1/48, f. 71; CO 1/51, f. 340; CO 1/52, f. 54; CO 1/55, ff. 105–106; CO 1/57, f. 300; CO 5/1311, no. 10.

[52] CO 1/30, ff. 114–115.

[53] CO 1/37, ff. 35–40.

[54] Vol. LXXVII, 144–46, Coventry Papers.

[55] Hening, *Statutes*, II, 448–54; CO 1/42, f. 178; CO 1/43, f. 29; CO 1/44, f. 398; CO 1/47, ff. 258–260, 267; CO 1/48, f. 46; vol. LXXVIII, 378–81, 386–87, 398–99, Coventry Papers.

[56] CO 1/48 *passim*.

[57] CO 1/43, ff. 359–365; CO 1/44, ff. 10–62; CO 1/47, f. 261; CO 1/48, ff. 87–96, 100–102, 185; CO 5/1305, no. 43; CO 5/1309, no. 74.

[58] Hening, *Statutes*, II, 113–14, 240.

[59] *Ibid.*, II, 266, 278.

[60] *Ibid.*, II, 116–17, 273–74, 277–78.

[61] For example, James Gray, absent twenty-two days, was required to serve fifteen months extra. Order Book 1666-1680, p. 163, Lancaster County Court Records.

[62] Hening, *Statutes*, II, 118.

[63] Order Book 1666-1680, p. 142, Lancaster County Court Records.

[64] Hening, *Statutes*, II, 280. It had been found, the preamble to the law said, that such persons "haveing little interest in the country doe oftner make tumults at the election to the disturbance of his majesties peace, then by their discretions in their votes provide for the conservasion thereof, by making choyce of persons fitly qualified for the discharge of soe great a trust. . . ."

[65] CO 1/39, f. 196; CO 1/48, f. 48; CO 5/1309, nos. 5, 9, 23; CO 5/1310, no. 83.

[66] Jordan, *White over Black*, 44–98.

[67] In 1700 they constituted half of the labor force (persons working for other men) in Surry County, the only county in which it is possible to ascertain the numbers. Robert Wheeler, "Social Transition in the Virginia Tidewater, 1650–1720: The Laboring Household as an Index," paper delivered at the Organization of American Historians' meeting, New Orleans, April 15, 1971. Surry County was on the south side of the James, one of the least wealthy regions of Virginia.

[68] See the letters of the Royal African Company to its ship captains, Oct. 23, 1701; Dec. 2, 1701; Dec. 7, 1704; Dec. 21, 1704; Jan. 25, 1704//5, T70 58 (Public Record Office, London).

[69] Abbot Emerson Smith, *Colonists in Bondage: White Servitude and Convict Labor in America 1607–1776* (Chapel Hill, 1947), 335. See also Thomas J. Wertenbaker, *The Planters of Colonial Virginia* (Princeton, 1922), 130–31, 134–35; Craven, *White, Red, and Black*, 17.

[70] CO 1/45, f. 138.

[71] Hening, *Statutes*, II, 481–82, 492–93; III, 86–88, 102–03, 179–80, 333–35, 447–62.

[72] For example, see William Byrd II to the Earl of Egmont, July 12, 1736, in Elizabeth Donnan, ed., *Documents Illustrative of the History of the Slave Trade to America* (4 vols., Washington, 1930–1935), IV, 131–32. But compare Byrd's letter to Peter Beckford, Dec. 6, 1735, "Letters of the Byrd Family," *Virginia Magazine of History and Biography*, XXXVI (April 1928), 121–23, in which he specifically denies any danger. The Virginia assembly at various times laid duties on the importation of slaves. See Donnan, ed., *Documents Illustrative of the History of the Slave Trade*, IV, 66–67, 86–88, 91–94, 102–17, 121–31, 132–42. The purpose of some of the acts was to discourage imports, but apparently the motive was to redress the colony's balance of trade after a period during which the planters had purchased far more than they could pay for. See also Wertenbaker, *The Planters of a Colonial Virginia*, 129.

[73] The Swiss traveler Francis Ludwig Michel noted in 1702 that "Both sexes are usually bought, which increase afterwards." William J. Hinke, trans. and ed., "Report of the Journey of Francis Louis Michel from Berne Switzerland to Virginia, October 2, (1) 1701–December 1, 1702: Part II," *Virginia Magazine of History and Biography*, XXIV (April 1916), 116. A sampling of the names identifiable by sex, for whom headrights were claimed in land patents in the 1680s and 1690s shows a much higher ratio of women to men among blacks than among whites. For example, in the years 1695–1699 (Patent Book 9) I count 818 white men and 276 white women, 376 black men and 220 black women (but compare Craven, *White, Red, and Black*, 99–100). In Northampton County in 1677, among seventy-five black tithables there were thirty-six men, thirty-eight women, and one person whose sex cannot be determined. In Surry County in 1703, among 211 black tithables there were 132 men, seventy-four women, and five persons whose sex cannot be determined. These are the only counties where the records yield such information. Northampton County Court Records, Order Book 10, 189–91; Surry County Court Records, Deeds, Wills, etc., No. 5, part 2, 287–90.

[74] Virginia disposed of so many this way in the campaign against Cartagena in 1741 that a few years later the colony was unable to scrape up any more for another expedition. Fairfax Harrison, "When the Convicts Came," *Virginia Magazine of History and Biography*, XXX (July 1922), 250–60, especially 256–57; John W. Shy, "A New Look at Colonial Militia," *William and Mary Quarterly*, XX (April 1963), 175–85. In 1736, Virginia had shipped another batch of unwanted freedmen to Georgia because of a rumored attack by the Spanish. Byrd II to Lord Egmont, July 1736, "Letters of the Byrd Family," *Virginia Magazine of History and Biography*, XXXVI (July 1928), 216–17. Observations by an English traveler who embarked on the same ship suggest that they did not go willingly: "our Lading consisted of all the Scum of Virginia, who had been recruited for the Service of Georgia, and who were ready at every Turn to mutiny, whilst they belch'd out the most shocking Oaths, wishing Destruction to the Vessel and every Thing in her." "Observations in Several Voyages and Travels in America in the Year 1736," *William and Mary Quarterly*, XV (April 1907), 224.

[75] Compare Lyon G. Tyler, "Virginians Voting in the Colonial Period," *William and Mary Quarterly*, VI (July 1897), 7–13.

[76] John C. Rainbolt, "The Alteration in the Relationship between Leadership and Constituents in Virginia, 1660 to 1720," *William and Mary Quarterly*, XXVII (July 1970), 411–34.

[77] William Berkeley to Richard Nicolls, May 20, 1666, May 4, 1667. Additional Mss. 28,218, ff. 14–17 (British Museum, London).

[78] Hening, *Statutes*, II, 517.

9

Selection from
Bound Labor: Slavery

Bound Labor: Slavery

Problems Created by the Use of Slave Labor

10. Runaways
A. Theoderick Bland Tries to Recapture Two Runaways, 1662

Charles City County Order Book, 1655–1665, 331.

It is ordered that Mr. Theoderick Bland by vertue hereof have power to require the sheriff of Charles Citty or James Citty (or any other) [county?] to raise such a Competent number of men and armes as shallbe needfull for the search and surprisall of two negroes runn away from the said Mr. Bland; And that the said Mr. Bland give such reasonable satisfaction to the men so imployed as their time and paines may deserve, and present a proposition to the next Assembly whether the said charge ought to be publick or private.

B. Punishment of a Runaway Slave, 1689

Charles City County Order Book, 1687–1695, 262.

Will a Negro slave belonging to Mrs. Mary Clarke being a runnaway thevish Rogue, and here accused of several injuries that he hath done to the People of the County in the tyme of his late absence from his service, It is ordered that he receive thirty nine lashes well layd, on his bare backe.

11. Slave Insurrections
A. A Rising on William Pierce's Plantation, 1640

"Decisions of the General Court," 1640, *Virginia Magazine of History and Biography*, V (1897–1898), 236–237.

July 22d, 1640. Whereas complaint has been made to this Board by Capt. William Pierce, Esqr., that six of his servants and a negro of Mr. Reginald's has plotted to run away unto the Dutch plantation from their said masters, and did assay to put the same in Execution upon

Saturday night, being the 8th day July, 1640, as appeared to the Board by the Examinations of Andrew Noxe, Richard Hill, Richard Cookeson and John Williams, and likewise by the confession of Christopher Miller, Peter Milcocke and Emanuel, the foresaid Negro, who had, at the foresaid time, taken the skiff of the said Capt. William Pierce, their master, and corn, powder and shot and guns to accomplish their said purposes, which said persons sailed down in the said skiff to Elizabeth river, where they were taken and brought back again, the court, taking the same into consideration as a dangerous precedent for the future time (if left unpunished), did order that Christopher Miller, a dutchman (a prime agent in the business), should receive the punishment of whipping, and to have thirty stripes and so be burnt in the cheek with the letter R and to work with a shackle on his legg for one whole year and longer if said master shall see cause, and after his full time of service is Expired with his said master to serve the colony for seven whole years, and the said Peter Milcocke to receive thirty stripes and to be Burnt in the cheek with the letter R, and after his term of service is Expired with his said master to serve the colony for three years, and the said Richard Cockson, after his full time Expired with his master, to serve the colony for two years and a half, and the said Richard Hill to remain upon his good behavior untill the next offence, and the said Andrew Noxe to receive thirty stripes, and the said John Williams, a dutchman and a chirurgeon after his full time of service is Expired with his master, to serve the colony for seven years, and Emanuel, the Negro, to receive thirty stripes and to be burnt in the cheek with the letter R and to work in shackles one year or more as his master shall see cause, and all those who are condemned to serve the colony after their time are Expired with their masters, then their said masters are required hereby to present to this board their said servants so condemned to the colony.

B. A Rising on the Northern Neck, 1680

> H. R. McIlwaine and Wilmer L. Hall, eds., *Executive Journals of the Council of Colonial Virginia* (Richmond, Va., 1925–1945), I, 86–87.

His Excellency was pleased this day in Councell to acquaint the Councell that he had even then received from Mr. Secretary Spencer Intelligence of the Discovery of a Negro Plott, formed in the Northern Neck for the Distroying and killing his Majesties Subjects the Inhabitants thereof, with a designe of Carrying it through the whole Collony of Virginia which being by Gods Providence timely discovered before any part of the designes were put in Execution, and thereby their whole Evill purposes for the present defeated, and Mr. Secretary Spencer haveing by his Care Secured some of the Principall Actors and Contrivers, and the Evill and fatall Consequences that might have hapned, being by this Board Seriously considered Have found fit to Order that the Negro Conspirators now in Custody be either safely Secured untill the next Generall Court, to the Intent they may then be proceeded against according to Law, or if it be found more Necessary for the present Safety of the Country that they be brought to a Speedy Tryall, that then his Excellency will be pleased to direct a Commission to Mr. Secretary Spencer, Col. Richard Lee, and Col. Isaac Allerton three of his Majesties Councell Inhabitants in the Northern Neck to Sitt heare and try according to Law the Negro Conspirators, and to proceed to Sentence of Condemnation and Execution, or to Such other punishments as according to Law they shall be found Guilty off, by such examples of Justice to deterr other Negroes from plotting or Contriveing either the Death wrongs or Injuries of any of his Majesties Subjects. And this Board haveing Considered that the great freedome and Liberty that has beene by many Masters given to their Negro Slaves for Walking on broad on Saterdays and Sundays and permitting them to meete in great Numbers in makeing and holding of Funeralls for Dead Negroes gives them the Opportunityes under pretention of such publique meetings to Consult and advise for the carrying on of their Evill and Wichked purposes and Contrivances, for prevention whereof for the future, It is by this Board thought fitt that a Proclamation doe forthwith Issue, requiring a Strickt observance of the Severall Laws of this Collony relateing to Negroes, and to require and Comand all Masters of families haveing any Negro Slaves, not to permitt them to hold or make any Solemnity or Funeralls for any deceased Negroes.

12. The Difficulty in Maintaining Racial Separation
A. Hugh Davis's Case, 1630

> William Waller Hening, ed., *The Statutes at Large; Being a Collection of All the Laws of Virgina, from the First Session of the Legislature, in the Year 1619* (Richmond, New York, and Philadelphia, 1809–1823), I, 146.

"September 17th, 1630. Hugh Davis to be soundly whipped, before an assembly of Negroes and others for abusing himself to the dishonor of God and shame of Christians, by defiling his body in lying with a negro; which fault he is to acknowledge next Sabbath day."

B. William Watts's and Mary's Case, 1649

> Lower Norfolk County Order Book, 1646–1650, 113a.

William Watts and Mary (Mr Cornelius Lloyds negro Woman) are ordered each of them to doe penance by standing in a white sheete with a white Rodd in theire hands in the Chappell of Elizabeth River in the face of the congregation on the next sabbath day that the minister shall make penince service and the said Watts to pay the court charges.

C. William's Case, 1681

> Lower Norfolk County Order Book, 1681–1686, 139.

Whereas upon the Information of mr. James Porter minister It hath appeared to this Court that Mary Williamson hath Comitted the filthy sin of fornication with William a negro belonging to William Basnett Squire It is therefore ordered that shee bee fined five hundred pounds of tobacco and Caske for the use of Linhaven parish, for which the said Basnet hath In open Court Ingaged himself etc. security.
Whereas It hath appeared to this Court that William a negro belonging to William Basnett Squire hath Comitted fornication with Mary Williams[on], and hath very arrogantly behaved himself in Linhaven Church in the face of the Congregation, It is therefore ordered that the Sherlff take the said William Into his Custody and give him thirty Lashes on his bare back.

D. Katherine Watkins's Case, 1681

> Henrico County Deed Book, 1677–1692, 192–195.

The examination of Katherine Watkins, the wife of Henry Watkins of Henrico County in Virginia had and taken this 13 of September 1681 before us William Byrd and John Farrar two of his Majesties Justices of the County aforesaid as followeth (vizt.)

The said Katherine aforesaid on her Oath and examination deposeth, That on fryday being in the Month of August aboute five weeks since, the said Katherine mett with John Long (a Mulatto belonging to Capt. Thomas Cocke) at or neare the pyney slash betweene the aforesaid Cockes and Henry Watkins house, and at the same tyme and place, the said John threw the said Katherine downe (He starting from behinde a tree) and stopped her Mouth with a handkerchief, and tooke up the said Katherines Coates [i.e., petticoats], and putt his yard into her and ravished her; Upon which she the said Katherine Cryed out (as she deposeth) and afterwards (being rescued by another Negroe of the said Cockes named Jack White) she departed home, and the said John departed to his Masters likewise, or that way; after which abuse she the said Katherine declares that her husband inclinable to the quakers, and therefore would not prosecute, and she being sicke and her Children likewise, she therefore did not make her complaint before she went to Lt. Col. Farrars (which was yesterday, Morning) and this day in the Morning she went to WIlliam Randolphs' and found him not at home, But at night met with the gentlemen Justices aforesaid at the house of the aforesaid Cocke in Henrico County in Virginia aforesaid before whom she hath made this complaint upon oath . . .

The deposition of John Aust aged 32 yeares or thereabouts Deposeth, That on fryday being the twelvth of August or thereabouts he came to the house of Mr. Thomas Cocke, and soe went into his Orchard where his servants were a cutting downe weeds, whoe asked the deponent to stay and drinke, soe the deponent stayed and dranke syder with them, and Jacke a Mulatto of the said Thomas Cocke went in to draw syder, and he stay'd something long whereupon the deponent followed him, and coming to the doore where the syder was, heard Katherine the wife of Henry Wakins say (Lord) Jacke what makes the[e] refraine our house that you come not oftner, for come when thou wilt thou shalt be as well come as any of My owne Children, and soe she tooke him about the necke and Kissed him, and Jacke went out and drawed Syder, and she said Jack wilt thou not drinke to me, who sayd yes if you will goe out where our Cupp is, and a little after she came out, where the said Thomas Cockes Negroes were a drinking and there dranke cupp for cupp with them (as others there did) and as she sett Negroe dirke passing by her she tooke up the taile of his shirt (saying) Dirke thou wilt have a good long thing, and soe did several tymes as he past [*sic*] by her; after this she went into the roome where the syder was and then came out againe, and between the two houses she mett Mulatto Jacke a going to draw more syder and putt her hand on his codpiece, at which he smil'd, and went on his way and drew syder and she came againe into the company but stay'd not long but went out to drinking with two of the said Thomas Cockes Negroes by the garden pale, And a while after she tooke Mingoe one of the said Cocke's Negroes about the Necke and fling on the bedd and Kissed him and putt her hand into his Codpeice, Awhile after Mulatto Jacke went into the Fish roome and she followed him, but what they did there this deponent knoweth not for it being near night this deponent left her and the Negroes together, (He thinking her to be much in drinke) and soe this deponent went home about one houre by sunn. . . .

The Deposition of William Harding aged about 35 yeares.

Deposeth,
That he came to the house of Mr. Thomas Cocke to speake with his brother, where he see Katherine the wife of Henry Watkins, and soe spoke to one there and sayd, that the said Henry Watkins wife had been a drinking; And that this deponent see the said Katherine Watkins turne up the taile of Negroe Dirks shirt, and said that he would have a good pricke, whereupon this deponent sayd is that the trick of a quaker, who made him answer, that what hast thou to say to quakers, It being acted on fryday the 12 of August or thereabouts and further saith not. . . .

The Deposition of Mary Winter aged about 22 years.

Deposeth,

That Mr. Thomas Cocks Negroes and others being in company with them a drinking of syder, Then came in Katherine Watkins the wife of Henry Watkins and went to drinking with them, and tooke Mulatto Jack by the hand in the outward roome and ledd him into the inward roome doore and then thrust him in before her and told him she loved him for his Fathers sake for his Father was a very hansome young Man, and afterwards the said Mulattoe went out from her, and then she fetched him into the roome againe and hugged and kist him. And further saith not. . . .

The Deposition of Lambert Tye aged about 26 yeares.

Deposeth,

That being at Worke at Mr. Thomas Cocks on fryday being the twelvth of August or there-abouts, and coming into the house with William Hobson and the rest of Mr. Thomas Cocks servants and others in Company with them to drinke syder, and being a drinking then comes in Katherine Watkins the wife of Henry Watkins having a very high Colour in her face whereupon this deponent asked Humphrey then servant to the said Thomas Cocke; what made his Countrywoman have such a high Colour; whereupon he made this answear; That the [said] Katherine was at Old Humphrey's a drinking and he gave her a Cupp or two that had turned her braines, and soe being a drinking with their company she went into the Chimney (as this deponent thinketh) to light her pipe, and soe made a posture with her body as if she would have gone to danceing, and then afterwards coming into their company againe, she told Mulatto Jack, that she loved him for his father's sake, And then having left the Company and she together a drinking, This deponent went home to his owne house, and afterwards coming from home towards the house of the said Thomas Cocke, he mett with the said Katherine Watkins about halfe an houre by sun in the pathway homewards neare to this deponents house. And further saith not. . . .

Humphrey Smith aged 26 yeares, deposeth,

That he heard John Aust say (about September last past) what Matter is it what I swore to and likewise the deponent saw Katherine's Mouth (the wife of Henry Watkins) torne and her lipps swell'd, And the handkerchief that she said the Mulatto Stopt her Mouth with very much bloody And the deponent heard the Mulatto confess that he had beene to aske the said Watkins wife forgiveness three tymes, and likewise the Mulatto sayd that Henry Watkins (the last tyme he went) bidd him keepe of[f] his plantation or else he would shoote him and further saith not. . . .

E. Rebecca Corney's Bastard, 1689

Charles City County Order Book, 1689–1695, 225.

John Baxter his servant wench namely Rebecca Corney being convicted in Courte of having a Mulatto bastard she is thereupon fined for her default as the law prescribes and the said Rebecca is ordered to reimburse her said Master in service upon his promise to pay this fine.

The Evolution of Slavery's Definition in the Law

17. *Acts of the General Assembly, 1640–1680*

A. An Act Preventing Negroes from Bearing Arms, 1640

"Acts of General Assembly, Jan. 6, 1639–40," *William and Mary Quarterly*, 2d Ser., IV (1924), 147.

It is likewise enacted that all masters of families shall use their best endeavours for the firnishing of themselves and all those of their families which shall be capable of arms (excepting negros) with arms both offensive and defensive (vizt) that all persons shall provide themselves as aforesaid with armes offensive the ensueing year, and with half armes both offensive and defensive the following year (vizt) in the year 1641 upon such penalty as shall be thought fitt by the Governor and council. And that for the present all persons shall cause their pieces to be fixed within three months upon such penalty as aforesaid.

B. An Act Taxing Negro Women, March 1642/43

Hening, ed., *Statues at Large*, I, 242.

Be it also enacted and confirmed That there be tenn pounds of tobacco per poll and a bushell of corne per poll paid to the ministers within the severall parishes of the collony for all tithable persons, that is to say, as well for all youths of sixteen years of age as upwards, as also for all negro women at the age of sixteen years. . . .

C. An Act Defining the Status of Mulatto Bastards, December 1662

Hening, ed., *Statutes at Large*, II, 170.

WHEREAS some doubts have arrisen whether children got by any Englishman upon a negro woman should be slave or Free, *Be it therefore enacted and declared by this present grand assembly,* that all children borne in this country shalbe held bond or free only according to the condition of the mother, *And* that if any christian shall committ Fornication with a negro man or woman, hee or shee soe offending shall pay double the Fines imposed by the former act.

D. An Act Declaring That Baptism Does Not Bring Freedom, September 1667

Hening, ed., *Statutes at Large*, II, 260.

WHEREAS some doubts have risen whether children that are slaves by birth, and by the charity and piety of their owners made pertakers of the blessed sacrament of baptisme, should by vertue of their baptisme be made Free; *It is enacted and declared by this grand assembly, and the authority thereof,* that the conferring of baptisme doth not alter the condition of the person as to his bondage or Freedome; that diverse masters, Freed from this doubt, may more carefully endeavour the propagation of christianity by permitting children, though slaves, or those of greater growth if capable to be admitted to that sacrament.

E. An Act Declaring How Negroes Belonging to Intestates Shall Be Disposed of, September 1671

Hening, ed., *Statutes at Large*, II, 288.

WHEREAS in the former act concerning the estates of persons dying intestate, it is provided that sheep, horses, and cattle should be delivered in kind to the orphant, when they came of age, according to the several ages the said cattle were of when the guardian tooke them into his possession, to which some have desired that negroes may be added; this assembly considering the difficulty of procureing negroes in kind as alsoe the value and hazard of their lives have doubted whither any suffitient men would be found who would engage themselves to deliver negroes of equall ages if the specificall negroes should dye, or become by age or accident unserviceable; *Be it therefore enacted and ordayned by this grand assembly and the authority thereof* that the consideration of this be referred to the county courts who are hereby authorized and impowred either to cause such negroes to be duly apprized, sold at an outcry, or preserved in kind, as they then find it most expedient for preservation, improvement or advancement of the estate and interest of such orphants.

F. An Act for Preventing Insurrections among Slaves, June 1680

Hening, ed., *Statutes at Large*, II, 481–482.

WHEREAS the frequent meeting of considerable numbers of negroe slaves under pretence of feasts and burialls is judged of dangerous consequence; for prevention whereof for the future, *Bee it enacted by the kings most excellent majestie by and with the consent of the generall assembly, and it is hereby enacted by the authority aforesaid,* that from and after the publication of this law, it shall not be lawfull for any negroe or other slave to carry or arme himselfe with any club, staffe, gunn, sword or any other weapon of defence or offence, nor to goe or depart from of his masters ground without a certificate from his master, mistris or overseer, and such permission not to be granted but upon perticuler and necessary occasions; and every negroe or slave soe offending not haveing a certificate as aforesaid shalbe sent to the next constable, who is hereby enjoyned and required to give the said negroe twenty lashes on his bare back well layd on, and soe sent home to his said master, mistris or overseer. *And it is further enacted by the authority aforesaid* that if any negroe or other slave shall presume to lift up his hand in opposition against any christian, shall for every such offence, upon due proofe made thereof by the oath of the party before a magistrate, have and receive thirty lashes on his bare back well laid on. *And it is hereby further enacted by the authority aforesaid* that if any negroe or other slave shall absent himself from his masters service and lye hid and lurking in obscure places, comitting injuries to the inhabitants, and shall resist any person or persons that shalby any lawful authority be imployed to apprehend and take the said negroe, that then in case of such resistance, it shalbe lawfull for such person or persons to kill the said negroe or slave soe lying out and resisting, and that this law be once every six months published at the respective county courts and parish churches within this colony.

10

"Evangelical Revolt: The Nature of the Baptists' Challenge to the Traditional Order in Virginia, 1765 to 1775"

Rhys Isaac

Reprinted by permission from "Evangelical Revolt: The Nature of the Baptists' Challenge to the Traditional Order in Virginia, 1765 to 1775," *William and Mary Quarterly*, 3rd ser., XXXI (1974), 345–368.

Evangelical Revolt: The Nature of the Baptists' Challenge to the Traditional Order in Virginia, 1765 to 1775

Rhys Isaac

An intense struggle for allegiance had developed in the Virginia countryside during the decade before the Revolution. Two eyewitness accounts may open to us the nature of the conflict.

First, a scene vividly remembered and described by the Reverend James Ireland etches in sharp profile the postures of the forces in contest. As a young man Ireland, who was a propertyless schoolmaster of genteel origin, had cut a considerable figure in Frederick County society. His success had arisen largely from his prowess at dancing and his gay facility as a satiric wit. Then, like many other young men at this time (ca. 1768), he came deeply "under conviction of sin" and withdrew from the convivialities of gentry society. When an older friend and patron of Ireland heard that his young protégé could not be expected at a forth-coming assembly, this gentleman, a leader in county society, sensed the challenge to his way of life that was implicit in Ireland's withdrawal. He swore instantly that "there could not be a dance in the settlement without [Ireland] being there, and if they would leave it to him, he would convert [him], and that to the dance, on Monday; and they would see [Ireland] lead the ball that day." Frederick County, for all its geographical spread, was a close community. Young James learned that his patron would call, and dreaded the coming test of strength:

> When I viewed him riding up, I never beheld such a display of pride arising from his deportment, attitude and jesture; he rode a lofty elegant horse, . . . his counte-nance appeared to me as bold and daring as satan himself, and with a commanding authority [he] called upon me, if I were there to come out, which I accordingly did, with a fearful and timorous heart. But O! how quickly can God level pride. . . . For no sooner did he behold my disconsolate looks, emaciated countenance and solemn aspect, than he . . . was riveted to the beast he rode on. . . . As soon as he could articulate a little his eyes fixed upon me, and his first address was this; "In the name of the Lord, what is the matter with you?"[1]

163

The evident overdramatization in this account is its most revealing feature for it is eloquent concerning the tormented convert's heightened awareness of the contrast between the social world he was leaving and the one he was entering.

The struggle for allegiance between these social worlds had begun with the Great Awakening in the 1740s, but entered into its most fierce and bitter phase with the incursions of the "New Light" Separate Baptists into the older parts of Virginia in the years after 1765.[2] The social conflict was not over the distribution of political power or of economic wealth, but over the ways of men and the ways of God. By the figures in the encounter described we may begin to know the sides drawn: on the one hand, a mounted gentleman of the world with "commanding authority" responding to challenge; on the other, a guilt-humbled, God-possessed youth with "disconsolate looks . . . and solemn aspect."

A second scene—this time in the Tidewater—reveals through actions some characteristic responses of the forces arrayed. From a diary entry of 1771 we have a description of the disruption of a Baptist meeting by some gentlemen and their followers, intent on upholding the cause of the established Church:

> Brother Waller informed us . . . [that] about two weeks ago on the Sabbath Day down in Caroline County he introduced the worship of God by singing. . . . The Parson of the Parish [who had ridden up with his clerk, the sheriff, and some others] would keep running the end of his horsewhip in [Waller's] mouth, laying his whip across the hymn book, etc. When done singing [Waller] proceeded to prayer. In it he was violently jerked off the stage; they caught him by the back part of his neck, beat his head against the ground, sometimes up, sometimes down, they carried him through a gate that stood some considerable distance, where a gentleman [the sheriff] gave him . . . twenty lashes with his horsewhip. . . . Then Bro. Waller was released, went back singing praise to God, mounted the stage and preached with a great deal of liberty.[3]

Violence of this kind had become a recurrent feature of social-religious life in Tidewater and Piedmont. We must ask: What kind of conflict was this? What was it that aroused such antagonism? What manner of man, what manner of movement, was it that found liberty in endurance under the lash?

The continuation of the account gives fuller understanding of the meaning of this "liberty" and of the true character of this encounter. Asked "if his nature did not interfere in the time of violent persecution, when whipped, etc.," Waller "answered that the Lord stood by him . . . and poured his love into his soul without measure, and the brethren and sisters about him singing praises . . . so that he could scarcely feel the stripes . . . rejoicing . . . that he was worthy to suffer for his dear Lord and Master."[4]

Again we see contrasted postures: on the one hand, a forceful, indeed brutal, response to the implicit challenge of religious dissidence; on the other, an acceptance of suffering sustained by shared emotions that gave release—"liberty." Both sides were, of course, engaged in combat, yet their modes of conducting themselves were diametrically opposite. If we are to understand the struggle that had developed, we must look as deeply as possible into the divergent styles of life, at the conflicting visions of what life should be like, that are reflected in this episode.

Opposites are intimately linked not only by the societal context in which they occur but also by the very antagonism that orients them to each other. The strength of the fascination that existed in this case is evident from the recurrent accounts of men drawn to Baptist meetings to make violent opposition, who, at the time or later, came "under conviction" and experienced conversion.[5] The study of a polarity such as we find in the Virginia pre-Revolutionary religious scene should illuminate not only the conflict but also some of the fundamental structures of the society in which it occurred. A profile of the style of the gentry, and of those for whom they were a pattern, must be attempted. Their values, and the system by which these values were maintained, must be sketched. A somewhat fuller contrasting picture of the less familiar Virginia Baptist culture must then be offered, so that its character as a radical social movement is indicated.

The gentry style, of which we have seen glimpses in the confrontation with Baptists, is best understood in relation to the concept of honor—the proving of prowess.[6] A formality of manners barely concealed adversary relationships; the essence of social exchange was overt self-assertion.

Display and bearing were important aspects of this system. We can best get a sense of the self-images that underlay it from the symbolic importance of horses. The figure of the gentleman who came to call Ireland back to society was etched on his memory as mounted on a "lofty . . . elegant horse." It was noted repeatedly in the eighteenth century that Virginians would "go five miles to catch a horse, to ride only one mile upon afterwards."[7] This apparent absurdity had its logic in the necessity of being mounted when making an entrance on the social scene. The role of the steed as a valuable part of proud self-presentation is suggested by the intimate identification of the gentry with their horses that was constantly manifested through their conversation. Philip Fithian, the New Jersey tutor, sometimes felt that he heard nothing but "Loud disputes concerning the Excellence of each others Colts . . . their Fathers, Mothers (for so they call the Dams) Brothers, Sisters, Uncles, Aunts, Nephews, Nieces, and Cousins to the fourth Degree!"[8]

Where did the essential display and self-assertion take place? There were few towns in Virginia; the outstanding characteristic of settlement was its diffuseness. Population was rather thinly scattered in very small groupings throughout a forested, river-dissected landscape. If there is to be larger community in such circumstances, there must be centers of action and communication. Insofar as cohesion is important in such an agrarian society, considerable significance must attach to the occasions when, coming together for certain purposes, the community realizes itself. The principal public centers in traditional Virginia were the parish churches and the county courthouses, with lesser foci established in a scatter of inns or "ordinaries." The principal general gatherings apart from these centers were for gala events such as horse race meetings and cockfights. Although lacking a specifically community character, the great estate house was also undoubtedly a very significant locus of action. By the operation of mimetic process and by the reinforcement of expectations concerning conduct and relationships, such centers and occasions were integral parts of the system of social control.[9]

The most frequently held public gatherings at generally distributed centers were those for Sunday worship in the Anglican churches and chapels. An ideal identification of parish and community had been expressed in the law making persistent absence from church punishable. The continuance of this ideal is indicated by the fact that prosecutions under the law occurred right up to the time of the Revolution.[10]

Philip Fithian has left us a number of vivid sketches of the typical Sunday scene at a parish church, sketches that illuminate the social nature and function of this institution. It was an important center of communication, especially among the elite, for it was "a general custom on Sundays here, with Gentlemen to invite one another home to dine, after Church; and to consult about, determine their common business, either before or after Service," when they would engage in discussing "the price of Tobacco, Grain etc. and settling either the lineage, Age, or qualities of favourite Horses." The occasion also served to demonstrate to the community, by visual representation, the rank structure of society. Fithian's further description evokes a dramatic image of haughty squires trampling past seated hoi polloi to their pews in the front. He noted that it was "not the Custom for Gentlemen to go into Church til Service is beginning, when they enter in a Body, in the same manner as they come out."[11]

Similarly, vestry records show that fifty miles to the south of Fithian's Westmoreland County the front pews of a King and Queen County church were allocated to the gentry, but the pressure for place and precedence was such that only the greatest dignitaries (like the Corbins) could be accommodated together with their families; lesser gentlemen represented the honor of their houses in single places while their wives were seated farther back.[12]

The size and composition of the ordinary congregations in the midst of which these representations of social style and status took place is as yet uncertain, but Fithian's description of a high festival is very suggestive on two counts: "This being Easter-Sunday, all the Parish seem'd to meet together High, Low, black, White all come out."[13] We learn both that such general attendance was unusual, and that at least once a year full expression of ritual community was achieved. The whole society was then led to see itself in order.

The county courthouse was a most important center of social action. Monthly court days were attended by great numbers, for these were also the times for markets and fairs. The facts of social dominance were there visibly represented by the bearing of the "gentlemen justices" and the respect they commanded. On court days economic exchange was openly merged with social exchange (both plentifully sealed by the taking of liquor) and also expressed in conventional forms of aggression—in banter, swearing and fighting.[14]

The ruling gentry, who set the tone in this society, lived scattered across broad counties in the midst of concentrations of slaves that often amounted to black villages. Clearly the great houses that they erected in these settings were important statements: they expressed a style, they asserted a claim to dominance. The lavish entertainments, often lasting days, which were held in these houses performed equally important social functions in maintaining this claim, and in establishing communication and control within the elite itself. Here the convivial contests that were so essential to traditional Virginia social culture would issue in their most elaborate and stylish performances.[15]

The importance of sporting occasions such as horse racing meets and cockfights for the maintenance of the values of self-assertion, in challenge and response, is strongly suggested by the comments of the marquis de Chastellux concerning cockfighting. His observations, dating from 1782, were that "when the principal promoters of this diversion [who were certainly gentry] propose to [match] their champions, they take great care to announce it to the public; and although there are neither posts, nor regular conveyances, this important news spreads with such facility, that the planters for thirty or forty miles round, attend, some with cocks, but all with money for betting, which is sometimes very considerable."[16] An intensely shared interest of this kind, crossing but not leveling social distinctions, has powerful effects in transmitting style and reinforcing the leadership of the elite that controls proceedings and excels in the display.

Discussion so far has focused on the gentry, for *there* was established in dominant form the way of life the Baptists appeared to challenge. Yet this way was diffused throughout the society. All the forms of communication and exchange noted already had their popular acceptances with variations appropriate to the context, as can be seen in the recollections of the young Devereux Jarratt. The son of a middling farmer-artisan, Jarratt grew up totally intimidated by the proximity of gentlemen, yet his marked preference for engagement "in keeping and exercising race-horses for the turf . . . in taking care of and preparing game-cocks for a match and main" served to bind him nonetheless into the gentry social world, and would, had he persisted, have brought him into contact—gratifying contact—with gentlemen. The remembered images of his upbringing among the small farmers of Tidewater New Kent County are strongly evocative of the cultural continuum between his humble social world and that of the gentry. In addition to the absorbing contest pastimes mentioned, there were the card play, the gathering at farmhouses for drinking (cider not wine), violin playing, and dancing.[17]

The importance of pastime as a channel of communication, and even as a bond, between the ranks of a society such as this can hardly be too much stressed. People were drawn together by occasions such as horse races, cockfights, and dancing as by no other, because here men would become "known" to each other—"known" in the ways which the culture defined as "real." Skill and daring in that violent duel, the "quarter race"; coolness in the "deep play" of the betting that necessarily went with racing, cockfighting, and cards—these were means whereby Virginia males could prove themselves.[18] Conviviality was an essential part of the social exchange, but through its soft coating pressed a harder structure of contest, or "emulation" as the contemporary phrase had it. Even in dancing this was so. Observers noted not only the passion for dancing—"*Virginians* are of genuine Blood—They will dance or die!"—but also the marked preference for the jig—in effect solo performances by partners of each sex, which were closely watched and were evidently competitive.[19] In such activities, in social contexts high or low, enhanced eligibility for marriage was established by young persons who emerged as virtuosos of the dominant style. Situations where so much could happen presented powerful images of the "good life" to traditional Virginians, especially young ones. It was probably true, as alleged, that religious piety was generally considered appropriate only for the aged.[20]

When one turns to the social world of the Baptists, the picture that emerges is so striking a negative of the one that has just been sketched that it must be considered to have been structured to an important extent by processes of reaction to the dominant culture.

Contemporaries were struck by the contrast between the challenging gaiety of traditional Virginia formal exchange and the solemn fellowship of the Baptists, who addressed each other as "Brother" and "Sister" and were perceived as "the most melancholy people in the world"—people who "cannot meet a man upon the road, but they must ram a text of Scripture down his throat."[21] The finery of a gentleman who might ride forth in a gold-lace hat, sporting a gleaming Masonic medal, must be contrasted with the strict dress of the Separate Baptist, his hair "cut off" and such "superfluous forms and Modes of Dressing . . . as cock't hatts" explicitly renounced.[22]

Their appearance was austere, to be sure, but we shall not understand the deep appeal of the evangelical movement, or the nature and full extent of its challenging contrast to the style and vision of the gentry-oriented social world, unless we look into the rich offerings beneath this somber exterior. The converts were proffered some escape from the harsh realities of disease, debt, overindulgence and deprivation, violence and sudden death, which were the common lot of small farmers. They could seek refuge in a close, supportive, orderly community, "a congregation of faithful persons, called out of the world by divine grace, who mutually agree to live together, and execute gospel discipline among them."[23] Entrance into this community was attained by the relation of a personal experience of profound importance to the candidates, who would certainly be heard with respect, however humble their station. There was a community resonance for deep feelings, since, despite their sober face to the outside world, the Baptists encouraged in their religious practice a sharing of emotion to an extent far beyond that which would elicit crushing ridicule in gentry-oriented society.[24] Personal testimonies of the experiences of simple folk have not come down to us from that time, but the central importance of the ritual of admission and its role in renewing the common experience of ecstatic conversion is powerfully evoked by such recurrent phrases in the church books as "and a dore was opened to experience." This search for deep fellow-feeling must be set in contrast to the formal distance and rivalry in the social exchanges of the traditional system.[25]

The warm supportive relationship that fellowship in faith and experience could engender appears to have played an important part in the spread of the movement. For example, about the year 1760 Peter Cornwell of Fauquier County sought out in the backcountry one Hays of pious repute, and settled him on his own land for the sake of godly companionship. "Interviews between these two families were frequent . . . their conversation religious . . . in so much that it began to be talked of abroad as a very strange thing. Many came to see them, to whom they related what God did for their souls . . . to the spreading of seriousness through the whole neighbourhood."[26]

A concomitant of fellowship in deep emotions was comparative equality. Democracy is an ideal, and there are no indications that the pre-Revolutionary Baptists espoused it as such, yet there can be no doubt that these men, calling each other brothers, who believed that the only authority in their church was the meeting of those in fellowship together, conducted their affairs on a footing of equality in sharp contrast to the explicit preoccupation with rank and precedence that characterized the world from which they had been called. Important Baptist church elections generally required unanimity and might be held up by the doubts of a few. The number of preachers who were raised from obscurity to play an epic role in the Virginia of their day is a clear indication of the opportunities for fulfillment that the movement opened up to men who would have found no other avenue for public achievement. There is no reason to doubt the contemporary reputation of the early Virginia Baptist movement as one of the poor and unlearned. Only isolated converts were made among the gentry, but many among the slaves.[27]

The tight cohesive brotherhood of the Baptists must be understood as an explicit rejection of the formalism of traditional community organization. The antithesis is apparent in the contrast between Fithian's account of a parish congregation that dispersed without any act of worship when a storm prevented the attendance of both parson and clerk, and the report of the Baptist David Thomas that "when no minister . . . is expected, our people meet notwithstanding; and spend . . . time in praying, singing, reading, and in religious conversation."[28]

The popular style and appeal of the Baptist Church found its most powerful and visible expression in the richness of its rituals, again a total contrast to the "prayrs read over in haste" of the colonial Church of England, where even congregational singing appears to have been a rarity.[29] The most prominent and moving rite practiced by the sect was adult baptism, in which the candidates were publicly sealed into fellowship. A scrap of Daniel Fristoe's journal for June 15–16, 1771, survives as a unique contemporary description by a participant:

> (Being sunday) about 2000 people came together; after preaching [I] heard others that proposed to be baptized. . . . Then went to the water where I preached and baptized 29 persons. . . . When I had finished we went to a field and making a circle in the center, there laid hands on the persons baptized. The multitude stood round weeping, but when we sang *Come we that love the lord* and they were so affected that they lifted up their hands and faces towards heaven and discovered such chearful countenances in the midst of flowing tears as I had never seen before.[30]

The warm emotional appeal at a popular level can even now be felt in that account, but it must be noted that the scene was also a vivid enactment of *a* community within and apart from *the* community. We must try to see that closed circle for the laying on of hands through the eyes of those who had been raised in Tidewater or Piedmont Virginia with the expectation that they would always have a monistic parish community encompassing all the inhabitants within its measured liturgical celebrations. The antagonism and violence that the Baptists aroused then also become intelligible.

The celebration of the Lord's Supper frequently followed baptism, in which circumstances it was a further open enactment of closed community. We have some idea of the importance attached to this public display from David Thomas's justification:

> . . . should we forbid even the worst of men, from viewing the solemn representation of his [the LORD JESUS CHRIST's] dying agonies? May not the sight of this mournful tragedy, have a tendency to alarm stupid creatures . . . when GOD himself is held forth . . . trembling, falling, bleeding, yea, expiring under the intollerable pressure of that wrath due to [sin]. . . . And therefore, this ordinance should not be put under a bushel, but on a candlestick, that all may enjoy the illumination.[31]

We may see the potency attributed to the ordinances starkly through the eyes of the abashed young John Taylor who, hanging back from baptism, heard the professions of seven candidates surreptitiously, judged them not saved, and then watched them go "into the water, and from thence, as I thought, seal their own damnation at the Lord's table. I left the meeting with awful horror of mind."[32]

More intimate, yet evidently important for the close community, were the rites of fellowship. The forms are elusive, but an abundance of ritual is suggested by the simple entry of Morgan Edwards concerning Falls Creek: "In this church are admitted, Evangelists, Ruling Elders, deaconesses, laying on of hands, feasts of charity, anointing the sick, kiss of charity, washing feet, right hand of fellowship, and devoting children. Far from being mere formal observances, these and other rites, such as the ordaining of "apostles" to "pervade" the churches, were keenly experimented with to determine their efficacy.[33]

Aspects of preaching also ought to be understood as ritual rather than as formal instruction. It was common for persons to come under conviction or to obtain ecstatic release "under preaching," and this established a special relationship between the neophyte and his or her "father in the gospel." Nowhere was the ritual character of the preaching more apparent than in the great meetings of the Virginia Separate Baptist Association. The messengers would preach to the people along the way to the meeting place and back; thousands would gather for the Sunday specially set aside for worship and preaching. There the close independent congregational communities found themselves merged in a great and swelling collective.[34] The varieties of physical manifestations such as crying out and falling down, which were frequently brought on by the ritualized emotionalism of such preaching, are too well known to require description.

Virginia Baptist sermons from the 1770s have not survived, perhaps another indication that their purely verbal content was not considered of the first importance. Ireland's account of his early ministry (he was ordained in 1769) reveals the ritual recurrence of the dominant themes expected to lead into repentance those who were not hardened: "I began first to preach . . . our awful apostasy by the fall; the necessity of repentance unto life, and of faith in the Lord Jesus Christ . . . our helpless incapacity to extricate ourselves therefrom I stated and urged."[35]

As "seriousness" spread, with fear of hell-fire and concern for salvation, it was small wonder that a gentleman of Loudoun County should find to his alarm "that the *Anabaptists* . . . growing very numerous . . . seem to be increasing in affluence [influence?]; and . . . quite destroying pleasure in the Country; for they encourage ardent Pray'r; strong and constant faith, and an intire Banishment of *Gaming, Dancing,* and Sabbath-Day Diversions."[36] That the Baptists were drawing away increasing numbers from the dominant to the insurgent culture was radical enough, but the implications of solemnity, austerity, and stern sobriety were more radical still, for they called into question the validity—indeed the propriety—of the occasions and modes of display and association so important in maintaining the bonds of

Virginia's geographically diffuse society. Against the system in which proud men were joined in rivalry and convivial excess was set a reproachful model of an order in which God-humbled men would seek a deep sharing of emotion while repudiating indulgence of the flesh. Yet the Baptist movement, although it must be understood as a revolt against the traditional system, was not primarily negative. Behind it can be discerned an impulse toward a tighter, more effective system of values and of exemplary conduct to be established and maintained within the ranks of the common folk.

In this aspect evangelicalism must be seen as a popular response to mounting social disorder. It would be difficult—perhaps even impossible—to establish an objective scale for measuring disorder in Virginia. What can be established is that during the 1760s and 1770s disorder was perceived by many as increasing. This has been argued for the gentry by Jack P. Greene and Gordon S. Wood, and need not be elaborated here. What does need to be reemphasized is that the gentry's growing perception of disorder was focused on those forms of activity which the Baptists denounced and which provided the main arenas for the challenge and response essential to the traditional "good life." It was coming to be felt that horse racing, cockfighting, and card play, with their concomitants of gambling and drinking, rather than serving to maintain the gentry's prowess, were destructive of it and of social order generally. Display might now be negatively perceived as "luxury."[37]

Given the absence of the restraints imposed by tight village community in traditional Virginia, disorder was probably an even more acute problem in the lower than in the upper echelons of society—more acute because it was compounded by the harshness and brutality of everyday life, and most acute in proportion to the social proximity of the lowest stratum, the enslaved. The last named sector of society, lacking sanctioned marriage and legitimated familial authority, was certainly disorderly by English Protestant standards, and must therefore have had a disturbing effect on the consciousness of the whole community.[38]

As the conversion experience was at the heart of the popular evangelical movement, so a sense of a great burden of guilt was at the heart of the conversion experience. An explanation in terms of social process must be sought for the sudden widespread intensification and vocal expression of such feelings, especially when this is found in areas of the Virginia Piedmont and Tidewater where no cultural tradition existed as preconditioning for the communal confession, remorse, and expiation that characterized the spread of the Baptist movement. The hypothesis here advanced is that the social process was one in which popular perceptions of disorder in society—and hence by individuals in themselves—came to be expressed in the metaphor of "sin." It is clear that the movement was largely spread by revolt from within, not by "agitators" from without. Commonly the first visit of itinerant preachers to a neighborhood was made by invitation of a group of penitents already formed and actively meeting together. Thus the "spread of seriousness" and alarm at the sinful disorder of the traditional world tended to precede the creation of an emotional mass movement "under preaching."[39] A further indication of the importance of order-disorder preoccupations for the spread of the new vision with its contrasted life style was the insistence on "works." Conversion could ultimately be validated among church members only by a radical reform of conduct. The Baptist church books reveal the close concern for the disciplinary supervision of such changes.[40]

Drunkenness was a persistent problem in Virginia society. There were frequent cases in the Baptist records where censure, ritual excommunication, and moving penitence were unable to effect a lasting cure. Quarreling, slandering, and disputes over property were other endemic disorders that the churches sought patiently and endlessly to control within their own communities.[41] With its base in slavery, this was a society in which contest readily turned into disorderly violence. Accounts of the occasion, manner, and frequency of wrestling furnish a horrifying testimony to the effects of combining a code of honor with the coarseness of life in the lower echelons of society. Hearing that "by appointment is to be fought this

Day . . . two fist Battles between four young Fellows," Fithian noted the common causes of such conflicts, listing numbers of trivial affronts such as that one "has in a merry hour call'd [another] a *Lubber*, . . . or a *Buckskin*, or a *Scotchman*, . . . or offered him a dram without wiping the mouth of the Bottle." He noted also the savagery of the fighting, including "Kicking, Scratching, Biting, . . . Throtling, Gouging [the eyes], Dismembring [the private parts]. . . . This spectacle . . . generally is attended with a crowd of People!" Such practices prevailed throughout the province.[42] An episode in the life of one of the great Baptist preachers, John, formerly "swearing Jack," Waller, illustrates both prevailing violence and something of the relationship between classes. Waller and some gentry companions were riding on the road when a drunken butcher addressed them in a manner they considered insolent. One of the gentlemen had a horse trained to rear and "paw what was before him," which he then had it do to frighten the butcher. The man was struck by the hooves and died soon after. Tried for manslaughter, the company of gentlemen were acquitted on a doubt as to whether the injury had indeed caused the butcher's death.[43] The episode may have helped prepare Waller for conversion into a radically opposed social world.

Nowhere does the radicalism of the evangelical reaction to the dominant values of self-assertion, challenge, and response of the gentry-oriented society reveal itself so clearly as in the treatment of physical aggression. In the Baptist community a man might come forward by way of confession with an accusation against himself for "Geting angry Tho in Just Defence of himself in Despute." The meeting of another church was informed that its clerk, Rawley Hazard, had been approached on his own land and addressed in "Very scurrilous language" and then assaulted, and that he then "did defend himself against this sd Violence, that both the Assailant and Defendent was much hurt." The members voted that the minister "do Admonish Brother Rawley . . . in the presents of the Church . . . saying that his defence was Irregular."[44]

A further mark of their radicalism, and without doubt the most significant aspect of the quest for a system of social control centered in the people, was the inclusion of slaves as "brothers" and "sisters" in their close community. When the Baptists sealed the slaves unto eternal life, leading them in white robes into the water and then back to receive the bread and wine, they were also laying upon them responsibility for godly conduct, demanding an internalization of strict Protestant Christian values and norms. They were seeking to create an orderly moral community where hitherto there had seemed to be none.

The slaves were members and therefore subject to church discipline. The incidence of excommunication of slaves, especially for the sin of adultery, points to the desire of the Baptists to introduce their own standards of conduct, including stable marital relationships, among slaves.[45] A revealing indication of the perception of the problem in this area is found in the recurrent phrase that was sometimes given as the sole reason for excommunication: "walking disorderly." Discipline was also clearly directed toward inculcating a sense of duty in the slaves, who could be excommunicated for "disobedience and Aggrevation to [a] master."[46]

The recurrent use of the words "order," "orderly," "disorderly" in the Baptist records reveals a preoccupation that lends further support to the hypothesis that concern for the establishment of a securer system of social control was a powerful impulse for the movement. "Is it orderly?" is the usual introduction to the queries concerning right conduct that were frequently brought forward for resolution at monthly meetings.[47]

With alarm at perceived disorder must also be associated the deep concern for Sabbath-day observance that is so strongly manifested in autobiographies, apologetics, and church books. It appears that the Virginia method of keeping the Sabbath "with sport, merriment, and dissipation" readily served to symbolize the disorder perceived in society. It was his observation of this that gave Ireland his first recorded shock. Conversely, cosmic order was affirmed and held up as a model for society in the setting aside on the Lord's Day of worldly pursuits, while men expressed their reverence for their Maker and Redeemer.[48]

When the Baptist movement is understood as a rejection of the style of life for which the gentry set the pattern and as a search for more powerful popular models of proper conduct, it can be seen why the ground on which the battle was mainly fought was not the estate or the great house, but the neighborhood, the farmstead, and the slave quarter. This was a contemporary perception, for it was generally charged that the Baptists were "continual fomenters of discord" who "not only divided good neighbours, but slaves and their masters; children and their parents . . . wives and their husbands." The only reported complaint against the first preachers to be imprisoned was of "their running into private houses and making dissensions."[49] The struggle for allegiance in the homesteads between a style of life modeled on that of the leisured gentry and that embodied in evangelicalism was intense. In humbler, more straitened circumstances a popular culture based on the code of honor and almost hedonist values was necessarily less securely established than among the more affluent gentry. Hence the anxious aggressiveness of popular anti-New Light feeling and action.[50]

The Baptists did not make a bid for control of the political system—still less did they seek a leveling or redistribution of worldly wealth. It was clearly a mark of the strength of gentry hegemony and of the rigidities of a social hierarchy with slavery at its base that the evangelical revolt should have been so closely restricted in scope. Yet the Baptists' salvation-ism and sabbatarianism effectively redefined morality and human relationships; their church leaders and organization established new and more popular foci of authority, and sought to impose a radically different and more inclusive model for the maintenance of order in society. Within the context of the traditional monistic, face-to-face, deferential society such a re-grouping necessarily constituted a powerful challenge.

The beginnings of a cultural disjunction between gentry and sections of the lower orders, where hitherto there had been a continuum, posed a serious threat to the traditional leaders of the community; their response was characteristic. The popular emotional style, the encouragement given to men of little learning to "exercise their gifts" in preaching, and the preponderance of humble folk in the movement gave to the proud gentry their readiest defense—contempt and ridicule. The stereotype of the Baptists as "an ignorant . . . set . . . of . . . the contemptible class of the people," a "poor and illiterate sect" which "none of the rich or learned ever join," became generally established. References in the *Virginia Gazette* to "ignorant enthusiasts" were common, and there could appear in its columns without challenge a heartless satire detailing "A Receipt to make an Anabaptist Preacher": "Take the Herbes of Hypocrisy and Ambition, . . . of the Seed of Dissention and Discord one Ounce, . . . one Pint of the Spirit of Self-Conceitedness."[51]

An encounter with some gentlemen at an inn in Goochland County is recorded by Morgan Edwards, a college-educated Pennsylvania Baptist minister. He noted the moderation of the gentry in this area, yet their arrogant scorn for dissenters in general, and for Baptists in particular, is unmistakable from the dialogue reported. Since Edwards had just come from Georgia, they began with ribald jests about "mr Whitefield's children . . . by the squaw" and continued as follows:

Esq[uire] U: Pray are you not a clergyman? . . .
Capt. L.: Of the church of England I presume?
N[orthern] M[inister]: No, Sir; I am a clergyman of a better church than that; for she is a persecutor.
Omnes: Ha! Ha! Ha! . . .
Esq. U: Then you are one of the fleabitten clergy?
N.M.: Are there fleas in this bed, Sir?
Esq. U: I ask, if you are a clergyman of the itchy true blue kirk of Scotland? . . .

CAPT. L. (whispers): He is ashamed to own her for fear you should scratch him 'Squire.' . . .

[When they have discovered that this educated man, who shows such address in fencing with words, is a Baptist minister, they discuss the subject bibulously among themselves.]

ESQ. U: He is no baptist . . . I take him to be one of the Georgia law[ye]rs.

MR. G: For my part I believe him to be a baptist minister. There are some clever fellows among them. . . .

MAJOR W: I confess they have often confounded me with their arguments and texts of Scripture; and if any other people but the baptists professed their religion I would make it my religion before tomorrow.[52]

The class of folk who filled the Baptist churches were a great obstacle to gentry participation. Behind the ridicule and contempt, of course, lay incomprehension, and behind that, fear of this menacing, unintelligible movement. The only firsthand account we have of a meeting broken up by the arrest of the preachers tells how they "were carried before the magistrate," who had them taken "one by one into a room and examined our pockets and wallets for firearms." He accused them of "carrying on a mutiny against the authority of the land." This sort of dark suspicion impelled David Thomas, in his printed defense of the Baptists, to reiterate several times that "We concern not ourselves with the government . . . we form no intrigues . . . nor make any attempts to alter the constitution of the kingdom to which as men we belong."[53]

Fear breeds fantasy. So it was that alarmed observers put a very crude interpretation on the emotional and even physical intimacy of this intrusive new society. Its members were associated with German Anabaptists, and a "historical" account of the erotic indulgences of that sect was published on the front page of the *Virginia Gazette.*[54]

Driven by uneasiness, although toughened by their instinctive contempt, some members of the establishment made direct moves to assert proper social authority and to outface the upstarts. Denunciations from parish pulpits were frequent. Debates were not uncommon, being sought on both sides. Ireland recalled vividly an encounter that reveals the pride and presumption of the gentlemen who came forward in defense of the Church of England. Captain M'Clanagan's place was thronged with people, some of whom had come forty miles to hear John Pickett, a Baptist preacher of Fauquier County. The rector of a neighboring parish attended with some leading parishioners "who were as much prejudiced . . . as he was." "The parson had a chair brought for himself, which he placed three or four yards in front of Mr. Pickett . . . taking out his pen, ink and paper, to take down notes of what he conceived to be false doctrine." When Pickett had finished, "the Parson called him a schismatick, a broacher of false doctrines . . . [who] held up damnable errors that day." Pickett answered adequately (it appeared to Ireland), but "when contradicted it would in a measure confuse him." So Ireland, who had been raised a gentleman, took it on himself to sustain the Baptist cause. The parson immediately "wheeled about on his chair . . . and let out a broadside of his eloquence, with an expectation, no doubt, that he would confound me with the first fire." However, Ireland "gently laid hold of a chair, and placed . . . it close by him, determined to argue." The contest was long, and "both gentlemen and ladies," who had evidently seated themselves near the parson, "would repeatedly help him to scripture, in order to support his arguments." When the debate ended (as the narrator recalled) in the refutation of the clergyman, Ireland "addressed one of the gentlemen who had been so officious in helping his teacher; he was a magistrate . . . 'Sir, as the dispute between the Parson and myself is ended, if you are disposed to argue the subject over again, I am willing to enter upon it with you.' He stretched out his arm straight before him, at that instant, and declared that I should not come nigher than that length." Ireland "concluded what the consequence would be, therefore made a peaceable retreat."[55] Such scenes of action are the stuff of social structure, as of social conflict, and require no further comment.

Great popular movements are not quelled, however, by outfacing, nor are they stemmed by the ridicule, scorn, or scurrility of incomprehension. Moreover, they draw into themselves members of all sections of society. Although the social worlds most open to proselytizing by the Baptists were the neighborhoods and the slave quarters, there were converts from the great houses too. Some of the defectors, such as Samuel Harris, played a leading role in the movement.[56] The squirearchy was disturbed by the realization that the contemptible sect was reaching among themselves. The exchanges between Morgan Edwards and the gentlemen in the Goochland inn were confused by the breakdown of the stereotype of ignorance and poverty. Edwards's cultured facility reminded the squires that "there are some clever fellows among [the Baptists]. I heard one Jery Walker support a petition of theirs at the assembly in such a manner as surprised us all, and [made] our wits draw in their horns."[57] The pride and assurance of the gentry could be engaged by awareness that their own members might withdraw from their ranks and choose the other way. The vigorous response of Ireland's patron to the challenge implicit in his defection provides a striking example.

The intensity of the conflict for allegiance among the people and, increasingly, among the gentry, makes intelligible the growing frequency of violent clashes of the kind illustrated at the beginning of this article. The violence was, however, one-sided and self-defeating. The episode of April 1771 in which the parson brutally interfered with the devotions of the preacher, who was then horsewhipped by the sheriff, must have produced a shock of revulsion in many quarters. Those who engaged in such actions were not typical of either the Anglican clergy or the country gentlemen. The extreme responses of some, however, show the anxieties to which all were subject, and the excesses in question could only heighten the tension.

Disquiet was further exacerbated by the fact that the law governing dissent, under which the repressive county benches were intent on acting, was of doubtful validity, and became the subject of public controversy in the fall of 1771.[58] This controversy, combined with the appalling scenes of disorder and the growing numbers of Separate Baptists, led the House of Burgesses to attempt action in its spring 1772 session. The Separates had shown renewed tendencies to intransigence as recently as May 1771, when a move was strongly supported to deny fellowship to all ministers who submitted to the secular authority by applying for permission to preach. The fact that eight months later the House of Burgesses received a petition for easier licensing conditions was a sign that a compromise was at last being sought. Nevertheless, prejudices were so strong that the bill that the Burgesses approved was considerably more restrictive than the English act that had hitherto been deemed law in the colony.[59]

The crisis of self-confidence which the evangelical challenges and the failure of forceful responses were inducing in the Virginia gentry was subtly revealed in March 1772 by the unprecedented decision of the House, ordinarily assertive of its authority, not to send the engrossed bill to the Council, but to have it printed and referred to the public for discussion. Nearly two years later, in January 1774, the young James Madison, exultant about the progress of the American cause in the aftermath of the Boston Tea Party, despaired of Virginia on account of religious intolerance. He wrote that he had "nothing to brag of as to the State and Liberty" of his "Country," where "Poverty and Luxury prevail among all sorts" and "that diabolical Hell conceived principle of persecution rages." In April of the same year he still had little hope that a bill would pass to ease the situation of dissenters. In the previous session "such incredible and extravagant stories" had been "told in the House of the monstrous effects of the Enthusiasm prevalent among the Sectaries and so greedily swallowed by their Enemies that . . . they lost footing by it." Burgesses "who pretend too much contempt to examine into their principles . . . and are too much devoted to the ecclesiastical establishment to hear of the Toleration of Dissentients" were likely to prevail once again.[60] Madison's foreboding was correct inasmuch as the old regime in Virginia never accomplished a legal resolution of the toleration problem.

The Revolution ultimately enshrined religious pluralism as a fundamental principle in Virginia. It rendered illegitimate the assumptions concerning the nature of community religious corporateness that underlay aggressive defense against the Baptists. It legitimated new forms of conflict, so that by the end of the century the popular evangelists were able to counterattack and symbolize social revolution in many localities by having the Episcopal Church's lands and even communion plate sold at auction. But to seek the conclusion to this study in such political-constitutional developments would be a deflection, for it has focused on a brief period of intense, yet deadlocked conflict in order to search out the social-cultural configurations of the forces that confronted each other. The diametrical opposition of the swelling Baptist movement to traditional mores shows it to have been indeed a radical social revolt, indicative of real strains within society.

Challenging questions remain. Can some of the appeal of the Revolution's republican ideology be understood in terms of its capacity to command the allegiance of both self-humbled evangelicals and honor-upholding gentry? What different meanings did the republican ideology assume within the mutually opposed systems of values and belief? And, looking forward to the post-Revolutionary period, what was the configuration—what the balance between antagonistic cultural elements—when confrontation within a monistic framework had given way to accommodation in a more pluralist republican society? These questions are closely related to the subject that this study has endeavored to illuminate—the forms and sources of popular culture in Virginia, and the relationship of popular culture to that of the gentry elite.

Notes

[1] James Ireland, *The Life of the Reverend James Ireland* . . . (Winchester, Va., 1819), 83, 84–85.

[2] For a valuable account of the triumph of evangelicalism in Virginia, 1740 to 1790, see Wesley M. Gewehr, *The Great Awakening in Virginia, 1740–1790* (Durham, N C., 1930). The rate at which the Separate Baptists were spreading may be seen by the following summary 1769— 7 churches, 3 north of the James River; May 1771—14 churches (1,335 members); May–Oct. 1774—54 churches (4,004 members); 24 north of the James River. *Ibid.*, 117. In the manuscript notes of Morgan Edwards references to *at least* 31 disruptions of meetings, by riot and/or arrest, occuring before 1772 can be identified; 13 of these appear to have been plebeian affairs, 8 gentry-led, and 10 unspecified. Morgan Edwards, Materials toward a History of the Baptists in the Province of Virginia, 1772 *passim*, MS, Furman University Library, Greenville, S.C. (microfilm kindly supplied by the Historical Commission, Southern Baptist Convention, Nashville, Tenn.).

[3] John Williams's Journal, May 10, 1771, in Lewis Peyton Little, *Imprisoned Preachers and Religious Liberty in Virginia* (Lynchburg, Va., 1938), 230–231. A similar account by Morgan Edwards indicates that the men were mounted and mentions who the principals were. Materials, 75–76.

[4] Williams, Journal, in Little, *Imprisoned Preachers*, 231.

[5] For examples see Edwards, Materials, 34, 54, 55, 73.

[6] For the sake of clarity a single "gentry style" is here characterized. Attention is focused on the forms that appear to have been most pervasive, perhaps because most adapted to the circumstances

of common life. It is not, however, intended to obscure the fact that there were divergent and more refined gentry ways of life. The development within the genteel elite of styles formed in negation of the predominant mores will be the subject of a full separate analysis. I am indebted to Jack P. Greene for advice on this point.

[7] J. F. D. Smyth, quoted in Jane Carson, *Colonial Virginians at Play* (Williamsburg, Va., 1965), 103–104. See also the comments of Hugh Jones and Edward Kimber, *ibid.*, 103.

[8] Hunter Dickinson Farish, ed., *Journal & Letters of Philip Vickers Fithian 1773–1774: A Plantation Tutor of the Old Dominion* (Williamsburg, Va., 1957), 177–178.

[9] I am unable to find a serviceable alternative for this much abused term. The concept has tended to be directed toward the operations of rules and sanctions, the restraint of the pursuit of self-interest, and the correction of deviant motivation. See *International Encyclopedia of the Social Sciences*, XIV (New York, 1968), 381–396. A different emphasis is adopted in this article, drawing attention to more fundamental aspects, namely, those processes by which cultural criteria of "proper" motivation and "true" self-interest are established and reinforced in a particular society. Closely related are the mechanisms whereby individuals' perceptions and valuations of their own and others' identities are shaped and maintained. My conceptualization derives from the ideas of "reality-maintenance" (almost of continuous socialization) which are fully developed in Peter L. Berger and Thomas Luckmann, *The Social Construction of Reality: A Treatise in the Sociology of Knowledge* (Garden City, N. J., 1966), 72–73, 84, 166–175, and *passim*.

[10] Little, *Imprisoned Preachers*, 265–266, 291.

[11] Farish, ed., *Journal of Fithian*, 29, 167.

[12] C. G. Chamberlayne, ed., *The Vestry Book of Stratton Major Parish, King and Queen County, Virginia, 1729–1783* (Richmond, Va., 1931), 167.

[13] Farish, ed., *Journal of Fithian*, 89. See also 137.

[14] Charles S. Sydnor, *American Revolutionaries in the Making: Political Practices in Washington's Virginia* (New York, 1965 [orig. publ. Chapel Hill, N. C., 1952]), 74–85. This is the incomparable authority for the nature and function of county court days, and for the rank, etc., of the justices. Chap. 4 makes clear the importance of liquor in social intercourse. That the custom of gentlemen establishing their "liberality" by "treating" their inferiors was not confined to the time of elections is suggested by Col. Wager's report "that he usually treated the members of his militia company with punch after the exercises were over." *Ibid.*, 58.

[15] Farish, ed., *Journal of Fithian*, *passim*; Carson, *Colonial Virginians at Play*, *passim*.

[16] Quoted in Carson, *Colonial Virginians at Play*, 160 and *passim*. For evidence of genteel patronage of the sport see *ibid.*, 156–157.

[17] Devereux Jarratt, *The Life of the Reverend Devereux Jarratt* . . . (Baltimore, 1806), 14, 19, 20, 23, 31, 42–44. It is interesting to note that although religious observance played a minimal part in Jarratt's early life, the Bible was the book from which he (and other small farmers' sons presumably) learned to read. A base was thereby prepared for evangelical culture. *Ibid.*, 20–21.

[18] Carson, *Colonial Virginians at Play*, *passim*. For an intensely illuminating discussion of the social significance of "deep play" in gambling see Clifford Geertz, "Deep Play: Notes on the Balinese Cockfight," *Daedalus*, CI (Winter, 1972), 1–37.

[19] Farish, ed., *Journal of Fithian*, 177; Carson, *Colonial Virginians at Play*, 21–35.

[20] Jarratt wrote of "*Church people*, that generally speaking, none went to the *table* [for communion] except a few of the more aged," *Life*, 102; and Ireland, "I . . . determined to pursue the pleasures . . . until I arrived to such an advance in years, that my nature would . . . enjoy no further relish. . . . A merciful God . . . would accept of a few days or weeks of my sincere repenting," *Life*, 59. Likewise it may be noted that religiosity only enters markedly into the old-man phase of Landon Carter's diary. Jack P. Greene, ed., *The Diary of Colonel Landon Carter of Sabine Hall, 1752–1778*, 2 vols. (Charlottesville, Va., 1965), *passim*.

[21] David Thomas, *The Virginian Baptist* . . . (Baltimore, 1774), 59; Robert B. Semple, *A History of the Rise and Progress of the Baptists in Virginia*, ed. G. W. Beale (Richmond, Va., 1894), 30.

[22] Farish, ed., *Journal of Fithian*, 69; Upper King and Queen Baptist Church, King and Queen County, Records, 1774–1816, Sept. 16, 1780. (Microfilm of this and subsequently cited Baptist church books kindly provided by the Virginia Baptist Historical Society, Richmond.)

[23] John Leland, *The Virginia Chronicle* (Fredericksburg, Va., 1790), 27. See also Thomas, *The Virginian Baptist*, 24–25.

[24] The Baptists, it was sneered, were "always sighing, groaning, weeping." To which Thomas replied, "It is true lively Christians are apt to weep much, but that is often with joy instead of sorrow." *The Virginian Baptist*, 59.

[25] Chestnut Grove Baptist Church, or Albemarle-Buck Mountain Baptist Church, Records, 1773–1779, 1792–1811, *passim*. Ireland tells how, when he had given the company of travelers to the Sandy Creek Association of 1769 an account of "what the Lord had done for my soul. . . . They were very much affected . . . so much so that one of the ministers embraced me in his arms." *Life*, 141.

[26] Edwards, Materials, 25–26.

[27] Thomas, *The Virginian Baptist*, 54. See also Semple, *History of the Baptists in Virginia*, 29, 270, and Leland, *Virginia Chronicle*, 23. I have not as yet been able to attempt wealth-status correlations for ministers, elders, deacons, and ordinary members of the churches. It must be noted that the role which the small group of gentry converts played (as one might expect from the history of other radical movements) assumed an importance out of all proportion to their numbers. See Morattico Baptist Church, Lancaster County, Records (1764), 1778–1814, *passim*, and Chesterfield Baptist Church, Lancaster County, Records, 1773–1788, for the role of the "rich" Eleazer Clay.

[28] Farish, ed., *Journal of Fithian*, 157; Thomas, *The Virginian Baptist*, 34.

[29] Farish, ed., *Journal of Fithian*, 167, 195.

[30] Morgan Edwards, Notes, in Little, *Imprisoned Preachers*, 243. See also Leland, *Virginia Chronicle*, 36: "At times appointed for baptism the people generally go singing to the water in grand procession: I have heard many souls declare they first were convicted or first found pardon going to, at, or coming from the water."

[31] Thomas, *The Virginian Baptist*, 35–36; Albemarle Baptist Church Book, June 18, 1774.

[32] John Taylor, *A History of Ten Baptist Churches* . . . (Frankfort, Ky., 1823), 296.

[33] Edwards, Materials, 56; Albemarle Baptist Church Book, Aug. 1776, Semple, *History of the Baptists in Virginia*, 81.

[34] Ireland, *Life*, 191; Taylor, *History of Ten Baptist Churches*, 7, 16; Semple, *History of the Baptists in Virginia*, 63; Garnett Ryland, *The Baptists of Virginia, 1699–1926* (Richmond, Va., 1955), 53–54.

[35] Ireland, *Life*, 185. Laboring day and night, "preaching three times a day very often, as well as once at night," he must have kept himself in an *exalté*, near trance-like condition. His instruction to those who came to him impressed with "their helpless condition" is also illuminating. "I would immediately direct them where their help was to be had, and that it was their duty to be as much engaged . . . as if they thought they could be saved by their own works, but not to rest upon such engagedness." *Ibid.*, 186.

[36] Farish, ed., *Journal of Fithian*, 72.

[37] Greene, ed., *Landon Carter Diary*, I, 14, 17–19, 21, 25, 33, 39, 44, 47, 52–53; Gordon S. Wood, "Rhetoric and Reality in the American Revolution," *William and Mary Quarterly*, 3d Ser., XXIII (1966), 27–31; Jack P. Greene, "Search for Identity: An Interpretation of the Meaning of Selected Patterns of Social Response in Eighteenth-Century America," *Journal of Social History*, III (1969–1970), 196–205.

[38] Gerald W. Mullin, *Flight and Rebellion: Slave Resistance in Eighteenth-Century Virginia* (New York, 1972), *passim*. This article owes an incalculable debt to Mullin's powerful and creative analysis of the dominant Virginia culture.

[39] Edwards, Materials, 25, 69, 89, 90; Semple, *History of the Baptists in Virginia*, 19–20, 25, 26, 32, 33, 227, 431.

[40] I have closely read the following Baptist church records for the period up to 1790: Broad Run Baptist Church, Fauquier County, Records, 1762–1837; Chesterfield Baptist Church Recs.; Chestnut Grove/Albemarle Church, Recs.; Hartwood-Potomac Baptist Church Book, Stafford County, 1771–1859; Mill Creek Baptist Church, Berkeley County, Records (1757), 1805–1928; Mill Swamp Baptist Church, Isle of Wight County, Records (1774), 1777–1790; Morattico Baptist Church, Recs.; Smith's Creek Baptist Church, Shenandoah and Rockingham counties, Records, 1779–1809 (1805); Upper King and Queen Baptist Church, Recs.

[41] Upper King and Queen Baptist Church, Recs., Jan. 20, 1781; Morattico Baptist Church, Recs., May 30, 1781, *et seq.*; Mill Swamp Baptist Church, Recs., Sept. 17, 1779; Broad Run Baptist Church, Recs., July 27, 1778.

[42] Farish, ed., *Journal of Fithian*, 183; Carson, *Colonial Virginians at Play*, 164–168.

[43] Edwards, Materials, 72.

[44] Chestnut Grove/Albemarle Baptist Church, Recs., Dec. 1776; Morattico Baptist Church, Recs., Feb. 17, 1783.

[45] Mill Swamp Baptist Church, Recs., Mar. 13, 1773.

[46] Morattico Baptist Church, Recs., Oct. 8, 1780. The role of the slaves in the 18th-century Baptist movement remains obscure. They always carried with them their slave identity, being designated "Gresham's Bob" or the like, or even "the property of." Yet it is reported that the slaves of William Byrd's great estates in Mecklenburg County were among the first proselytes to the Separate Baptists in Virginia. "Many of these poor slaves became bright and shining Christians. The breaking up of Byrd's quarters scattered these blacks into various parts. It did not rob them of their religion. It is said that through their labors in the different neighborhoods . . . many persons were brought to the knowledge of the truth, and some of them persons of distinction." Semple, *History of the Baptists in Virginia*, 291–292. The valuable researches of W. Harrison Daniel show that hearing of experience, baptism, and disciplining of whites and blacks took place in common. Black preachers were not uncommon and swayed mixed congregations. "In the 1780s one predominantly white congregation in Gloucester County chose William Lemon, a Negro, as its pastor." Segregation of the congregation does not begin to appear in the records until 1811. Daniel, "Virginia Baptists and the Negro in the Early Republic," *Virginia Magazine of History and Biography*, LXXX (1972), 62, 60–69.

[47] Mill Swamp Baptist Church, Recs., Mar. 13, June 9, 1778; Hartwood-Potomac Baptist Church, Recs., 1776, 9–10.

[48] Ireland, *Life*, 44; Thomas, *The Virginian Baptist*, 34–35.

[49] Thomas, *The Virginian Baptist*, 57: John Blair to the King's Attorney in Spotsylvania County, July 16, 1768, in Little, *Imprisoned Preachers*, 100–101.

[50] Jarratt, *Life*, 23, 31, 38; Farish, ed., *Journal of Fithian*, 73; Semple, *History of the Baptists in Virginia, passim*.

[51] Little, *Imprisoned Preachers*, 36; Thomas, *The Virginian Baptist*, 54. See also Semple, *History of the Baptists in Virginia*, 29; Leland, *Virginia Chronicle*, 23; *Virginia Gazette* (Purdie and Dixon), Oct. 31, 1771.

[52] Edwards, Materials, 86–88.

[53] John Waller to an unknown fellow Baptist, Aug. 12, 1771, in Little, *Imprisoned Preachers*, 276; Thomas, *The Virginian Baptist*, 33, 36.

[54] *Va. Gaz.* (Purdie and Dixon), Oct. 4, 1770. Thomas states that there is no evil which "has not been reported of us." *The Virginian Baptist,* 6. There is in a letter of James Madison a reference to the "Religion . . . of some enthusiasts, . . . of such a nature as to fan the amorous fire." Madison to William Bradford, Apr. 1, 1774, in William T. Hutchinson and William M. E. Rachal, eds., *The Papers of James Madison,* I (Chicago, 1962), 112. See also Richard J. Hooker, ed., *The Carolina Backcountry on the Eve of the Revolution* (Chapel Hill, N.C., 1953), 98, 100–104, 113–117, for more unrestrained fantasies concerning the emergent Southern Baptists.

[55] Ireland, *Life,* 129–134.

[56] Although Samuel Harris, renouncing the world, gave up his newly built country seat to be a meetinghouse for his church, the role of patron died hard. He would kill cattle for love feasts that were held there. Edwards, Materials, 57.

[57] *Ibid.,* 88. The scene was concluded by the genteel Baptist being offered and accepting hospitality. He finally left the neighborhood with an assurance from his host "that he would never talk any more against the Baptists." *Ibid.,* 89.

[58] *Va. Gaz.* (Purdie and Dixon), Aug. 15, 22, 1771; *Va. Gaz.* (Rind), Aug. 8, 1771.

[59] *Va. Gaz.* (Rind), Mar. 26, 1772. Especially severe were provisions designed to curb activities among the slaves.

[60] Madison to Bradford, Jan. 24, Apr. 1, 1774, in Hutchinson and Rachal, eds., *Madison Papers,* 1, 106, 112.

11

"Social Change and the Growth of Prerevolutionary Urban Radicalism"

Gary B. Nash

Reprinted with permission from *The American Revolution: Explorations in the History of American Radicalism* by Alfred F. Young; © 1976 Northern Illinois University Press. All rights reserved.

Social Change and the Growth of Prerevolutionary Urban Radicalism

Gary B. Nash

The symbol of mechanic pride in the "productive arts," which appeared as the central motif on the membership certificate of the General Society of Mechanics and Tradesmen of New York City, organized in 1786. Taken from a reissue of the certificate by the Society.

Recent studies of the American Revolution have relied heavily on the role of ideas to explain the advent of the American rebellion against England.[1] The gist of the ideological interpretation of the Revolution is that colonists, inheriting a tradition of protest against arbitrary rule, became convinced in the years after 1763 that the English government meant to impose in America "not merely misgovernment and not merely insensitivity to the reality of life in the British overseas provinces but a deliberate design to destroy the constitutional safeguards of liberty, which only concerted resistance—violent resistance if necessary—could effectively oppose."[2] It was this conspiracy against liberty that "above all else . . . propelled [the colonists] into Revolution."[3]

An important corollary to this argument, which stresses the colonial defense of constitutional rights and liberties, is the notion that the material conditions of life in America were so generally favorable that social and economic factors deserve little consideration as a part of the impetus to revolution. "The outbreak of the Revolution," writes Bernard Bailyn, a leading proponent of the ideological school, "was not the result of social discontent, or of economic disturbances, or of rising misery, or of those mysterious social strains that seem to beguile the imaginations of historians straining to find peculiar predispositions to upheaval." Nor, asserts Bailyn, was there a "transformation of mob behavior or of the lives of the 'inarticulate' in the pre-Revolutionary years that accounts for the disruption of Anglo-American politics."[4] Another historian, whose focus is economic change and not ideas, writes that "whatever it might have been, the American Revolution was not a rising of impoverished masses—or merchants—in search of their share of the wealth. The 'predicament of poverty,' in Hannah Arendt's phrase, was absent from the American scene"—so much so that even though the "secular trend in the concentration of wealth created an increasing gulf between the rich and the poor over the years separating 1607 and 1775, the fact remains that not only were the rich getting richer but the poor were also, albeit at a slower rate."[5]

One of the purposes of this essay is to challenge these widely accepted notions that the "predicament of poverty" was unknown in colonial America, that the conditions of everyday life among "the inarticulate" had not changed in ways that led toward a revolutionary predisposition, and that "social discontent," "economic disturbances," and "social strains" can generally be ignored in searching for the roots of the Revolution. I do not suggest that we replace an ideological construction with a mechanistic economic interpretation, but argue that a popular ideology, affected by rapidly changing economic conditions in American cities, dynamically interacted with the more abstract Whig ideology borrowed from England. These two ideologies had their primary appeal within different parts of the social structure, were derived from different sensibilities concerning social equity, and thus had somewhat different goals. The Whig ideology, about which we know a great deal through recent studies, was drawn from English sources, had its main appeal within upper levels of colonial society, was limited to a defense of constitutional rights and political liberties, and had little to say about changing social and economic conditions in America or the need for change in the future. The popular ideology, about which we know very little, also had deep roots in English culture, but it resonated most strongly within the middle and lower strata of society and went far beyond constitutional rights to a discussion of the proper distribution of wealth and power in the social system. It was this popular ideology that undergirded the politicization of the artisan and laboring classes in the cities and justified the dynamic role they assumed in the urban political process in the closing decades of the colonial period.

It is toward understanding this popular ideology and its role in the upsurge of revolutionary sentiment and action in the 1760s that this essay is devoted. Our focus will be on the three largest colonial cities—Boston, New York, and Philadelphia. Other areas, including the older, settled farming regions and backcountry, were also vitally important to the upwelling of revolutionary feeling in the fifteen years before 1776 and in the struggle that followed. But the northern cities were the first areas of revolutionary ferment, the communication centers where newspapers and pamphlets spread the revolutionary message, and the arenas of change in British North America where most of the trends overtaking colonial society in the eighteenth century were first and most intensely felt.

To understand how this popular ideology swelled into revolutionary commitment within the middle and lower ranks of colonial society, we must first comprehend how the material conditions of life were changing for city dwellers during the colonial period and how people at different levels of society were affected by these alterations. We cannot fathom this process by consulting the writings of merchants, lawyers, and upper-class politicians, because their business and political correspondence and the tracts they wrote tell us almost nothing about those below them in the social hierarchy. But buried in more obscure documents are glimpses of the lives of both ordinary and important people—shoemakers and tailors as well as lawyers and merchants. The story of changing conditions and how life in New York, Philadelphia, and Boston was experienced can be discerned, not with perfect clarity but in general form, from tax, poor relief, and probate records.

I

The most generally recognized alteration in eighteenth-century urban social structures is the long-range trend toward a less even distribution of wealth. Tax lists for Boston, Philadelphia, and New York, ranging over nearly a century prior to the Revolution, make this clear. By the early 1770s the top 5 percent of Boston's taxpayers controlled 49 percent of the taxable assets of the community, whereas they had held only 30 percent in 1687. In Philadelphia the top twentieth increased its share of wealth from 33 to 55 percent between 1693 and 1774. Those in the lower half of society, who in Boston in 1687 had commanded 9 percent of the taxable wealth, were left collectively with a mere 5 percent in 1771. In Philadelphia, those in the lower half of the wealth spectrum saw their share of wealth drop from 10.1 to 3.3 percent in the same period. It is now evident that the concentration of wealth had proceeded very far in the eighteenth-century cities.[6]

Though city dwellers from the middle and lower ranks could not measure this redistribution of economic resources with statistical precision, they could readily discern the general trend. No one could doubt that upper-class merchants were amassing fortunes when four-wheeled coaches, manned by liveried Negro slaves, appeared in Boston's crooked streets, or when urban mansions, lavishly furnished in imitation of the English aristocracy, rose in Philadelphia and New York.[7] Colonial probate records reveal that personal estates of £5000 sterling were rare in the northern cities before 1730, but by 1750 the wealthiest town dwellers were frequently leaving assets of £20,000 sterling, exclusive of real estate, and sometimes fortunes of more than £50,000 sterling—equivalent in purchasing power to about 2.5 million dollars today.[8] Wealth of this magnitude was not disguised in cities with populations ranging from about 16,000 in Boston to about 25,000 in New York and Philadelphia and with geographical expanses half as large as public university campuses today.

While urban growth produced a genuinely wealthy upper class, it simultaneously created a large class of impoverished city dwellers. All of the cities built almshouses in the 1730s in order to house under one roof as many of the growing number of poor as possible. This was the beginning of a long trend toward substituting confinement in workhouses and almshouses for the older familial system of direct payments to the poor at home. The new system was designed to reduce the cost of caring for a growing number of marginal persons—people who, after the 1730s, were no longer simply the aged, widowed, crippled, incurably ill, or orphaned members of society, but also the seasonally unemployed, war veterans, new immigrants, and migrants from inland areas seeking employment in the cities. These persons, whose numbers grew impressively in the 1750s and 1760s, were now expected to contribute to their own support through cloth weaving, shoemaking, and oakum picking in city workhouses.[9]

Beginning in Boston in the 1740s and in New York and Philadelphia somewhat later, poverty scarred the lives of a growing part of the urban populations. Among its causes were periodic unemployment, rising prices that outstripped wage increases, and war taxes which fell with unusual severity on the lower classes. In Boston, where the Overseers of the Poor had expended only £25–35 sterling per thousand inhabitants in the 1720s and 1730s, per capita expenditures for the poor more than doubled in the 1740s and 1750s, and then doubled again in the last fifteen years of the colonial period. Poor relief rose similarly in Philadelphia and New York after 1750.

In the third quarter of the eighteenth century poverty struck even harder at Boston's population and then blighted the lives of the New York and Philadelphia laboring classes to a degree unparalleled in the first half of the century. In New York, the wartime boom of 1755–1760 was followed by postwar depression. High rents and unemployment brought hundreds of families to the edge of indigency. The incidence of poverty jumped more than fourfold between 1750 and 1775. By 1772 a total of 425 persons jostled for space in the city's almshouse, which had been built to accommodate about 100 indigents. In Philadelphia, in the decade before the Revolution, more than 900 persons each year were admitted to the city's institutions for the impoverished—the almshouse, workhouse, and Hospital for the Sick Poor.[10] The data on poor relief leaves little room for doubt that the third quarter of the eighteenth century was an era of severe economic and social dislocation in the cities, and that by the end of the colonial period a large number of urban dwellers were without property, without opportunity, and, except for public aid, without the means of obtaining the necessities of life.

The economic changes that redistributed wealth, filled the almshouses to overflowing, and drove up poor rates, also hit hard at the lower part of the middle class in the generation before the Revolution. These people—master artisans rather than laborers, skilled shipwrights rather than merchant seamen, shopkeepers rather than peddlers—were financially humbled in substantial numbers in Boston beginning in the 1740s and in Philadelphia and New York a dozen years later.

In Boston, this crumbling of middle-class economic security can be traced in individual cases through the probate records and in aggregate form in the declining number of "taxables." In that city, where the population remained nearly static, at about 15,500 from 1735 to the Revolution, the number of "rateable polls" declined from a high of more than 3,600 in 1735, when the city's economy was at its peak, to a low of about 2,500 around mid-century. By 1771, Boston's taxables still numbered less than 2,600.[11] This decline of more than a thousand taxable adults was not caused by loss of population but by the sagging fortunes of more than 1,000 householders—almost one-third of the city's taxpaying population. Boston's selectmen made this clear in 1757 when they pointed out that "besides a great Number of Poor . . . who are either wholly or in part maintained by the Town, & so are exempt from being Taxed, there are many who are Rateable according to Law . . . who are yet in such poor Circumstances that Considering how little business there is to be done in Boston they can scarcely procure from day to day daily Bread for themselves & Families."[12]

In Philadelphia, the decay of a substantial part of the "middling sort" similarly altered the urban scene, though the trend began later and did not proceed as far as in Boston. City tax collectors reported the names of each taxable inhabitant from whom they were unable to extract a tax, and the survival of their records allows for some precision in tracing this phenomenon. Taxpayers dropped from the rolls because of poverty represented less than 3 percent of the taxables in the period before 1740, but they increased to about 6 to 7 percent in the two decades beginning in 1740, and then to one in every ten taxpayers in the fifteen years before the Revolution.[13]

The probate records of Boston and Philadelphia tell a similar tale of economic insecurity hovering over the middle ranges of urban society.[14] Among these people in Boston, median wealth at death dropped sharply between 1685 and 1735 and then made a partial but uneven recovery as the Revolution approached. The average carpenter, baker, shopkeeper, shipwright, or tavernkeeper dying in Boston between 1735 and 1765 had less to show for a lifetime's work than his counterpart of a half century before. In Philadelphia, those in the lower ranges of the middle class also saw the value of their assets, accumulated over a lifetime's labor, slowly decline during the first half of the eighteenth century, though not so severely as in Boston. The startling conclusion that must be drawn from a study of nearly 4,500 Boston and Philadelphia inventories of estates at probate is that population growth and economic development in the colonial cities did not raise the standard of living and broaden opportunities for the vast majority of people, but instead conferred benefits primarily upon those at the top of the social pyramid. The long-range effect of growth was to erode the personal assets held at death by those in the lower 75 percent of Boston society and the lower 60 percent of Philadelphia society. Though many city dwellers had made spectacular individual ascents from the bottom, in the manner of Benjamin Franklin of Philadelphia or Isaac Sears of New York, the statistical chances of success for those beginning beneath the upper class were considerably less after the first quarter of the eighteenth century than before. The dominating fact of late colonial life for many middle-class as well as most lower-class city folk was not economic achievement but economic frustration.

II

Understanding that the cities were becoming centers of frustrated ambition, propertylessness, genuine distress for those in the lower strata, and stagnating fortunes for many in the middle class makes comprehensible much of the violence, protest, and impassioned rhetoric that occurred in the half-generation before the colonial challenge to British regulations began in 1764. Upper-class colonists typically condemned these verbal attacks and civil disorders as the work of the "rabble," the "mob," the "canaille," or individuals "of turbulent disposition." These labels were used to discredit crowd activity, and historians have only recently recognized that the "rabble" often included a broad range of city dwellers, from slaves and servants through laborers and seamen to artisans and shopkeepers—all of whom were directly or indirectly expressing grievances.[15] Cutting across class lines, and often unified by economic conditions that struck at the welfare of both the lower and middle classes, these crowds began to play a larger role in a political process that grew more heated as the colonial period came to an end.[16] This developing consciousness and political sophistication of ordinary city dwellers came rapidly to fruition in the early 1760s and thereafter played a major role in the advent of the Revolution.

Alienation and protest had been present in the northern cities, especially during periods of economic difficulty, since the early eighteenth century. In Boston, between 1709 and 1713, townspeople protested vigorously and then took extralegal action when Andrew Belcher, a wealthy merchant, refused to stop exporting grain during a bread shortage in the city. Belcher had grown fat on war contracts during Queen Anne's War, and when he chose to export grain to the Caribbean, at a handsome profit, rather than sell it for a smaller profit to hungry townspeople, his ships were attacked and his warehouses emptied by an angry crowd. Rank had no privileges, as even the lieutenant-governor was shot when he tried to intervene. Bostonians of meagre means learned that through concerted action, the powerless could become powerful, if only for the moment. Wealthy merchants who would not listen to pleas from the community could be forced through collective action to subordinate profits to the public need.[17]

After the end of Queen Anne's War, in 1713, Boston was troubled by postwar recession and inflation, which cut into the wages of working people. Attempts to organize a land bank in order to increase the scarce circulating medium in Boston were opposed by wealthy men, many of them former war contractors. Gathering around the unpopular governor, Paul Dudley, these fiscal conservatives blamed the hard times on the extravagant habits of "the Ordinary sort" of people, who squandered their money on a "foolish fondness of Forreign Commodities & Fashions" and on too frequent tippling in the town's taverns.[18] But such explanations did not deceive returning war veterans, the unemployed, or those caught in an inflationary squeeze. They protested openly against men who made their fortunes "by grinding the poor," as one writer expressed it, and who studied "how to oppress, cheat, and overreach their neighbours." "The Rich, Great, and Potent," stormed this angry spokesman, "with rapacious violence bear down all before them, who have not wealth, or strength to encounter or avoid their fury."[19] Although the land bank movement failed in 1720, it was out of this defeat that the Boston Caucus, the political organization designed to mobilize the middle- and lower-class electorate in the decades to come, arose.[20]

In Philadelphia, economic issues also set the mechanic and laborer against the rich as early as the 1720s. When a business recession brought unemployment and a severe shortage of specie (the only legal circulating medium), leading merchant-politicans argued that the problem was moral in nature. If the poor were unemployed or hungry, they had their own lack of industry and prudence to thank, wrote James Logan, a thriving merchant and land speculator. "The Sot, the Rambler, the Spendthrift, and the Slip Season," he charged, were at the heart of the slump. Schemes for reviving the economy with emissions of paper money were reckless attempts to cheat those who worked for their money instead of drinking their time away.[21]

But, as in Boston, the majority of people were not fooled by such high-toned arguments. Angry tracts appeared on both sides of the debate concerning the causes and cure for recession. Those who favored paper money and called for restrictions on land speculators and monopolizers of the money market made an attack on wealth itself an important theme. Logan found bricks flying through his windows and a crowd threatening to level his house. Meanwhile, he looked on in disgust as Governor William Keith organized a political caucus, encouraged labouring men to participate in politics, and conducted a campaign aimed at discrediting Logan and other wealthy merchants.[22] "It is neither the Great, the Rich, nor the Learned, that compose the Body of any People, and . . . civil Government ought carefully to protect the poor, laborious and industrious Part of Mankind," Keith cautioned the Assembly in 1723.[23] Logan, formerly respected as William Penn's chief proprietary officeholder, a member of council, a judge of the colony's highest court, and Pennsylvania's most educated man, now found himself reviled in widely distributed tracts as "Pedagogus Mathematicus"— an ambitious, ruthless elitist. He and his henchmen, cried the pamphleteers, deserved to be called "petty Tyrants of this Province," "Serpents in the Grass," "Rich Misers," "Phenomena of Aristocracy," "Infringers of our Priviledges," and "Understrappers of Government."[24]

In a striking inversion of the conventional eighteenth-century thinking that only the rich and educated were equipped to hold high political offices, the Keithian faction urged the voters to recognize that "a mean Man, of small Interest, devoted to the faithful Discharge of his Trust and Duty to the Government" was far more to be valued than rich and learned men.[25] For the rest of the decade the anti-Logan forces, organized into political clubs in Philadelphia, held sway at the annual elections and passed legislation to relieve the distress of the lower-class unemployed and middle-class debtors. Members of the Philadelphia elite, such as Logan and merchant Isaac Norris, hated the "new vile people [who] may be truly called a mob," and deplored Keith's "doctrine of reducing all to a level."[26] But they could no longer manage politics from the top. The "moral economy of the crowd," as E. P. Thompson has called it—the people's sense that basic rules of equity in social relations had been breached—had intervened when the rich would do nothing to relieve suffering in a period of economic decline.[27]

When an economic slump beset New York in the 1730s, causing unemployment and an increase in suits for debt, the reaction was much the same as in the other cities. The John Peter Zenger trial of this era is best remembered as a chapter in the history of the freedom of the press. But central to the campaign organized by Zenger's supporters were the indictment of the rich and the mobilization of the artisanry against them. A 1734 election tract reminded the New York electorate that the city's strength—and its future—lay with the fortunes of "Shuttle" the weaver, "Plane" the joiner, "Drive" the carter, "Mortar" the mason, "Tar" the mariner, "Snip" the tailor, "Smallrent" the fair-minded landlord, and "John Poor" the tenant. Pitted against them were "Gripe the Merchant, Squeeze the Shopkeeper, Spintext and Quible the Lawyer."[28] In arguments reminiscent of those in Philadelphia a decade before, the Lewis Morris faction counseled the people that "A poor honest Man [is] preferable to a rich Knave." Only by electing men responsive to the needs of the whole community, the Morrisites advised, could New Yorkers arrest the forces that were impoverishing the artisan class while fattening the purses of merchants and moneylenders. The conservative clergy of the city advised working people to pray harder in difficult times, but the Morrisite pamphleteers urged the electorate to throw out of office those "people in Exalted Stations" who looked with disdain upon "those they call the Vulgar, the Mob, the herd of Mechanicks."[29]

Attacks on wealth and concentrated power continued in New York through 1737. The opulent and educated of the city were exposed as self-interested and oppressive men, not the public-minded community servants that conventional political philosophy prescribed. Though the leaders of the Morris faction were themselves men of substantial wealth, and though they never advocated a truly popular form of politics, their attacks on the rich and their organization of artisan voters became imbedded in the structure and ideology of politics.[30]

A decade later, political contention broke out again in New York City and attacks on the wealthy and well-born were revived. To some extent the political factionalism in the period from 1747 to 1755 represented a competition for power and profit between different elements of the elite. DeLanceys were pitted against Coldens, and Alexanders against Bayards, in a game where the stakes were control of land in neighboring New Jersey, the profits of the Iroquois fur trade, and the power of the assembly in opposition to the governor and his clique of officeholders. But as in earlier decades, the success of these intra-elite struggles depended upon gaining support from below. In appealing to the artisans and tradesmen, especially during periods of economic decline, bitter charges surfaced about the selfishness of wealthy men and the social inequities in society which they promoted.[31] Cadwallader Colden's *Address to the Freeholders* in 1747 inveighed against the rich, who did not build their fortunes "by the honestest means" and who had no genuine concern for the "publick spirit." Colden attacked the wealthy, among whose ranks he figured importantly, as tax dodgers who indulged in wanton displays of wealth and gave little thought to the welfare of those below them. "The midling rank of mankind," argued Colden, was far more honest, dependable, sober, and public spirited "in all Countries," and it was therefore best to trust "our Liberty & Property" to them rather than to New York's "rich jolly or swaggering companions."[32]

In Boston, resentment against the rich, focusing on specific economic grievances, continued to find voice in the middle third of the century. Moreover, since the forming of the caucus a generation before, well-coordinated street action channeled the wrath of townspeople against those who were thought to act against the interest of the commonality. In the 1730s an extended debate erupted on establishing a public market where prices and marketing conditions would be controlled. Many Bostonians in the lower and middle strata regarded a regulated public market as a device of merchants and fiscal conservatives to drive small retailers from the field and reap the profits of victualing Boston themselves. Though they lost their cause after a number of bitter debates and close votes at the town meeting in the mid-1730s, these humbler people, who probably included many without a vote, ultimately prevailed by demolishing the public market on Dock Square in 1737.[33] The attack was accompanied by much "murmuring agt the Government & the rich people," lamented Benjamin Colman, an advocate of the regulated market and a member of the conservative faction. Worse yet, "none of the Rioters or Mutineers" could be discovered. Their support was so broad that they promised that any attempt to arrest or arraign the saboteurs would be met by "Five Hundred Men in Solemn League and Covenant," who would resist the sheriff and destroy any other markets erected by wealthy merchants. The timbers of the public market which fell before the night raiders in 1737 showed how widely held was the conviction that only this kind of civil disobedience would "deliver the poor oppressed and distressed People out of the Hands of the Rich and Mighty."[34]

The Land Bank controversy from 1740 to 1742 further inflamed a wide segment of Boston society. Most of the colony, including Boston, favored a land bank which would relieve the economic distress of the period by issuing more paper money and thus continuing the inflationist policies of the last twenty years. In opposition stood a group of Boston merchants, who "had railed against the evils of paper money" for years and now "damned the Bank as merely a more invidious form of the soft money panacea typically favored by the province's poor and unsuccessful."[35] One of their spokesman, William Douglass, reflected the elitist view by characterizing the dispute as a struggle between the "Idle & Extravagant who want to borrow money at any bad lay" and "our considerable Foreign Traders and rich Men."[36]

Even though the inflationists swept the Massachusetts assembly elections of 1740 and 1741, they could not overcome the combined opposition of Governor Jonathan Belcher, a group of wealthy merchants, and officials in England. In the end, the Land Bank movement was thwarted. The defeat was not lightly accepted or quickly forgotten by debtors and Bostonians of modest means. Three years later, a committee of the Boston town meeting, which had consistently promoted inflated paper currency as a means of relief for Boston's numerous debtors, exploded with angry words at another deflationist proposal of the mercantile elite: "We cannot suppose, because in some extraordinary Times when a Party Spirit has run high there have been some Abuses of Our Liberties and Priviledges, that therefore We should in a Servile Manner give them all up. And have our Bread & Water measured out to Us by those Who Riot in Luxury & Wantonness on Our Sweat & Toil and be told by them that we are too happy, because we are not reduced to Eat Grass with the Cattle."[37]

The crowning blow to ordinary Bostonians came in 1748 when Thomas Hutchinson, the principal architect of the monetary policy favored by the wealthiest merchants, engineered a merciless devaluation of Massachusetts currency as a cure to the continuing inflation, which by now had reduced the value of paper money to a fraction of its face value. With many persons unemployed, with poverty afflicting hundreds of families, and with Hutchinson personifying the military contractors who had reaped fortunes from King George's War (1739–1747) while common people suffered, popular sentiment exploded. The newspapers carried a rancorous debate on the proposed devaluation, street fights broke out when the new policy was instituted, and Hutchinson was personally threatened on several occasions.[38] An anonymous pamphleteer put into words the sentiment of many in the city who had watched the gap widen between rich and poor during hard times. "Poverty and Discontent appear in every Face, (except the Countenances of the Rich), and dwell upon every Tongue." A few men, fed by "Lust of Power, Lust of Fame, Lust of Money," had grown rich by supplying military expeditions during the last war and had now cornered the paper money market and manipulated the rates of exchange for English sterling to their own profit. "No Wonder such Men can build Ships, Houses, buy Farms, set up their Coaches, Chariots, live very splendidly, purchase Fame, Posts of Honour," railed the pamphleteer. But such "Birds of prey . . . are Enemies to all Communities—wherever they live."[39]

The growing sentiment in the cities against the wealthy was nourished by the Great Awakening—the outbreak of religious enthusiasm throughout the colonies beginning in the late 1730s. Although this eruption of evangelical fervor is primarily identified as a rural phenomenon, it also had powerful effects in the cities, where fiery preachers such as George Whitefield and Gilbert Tennant had their greatest successes. We have no study as yet of the Great Awakening in the cities, but clues abound that one important reason for its urban appeal was the fact that the evangelists took as one of their primary targets the growth of wealth and extravagance, accompanied by a dwindling of social concern in colonial America. Nowhere was this manifested more noticeably than in the cities.[40]

The urban dwellers who thronged to hear George Whitefield in Philadelphia in 1739 and 1741 and those who crowded the Common in Boston to hear Whitefield and the vituperative James Davenport in the early 1740s were overwhelmingly from the "lower orders," so far as we can tell. What accounts for their "awakening" is the evangelists' presentation of a personal religion where humble folk might find succor from debt, daily toil, sickness, and want, and might express deeply felt emotions in an equality of fellowship. At the same time, the revivalist preachers spread a radical message concerning established authority. City dwellers were urged to partake in mass revivals, where the social distance between clergyman and parishioner and among worshippers themselves was obliterated. They were exhorted to be skeptical toward dogma and to participate in ecclesiastical affairs rather than bow passively to established hierarchy.[41]

Through the Great Awakening, doctrinal controversy and attacks on religious leaders became widely accepted in the 1740s. In Boston the itinerant preachers James Davenport hotly indicted the rich and powerful and advised ordinary people to break through the crust of tradition in order to right the wrongs of a decaying society. It was the spectre of unlearned artisans and laborers assuming authority in this manner that frightened many upper-class city dwellers and led them to charge the revivalists with preaching levelism and anarchy. "It is . . . an exceedingly difficult, gloomy time with us . . . ," wrote one conservative clergyman from Boston. "Such an enthusiastic, factious, censorious Spirit was never known here. . . . Every low-bred, illiterate Person can resolve Cases of Conscience and settle the most difficult Points of Divinity better than the most learned Divines."[42]

Such charges were heard repeatedly during the Great Awakening, revealing the fears of those who trembled to see the "unthinking multitude" invested with a new dignity and importance. Nor could the passing of the Awakening reverse the tide, for this new sense of power remained a part of the social outlook of ordinary people. In fact, the radical transformation of religious feeling overflowed into civil affairs. The new feeling of autonomy and importance was bred in the churches, but now it was carried into the streets. Laboring people in the city learned "to identify the millenium with the establishment of governments which derived their power from the people, and which were free from the great disparities of wealth which characterized the old world."[43]

III

The crescendo of urban protest and extralegal activity in the prerevolutionary decades cannot be separated from the condition of people's lives. Of course those who authored attacks on the growing concentration of wealth and power were rarely artisans or laborers; usually they were men who occupied the middle or upper echelons of society, and sometimes they were men who sought their own gain—installment in office, or the defeat of a competitor for government favors. But whatever their motives, their sharp criticisms of the changes in urban society were widely shared among humbler townspeople. It is impossible to say how much they shaped rather than reflected the views of those in the lower half of the social structure—urban dwellers whose opportunities and daily existence had been most adversely affected by the structural changes overtaking the colonial cities. But the willingness of broad segments of urban society to participate in attacks on narrowly concentrated wealth and power—both at the polls where the poor and propertyless were excluded, and in the streets where everyone, including women, apprentices, indentured servants, and slaves, could engage in action—should remind us that a rising tide of class antagonism and political consciousness, paralleling important economic changes, was a distinguishing feature of the cities at the end of the colonial period.

It is this organic link between the circumstances of people's lives and their political thought and action that has been overlooked by historians who concentrate on Whig ideology, which had its strongest appeal among the educated and well-to-do. The link had always been there, as detailed research into particular communities is beginning to show. But it became transparently clear in the late colonial period, even before England began demanding greater obedience and greater sacrifices in the colonies for the cause of the British Empire. The connection can be seen in New York in the 1760s, where the pleas of the impoverished against mercenary landlords were directly expressed in 1762, and where five years later the papers were pointing out that while the poor had vastly increased in recent years and while many families were selling their furniture at vendue to pay their rent, carriage owners in the city had grown from five to seventy.[44] The link can also be seen in Philadelphia, where growing restlessness at unemployment, bulging almshouses, rising poor taxes, and soaring prices for food and firewood helped to politicize the electorate and drew unprecedented numbers of people to the polls in the last decade of the colonial period.[45]

However, it was in Boston, where poverty had struck first, cut deepest, and lasted longest, that the connection between changing urban conditions and rising political radicalism is most obvious. That it preceded the post-1763 imperial debate, rather than flowing from it, becomes apparent in a close examination of politics in that city between 1760 and 1765.

The political factionalism of these years has usually been seen as a product of the accession of Francis Bernard to the governorship in 1760 and the subsequent appointment of Thomas Hutchinson to the chief justiceship of the colony over the claims of James Otis, Sr., who thought he had been promised the position. Hutchinson, already installed as lieutenant-governor, judge of probate, president of the provincial council, and captain of Castle William, now held high office in all three branches of government—executive, judicial, and legislative. The issues, as historians have portrayed them, were plural officeholding, prosecution of the colony's illegal traders under writs of assistance, and, ultimately, the right of England to fasten new imperial regulations on the colony.[46] But running beneath the surface of these arguments, and almost entirely overlooked by historians, were issues that had far greater relevance to Boston's commonality.

For ordinary Bostonians, Thomas Hutchinson had long been regarded as a man who claimed to serve the community at large but devised policies which invariably benefitted the rich and hurt the poor. As far back as 1738, Hutchinson had disregarded instructions from the town meeting and pressed the General Court to pass deflationary measures which hurt the pocketbooks of common people, particularly those in debt. Hutchinson continued his hard money campaign in the 1740s. During the 1747 impressment riot, when an angry crowd took control of Boston and demanded the release of some fifty of the town's citizens seized for service in His Majesty's ships, Hutchinson lined up behind the governor in defense of law and order. Alongside other merchants who were chalking up handsome profits on war contracts issued by Governor William Shirley, Hutchinson now stood at the governor's side as his house was surrounded by a jeering, hostile crowd that battered the sheriff and then "swabb'd in the gutter" and locked in the town stocks a deputy sheriff who attempted to disperse them. Hutchinson and his future brother-in-law, Andrew Oliver, joined two other merchants in drafting a report condemning the impressment proceedings as a "Riotous Tumultuous Assembly" of "Foreign Seamen, Servants, Negroes, and Other Persons of Mean and Vile Condition."[47]

One year later, Hutchinson became the designer and chief promoter of a plan for drastically devaluing Massachusetts currency. Enacted into law after bitter debate, the hard money plan was widely seen as a cause of the trade paralysis and economic recession that struck Boston in the early 1750s. Hutchinson's conservative fiscal measure was roundly attacked in the Boston press and specifically criticized for discriminating against the poor. Four months after the Hutchinson plan became law, Boston's voters turned him out of the House. Shortly thereafter, when his home mysteriously caught fire, a crowd gathered in the street, cursing Hutchinson and crying, "Let it burn!" A rump town meeting sardonically elected Hutchinson tax collector, a job which would take him out of his mansion and into the streets where he might personally see how laboring-class Bostonians were faring during hard times.[48]

The animosity against Hutchinson continued during the next decade, because he aligned himself with a series of unpopular issues—the excise tax of 1754, the Albany Plan of the same year, and another devaluation scheme in 1761.[49] More than anyone in Boston in the second third of the eighteenth century, Thomas Hutchinson stood in the common people's view as the archetype of the cold, grasping, ambitious, aristocratic merchant-politician who had lost touch with his humbler neighbors and cared little whether they prospered or failed.

Fanning the flames of rancor toward Hutchinson in the early 1760s was his leadership of a small group of conservative merchants and lawyers, known in the popular press as the "Junto." These men were known not only for fiscal conservatism but for their efforts to dismantle the town meeting system of government in Boston in order to enlarge their power while curbing that of the middle and lower classes. Most of them were friends of the new governor, Francis Bernard, enjoyed appointments in the provincial government, belonged to the Anglican church, and were related by blood or marriage. Among them were Hutchinson, Andrew and Peter Oliver, Eliakim Hutchinson, Charles Apthorp, Robert Auchmuty, Samuel Waterhouse, Charles Paxton, Thomas Flucker, John Erving, Jr., Edmund Trowbidge, and Chambers Russell.

The move to overthrow the town meeting in 1760 had deep roots. In 1715 and again in the early 1730s conservative merchants had argued that Boston should substitute a borough government for the town meeting. Under municipal incorporation, a system of town government widely used in England as well as in Philadelphia, appointed alderman would serve life terms and would elect the mayor. Under such a plan most municipal officers would be appointed rather than elected. The proposal was designed to limit popular participation in government and transfer control of the city to the elite, whose members argued that they would institute greater order and efficiency.[50]

Both earlier attempts to scrap the town meeting had been staunchly attacked by pamphleteers, who warned that such "reforms" would give exorbitant power to men whose wealth and elevated social status were frail guarantees that they would act in the public interest. The gulf between the rulers and the ruled, between the rich and poor, would only increase, they prophesied, and the people would pay a fearful price for abdicating their political rights. Those who favored incorporation, argued a pamphleteer in 1715, despised "Mobb Town Meetings," where the rich, if they wished to participate, had to mingle with less elevated townspeople. They wished to substitute the rule of the few so that "the Great Men will no more have the Dissatisfaction of seeing their Poorer Neighbours stand up for equal Privilege with them." But neither in 1715 nor in the early 1730s could the elite push through their reorganization of town government.[51]

The town meeting continued to rankle those who regarded laboring people as congenitally turbulent, incapable of understanding economic issues, and moved too much by passion and too little by reason to make wise political choices. Governor Shirley expressed this view most cogently after the demonstration against British impressment of Boston citizens in 1747: "What I think may be esteemed the principal cause of the Mobbish turn in this Town is its Constitution; by which the Management of it is devolv'd upon the populace assembled in their Town Meetings . . . where the meanest Inhabitants . . . by their constant Attendence there generally are the majority and outvote the Gentlemen, Merchants, Substantial Traders and all the better part of the Inhabitants; to whom it is irksome to attend." When so many workingmen, merchant seamen, and "low sort of people" could participate in town meetings, the governor lamented, what could be expected but "a factious and Mobbish Spirit" that kept educated and respectable people away?[52]

In 1760, five months before Hutchinson's appointment as chief justice, the conservative "Junto" made another attempt to gain control of the town government. Realizing that common Bostonians could not be gulled into surrendering their political rights, the "Junto" plotted a strategy for swinging the May elections in Boston and sending to the General Court four representatives who would convince the House to pass a law for incorporating Boston. A "Combination of Twelve Strangers," who called themselves "The New and Grand Corcas," warned the populist *Boston Gazette*, were designing to "overthrow the ancient Constitution of our Town-Meeting, as being popular and mobbish; and to form a Committee to transact the whole Affairs of the Town for the future." In order to control the elections, the article continued, the "Junto" would attempt to keep "tradesmen, and those whom in Contempt they usually term the Low lived People," from voting. They would challenge their eligibility at the polls, attempt to buy their votes, and threaten them with arrest and loss of their jobs.[53] As Samuel Adams later remarked, it was obvious that Hutchinson was bent on destroying the "Democratic part" of government.[54] On the eve of the election, the "Committee of Tradesmen," working with the "old and true Corcas," used the press to urge Boston's working people to stand up to these threats. The artisans should "put on their Sabbath Cloathes . . . wash their Hands and faces that they may appear neat and cleanly," spurn the vote-buying tactics of the "Junto," and elect men who represented their interests.[55]

A record number of voters turned out on 13 May 1760, as both factions courted the electorate. The result was indecisive. Royall Tyler, vociferously opposed by the Anglican "Junto," was reelected. But Benjamin Prat and John Tyng, who during the preceding year had taken an unpopular stand on sending the province ship to England, lost their seats to two moderates, Samuel Welles and John Phillips, who were supported by the Hutchinsonians. The conservatives had succeeded to this extent in creating a "popular" issue and using it to rally the electorate against two of the Caucus's candidates. It was enough to hearten the Hutchinsonians, who now had reason to anticipate other electoral successes, and to galvanize the anti-Hutchinsonians into redoubling their efforts among Boston's electorate.

In the period immediately after the 1760 election, James Otis made his meteoric rise in the "popular" party in Boston, leading the fight to curb the growing power of the Hutchinsonian circle. The Otis-Hutchinson struggle has usually been interpreted as a fight over the regulation of trade and oligarchic officeholding, or, more recently, as the culmination of a long-standing interfamily competition. In both interpretations Otis appears as a sulphurous orator and writer (either brilliant or mad according to one's views), who molded laboring-class opinion, called the "mob" into action, and shaped its behavior. To a large extent, however, Otis was only reflecting the perceptions and interests of common Bostonians in his abusive attacks on the lieutenant governor and his allies. For two years after the 1760 elections, which were dangerously indecisive from the viewpoint of the "popular" party, Otis filled the *Gazette* with vitriolic assaults on the Hutchinson clique, each fully answered in the conservative *Evening-Post*. Woven into Otis's offensive was the theme of resentment against wealth, narrowly concentrated political power, and arbitrary political actions which adversely affected Boston's ordinary people. But rather than seeing this campaign solely as an attempt to mobilize the artisans and laborers, we should also understand it as a reflection of opinion already formed within these groups. For years Boston's common people had shown their readiness to act against such oppression—in preventing the exportation of grain, in destroying the public market, and in harassing arbitrary officeholders. Otis, keenly aware of the declining fortunes and the resentment of ordinary townspeople, was mirroring as well as molding popular opinion.

In 1763 the Hutchinson circle made another attempt to strike at the town meeting system of politics, which was closely interwoven with the Boston Caucus. Election messages in the *Evening-Post* urged the electorate to "keep the Public Good only in View" while burying "in everlasting Oblivion" old prejudices and animosities. But this much said, the paper ran a scathing "expose" of the Caucus, which read like the confessions of an ex-Communist. Allegedly written by a former member of the Caucus, it explained how Caucus leaders conducted all political affairs behind closed doors and in smoke-filled rooms. Then, "for form sake," the leaders "prepared a number of warm disputes . . . to entertain the lower sort; who are in an ecstasy to find the old Roman Patriots still surviving." All townspeople were invited to speak at these open meetings, it was claimed, but to oppose Caucus leaders was to earn their "eternal animosity" and end forever any chance of obtaining town office. Democracy, as practiced by the Caucus, was nothing but sham, mocked the *Evening-Post* writer.[56]

The attempt to "expose" the Caucus as a dictatorial clique, with little genuine interest in the laboring classes, failed miserably. The Caucus responded by organizing its most successful roundup of voters in Boston's colonial history. On election day, 1,089 voters went to the poll, a number never to be exceeded even in the tumultuous years of the following decade. They drubbed the candidates favored by the Hutchinsonians. James Otis, the leading anti-Hutchinsonian, got the largest number of votes and was installed as moderator of the town meeting—a token of the confidence in which he was held for his open-handed attacks on Hutchinson.[57]

The bitter Otis-Hutchinson fight of the early 1760s, carried on *before* English imperial policy became an issue in Massachusetts, revolved around a number of specific issues, including the replacement of William Bollan as provincial agent, the establishment of an Anglican mission in the shadow of Harvard College, the multiple offices held by Hutchinson and his relatives, the writs of assistance, and other problems. But more fundamentally, the struggle matched two incompatible conceptions of government and society. Developed during the controversies of preceding decades, these conceptions were spelled out in an outpouring of political rhetoric in the early 1760s and in the crystallization of two distinct factions.

James Otis, Samuel Adams, Royall Tyler, Oxenbridge Thacher, and a host of other Bostonians, linked to the artisans and laborers through a network of neighborhood taverns, fire companies, and the Caucus, espoused a vision of politics that gave credence to laboring-class views and regarded as entirely legitimate the participation of artisans and even laborers in the political process.[58] This was not a new conception of the rightful political economy, but a very old one. The leaders of this movement were merely following in the footsteps of earlier popular leaders—from John Noyes to Elisha Cooke to James Allen. The town meeting, open to almost all property owners in the city and responsive to the propertyless as well, was the foundation of this system. By no means narrowly based, the "popular" party included many of the city's merchants, shopkeepers, lawyers, doctors, clergymen, and other well-to-do men. They provided leadership and filled the most important elective offices—overseers of the poor, tax assessors, town selectmen, and delegates to the House of Representatives. Lesser people filled minor offices and voiced their opinions at the town meetings where they were numerically dominant.

For the conservative merchants and lawyers, led and personified by Thomas Hutchinson, the old system spelled only chaos. "Reform" for these men meant paring back the responsibilities of the town meeting, substituting appointive for elective officeholders, restricting the freedom of the press, and breaking down the virulent anti-Anglican prejudice that still characterized the popular party. Like their opponents, members of the "prerogative" party had suffered as Boston's economy stagnated after 1740. But they saw the best hope for reviving the economy in handing over the management of town government to the wealthy and well-born exclusively. To see Otis address the crowd and to witness "the Rage of Patriotism . . . spread so violently . . . thro' town and country, that there is scarce a cobler or porter but has turn'd mountebank in politicks and erected his stage near the printing-press" was their vision of hell.[59]

Between 1761 and 1764 proponents of the "popular" and "prerogative" conceptions of politics engaged in a furious battle of billingsgate that filled the columns of the *Gazette* and *Evening-Post*. It is easy to be diverted by the extreme forms which the scurrility took. Charges of "Racoon," "stinking Skunk," "Pimp," "wild beast," "drunkard," and dozens of other choice titles were traded back and forth in verbal civil war. But more important than this stream of epithets was the deep-seated, class-tinged animosity which the polemical pieces exposed: hatred and suspicion of laboring people on the part of the Hutchinsonians; suspicion and hatred of the wealthy, Anglican, prerogative elite held by the common people.

Thus, Thomas Pownall, the popular governor from 1757 to 1760, was satirized by a conservative for confusing class lines by going aboard ships in Boston harbor to talk with "common people about ship-affairs" and mingling in the streets with the "dirtiest, most lubberly, mutinous, and despised part of the people."[60] The anti-Hutchinsonians, on the other hand, urged Bostonians to oppose "The Leviathan in power [Hutchinson], or those other overgrown Animals, whose influence and importance is only in exact mathematical proportion to the weight of their purses."[61] The Caucus, decried a Hutchinsonian, talked incessantly about the right "for every dabbler in politicks to say and print whatever his shallow understanding, or vicious passions may suggest, against the wisest and best men—a liberty for fools and madmen to spit and throw firebrands at those of the most respectable and most amiable character."[62] In retort, Otis, speaking as a mechanic, poured out his resentment: "I am forced to get my living by the labour of my hand; and the sweat of my brow, as most of you are and obliged to go thro' good report and evil report, for bitter bread, earned under the frowns of some who have no natural or divine right to be above me, and entirely owe their grandeur and honor to grinding the faces of the poor, and other acts of ill gotten gain and power."[63] In reply, the conservatives charged anarchy: "The day is hastening, when some who are now, or, have lately been the darling idols of a dirty very dirty witless rabble commonly called the little vulgar, are to sink and go down with deserved infamy, to all posterity."[64] This was doubtful, retorted a writer in the *Gazette*: the problem was that the rich were obsessed with money and "couldn't have the idea of riches without that of poverty. They must see others poor in order to form a notion of their own happiness." Thus, in what was once a flourishing town, "a few persons in power" attempted to monopolize politics, and promoted projects "for keeping the people poor in order to make them humble. . . ."[65]

This reciprocal animosity and mistrust, suffusing the newspapers and pamphlets of the late colonial period, reveals the deeply rooted social tensions that Bostonians would carry into the revolutionary era. These tensions shaped the ways in which different social groups began to think about *internal* political goals once the conflict against *external* authority began. In the end, the Hutchinson faction, looking not to the future but staring into the distant past, faced an impossible task—to convince a broad electorate that the very men who had accumulated fortunes in an era when most had suffered were alone qualified to govern in the interest of the whole community. Lower- and middle-class Bostonians had heard fiscal conservatives and political elitists pronounce the same platitudes for half a century. Even now, a generation before James Madison formally enunciated an interest-group theory of politics, they understood that each group had its particular interest to promote and that aristocratic politicians who claimed to work for the commonweal were not to be trusted. Such men employed the catchwords of the traditional system of politics—"public good," "community," "harmony," and "public virtue"—to cloak their own ambitions for aggrandizing wealth and power.[66] The growing inequalities of wealth in Boston, which could be readily seen in the overcrowded almshouse and flocks of outreliefers in contrast to the urban splendor of men like Hutchinson and Oliver, were proof enough of that.

IV

Only by understanding the long animosity that the common people of Boston held for Thomas Hutchinson and his clique can sense be made of the extraordinary response to the Stamp Act in Boston in August 1765—the systematic destruction of the houses of Hutchinson and other wealthy and conservative Boston officials—and of the course of revolutionary politics in the city in the years that followed. It is possible, of course, to revert to the explanation of Peter Oliver, who, at the time, argued that "the People in general . . . were like the Mobility of all Countries, perfect Machines, wound up by any Hand who might first take the winch."[67] In this view, the crowd was led by the nose by middle- and upper-class manipulators such as Otis and Samuel Adams, and used to further their own political ambitions. In this Newtonian formulation, the crowd could never be self-activating, for thought and planned action could have their source only in the minds of educated persons.[68]

Such explanations, however, bear no relationship to the social realities in Boston at the time or to the long history of popular protest in the city. Again and again in the eighteenth century the Boston crowd had considered its interest, determined its enemies, and moved in a coordinated and discriminating way to gain its ends through street action. It was frequently supported in this by men higher up on the social scale—men who shielded the crowd leaders from subsequent attempts of the authorities to punish them.[69] Thus, several socioeconomic groups, with interests that often coincided but sometimes diverged, found it profitable to coordinate their actions.

The attacks on Andrew Oliver's house on the evening of 14 August 1765, and on Hutchinson's house twelve days later, were entirely consistent with this pattern of politics. On the evening of 14 August, the crowd, led by the shoemaker Ebenezer MacIntosh, culminated a day of protest against the Stamp Act by reducing Oliver's mansion to a shambles. Accompanied by the sheriff, Hutchinson attempted to stop the property destruction. For his trouble, he was driven off with a hailstorm of stones. Less than two weeks later it was Hutchinson's turn. Forcing him and his family to flee, the crowd smashed in the doors with axes, reduced the furniture to splinters, stripped the walls bare, chopped through inner partitions until the house was a hollow shell, destroyed the formal gardens behind the house, drank the contents of the wine cellar, and carried off every moveable object of value except some of Hutchinson's books and papers, which were left to scatter in the wind. Not a person in Boston, neither private citizen nor officer of the law, attempted to stop the crowd. Its members worked through the night with almost military precision to raze the building, spending three hours alone "at the cupola before they could get it down," according to Governor Bernard.[70]

Historians agree that in destroying the Boston mansions of Oliver and Hutchinson, the crowd was demonstrating against the Stamp Act. Oliver had been appointed Stamp Collector, and Hutchinson, though he publicly expressed his view that the act was unwise, had vowed to use his authority as lieutenant-governor to see it executed. But in conducting probably the most ferocious attack on private property in the history of the English colonies, the crowd was demonstrating against far more than Parliamentary policy. Stamp collectors were intimidated and handled roughly in many other cities. But nowhere else did the crowd choose to destroy property on such a grand scale and with such exacting thoroughness. The full meaning of these attacks can be extracted only by understanding the long-standing animus against the Oliver-Hutchinson circle. Beyond intimidating British officialdom, the crowd was giving vent to years of hostility at the accumulation of wealth and power by the aristocratic, Hutchinson-led prerogative faction. Behind every swing of the ax and every hurled stone, behind every shattered plate and splintered mahogany chair lay the fury of a Bostonian who had read or heard the repeated references to the people as "rabble," and who had suffered economic hardship while others grew rich. The handsome furnishings in the houses of Hutchinson, Oliver, and others that fell before the "Rage-intoxicated rabble," as one young upper-class lawyer put it, provided psychological recompense for those Bostonians who had lost faith that opportunity or equitable relationships any longer prevailed in their city.[71]

The political consciousness of the crowd and its use of the Stamp Act protests as an opportunity for an attack on wealth itself were remarked upon again and again in the aftermath of the August crowd actions. Fifteen houses were targeted for destruction on the night of 27 August, according to Governor Bernard, in what he thought had become "a War of Plunder, of general levelling and taking away the Distinction of rich and poor." "Everything that for years past, had been the cause of any unpopular discontent was revived," he explained; "and private resentments against persons in office worked themselves in, and endeavoured to exert themselves under the mask of the public cause."[72] On the same day, the governor warned that unless "persons of property and consideration did not unite in support of government"—by which he meant that a way must be found to employ the militia or some kind of *posse comitatus* to control crowd actions—"anarchy and confusion" would continue in "an insurrection of the poor against the rich, those that want the necessities of life against those that have them."[73] On 10 September, two weeks after the destruction of Hutchinson's house, another Boston merchant wrote that "the rich men in the town" were seized with apprehension and "were moveing their cash & valuable furniture,&c" to the homes of poorer friends who were above suspicion.[74]

Seen in the context of three generations of social and economic change in Boston, and set against the drive for power of the Hutchinson-Oliver faction in Massachusetts, the Stamp Act riots provide a revealing example of the "moral economy of the crowd" in the early stages of the revolutionary movement. Members of the Boston "mob" needed no upper-class leaders to tell them about the economic stagnation of the late colonial period that had been affecting their lives and the structure of opportunity in the town. Nor did they need to destroy the homes of Oliver and Hutchinson in order to obtain the promise of these officeholders to hold the Stamp Act in abeyance. Instead, the crowd paid off some old debts and served notice on those whom it regarded as enemies of its interests.[75] It was the culminating event of an era of protest against wealth and oligarchic power that had been growing in all the cities. In addition, it demonstrated the fragility of the union between protesting city dwellers of the laboring classes and their more bourgeois partners, for in the uninhibited August attacks on property, the Boston crowd went much farther than Caucus leaders such as James Otis and Samuel Adams had reckoned or wished to countenance.[76]

V

In the other cities the growing resentment of wealth, the rejection of an elitist conception of politics, and the articulation of artisan- and laboring-class interests also gained momentum after 1765. These were vital developments in the revolutionary period. Indeed, it was the extraordinary new vigor of urban laboring people in defining and pursuing their goals that raised the frightening spectre of a radicalized form of politics and a radically changed society in the minds of many upper-class city dwellers, who later abandoned the resistance movement against England that they had initially supported and led.

That no full-fledged proletarian radical ideology emerged in the decade before the Revolution should not surprise us, for this was a preindustrial society in which no proletariat yet existed. Instead, we can best understand the long movement of protest against concentrated wealth and power, building powerfully as social and economic conditions changed in the cities, as a reflection of the disillusionment of laborers, artisans, and many middle-class city dwellers against a system that no longer delivered equitable rewards to the industrious. "Is it equitable that 99, rather 999, should suffer for the Extravagance or Grandeur of one," asked a New Yorker in 1765, "especially when it is considered that Men frequently owe their Wealth to the impoverishment of their Neighbors?"[77] Such thoughts, cutting across class lines, were gaining force among large parts of the urban population in the late colonial period. They were directed squarely at outmoded notions that only the idle and profligate could fail in America and that only the educated and wealthy were entitled to manage political affairs.

But the absence of clearly identifiable class consciousness and of organized proletarian radicalism does not mean that a radical ideology, nurtured within the matrix of preindustrial values and modes of thought, failed to emerge during the Revolution. Though this chapter in the history of the Revolution is largely unwritten, current scholarship is making it clear that the radicalization of thought in the cities, set in motion by economic and social change, advanced very rapidly once the barriers of traditional thought were broken down. A storm of demands, often accompanied by crowd action to insure their implementation, rose from the urban "tradesmen" and "mechanicks": for the end of closed assembly debates and the erection of public galleries in the legislative houses; for published roll-call votes which would indicate how faithfully elected legislators followed the wishes of their constituents; for open-air meetings where laboring men could help devise and implement public policy; for more equitable laying of taxes; for price controls instituted by and for the laboring classes to shield them from avaricious men of wealth; and for the election of mechanics and other ordinary people at all levels of government.[78]

How rapidly politics and political ideology could be transformed, as colonists debated the issue of rebellion, is well illustrated by the case of Philadelphia. In one brief decade preceding the Revolution the artisanry and laboring poor of the city moved from a position of clear political inferiority to a position of political control. They took over the political machinery of the city, pushed through the most radical state constitution of the period, and articulated concepts of society and political economy that would have stunned their predecessors. By mid-1776, laborers, artisans, and small tradesmen, employing extralegal measures when electoral politics failed, were in clear command in Philadelphia. Working with middle-class leaders such as James Cannon, Timothy Matlack, Thomas Young, and Thomas Paine, they launched a full-scale attack on wealth and even on the right to acquire unlimited private property. By the summer of 1776 the militant Privates Committee, which probably represented the poorest workers, became the foremost carrier of radical ideology in Pennsylvania. It urged the voters, in electing delegates for the constitutional convention, to shun "great and overgrown rich men [who] will be improper to be trusted, [for] they will be too apt to be framing distinctions in society, because they will reap the benefits of all such distinctions."[79] Going even further, they drew up a bill of rights for consideration by the convention, which included the proposition that "an enormous proportion of property vested in a few individuals is dangerous to the rights, and destructive of the common happiness, of mankind; and therefore every free state hath a right by its laws to discourage the possession of such property."[80] For four years, in an extremely fluid political scene, a radicalized artisanry shaped—and sometimes dominated—city and state politics, while setting forth the most fully articulated ideology of reform yet heard in America.[81]

These calls for reform varied from city to city, depending on differing conditions, past politics, and the qualities of particular leaders. Not all the reforms were implemented, especially those that went to the heart of the structural problems in the economy. Pennsylvania, for example, did not adopt the radical limitation on property holding. But that we know from hindsight that the most radical challenges to the existing system were thwarted, or enjoyed only a short period of success, does not mean that they are not a vital part of the revolutionary story. At the time, the disaffected in the cities were questioning some of the most fundamental tenets of colonial thought. Ordinary people, in bold opposition to their superiors, to whom custom required that they defer, were creating power and suggesting solutions to problems affecting their daily lives. As other essays in this book explain, how far these calls for radical reform extended and the success they achieved are matters that historians have begun to investigate only lately. But this much is clear: even though many reforms were defeated or instituted briefly and then abandoned, political thought and behavior would never again be the same in America.

In preparing this essay I profited greatly from the criticism of James A. Henretta, Jesse Lemisch, Stephen Patterson, and Alfred Young.

Notes

[1] See, for example, Bernard Bailyn, *The Ideological Origins of the American Revolution* (Cambridge: Harvard University Press, 1967); Bailyn, *The Ordeal of Thomas Hutchinson* (Cambridge: Harvard University Press, 1974); Pauline Maier, *From Resistance to Revolution: Colonial Radicals and the Development of American Opposition to Britain, 1765–1776* (New York: Alfred A. Knopf, 1972); Richard D. Brown, *Revolutionary Politics in Massachusetts: The Boston Committee of Correspondence and the Towns, 1772–1774* (Cambridge: Harvard University Press, 1970).

[2] Bailyn, "The Central Themes of the American Revolution: An Interpretation," in Stephen G. Kurtz and James H. Hutson, eds., *Essays on the American Revolution* (Chapel Hill: University of North Carolina Press, 1973), p. 12.

[3] Bailyn, *Ideological Origins of the Revolution*, p. 95.

[4] Bailyn, "Central Themes of the American Revolution," p. 12.

[5] John J. McCusker, "Sources of Investment Capital in the Colonial Philadelphia Shipping Industry," *Journal of Economic History* 32 (1972): 156–57.

[6] For Boston, see James A. Henretta, "Economic Development and Social Structure in Colonial Boston," *William and Mary Quarterly*, 3d ser. 22 (1965): 75–92. The Boston data has been reexamined and compared with similar data from New York and Philadelphia in Gary B. Nash, "Wealth and Poverty in Three Colonial Cities: The Social Background to Revolution," *Journal of Interdisciplinary History* 8 (1976).

[7] For the rise of urban affluence, see Carl Bridenbaugh, *Cities in Revolt: Urban Life in America, 1743–1776* (New York: Alfred A. Knopf, 1955), chap. 6. A revealing individual case is studied in Nicholas B. Wainwright, *Colonial Grandeur in Philadelphia: the House and Furniture of General John Cadwalader* (Philadelphia: Historical Society of Pennsylvania, 1964).

[8] Wills and inventories for almost 1,400 eighteenth-century Philadelphians are in the Office of the Recorder of Wills, City Hall Annex, Philadelphia. More than twice that number are available for Boston at the Office of the Recorder of Wills, Suffolk County Court House, Boston.

[9] Raymond A. Mohl, "Poverty in Early America, A Reappraisal: The Case of Eighteenth-Century New York City," *New York History* 50 (1969): 5–27. The data and conclusions on poverty and poor relief in the following paragraphs are discussed more fully in Nash, "Wealth and

Poverty," and Gary B. Nash, "Poverty and Poor Relief in Pre-Revolutionary Philadelphia," *William and Mary Quarterly*, 3d ser. 33 (1976).

[10] Data derived from Records of the Pennsylvania Hospital for the Sick Poor, 1751–1828, American Philosophical Society (microfilms); and Records of the Contributors for the Better Relief and Employment of the Poor, 1767–1778, City Archives, Philadelphia.

[11] William H. Whitmore et al., eds., *Reports of the Record Commissioners of Boston*, 39 vols. (Boston, 1878–1902), 14:13, 100, 280; Lemuel Shattuck, *Report to the Committee of the City Council Appointed to Obtain a Census of Boston for the Year 1845* (Boston, 1846), p. 5; G. B. Warden, *Boston, 1689–1776* (Boston: Little, Brown, and Co., 1970), pp. 128, 325n.

[12] *Record Commissioners of Boston*, 12:178; 14:302.

[13] County Commissioners of Philadelphia, Minutes, 1718–1766, City Archives, Philadelphia; Minutes, 1771–1774, Historical Society of Pennsylvania; Minutes, 1774–1776, Pennsylvania State Archives, Harrisburg.

[14] The following discussion of probated wealth is drawn from a much fuller treatment in Nash, "Wealth and Poverty."

[15] Gordon S. Wood, "A Note on Mobs in the American Revolution," *William and Mary Quarterly* 23 (1966): 635–42; Pauline Maier, "Popular Uprisings and Civil Authority in Eighteenth-Century America," ibid., 27 (1970): 3–35.

[16] Jesse Lemisch, "Jack Tar in the Street: Merchant Seamen in the Politics of Revolutionary America," *William and Mary Quarterly* 25 (1968): 371–407; Warden, *Boston*, chaps. 6–8; Gary B. Nash, "The Transformation of Urban Politics, 1700–1765," *Journal of American History* 60 (1973): 605–32.

[17] *Record Commissioners of Boston*, 8:99–104; 11:194–97; Warden, *Boston*, p. 66.

[18] *The Present Melancholy Circumstances of the Province . . .* (Boston, 1719); Everett Kimball, *The Public Life of Joseph Dudley: A Study of the Colonial Policy of the Stuarts in New England, 1660–1715* (New York: Longmans, Green and Co., 1911), pp. 161–78.

[19] *A Letter to an Eminent Clergy-Man . . .* [Boston, 1721]; see also the series of pamphlets published from 1719 to 1721 reprinted in Andrew McFarland Davis, *Colonial Currency Reprints, 1682–1751*, 4 vols. (Boston: The Prince Society, 1910–1911), 1:367–452; 2:3–334.

[20] Warden, *Boston*, pp. 91–96; Warden, "The Caucus and Democracy in Colonial Boston," *New England Quarterly* 43 (1970): 19–33.

[21] Logan, *A Dialogue Showing What's Therein to be Found* (Philadelphia, 1725); in *A Charge From the Bench to the Grand Jury* (Philadelphia, 1723), Logan argued that the high wages demanded by artisans and laboring men were also a cause of the depression.

[22] Thomas Wendel, "The Keith-Lloyd Alliance: Factional and Coalition Politics in Colonial Pennsylvania," *Pennsylvania Magazine of History and Biography* 92 (1968): 289–305; Nash, "Transformation of Urban Politics," pp. 606–8.

[23] Gertrude MacKinney, ed., *Votes and Proceedings of the House of Representatives of the Province of Pennsylvania, Pennsylvania Archives*, 8th ser. (Harrisburg, 1931–1935), 2:1459. For the attack on Logan's house, see Logan to James Alexander, 23 October 1749, Logan Letter Book, 1748–1750, Historical Society of Pennsylvania.

[24] *The Triumverate of Pennsylvania: In a Letter to a Friend in the Country* (Philadelphia, 1728); also *A Dialogue Between Mr. Robert Rich and Roger Plowman* (Philadelphia, 1725).

[25] David Lloyd, *A Vindication of the Legislative Power* (Philadelphia, 1725); the attacks on accumulated wealth and power were continued in [William Keith], *The Observators Trip to America* (Philadelphia, 1725); Keith, *A Modest Reply to the Speech of Isaac Norris . . .* (Philadelphia, 1727); [Keith], *Remarks upon the Advice to the Freeholders* of the Triumvirate . . . (Philadelphia, 1729).

[26] Logan to John Penn, 17 November 1729, *Pennsylvania Magazine of History and Biography* 34 (1910): 122–23; Norris to Joseph Pike, 28 August 1728, Norris Letter Book, 1716–1730; David Barclay to Thomas Penn, [1727], Penn Papers; Official Correspondence, 2:43, Historical Society of Pennsylvania.

[27] Thompson, "The Moral Economy of the English Crowd in the Eighteenth Century," *Past and Present*, no. 50 (1971), pp. 76–136.

[28] Timothy Wheelwright [pseud.], *Two Letters on Election of Alderman* [New York, 1734].

[29] *New-York Journal*, 18 March, 20 May, 8 July 1734; for a general consideration of New York City politics in this era, see Patricia U. Bonomi, *A Factious People: Politics and Society in Colonial New York* (New York: Columbia University Press, 1971), pp. 112–34.

[30] *New-York Journal*, 8, 15 July 1734; 3 March 1735; 30 May 1737. The fullest discussion of this era is Beverly McAnear, "Politics in Provincial New York, 1689–1761," (Ph.D. diss., Stanford University, 1935), pp. 420–88.

[31] Bonomi, *A Factious People*, chap. 5; *New-York Gazette, or the Weekly Post-Boy*, 25 January 1747/48.

[32] Colden, *An Address to the Freeholders* (New York, 1747); *New-York Evening Post*, 21 December 1747; *New-York Mercury*, 7, 21 January 1754; *New-York Gazette*, 14 January 1754; *New-York Post-Boy*, 22 April 1754; McAnear, "Politics in Provincial New York," pp. 535–36.

[33] Warden, *Boston*, pp. 116–22; Dirk Hoerder, "People and Mobs: Crowd Action in Massachusetts during the American Revolution, 1765–1780," (Inaugural-diss., University of Berlin, 1971), pp. 94–102.

[34] Warden, *Boston*, p. 122; *The Melancholy State of this Province . . .* ([Boston], 1736), p. 9.

[35] Robert Zemsky, *Merchants, Farmers, and River Gods: An Essay on Eighteenth-Century American Politics* (Boston: Gambit, 1971), pp. 118–19; for the Land Bank, see also George A. Billias, *The Massachusetts Land Bankers of 1740* (Orono, Me.: University of Maine, 1959).

[36] [Douglass], *Postscript To a Discourse concerning the Currencies of the British Plantations in America* ([Boston, 1740]), pp. 59–60.

[37] Minutes of the Boston Town Meeting, in Justin Winsor et al., *The Memorial History of Boston*, 3 vols. (Boston, 1880–1883), 2:489–90.

[38] *Boston Gazette*, 4, 11 December 1749; 9 January, 13, 20 March 1750; *Boston Evening-Post*, 18 December 1749; 12, 19 March 1750; *Boston Independent Advertiser*, 18, 25 September 1749; *Boston Weekly News-Letter*, 1 February 1750; Warden, *Boston*, pp. 139–41; Peter Orlando Hutchinson, ed., *The Diary and Letters of His Excellency Thomas Hutchinson*, 2 vols. (London, 1883–1886), 1:54. Hutchinson's account of his role in the devaluation is in his *History of the Colony and Province of Massachusetts-Bay*, ed. Lawrence Shaw Mayo, 3 vols. (Cambridge: Harvard University Press, 1936), 2:334–37; 3:6–7. Hutchinson later recounted that his friend, William Bollan, warned him to retire to his summer mansion at Milton in order to avoid being mobbed by his townsmen. Hutchinson to Bollan, 27 December 1765, Massachusetts Archives, 26:187.

[39] Vincent Centinel [pseud.], *Massachusetts in Agony: Or, Important Hints To the Inhabitants of the Province: Calling aloud For Justice to be done to the Oppressed . . .* (Boston, 1750), pp. 3–5, 8, 12–13. The best account of Hutchinson's hard money policy and its repercussions in Boston is Malcom Freiberg, "Thomas Hutchinson and the Province Currency," *New England Quarterly* 30 (1957): 196–206.

[40] The best places to begin a study of the urban dimension of the Great Awakening are Alan Heimert, *Religion and the American Mind from the Great Awakening to the Revolution* (Cambridge: Harvard University Press, 1966); and Dietmar Rothermund, *The Layman's Progress: Religious and Political Experience in Colonial Pennsylvania, 1740–1770* (Philadelphia: University of Pennsylvania Press, 1961).

[41] Rothermund, *Layman's Progress*, pp. 55–60, 81–82; Heimert, *Religion and the American Mind*, pp. 27–58, 239–93. The process of mental transformation was not confined to the cities of course. See Richard L. Bushman, *From Puritan to Yankee: Character and the Social Order in Connecticut, 1690–1765* (Cambridge: Harvard University Press, 1967); and Rhys Isaac, "Preachers and Patriots: Explorations in Popular Culture and Revolution in Virginia, 1774–1776," in this volume.

[42] For Davenport, see *Boston Evening-Post*, 2 August 1742. The response of the frightened Charles Chauncy is quoted in John C. Miller, "Religion, Finance, and Democracy in Massachusetts," *New England Quarterly* 6 (1933): 52–53.

[43] Eric Foner, "Tom Paine's Republic: Radical Ideology and Social Change," in this volume.

[44] *New-York Gazette or Weekly Post-Boy*, 26 August 1762; 13, 20 August 1767; *New-York Journal*, 18 November, 17, 24, 31 December 1767; 7, 21 January 1768; Pierre Du Simitiere Papers, Historical Society of Pennsylvania, for carriage owners.

[45] Nash, "Transformation of Urban Politics," pp. 626–29.

[46] The most important contributions are Malcolm Freiberg, "Thomas Hutchinson: The First Fifty Years (1711–1761)," *William and Mary Quarterly* 15 (1958): 35–55; John A. Schutz, *Thomas Pownall, British Defender of American Liberty: A Study of Anglo-American Relations in the Eighteenth Century* (Glendale, Calif.: A. H. Clark Co., 1951); Ellen E. Brennan, *Plural Office-Holding in Massachusetts, 1760–1780: Its Relation to the "Separation" of Departments of Government* (Chapel Hill: University of North Carolina Press, 1945); John J. Waters, Jr., *The Otis Family in Provincial and Revolutionary Massachusetts* (Chapel Hill: University of North Carolina Press, 1968); and Waters and Schutz, "Patterns of Massachusetts Colonial Politics: The Writs of Assistance and the Rivalry between the Otis and Hutchinson Families," *William and Mary Quarterly* 24 (1967): 543–67.

[47] Warden, *Boston*, p. 136; *Boston Record Commissioners* 14:127.

[48] *Boston Gazette*, 9 January 1750; *Boston Weekly News-Letter*, 7 July 1748; *Boston Evening-Post*, 11, 18 December 1749. See also Herman J. Belz, "Currency Reform in Massachusetts, 1749–50," *Essex Institute Historical Collections*, 103 (1967): 66–84; and Freiberg, "Thomas Hutchinson and the Province Currency," pp. 199–206. The election of Hutchinson as tax collector, an office from which he was exempt by law as a member of the governor's council, was reported in *Boston Weekly Post-Boy*, 25 December 1749.

[49] In 1759 Hutchinson himself noted the bitter opposition to him in Boston. Hutchinson to Israel Williams, 14 June 1759, Israel Williams Letters, Massachusetts Historical Society, 2:150. The attacks on Hutchinson's 1761 devaluation scheme are in *Boston Gazette*, 21, 28 December 1761; 11 January 1762; and [Oxenbridge Thacher], *Considerations on Lowering the Value of Gold Coins . . .* [Boston, 1762]. See also Hugh F. Bell, "A Personal Challenge: the Otis-Hutchinson Currency Controversy of 1761–1762," *Essex Institute Historical Collections* 106 (1970): 297–323.

[50] Warden, *Boston*, pp. 73–77, 104–11.

[51] *A Dialogue Between a Boston Man and A Country Man* ([Boston], 1715); *Trade and Commerce Inculcated . . .* (Boston, 1731).

[52] Charles H. Lincoln ed., *Correspondence of William Shirley*, 2 vols (New York, 1912), 1:418–22.

[53] *Boston Gazette*, 5, 12 May 1760.

[54] Quoted in John C. Miller, *Sam Adams; Pioneer in Propaganda* (Stanford, Calif.: Stanford University Press, 1936), p. 27.

[55] *To the Freeholders of the Town of Boston* (Boston, 1760); *Boston Gazette*, 12 May 1760.

[56] *Boston Evening-Post*, 21 March 1763.

[57] *Boston Gazette*, 16 May 1763.

58 On the Caucus, see Warden, "The Caucus and Democracy in Colonial Boston"; and Alan and Katherine Day, "Another Look at the Boston 'Caucus,'" *Journal of American Studies* 5 (1971): 19–42.

59 *Boston Evening-Post*, 7 March 1763.

60 Tom Thumb [Samuel Waterhouse], *Proposals for Printing . . . by Subscription the History of Vice-Admiral Thomas Brazen . . .* ([Boston], 1760).

61 *Boston Gazette*, 28 December 1761. See also [Oxenbridge Thacher], *Considerations on the Election of Counsellors, Humbly Offered to the Electors* ([Boston], 1761).

62 *Boston Evening-Post*, 14 March 1763.

63 *Boston Gazette*, 11 January 1762, Supplement.

64 *Boston Evening-Post*, 14 March 1763.

65 *Boston Gazette*, 28 February 1763.

66 The best explication of coexisting "antipartisan theory and partisan reality" during this period is in Stephen E. Patterson, *Political Parties in Revolutionary Massachusetts* (Madison, Wis.: University of Wisconsin Press, 1973), chap. 1.

67 Peter Oliver, *Origins & Progress of the American Rebellion: A Tory View*, eds. Douglass Adair and John A. Schutz (Stanford, Calif.: Stanford University Press, 1967), p. 65. This is a view found in most modern histories of the period.

68 In most of the recent literature of the early revolutionary period in Boston, and especially in John C. Miller, *Sam Adams;* and Hiller Zobel, *The Boston Massacre* (Boston: W. W. Norton and Co., 1970), the crowd is characterized as mindless, manipulable, and antirational. For a discussion of how the crowd is treated in Zobel's book and several other recent works, see Jesse Lemisch, "Radical Plot in Boston (1770): A Study in the Use of Evidence," *Harvard Law Review* 84 (1970): 485–504; and Edward Countryman, "The Problem of the Early American Crowd," *Journal of American Studies* 7 (1973): 77–90.

69 Pauline Maier, "Popular Uprisings and Civil Authority in Eighteenth-Century America," *William and Mary Quarterly* 27 (1970): 3–35; in many ways the Boston crowd resembles the preindustrial "city mob" described by E. J. Hobsbawm in *Primitive Rebels: Studies in Archaic Forms of Social Movement in the 19th and 20th Centuries* (New York: W. W. Norton and Co., 1965), chap. 7. Nothing illustrates better the support which the lower-class participants in crowd action received from those above them than the consistent refusal of the grand jury in Boston to indict rioters.

70 The Stamp Act riots are best described, though analyzed differently, in Edmund S. and Helen M. Morgan, *The Stamp Act Crisis; Prologue to Revolution* (Chapel Hill: University of North Carolina Press, 1953), pp. 160–69; Warden, *Boston*, pp. 165–69; Zobel, *Boston Massacre*, pp. 24–47; and George P. Anderson, "Ebenezer Mackintosh: Stamp Act Rioter and Patriot," *Publications* of the Colonial Society of Massachusetts, 26 (1924–1926): 15–64.

71 Josiah Quincy, Jr., *Reports of Cases Argued in the Superior Court . . . Between 1761 and 1772 . . .* , Samuel M. Quincy, ed. (Boston, 1865), p. 169.

72 Bernard to the Board of Trade, 31 August 1765, in William Cobbett, ed., *The Parliamentary History of England*, 16 (London, 1813), pp. 129–31.

73 Bernard to Halifax, 31 August 1765, Francis Bernard Papers, 4:158ff, Houghton Library, Harvard University, quoted in Bailyn, *Hutchinson*, p. 37n.

74 James Gordon to William Martin, 10 September 1765, Massachusetts Historical Society *Proceedings*, 2d ser. 13 (1899–1900): 393.

75 A month after the destruction of his house Hutchinson admitted that some of those who in 1749 and 1750 had "threatened me with destruction" had "retained their rancor ever since and are supposed to have been aiders and abettors if not actors in the late riot." Hutchinson to Henry Seymour Conway, 1 October 1765, Massachusetts Archives 26:155. Four years earlier Hutchin-

son had noted that his unpopularity was largely attributable to his hard money policy in the late 1740s. Hutchinson to William Bollan, 14 December 1761, ibid., 26:24.

[76] Patterson, *Political Parties in Revolutionary Massachusetts*, chap. 3.

[77] *New-York Gazette*, 11 July 1765, quoted in Bernard Friedman, "The Shaping of the Radical Consciousness in Provincial New York," *Journal of American History* 56 (1970): 794.

[78] The calls for political reform are best treated in J. R. Pole, *Political Representation in England and the Origins of the American Republic* (New York: MacMillan and Co., 1966); for price controls, Hoerder, "People and Mobs: Crowd Action in Massachusetts"; John K. Alexander, "The Fort Wilson Incident of 1779: A Case Study of the Revolutionary Crowd," *William and Mary Quarterly* 31 (1974): 589–612; and Anne Bezanson, "Inflation and Controls During the American Revolution in Pennsylvania, 1774–1779," *Journal of Economic History* 8, Supplement (1948): 1–20.

[79] *To the Several Battalions of Military Associators in the Province of Pennsylvania* (Philadelphia, 1776), quoted in Merrill Jensen, "The American People and the American Revolution," *Journal of American History* 57 (1970): 29. Four months later, the radical party in Philadelphia urged the voters "to chuse no rich men and [as] few learned men possible to represent them in the [state constitutional] Convention." *Pennsylvania Packet*, 26 November 1776. The best accounts of the Privates Committee are in David Hawke, *In the Midst of a Revolution* (Philadelphia: University of Pennsylvania Press, 1961); R. A. Ryerson, "Political Mobilization and the American Revolution: The Resistance Movement in Philadelphia, 1765 to 1776," *William and Mary Quarterly* 31 (1974): 565–88.

[80] *An Essay of a Declaration of Rights . . .* (Philadelphia, 1776), quoted in Jensen, "The American People and the American Revolution," pp. 32–33.

[81] The standard account of this process is J. Paul Selsam, *The Pennsylvania Constitution of 1776: A Study in Revolutionary Democracy* (Philadelphia: University of Pennsylvania Press, 1936). Recent work is extending and revising Selsam's analysis; see especially, Ryerson, "Political Mobilization"; Alexander, "The Fort Wilson Incident of 1779"; and the essay on Thomas Paine by Eric Foner in this volume.

12

Common Sense

Thomas Paine

Introduction

PERHAPS the sentiments contained in the following pages, are not yet sufficiently fashionable to procure them general favor; a long habit of not thinking a thing *wrong*, gives it a superficial appearance of being *right*, and raises at first a formidable outcry in defence of custom. But the tumult soon subsides. Time makes more converts than reason.

As a long and violent abuse of power, is generally the Means of calling the right of it in question (and in matters too which might never have been thought of, had not the Sufferers been aggravated into the inquiry) and as the K— of England had undertaken in his *own Right*, to support the Parliament in what he calls *Theirs*, and as the good people of this country are grievously oppressed by the combination, they have an undoubted privilege to inquire into the pretensions of both, and equally to reject the usurpation of either.

In the following sheets, the author hath studiously avoided every thing which is personal among ourselves. Compliments as well as censure to individuals make no part thereof. The wise, and the worthy, need not the triumph of a pamphlet; and those whose sentiments are injudicious, or unfriendly, will cease of themselves unless too much pains are bestowed upon their conversion.

The cause of America is in a great measure the cause of all mankind. Many circumstances hath, and will arise, which are not local, but universal, and through which the principles of all Lovers of Mankind are affected, and in the Event of which, their Affections are interested. The laying a Country desolate with Fire and Sword, declaring War against the natural rights of all Mankind, and extirpating the Defenders thereof from the Face of the Earth, is the Concern of every Man to whom Nature hath given the Power of feeling; of which Class, regardless of Party Censure, is the

AUTHOR.

P.S. The Publication of this new Edition hath been delayed, with a View of taking notice (had it been necessary) of any Attempt to refute the Doctrine of Independance: As no Answer hath yet appeared, it is now presumed that none will, the Time needful for getting such a Performance ready for the Public being considerably past.

Who the Author of this Production is, is wholly unnecessary to the Public, as the Object for Attention is the *Doctrine itself*, not the *Man*. Yet it may not be unnecessary to say, That he is unconnected with any Party, and under no sort of Influence public or private, but the influence of reason and principle.

Philadelphia, February 14, 1776.

Common Sense

Thomas Paine

————•————•————•————

OF THE ORIGIN AND DESIGN OF GOVERNMENT IN GENERAL. WITH CONCISE REMARKS ON THE ENGLISH CONSTITUTION.

SOME writers have so confounded society with government, as to leave little or no distinction between them; whereas they are not only different, but have different origins. Society is produced by our wants, and government by our wickedness; the former promotes our happiness *positively* by uniting our affections, the latter *negatively* by restraining our vices. The one encourages intercourse, the other creates distinctions. The first is a patron, the last a punisher.

Society in every state is a blessing, but government even in its best state is but a necessary evil; in its worst state an intolerable one; for when we suffer, or are exposed to the same miseries *by a government*, which we might expect in a country *without government*, our calamities is heightened by reflecting that we furnish the means by which we suffer. Government, like dress, is the badge of lost innocence; the palaces of kings are built on the ruins of the bowers of paradise. For were the impulses of conscience clear, uniform, and irresistibly obeyed, man would need no other lawgiver; but that not being the case, he finds it necessary to surrender up a part of his property to furnish means for the protection of the rest; and this he is induced to do by the same prudence which in every other case advises him out of two evils to choose the least. *Wherefore*, security being the true design and end of government, it unanswerably follows that whatever *form* thereof appears most likely to ensure it to us, with the least expence and greatest benefit, is preferable to all others.

In order to gain a clear and just idea of the design and end of government, let us suppose a small number of persons settled in some sequestered part of the earth, unconnected with the rest, they will then represent the first peopling of any country, or of the world. In this state of natural liberty, society will be their first thought. A thousand motives will excite them thereto, the strength of one man is so unequal to his wants, and his mind so unfitted for perpetual solitude, that he is soon obliged to seek assistance and relief of another, who in his turn requires the same. Four or five united would be able to raise a tolerable dwelling in the midst of a wilderness, but *one* man might labour out the common period of life without accomplishing any thing; when he had felled his timber he could not remove it, nor erect it after it was removed; hunger in the mean time would urge him from his work, and every different want call him a different way. Disease, nay even misfortune would be death, for though neither

210

might be mortal, yet either would disable him from living, and reduce him to a state in which he might rather be said to perish than to die.

Thus necessity, like a gravitating power, would soon form our newly arrived emigrants into society, the reciprocal blessings of which, would supercede, and render the obligations of law and government unnecessary while they remained perfectly just to each other; but as nothing but heaven is impregnable to vice, it will unavoidably happen, that in proportion as they surmount the first difficulties of emigration, which bound them together in a common cause, they will begin to relax in their duty and attachment to each other; and this remissness, will point out the necessity, of establishing some form of government to supply the defect of moral virtue.

Some convenient tree will afford them a State-House, under the branches of which, the whole colony may assemble to deliberate on public matters. It is more than probable that their first laws will have the title only of REGULATIONS, and be enforced by no other penalty than public disesteem. In this first parliament every man, by natural right will have a seat.

But as the colony increases, the public concerns will increase likewise, and the distance at which the members may be separated, will render it too inconvenient for all of them to meet on every occasion as at first, when their number was small, their habitations near, and the public concerns few and trifling. This will point out the convenience of their consenting to leave the legislative part to be managed by a select number chosen from the whole body, who are supposed to have the same concerns at stake which those have who appointed them, and who will act in the same manner as the whole body would act were they present. If the colony continue increasing, it will become necessary to augment the number of the representatives, and that the interest of every part of the colony may be attended to, it will be found best to divide the whole into convenient parts, each part sending its proper number; and that the *elected* might never form to themselves an interest separate from the *electors*, prudence will point out the propriety of having elections often; because as the *elected* might by that means return and mix again with the general body of the *electors* in a few months, their fidelity to the public will be secured by the prudent reflexion of not making a rod for themselves. And as this frequent interchange will establish a common interest with every part of the community, they will mutually and naturally support each other, and on this (not on the unmeaning name of king) depends the *strength of government, and the happiness of the governed.*

Here then is the origin and rise of government; namely, a mode rendered necessary by the inability of moral virtue to govern the world; here too is the design and end of government, viz. freedom and security. And however our eyes may be dazzled with snow, or our ears deceived by sound; however prejudice may warp our wills, or interest darken our understanding, the simple voice of nature and of reason will say, it is right.

I draw my idea of the form of government from a principle in nature, which no art can overturn, viz. that the more simple any thing is, the less liable it is to be disordered, and the easier repaired when disordered; and with this maxim in view, I offer a few remarks on the so much boasted constitution of England. That it was noble for the dark and slavish times in which it was erected is granted. When the world was over-run with tyranny the least remove therefrom was a glorious rescue. But that it is imperfect, subject to convulsions, and incapable of producing what it seems to promise, is easily demonstrated.

Absolute governments (tho' the disgrace of human nature) have this advantage with them, that they are simple; if the people suffer, they know the head from which their suffering springs, know likewise the remedy, and are not bewildered by a variety of causes and cures. But the constitution of England is so exceedingly complex, that the nation may suffer for years together without being able to discover in which part the fault lies, some will say in one and some in another, and every political physician will advise a different medicine.

I know it is difficult to get over local or long standing prejudices, yet if we will suffer ourselves to examine the component parts of the English constitution, we shall find them to be the base remains of two ancient tyrannies, compounded with some new republican materials.

First.—The remains of monarchical tyranny in the person of the king.

Secondly.—The remains of aristocratical tyranny in the persons of the peers.

Thirdly.—The new republican materials, in the persons of the commons, on whose virtue depends the freedom of England.

The two first, by being hereditary, are independent of the people; wherefore in a *constitutional sense* they contribute nothing towards the freedom of the state.

To say that the constitution of England is a *union* of three powers reciprocally *checking* each other, is farcical, either the words have no meaning, or they are flat contradictions.

To say that the commons is a check upon the king, presupposes two things.

First.—That the king is not to be trusted without being looked after, or in other words, that a thirst for absolute power is the natural disease of monarchy.

Secondly.—That the commons, by being appointed for that purpose, are either wiser or more worthy of confidence than the crown.

But as the same constitution which gives the commons a power to check the king by withholding the supplies, gives afterwards the king a power to check the commons, by empowering him to reject their other bills; it again supposes that the king is wiser than those whom it has already supposed to be wiser than him. A mere absurdity!

There is something exceedingly ridiculous in the composition of monarchy; it first excludes a man from the means of information, yet empowers him to act in cases where the highest judgment is required. The state of a king shuts him from the world, yet the business of a king requires him to know it thoroughly; wherefore the different parts, unnaturally opposing and destroying each other, prove the whole character to be absurd and useless.

Some writers have explained the English constitution thus; the king, say they, is one, the people another; the peers are an house in behalf of the king; the commons in behalf of the people; but this hath all the distinctions of an house divided against itself; and though the expressions be pleasantly arranged, yet when examined they appear idle and ambiguous; and it will always happen, that the nicest construction that words are capable of, when applied to the description of some thing which either cannot exist, or is too incomprehensible to be within the compass of description, will be words of sound only, and though they may amuse the ear, they cannot inform the mind, for this explanation includes a previous question, viz. *How came the king by a power which the people are afraid to trust, and always obliged to check?* Such a power could not be the gift of a wise people, neither can any power, *which needs checking*, be from God; yet the provision, which the constitution makes, supposes such a power to exist.

But the provision is unequal to the task; the means either cannot or will not accomplish the end, and the whole affair is a *felo de se;* for as the greater weight will always carry up the less, and as all the wheels of a machine are put in motion by one, it only remains to know which power in the constitution has the most weight, for that will govern; and though the others, or a part of them, may clog, or, as the phrase is, check the rapidity of its motion, yet so long as they cannot stop it, their endeavours will be ineffectual; the first moving power will at last have its way, and what it wants in speed is supplied by time.

That the crown is this overbearing part in the English constitution needs not be mentioned, and that it derives its whole consequence merely from being the giver of places and pensions is self-evident, wherefore, though we have been wise enough to shut and lock a door against absolute monarchy, we at the same time have been foolish enough to put the crown in possession of the key.

The prejudice of Englishmen, in favour of their own government by king, lords, and commons, arises as much or more from national pride than reason. Individuals are undoubtedly safer in England than in some other countries, but the *will* of the king is as much the *law* of the land in Britain as in France, with this difference, that instead of proceeding directly from his mouth, it is handed to the people under the most formidable shape of an act of parliament. For the fate of Charles the First, hath only made kings more subtle—not more just.

Wherefore, laying aside all national pride and prejudice in favour of modes and forms, the plain truth is, that *it is wholly owing to the constitution of the people, and not to the constitution of the government* that the crown is not as oppressive in England as in Turkey.

An inquiry into the *constitutional errors* in the English form of government is at this time highly necessary; for as we are never in a proper condition of doing justice to others, while we continue under the influence of some leading partiality, so neither are we capable of doing it to ourselves while we remain fettered by any obstinate prejudice. And as a man, who is attached to a prostitute, is unfitted to choose or judge of a wife, so any prepossession in favour of a rotten constitution of government will disable us from discerning a good one.

Of Monarchy and Hereditary Succession.

MANKIND being originally equals in the order of creation, the equality could only be destroyed by some subsequent circumstance; the distinctions of rich, and poor, may in a great measure be accounted for, and that without having recourse to the harsh, ill-sounding names of oppression and avarice. Oppression is often the *consequence*, but seldom or never the *means* of riches; and though avarice will preserve a man from being necessitously poor, it generally makes him too timorous to be wealthy.

But there is another and greater distinction for which no truly natural or religious reason can be assigned, and that is, the distinction of men into KINGS and SUBJECTS. Male and female are the distinctions of nature, good and bad the distinctions of heaven; but how a race of men came into the world so exalted above the rest, and distinguished like some new species, is worth enquiring into, and whether they are the means of happiness or of misery to mankind.

In the early ages of the world, according to the scripture chronology, there were no kings; the consequence of which was there were no wars; it is the pride of kings which throw mankind into confusion. Holland without a king hath enjoyed more peace for this last century than any of the monarchial governments in Europe. Antiquity favors the same remark; for the quiet and rural lives of the first patriarchs hath a happy something in them, which vanishes away when we come to the history of Jewish royalty.

Government by kings was first introduced into the world by the Heathens, from whom the children of Israel copied the custom. It was the most prosperous invention the Devil ever set on foot for the promotion of idolatry. The Heathens paid divine honors to their deceased kings, and the christian world hath improved on the plan by doing the same to their living ones. How impious is the title of *sacred majesty* applied to a worm, who in the midst of his splendor is crumbling into dust.

As the exalting one man so greatly above the rest cannot be justified on the equal rights of nature, so neither can it be defended on the authority of scripture; for the will of the Almighty, as declared by Gideon and the prophet Samuel, expressly disapproves of government by kings. All anti-monarchial parts of scripture have been very smoothly glossed over in monarchial governments, but they undoubtedly merit the attention of countries which have their governments yet to form. 'Render unto Cæsar the things which are Cæsar's' is the scriptural doctrine of courts, yet it is no support of monarchial government, for the Jews at that time were without a king, and in a state of vassalage to the Romans.

Near three thousand years passed away from the Mosaic account of the creation, till the Jews under a national delusion requested a king. Till then their form of government (except in extraordinary cases, where the Almighty interposed) was a kind of republic administered by a judge and the elders of the tribes. Kings they had none, and it was held sinful to acknowledge any being under that title but the Lords of Hosts. And when a man seriously reflects on the idolatrous homage which is paid to the persons of Kings, he need not wonder, that the Almighty, ever jealous of his honor, should disapprove of a form of government which so impiously invades the prerogative of heaven.

Monarchy is ranked in scripture as one of the sins of the Jews, for which a curse in reserve is denounced against them. The history of that transaction is worth attending to.

The children of Israel being oppressed by the Midianites, Gideon marched against them with a small army, and victory, thro' the divine interposition, decided in his favour. The Jews elate with success, and attributing it to the generalship of Gideon, proposed making him a king, saying, *Rule thou over us, thou and thy son and thy son's son.* Here was temptation in its fullest extent; not a kingdom only, but an hereditary one, but Gideon in the piety of his soul replied, *I will not rule over you, neither shall my son rule over you,* THE LORD SHALL RULE OVER YOU. Words need not be more explicit; Gideon doth not *decline* the honor but denieth their right to give it; neither doth he compliment them with invented declarations of his thanks, but in the positive stile of a prophet charges them with disaffection to their proper sovereign, the King of Heaven.

About one hundred and thirty years after this, they fell again into the same error. The hankering which the Jews had for the idolatrous customs of the Heathens, is something exceedingly unaccountable; but so it was, that laying hold of the misconduct of Samuel's two sons, who were entrusted with some secular concerns, they came in an abrupt and clamourous manner to Samuel, saying, *Behold thou art old, and thy sons walk not in thy ways, now make us a king to judge us like all the other nations.* And here we cannot but observe that their motives were bad, viz. that they might be *like* unto other nations, i. e. the Heathens, whereas their true glory laid in being as much *unlike* them as possible. *But the thing displeased Samuel when they said, give us a king to judge us; and Samuel prayed unto the Lord, and the Lord said unto Samuel, Hearken unto the voice of the people in all that they say unto thee, for they have not rejected thee, but they have rejected me,* THAT I SHOULD NOT REIGN OVER THEM. *According to all the works which they have done since the day that I brought them up out of Egypt, even unto this day; wherewith they have forsaken me and served other gods; so do they also unto thee. Now therefore hearken unto their voice, howbeit, protest solemnly unto them and shew them the manner of the king that shall reign over them,* i. e. not of any particular king, but the general manner of the kings of the earth, whom Israel was so eagerly copying after. And notwithstanding the great distance of time and difference of manners, the character is still in fashion, *And Samuel told all the words of the Lord unto the people, that asked of him a king. And he said, This shall be the manner of the king that shall reign over you; he will take your sons and appoint them for himself for his chariots, and to be his horsemen, and some shall run before his chariots* (this description agrees with the present mode of impressing men) *and he will appoint him captains over thousands and captains over fifties, and will set them to ear his ground and to reap his harvest, and to make his instruments of war, and instruments of his chariots; and he will take your daughters to be confectionaries and to be cooks and to be bakers* (this describes the expence and luxury as well as the oppression of kings) *and he will take your fields and your olive yards, even the best of them, and give them to his servants; and he will take the tenth of your seed, and of your vineyards, and give them to his officers and to his servants* (by which we see that bribery, corruption, and favoritism are the standing vices of kings) *and he will take the tenth of your men servants, and your maid servants, and your goodliest young men and your asses, and put them to his work; and he will take the tenth of your sheep, and ye shall be his servants, and ye shall cry out in that day because of your king which ye shall have chosen,* AND THE LORD

WILL NOT HEAR YOU IN THAT DAY. This accounts for the continuation of monarchy; neither do the characters of the few good kings which have lived since, either sanctify the title, or blot out the sinfulness of the origin; the high encomium given of David takes no notice of him *officially as a king*, but only as a *man* after God's own heart. *Nevertheless the People refused to obey the voice of Samuel, and they said, Nay, but we will have a king over us, that we may be like all the nations, and that our king may judge us, and go out before us and fight our battles.* Samuel continued to reason with them, but to no purpose; he set before them their ingratitude, but all would not avail; and seeing them fully bent on their folly, he cried out, *I will call unto the Lord, and he shall send thunder and rain* (which then was a punishment, being the time of wheat harvest) *that ye may perceive and see that your wickedness is great which ye have done in the sight of the Lord,* IN ASKING YOU A KING. *So Samuel called unto the Lord, and the Lord sent thunder and rain that day, and all the people greatly feared the Lord and Samuel. And all the people said unto Samuel, Pray for thy servants unto the Lord thy God that we die not, for* WE HAVE ADDED UNTO OUR SINS THIS EVIL, TO ASK A KING. These portions of scripture are direct and positive. They admit of no equivocal construction. That the Almighty hath here entered his protest against monarchial government is true, or the scripture is false. And a man hath good reason to believe that there is as much of king-craft, as priest-craft in withholding the scripture from the public in Popish countries. For monarchy in every instance is the Popery of government.

To the evil of monarchy we have added that of hereditary succession; and as the first is a degredation and lessening of ourselves, so the second, claimed as a matter of right, is an insult and an imposition on posterity. For all men being originally equal, no *one* by *birth* could have a right to set up his own family in perpetual preference to all others for ever, and though himself might deserve *some* decent degree of honors of his contemporaries, yet his descendants might be far too unworthy to inherit them. One of the strongest *natural* proofs of the folly of hereditary right in kings, is, that nature disapproves it, otherwise she would not so frequently turn it into ridicule by giving mankind an *ass for a lion.*

Secondly, as no man at first could possess any other public honors than were bestowed upon him, so the givers of those honors could have no power to give away the right of posterity, and though they might say 'We choose you for *our* head,' they could not, without manifest injustice to their children, say 'that your children and your children's children shall reign over *ours* for ever.' Because such an unwise, unjust, unnatural compact might (perhaps) in the next succession put them under the government of a rogue or a fool. Most wise men, in their private sentiments, have ever treated hereditary right with contempt; yet it is one of those evils, which when once established is not easily removed; many submit from fear, others from superstition, and the more powerful part shares with the king the plunder of the rest.

This is supposing the present race of kings in the world to have had an honourable origin; whereas it is more than probable, that could we take off the dark covering of antiquity, and trace them to their first rise, that we should find the first of them nothing better than the principal ruffian of some restless gang, whose savage manners or pre-eminence in subtilty obtained him the title of chief among plunderers; and who by increasing in power, and extending his depredations, over-awed the quiet and defenceless to purchase their safety by frequent contributions. Yet his electors could have no idea of giving hereditary right to his descendants, because such a perpetual exclusion of themselves was incompatible with the free and unrestrained principles they professed to live by. Wherefore, hereditary succession in the early ages of monarchy could not take place as a matter of claim, but as something casual or complimental; but as few or no records were extant in those days, and traditionary history stuffed with fables, it was very easy, after the lapse of a few generations, to trump up some superstitious tale, conveniently timed, Mahomet like, to cram hereditary right down the throats of the vulgar. Perhaps the disorders which threatened, or seemed to threaten on the decease of a leader and the choice of a new one (for elections among ruffians could not be very orderly) induced many at first to favor hereditary pretentions; by which means it happened, as it hath happened since, that what at first was submitted to as a convenience, was afterwards claimed as a right.

England, since the conquest, hath known some few good monarchs, but groaned beneath a much larger number of bad ones, yet no man in his senses can say that their claim under William the Conqueror is a very honorable one. A French bastard landing with an armed banditti, and establishing himself king of England against the consent of the natives, is in plain terms a very paltry rascally original.—It certainly hath no divinity in it. However, it is needless to spend much time in exposing the folly of hereditary right, if there are any so weak as to believe it, let them promiscuously worship the ass and lion, and welcome. I shall neither copy their humility, nor disturb their devotion.

Yet I should be glad to ask how they suppose kings came at first? The question admits but of three answers, viz. either by lot, by election, or by usurpation. If the first king was taken by lot, it establishes a precedent for the next, which excludes hereditary succession. Saul was by lot yet the succession was not hereditary, neither does it appear from that transaction there was any intention it ever should. If the first king of any country was by election, that likewise establishes a precedent for the next; for to say, that the *right* of all future generations is taken away, by the act of the first electors, in their choice not only of a king, but of a family of kings for ever, hath no parallel in or out of scripture but the doctrine of original sin, which supposes the free will of all men lost in Adam; and from such comparison, and it will admit of no other, heredity succession can derive no glory. For as in Adam all sinned, and as in the first electors all men obeyed; as in the one all mankind were subjected to Satan, and in the other to Sovereignty; as our innocence was lost in the first, and our authority in the last; and as both disable us from re-assuming some former state and privilege, it unanswerably follows that original sin and heredity succession are parallels. Dishonourable rank! Inglorious connexion! Yet the most subtile sophist cannot produce a juster simile.

As to usurpation, no man will be so hardy as to defend it; and that William the Conqueror was an usurper is a fact not to be contradicted. The plain truth is, that the antiquity of English monarchy will not bear looking into.

But it is not so much the absurdity as the evil of hereditary succession which concerns mankind. Did it ensure a race of good and wise men it would have the seal of divine authority, but as it opens a door to the *foolish*, the *wicked*, and the *improper*, it hath in it the nature of oppression. Men who look upon themselves born to reign, and others to obey, soon grow insolent; selected from the rest of mankind their minds are early poisoned by importance; and the world they act in differs so materially from the world at large, that they have but little opportunity of knowing its true interests, and when they succeed to the government are frequently the most ignorant and unfit of any throughout the dominions.

Another evil which attends hereditary succession is, that the throne is subject to be possessed by a minor at any age; all which time the regency, acting under the cover of a king, have every opportunity and inducement to betray their trust. The same national misfortune happens, when a king worn out with age and infirmity, enters the last stage of human weakness. In both these cases the public becomes a prey to every miscreant, who can tamper successfully with the follies either of age or infancy.

The most plausible plea, which hath ever been offered in favour of hereditary succession, is, that it preserves a nation from civil wars; and were this true, it would be weighty; whereas, it is the most barefaced falsity ever imposed upon mankind. The whole history of England disowns the fact. Thirty kings and two minors have reigned in that distracted kingdom since the conquest, in which time there have been (including the Revolution) no less than eight civil wars and nineteen rebellions. Wherefore instead of making for peace, it makes against it, and destroys the very foundation it seems to stand on.

The contest for monarchy and succession, between the houses of York and Lancaster, laid England in a scene of blood for many years. Twelve pitched battles, besides skirmishes and sieges, were fought between Henry and Edward. Twice was Henry prisoner to Edward, who in his turn was prisoner to Henry. And so uncertain is the fate of war and the temper of a nation, when nothing but personal matters are the ground of a quarrel, that Henry was taken in triumph from a prison to a palace, and Edward obliged to fly from a palace to a foreign land; yet, as sudden transitions of temper are seldom lasting, Henry in his turn was driven from the throne, and Edward recalled to succeed him. The parliament always following the strongest side.

This contest began in the reign of Henry the Sixth, and was not entirely extinguished till Henry the Seventh, in whom the families were united. Including a period of 67 years, viz. from 1422 to 1489.

In short, monarchy and succession have laid (not this or that kingdom only) but the world in blood and ashes. 'Tis a form of government which the word of God bears testimony against, and blood will attend it.

If we inquire into the business of a king, we shall find that in some countries they have none; and after sauntering away their lives without pleasure to themselves or advantage to the nation, withdraw from the scene, and leave their successors to tread the same idle round. In absolute monarchies the whole weight of business civil and military, lies on the king; the children of Israel in their request for a king, urged this plea 'that he may judge us, and go out before us and fight our battles.' But in countries where he is neither a judge nor a general, as in E—d, a man would be puzzled to know what *is* his business.

The nearer any government approaches to a republic the less business there is for a king. It is somewhat difficult to find a proper name for the government of E—. Sir William Meredith calls it a republic; but in its present state it is unworthy of the name, because the corrupt influence of the crown, by having all the places in its disposal, hath so effectually swallowed up the power, and eaten out the virtue of the house of commons (the republican part in the constitution) that the government of England is nearly as monarchical as that of France or Spain. Men fall out with names without understanding them. For it is the republican and not the monarchical part of the constitution of England which Englishmen glory in, viz. the liberty of choosing an house of commons from out of their own body—and it is easy to see that when the republican virtue fails, slavery ensues. Why is the constitution of E—d sickly, but because monarchy hath poisoned the republic, the crown hath engrossed the commons?

In England a k— hath little more to do than to make war and give away places; which in plain terms, is to impoverish the nation and set it together by the ears. A pretty business indeed for a man to be allowed eight hundred thousand sterling a year for, and worshipped into the bargain! Of more worth is one honest man to society, and in the sight of God, than all the crowned ruffians that ever lived.

Thoughts on the Present State of American Affairs.

IN the following pages I offer nothing more than simple facts, plain arguments, and common sense; and have no other preliminaries to settle with the reader, than that he will divest himself of prejudice and prepossession, and suffer his reason and his feelings to determine for themselves; that he will put *on*, or rather that he will not put *off*, the true character of a man, and generously enlarge his views beyond the present day.

Volumes have been written on the subject of the struggle between England and America. Men of all ranks have embarked in the controversy, from different motives, and with various designs; but all have been ineffectual, and the period of debate is closed. Arms, as the last resource, decide the contest; the appeal was the choice of the king, and the continent hath accepted the challenge.

It hath been reported of the late Mr Pelham (who tho' an able minister was not without his faults) that on his being attacked in the house of commons, on the score, that his measures were only of a temporary kind, replied, '*they will last my time.*' Should a thought so fatal and unmanly possess the colonies in the present contest, the name of ancestors will be remembered by future generations with detestation.

The sun never shined on a cause of greater worth. 'Tis not the affair of a city, a country, a province, or a kingdom, but of a continent—of at least one eighth part of the habitable globe. 'Tis not the concern of a day, a year, or an age; posterity are virtually involved in the contest, and will be more or less affected, even to the end of time, by the proceedings now. Now is the seed time of continental union, faith and honor. The least fracture now will be like a name engraved with the point of a pin on the tender rind of a young oak; the wound will enlarge with the tree, and posterity read it in full grown characters.

By referring the matter from argument to arms, a new æra for politics is struck; a new method of thinking hath arisen. All plans, proposals, &c. prior to the nineteenth of April, *i. e.* to the commencement of hostilities, are like the almanacks of the last year; which, though proper then, are superceded and useless now. Whatever was advanced by the advocates on either side of the question then, terminated in one and the same point, viz. a union with Great Britain; the only difference between the parties was the method of effecting it; the one proposing force, the other friendship; but it hath so far happened that the first hath failed, and the second hath withdrawn her influence.

As much hath been said of the advantages of reconciliation, which, like an agreeable dream, hath passed away and left us as we were, it is but right, that we should examine the contrary side of the argument, and inquire into some of the many material injuries which these colonies sustain, and always will sustain, by being connected with, and dependant on Great Britain. To examine that connexion and dependance, on the principles of nature and common sense, to see what we have to trust to, if separated, and what we are to expect, if dependant.

I have heard it asserted by some, that as America hath flourished under her former connexion with Great-Britain, that the same connexion is necessary towards her future happiness, and will always have the same effect. Nothing can be more fallacious than this kind of argument. We may as well assert, that because a child has thrived upon milk, that it is never to have meat; or that the first twenty years of our lives is to become a precedent for the next twenty. But even this is admitting more than is true, for I answer roundly, that America would have flourished as much, and probably much more, had no European power had any thing to do with her. The commerce by which she hath enriched herself are the necessaries of life, and will always have a market while eating is the custom of Europe.

But she has protected us, say some. That she hath engrossed us is true, and defended the continent at our expence as well as her own is admitted, and she would have defended Turkey from the same motive, viz. the sake of trade and dominion.

Alas, we have been long led away by ancient prejudices, and made large sacrifices to superstition. We have boasted the protection of Great-Britain, without considering, that her motive was *interest* not *attachment;* that she did not protect us from *our enemies* on *our account,* but from *her enemies* on *her own account,* from those who had no quarrel with us on any *other account,* and who will always be our enemies on the *same account.* Let Britain wave her pretensions to the continent, or the continent throw off the dependance, and we should be at peace with France and Spain were they at war with Britain. The miseries of Hanover last war ought to warn us against connexions.

It hath lately been asserted in parliament, that the colonies have no relation to each other but through the parent country, *i. e.* that Pennsylvania and the Jerseys, and so on for the rest, are sister colonies by the way of England; this is certainly a very round-about way of proving relationship, but it is the nearest and only true way of proving enemyship, if I may so call it. France and Spain never were, nor perhaps ever will be our enemies as *Americans*, but as our being the *subjects of Great Britain*.

But Britain is the parent country, say some. Then the more shame upon her conduct. Even brutes do not devour their young, nor savages make war upon their families; wherefore the assertion, if true, turns to her reproach; but it happens not to be true, or only partly so, and the phrase *parent* or *mother country* hath been jesuitically adopted by the — and his parasites, with a low papistical design of gaining an unfair bias on the credulous weakness of our minds. Europe, and not England, is the parent country of America. This new world hath been the asylum for the persecuted lovers of civil and religious liberty from *every part* of Europe. Hither have they fled, not from the tender embraces of the mother, but from the cruelty of the monster; and it is so far true of England, that the same tyranny which drove the first emigrants from home, pursues their descendants still.

In this extensive quarter of the globe, we forget the narrow limits of three hundred and sixty miles (the extent of England) and carry our friendship on a larger scale; we claim brotherhood with eve-European christian, and triumph in the generosity of the sentiment.

It is pleasant to observe by what regular gradations we surmount the force of local prejudice, as we enlarge our acquaintance with the world. A man born in any town in England divided into parishes, will naturally associate most with his fellow parishioners (because their interests in many cases will be common) and distinguish him by the name of *neighbour;* if he meet him but a few miles from home, he drops the narrow idea of a street, and salutes him by the name of *townsman;* if he travels out of the county, and meet him in any other, he forgets the minor divisions of street and town, and calls him *countryman, i.e. countyman;* but if in their foreign excursions they should associate in France or any other part of *Europe*, their local remembrance would be enlarged into that of *Englishmen.* And by a just parity of reasoning, all Europeans meeting in America, or any other quarter of the globe, are *countrymen;* for England, Holland, Germany, or Sweden, when compared with the whole, stand in the same places on the larger scale, which the divisions of street, town, and county do on the smaller ones; distinctions too limited for continental minds. Not one third of the inhabitants, even of this province, are of English descent. Wherefore I reprobate the phrase of parent or mother country applied to England only, as being false, selfish, narrow and ungenerous.

But admitting that we were all of English descent, what does it amount to? Nothing. Britain, being now an open enemy, extinguishes every other name and title: And to say that reconciliation is our duty, is truly farcical. The first king of England, of the present line (William the Conqueror) was a Frenchman, and half the peers of England are descendants from the same country; wherefore by the same method of reasoning, England ought to be governed by France.

Much hath been said of the united strength of Britain and the colonies, that in conjunction they might bid defiance to the world. But this is mere presumption; the fate of war is uncertain, neither do the expressions mean any thing; for this continent would never suffer itself to be drained of inhabitants to support the British arms in either Asia, Africa, or Europe.

Besides, what have we to do with setting the world at defiance? Our plan is commerce, and that, well attended to, will secure us the peace and friendship of all Europe; because it is the interest of all Europe to have America a *free port.* Her trade will always be a protection, and her barrenness of gold and silver secure her from invaders.

I challenge the warmest advocate for reconciliation, to shew, a single advantage that this continent can reap, by being connected with Great Britain. I repeat the challenge, not a single advantage is derived. Our corn will fetch its price in any market in Europe, and our imported goods must be paid for buy them where we will.

But the injuries and disadvantages we sustain by that connection, are without number; and our duty to mankind at large, as well as to ourselves, instruct us to renounce the alliance:

Because, any submission to, or dependance on Great Britain, tends directly to involve this continent in European wars and quarrels; and sets us at variance with nations, who would otherwise seek our friendship, and against whom, we have neither anger nor complaint. As Europe is our market for trade, we ought to form no partial connection with any part of it. It is the true interest of America to steer clear of European contentions, which she never can do, while by her dependance on Britain, she is made the make-weight in the scale of British politics.

Europe is too thickly planted with kingdoms to be long at peace, and whenever a war breaks out between England and any foreign power, the trade of America goes to ruin, *because of her connection with Britain.* The next war may not turn out like the last, and should it not, the advocates for reconciliation now will be wishing for separation then, because, neutrality in that case, would be a safer convoy than a man of war. Every thing that is right or natural pleads for separation. The blood of the slain, the weeping voice of nature cries, 'TIS TIME TO PART. Even the distance at which the Almighty hath placed England and America, is a strong and natural proof, that the authority of the one, over the other, was never the design of Heaven. The time likewise at which the continent was discovered, adds weight to the argument, and the manner in which it was peopled encreases the force of it. The reformation was preceded by the discovery of America, as if the Almighty graciously meant to open a sanctuary to the persecuted in future years, when home should afford neither friendship nor safety.

The authority of Great-Britain over this continent, is a form of government, which sooner or later must have an end: And a serious mind can draw no true pleasure by looking forward, under the painful and positive conviction, that what he calls 'the present constitution' is merely temporary. As parents, we can have no joy, knowing that *this government* is not sufficiently lasting to ensure any thing which we may bequeath to posterity: And by a plain method of argument, as we are running the next generation into debt, we ought to do the work of it, otherwise we use them meanly and pitifully. In order to discover the line of our duty rightly, we should take our children in our hand, and fix our station a few years farther into life; that eminence will present a prospect, which a few present fears and prejudices conceal from our sight.

Though I would carefully avoid giving unnecessary offence, yet I am inclined to believe, that all those who espouse the doctrine of reconciliation, may be included within the following descriptions. Interested men, who are not to be trusted; weak men who *cannot* see; prejudiced men who *will not* see; and a certain set of moderate men who think better of the European world than it deserves; and this last class by an ill-judged deliberation, will be the cause of more calamities to this continent than all the other three.

It is the good fortune of many to live distant from the scene of sorrow; the evil is not sufficiently brought to *their* doors to make *them* feel the precariousness with which all American property is possessed. But let our imaginations transport us for a few moments to Boston, that seat of wretchedness will teach us wisdom, and instruct us for ever to renounce a power in whom we can have no trust. The inhabitants of that unfortunate city, who but a few months ago were in ease and affluence, have now no other alternative than to stay and starve, or turn out to beg. Endangered by the fire of their friends if they continue within the city, and plundered by the soldiery if they leave it. In their present condition they are prisoners without the hope of redemption, and in a general attack for their relief, they would be exposed to the fury of both armies.

Men of passive tempers look somewhat lightly over the offences of Britain, and, still hoping for the best, are apt to call out, *'Come we shall be friends again for all this.'* But examine the passions and feelings of mankind. Bring the doctrine of reconciliation to the touchstone of nature, and then tell me, whether you can hereafter love, honour, and faithfully serve the power that hath carried fire and sword into your land? If you cannot do all these, then are you only deceiving yourselves, and by your delay bringing ruin upon posterity. Your future connection with Britain, whom you can neither love nor honour, will be forced and unnatural, and being formed only on the plan of present convenience, will in a little time fall into a relapse more wretched than the first. But if you say, you can still pass the violations over, then I ask, Hath your house been burnt? Hath your property been destroyed before your face? Are your wife and children destitute of a bed to lie on, or bread to live on? Have you lost a parent or a child by their hands, and yourself the ruined and wretched survivor? If you have not, then are you not a judge of those who have. But if you have, and can still shake hands with the murderers, then are you unworthy the name of husband, father, friend, or lover, and whatever may be your rank or title in life, you have the heart of a coward, and the spirit of a sycophant.

This is not inflaming or exaggerating matters, but trying them by those feelings and affections which nature justifies, and without which, we should be incapable of discharging the social duties of life, or enjoying the felicities of it. I mean not to exhibit horror for the purpose of provoking revenge, but to awaken us from fatal and unmanly slumbers, that we may pursue determinately some fixed object. It is not in the power of Britain or of Europe to conquer America, if she do not conquer herself by *delay* and *timidity*. The present winter is worth an age if rightly employed, but if lost or neglected, the whole continent will partake of the misfortune; and there is no punishment which that man will not deserve, be he who, or what, or where he will, that may be the means of sacrificing a season so precious and useful.

It is repugnant to reason, to the universal order of things, to all examples from the former ages, to suppose, that this continent can longer remain subject to any external power. The most sanguine in Britain does not think so. The utmost stretch of human wisdom cannot, at this time compass a plan short of separation, which can promise the continent even a year's security. Reconciliation is was a falacious dream. Nature hath deserted the connexion, and Art cannot supply her place. For, as Milton wisely expresses, 'never can true reconcilement grow where wounds of deadly hate have pierced so deep.'

Every quiet method for peace hath been ineffectual. Our prayers have been rejected with disdain; and only tended to convince us, that nothing flatters vanity, or confirms obstinancy in Kings more than repeated petitioning—and nothing hath contributed more than that very measure to make the Kings of Europe absolute: Witness Denmark and Sweden. Wherefore since nothing but blows will do, for God's sake, let us come to a final separation, and not leave the next generation to be cutting throats, under the violated unmeaning names of parent and child.

To say, they will never attempt it again is idle and visionary, we thought so at the repeal of the stamp-act, yet a year or two undeceived us; as well we may suppose that nations, which have been once defeated, will never renew the quarrel.

As to government matters, it is not in the power of Britain to do this continent justice: The business of it will soon be too weighty, and intricate, to be managed with any tolerable degree of convenience, by a power, so distant from us, and so very ignorant of us; for if they cannot conquer us, they cannot govern us. To be always running three or four thousand miles with a tale or a petition, waiting four or five months for an answer, which when obtained requires five or six more to explain it in, will in a few years be looked upon as folly and childishness—There was a time when it was proper, and there is a proper time for it to cease.

Small islands not capable of protecting themselves, are the proper objects for kingdoms to take under their care; but there is something very absurd, in supposing a continent to be perpetually governed by an island. In no instance hath nature made the satellite larger than its primary planet, and as England and America, with respect to each other, reverses the common order of nature, it is evident they belong to different systems: England to Europe, America to itself.

I am not induced by motives of pride, party, or resentment to espouse the doctrine of separation and independance; I am clearly, positively, and conscientiously persuaded that it is the true interest of this continent to be so; that every thing short of *that* is mere patchwork, that it can afford no lasting felicity,—that it is leaving the sword to our children, and shrinking back at a time, when, a little more, a little farther, would have rendered this continent the glory of the earth.

As Britain hath not manifested the least inclination towards a compromise, we may be assured that no terms can be obtained worthy the acceptance of the continent, or any ways equal to the expence of blood and treasure we have been already put to.

The object contended for, ought always to bear some just proportion to the expence. The removal of N—, or the whole detestable junto, is a matter unworthy the millions we have expended. A temporary stoppage of trade, was an inconvenience, which would have sufficiently ballanced the repeal of all the acts complained of, had such repeals been obtained; but if the whole continent must take up arms, if every man must be a soldier, it is scarcely worth our while to fight against a contemptible ministry only. Dearly, dearly, do we pay for the repeal of the acts, if that is all we fight for; for in a just estimation, it is as great a folly to pay a Bunker-hill price for law, as for land. As I have always considered the independancy of this continent, as an event, which sooner or later must arrive, so from the late rapid progress of the continent to maturity, the event could not be far off. Wherefore, on the breaking out of hostilities, it was not worth the while to have disputed a matter, which time would have finally redressed, unless we meant to be in earnest; otherwise, it is like wasting an estate on a suit at law, to regulate the trespasses of a tenant, whose lease is just expiring. No man was a warmer wisher for reconciliation than myself, before the fatal nineteenth of April 1775*, but the moment the event of that day was made known, I rejected the hardened, sullen tempered Pharoah of — for ever; and disdain the wretch, that with the pretended title of FATHER OF HIS PEOPLE can unfeelingly hear of their slaughter, and composedly sleep with their blood upon his soul.

But admitting that matters were now made up, what would be the event? I answer, the ruin of the continent. And that for several reasons.

First. The powers of governing still remaining in the hands of the k—, he will have a negative over the whole legislation of this continent. And as he hath shewn himself such an inveterate enemy to liberty, and discovered such a thirst for arbitrary power; is he, or is he not, a proper man to say to these colonies, *'You shall make no laws but what I please.'* And is there any inhabitants in America so ignorant, as not to know, that according to what is called the *present constitution*, that this continent can make no laws but what the king gives leave to; and is there any man so unwise, as not to see, that (considering what has happened) he will suffer no Law to be made here, but such as suit his purpose. We may be as effectually enslaved by the want of laws in America, as by submitting to laws made for us in England. After matters are made up (as it is called) can there be any doubt but the whole power of the crown will be exerted, to keep this continent as low and humble as possible? Instead of going forward we shall go backward, or be perpetually quarrelling or ridiculously petitioning.—We are already greater than the king wishes us to be, and will he not hereafter endeavour to make us less? To bring the matter to one point. Is the power who is jealous of our prosperity, a proper power to govern us? Whoever says *No* to this question is an *independant*, for independancy means no more, than, whether we shall make our own laws, or, whether the —, the greatest enemy this continent hath, or can have, shall tell us *'there shall be no laws but such as I like.'*

But the k— you will say has a negative in England; the people there can make no laws without his consent. In point of right and good order, there is something very ridiculous, that

---

* Massacre at Lexington.

a youth of twenty-one (which hath often happened) shall say to several millions of people, older and wiser than himself, I forbid this or that act of yours to be law. But in this place I decline this sort of reply, tho' I will never cease to expose the absurdity of it, and only answer, that England being the king's residence, and America not so, makes quite another case. The k—'s negative *here* is ten times more dangerous and fatal than it can be in England, for *there* he will scarcely refuse his consent to a bill for putting England into as strong a state of defence as possible, and in America he would never suffer such a bill to be passed.

America is only a secondary object in the system of British politics. England consults the good of *this* country, no farther than it answers her *own* purpose. Wherefore, her own interest leads her to suppress the growth of *ours* in every case which doth not promote her advantage, or in the least interfere with it. A pretty state we should soon be in under such a second-hand government, considering what has happened! Men do not change from enemies to friends by the alteration of a name: And in order to shew that reconciliation *now* is a dangerous doctrine, I affirm, *that it would be policy in the k— at this time, to repeal the acts for the sake of reinstating himself in the government of the provinces;* in order, that HE MAY ACCOMPLISH BY CRAFT AND SUBTILTY, IN THE LONG RUN, WHAT HE CANNOT DO BY FORCE AND VIOLENCE IN THE SHORT ONE. Reconciliation and ruin are nearly related.

Secondly, That as even the best terms, which we can expect to obtain, can amount to no more than a temporary expedient, or a kind of government by guardianship, which can last no longer than till the colonies come of age, so the general face and state of things, in the interim, will be unsettled and unpromising. Emigrants of property will not choose to come to a country whose form of government hangs but by a thread, and who is every day tottering on the brink of commotion and disturbance; and numbers of the present inhabitants would lay hold of the interval, to dispose of their effects, and quit the continent.

But the most powerful of all arguments, is, that nothing but independance, i. e. a continental form of government, can keep the peace of the continent and preserve it inviolate from civil wars. I dread the event of a reconciliation with Britain now, as it is more than probable, that it will be followed by a revolt somewhere or other, the consequences of which may be far more fatal than all the malice of Britain.

Thousands are already ruined by British barbarity; (thousands more will probably suffer the same fate.) Those men have other feelings than us who have nothing suffered. All they *now* possess is liberty, what they before enjoyed is sacrificed to its service, and having nothing more to lose, they disdain submission. Besides, the general temper of the colonies, towards a British government, will be like that of a youth, who is nearly out of his time, they will care very little about her. And a government which cannot preserve the peace, is no government at all, and in that case we pay our money for nothing; and pray what is it that Britain can do, whose power will be wholly on paper, should a civil tumult break out the very day after reconciliation? I have heard some men say, many of whom I believe spoke without thinking, that they dreaded an independance, fearing that it would produce civil wars. It is but seldom that our first thoughts are truly correct, and that is the case here; for there are ten times more to dread from a patched up connexion than from independance. I make the sufferers case my own, and I protest, that were I driven from house and home, my property destroyed, and my circumstances ruined, that as man, sensible of injuries, I could never relish the doctrine of reconciliation, or consider myself bound thereby.

The colonies have manifested such a spirit of good order and obedience to continental government, as is sufficient to make every reasonable person easy and happy on that head. No man can assign the least pretence for his fears, on any other grounds, that such as are truly childish and ridiculous, that one colony will be striving for superiority over another.

Where there are no distinctions there can be no superiority, perfect equality affords no temptation. The republics of Europe are all (and we may say always) in peace. Holland and

Swisserland are without wars, foreign or domestic: Monarchical governments, it is true, are never long at rest; the crown itself is a temptation to enterprizing ruffians at *home;* and that degree of pride and insolence ever attendant on regal authority, swells into a rupture with foreign powers, in instances, where a republican government, by being formed on more natural principles, would negociate the mistake.

If there is any true cause of fear respecting independance, it is because no plan is yet laid down. Men do not see their way out—Wherefore, as an opening into that business, I offer the following hints; at the same time modestly affirming, that I have no other opinion of them myself, than that they may be the means of giving rise to something better. Could the straggling thoughts of individuals be collected, they would frequently form materials for wise and able men to improve to useful matter.

LET the assemblies be annual, with a President only. The representation more equal. Their business wholly domestic, and subject to the authority of a Continental Congress.

Let each colony be divided into six, eight, or ten, convenient districts, each district to send a proper number of delegates to Congress, so that each colony send at least thirty. The whole number in Congress will be at least 390. Each Congress to sit and to choose a president by he following method. When the delegates are met, let a colony be taken from the whole thirteen colonies by lot, after which let the whole Congress choose (by ballot) a president from out of the delegates of *that* province. In the next Congress, let a colony be taken by lot from twelve only, omitting that colony from which the president was taken in the former Congress, and so proceeding on till the whole thirteen shall have had their proper rotation. And in order that nothing may pass into a law but what is satisfactorily just, not less than three fifths of the Congress to be called a majority.—He that will promote discord, under a government so equally formed as this, would join Lucifer in his revolt.

But as there is a peculiar delicacy, from whom, or in what manner, this business must first arise, and as it seems most agreeable and consistent, that it should come from some intermediate body between the governed and the governors, that is between the Congress and the people, let a CONTINENTAL CONFERENCE be held, in the following manner, and for the following purpose.

A committee of twenty-six members of Congress, viz. two for each colony. Two members for each house of assembly, or Provincial convention; and five representatives of the people at large, to be chosen in the capital city or town of each province, for, and in behalf of the whole province, by as many qualified voters as shall think proper to attend from all parts of the province for that purpose; or, if more convenient, the representatives may be chosen in two or three of the most populous parts thereof. In this conference, thus assembled, will be united, the two grand principles of business, *knowledge* and *power.* The members of Congress, Assemblies, or Conventions, by having had experience in national concerns, will be able and useful counsellors, and the whole, being impowered by the people will have a truly legal authority.

The conferring members being met, let their business be to frame a CONTINENTAL CHARTER, or Charter of the United Colonies; (answering to what is called the Magna Charta of England) fixing the number and manner of choosing members of Congress, members of Assembly, with their date of sitting, and drawing the line of business and jurisdiction between them: (Always remembering, that our strength is continental, not provincial:) Securing freedom and property to all men, and above all things the free exercise of religion, according to the dictates of conscience; with such other matter as is necessary for a charter to contain. Immediately after which, the said conference to dissolve, and the bodies which shall be chosen conformable to the said charter, to be the legislators and governors of this continent for the time being: Whose peace and happiness, may God preserve, Amen.

Should any body of men be hereafter delegated for this or some similar purpose, I offer them the following extracts from that wise observer on governments *Dragonetti.* 'The science' says he, 'of the politician 'consists in fixing the true point of happiness and freedom. 'Those men would deserve the gratitude of ages, who 'should discover a mode of government that contained the 'greatest sum of individual happiness, with the least 'national expence.

Dragonetti on Virtue and Rewards.'

But where says some is the King of America? I'll tell you Friend, he reigns above, and doth not make havock of mankind like the Royal — of Britain. Yet that we may not appear to be defective even in earthly honors, let a day be solemnly set apart for proclaiming the charter; let it be brought forth placed on the divine law, the word of God; let a crown be placed thereon, by which the world may know, that so far as we approve of monarchy, that in America THE LAW IS KING. For as in absolute governments the King is law, so in free countries the law *ought* to be King; and there ought to be no other. But lest any ill use should afterwards arise, let the crown at the conclusion of the ceremony be demolished, and scattered among the people whose right it is.

A government of our own is our natural right: And when a man seriously reflects on the precariousness of human affairs, he will become convinced, that it is infinitely wiser and safer, to form a constitution of our own in a cool deliberate manner, while we have it in our power, than to trust such an interesting event to time and chance. If we omit it now, some *Massenello may hereafter arise, who laying hold of popular disquietudes, may collect together the desperate and the discontented, and by assuming to themselves the powers of government, may sweep away the liberties of the continent like a deluge. Should the government of America return again into the hands of Britain, the tottering situation of things, will be a temptation for some desperate adventurer to try his fortune; and in such a case, what relief can Britain give? Ere she could hear the news the fatal business might be done, and ourselves suffering like the wretched Britons under the oppression of the Conqueror. Ye that oppose independance now, ye know not what ye do; ye are opening a door to eternal tyranny, by keeping vacant the seat of government. There are thousands and tens of thousands, who would think it glorious to expel from the continent, that barbarous and hellish power, which hath stirred up the Indians and Negroes to destroy us; the cruelty hath a double guilt, it is dealing brutally by us, and treacherously by them.

To talk of friendship with those in whom our reason forbids us to have faith, and our affections wounded through a thousand pores instruct us to detest, is madness and folly. Every day wears out the little remains of kindred between us and them, and can there be any reason to hope, that as the relationship expires, the affection will increase, or that we shall agree better, when we have ten times more and greater concerns to quarrel over than ever?

Ye that tell us of harmony and reconciliation, can ye restore to us the time that is past? Can ye give to prostitution its former innocence? Neither can ye reconcile Britain and America. The last cord now is broken, the people of England are presenting addresses against us. There are injuries which nature cannot forgive; she would cease to be nature if she did. As well can the lover forgive the ravisher of his mistress, as the continent forgive the murders of Britain. The Almighty hath implanted in us these inextinguishable feelings for good and wise purposes. They are the guardians of his image in our hearts. They distinguish us from the herd of common animals. The social compact would dissolve, and justice be extirpated the earth, or have only a casual existence were we callous to the touches of affection. The robber and the murderer, would often escape unpunished, did not the injuries which our tempers sustain, provoke us into justice.

O ye that love mankind! Ye that dare oppose, not only the tyranny, but the tyrant, stand

---

* Thomas Anello, otherwise Massenello, a fisherman of Naples, who after spiriting up his countrymen in the public market place, against the oppression of the Spaniards, to whom the place was then subject, prompted them to revolt, and in the space of a day became King.

forth! Every spot of the old world is over-run with oppression. Freedom hath been hunted round the globe. Asia, and Africa, have long expelled her.—Europe regards her like a stranger, and England hath given her warning to depart. O! receive the fugitive, and prepare in time an asylum for mankind.

Of the Present Ability of America, with Some Misellaneous Reflexions.

I have never met with a man, either in England or America, who hath not confessed his opinion, that a separation between the countries, would take place one time or other. And there is no instance in which we have shewn less judgment, than in endeavouring to describe, what we call, the ripeness or fitness of the Continent for independance.

As all men allow the measure, and vary only in their opinion of the time, let us, in order to remove mistakes, take a general survey of things and endeavour if possible, to find out the *very* time. But we need not go far, the inquiry ceases at once, for the *time hath found us.* The general concurrence, the glorious union of all things prove the fact.

It is not in numbers but in unity, that our great strength lies; yet our present numbers are sufficient to repel the force of all the world. The Continent hath, at this time, the largest body of armed and disciplined men of any power under Heaven; and is just arrived at that pitch of strength, in which no single colony is able to support itself, and the whole, when united can accomplish the matter, and either more, or, less than this, might be fatal in its effects. Our land force is already sufficient, and as to naval affairs, we cannot be insensible, that Britain would never suffer an American man of war to be built while the continent remained in her hands. Wherefore we should be no forwarder an hundred years hence in that branch, than we are now; but the truth is, we should be less so, because the timber of the country is every day diminishing, and that which will remain at last, will be far off and difficult to procure.

Were the continent crowded with inhabitants, her sufferings under the present circumstances would be intolerable. The more sea port towns we had, the more should we have both to defend and to loose. Our present numbers are so happily proportioned to our wants, that no man need be idle. The diminution of trade affords an army, and the necessities of an army create a new trade.

Debts we have none; and whatever we may contract on this account will serve as a glorious memento of our virtue. Can we but leave posterity with a settled form of government, an independant constitution of its own, the purchase at any price will be cheap. But to expend millions for the sake of getting a few vile acts repealed, and routing the present ministry only, is unworthy the charge, and is using posterity with the utmost cruelty; because it is leaving them the great work to do, and a debt upon their backs, from which they derive no advantage. Such a thought is unworthy a man of honor, and is the true characteristic of a narrow heart and a pedling politician.

The debt we may contract doth not deserve our regard if the work be but accomplished. No nation ought to be without a debt. A national debt is a national bond; and when it bears no interest, is in no case a grievance. Britain is oppressed with a debt of upwards of one hundred and forty millions sterling, for which she pays upwards of four millions interest. And as a compensation for her debt, she has a large navy; America is without a debt, and without a navy; yet for the twentieth part of the English national debt, could have a navy as large again. The navy of England is not worth, at this time, more than three millions and a half sterling.

The first and second editions of this pamphlet were published without the following calculations, which are now given as a proof that the above estimation of the navy is a just one. *See Entic's naval history, intro.* page 56.

The charge of building a ship of each rate, and furnishing her with masts, yards, sails and rigging, together with a proportion of eight months boatswain's and carpenter's sea-stores, as calculated by Mr Burchett, Secretary to the navy.

		£.
For a ship of 100 guns	——	35,553
90	— —	29,886
80	—— ——	23,638
70	——	17,785
60	— —	14,197
50	——	10,606
40	— —	7,558
30	—— ——	5,846
20	——	3,710

And from hence it is easy to sum up the value, or cost rather, of the whole British navy, which in the year 1757, when it was as its greatest glory consisted of the following ships and guns:

Ships.		Guns.		Cost of one.		Cost of all.
6	—	100	—	35,553 *l.*	—	213,318 *l.*
12	—	90	—	29,886	—	358,632
12	—	80	—	23,638	—	283,656
43	—	70	—	17,785	—	746,755
35	—	60	—	14,197	—	496,895
40	—	50	—	10,606	—	424,240
45	—	40	—	7,558	—	340,110
58	—	20	—	3,710	—	215,180
85 Sloops, bombs, and fireships, one with another, at				2,000	—	170,000
					Cost	3,266,786
Remains for guns,			——			233,214
					Total,	3,500,000

No country on the globe is so happily situated, so internally capable of raising a fleet as America. Tar, timber, iron, and cordage are her natural produce. We need go abroad for nothing. Whereas the Dutch, who make large profits by hiring out their ships of war to the Spaniards and Portuguese, are obliged to import most of the materials they use. We ought to view the building a fleet as an article of commerce, it being the natural manufactory of this country. It is the best money we can lay out. A navy when finished is worth more than it cost. And is that nice point in national policy, in which commerce and protection are united. Let us build; if we want them not, we can sell; and by that means replace our paper currency with ready gold and silver.

In point of manning a fleet, people in general run into great errors; it is not necessary that one-fourth part should be sailors. The Terrible privateer, Captain Death, stood the hottest engagement of any ship last war, yet had not twenty sailors on board, though her complement of men was upwards of two hundred. A few able and social sailors will soon instruct a sufficient number of active land-men in the common work of a ship. Wherefore, we never can be more capable to begin on maritime matters than now, while our timber is standing, our fisheries blocked up, and our sailors and shipwrights out of employ. Men of war of seventy and 80 guns were built forty years ago in New-England, and why not the same now? Ship-building is America's greatest pride, and in which, she will in time excel the whole world. The great empires of the east are mostly inland, and consequently excluded from the possibility of rivalling her. Africa is in a state of barbarism; and no power in Europe, hath either such an extent or coast, or such an internal supply of materials. Where nature hath given the one, she has withheld the other; to America only hath she been liberal of both. The vast empire of Russia is almost shut out from the sea; wherefore, her boundless forests, her tar, iron, and cordage are only articles of commerce.

In point of safety, ought we to be without a fleet? We are not the little people now, which we were sixty years ago; at that time we might have trusted our property in the streets, or fields rather; and slept securely without locks or bolts to our doors or windows. The case now is altered, and our methods of defence ought to improve with our increase of property. A common pirate, twelve months ago, might have come up the Delaware, and laid the city of Philadelphia under instant contribution, for what sum he pleased; and the same might have happened to other places. Nay, any daring fellow, in a brig of fourteen or sixteen guns, might have robbed the whole Continent, and carried off half a million of money. These are circumstances which demand our attention, and point out the necessity of naval protection.

Some, perhaps, will say, that after we have made it up with Britain, she will protect us. Can we be so unwise as to mean, that she shall keep a navy in our harbours for that purpose? Common sense will tell us, that the power which hath endeavoured to subdue us, is of all others the most improper to defend us. Conquest may be effected under the pretence of friendship; and ourselves, after a long and brave resistance, be at last cheated into slavery. And if her ships are not to be admitted into our harbours, I would ask, how is she to protect us? A navy three or four thousand miles off can be of little use, and on sudden emergencies, none at all. Wherefore, if we must hereafter protect ourselves, why not do it for ourselves? Why do it for another?

The English list of ships of war is long and formidable, but not a tenth part of them are at any one time fit for service, numbers of them not in being; yet their names are pompously continued in the list, if only a plank be left of the ship: and not a fifth part, of such as are fit for service, can be spared on any one station at one time. The East, and West Indies, Mediterranean, Africa, and other parts over which Britain extends her claim, make large demands upon her navy. From a mixture of prejudice and inattention, we have contracted a false notion respecting the navy of England, and have talked as if we should have the whole of it to encounter at once, and for that reason, supposed that we must have one as large; which not being instantly practicable, have been made use of by a set of disguised Tories to discourage our beginning thereon. Nothing can be farther from truth than this; for if America had only a twentieth part of the naval force of Britain, she would be by far an over match for her; because, as we neither have, nor claim any foreign dominion, our whole force would be employed on our own coast, where we should, in the long run, have two to one the advantage of those who had three or four thousand miles to sail over, before they could attack us, and the same distance to return in order to refit and recruit. And although Britain by her fleet, hath a check over our trade to Europe, we have as large a one over her trade to the West-Indies, which, by laying in the neighbourhood of the Continent, is entirely at its mercy.

Some method might be fallen on to keep up a naval force in time of peace, if we should not judge it necessary to support a constant navy. If premiums were to be given to merchants, to build and employ in their service, ships mounted with twenty, thirty, forty, or fifty guns, (the premiums to be in proportion to the loss of bulk to the merchants) fifty or sixty of those ships, with a few guard ships on constant duty, would keep up a sufficient navy, and that without burdening ourselves with the evil so loudly complained of in England, of suffering their fleet, in time of peace to lie rotting in the docks. To unite the sinews of commerce and defence is sound policy; for when our strength and our riches, play into each other's hand, we need fear no external enemy.

In almost every article of defence we abound. Hemp flourishes even to rankness, so that we need not want cordage. Our iron is superior to that of other countries. Our small arms equal to any in the world. Cannon we can cast at pleasure. Saltpetre and gunpowder we are every day producing. Our knowledge is hourly improving. Resolution is our inherent character, and courage hath never yet forsaken us. Wherefore, what is it that we want? Why is it that we hesitate? From Britain we can expect nothing but ruin. If she is once admitted to the government of America again, this Continent will not be worth living in. Jealousies will be always arising; insurrections will be constantly happening; and who will go forth to quell them? Who will venture his life to reduce his own countrymen to a foreign obedience? The difference between Pennsylvania and Connecticut, respecting some unlocated lands, shews the insignificance of a B—sh government, and fully proves, that nothing but Continental authority can regulate Continental matters.

Another reason why the present time is preferable to all others, is, that the fewer our numbers are, the more land there is yet unoccupied, which instead of being lavished by the k— on his worthless dependants, may be hereafter applied, not only to the discharge of the present debt, but to the constant support of government. No nation under heaven hath such an advantage as this.

The infant state of the Colonies, as it is called, so far from being against, is an argument in favor of independance. We are sufficiently numerous, and were we more so, we might be less united. It is a matter worthy of observation, that the more a country is peopled, the smaller their armies are. In military numbers, the ancients far exceeded the moderns: and the reason is evident, for trade being the consequence of population, men become too much absorbed thereby to attend to any thing else. Commerce diminishes the spirit, both of patriotism and military defence. And history sufficiently informs us, that the bravest atchievements were always accomplished in the non-age of a nation. With the increase of commerce, England hath lost its spirit. The city of London, notwithstanding its numbers, submits to continued insults with the patience of a coward. The more men have to lose, the less willing are they to venture. The rich are in general slaves to fear, and submit to courtly power with the trembling duplicity of a spaniel.

Youth is the seed time of good habits, as well in nations as in individuals. It might be difficult, if not impossible, to form the Continent into one government half a century hence. The vast variety of interests, occasioned by an increase of trade and population, would create confusion. Colony would be against colony. Each being able might scorn each other's assistance: and while the proud and foolish gloried in their little distinctions, the wise would lament that the union had not been formed before. Wherefore, the *present time* is the *true time* for establishing it. The intimacy which is contracted in infancy, and the friendship which is formed in misfortune, are, of all others, the most lasting and unalterable. Our present union is marked with both these characters: we are young, and we have been distressed; but our concord hath withstood our troubles, and fixes a memorable æra for posterity to glory in.

The present time, likewise, is that peculiar time, which never happens to a nation but once, *viz.* the time of forming itself into a government. Most nations have let slip the opportunity, and by that means have been compelled to receive laws from their conquerors, instead of making laws for themselves. First, they had a king, and then a form of government; whereas, the articles or charter of government, should be formed first, and men delegated to execute them afterward: but from the errors of other nations, let us learn wisdom, and lay hold of the present opportunity—*To begin government at the right end.*

When William the conqueror subdued England he gave them law at the point of the sword; and until we consent that the seat of government in America, be legally and authoritatively occupied, we shall be in danger of having it filled by some fortunate ruffian, who may treat us in the same manner, and then, where will be our freedom? where our property?

As to religion, I hold it to be the indispensible duty of all government, to protect all conscientious professors thereof, and I know of no other business which government hath to do therewith. Let a man throw aside that narrowness of soul, that selfishness of principle, which the niggards of all professions are so unwilling to part with, and he will be at once delivered of his fears on that head. Suspicion is the companion of mean souls, and the bane of all good society. For myself I fully and conscientiously believe, that it is the will of the Almighty, that there should be diversity of religious opinions among us: It affords a larger field for our christian kindness. Were we all of one way of thinking, our religious dispositions would want matter for probation; and on this liberal principle, I look on the various denominations among us, to be like children of the same family, differing only, in what is called their Christian names.

In page fifty-four,* I threw out a few thoughts on the propriety of a Continental Charter, (for I only presume to offer hints, not plans) and in this place, I take the liberty of rementioning the subject, by observing, that a charter is to be understood as a bond of solemn obligation, which the whole enters into, to support the right of every separate part, whether of religion, personal freedom, or property, A firm bargain and a right reckoning make long friends.

In a former page I likewise mentioned the necessity of a large and equal representation; and there is no political matter which more deserves our attention. A small number of electors, or a small number of representatives, are equally dangerous. But if the number of the representatives be not only small, but unequal, the danger is increased. As an instance of this, I mention the following; when the Associators petition was before the House of Assembly of Pennsylvania; twenty-eight members only were present, all the Bucks county members, being eight, voted against it, and had seven of the Chester members done the same, this whole province had been governed by two counties only, and this danger it is always exposed to. The unwarrantable stretch likewise, which that house made in their last sitting, to gain an undue authority over the Delegates of that province, ought to warn the people at large, how they trust power out of their own hands. A set of instructions for the Delegates were put together, which in point of sense and business would have dis-honored a school-boy, and after being approved by a *few*, a *very few* without doors, were carried into the House, and there passed *in behalf of the whole colony*; whereas, did the whole colony know, with what ill-will that House hath entered on some necessary public measures, they would not hesitate a moment to think them unworthy of such a trust.

Immediate necessity makes many things convenient, which if continued would grow into oppressions. Expedience and right are different things. When the calamities of America required a consultation, there was no method so ready, or at that time so proper, as to appoint persons from the several Houses of Assembly for that purpose and the wisdom with which they have proceeded hath preserved this continent from ruin. But as it is more than probable that we shall never be without a CONGRESS, every well wisher to good order, must own, that the mode for choosing members of that body, deserves consideration. And I put it as a question to those, who make a study of mankind, whether *representation and election* is not too great a power for one and the same body of men to possess? When we are planning for posterity, we ought to remember that virtue is not hereditary.

It is from our enemies that we often gain excellent maxims, and are frequently surprised into reason by their mistakes. Mr Cornwall (one of the Lords of the Treasury) treated the petition of the New-York Assembly with contempt, because *that* House, he said, consisted

*[Page 224 in this edition.]

but of twenty-six members, which trifling number, he argued, could not with decency be put for the whole. We thank him for his involuntary honesty*.

TO CONCLUDE, however strange it may appear to some, or however unwilling they may be to think so, matters not, but many strong and striking reasons may be given, to shew, that nothing can settle our affairs so expeditiously as an open and determined declaration for independance. Some of which are,

First.—It is the custom of nations, when any two are at war, for some other powers, not engaged in the quarrel, to step in as mediators, and bring about the preliminaries of a peace: but while America calls herself the subject of Great Britain, no power, however well disposed she may be, can offer her mediation. Wherefore, in our present state we may quarrel on for ever.

Secondly.—It is unreasonable to suppose, that France or Spain will give us any kind of assistance, if we mean only to make use of that assistance for the purpose of repairing the breach, and strengthening the connection between Britain and America; because, those powers would be sufferers by the consequences.

Thirdly.—While we profess ourselves the subjects of Britain, we must, in the eye of foreign nations, be considered as rebels. The precedent is somewhat dangerous to *their peace*, for men to be in arms under the name of subjects; we on the spot, can solve the paradox: but to unite resistance and subjection, requires an idea much too refined for common understanding.

Fourthly.—Were a manifesto to be published, and despatched to foreign courts, setting forth the miseries we have endured, and the peaceable methods we have ineffectually used for redress; declaring, at the same time, that not being able, any longer to live happily or safely under the cruel disposition of the B—sh court, we had been driven to the necessity of breaking off all connection with her; at the same time assuring all such courts of our peaceable disposition towards them, and of our desire of entering into trade with them: Such a memorial would produce more good effects to this Continent, than if a ship were freighted with petitions to Britain.

Under our present denomination of British subjects we can neither be received nor heard abroad: The custom of all courts is against us, and will be so, until, by an independance, we take rank with other nations.

These proceedings may at first appear strange and difficult; but, like all other steps which we have already passed over, will in a little time become familiar and agreeable; and, until an independance is declared, the Continent will feel itself like a man who continues putting off some unpleasant business from day to day, yet knows it must be done, hates to set about it, wishes it over, and is continually haunted with the thoughts of its necessity.

Appendix

SINCE the publication of the first edition of this pamphlet, or rather, on the same day on which it came out, the —'s Speech made its appearance in this city. Had the spirit of prophecy directed the birth of this production, it could not have brought it forth, at a more seasonable juncture, or a more necessary time. The bloody mindedness of the one, shew the necessity of pursuing the doctrine of the other. Men read by way of revenge. And the speech instead of terrifying, prepared a way for the manly principles of Independence.

Ceremony, and even, silence, from whatever motive they may arise, have a hurtful tendency, when they give the least degree of countenance to base and wicked performances; wherefore, if this maxim be admitted, it naturally follows, that the —'s speech, as being a piece of finished villainy, deserved, and still deserves, a general execration both by the Congress and the people. Yet as the domestic tranquility of a nation, depends greatly on the

---

* Those who would fully understand of what great consequence a large and equal representation is to a state, should read Burgh's political Disquisitions.

chastity of what may properly be called NATIONAL MATTERS, it is often better, to pass some things over in silent disdain, than to make use of such new methods of dislike, as might introduce the least innovation, on that guardian of our peace and safety. And perhaps, it is chiefly owing to this prudent delicacy, that the —'s Speech, hath not before now, suffered a public execution. The Speech if it may be called one, is nothing better than a wilful audacious libel against the truth, the common good, and the existence of mankind; and is a formal and pompous method of offering up human sacrifices to the pride of tyrants. But this general massacre of mankind, is one of the privileges, and the certain consequences of K—s; for as nature knows them *not*, they know *not her*, and although they are beings of our *own* creating, they know not *us*, and are become the gods of their creators. The speech hath one good quality, which is, that it is not calculated to deceive, neither can we, even if we would, be deceived by it. Brutality and tyranny appear on the face of it. It leaves us at no loss: And every line convinces, even in the moment of reading, that He, who hunts the woods for prey, the naked and untutored Indian, is less a Savage than the — of B—.

Sir J—n D—e, the putative father of a whining jesuitical piece, fallaciously called, '*The Address of the people of* ENGLAND *to the inhabitants of* AMERICA,' hath, perhaps from a vain supposition, that the people *here* were to be frightened at the pomp and description of a king, given, (though very unwisely on his part) the real character of the present one: 'But,' says this writer, 'if you are inclined to pay compliments to an administration, which we do not complain of,' (meaning the Marquis of Rockingham's at the repeal of the Stamp Act) 'it is very unfair in you to withold them from that prince, *by whose* NOD ALONE *they were permitted to do any thing*.' this is toryism with a witness! Here is idolatry even without a mask: And he who can calmly hear, and digest such doctrine, hath forfeited his claim to rationality—an apostate from the order of manhood; and ought to be considered—as one, who hath, not only given up the proper dignity of a man, but sunk himself beneath the rank of animals, and contemptibly crawl through the world like a worm.

However, it matters very little now, what the — of E— either says or does; he hath wickedly broken through every moral and human obligation, trampled nature and conscience beneath his feet; and by a steady and constitutional spirit of insolence and cruelty, procured for himself an universal hatred. It is *now* the interest of America to provide for herself. She hath already a large and young family, whom it is more her duty to take care of, than to be granting away her property, to support a power who is become a reproach to the names of men and christians—YE, whose office it is to watch over the morals of a nation, of whatsoever sect or denomination ye are of, as well as ye, who are more immediately the guardians of the public liberty, if ye wish to preserve your native country uncontaminated by European corruption, ye must in secret wish a separation—But leaving the moral part to private reflection, I shall chiefly confine my farther remarks to the following heads.

First, That it is the interest of America to be separated from Britain.

Secondly. Which is the easiest and most practicable plan, RECONCILIATION or INDEPENDANCE? with some occasional remarks.

In support of the first, I could, if I judged it proper, produce the opinion of some of the ablest and most experienced men on this continent; and whose sentiments, on that head, are not yet publickly known. It is in reality a self-evident position: For no nation in a state of foreign dependance, limited in its commerce, and cramped and fettered in its legislative powers, can ever arrive at any material eminence. America doth not yet know what opulence is; and although the progress which she hath made stands unparalleled in the history of other nations, it is but childhood, compared with what she would be capable of arriving at, had she, as she ought to have, the legislative powers in her own hands. England is, at this time, proudly coveting what would do her no good, were she to accomplish it; and the Continent hesitating on a matter, which will be her final ruin if neglected. It is the commerce and not the conquest of America, by which England is to be benefited, and that would in a great measure continue, were the countries as independant of each other as France and Spain; because in many articles, neither can go to a better market. But it is the independance of this country on Britain or any other, which is now the main and only object worthy of contention, and which, like all other truths discovered by necessity, will appear clearer and stronger every day.

First. Because it will come to that one time or other.

Secondly. Because the longer it is delayed the harder it will be to accomplish.

I have frequently amused myself both in public and private companies, with silently remarking the spacious errors of those who speak without reflecting. And among the many which I have heard, the following seems the most general, viz. that had this rupture happened forty or forty years hence, instead of *now*, the Continent would have been more able to have shaken off the dependance. To which I reply, that our military ability *at this time*, arises from the experience gained in the last war, and which in forty or fifty years time, would have been totally extinct. The Continent, would not, by that time, have had a General, or even a military officer left; and we, or those who may succeed us, would have been as ignorant of martial matters as the ancient Indians: And this single position, closely attended to, will unanswerably prove, that the present time is preferable to all others: The argument turns thus—at the conclusion of the last war, we had experience, but wanted numbers; and forty or fifty years hence, we should have numbers, without experience; wherefore, the proper point of time, must be some particular point between the two extremes, in which a sufficiency of the former remains, and a proper increase of the latter is obtained: And that point of time is the present time.

The reader will pardon this digression, as it does not properly come under the head I first set out with, and to which I again return by the following position, viz.

Should affairs be patched up with Britain, and she to remain the governing and sovereign power of America, (which as matters are now circumstanced, is giving up the point entirely) we shall deprive ourselves of the very means of sinking the debt we have or may contract. The value of the back lands which some of the provinces are clandestinely deprived of, by the unjust extention of the limits of Canada, valued only at five pounds sterling per hundred acres, amount to upwards of twenty-five millions, Pennsylvania currency; and the quit-rents at one penny sterling per acre, to two millions yearly.

It is by the sale of those lands that the debt may be sunk, without burthen to any, and the quit-rent reserved thereon, will always lessen, and in time, will wholly support the yearly expence of government. It matters not how long the debt is in paying, so that the lands when sold be applied to the discharge of it, and for the execution of which, the Congress for the time being, will be the continental trustees.

I proceed now to the second head, viz. Which is the earliest and most practicable plan, RECONCILIATION or INDEPENDANCE? with some occasional remarks.

He who takes nature for his guide is not easily beaten out of his argment, and on that ground, I answer *generally—That* INDEPENDANCE *being a* SINGLE SIMPLE LINE, *contained within ourselves; and reconciliation, a matter exceedingly perplexed and complicated, and in which, a treacherous capricious court is to interfere, gives the answer without a doubt.*

The present state of America is truly alarming to every man who is capable of reflexion. Without law, without government, without any other mode of power than what is founded on, and granted by courtesy. Held together by an unexampled concurrence of sentiment, which is nevertheless subject to change, and which every secret enemy is endeavouring to dissolve. Our present condition, is, Legislation without law; wisdom without a plan; a constitution without a name; and, what is strangely astonishing, perfect Independance contending for Dependance. The instance is without a precedent; the case never existed before; and who can tell what may be the event? The property of no man is secure in the present unbraced system of things. The mind of the multitude is left at random, and feeling no fixed object before them, they pursue such as fancy or opinion starts. Nothing is criminal; there is no such thing as treason; where-fore, every one thinks himself at liberty to act as he pleases. The Tories dared not to have assembled offensively, had they known that their lives, by that act were forfeited to the laws of the state. A line of distinction should be drawn, between English soldiers taken in battle, and inhabitants of America taken in arms. The first are prisoners, but the latter traitors. The one forfeits his liberty the other his head.

Notwithstanding our wisdom, there is a visible feebleness in some of our proceedings which gives encouragement to dissentions. The Continental belt is too loosely buckled. And if something is not done in time, it will be too late to do any thing, and we shall fall into a state, in which, neither *reconciliation* nor *independance* will be practicable. The — and his worthless adherents are got at their old game of dividing the Continent, and there are not wanting among us, Printers, who will be busy spreading specious falsehoods. The artful and hypocritical letter which appeared a few months ago in two of the New-York papers, and likewise in two others, is an evidence that there are men who want either judgement or honesty.

It is easy getting into holes and corners and talking of reconciliation: But do such men seriously consider, how difficult the task is, and how dangerous it may prove, should the Con-tinent divide thereon. Do they take within their view, all the various orders of men whose sit-uation and circumstances, as well as their own, are to be considered therein. Do they put themselves in the place of the sufferer whose *all* is *already* gone, and of the soldier, who hath quitted *all* for the defence of his country. If their ill-judged moderation be suited to their own private situations *only*, regardless of others, the event will convince them, that 'they are reck-oning without their Host.'

Put us, says some, on the footing we were on in sixty-three: To which I answer, the request is not *now* in the power of Britain to comply with, neither will she propose it; but if it were, and even should be granted, I ask, as a reasonable question, By what means is such a corrupt and faithless court to be kept to its engagements? Another parliament, nay, even the present, may hereafter repeal the obligation, on the pretence of its being violently obtained, or unwisely granted; and in that case, Where is our redress?—No going to law with nations; cannon are the barristers of crowns; and the sword, not of justice, but of war, decides the suit. To be on the footing of sixty-three, it is not sufficient, that the laws only be put on the same state, but, that our circumstances, likewise, be put on the same state; our burnt and destroyed towns repaired or built up, our private losses made good, our public debts (contracted for defence) discharged; otherwise, we shall be millions worse than we were at that enviable period. Such a request had it been complied with a year ago, would have won the heart and soul of the Continent—but now it is too late, 'The Rubicon is passed.'

Besides the taking up arms, merely to enforce the repeal of a pecuniary law, seems as unwarrantable by the divine law, and as repugnant to human feelings, as the taking up arms to enforce obedience thereto. The object, on either side, doth not justify the ways and means; for the lives of men are too valuable to be cast away on such trifles. It is the violence which is done and threatened to our persons; the destruction of our property by an armed force; the invasion of our country by fire and sword, which conscientiously qualifies the use of arms: And the instant, in which such a mode of defence became necessary, all subjection to Britain ought to have ceased; and the independancy of America should have been considered, as dat-ing its æra from, and published by, *the first musket that was fired against her.* This line is a line of consistency; neither drawn by caprice, nor extended by ambition; but produced by a chain of events, of which the colonies were not the authors.

I shall conclude these remarks, with the following timely and well intended hints, We ought to reflect, that there are three different ways by which an independancy may hereafter be effected; and that *one* of those *three*, will one day or other, be the fate of America, viz. By the legal voice of the people in Congress; by a military power; or by a mob: It may not always happen that our soldiers are citizens, and the multitude a body of reasonable men; virtue, as I have already remarked, is not hereditary, neither is it perpetual. Should an independancy be brought about by the first of those means, we have every opportunity and every encouragement before us, to form the noblest, purest constitution on the face of the earth. We have it in our power to begin the world over again. A situation, similar to the present, hath not happened since the days of Noah until now. The birth-day of a new world is at hand, and a race of men perhaps as numerous as all Europe contains, are to receive their portion of freedom from the event of a few months. The Reflexion is awful—and in this point of view, How trifling, how ridiculous, do the little, paltry cavellings, of a few weak or interested men appear, when weighed against the business of a world.

Should we neglect the present favorable and inviting period, and an independance be hereafter effected by any other means, we must charge the consequence to ourselves, or to those rather, whose narrow and prejudiced souls, are habitually opposing the measure, without either inquiring or reflecting. There are reasons to be given in support of Independance, which men should rather privately think of, than be publicly told of. We ought not now to be debating whether we shall be independant or not, but, anxious to accomplish it on a firm, secure, and honorable basis, and uneasy rather that it is not yet began upon. Every day convinces us of its necessity. Even the Tories (if such beings yet remain among us) should, of all men, be the most solicitous to promote it; for, as the appointment of committees at first, protected them from popular rage, so, a wise and well established form of government, will be the only certain means of continuing it securely to them. *Wherefore*, if they have not virtue enough to be WHIGS, they ought to have prudence enough to wish for Independance.

In short, Independance is the only BOND that can tye and keep us together. We shall then see our object, and our ears will be legally shut against the schemes of an intriguing, as well as a cruel enemy. We shall then too, be on a proper footing, to treat with Britain; for there is reason to conclude, that the pride of that court, will be less hurt by treating with the American states for terms of peace, than with those, whom she denominates, 'rebellious subjects,' for terms of accommodation. It is our delaying it that encourages her to hope for conquest, and our backwardness tends only to prolong the war. As we have, without any good effect therefrom, with-held our trade to obtain a redress of our grievances, let us *now* try the alternative, by *independantly* redressing them ourselves, and then offering to open the trade. The mercantile and reasonable part of England will be still with us; because, peace *with* trade, is preferable to war *without* it. And if this offer be not accepted, other courts may be applied to.

On these grounds I rest the matter. And as no offer hath yet been made to refute the doctrine contained in the former editions of this pamphlet, it is a negative proof, that either the doctrine cannot be refuted, or, that the part in favour of it are too numerous to be opposed. WHEREFORE, instead of gazing at each other with suspicious or doubtful curiosity, let each of us, hold out to his neighbour the hearty hand of friendship, and unite in drawing a line, which, like an act of oblivion, shall bury in forgetfulness every former dissention. Let the names of Whig and Tory be extinct; and let none other be heard among us, than those of *a good citizen, an open and resolute friend, and a virtuous supporter of the* RIGHTS *of* MANKIND *and of the* FREE AND INDEPENDANT STATES OF AMERICA.

*

To the Representatives of the Religious Society of the People called Quakers, or to so many of them as were concerned in publishing a late piece, entitled 'The Ancient Testimony and 'Principles of the people called Quakers renewed, with respect to 'the King and Government, and Touching the Commotions now 'prevailing in these and other parts of America, addressed to the 'people in general.'

THE Writer of this, is one of those few, who never dishonors religion either by ridiculing, or cavilling at any denomination whatsoever. To God, and not to man, are all men accountable on the score of religion. Wherefore, this epistle is not so properly addressed to you as a religious, but as a political body, dabbling in matters, which the professed Quietude of your Principles instruct you not to meddle with.

As you have, without proper authority for so doing, put yourselves in the place of the whole body of the Quakers, so, the writer of this, in order to be on an equal rank with yourselves, is under the necessity, of putting himself in the place of all those who approve the very writings and principles, against which your testimony is directed: And he hath chosen their singular situation, in order that you might discover in him, that presumption of character which you cannot see in yourselves. For neither he nor you have any claim or title to *Political Representation*.

When men have departed from the right way, it is no wonder that they stumble and fall. And it is evident from the manner in which ye have managed your testimony, that politics, (as a religious body of men) is not your proper Walk; for however well adapted it might appear to you, it is, nevertheless, a jumble of good and bad put unwisely together, and the conclusion drawn therefrom, both unnatural and unjust.

The two first pages, (and the whole doth not make four) we give you credit for, and expect the same civility from you, because the love and desire of peace is not confined to Quakerism, it is the *natural*, as well as the religious wish of all denominations of men. And on this ground, as men labouring to establish an Independant Constitution of our own, do we exceed all others in our hope, end, and aim. *Our plan is peace for ever.* We are tired of contention with Britain, and can see no real end to it but in a final separation. We act consistently, because for the sake of introducing an endless and uninterrupted peace, do we bear the evils and burthens of the present day. We are endeavouring, and will steadily continue to endeavor, to separate and dissolve a connexion which hath already filled our land with blood; and which, while the name of it remains, will be the fatal cause of future mischiefs to both countries.

We fight neither for revenge nor conquest; neither from pride nor passion; we are not insulting the world with our fleets and armies, nor ravaging the globe for plunder. Beneath the shade of our own vines are we attacked; in our own houses, and on our own lands, is the violence committed against us. We view our enemies in the characters of Highwaymen and Housebreakers, and having no defence for ourselves in the civil law, are obliged to punish them by the military one, and apply the sword, in the very case, where you have before now, applied the halter.—Perhaps we feel for the ruined and insulted sufferers in all and every part of the continent, and with a degree of tenderness which hath not yet made its way into some of your bosoms. But be ye sure that ye mistake not the cause and ground of your Testimony. Call not coldness of soul, religion; nor put the *Bigot* in the place of the *Christian*.

O ye partial ministers of your own acknowledged principles. If the bearing arms be sinful, the first going to war must be more so, by all the difference between wilful attack and unavoidable defence. Wherefore, if ye really preach from conscience, and mean not to make a political hobby-horse of your religion, convince the world thereof, by proclaiming your doctrine to our enemies, *for they likewise bear* ARMS. Give us proof of your sincerity by publishing it at St. James's, to the commanders in chief at Boston, to the Admirals and Captains who are piratically ravaging our coasts, and to all the murdering miscreants who are acting in authority under HIM whom ye profess to serve. Had ye the honest soul of *Barclay* ye would preach repentance to *your* king; Ye would tell the Royal — his sins, and warn him of eternal ruin. Ye would not spend your partial invectives against the injured and the insulted only, but like faithful ministers, would cry aloud and *spare none*. Say not that ye are persecuted, neither endeavour to make us the authors of that reproach, which, ye are bringing upon yourselves; for we testify unto all men, that we do not complain against you because ye are *Quakers*, but because ye pretend to *be* and are NOT Quakers.

Alas! it seems by the particular tendency of some part of your testimony, and other parts of your conduct, as if all sin was reduced to, and comprehended in *the act of bearing arms*, and that by the *people only*. Ye appear to us, to have mistaken party for conscience, because the general tenor of your actions wants uniformity: And it is exceedingly difficult to us to give credit to many of your pretended scruples; because we see them made by the same men, who, in the very instant that they are exclaiming against the mammon of this world, are nevertheless, hunting after it with a step as steady as Time, and an appetite as keen as Death.

The quotation which ye have made from Proverbs, in the third page of your testimony, that, 'when a man's ways please the Lord, he maketh even his enemies to be at peace with him'; is very unwisely chosen on your part; because it amounts to a proof, that the king's ways (whom ye are so desirous of supporting) do *not* please the Lord, otherwise, his reign would be in peace.

I now proceed to the latter part of your testimony, and that, for which all the foregoing seems only an introduction, viz.

'It hath ever been our judgment and principle, since we 'were called to profess the light of Christ Jesus, mani'fested in our consciences unto this day, that the setting up 'and putting down kings and governments, is God's 'peculiar prerogative; for causes best known to himself: 'And that it is not our business to have any hand or 'contrivance therein; nor to be busy bodies above our 'station, much less to plot and contrive the ruin, or over'turn any of them, but to pray for the king, and safety of 'our nation, and good of all men: That we may live a 'peaceable and quiet life, in all goodliness and honesty; *'under the government which God is pleased to set over us.'*—If these are *really* your principles why do ye not abide by them? Why do ye not leave that, which ye call God's Work, to be managed by himself? These very principles instruct you to wait with patience and humility, for the event of all public measures, and to receive *that event* as the divine will towards you. *Wherefore*, what occasion is there for your *political testimony* if you fully believe what it contains? And the very publishing it proves, that either, ye do not believe what ye profess, or have not virtue enough to practise what ye believe.

The principles of Quakerism have a direct tendency to make a man the quiet and inoffensive subject of any, and every government *which is set over him*. And if the setting up and putting down of kings and governments is God's peculiar prerogative, he most certainly will not be robbed thereof by us; wherefore, the principle itself leads you to approve of every thing, which ever happened, or may happen to kings as being his work, OLIVER CROMWELL

---

* 'Thou hast tasted of prosperity and adversity; thou knowest 'what it is to be banished thy native country, to be over-ruled as 'well as to rule, and set upon the throne; and being *oppressed* thou 'hast reason to know now *hateful* the *oppressor* is both to God and 'man: If after all these warnings and advertisements, thou dost not 'turn unto the Lord with all thy heart, but forget him who remem'bered thee in thy distress, and give up thyself to follow lust and 'vanity, surely great will be thy condemnation.—Against which 'snare, as well as the temptation of those who may or do feed thee, 'and prompt thee to evil, the most excellent and prevalent remedy 'will be, to apply thyself to that light of Christ which shineth in thy 'conscience and which neither can, nor will flatter thee, nor suffer 'thee to be at ease in thy sins.'

Barclay's Address to Charles II.

thanks you.—CHARLES, then, died not by the hands of man; and should the present Proud Imitator of him, come to the same untimely end, the writers and publishers of the testimony, are bound by the doctrine it contains, to applaud the fact. Kings are not taken away by miracles, neither are changes in governments brought about by any other means than such as are common and human; and such as we are now using. Even the dispersing of the Jews, though foretold by our Saviour, was effected by arms. Wherefore, as ye refuse to be the means on one side, ye ought not to be meddlers on the other; but to wait the issue in silence; and unless you can produce divine authority, to prove, that the Almighty who hath created and placed this *new* world, at the greatest distance it could possibly stand, east and west, from every part of the old, doth, nevertheless, disapprove of its being independant of the corrupt and abandoned court of B—n, unless I say, ye can show this, how can ye, on the ground of your principles, justify the exciting and stirring up of the people 'firmly to unite in the *abhorrence* of all such *writings*, and '*measures*, as evidence a desire and design to break off the '*happy* connexion we have hitherto enjoyed, with the 'kingdom of Great-Britain, and our just and necessary 'subordination to the king, and those who are lawfully 'placed in authority under him.' What a slap in the face is here! the men, who, in the very paragraph before, have quietly and passively resigned up the ordering, altering, and disposal of kings and governments, into the hands of God, are now recalling their principles, and putting in for a share of the business. Is it possible, that the conclusion, which is here justly quoted, can any ways follow from the doctrine laid down? The inconsistency is too glaring not to be seen; the absurdity too great not to be laughed at; and such as could only have been made by those, whose understandings were darkened by the narrow and crabby spirit of a despairing political party; for ye are not to be considered as the whole body of the Quakers but only as a factional and fractional part thereof.

Here ends the examination of your testimony; (which I call upon no man to abhor, as ye have done, but only to read and judge of fairly;) to which I subjoin the following remark; 'That the setting up and putting down of kings,' most certainly mean, the making him a king, who is yet not so, and the making him no king who is already one. And pray what hath this to do in the present case? We neither mean to *set up* nor to *put down*, neither to *make* nor to *unmake*, but to have nothing to *do* with them. Wherefore, your testimony in whatever light it is viewed serves only to dishonour your judgment, and for many other reasons had better have been let alone than published.

First. Because it tends to the decrease and reproach of all religion whatever, and is of the utmost danger to society, to make it a party in political disputes.

Secondly. Because it exhibits a body of men, numbers of whom disavow the publishing political testimonies, being concerned therein and approvers thereof.

Thirdly. Because it hath a tendency to undo that continental harmony and friendship which yourselves by your late liberal and charitable donations hath lent a hand to establish; and the preservation of which, is of the utmost consequence to us all.

And here without anger or resentment I bid you farewell. Sincerely wishing, that as men and christians, ye may always fully and uninterruptedly enjoy every civil and religious right; and be, in your turn, the means of securing it to others; but that the example which ye have unwisely set, of mingling religion with politics, *may be disavowed and reprabated by every inhabitant of* AMERICA.

FINIS

13

The Declaration of Independence

The Declaration of Independence

In Congress, July 4, 1776

The Unanimous Declaration of the thirteen United States of America,

When, in the course of human events, it becomes necessary for one people to dissolve the political bonds which have connected them with another, and to assume, among the powers of the earth, the separate and equal station to which the laws of nature and of nature's God entitle them, a decent respect to the opinions of mankind requires that they should declare the causes which impel them to the separation.

We hold these truths to be self-evident: That all men are created equal; that they are endowed by their Creator with certain unalienable rights; that among these are life, liberty, and the pursuit of happiness; that, to secure these rights, governments are instituted among men, deriving their just powers from the consent of the governed; that whenever any form of government becomes destructive of these ends, it is the right of the people to alter or to abolish it, and to institute new government, laying its foundation on such principles, and organizing its powers in such form, as to them shall seem most likely to effect their safety and happiness. Prudence, indeed, will dictate that governments long established should not be changed for light and transient causes; and accordingly all experience hath shown that mankind are more disposed to suffer, while evils are sufferable, than to right themselves by abolishing the forms to which they are accustomed. But when a long train of abuses and usurpations, pursuing invariably the same object, evinces a design to reduce them under absolute despotism, it is their right, it is their duty, to throw off such government, and to provide new guards for their future security. Such has been the patient sufferance of these colonies; and such is now the necessity which constrains them to alter their former systems of government. The history of the present King of Great Britain is a history of repeated injuries and usurpations, all having in direct object the establishment of an absolute tyranny over these states. To prove this, let facts be submitted to a candid world.

He has refused his assent to laws, the most wholesome and necessary for the public good.

He has forbidden his governors to pass laws of immediate and pressing importance, unless suspended in their operation till his assent should be obtained; and, when so suspended, he has utterly neglected to attend to them.

He has refused to pass other laws for the accommodation of large districts of people, unless those people would relinquish the right of representation in the legislature, a right inestimable to them, and formidable to tyrants only.

He has called together legislative bodies at places unusual, uncomfortable, and distant from the depository of their public records, for the sole purpose of fatiguing them into compliance with his measures.

He has dissolved representative houses repeatedly, for opposing, with manly firmness, his invasions on the rights of the people.

He has refused for a long time, after such dissolutions, to cause others to be elected; whereby the legislative powers, incapable of annihilation, have returned to the people at large for their exercise; the state remaining, in the mean time, exposed to all the dangers of invasions from without and convulsions within.

He has endeavored to prevent the population of these states; for that purpose obstructing the laws for naturalization of foreigners; refusing to pass others to encourage their migration hither, and raising the conditions of new appropriations of lands.

He has obstructed the administration of justice, by refusing his assent to laws for establishing judiciary powers.

He has made judges dependent on his will alone, for the tenure of their offices, and the amount and payment of their salaries.

He has erected a multitude of new offices, and sent hither swarms of officers to harass our people and eat out their substance.

He has kept among us, in times of peace, standing armies, without the consent of our legislatures.

He has affected to render the military independent of, and superior to, the civil power.

He has combined with others to subject us to a jurisdiction foreign to our constitution, and unacknowledged by our laws, giving his assent to their acts of pretended legislation:

For quartering large bodies of armed troops among us;

For protecting them, by a mock trial, from punishment for any murder which they should commit on the inhabitants of these states;

For cutting off our trade with all parts of the world;

For imposing taxes on us without our consent;

For depriving us, in many cases, of the benefits of trial by jury;

For transporting us beyond seas, to be tried for pretended offenses;

For abolishing the free system of English laws in a neighboring province, establishing therein an arbitrary government, and enlarging its boundaries, so as to render it at once an example and fit instrument for introducing the same absolute rule into these colonies;

For taking away our charters, abolishing our most valuable laws, and altering fundamentally the forms of our governments;

For suspending our own legislatures, and declaring themselves invested with power to legislate for us in all cases whatsoever.

He has abdicated government here, by declaring us out of his protection and waging war against us.

He has plundered our seas, ravaged our coasts, burned our towns, and destroyed the lives of our people.

He is at this time transporting large armies of foreign mercenaries to complete the works of death, desolation, and tyranny already begun with circumstances of cruelty and perfidy scarcely paralleled in the most barbarous ages, and totally unworthy the head of a civilized nation.

He has constrained our fellow-citizens, taken captive on the high seas, to bear arms against their country, to become the executioners of their friends and brethren, or to fall themselves by their hands.

He has excited domestic insurrection among us, and has endeavored to bring on the inhabitants of our frontiers the merciless Indian savages, whose known rule of warfare is an undistinguished destruction of all ages, sexes, and conditions.

In every stage of these oppressions we have petitioned for redress in the most humble terms; our repeated petitions have been answered only by repeated injury. A prince, whose character is thus marked by every act which may define a tyrant, is unfit to be the ruler of a free people.

Nor have we been wanting in our attentions to our British brethren. We have warned them, from time to time, of attempts by their legislature to extend an unwarrantable jurisdiction over us. We have reminded them of the circumstances of our emigration and settlement here. We have appealed to their native justice and magnanimity; and we have conjured them, by the ties of our common kindred, to disavow these usurpations, which would inevitably interrupt our connections and correspondence. They, too, have been deaf to the voice of justice and of consanguinity. We must, therefore, acquiesce in the necessity which denounces our separation, and hold them, as we hold the rest of mankind, enemies in war, in peace friends.

We, therefore, the representatives of the United States of America, in General Congress assembled, appealing to the Supreme Judge of the world for the rectitude of our intentions, do, in the name and by the authority of the good people of these colonies, solemnly publish and declare, that these United Colonies are, and of right ought to be, FREE AND INDEPENDENT STATES; that they are absolved from all allegiance to the British crown, and that all political connection between them and the state of Great Britain is, and ought to be, totally dissolved; and that, as free and independent states, they have full power to levy war, conclude peace, contract alliances, establish commerce, and do all other acts and things which independent states may of right do. And for the support of this declaration, with a firm reliance on the protection of Divine Providence, we mutually pledge to each other our lives, our fortunes, and our sacred honor.

JOHN HANCOCK

BUTTON GWINNETT
LYMAN HALL
GEO. WALTON
WM. HOOPER
JOSEPH HEWES
JOHN PENN
EDWARD RUTLEDGE
THOS. HEYWARD, JUNR.
THOMAS LYNCH, JUNR.
ARTHUR MIDDLETON
SAMUEL CHASE
WM. PACA
THOS. STONE
CHARLES CARROLL OF
    CARROLLTON
GEORGE WYTHE
RICHARD HENRY LEE
TH. JEFFERSON
BENJ. HARRISON

THOS. NELSON, JR.
FRANCIS LIGHTFOOT LEE
CARTER BRAXTON
ROBT. MORRIS
BENJAMIN RUSH
BENJA. FRANKLIN
JOHN MORTON
GEO. CLYMER
JAS. SMITH
GEO. TAYLOR
JAMES WILSON
GEO. ROSS
CAESAR RODNEY
GEO. READ
THO. M'KEAN
WM. FLOYD
PHIL. LIVINGSTON
FRANS. LEWIS
LEWIS MORRIS

RICHD. STOCKTON
JNO. WITHERSPOON
FRAS. HOPKINSON
JOHN HART
ABRA. CLARK
JOSIAH BARTLETT
WM. WHIPPLE
SAML. ADAMS
JOHN ADAMS
ROBT. TREAT PAINE
ELBRIDGE GERRY
STEP. HOPKINS
WILLIAM ELLERY
ROGER SHERMAN
SAM'EL HUNTINGTON
WM. WILLIAMS
OLIVER WOLCOTT
MATTHEW THORNTON

14

Selection from The Diary of Elizabeth Drinker

Elaine Forman Crane, ed.

Reprinted from *The Diary of Elizabeth Drinker: The Life Cycle of an Eighteenth-Century Woman*; © 1994 by Elaine Forman Crane. By permission of Northeastern University Press.

The Diary of Elizabeth Drinker: The Life Cycle of an Eighteenth-Century Woman

Elaine Forman Crane, ed.

3. Middle Age in Years of Crisis, 1776–1793

Two major public events bookend the central phase of Elizabeth Drinker's life: a violent War for Independence and a virulent yellow fever epidemic. Both episodes threatened the Drinkers' well-being, although neither claimed the life of immediate family members.

During the Revolution, zealous rebel leaders banished Henry Drinker and other fellow Quakers to Virginia, leaving Elizabeth and "Aunty" to cope as best they could. With the children's health at an all-time low and inflationary prices at an all-time high, servants running away and armies drawing near, Elizabeth found it difficult to maintain her equanimity in a war zone and occupied city. Nevertheless, she dealt with each potential disaster as it arose, and in the spring of 1778 she and several other wives journeyed to Lancaster to confront the radical leaders and plead for their husbands' release. Elizabeth's passion for privacy prevented her from revealing the intimate nature of Henry's homecoming, but the Drinker children doubtless welcomed their affectionate "Daddy" with great joy.

Ten years arter the war's end, yellow fever struck Philadelphia with such force that Drinker titled her journal for that half year the "Book of Mortality." The disease claimed at least 10 percent of the city's population of forty thousand, while seventeen thousand terrified citizens fled until the epidemic subsided—the Drinkers among them.

When Elizabeth Drinker's oldest daughter was nearly twenty, Elizabeth gave birth to her last child, a son who died in 1784 at age two and a half. Four years later, she became a grandmother. Entries for the 1780s are sparse, but despite their meagerness recount the progression of Sally's and Nancy's courtships. Suitors visited the two older Drinker sisters on a regular basis and spoke to Henry Drinker "on account of" his daughters. Sally and Jacob Downing married in 1787, and John Skyrin became Nancy's husband in 1791. Both Sally and Nancy named their first daughters after their mother, and by the end of 1793 Elizabeth Drinker was a grandmother three times over.

It is at the end of this chapter, when Drinker was in her late fifties, that now and then she found herself free from the continual beck and call of others—a circumstance reflected by the notation "no of our Children at home . . . myself alone."

1776

Janry. 25 ED—M.

Janry. 30. JD call'd before the Committee.[1]

[Feb.] 12 had a very bad Night, got up with my Forehead very much swel'd discover'd it to be St Antoys Fire[2]—sent for Dr. Redman—Jacob Shoemaker call'd, a man for poor Tax—H Sanson, Becky Waln, Rachel and Henry Drinker here to Day:—fine Weather.

15th. John Drinkers Store shet up by the Committe[3]—. HD. JD. return'd the 18th.

1776 March 2. HD. left home Sammy Sansom—call'd,[4] din'd A Benezet; Salors Wife, G. Churchman, call'd—Cheese from Burlington, fell on Sisters Toes—Ellection[5]—MS. out this Morning at R Stevensons &c.

May 8th. HD. this Morning Henry Mitchel and Jos James went to Atsion—the Town has been in Confusion this afternoon on account of an engagement between the Rowbuck Man of War and the Gondelows[6]—the 9 another fight below, without much Damage—HD, return'd the 10th—sixth Day.

July 16. Friends Meeting-House at Market-Street Corner broke open by the American Soldiers, where they have taken up their Abode.[7]

Augt. 13. third Day—HD. Nancy and, little Henry—in the Chaise, George James on Horseback.—left home for the Iron, Works—Nancy to be left at J. Hopkins Haddonfield—An Account this afternoon of 104 sail of Vessels having joyn'd Lord How[8]—Sister went this Afternoon with S Wharton to Visit Joseph Whartons Widdow HD return'd the 17th—Nancy stay'd at Haddonfield 'till the 21st—then came home, with Betsy Mickel and Hannah Hopkins, who, went back in the Afternoon.

Augt. 28. fourth day, Susanna Swett, left us, and went to House-Keeping near Cabble Lane.

1777

1777 Janry. 25. We had 5 American Soliders quartered upon us by order of the Counsel of Safty[1]—the Soliders named Adam Wise, Henry Feating, these two stay'd 2 or 3 days with us, the rest went of in an hour or two after they came.

March 5. Thos. Wharton, was proclaimed; Esqr., President of the Supreme Executive Council of the commonwealth of Pennsylvania,[2] Capt. General and Commander in Chief in and over the Same—some call him Governour.

March a Young Man of the Name of Molsworth was hang'd on the Commons by order of our present ruling Gentr'y.[3]

March Our little Henry was run over by a Horse in the Street, his Knee was Brused, but not meterially hurt.

April 12 Bill Gardiner push'd little Henry of a Carpenters Bench, in Carlilse's Shop, and hurt his arm very much—we sent for Docr. Redman who after examineing it, found the Bones were not broak but the Arm badly strain'd.

June the 5 an Officer with 2 Constables call'd on us for Blankets,[4] went away without any—as others had done 3 or 4 times before.

1777 July 4—the Town Illuminated and a great number of Windows Broke on the Anniversary of Independence and Freedom.[5]

Augt. 20 or 21 our dear little Henry was taken ill with a vomiting and disordred Bowels, occasion'd by eating watermellon too close to the Rine—he voided in the course of his Sickness, (which turnd out to be an inviterate Bloody and white Flux) 3 large Worms, and vomited one alive—for 12 Days he eat nothing—and is now Sepr. the 6 in a very poor way, reduced almost to a Skelaton with a constant fever hanging about him, tho' the disorder seems to be somewhat check'd, and he has an appetite in the Morning—he has taken 8 Clysters and many doses of Physick—his Body comes down and he is so weak that he cannot sit up alone.

Some day since the illness of our Child, we had a valuable pair of large End-Irons seazed and taken from us, by Philip Mause.

1777 Sepr. the 2 third Day—HD. having been, and continuing to be unwell, stay'd from meeting this morning. he went towards Noon into the front Parlor to copy the Monthly meeting minuits—the Book on the Desk—and the Desk unlock'd, when Wm. Bradford; one [Bluser] and Ervin, entred, offering a Parole for him to sign—which was refus'd. they then seiz'd on the Book and took several papers out of the Desk and carried them off; intimating their design of calling the next morning at 9 o'clock; and desireing HD to stay at home for that time, which as he was unwell, was necessary; they according calld the 4th, in the morning and took my Henry to the [Massons] lodge—in an illegeal, unpredesented manner—where are several, other Friends with some of other proswasions, made prisoners;—Isreal Pemberton, John Hunt, James Pemberton, John Pemberton, Henry Drinker, Saml. Pleasants, Thos. Fisher, Saml. Fisher, Thos. Gillpin, Edward Penington; Thos. Wharton, Charles Jervis, Ellijah Brown, Thos. Afflick, Phineas Bond, Wm. Pike, Mires Fisher, Charles Eddy, Wm. Smith, Broker—Wm. D Smith, Thos. Comb, &c I went this Even'g to see my HD. where I mett with the Wives & Children of our dear Friends and other visitors in great numbers—upwards of 20 of our Friends call'd to see us this Day—my little Henry very low and Feverish.

8th. my little Henry very unwell this Day could not go to see his Daddy untill the Afternoon, who I found with the other Friends pritty-well. they have sent several Remonsterances to the Congress and Consel.[6] . . .

9 . . . My self Sally and little Molly went this Afternoon to the Lodge, during my stay there, word was brought from the Conscil that their Banishment was concluded to be on the Morrow,[7] the Waggons were preparing to carry them off—I came home in great distress. . . .

11 The sending off our Friends is put of till 3 this Afternoon, they find it difficult to procure Waggons and Men—My Henry Breakfasted with us; then went to the Lodge. I went there about 10 o'clock, R Drinker with me, I step'd over to S. Pleasants, then back to the Lodge HD—not there when I return'd—the Town is in great Confusion at present a great fireing heard below[8] it is supos'd the Armies are Engag'd, 'tis also reported that several Men of War are [ ] up the River—Jos. Howell, R. Scattergood, S Swett, R Drinker &c here this Morning.—Some time after dinner Harry came in a hurry for his Master Horse for a Servent to ride, informing me that the waggons were waiting at the Lodge to take our dear Friends away. I quickly went there; and as quickly came away finding great a number of People there but few women, bid my dearest Husband farewell, and went in great distress to James Pembertons, Sally with me. . . .

12 . . . this has been a day of Great Confusion to many in this City; which I have in great measure been kept out of by my constant attension on my sick Child. part of Washingtons

Army has been routed, and have been seen coming into Town in Great Numbers; the perticulars of the Battle, I have not attended to, the slain is said to be very numerous.—hundreds of their muskets laying in the road, which those that made off have thrown down . . . the Wounded have been brought in this Afternoon, to what amount I have not learnt. . . .

13 Wrote to HD. by Isaac Zane Junr.—our Child appears to be better.—they have Chang'd the place of Banishment of our Friends to Winchester, as I understand. . . .

15, I have heard no News from abroad this Morning but Carriages constantly passing with the Inhabitants going away . . . last night I heard of several Friends having lost their Horses, taken from the Stables,—for which reason I ordred our Horse, and Cow to be put into the Washhouse, where they at present remain—several of my Sisters in Affliction, have this Day received Letters from their Husbands, I make no doubt but I should also have had one, but for some good reason. . . .

16 I read a letter this Morning from my HD to JD—our Stable seller was last Night broak open, and several of Jos. Scotts Barrels of Flour stolen—I rote to my HD. this Morning by Nisbet—our child seem'd better, this forenoon, but more unwell towards Evening a great weight upon my Spirits most of this day: Nancy and little Molly both complaining—this is a Sickly season, many taken down with Fevers. May it please kind Providence to preserve my dearest Husband. . . .

19 Jenny awoke us this Morning about 7 o'clock, with the News that the English were near; we find that most of our Neighbors and almost all the Town have been up since one in the Morning The account is that the British Army cross'd the [S]weeds-Foard last night, and are now on their way heather; Congress, Counsil &c are flown,[9] Boats, Carriages, and foot Padds going off all Night; Town in great Confusion. . . .

20 The Town has been very quiet all this day, I believe; it is said that Washingtons Army has cross'd the Foard and are at present on this side—some expect a battle hourly; as the English are on the opposite side—I received a Letter this Evening from my dear, a long letter . . . all the boats, Ferry boats excepted, are put away—and the Shiping all ordred up the River, the next tide, on pain of being burnt, should G. Howes Vesels approach. . . .

21. . . . Sammy read aloud my dear Henrys long letter of the 17th Instant and was very much affected thereby.—after which we had a setting togeather, and Sammy was led to speak comfort to us. . . . this Evening our little sick Son received a letter from his dear Father, which is well worth the store he sits by it, he has ordred it to be put in his Pocket-Book Wile he larns to read writing. . . .

22 . . . Nanny Oat call'd to day, to demand her freedom dues,[10] and was very impertinent and Saucy. . . .

23. . . . Our dear Child has walk'd several times across the Room, with Jennys help to day. those men that collected Blankets &c in our Ward, were this Afternoon at each of our Neighbours, but did not call on us. it is reported and gains credit, that the English have actually cross'd Schuylkill and are on their way towards us,[11]—I received two letters after meeting from my dear Husband; which at the same time that they made my Heart ake, gave me comfort. . . .

24. . . . the Sign (Over tbe Way) of G. Washingn. taken down this Afternoon—talk of the City being set on fire—Joseph Ingel, call'd to pay, for 2 or 3 Tonns of Hay, but as I had not my Husbands papers, could not receive the money. . . .

25 . . . most of our warm people are gone of, tho there are many continue here that I should not have expected. Things seem very quiate and still, and if we come of so, we shall have great

cause of thankfullness—should any be so wicked as to attempt fireing the Town, Rain which seems to be coming on, may Providentially, prevent it—a great number of the lower sort of the People are gone out to them. . . .

26 Well, here are the English in earnest,[12] about 2 or 3000, came in, through second street, without oppossition or interruption, no plundering on the one side or the other, what a satisfaction would it be to our dear Absent Friends, could they but be inform'd of it. . . .

27 About 9 o'clock this Morning the Province, and Delaware Frigets, with several Gondelows came up the River, with a design to fire on the[13] they were attac'd by a Battry[14] which the English have errected[15] the engagement lasted about half an hour when many shots were exchang'd; one House struck, but not much damaged; no body, that I have heard, hurt on shore. . . .

28 First Day: Sister and the Children went to Meeting this Morning this is our Yearly Meeting, and many more Friends in Town than could have been expected, the Situation of things considred. . . . I hear this Evening that they are building Battrys on the Jersey shore, opposite Arch and Market Streets. The Ameriacans I mean.

29 . . . a Number of the [Citysans] taken up, and imprison'd.[16] . . .

[Oct.] 6 . . . The heaviest fireing that I think I ever heard, was this Evening, for upwards of two hours, thought to be the English troops, engag'd with the Mud-Island Battry,[17]—an Officer call'd this Afternoon to ask if we could take in a Sick or Wounded Captain; I put him off by saying that as my Husband was from me, I should be pleas'd if he could provide some other convenient place, he hop'd no offence, and departed. . . . two of the Presbytearan Meeting Houses, are made Hospitals of, for the Wounded Soliders, of which there are a great Number.

8 . . . Sister with Billy and the two Hannah Catherels & M Pleasants, went to the Play-House, the State-House, and one of the Presbytearn's Meeting Houses, to see the Wounded Soliders.

9 fireing last night, and heavey fireing this Morning from 5 o'clock 'till between 6 & 7, it was the Frigit and Gondelows, playing upon the English, who were errecting a Battry on, or near the Banks of Schuylkill,[18] one Englishman slain and two Wounded, 2 Horses kill'd—Jenney and Harry went this Afternoon in the rain, to the Play House &c. with a Jugg of Wine-Whey and a Tea-Kittle of Coffee, for the Wounded Men. . . .

12 First Day: We were awaked this Morning at about 2 o'clock, by H Drinker, knocking at my Chamber door, and asking for a light, as there was a cry of fire, it prov'd to be a Stable at the upper end of Second Street, where 3 or 4 Horses were burnt to Death. . . .

16 . . . 5 Weeks this day since my dearest Henry left us, the thoughts of the approaching cold season, and the uncertainty when we shall meet again, is at times hard to bare; yet at other times I am sustain'd with a Lively hope, that I shall see that time, and prehaps it may be sooner than we seem to expect. . . .

our little Molly went alone when she was, between 14 and 15 months—May—1775.[19]

little Molly began to Chatter, when she was about 20 months old.

Novr. the 20. 1775. second Day, I began to Wean my little Molly—she is very good natur'd, and bares it well, tho' she seems in trouble about it—20 months old and upwards, when she was Wean'd.

18th. . . . The Troops at Germington are coming within 2 or 3 miles of this City to encamp—provisions are so scarce with us now, that Jenney gave 2/6 p. lb. for mutton this Morning—

The people round the Country dose not come near us with any thing, what little butter is brought is 7/6—The fleet not yet up, nor likely to be soon, I [fear]. Jenney and Billy, went this Afternoon, with coffee and whey for the Soliders.

20th. Chalkley James Breakfasted with us—Billy began a quarters Schooling, whole Days, at Joseph Yerkess the first of his going since his dear Daddy left us, and for a long time before, Henry went this morning for the first time since his illness, little Molly also, I put to school with Henry, to H. Catheral, the first of her ever going unless on a visit . . . if things dont change 'eer long, we shall be in poor plight, everything scarce and dear, and nothing suffer'd to be brought in to us. . . .

23 this day will be remember'd by many; the 2500 Hessions who cross'd the River the day before yesterday, were last Night driven back 2 or 3 times, in endeavouring to Storm the fort on Red Bank,[20] 200 slain and great Numbers wounded, the fireing this Morning seem'd to be incesant, from the Battry, the Gondelows, and the Augustia Man of War, of 64 Guns, she took fire, and after burning near 2 hours, blew up . . . The Hessians and other of the British Troops are encamp'd in the Jersyes, this Night, we can see their fiers for a considerable distance along the shore. . . .

25 . . . An Officer call'd to Day to know if Genl. Grant could have quarters with us; I told him as my Husband was from me, and a Number of Young Children round me, I should be glad to be excus'd—he reply'd, as I desir'd it, it should be so. . . .

Novr 1. . . . a poor Solider was hang'd this Afternoon on the Common, for striking his Officer; The Hessians go on plundring at a great rate, such things as, Wood, Potatoes, Turnips &c—Provisions are scarce among us. . . .

5 . . . A Solider came to demand Blankets, which I did not in any wise agree to, notwithstanding my refusial he went up stairs and took one, and with seeming good Nature beg'd I would excuse his borrowing it, as it was G. Howes orders. . . .

8 We had a Stove put up in the back Parlor; this Morning Wood is so very scarce, that unless thing mend there is no likelyhood of a Supply, and we have no more then 4 or 5 Cord, in the Celler. . . .

11 . . . it is two months this day since my dear Henry left me, and I have not heard directly from himself since he left Reading, except one Letter from Carlile to J Drinker. . . .

12 great part of last Night and most of this day at times, we have heard the Cannon below; Mud-Island Battry not yet taken.—they say that it is reported in the Country that 5/- is given here for a Rat: it is bad enough indeed, but far from being so, I trust it will not. . . .

15 . . . I had the great Satisfaction this Evening of receiving two Letters from my dearest Henry, the first I have received from him since he left Reading, he mentions 2 others, wrote before these, that have not come to hand, several since I doubt not,—if I can judge of my dear by his Letters, he is in good Spirits, which thought is pleasing to me. . . .

18 . . . Nanny Oat came while I was out, to ask pardon for her former conduct, which has been vastly impudent. . . .

19 . . . G. Corn Walace left this City the Day before Yesterday at 2 o'clock in the Morning with 3000 men.[21] . . .

20 . . . Wm. Jackson and Benjn. Mason call'd and brought me two letters from my dear Henry—dated the 1 and 11th. Instant—tis a great comfort to know that he was so lately well—they left others litters for us poor women. . . .

22 . . . one thousand Men, attack'd the Picquet guard this Morning about 11 o'clock, they drove them off, when some took Shelter in J. Dickensons House, and other Houses thereabouts, the English immeadatly set fire to said Houses and burnt them to the Ground,—the burning those Houses tis said is a premeditated thing, as they serve for skulking places; and much anoy the Guards. . . .

23 . . . William Jackson proposes, paying a visit to Winchester next month, he leaves Town tomorrow Morning I gave him this Afternoon £61. 11. 3. Continenl. Cury.—and 2 pair of worsted Stockings for my dear Henry. . . .

24 Wm. Jackson call'd this Morning to let me know, that he was not free to take the continental money with him, I must therefore seek another conveyance. . . . the poor people have been allow'd for some time past to go to Frankford Mill, and other Mills that way, for Flour, Abraham Carlile who gives them passes, has his Door very much crouded every morning. . . .

25 . . . We were very much affrighted this Evening before 9 o'clock, Jenney happen'd to go into the Yard, where she saw a Man with Ann—she came in and wisper'd to Sister, who immediately went out, and discoverd a Young Officer with Ann coming out from the little House, Sister held the Candle up to his Face and ask'd him who he was, his answer was whats that to you, the Gate was lock'd and he followd Ann and Sister into the Kitchen, where he swore he had mistaken the House, but we could not get him out,—Chalkley James who happen'd to be here, came into the Kitchen and ask'd him what busyness he had there he dam'd him and ask'd whats that to you, shook his Sword, which he held in his Hand and seem'd to threaten, when Chalkly with great resolution twisted it out of his Hands and Collor'd him—Sister took the Sword from Chalkly and lock'd it up in the draw in the parlor, all his outcry was for his Sword, and swore he would not stir a foot untill he had it. I then sent in for Josa. Howel, when he declar'd that he knew we were peaceable people, and that he gave up his Sword on that account out of pure good natur'd, which he had said to us before. he told Chalkley in the Kitchen that he would be the death of him tomorrow,—Josa. got him to the door, and then gave him his Sword, expecting he would go of, but he continu'd swaring there, where Josa. left him and went to call Abel James; in the mean time the impudent Fellow came in again swareing in the entry with the Sword in his hand. Sister had lock'd Chalkly up in the Middle Room, and we shut ourselves in the parlor, where he knock'd, and swore desireing entrance, our poor dear Children was never so frightend, to have an enrag'd, drunken Man, as I believe he was, with a Sword in his Hand swareing about the House, after going to or 3 times up and down the Entry, desireing we would let him in to drink a Glass of Wine with us—he went to the end of the Alley—when Harry lock'd the Front door on him, he knock and desir'd to come in, when J. Howel, and A James whome Josa. had been for, came to him, they had some talk with him, and he went off as I supose'd—I had all the back doors boulted, the Gate and[22] Front door lock'd, when in about 10 minuts after Harry came out of the Kitchen, and told us he was there I then lock'd the parlor door, and would not let Chalkley go out, Harry run into Howels for Josa. who did not come 'till some time after the Fellow was gone, and Ann with him he came over the Fence, and they went out the same way; 'tis not near one in the Morning and I have not yet recoverd the fright,—Ann call'd him Capt. Tape, or John Tape. . . .

28 sent Harry to M. Hains, with 9 Bottls of Sider for Thos. Gothrope, Sally Logan spent this Afternoon with us—Nr. Waln and myself took a walk this Morning to see Polly Brown, we call'd at Sally Lewiss at Eliza Armitts, came home to dinner, I took a walk in the Afternoon to Uncle Jerviss came home to Coffee. . . .

[Dec.] 2 . . . Our Saucy Ann came while I was at meeting desereing to know what I would take for hir time and she would bring the money in a minuit Sister told her she did not know, but that she heard me talk of puting her in the Work House, she reply'd if you talk so, you shall neither have me nor the Money, Sister then ordred her to come again at 12 o'clock, but she has not been since. . . .

4th. . . . I went with Nancy to H Pembertons, to carry my Letter &c to T Lightfoot, I sent lap'd up in[23] HDs Shirts £61. 11. 3 in Conti. . . .

7 . . . I drank Tea at Neigr. Howell's who was last Night Robed of a Bed from one of their 2 [p'r.] Stairs Chambers, the Fellow being surpris'd got of, without the rest of the Bootey which he had lay'd out of the Drawers ready to take away—there has been many roberies committed lately in Town. . . . we have but [9] Persons in Family this Winter we have not had less then 13 or 14 for many years past.

11 Catty Howell came in to show us, some things that she had purchas'd, Sister went out upon the Strength of it and bought a piece of Lennen &c, its a long time since we have done such a thing—goods will soon be plenty in all probobility, nothing but hard mony will pass; 40 or 50 Sail below with goods . . . Isaac Zane call'd here this Morning to see us. he is going to Winchester to see our dear Frds. he takes no letters, I sent by him a under Jacket and pair Gloves, and lap a letter up in them from Billy. . . . these are sad times for Thiveing & plundering, tis hardly safe to leave the door open a minuet. . . .

13 . . . John Gillingham was lately stop'd in the Street, after Night, and his Watch taken from him. we daily hear of enormitys of one kind or other, being committed by those from whome, we ought to find protection.

18th. . . . An Officer who calls himself Major Carmon or Carmant, call'd this Afternoon, to look for Quarters for some Oiffecer of distinction, I plead off, he would have preswaded me that it was a necessary prtiction at these times to have one in the House; said I must consider of it, that he would call in a day or two, I desir'd to be excus'd, and after some more talk we parted, he behaved with much politeness, which has not been the case at many other places; they have been very rude and impudent at some houses,—I wish I may come of so; but at same time fear we must have some with us, as many Friends have them, and it seems likely to be a general thing. This has been a trying day to my Spirits—E. Edwards had a number of Letters stolen from him, which was for us poor destitutes. I have just finish'd a Letter to my dearest tis now past 12 o'clock, and Watch has put me in a flutter, by his violent barking, as if some one was in the Alley, which I believe was the case—hail since Night.

22 . . . Thos. Pleasants and Ezekill Edwards, came this Morning stayed [above] an hour, conferms the Sorrowful account that my dear is to be sent further from me. . . . the night before, I heard somebody down stairs, upon enquiry found it was Harry who had been up; every[24] noise now seems alarming, that happns in the Night.

23 . . . the Soliders Wife who lives in our House in Water Street came to me this Morning to inform that some were taring down the Shed &c. Sister went down after Meeting and desir'd 'em to desist, they said they would not for it was a Rebels House, she assur'd 'em it was not, and after more talk, proms'd if she would let 'em take the large Gate they would desist, she agreed thereto, and came [away]. . . .

29 very clear and cold, Cramond here this morning, we have at last agreed on his coming to take up his aboud with us, I hope it will be no great inconvenience, tho I have many fears, he came again in the Afternoon with a servant to look at the Stable, stay'd Tea, Thos. Masterman also, C. West and Reba. Waln here, the Troops are all return'd from Forageing—tis now 19 days since the date of my dears last letter; my mind is greatly troubled.

31st. J. Cramond who is now become one of our Family, appears to be a thoughtful sober young man, his Servant also sober and orderly; which is a great favour to us. . . .

1778

[Jan.] 4 First Day: I forgot to mention Yesterday, that I had a conferance with the officer who took away Ann; I stop'd him as he past the door—and after desiring him to stand still, 'till a noisey Waggon which was going by had past, (as he said he was in a hurry) I then adress'd him; if thee has no sense of Religion or Virtue, I should think that what you Soliders call Honor would have dictated to thee what was thy duty after thy behaviour some time ago in this House, who me! Yes I know thee very well, I have as yet been carefull of exposeing thee, but if thee dont very soon pay me for my Servants time; as there is officers quarterd among Numbers of my acquaintance, I will tell all I meet with, he stutter'd and said I han't got your Servant, I dont care who has her, it was thee that stole her; well said he a little impudently if you'l come up to my quarters up Town, I told him If he did not bring the Mony or send it soon he should hear further from me; well, well well said he and away he went seemingly confus'd. . . .

10th. I went this Morning to H Pembertons found her smoking her pipe with 2 officers one of 'em is quarter'd there, after they were gone Hannah and myself were comparing notes, and reading our last Letters, we were neither of us so happy in our expectations as some others— I left Hannah near 1 o'clock and as I was returning I mett Susanna Jones and Richd. Wister talking together. I stop'd and heard him tell that he had just parted with Billy Lewis who told him that Andrew Roberson was come from Lancaster this Morning, and assures him that our dear Friends were actualy discharg'd—I have heard the same report several times since Morning and I know not what ails me that I cannot believe such good news—so much has however laid hold on me that I shall be grievously disoponined if it should fall through, a Letter from my dearest confirming it would rejoyce my Heart. . . .

19 This Morning our officer mov'd his lodgings from the bleu Chamber to the little front parlor, so that he has the two front Parlors, a Chamber up two pair of stairs for his bagage, and the Stable wholly to himself, besides the use of the Kitchen, his Camp Bed is put up. . . .

[Feb.] 3 . . . I took a walk this Morning to see Hannah Pemberton; stay'd till near dinner time mett Sucky Jones in my return who told me her mammy wanted to speak with me; she intends to go before long to G. Washington, on account of her Son; she hinted as if she would like me to go with her,—which I think will not suit me; tho' my Heart is full of some such thing, but I dont see the way clear yet. . . .

5 . . . our dear Friends are to be continu'd at Winchester 'till further orders, and that the Congress have again offred them their Liberty on taken a Test,[1] which is all sham, as they know they will not do it. . . .

7 . . . I have been much distress'd at times, when I have thought of my being still here, when prehaps it might be in my power to do something for my dear Husband; which uneasyness I communicated to MP. who then show'd me a Letter from her Father; intimating something of the kind to her Mother and herself—I hope it will please the Lord to direct us to do that which is right. it would be a tryal on us to leave our Young Familys at this time, but that I belive, if we could conclude on the matter we should leave, and trust in kind providence—it is now between 11 and 12 o'clock, and our Officer has company at Supper with him; the late hours he keeps is the greatest inconvenienc we have as yet suffer'd by having him in the House.

11 dull rainy weather and a great thaw, very foggy—several in our Family and in many other Families have got Colds—Robt. Waln and J. Drinker call'd—J.C—drank Tea with us—5 month this day since my dear Henry left me.

17 . . . our major had 8 or 10 to dine with him, they broke up in good time, but he's gone of with them and when he'l return I know not, I gave him some hints 2 or 3 days ago, and he has behav'd better since. . . .

27 . . . going into the Kitchen to night, I met Heritta the Hession Stable—Boy, in the dark, I ran against him and hurt my Eye, my Cheek is much swell'd and painful. . . .

28th. Rain and Snow all day, clear to night the Blood has settled round my eye, and it looks very ugly, my Cheek much swell'd. Capt. Harper Son from Alexandria call'd this Morning said that he was at Lancaster 3 Week ago, and heard then that the Friends at Winchester were well—Becky Jones call'd this Evening—a Number of the Troops are gone in to the Jersys, tis said that the Rebels there, are burning and destroying all before them.

March 1st. First Day: Sally and Billy went to meeting this morning—Nancy still unwell with a cough and pain in her side, little Henrys face swell'd with the Tooth Ach—Abey Parish, S. Swett, Jos. Scott, Danl. Drinker, Anthony Benezet and the Major drank tea with us—Sarah Fisher and her Son James here this Evening—a fine clear day, Moonlight evening a Snow Storm Since night—a number of prisoners brought from the Jersys to day, 18 or 20 they say.

14 I took a walk to H Pembertons before dinner, Our Major din'd with us to day, for the first time; Saml. Emlen, Chackly James, call'd—Molly Pleasants junr. spent this Afternoon with our Children—I call'd while I was out this Morning at O. Jones, Susy full of the notion of going to Congress, gave me several broad hints, which I could not give into. . . .

25th. Dr. Parke call'd this Morning he seems to think it somthing strange that we have no letters—Caty Howel here after dinner—Phebe Pemberton, M Pleasants, R. Drinker, Hannah Drinker, Polly Drinker and Sally Pleasants, drank tea with us—PP. and MP. came to consult me about drawing up something to present to those who shall acknowledge our dear Friends as their prisoners; I had sometime ago mentiond JD. as a sutiable person to assist us in such an undertaking—We went in the Evening to JDs.—he appeard rather reluctant, but tis likely he will think of it—our intention is, tho we do not yet say so, to take it ourselves, 2 or 4 of us—when we can hear how, matters stand with our dear absent Friends . . . our Hay is out, and I beleive I must sell our poor Cow. . . .

28 . . . Mary Eddy and her Son George came this Evening to consult about sending provisions &c to our Friends John Drinker went to O Joness to consult him on the matter—Our Children are all through Mercy in good Health at present—but little Henry swallow'd a pin Yesterday which adds something to my uneasyness.

31 . . . M. Pleasants sent for me before dinner, I went, she showd me a paper drawn up to send or take to Congress, she had drawn it up, and her Mammy had added somthing to it, Nics. Waln had also made out one for us, which was not approv'd—in the Afternoon O. Jones came to desire I would meet the rest of the Women concern'd at 5 o'clock at M. Pembertons, which I did, they were all there except R. Hunt, Hetty Fisher and T. Afflicks wife—Josa. Fisher O. Jones, A. Benezet, J Drinker and Nichs. Waln, were also there—Nicholas read the Address, and the Women all sign'd it—it is partly concluded that Sush. Jones, P. Pemberton M. Pleasants and E. Drinker is to take it—I wish I felt better both in Body and mind for such an undertaking. . . .

April 1st. . . . I sent Billy for John Burket, who came, I demanded the Money which has been so long owing, he promis'd to pay it next seventh Day—I took a walk to look for Shoes, but did not succeed—Sally Logan drank Tea with us, I step'd down to Abels to ask for J. Burkets account he say'd it was not in the Company Books—Sally Zane Becky Jones call'd—I had promisd to meet R Pemberton and M. Pleasants at H. Pembertons this Afternoon, but Sister declin'd taking the weight of the Family on her during my absence, which prevented my meeting them according to Promise, and distresses me much. . . .

2d. . . . I went to Rachl. Hunts who I found writeing to her Husband, she had flattred herself from some of the letters that he was getting better and that his disorder had terminated in a Rumitisam. when I came from their door, Patty Hudson call'd me, and told me, that John Hunt was no more—that the Account of his death was just come to Town, I then went to M. Pleasants, who had sent for me, to meet at O. Jones, to settle matters for our journey; I had reason to think that it would be no easy matter to get of, therefore say'd but little about it, but concluded in my mind, that to the care of kind providence, and my dear Sister I must leave my dear little ones, and the Family generaly—it will be a great care on Sister, as we have an Officer and his Servants in the House, but I hope she will be strengthen'd. . . .

3 . . . O. Jones call'd to tell me, that Isreal Morris had been to offer himself to accompany us on our journey, Owen seems inclin'd to favour his applycation, for my part I do not approve of it, however we are to meet at 3 o'clock at O Jones to consider of it. Johnny Drinker call'd—and Josey Fox—I went accordingly after dinner to O. Jones mett the other women there—it was agreed to except of Isreal if he would come into our terms, he was sent for, and came, said that he had had a concern for some time to go to Congress on account of our dear Friends and that he look'd upon this as the proper time, we told him that, we could not agree to unite with him in the busyness, we spoke very freely to him, that is MP and myself—that if he could be willing to escort us, and advise when we ask'd it, we should be oblig'd to him for his company, to which he consented—but hinted that he thought it necessary that he should appear with us before Congress, which we by no means consented to—and he acques'd—I hope that his going with us, may turn out more satisfactory then it at present appears to me. . . .

5 . . . I left home after dinner went to M. Pleasants where were a great Number of our Friends mett to take leave of us, We took Coach at about 2 o'clock, S. Jones, Phebe Pemberton, M. Pleasants and Myself—with 4 Horses, and two Negros who rode Postilion. . . .

6 left J. Roberts after Breakfast, and proceeded on to the American Picket guard, who upon hearing that we were going to head-quarters, sent 2 or 3 to guard us further on to another guard where Colll. Smith gave us a pass for Head Quarters where we arriv'd at about 1/2 past one;[2] requested an audience with the General—set with his Wife, (a sociable pretty kind of Woman) untill he came in; a number of Officers there, who were very complient, Tench Tillman, among the rest, it was not long before GW. came and discoarsd with us freely, but not so long as we could have wish'd, as dinner was serv'd in, to which he had invited us, there was 15 of the Officers besides the General and his Wife, Gen. Green, and G. Lee we had an eligant dinner, which was soon over; when we went out with the General Wife up to her Chamber, and saw no more of him,—he told us, he could do nothing in our busyness further than granting us a pass to Lancaster, which he did. . . .

9 . . . We set of after on our journey till we arrived at James Gibbons, where we din'd, his Wife is lyeing in, while we were at Dinner JG. and several other Friends came there from meeting . . . here we understood that our Friends were by an order of Council to be brought to Shipensburgh, and there discharged. . . .

10 we arose by times this Morning dress'd ourselves, and after Breakfast, went to Lancaster, several Friends went with us, I. Morris also . . . we were this day waited upon by T Matlack, who undertook to advise us, and prehaps with sincerety—we paid a visit to 3 of the Councilors . . . after the council had set some time, T.M. came for our address, which was sign'd by all the Women concern'd, he say'd he would come for us, when it was proper, but after above an hour waiting, he inform'd us, that our presence was not necessary, and put us of in that

way. We sent for Capt Lang who is one of the Guards that is to conduct our Friends to Lancaster, or any place nearer home, that we shall chuse, Shippensburg was to have been the place, but to oblidge us it was chang'd. . . .

14 went to Town before Breakfast, to look for Jos. Reed, who we mett with at one Attleys, with Thos. McClane and 2 others,—he conferm'd the account of the death of J Hunt &c— we discourc'd with 'em for some time, they appear kind, but I fear tis from teeth outwards . . . in our journey to day we found the roads so bad, that we walk'd part of the way, and clim'd 3 fences, to get clear of the mud, Isreal has enough to do with us.

19 First Day: . . . We went to Lampater meeting and return'd to A Gibbons to Dinner, after which set of for James Webbs. . . .

20 fine clear windy weather such as will dry the roads,—Billy Lewis, Owen Biddle, T. Afflick, and Danl. la Fever came this Morning to JWs After dinner John Musser return'd from Winchester with Letters from our Husbands, giving us expectation that they would be with us, here, the latter end of this Week. . . .

21st. . . . we took a walk to Thos. Whartons, had a conference with him, not altogeather agreeable . . . din'd at Danl. Whitelocks . . . while we were at Whitelocks, T. Matlack came with our dear Friends sham release, and said that was the conclusion Council had come to, (of this order we each took a Copy).

24 James Gibbon call'd this Morning—we went to Town after Breakfast, drove directly to the Coart-House, where we mett with George Brion and Tim Matlack, going up to Council, we presented our second address, (requesting a pass for our Friends) as the first was not answ'd to our minds, GB. said that all was granted that could be, he would not feed us up with false Hopes, we desir'd they would reconcider the matter, which he did not refuse. . . . TM came from Council, saying he was sorry to tell us, that nothing further could be done, towards granting our request. . . .

25 I can recollect nothing of the occurances of this Morning—about one o'clock my Henry arrived at J Webbs, just time enough to dine with us; all the rest of our Friends came this day to Lancaster; HD. much hartier than I expected, he look fat and well.

27 . . . our Friends apply'd to Counsil this Morning for a proper discharge, which was not comply'd with, but a permission to pass to Potts-Grove, in the County of Philada. was all they would grant. . . .

30 After Breakfast we had a setting at John Robertss John Pemberton, speak to the Family, we set of after 8 o'clock, and traveled on without interuption, were wellcom'd by many before, and on our entrence into the City—where we arrived about 11 o'clock, and round our dear Families all well, for which favour and Blessing and the restoration of my dear Husband, may I ever be thankful—We have had such a number of our Friends to see us this day, that it is not in my power to enumerate them.

[May] 4 Went to Quarterly Meeting, call'd at Uncle Jerviss and at several Shops,—went out again after dinner to Shops, bought merceals Quilting[3] for Peticoats for the Girls—Campany here this Afternoon.

23 little Molly sick and feverish, her Mouth sore this evening I am fearful of an Aptha Fever which she was bad with while I was absent last Month at Lancaster—the Army tis thought are going in reality to leave us—to evacuate the City[4]—some hope tis not the case, tho' things look like it—many of the Inhabitants are preparing to go with them,—Robt. Waln, Reba.

Waln, Richd. Waln, Abel James, Saml. Emlen, Reba. Jones, Molly Pleasants, Sucky Jones, here to day—fine weather.

30 Henry better, Molly still poorly—tis reported that the British Army are giving the remainder of their Stores of Wood and Hay, to the poor, which seems to prove they intend 'eer long to leave us. . . .

[June] 9 The Major left us at a little past one, this Morning, was very dull at takeing leave,—Sister and self stay'd at the Door untill the two Regiments, (which quarter'd up Town) had past—J.C. bid us adieu as they went by—and we saw no more of them, a fine moon-light Morning. . . .

14 First Day: . . . I wrote a few lines to J.C—in order to send by Christopher, who expects to go early in the Morning. . . .

18 last night it was said there was 9000 of the British Troops left in Town 11,000 in the Jersyes: this Morning when we arose, there was not one Red-Coat to be seen in Town; and the encampment, in the Jersys vanish'd[5]—Colll. Gordon and some others, had not been gone a quarter of an hour before the American Light-Horse enter'd the City, not many of them, they were in and out all day A Bell-Man went about this evening by order of one Coll. Morgan, to desire the Inhabatants, to stay within doors after Night, that if any were found in the street by the Partrole, they should be punish'd—the few that came in today, had drawn Swords in their Hands, Gallop'd about the Streets in a great hurry, many were much frightn'd at their appearance. . . .

22 dull rainy weather an account of a Battle in the Jersyes, the perticulars not known, no great one—the Store and Shop-keepers, orderd to shut up, and render an account of their goods[6]—Reb Waln and John Drinker call'd.

30 very warm, Robt. Valentine, Becky Jones, Sus. Lightfoot, Saml. Trimble, Sam Emlen, here before meeting. I went to meeting—SL—and S Emlen appeard in testimony, James Bringhurst and Hannah Peters were married—Lawrance and Dolly Salter din'd with us—Nany Oat here this Evening—gave her part of her Cloths—she is to call again for the rest,—Reba. Waln, and Capt. Spains widdow call'd—it is said that there has been a great Battle on First day last,[7] that great numbers of the British Troops were slain and taken, a young Solider that is disorderd in his senses, went up our Stairs this Afternoon, we had no man, in the House: Isaac Catheral came in and went up after him, found him in the entry up two pair Stairs, saying his prayers—he readly came down with him. Jenny up stairs all day, unwel with the Collick.

[July] 2 The Congress came in to day: fireing of Cannon on the Occasion—rain and thunder this Afternoon. . . .

4 . . . A great fuss this evening it being the Annavarsary of Independance, fireing of Guns, Sky Rockets &c—Candles were too scarce and dear, for Alluminations, which prehaps sav'd some of our Windows—A very high Head dress was exhibited thro the Streets, this Afternoon on a very dirty Woman with a mob after her, with Drums &c. by way of rediculing that very foolish fashon—a Number of Prisoners brought in to day: moderate weather.

8 very warm to day: Sally very ill, with the vomitting and Flux, above 30 stools to day, she took a vomitt this Morning and I gave her a Clyster this Evening she has a great deal of fever. . . .

10 exceeding Hott my poor Child very ill, continues sick at her Stomach, and frequently vomitts quantities of dark green Boile, which as the Weather is so warm, gives me great

uneasyness, she took to day 3 Spoonfulls of Castor-Oyl—one of which she vomitted up, it work'd her twice, she is very low this evening—I have not had my cloaths of since 3d. day Night, and tis now sixth day: little Henry and Billy are both unwell,—Lidia Stretch was bury'd Yesterday, she dy'd of the Flux. . . .

15 Sally took a dose of Rheubarb to day she is still very bad. . . .

20 Sally more unwel to day, with greater pain in her Bowels, and vomitting—many call'd to day.

24 Sally more unwell than Yesterday—John Drinker, E. Clever, Saml. Esborn, Docr, Nancy Waln, Nics. Waln, C. West and Wife, Peggy Hart, call'd—Robt Willis din'd—John Balderston call'd—HD. went to the Burial of the Widdow Gordon, who dyed of the Flux, we did not hear of her sickness or death, untill invited to the Funeral—warmer to day, our little Molly went to meeting for the first time, with her Sister Nancy, to the Childrens meeting, which is held at the Bank.[8]

27 Sallys disorder continues bad, tho' something abated. . . .

Augt. the 1st. The weather very warm,—our Neighbor Abraham Carlile was yesterday taken up, and put into Jail,[9]—several here to day—Sally, not much change in her.

3d. Sally much better, she eat her Breakfast down Stairs . . . Ann Carlile call'd, she had been to the Old Prison to visit her Husband.

5 HD. at meeting most of the day: Thos. Watson Breakfasted with us—Jas. Logan at Tea—Wm. Smith, Warner Mifflin, John Drinker call'd—weather more moderate—Sally very weak, her Bowels still disordred—S Swett and Doctor call'd—tis a month tomorrow since Sally was taken ill.

19 many Showers to day with Sun-shine—HD. went over the river, with T. Masterman and I. Catheral this Morning—I spent the Afternoon at Neigr. Walns—Parson Murry, Wm. Smith, Polly Gordon, Lawrence Salter &c call'd—Sister went down to Abels, for a peice Linnen and some Tea—Janney Boon left us this Evening and went to stay a week with her Cozin Jacob James's wife, and then to go to her aunts at Willmington who has wrote for her—she has been with us, 3 years and near nine months—Molly Lahew came to day in her place—a great noise last night or the night before at the Bakers, William crying Murder, while the Baker beat him.

21st. . . . Billy help'd to carry Wm. Norton junrs. Child to the Grave this Afternoon, Becky Shoemaker was again ordred out of her House last night.[10] . . .

25 . . . Joseph Yerkes was had up yesterday before a Magistrate for keeping School;[11] his School is stop'd, and our Son Billy is at a loss for employment, as well as many others, in consiquence of it; sad doings. . . .

[Sept.] 7 . . . Reba. Waln, myself, my two Sons, Bob Waln, Neddy Howell and Anna Waln, took a walk this Afternoon to Springsbury to see the Aloes Tree[12]—stop'd in our return at Bush-Hill and walk'd in the Garden,—came home after Sun Set, very much tired. . . .

10 I spent this Afternoon at Sarah Lewiss Sally Logan drank tea with Sister,—we are reduc'd from 5 Servants to one, which wont do long, if we can help ourselves, it is the case with many at present, good Servants are hard to be had, such a time was never known here I beleive in that respect. . . .

23 Stay'd within all day—cloudy with rain—Robt. and Reba. Waln, Wm. Smith, call'd—HDs allmost all night awake with the toothach—which he had had greatest part of the day.

24th HD. sent for Fredrick this Morning and had a tooth drawn which requir'd a strong pull; Neigr. Waln spent this Afternoon helping me to cut out a Satten Cloak for Nancy. . . .

25 Abraham Carliles tryal came on to day and is not yet concluded, are at a loss to judge how it will go with him. . . . James and Joseph Stear, from Virginia, came this evening to stay with us during the Meeting—HD. at home all day, a pain in his Face. . . .

26 . . . I went in this Afternoon to visit our depress'd Neigr Carlile, whose Husband they have brought in gilty of High treason, tho' it is hop'd by many that he will not suffer what some others fear he will. . . .

28 . . . we have nine with us this Night a great number in and out to day—I went to meeting Morning and Afternoon. . . .

[Oct.] 2. . . . John Roberts is brought in gilty at which some are surpris'd as they did not expect it, who had attended the court. . . .

3 . . . the womans meeting is concluded,[13] the Men have adjornd till second day—which I never rembember to have been the case before. . . .

6. . . . HD gone to Meeting, he is with Robt. Waln, to attend the marriage of Dl. Mifflin and Debby Howel, Sally Zane, and 5 or 6 of the wedding Guest came here after meeting,—we were just inform'd that our poor neighbor Abram. Carlile, has received sentence of Death. . . .

7 . . . fine weather, [sev]eral Friends went today to visit Neigr. Carlile in the Dungon.

1778 Octor. 17. . . . John Robarts Miller condem'd to die,[14] Shocking doings!—I spent this Afternoon with R Waln &c at Neigr. Howels, on a visit to Debbe Mifflin.

Novr. 3 This afternoon I spent at Catre. Greenleafs, the Evening at S. Pleasants, where I was inform'd that preparations were making this evening for the Execution of our poor Friends tomorrow Morning—Notwithstanding the many pertitions that have been sent in, and the Personal appearance of the Destress'd wives and Children; before the Council,—much Compy. here. I am still of the mind, that they will not be permitted, to carry this matter to the last extremity. . . .

Novr. 4. they have actually put to Death; Hang'd on the Commons, John Robarts and Am. Carlisle this moring or about noon[15]—an awful Solemn day it has been—I went this evening with my HD. to Neigr. Carliles, the Body is brought home, and laid out—looks placid & Serene—no marks of agony or distortion, the poor afflicted widdows, are wonderfully upheld and suported, under their very great tryal—they have many simpathizing Friends.

19th. . . . I had a fainty fitt this morning which lasted 10 or 15 minits, and continued poorly afterwards.

Novr. 25. . . . I have been all day very ill with the sick headach. . . .

26. . . . Sister has been very busy all day in the Kitchen with Isaac Catheral and Molly, cutting up and salting a Beef—rendring the Tallow, [&c.]

29 First Day: . . . our maid Molly went out last night, and has not return'd yet, so that we have had none other than little John Pope, to assist us this day; we were never so situate before; tis the case with many others. . . .

Dec. 18 Josa. and Caty Howel and their Daughr. Caty spent the Afternoon with us—HD— received a Letter from J. Cramound—our new Maid has had a visitor all day and has invited hir to lodge with her, without asking leave, times are much changed, and Maids are become mistresses.

Decr. 19. P. Pemberton and M. Pleasants sent Molly this Morning to ask my Company with them, to see G. Washingtons Wife:[16] which visit I declin'd.

Notes

1776

[1] John Drinker and Thomas and Samuel Fisher were called before the Committee of Observation and Inspection for the City and Liberties of Philadelphia on Jan. 30 for refusing to accept continental bills of credit. On Feb. 5 the committee issued a statement condemning them as enemies of their country; the three men neither denied nor appealed the charges. The committee also precluded them from all trade with the inhabitants of the colonies (*Pa. Journal*, Feb. 7, 1776; *Col. Recs. Pa.* 10:486–87).

[2] St. Anthony's Fire, also known as erysipelas or the rose, is characterized by red swellings on the face, the legs and face, or the whole body, and is caused by streptococci. Some forms attacked women in childbearing years (Buchan, *Domestic Medicine* [1799], 188–91; Gould, *Dictionary of Medicine*).

[3] On Feb. 15 the Council of Safety directed the Philadelphia Committee of Observation and Inspection to seize all of John Drinker's books and papers and deposit them in a locked and sealed chest or trunk in his ship and to lock up the windows and doors of his stores and warehouses and nail them shut (*Col. Recs. Pa.* 10:486–87).

[4] The name "Tommy James" crossed out.

[5] A by-election for the seat held by Benjamin Franklin in the Pennsylvania Assembly. Franklin, who had never occupied the seat, resigned on Feb. 27, giving Philadelphians an opportunity to elect another representative to the assembly in his place (Ryerson, *Revolution Is Now Begun*, 159).

[6] On this day two heavily armed British ships, the *Roebuck*, a man of war, and the *Liverpool*, a frigate, were prevented from sailing up the Delaware River to Pennsylvania by colonial forces stationed at Fort Island. Fire was exchanged, but neither side was able to inflict much damage (*Pa. Gaz.*, May 15, 1776).

[7] In 1776 several Friends' meetinghouses in the Philadelphia area were seized by local agencies and used to quarter soldiers and for other military purposes. American soldiers en route to New York from Maryland broke into the Market Street Meetinghouse and seized it for their quarters. After discussions, the officer in charge allowed Quakers to use the meetinghouse for worship, but the army retained possession of it (Mekeel, *Relation of the Quakers*, 167).

[8] Philadelphia newspapers reported various sightings of British and Hessian ships off Perth Amboy, Bermuda, and Annapolis in August. Some of these vessels carried the remnants of the British army following its defeat in Charleston and survivors of Lord Dunmore's raids in Virginia. The ships were bound for New York to join Gen. William Howe and Adm. Richard Howe, whose forces had arrived in New York in July (*Pa. Journal*, Aug. 14, 1776; *Pa. Gaz.*, Aug. 14, 1776; Boatner, *American Revolution*, 472–73, 798).

1777

[1] In the winter of 1777 various colonial militia groups passed through Philadelphia. As the available barracks in Philadelphia filled up, the Council of Safety on Jan. 22 directed the barracks master to quarter the militia in the private homes of people who had not joined the campaign against England. Quarters in private homes were to be based on the size of the house and the convenience of the families (*Pa. Ev. Post*, Jan. 25, 1777).

[2] On Mar. 5 Thomas Wharton, Jr., was elected president of Pennsylvania's Supreme Executive Council. Wharton, a merchant, was a younger cousin of Thomas Wharton, Sr., a Quaker who was later exiled to Virginia with HD. Wharton Jr., unlike his cousin, was an enthusiastic supporter of the rebel cause and had been the head of Pennsylvania's Council of Safety, which ran the state from July 1776 until this date, when the new constitution went into effect. The 1776 state constitution created a plural executive branch called the Supreme Executive Council, made up of one representative of the city of Philadelphia and one representative from each county. The representatives served three-year terms. At the head of the council was a president elected jointly by the council and the assembly. Wharton was its first elected president, and George Bryan was the vice president. Five members of the Supreme Executive Council constituted a quorum (*DAB*, s.v. "Thomas Wharton"; Robert L. Brunhouse, *The Counter-Revolution in Pennsylvania 1776–1790* [1942; 2d ptg. Harrisburg, Pa.: The Pennsylvania Historical and Museum Commission, 1971], 10–15, 22).

[3] James Molesworth was hanged following his conviction for treasonable practices against the state. He was accused of trying to hire men to pilot the British fleet up the Delaware River (Reed, *Joseph Reed*, 2:30–34; Marshall, *Diary Extracts*, 118, 201; *Pa. Archives*, ser. 1, 5:270–82; *Col. Recs. Pa.*, 11:197).

[4] On Mar. 12 the Continental Congress had passed a resolution requesting the states to supply blankets to colonial troops. The commissary of the continental army then requested the Pennsylvania Board of War to supply blankets, and on May 2 Pennsylvania's ruling body, the Supreme Executive Council, authorized the requisition of 4,000 blankets from the state, 667 of them to come from the city of Philadelphia, where twelve men, including the artist Charles Willson Peale, were appointed commissioners to collect the blankets. Quakers were apparently singled out for this and other requisitions (*Pa. Ev. Post*, Mar. 13, 1777; *Pa. Gaz.*, May 7, 1777; Mekeel, *Relation of the Quakers*, 167).

[5] Quaker shopkeepers refused to close their shops on holidays like July 4 or days appointed to celebrate American military victories. In retaliation, Philadelphians broke the windows of many Quaker shops (Mekeel, *Relation of Quakers*, 167).

[6] The prisoners sent remonstrances to the Continental Congress and the Supreme Executive Council, protesting that their arrests were arbitrary, unjust, and illegal. Upon receiving the remonstrances, the Continental Congress requested that the Supreme Executive Council give the prisoners a hearing. The council replied that in the press of events it had no time to listen to the prisoners' claims. The Congress then disassociated itself from the matter by saying that the prisoners were subject to the Supreme Executive Council and that Congress would not interfere in the state's internal affairs (remonstrances are printed in Gilpin, *Exiles in Virginia*, 77–85, 96–97, 103–4; Congress's response is in *JCC*, 8:718–19, 722–23; for a discussion of the confusion regarding authority over the prisoners, see Thayer, *Israel Pemberton*, 225–31).

[7] The instructions of the Continental Congress to Pennsylvania were only to secure and disarm disaffected persons. On September 3, however, Congress noted a letter from George Bryan, vice president of the Supreme Executive Council of Pennsylvania, requesting the approval of Congress for Pennsylvania's plan to send those arrested, particularly Quakers who refused to make any promises or affirmations of allegiance, to Staunton, Virginia. Congress approved the request (*JCC*, 8:707–8; *Col. Recs. Pa.* 11:264, 265; Oaks, "Philadelphians in Exile," 309).

[8] A reference to the Battle of Brandywine, at which Washington unsuccessfully attempted to halt the British advance on Philadelphia (Boatner, *American Revolution*, 104–10).

[9] Members of the Continental Congress, expecting Philadelphia to fall to the British, left Philadelphia on Sept. 19 for Lancaster, Pa. (Boatner, *American Revolution*, 860).

[10] Legislation passed in 1700 by the colonial assembly gave indentured servants two suits of clothes, a new axe, a grubbing hoe, and a weeding hoe as freedom dues (the axe and hoes were eliminated in 1771 legislation), but the actual composition of freedom dues varied greatly over

time and place in eighteenth-century Pennsylvania. By the 1770s many indentured servants in Philadelphia received clothes and a cash settlement upon the completion of their service (Cheesman A. Herrick, *White Servitude in Pennsylvania* [Philadelphia, 1926; reprint, New York: Negro Universities Press, 1969], 205–11, 293; *Statutes at Large*, 8:30–31; Salinger, *Labor and Indentured Servants*, 134–35).

[11] The word "they" crossed out.

[12] On Sept. 26 three thousand British troops under Lord Charles Cornwallis took possession of Philadelphia. The main body of the British army remained in Germantown, five miles north of the city, where they had camped on Sept. 25 with their commander-in-chief, General Howe (Frederick D. Stone, "The Struggle for the Delaware: Philadelphia under Howe and Arnold," in *Narrative and Critical History of America*, ed. Justin Winsor [Boston: Houghton Mifflin, 1887], 6:383–84).

[13] "Town" crossed out.

[14] On Sept. 27, a day after the British occupation of Philadelphia, British soldiers began erecting batteries to protect the city against the American navy anchored a short distance below in the Delaware River. The British succeeded in mounting only four guns when the American frigate *Delaware*, with Capt. Charles Alexander in command, the ship *Montgomery*, the sloop *Fly*, and four galleys began firing on the British at nine in the morning. The battle lasted about an hour, when the *Delaware's* foremast was shot away and the ship ran aground. The *Fly* also ran aground shortly thereafter. The other American vessels slipped away safely. The British boarded the *Delaware* and captured those of the crew who did not escape to other vessels or the Jersey shore (Stryker, *Forts on the Delaware*, 3–4).

[15] The words "at the upper lower end of the Town" crossed out.

[16] Loyalists were rounding up American sympathizers, subjecting them to a "Loyalist citizen arrest," and incarcerating them in the Walnut Street jail. After questioning, British authorities released most of the several hundred persons arrested (Jackson, *With the British Army*, 17).

[17] Mud Island, situated in the Delaware River a little below the mouth of the Schuylkill River, south of Philadelphia, had a commanding position over the navigable channel between the island and the Pennsylvania shore. American forces built Fort Mifflin there and placed barricades in the river to hinder British vessels. The British, who had entered the lower Delaware on Oct. 4, knew they had to incapacitate the American batteries and river barricades in advance. The gunfire to which ED refers may have had some connection with the British troops who began building batteries on nearby Province Island in the Schuylkill River on Oct. 7. The British hoped that the Province Island location would give them a commanding position over Mud Island so they could silence the batteries at Fort Mifflin and remove the barricades (Stryker, *Forts on the Delaware*, 7–11).

[18] An attack by nine American galleys on British grenadiers who were building batteries at Webb's Ferry, a crossing point of the Schuylkill River to Province Island (Jackson, *Pennsylvania Navy*, 143, 139).

[19] The three entries "our little Molly . . . when she was wean'd" were written on loose, mispaginated leaves in the manuscript volume.

[20] A reference to the Battle of Fort Mercer on Oct. 22. Fort Mercer, another of the Delaware River fortifications (see above, Oct. 6), was located at Red Bank in Gloucester County, N.J. Four hundred American troops led by Col. Christopher Greene repulsed an attack by three battalions and one artillery regiment of Hessian soldiers. The Hessians suffered many casualties. The naval action concerning the *Augustia* took place on Oct. 23 in the vicinity of Fort Mifflin at Mud Island, where a five-hour battle transpired between the British and American fleets (Stryker, *Forts on the Delaware*, 15–26).

[21] Lord Cornwallis left Philadelphia with two thousand troops to attempt another assault on Fort Mercer (see above, Oct. 23). After the fall of Fort Mifflin on Nov. 16 further defense of Fort

Mercer was untenable, and Col. Christopher Greene evacuated the fort the night of Nov. 20–21, thus opening the Delaware River to British shipping (Boatner, *American Revolution*, 383).

[22] The word "back" crossed out.

[23] The word "his" crossed out.

[24] The word "thing" crossed out.

1778

[1] On Jan. 29 the Continental Congress ordered the release of the prisoners on condition that they take an oath or affirmation to the state of Pennsylvania whereby each man agreed to be "a good and faithful subject" (Gilpin, *Exiles in Virginia*, 188–93, 198–200; see also *Col. Recs. Pa.*, 11:395; *JCC*, 10:85, 98; Jonathan Bayard Smith to Timothy Matlack, Jan. 19, 1778, in P. H. Smith, *Letters of the Delegates*, 8:615, n.3).

[2] General Washington and the American forces spent the winter of 1777–78 and the spring of 1778 at Valley Forge, Pa. (Boatner, *American Revolution*, 1136–37).

[3] Cloth associated with Marseilles, France, a center for fine quilted petticoats and coverlets consisting of two layers of cloth, with backing in between for the raised pattern on the quilt or petticoat. Similar cloth, known as Marseilles, Marcella, or Marsella, was also imported from England in the eighteenth century (Montgomery, *Textiles*, 289–92).

[4] After negotiations with colonial forces, the British army, under the command of General Clinton, agreed to turn control of the city over to General Washington and withdraw their troops on June 18 (George M. Wrong, *Washington and His Comrades in Arms* [New Haven, Conn.: Yale University Press, 1921], 196).

[5] After withdrawing from Philadelphia on June 18, Clinton began to move his troops through New Jersey toward New York. Washington broke camp at Valley Forge on June 19 and pursued the British forces (William B. Willcox, "British Strategy in America, 1778," *Journal of Modern History* 19 [1947]: 110).

[6] On June 4 Washington had ordered that once Philadelphia was occupied by American troops, measures should be taken to prevent the removal, transfer, and sale of all British goods and merchandise in the possession of the inhabitants. Gen. Benedict Arnold, who became the city's military governor following the American reentry on June 18, issued these orders as a proclamation on June 19, in effect closing all private shops until individual owners could make lists of their goods. The shops reopened a week later (*JCC*, 11:571; *Pa. Archives*, ser. 1, 6:606; Scharf and Westcott, *Philadelphia*, 1:385–86).

[7] The Battle of Monmouth, N.J., June 28, in which each side lost approximately three hundred men. More than six hundred British soldiers deserted and made their way to Philadelphia (Boatner, *American Revolution*, 716–25).

[8] The Bank Meeting, established in 1865, held meetings at a building on Front Street between Arch and Race streets that had been constructed in 1702. This building stood until 1790, when the Philadelphia Northern District built a new meetinghouse at Keys Alley (Edwin B. Bronner, "The Center Square Meetinghouse and other Meetinghouses of Early Philadelphia," *Bulletin of the Friends Historical Association* 44 [1955]: 67–74).

[9] Abraham Carlisle, a Philadelphia Quaker, was first named as a traitor in May 1778, along with more than fifty other Pennsylvanians. Against the advice of Friends, he had accepted a post from the British to grant passes in and out of the city (see above, Nov. 24, 1777; *Col. Recs. Pa.*, 11:481–86, 603–605; Mekeel, *Relation of the Quakers*, 193; notes on Carlisle's trial and petitions on his behalf are in *Pa. Archives*, ser. 1, 7:44–52 and 53–58, respectively).

[10] Charles Willson Peale and other confiscation agents took possession of the Shoemaker home on Arch Street and ordered Rebecca Shoemaker out. Many years later, Peale recalled that

the confiscation agents began with the property of those "who were of most consideration among those named in the Proclamation" and so accordingly they went first to the Joseph Galloway and Samuel Shoemaker homes (Coleman, "Joseph Galloway," 288, 289 n. 51; "Memoirs of Charles Willson Peale: From his Original Ms. with Notes by Horace Wells Sellers" [1896], typescript, Peale-Sellers Papers, APS, Philadelphia, 67).

[11] Joseph Yerkes was called before a magistrate because he did not conform to legislation passed in April requiring all schoolmasters to take an oath or affirmation of allegiance. Those who failed to do so by June 1 could be removed from their positions and subject to a penalty of five hundred pounds plus costs. Yerkes was not the only Quaker schoolmaster who ran afoul of this legislation: some Quaker schoolmasters were imprisoned (*Laws Enacted in the Second Sitting*, 127–30; Mekeel, *Relation of the Quakers*, 189–90, 180, 187 n. 40).

[12] Springettsbury Manor, a tract of land along the Schuylkill River in Philadelphia County, held two large country homes: Bush Hill, built by James Logan, and Springettsbury, built by Thomas Penn in the 1730s. A popular place to visit, Springettsbury was noted for its flowers, formal gardens, and greenhouse where the great American aloe tree was nurtured (J. F. Watson, *Annals*, 2:478–79).

[13] The Society of Friends, believing strongly that women's faith and gifts in the service of the church were as valuable as men's, set up parallel women's meetings to the men's monthly, quarterly, and yearly meetings. The difference in these meetings supposedly related to function rather than status, but in practice, women's meetings, at least in Philadelphia, had less power over discipline than the men's meetings. They were required to obtain the approval of the men's meetings before disowning women for marrying out or accepting their statements of apology before readmitting them to full standing. In neighboring Bucks County, the women's monthly meetings appear to have exercised full disciplinary functions without the approval of the men's meetings (L. Hugh Doncaster, *Quaker Organization and Business Meetings* [London: Friends Home Service Committee, 1952], 17–18; Frost, *Quaker Family*, 55–57; on Bucks County see Jack D. Marietta, *The Reformation of American Quakerism 1748–1783* [Philadelphia: University of Pennsylvania Press, 1984], 28–29).

[14] John Roberts, a Quaker miller from Merion who had originally sought the intervention of the British because of his distress over the banishment of the Quaker exiles, had been forced to act as a guide and informer for the British, then advancing on Philadelphia. Roberts was tried with Abraham Carlisle at the Philadelphia Court of Oyer and Terminer on Sept. 27, 1778; both men were found guilty of treason and executed on Nov. 4 (*Col. Recs. Pa.*, 11:481–86, 600–605; petitions for Roberts in *Pa. Archives*, ser. 1, 7:21–43; Mekeel, *Relation of the Quakers*, 193; Judge Thomas McKean's pronouncement of the death sentence despite the jury recommendation for mercy is in *Pa. Packet*, Nov. 7, 1778).

[15] *Pa. Ev. Post*, Nov. 6, 1778.

[16] The word "the" crossed out.

15

The Constitution of the United States of America and Related Documents

The Constitution of the United States of America

We the People of the United States, in Order to form a more perfect Union, establish Justice, insure domestic Tranquility, provide for the common defence, promote the general Welfare, and secure the Blessings of Liberty to ourselves and our Posterity, do ordain and establish this Constitution for the United States of America.

Article. I.

Section. 1. All legislative Powers herein granted shall be vested in a Congress of the United States, which shall consist of a Senate and House of Representatives.

Section. 2. The House of Representatives shall be composed of Members chosen every second Year by the People of the several States, and the Electors in each State shall have the Qualifications requisite for Electors of the most numerous Branch of the State Legislature.

No Person shall be a Representative who shall not have attained to the Age of twenty five Years, and been seven Years a Citizen of the United States, and who shall not, when elected, be an Inhabitant of that State in which he shall be chosen.

Representatives and direct Taxes shall be apportioned among the several States which may be included within this Union, according to their respective Numbers, which shall be determined by adding to the whole Number of free Persons, including those bound to Service for a Term of Years, and excluding Indians not taxed, three fifths of all other Persons. The actual Enumeration shall be made within three Years after the first Meeting of the Congress of the United States, and within every subsequent Term of ten Years, in such Manner as they shall by Law direct. The Number of Representatives shall not exceed one for every thirty Thousand, but each State shall have at Least one Representative; and until such enumeration shall be made, the State of New Hampshire shall be entitled to chuse three, Massachusetts eight, Rhode-Island and Providence Plantations one, Connecticut five, New-York six, New Jersey four, Pennsylvania eight, Delaware one, Maryland six, Virginia ten, North Carolina five, South Carolina five, and Georgia three.

When vacancies happen in the Representation from any State, the Executive Authority thereof shall issue Writs of Election to fill such Vacancies.

The House of Representatives shall chuse their Speaker and other Officers; and shall have the sole Power of Impeachment.

Section. 3. The Senate of the United States shall be composed of two Senators from each State, chosen by the Legislature thereof, for six Years; and each Senator shall have one Vote.

Immediately after they shall be assembled in Consequence of the first Election, they shall be divided as equally as may be into three Classes. The Seats of the Senators of the first class shall be vacated at the Expiration of the second Year, of the second Class at the Expiration of the fourth Year, and of the third Class at the Expiration of the sixth Year, so that one third may be chosen every second Year; and if Vacancies happen by Resignation, or otherwise, during the Recess of the Legislature of any State, the Executive thereof may make temporary Appointments until the next Meeting of the Legislature, which shall then fill such Vacancies.

No Person shall be a Senator who shall not have attained to the Age of thirty Years, and been nine Years a Citizen of the United States, and who shall not, when elected, be an Inhabitant to that State for which he shall be chosen.

The Vice President of the United States shall be President of the Senate, but shall have no Vote, unless they be equally divided.

The Senate shall chuse their other Officers, and also a President pro tempore, in the Absence of the Vice President, or when he shall exercise the Office of President of the United States.

The Senate shall have the sole Power to try all Impeachments. When sitting for that Purpose, they shall be on Oath or Affirmation. When the President of the United States is tried, the Chief Justice shall preside: And no Person shall be convicted without the Concurrence of two thirds of the Members present.

Judgment in Cases of Impeachment shall not extend further than to removal from Office, and disqualification to hold and enjoy any Office of honor, Trust or Profit under the United States: but the Party convicted shall nevertheless be liable and subject to Indictment, Trial, Judgment and Punishment, according to Law.

Section. 4. The Times, Places and Manner of holding Elections for Senators and Representatives, shall be prescribed in each State by the Legislature thereof; but the Congress may at any time by Law make or alter such Regulations, except as to the Places of chusing Senators.

The Congress shall assemble at least once in every Year, and such Meeting shall be on the first Monday in December, unless they shall by Law appoint a different Day.

Section. 5. Each House shall be the Judge of the Elections, Returns and Qualifications of its own Members, and a Majority of each shall constitute a Quorum to do Business; but a smaller Number may adjourn from day to day, and may be authorized to compel the Attendance of absent Members, in such Manner, and under such Penalties as each House may provide.

Each House may determine the Rules of its Proceedings, punish its members for disorderly Behaviour, and, with the Concurrence of two thirds, expel a Member.

Each House shall keep a Journal of its Proceedings, and from time to time publish the same, excepting such Parts as may in their Judgment require Secrecy; and the Yeas and Nays of the Members of either House on any question shall, at the Desire of one fifth of those Present, be entered on the Journal.

Neither House, during the Session of Congress, shall, without the Consent of the other, adjourn for more than three days, nor to any other Place than that in which the two Houses shall be sitting.

Section. 6. The Senators and Representatives shall receive a Compensation for their Services, to be ascertained by Law, and paid out of the Treasury of the United States. They shall in all Cases, except Treason, Felony and Breach of the Peace, be privileged from Arrest during their Attendance at the Session of their respective Houses, and in going to and returning from the same; and for any Speech or Debate in either House, they shall not be questioned in any other Place.

No Senator or Representative shall, during the Time for which he was elected, be appointed to any civil Office under the Authority of the United States which shall have been created, or the Emoluments whereof shall have been encreased during such time; and no Person holding any Office under the United States, shall be a Member of either House during his Continuance in Office.

Section. 7. All Bills for raising Revenue shall originate in the House of Representatives; but the Senate may propose or concur with Amendments as on other Bills.

Every Bill which shall have passed the House of Representatives and the Senate shall, before it become a Law, be presented to the President of the United States; If he approve he shall sign it, but if not he shall return it, with his Objections to that House in which it shall have originated, who shall enter the Objections at large on their Journal, and proceed to reconsider it. If after such Reconsideration two thirds of that House shall agree to pass the Bill, it shall be sent, together with the Objections, to the other House, by which it shall likewise be reconsidered, and if approved by two thirds of that House, it shall become a Law. But in all such Cases the Votes of both Houses shall be determined by yeas and Nays, and the Names of the Persons voting for and against the Bill shall be entered on the Journal of each House respectively. If any Bill shall not be returned by the President ten Days (Sundays excepted) after it shall have been presented to him, the Same shall be a Law, in like Manner as if he had signed it, unless the Congress by their Adjournment prevent its Return, in which Case it shall not be a Law.

Every Order, Resolution, or Vote to which the Concurrence of the Senate and House of Representatives may be necessary (except on a question of Adjournment) shall be presented to the President of the United States; and before the Same shall take Effect, shall be approved by him, or being disapproved by him, shall be repassed by two thirds of the Senate and House of Representatives, according to the Rules and Limitations prescribed in the Case of a Bill.

Section. 8. The Congress shall have Power To lay and collect Taxes, Duties, Imposts and Excises, to pay the Debts and provide for the common Defence and general Welfare of the United States; but all Duties, Imposts and Excises shall be uniform throughout the United States;

To borrow Money on the credit of the United States;

To regulate Commerce with foreign Nations, and among the several States, and with the Indian Tribes;

To establish an uniform Rule of Naturalization, and uniform Laws on the subject of Bankruptcies throughout the United States;

To coin Money, regulate the Value thereof, and of foreign Coin, and fix the Standard of Weights and Measures;

To provide for the Punishment of counterfeiting the Securities and current Coin of the United States;

To establish Post Offices and post Roads;

To promote the Progress of Science and useful Arts, by securing for limited Times to Authors and Inventors the exclusive Right to their respective Writings and Discoveries;

To constitute Tribunals inferior to the supreme Court;

To define and punish piracies and Felonies committed on the high Seas, and Offences against the Law of Nations;

To declare War, grant Letters of Marque and Reprisal, and make Rules concerning Captures on Land and Water;

To raise and support Armies, but no Appropriation of Money to that Use shall be for a longer Term than two Years;

To provide and maintain a Navy;

To make Rules for the Government and Regulation of the land and naval Forces;

To provide for calling forth the Militia to execute the Laws of the Union, suppress Insurrections and repel Invasions;

To provide for organizing, arming, and disciplining, the Militia, and for governing such Part of them as may be employed in the Service of the United States, reserving to the States respectively, the Appointment of the Officers, and the Authority of training the Militia according to the discipline prescribed by Congress;

To exercise exclusive Legislation in all Cases whatsoever, over such District (not exceeding ten Miles square) as may, by Cession of particular States, and the Acceptance of Congress, become the Seat of the Government of the United States, and to exercise like Authority over all Places purchased by the Consent of the Legislature of the State in which the same shall be, for the Erection of Forts, Magazines, Arsenals, dock-Yards, and other needful Buildings;—And

To make all Laws which shall be necessary and proper for carrying into Execution the foregoing Powers, and all other Powers vested by this Constitution in the Government of the United States, or in any Department or Officer thereof.

Section. 9. The Migration or Importation of such Persons as any of the States now existing shall think proper to admit, shall not be prohibited by the Congress prior to the Year one thousand eight hundred and eight, but a Tax or duty may be imposed on such Importation, not exceeding ten dollars for each Person.

The Privilege of the Writ of Habeas Corpus shall not be suspended, unless when in Cases of Rebellion or Invasion the public Safety may require it.

No Bill of Attainder or ex post facto Law shall be passed.

No Capitation, or other direct, Tax shall be laid, unless in Proportion to the Census or Enumeration herein before directed to be taken.

No Tax or Duty shall be laid on Articles exported from any State.

No Preference shall be given by any Regulation of Commerce or Revenue to the Ports of one State over those of another: nor shall Vessels bound to, or from, one State, be obliged to enter, clear, or pay Duties in another.

No Money shall be drawn from the Treasury, but in Consequence of Appropriations made by Law; and a regular Statement and Account of the Receipts and Expenditures of all public Money shall be published from time to time.

No Title of Nobility shall be granted by the United States: And no Person holding any Office of Profit or Trust under them, shall, without the Consent of the Congress, accept of any present, Emolument, Office, or Title, of any kind whatever, from any King, Prince, or foreign State.

Section. 10. No State shall enter into any Treaty, Alliance, or Confederation; grant Letters of Marque and Reprisal; coin Money; emit Bills of Credit; make any Thing but gold and silver Coin a Tender in Payment of Debts; pass any Bill of Attainder, ex post facto Law, or Law impairing the Obligation of Contracts, or grant any Title of Nobility.

No State shall, without the Consent of the Congress, lay any Imposts or Duties on Imports or Exports, except what may be absolutely necessary for executing its inspection Laws: and the net Produce of all Duties and Imposts, laid by any State on Imports or Exports, shall be for the Use of the Treasury of the United States; and all such Laws shall be subject to the Revision and Controul of the Congress.

No State shall, without the Consent of Congress, lay any Duty of Tonnage, keep Troops, or Ships of War in time of Peace, enter into any Agreement or Compact with another State, or with a foreign Power, or engage in War, unless actually invaded, or in such imminent Danger as will not admit of delay.

Article. II.

Section. 1. The executive Power shall be vested in a President of the United States of America. He shall hold his Office during the Term of four Years, and, together with the Vice President, chosen for the same Term, be elected, as follows.

Each State shall appoint, in such Manner as the Legislature thereof may direct, a Number of Electors, equal to the whole Number of Senators and Representatives to which the State may be entitled in the Congress: but no Senator or Representative, or Person holding an Office of Trust or Profit under the United States, shall be appointed an Elector.

The Electors shall meet in their respective States and vote by Ballot for two Persons, of whom one at least shall not be an Inhabitant of the same State with themselves. And they shall make a List of all the Persons voted for, and of the Number of Votes for each; which List they shall sign and certify, and transmit sealed to the Seat of the Government of the United States, directed to the President of the Senate. The President of the Senate shall, in the Presence of the Senate and House of Representatives, open all the Certificates, and the Votes shall then be counted. The Person having the greatest Number of Votes shall be the President, if such Number be a Majority of the whole Number of Electors appointed; and if there be more than one who have such Majority, and have an equal Number of Votes, then the House of Representatives shall immediately chuse by Ballot one of them for President; and if no Person have a Majority, then from the five highest on the List the said House shall in like Manner chuse the President. But in chusing the President, the Votes shall be taken by States, the Representation from each State having one Vote; A quorum for this Purpose shall consist of a Member or Members from two thirds of the States, and a Majority of all the States shall be necessary to a Choice. In every Case, after the Choice of the President, the Person having the greatest Number of Votes of the Electors shall be the Vice President. But if there should remain two or more who have equal Votes, the Senate shall chuse from them by Ballot the Vice President.

The Congress may determine the Time of chusing the Electors, and the Day on which they shall give their Votes; which Day shall be the same throughout the United States.

No Persons except a natural born Citizen, or a Citizen of the United States, at the time of the Adoption of this Constitution, shall be eligible to the Office of President; neither shall any Person be eligible to that Office who shall not have attained to the Age of thirty five Years, and been fourteen Years a Resident within the United States.

In Case of the Removal of the President from Office, or of his Death, Resignation, or Inability to discharge the Powers and Duties of the said Office, the Same shall devolve on the Vice President, and the Congress may by Law provide for the Case of Removal, Death, Resignation or Inability, both of the President and Vice President, declaring what Officer shall then act as President, and such Officer shall act accordingly, until the Disability be removed, or a President shall be elected.

The President shall, at stated Times, receive for his Services, a Compensation, which shall neither be encreased nor diminished during the Period for which he shall have been elected, and he shall not receive within that period any other Emolument from the United States, or any of them.

Before he enter on the Execution of his Office, he shall take the following Oath or Affirmation:—"I do solemnly swear (or affirm) that I will faithfully execute the Office of President of the United States, and will to the best of my Ability, preserve, protect and defend the Constitution of the United States."

Section. 2. The President shall be Commander in Chief of the Army and Navy of the United States, and of the Militia of the several States, when called into the actual Service of the United States; he may require the Opinion, in writing, of the principal Officer in each of the executive Departments, upon any Subject relating to the Duties of their respective Offices, and he shall have Power to grant Reprieves and Pardons for Offences against the United States, except in Cases of Impeachment.

He shall have Power, by and with the Advice and Consent of the Senate, to make Treaties, provided two thirds of the Senators present concur; and he shall nominate, and by and with the Advice and Consent of the Senate, shall appoint Ambassadors, other public Ministers and Consuls, Judges of the supreme Court, and all other Officers of the United States, whose Appointments are not herein otherwise provided for, and which shall be established by Law: but the Congress may by Law vest the Appointment of such inferior Officers, as they think proper, in the President alone, in the Courts of Law, or in the Heads of Departments.

The President shall have Power to fill up all Vacancies that may happen during the Recess of the Senate, by granting Commissions which shall expire at the End of their next Session.

Section. 3. He shall from time to time give to the Congress Information of the State of the Union, and recommend to their Consideration such Measures as he shall judge necessary and expedient; he may, on extraordinary Occasions, convene both Houses, or either of them, and in Case of Disagreement between them, with Respect to the Time of Adjournment, he may adjourn them to such Time as he shall think proper; he shall receive Ambassadors and other public Ministers; he shall take Care that the Laws be faithfully executed, and shall Commission all the Officers of the United States.

Section. 4. The President, Vice President and all civil Officers of the United States, shall be removed from Office on Impeachment for, and Conviction of Treason, Bribery, or other high Crimes and Misdemeanors.

Article. III.

Section. 1. The judicial Power of the United States, shall be vested in one supreme Court, and in such inferior Courts as the Congress may from time to time ordain and establish. The Judges, both of the supreme and inferior Courts, shall hold their Offices during good Behaviour, and shall, at stated Times, receive for their Services, a Compensation, which shall not be diminished during their Continuance in Office.

Section. 2. The judicial Power shall extend to all Cases, in Law and Equity, arising under this Constitution, the Laws of the United States, and Treaties made, or which shall be made, under their Authority;—to all Cases affecting Ambassadors, other public Ministers and Consuls;—to all Cases of admiralty and maritime Jurisdiction;—to Controversies to which the United States shall be a Party;—to Controversies between two or more States;—between a State and Citizens of another State;—between Citizens of different States,—between Citizens of the same State claiming Lands under Grants of different States, and between a State, or the Citizens thereof, and foreign States, Citizens or Subjects.

In all Cases affecting Ambassadors, other public Ministers and Consuls, and those in which a State shall be Party, the supreme Court shall have original Jurisdiction. In all the other Cases before mentioned, the supreme Court shall have appellate Jurisdiction, both as to Law and Fact, with such Exceptions, and under such Regulations as the Congress shall make.

The Trial of all Crimes, except in Cases of Impeachment, shall be by Jury; and such Trial shall be held in the State where the said Crimes shall have been committed; but when not committed within any State, the Trial shall be at such Place or Places as the Congress may by Law have directed.

Section. 3. Treason against the United States, shall consist only in levying War against them, or in adhering to their Enemies, giving them Aid and Comfort. No Person shall be convicted of Treason unless on the Testimony of two Witnesses to the same overt Act, or on Confession in open Court.

The Congress shall have Power to declare the Punishment of Treason, but no Attainder of Treason shall work Corruption of Blood, or Forfeiture except during the Life of the Person attainted.

Article. IV.

Section. 1. Full Faith and Credit shall be given in each State to the public Acts, Records, and judicial Proceedings of every other State. And the Congress may by general Laws prescribe the Manner in which such Acts, Records and Proceedings shall be proved, and the Effect thereof.

Section. 2. The Citizens of each State shall be entitled to all privileges and Immunities of Citizens in the several States.

A Person charged in any State with Treason, Felony, or other Crime, who shall flee from Justice, and be found in another State, shall on Demand of the executive Authority of the State from which he fled, be delivered up, to be removed to the State having Jurisdiction of the Crime.

No Person held to Service or Labour in one State, under the Laws thereof, escaping into another, shall, in Consequence of any Law or Regulation therein, be discharged from such Service or Labour, but shall be delivered up on Claim of the Party to whom such Service or Labour may be due.

Section. 3. New States may be admitted by the Congress into this Union; but no new State shall be formed or erected within the Jurisdiction of any other State; nor any State be formed by the Junction of two or more States, or Parts of States, without the Consent of the Legislatures of the States concerned as well as of the Congress.

The Congress shall have Power to dispose of and make all needful Rules and Regulations respecting the Territory or other Property belonging to the United States; and nothing in this Constitution shall be so construed as to Prejudice any Claims of the United States, or of any particular State.

Section. 4. The United States shall guarantee to every State in this Union a Republican Form of Government, and shall protect each of them against Invasion; and on Application of the Legislature, or of the Executive (when the Legislature cannot be convened) against domestic Violence.

Article. V.

The Congress, whenever two thirds of both Houses shall deem it necessary, shall propose Amendments to this Constitution, or, on the Application of the Legislatures of two thirds of the several States, shall call a Convention for proposing Amendments, which, in either Case, shall be valid to all Intents and Purposes, as Part of this Constitution, when ratified by the Legislatures of three fourths of the several States, or by Conventions in three fourths thereof, as the one or the other Mode of Ratification may be proposed by the Congress; Provided that no Amendment which may be made prior to the Year One thousand eight hundred and eight shall in any Manner affect the first and fourth Clauses in the Ninth Section of the first Article; and that no State, without its Consent, shall be deprived of its equal Suffrage in the Senate.

Article. VI.

All Debts contracted and Engagements entered into, before the Adoption of this Constitution, shall be as valid against the United States under this Constitution, as under the Confederation.

This Constitution, and the Laws of the United States which shall be made in Pursuance thereof; and all Treaties made, or which shall be made, under the Authority of the United States, shall be the supreme Law of the Land; and the Judges in every State shall be bound thereby, any Thing in the Constitution or Laws of any State to the Contrary notwithstanding.

The Senators and Representatives before mentioned, and the Members of the several State Legislatures, and all executive and judicial Officers; both of the United States and of the several States, shall be bound by Oath or Affirmation, to support this Constitution; but no religious test shall ever be required as a Qualification to any Office or public Trust under the United States.

Article. VII.

The Ratification of the Conventions of nine States, shall be sufficient for the Establishment of this Constitution between the States so ratifying the Same.

done in Convention by the Unanimous Consent of the States present the Seventeenth Day of September in the Year of our Lord one thousand seven hundred and Eighty seven and of the Independance of the United States of America the Twelfth In Witness whereof We have hereunto subscribed our Names,

Attest William Jackson Secretary

Delaware	Geo: Read Gunning Bedford junr John Dickinson Richard Bassett Jaco: Broom	**New Hampshire**	John Langdon Nicholas Gilman
Maryland	James McHenry Dan of St Thos. Jenifer Danl Carroll	**Massachusetts**	Nathaniel Gorham Rufus King
		Connecticut	Wm: Saml. Johnson Roger Sherman
Virginia	John Blair— James Madlson Jr.	**New York . . .**	Alexander Hamilton
North Carolina	Wm. Blount Richd. Dobbs Spaight. Hu Williamson	**New Jersey**	Wil: Livingston David Brearley Wm. Paterson. Jona: Dayton
South Carolina	J. Rutledge Charles Cotesworth Pinckney Charles Pinckney Pierce Butler	**Pennsylvania**	B Franklin Thomas Mifflin Robt Morris Geo. Clymer Thos. FitzSimons Jared Ingersoll James Wilson Gouv. Morris
Georgia	William Few Abr Baldwin		

Go: Washington—Presidt. and deputy from Virginia

The Federalist No. 1
[Alexander Hamilton]

October 27, 1787

After an unequivocal experience of the inefficacy of the subsisting Fœderal Government, you are called upon to deliberate on a new Constitution for the United States of America. The subject speaks its own importance; comprehending in its consequences, nothing less than the existence of the UNION, the safety and welfare of the parts of which it is composed, the fate of an empire, in many respects, the most interesting in the world. It has been frequently remarked, that it seems to have been reserved to the people of this country, by their conduct and example to decide the important question, whether societies of men are really capable or not, of establishing good government from reflection and choice, or whether they are forever destined to depend, for their political constitutions, on accident and force. If there be any truth in the remark, the crisis, at which we are arrived, may with propriety be regarded as the æra in which that decision is to be made; and a wrong election of the part we shall act, may, in this view, deserve to be considered as the general misfortune of mankind.

This idea will add the inducements of philanthropy to those of patriotism to heighten the solicitude, which all considerate and good men must feel for the event. Happy will it be if our choice should be directed by a judicious estimate of our true interests, unperplexed and unbiassed by considerations not connected with the public good. But this is a thing more ardently to be wished, than seriously to be expected. The plan offered to our deliberations, affects too many particular interests, innovates upon too many local institutions, not to involve in its discussion a variety of objects foreign to its merits, and of views, passions and prejudices little favourable to the discovery of truth.

Among the most formidable of the obstacles which the new Constitution will have to encounter, may readily be distinguished the obvious interest of a certain class of men in every State to resist all changes which may hazard a diminution of the power, emolument and consequence of the offices they hold under the State-establishments—and the perverted ambition of another class of men, who will either hope to aggrandise themselves by the confusions of their country, or will flatter themselves with fairer prospects of elevation from the subdivision of the empire into several partial confederacies, than from its union under one government.

It is not, however, my design to dwell upon observations of this nature. I am well aware that it would be disingenuous to resolve indiscriminately the opposition of any set of men (merely because their situations might subject them to suspicion) into interested or ambitious views: Candour will oblige us to admit, that even such men may be actuated by upright intentions; and it cannot be doubted that much of the opposition which has made its appearance, or may hereafter make its appearance, will spring from sources, blameless at least, if not respectable, the honest errors of minds led astray by preconceived jealousies and fears. So numerous indeed and so powerful are the causes, which serve to give a false bias to the judgment, that we upon many occasions, see wise and good men on the wrong as well as on the right side of questions, of the first magnitude to society. This circumstance, if duly attended to, would furnish a lesson of moderation to those, who are ever so much persuaded of their being in the right, in any controversy. And a further reason for caution, in this respect, might be drawn from the reflection, that we are not always sure, that those who advocate the truth are influenced by purer principles than their antagonists. Ambition, avarice, personal animosity, party opposition, and many other motives, not more laudable than these, are apt to operate as well upon those who support as upon those who oppose the right side of a question. Were there not even these inducements to moderation, nothing could be more illjudged than that intolerant spirit, which has, at all times, characterised political parties. For, in politics as in religion, it is equally absurd to aim at making proselytes by fire and sword. Heresies in either can rarely be cured by persecution.

And yet however just these sentiments will be allowed to be, we have already sufficient indications, that it will happen in this as in all former cases of great national discussion. A torrent of angry and malignant passions will be let loose. To judge from the conduct of the opposite parties, we shall be led to conclude, that they will mutually hope to evince the justness of their opinions, and to increase the number of their converts by the loudness of their declamations, and by the bitterness of their invectives. An enlightened zeal for the energy and efficiency of government will be stigmatized, as the off-spring of a temper fond of despotic power and hostile to the principles of liberty. An overscrupulous jealousy of danger to the rights of the people, which is more commonly the fault of the head than of the heart, will be represented as mere pretence and artifice; the bait for popularity at the expence of public good. It will be forgotten, on the one hand, that jealousy is the usual concomitant of violent love, and that the noble enthusiasm of liberty is too apt to be infected with a spirit of narrow and illiberal distrust. On the other hand, it will be equally forgotten, that the vigour of government is essential to the security of liberty; that, in the contemplation of a sound and well informed judgement, their interest can never be separated; and that a dangerous ambition more often lurks behind the specious mask of zeal for the rights of the people, than under the forbidding appearance of zeal for the firmness and efficiency of government. History will teach us, that the former has been found a much more certain road to the introduction of despotism, than the latter, and that of those men who have overturned the liberties of republics the greatest number have begun their carreer, by paying an obsequious court to the people, commencing Demagogues and ending Tyrants.

In the course of the preceeding observations I have had an eye, my Fellow Citizens, to putting you upon your guard against all attempts, from whatever quarter, to influence your decision in a matter of the utmost moment to your welfare by any impressions other than those which may result from the evidence of truth. You will, no doubt, at the same time, have collected from the general scope of them that they proceed from a source not unfriendly to the new Constitution. Yes, my Countrymen, I own to you, that, after having given it an attentive consideration, I am clearly of opinion, it is your interest to adopt it. I am convinced, that this is the safest course for your liberty, your dignity, and your happiness. I effect not reserves, which I do not feel. I will not amuse you with an appearance of deliberation, when I have decided. I frankly acknowledge to you my convictions, and I will freely lay before you the reasons on which they are founded. The consciousness of good intentions disdains ambiguity. I shall not however multiply professions on this head. My motives must remain in the depository of my own breast: My arguments will be open to all, and may be judged of by all. They shall at least be offered in a spirit, which will not disgrace the cause of truth.

I propose in a series of papers to discuss the following interesting particulars—*The utility of this* UNION *to your political prosperity—The insufficiency of the present Confederation to preserve that Union—The necessity of a government at least equally energetic with the one proposed to the attainment of this object—The conformity of the proposed constitution to the true principles of republican government—Its analogy to your own state constitution—and lastly, The additional security, which its adoption will afford to the preservation of that species of government, to liberty and to property.*

In the progress of this discussion I shall endeavour to give a satisfactory answer to all the objections which shall have made their appearance that may seem to have any claim to your attention.

It may perhaps be thought superfluous to offer arguments to prove the utility of the UNION, a point, no doubt, deeply engraved on the hearts of the great body of the people in every state, and one, which it may be imagined has no adversaries. But the fact is, that we already hear it whispered in the private circles of those who oppose the new constitution, that the Thirteen States are of too great extent for any general system, and that we must of necessity resort to separate confederacies of distinct portions of the whole.* This doctrine will, in all probability, be gradually propagated, till it has votaries enough to countenance an open avowal of it. For nothing can be more evident, to those who are able to take an enlarged view of the subject, than the alternative of an adoption of the new Constitution, or a dismemberment of the Union. It will therefore be of use to begin by examining the advantages of that Union, the certain evils and the probable dangers, to which every State will be exposed from its dissolution. This shall accordingly constitute the subject of my next address.

The Federalist No. 2
[John Jay]

October 31, 1787

When the people of America reflect that they are now called upon to decide a question, which, in its consequences, must prove one of the most important, that ever engaged their attention, the propriety of their taking a very comprehensive, as well as a very serious view of it, will be evident.

Nothing is more certain than the indispensable necessity of Government, and it is equally undeniable, that whenever and however it is instituted, the people must cede to it some of their natural rights, in order to vest it with requisite powers. It is well worthy of consideration therefore, whether it would conduce more to the interest of the people of America, that they should, to all general purposes, be one nation, under one fœderal Government, than that they should divide themselves into separate confederacies, and give to the head of each, the same kind of powers which they are advised to place in one national Government.

It has until lately been a received and uncontradicted opinion, that the prosperity of the people of America depended on their continuing firmly united, and the wishes, prayers, and efforts of our best and wisest Citizens have been constantly directed to that object. But Politicians now appear, who insist that this opinion is erroneous, and that instead of looking for safety and happiness in union, we ought to seek it in a division of the States into distinct confederacies or sovereignties. However extraordinary this new doctrine may appear, it nevertheless has its advocates; and certain characters who were much opposed to it formerly, are at present of the number. Whatever may be the arguments or inducements, which have wrought this change in the sentiments and declarations of these Gentlemen, it certainly would not be wise in the people at large to adopt these new political tenets without being fully convinced that they are founded in truth and sound Policy.

It has often given me pleasure to observe, that Independent America was not composed of detached and distant territories, but that one connected, fertile, wide spreading country was the portion of our western sons of liberty. Providence has in a particular manner blessed it with a variety of soils and productions, and watered it with innumerable streams, for the delight and accommodation of its inhabitants. A succession of navigable waters forms a kind of chain round its borders, as if to bind it together; while the most noble rivers in the world, running at convenient distances, present them with highways for the easy communication of friendly aids, and the mutual transportation and exchange of their various commodies.

With equal pleasure I have as often taken notice, that Providence has been pleased to give this one connected country, to one united people, a people descended from the same ancestors, speaking the same language, professing the same religion, attached to the same

---

* The same idea, tracing the arguments to their consequences, is held out in several of the late publications against the New Constitution.

principles of government, very similar in their manners and customs, and who, by their joint counsels, arms and efforts, fighting side by side throughout a long and bloody war, have nobly established their general Liberty and Independence.

This country and this people seem to have been made for each other, and it appears as if it was the design of Providence, that an inheritance so proper and convenient for a band of brethren, united to each other by the strongest ties, should never be split into a number of unsocial, jealous and alien sovereignties.

Similar sentiments have hitherto prevailed among all orders and denominations of men among us. To all general purposes we have uniformly been one people—each individual citizen every where enjoying the same national rights, privileges, and protection. As a nation we have made peace and war—as a nation we have vanquished our common enemies—as a nation we have formed alliances and made treaties, and entered into various compacts and conventions with foreign States.

A strong sense of the value and blessings of Union induced the people, at a very early period, to institute a Fœderal Government to preserve and perpetuate it. They formed it almost as soon as they had a political existence; nay at a time, when their habitations were in flames, when many of their Citizens were bleeding, and when the progress of hostility and desolation left little room for those calm and mature enquiries and reflections, which must ever precede the formation of a wise and well balanced government for a free people. It is not to be wondered at that a Government instituted in times so inauspicious, should on experiment be found greatly deficient and inadequate to the purpose it was intended to answer.

This intelligent people perceived and regretted these defects. Still continuing no less attached to union, than enamoured of liberty, they observed the danger, which immediately threatened the former and more remotely the later; and being persuaded that ample security for both, could only be found in a national Government more wisely framed, they, as with one voice, convened the late Convention at Philadelphia, to take that important subject under consideration.

This Convention, composed of men, who possessed the confidence of the people, and many of whom had become highly distinguished by their patriotism, virtue and wisdom, in times which tried the minds and hearts of men, undertook the arduous task. In the mild season of a peace, with minds unoccupied by other subjects, they passed many months in cool uninterrupted and daily consultations: and finally, without having been awed by power, or influenced by any passions except love for their Country, they presented and recommended to the people the plan produced by their joint and very unanimous counsels.

Admit, for so is the fact, that this plan is only *recommended*, not imposed, yet let it be remembered, that it is neither recommended to *blind* approbation, nor to *blind* reprobation; but to that sedate and candid consideration, which the magnitude and importance of the subject demand, and which it certainly ought to receive. But this, (as was remarked in the foregoing number of this Paper,) is more to be wished than expected that it may be so considered and examined. Experience on a former occasion teaches us not to be too sanguine in such hopes. It is not yet forgotten, that well grounded apprehensions of imminent danger induced the people of America to form the Memorable Congress of 1774. That Body recommended certain measures to their Constituents, and the event proved their wisdom; yet it is fresh in our memories how soon the Press began to teem with Pamphlets and weekly Papers against those very measures. Not only many of the Officers of Government who obeyed the dictates of personal interest, but others from a mistaken estimate of consequences, or the undue influence of former attachments, or whose ambition aimed at objects which did not correspond with the public good, were indefatigable in their endeavours to persuade the people to reject the advice of that Patriotic Congress. Many indeed were deceived and deluded, but the great majority of the people reasoned and decided judiciously; and happy they are in reflecting that they did so.

They considered that the Congress was composed of many wise and experienced men. That being convened from different parts of the country, they brought with them and communicated to each other a variety of useful information. That in the course of the time they passed together in enquiring into and discussing the true interests of their country, they must have acquired very accurate knowledge on that head. That they were individually interested in the public liberty and prosperity, and therefore that it was not less their inclination, than their duty, to recommend only such measures, as after the most mature deliberation they really thought prudent and adviseable.

These and similar considerations then induced the people to rely greatly on the judgment and integrity of the Congress; and they took their advice, notwithstanding the various arts and endeavours used to deter and disuade them from it. But if the people at large had reason to confide in the men of that Congress, few of whom had then been fully tried or generally known, still greater reason have they now to respect the judgment and advice of the Convention, for it is well known that some of the most distinguished members of that Congress, who have been since tried and justly approved for patriotism and abilities, and who have grown old in acquiring political information, were also members of this Convention and carried into it their accumulated knowledge and experience.

It is worthy of remark that not only the first, but every succeeding Congress, as well as the late Convention, have invariably joined with the people in thinking that the prosperity of America depended on its Union. To preserve and perpetuate it, was the great object of the people in forming that Convention, and it is also the great object of the plan which the Convention has advised them to adopt. With what propriety therefore, or for what good purposes, are attempts at this particular period, made by some men, to depreciate the importance of the Union? or why is it suggested that three or four confederacies would be better than one? I am persuaded in my own mind, that the people have always thought right on this subject, and that their universal and uniform attachment to the cause of the Union, rests on great and weighty reasons, which I shall endeavour to develope and explain in some ensuing papers. They who promote the idea of substituting a number of distinct confederacies in the room of the plan of the Convention, seem clearly to foresee that the rejection of it would put the continuance of the Union in the utmost jeopardy. That certainly would be the case, and I sincerely wish that it may be as clearly foreseen by every good Citizen, that whenever the dissolution of the Union arrives, America will have reason to exclaim in the words of the Poet, "FAREWELL, A LONG FAREWELL, TO ALL MY GREATNESS."

The Federalist No. 10
[James Madison]

November 22, 1787

Among the numerous advantages promised by a well constructed Union, none deserves to be more accurately developed than its tendency to break and control the violence of faction. The friend of popular governments, never finds himself so much alarmed for their character and fate, as when he contemplates their propensity to this dangerous vice. He will not fail therefore to set a due value on any plan which, without violating the principles to which he is attached, provides a proper cure for it. The instability, injustice and confusion introduced into the public councils, have in truth been the mortal diseases under which popular governments have every where perished; as they continue to be the favorite and fruitful topics from which the adversaries to liberty derive their most specious declamations. The valuable improvements made by the American Constitutions on the popular models, both ancient and modern, cannot certainly be too much admired; but it would be an unwarrantable partiality, to contend that they have as effectually obviated the danger on this side as was wished and expected. Complaints are every where heard from our most considerate and virtuous citizens, usually the friends of public and private faith, and of public and personal liberty; that our governments are too unstable; that the public good is disregarded in the conflicts of rival parties; and that measures are too often decided, not according to the rules of justice, and the rights of the minor party; but by the superior force of an interested and over-bearing majority. However anxiously we may wish that these complaints had no foundation, the evidence of known facts will not permit us to deny that they are in some degree true. It will be found indeed, on a candid review of our situation, that some of the distresses under which we labor, have been erroneously charged on the operation of our governments; but it will be found, at the same time, that other causes will not alone account for many of our heaviest misfortunes; and particularly, for that prevailing and increasing distrust of public engagements, and alarm for private rights, which are echoed from one end of the continent to the other. These must be chiefly, if not wholly, effects of the unsteadiness and injustice, with which a factious spirit has tainted our public administrations.

By a faction I understand a number of citizens, whether amounting to a majority or minority of the whole, who are united and actuated by some common impulse of passion, or of interest, adverse to the rights of other citizens, or to the permanent and aggregate interests of the community.

There are two methods of curing the mischiefs of faction: the one, by removing its causes; the other, by controling its effects.

There are again two methods of removing the causes of faction: the one by destroying the liberty which is essential to its existence; the other, by giving to every citizen the same opinions, the same passions, and the same interests.

It could never be more truly said than of the first remedy, that it is worse than the disease. Liberty is to faction, what air is to fire, an aliment without which it instantly expires. But it could not be a less folly to abolish liberty, which is essential to political life, because it nourishes faction, than it would be to wish the annihilation of air, which is essential to animal life, because it imparts to fire its destructive agency.

The second expedient is as impracticable, as the first would be unwise. As long as the reason of man continues fallible, and he is at liberty to exercise it, different opinions will be formed. As long as the connection subsists between his reason and his self-love, his opinions and his passions will have a reciprocal influence on each other; and the former will be objects to which the latter will attach themselves. The diversity in the faculties of men from which the rights of property originate, is not less an insuperable obstacle to a uniformity of interests. The protection of these faculties is the first object of Government. From the protection of different and unequal faculties of acquiring property, the possession of different degrees and kinds of property immediately results: and from the influence of these on the sentiments and views of the respective proprietors, ensues a division of the society into different interests and parties.

The latent causes of faction are thus sown in the nature of man; and we see them every where brought into different degrees of activity, according to the different circumstances of civil society. A zeal for different opinions concerning religion, concerning Government and many other points, as well of speculation as of practice; an attachment of different leaders ambitiously contending for preeminence and power; or to persons of other descriptions whose fortunes have been interesting to the human passions, have in turn divided mankind into parties, inflamed them with mutual animosity, and rendered them much more disposed to vex and oppress each other, than to co-operate for their common good. So strong is this propensity of mankind to fall into mutual animosities, that where no substantial occasion presents itself, the most frivolous and fanciful distinctions have been sufficient to kindle their unfriendly passions, and excite their most violent conflicts. But the most common and durable source of factions, has been the various and unequal distribution of property. Those who hold, and those who are without property, have ever formed distinct interests in society. Those who are creditors, and those who are debtors, fall under a like discrimination. A landed interest, a manufacturing interest, a mercantile interest, a monied interest, with many lesser interests, grow up of necessity in civilized nations, and divide them into different classes, actuated by different sentiments and views. The regulation of these various and interfering interests forms the principal task of modern Legislation, and involves the spirit of party and faction in the necessary and ordinary operations of Government.

No man is allowed to be a judge in his own cause; because his interest would certainly bias his judgment, and, not improbably, corrupt his integrity. With equal, nay with greater reason, a body of men, are unfit to be both judges and parties, at the same time; yet, what are many of the most important acts of legislation, but so many judicial determinations, not indeed concerning the rights of single persons, but concerning the rights of large bodies of citizens; and what are the different classes of legislators, but advocates and parties to the causes which they determine? Is a law proposed concerning private debts? It is a question to which the creditors are parties on one side, and the debtors on the other. Justice ought to hold the balance between them. Yet the parties are and must be themselves the judges; and the most numerous party, or, in other words, the most powerful faction must be expected to prevail. Shall domestic manufactures be encouraged, and in what degree, by restrictions on foreign manufactures? are questions which would be differently decided by the landed and the manufacturing classes; and probably by neither, with a sole regard to justice and the public good. The apportionment of taxes on the various descriptions of property, is an act which seems to require the most exact impartiality; yet, there is perhaps no legislative act in which greater opportunity and temptation are given to a predominant party, to trample on the rules of justice. Every shilling with which they overburden the inferior number, is a shilling saved to their own pockets.

It is in vain to say, that enlightened statesmen will be able to adjust these clashing interests, and render them all subservient to the public good. Enlightened statesmen will not always be at the helm: Nor, in many cases, can such an adjustment be made at all, without taking into view indirect and remote considerations, which will rarely prevail over the immediate interest which one party may find in disregarding the rights of another, or the good of the whole.

The inference to which we are brought is, that the *causes* of faction cannot be removed; and that relief is only to be sought in the means of controling its *effects*.

If a faction consists of less than a majority, relief is supplied by the republican principle, which enables the majority to defeat its sinister views by regular vote: It may clog the administration, it may convulse the society; but it will be unable to execute and mask its violence under the forms of the Constitution. When a majority is included in a faction, the form of popular government on the other hand enables it to sacrifice to its ruling passion or interest, both the public good and the rights of other citizens. To secure the public good, and private rights, against the danger of such a faction, and at the same time to preserve the spirit and the form of popular government, is then the great object to which our enquiries are directed: Let me add that it is the great desideratum, by which alone this form of government can be rescued from the opprobrium under which it has so long labored, and be recommended to the esteem and adoption of mankind.

By what means is this object attainable? Evidently by one of two only. Either the existence of the same passion or interest in a majority at the same time, must be prevented; or the majority, having such co-existent passion or interest, must be rendered, by their number and local situation, unable to concert and carry into effect schemes of oppression. If the impulse and the opportunity be suffered to coincide, we well know that neither moral nor religious motives can be relied on as an adequate control. They are not found to be such on the injustice and violence of individuals, and lose their efficacy in proportion to the number combined together; that is, in proportion as their efficacy becomes needful.

From this view of the subject, it may be concluded, that a pure Democracy, by which I mean, a Society, consisting of a small number of citizens, who assemble and administer the Government in person, can admit of no cure for the mischiefs of faction. A common passion or interest will, in almost every case, be felt by a majority of the whole; a communication and concert results from the form of Government itself; and there is nothing to check the inducements to sacrifice the weaker party, or an obnoxious individual. Hence it is, that such Democracies have ever been spectacles of turbulence and contention; have ever been found incompatible with personal security, or the rights of property; and have in general been as short in their lives, as they have been violent in their deaths. Theoretic politicians, who have patronized this species of Government, have erroneously supposed, that by reducing mankind to a perfect equality in their political rights, they would, at the same time, be perfectly equalized and assimilated in their possessions, their opinions, and their passions.

A Republic, by which I mean a Government in which the scheme of representation takes place, opens a different prospect, and promises the cure for which we are seeking. Let us examine the points in which it varies from pure Democracy, and we shall comprehend both the nature of the cure, and the efficacy which it must derive from the Union.

The two great points of difference between a Democracy and a Republic are, first, the delegation of the Government, in the latter, to a small number of citizens elected by the rest: secondly, the greater number of citizens, and greater sphere of country, over which the latter may be extended.

The effect of the first difference is, on the one hand to refine and enlarge the public views, by passing them through the medium of a chosen body of citizens, whose wisdom may best discern the true interest of their country, and whose patriotism and love of justice, will be least likely to sacrifice it to temporary or partial considerations. Under such a regulation, it may well happen that the public voice pronounced by the representatives of the people, will be more consonant to the public good, than if pronounced by the people themselves convened for the purpose. On the other hand, the effect may be inverted. Men of factious tempers, of local prejudices, or of sinister designs, may by intrigue, by corruption or by other means, first obtain the suffrages, and then betray the interests of the people. The question resulting is, whether small or extensive Republics are most favorable to the election of proper guardians of the public weal; and it is clearly decided in favor of the latter by two obvious considerations

In the first place it is to be remarked that however small the Republic may be, the Representatives must be raised to a certain number, in order to guard against the cabals of a few; and that however large it may be, they must be limited to a certain number, in order to guard against the confusion of a multitude. Hence the number of Representatives in the two cases, not being in proportion to that of the Constituents, and being proportionally greatest in the small Republic, it follows, that if the proportion of fit characters, be not less, in the large than in the small Republic, the former will present a greater option, and consequently a greater probability of a fit choice.

In the next place, as each Representative will be chosen by a greater number of citizens in the large than in the small Republic, it will be more difficult for unworthy candidates to practise with success the vicious arts, by which elections are too often carried; and the suffrages of the people being more free, will be more likely to centre on men who possess the most attractive merit, and the most diffusive and established characters.

It must be confessed, that in this, as in most other cases, there is a mean, on both sides of which inconveniencies will be found to lie. By enlarging too much the number of electors, you render the representative too little acquainted with all their local circumstances and lesser interests; as by reducing it too much, you render him unduly attached to these, and too little fit to comprehend and pursue great and national objects. The Federal Constitution forms a happy combination in this respect; the great and aggregate interests being referred to the national, the local and particular, to the state legislatures.

The other point of difference is, the greater number of citizens and extent of territory which may be brought within the compass of Republican, than of Democratic Government; and it is this circumstance principally which renders factious combinations less to be dreaded in the former, than in the latter. The smaller the society, the fewer probably will be the distinct parties and interests composing it; the fewer the distinct parties and interests, the more frequently will a majority be found of the same party; and the smaller the number of individuals composing a majority, and the smaller the compass within which they are placed, the more easily will they concert and execute their plans of oppression. Extend the sphere, and you take in a greater variety of parties and interests; you make it less probable that a majority of the whole will have a common motive to invade the rights of other citizens; or if such a common motive exists, it will be more difficult for all who feel it to discover their own strength, and to act in unison with each other. Besides other impediments, it may be remarked, that where there is a consciousness of unjust or dishonorable purposes, a communication is always checked by distrust, in proportion to the number whose concurrence is necessary.

Hence it clearly appears, that the same advantage, which a Republic has over a Democracy, in controling the effects of faction, is enjoyed by a large over a small Republic—is enjoyed by the Union over the States composing it. Does this advantage consist in the substitution of Representatives, whose enlightened views and virtuous sentiments render them superior to local prejudices, and to schemes of injustice? It will not be denied, that the Representation of the Union will be most likely to possess these requisite endowments. Does it consist in the greater security afforded by a greater variety of parties, against the event of any one party being able to outnumber and oppress the rest? In an equal degree does the encreased variety of parties, comprised within the Union, encrease this security. Does it, in fine, consist in the greater obstacles opposed to the concert and accomplishment of the secret wishes of an unjust and interested majority? Here, again, the extent of the Union gives it the most palpable advantage.

The influence of factious leaders may kindle a flame within their particular States, but will be unable to spread a general conflagration through the other States: a religious sect, may degenerate into a political faction in a part of the Confederacy; but the variety of sects dispersed over the entire face of it, must secure the national Councils against any danger from that source: a rage for paper money, for an abolition of debts, for an equal division of property, or for any other improper or wicked project, will be less apt to pervade the whole body of the Union, than a particular member of it; in the same proportion as such a malady is more likely to taint a particular county or district, than an entire State.

In the extent and proper structure of the Union, therefore, we behold a Republican remedy for the diseases most incident to Republican Government. And according to the degree of pleasure and pride, we feel in being Republicans, ought to be our zeal in cherishing the spirit, and supporting the character of Federalists.

The Federalist No. 39
[Madison]

January 16, 1788

The last paper having concluded the observations which were meant to introduce a candid survey of the plan of government reported by the Convention, we now proceed to the execution of that part of our undertaking. The first question that offers itself is, whether the general form and aspect of the government be strictly republican? It is evident that no other form would be reconcilable with the genius of the people of America; with the fundamental principles of the revolution; or with that honorable determination, which animates every votary of freedom, to rest all our political experiments on the capacity of mankind for self-government. If the plan of the Convention therefore be found to depart from the republican character, its advocates must abandon it as no longer defensible.

What then are the distinctive characters of the republican form? Were an answer to this question to be sought, not by recurring to principles, but in the application of the term by political writers, to the constitutions of different States, no satisfactory one would ever be found. Holland, in which no particle of the supreme authority is derived from the people, has passed almost universally under the denomination of a republic. The same title has been bestowed on Venice, where absolute power over the great body of the people, is exercised in the most absolute manner, by a small body of hereditary nobles. Poland, which is a mixture of aristocracy and of monarchy in their worst forms, has been dignified with the same appellation. The government of England, which has one republican branch only, combined with a hereditary aristocracy and monarchy, has with equal impropriety been frequently placed on the list of republics. These examples, which are nearly as dissimilar to each other as to a genuine republic, shew the extreme inaccuracy with which the term has been used in political disquisitions.

If we resort for a criterion, to the different principles on which different forms of government are established, we may define a republic to be, or at least may bestow that name on, a government which derives all its powers directly or indirectly from the great body of the people; and is administered by persons holding their offices during pleasure, for a limited period, or during good behaviour. It is *essential* to such a government, that it be derived from the great body of the society, not from an inconsiderable proportion, or a favored class of it; otherwise a handful of tyrannical nobles, exercising their oppressions by a delegation of their powers, might aspire to the rank of republicans, and claim for their government the honorable title of republic. It is *sufficient* for such a government, that the persons administering it be appointed, either directly or indirectly, by the people; and that they hold their appointments by either of the tenures just specified; otherwise every government in the United States, as well as every other popular government that has been or can be well organized or well executed, would be degraded from the republican character. According to the Constitution of every State in the Union, some or other of the officers of government are appointed indirectly only by the people. According to most of them the chief magistrate himself is so appointed. And according to one, this mode of appointment is extended to one of the coordinate branches of the legislature. According to all the Constitutions also, the tenure of the highest offices is extended to a definite period, and in many instances, both within the legislative and executive departments, to a period of years. According to the provisions of most of the constitutions, again, as well as according to the most respectable and received opinions on the subject, the members of the judiciary department are to retain their offices by the firm tenure of good behaviour.

On comparing the Constitution planned by the Convention, with the standard here fixed, we perceived at once that it is in the most rigid sense conformable to it. The House of

Representatives, like that of one branch at least of all the State Legislatures, is elected immediately by the great body of the people. The Senate, like the present Congress, and the Senate of Maryland, derives its appointment indirectly from the people. The President is indirectly derived from the choice of the people, according to the example in most of the States. Even the judges, with all other officers of the Union, will, as in the several States, be the choice, though a remote choice, of the people themselves. The duration of the appointments is equally conformable to the republican standard, and to the model of the State Constitutions. The House of Representatives is periodically elective as in all the States: and for the period of two years as in the State of South-Carolina. The Senate is elective for the period of six years; which is but one year more than the period of the Senate of Maryland; and but two more than that of the Senates of New-York and Virginia. The President is to continue in office for the period of four years; as in New-York and Delaware, the chief magistrate is elected for three years, and in South-Carolina for two years. In the other States the election is annual. In several of the States however, no constitutional provision is made for the impeachment of the Chief Magistrate. And in Delaware and Virginia, he is not impeachable till out of office. The President of the United States is impeachable at any time during his continuance in office. The tenure by which the Judges are to hold their places, is, as it unquestionably ought to be, that of good behaviour. The tenure of the ministerial offices generally will be a subject of legal regulation, conformably to the reason of the case, and the example of the State Constitutions.

Could any further proof be required of the republican complextion of this system, the most decisive one might be found in its absolute prohibition of titles of nobility, both under the Federal and the State Governments; and in its express guarantee of the republican form to each of the latter.

But it was not sufficient, say the adversaries of the proposed Constitution, for the Convention to adhere to the republican form. They ought, with equal care, to have preserved the *federal* form, which regards the union as a *confederacy* of sovereign States; instead of which, they have framed a *national* government, which regards the union as a *consolidation* of the States. And it is asked by what authority this bold and radical innovation was undertaken. The handle which has been made of this objection requires, that it should be examined with some precision.

Without enquiring into the accuracy of the distinction on which the objection is founded, it will be necessary to a just estimate of its force, first to ascertain the real character of the government in question; secondly, to enquire how far the Convention were authorised to propose such a government; and thirdly, how far the duty they owed to their country, could supply any defect of regular authority.

First. In order to ascertain the real character of the government it may be considered in relation to the foundation on which it is to be established; to the sources from which its ordinary powers are to be drawn; to the operation of those powers; to the extent of them; and to the authority by which future changes in the government are to be introduced.

On examining the first relation, it appears on one hand that the Constitution is to be founded on the assent and ratification of the people of America, given by deputies elected for the special purpose; but on the other, that this assent and ratification is to be given by the people, not as individuals composing one entire nation; but as composing the distinct and independent States to which they respectively belong. It is to be the assent and ratification of the several States, derived from the supreme authority in each State, the authority of the people themselves. The act therefore establishing the Constitution, will not be a *national* but a *federal* act.

That it will be a federal and not a national act, as these terms are understood by the objectors, the act of the people as forming so many independent States, not as forming one aggregate nation, is obvious from this single consideration that it is to result neither from the decision of a *majority* of the people of the Union, nor from that of a *majority* of the States. It must result from the *unanimous* assent of the several States that are parties to it, differing no other wise from their ordinary assent than in its being expressed, not by the legislative authority, but by that of the people themselves. Were the people regarded in this transaction as forming one nation, the will of the majority of the whole people of the United States, would bind the minority; in the same manner as the majority in each State must bind the minority; and the will of the majority must be determined either by a comparison of the individual votes; or by considering the will of a majority of the States, as evidence of the will of a majority of the people of the United States. Neither of these rules has been adopted. Each State in ratifying the Constitution, is considered as a sovereign body independent of all others, and only to be bound by its own voluntary act. In this relation then the new Constitution will, if established, be a *federal* and not a *national* Constitution.

The next relation is to the sources from which the ordinary powers of government are to be derived. The house of representatives will derive its powers from the people of America; and the people will be represented in the same proportion, and on the same principle, as they are in the Legislature of a particular State. So far the Government is *national* not *federal*. The Senate on the other hand will derive its powers from the States, as political and co-equal societies; and these will be represented on the principle of equality in the Senate, as they now are in the existing Congress. So far the government is *federal*, not *national*. The executive power will be derived from a very compound source. The immediate election of the President is to be made by the States in their political characters. The votes allotted to them, are in a compound ratio, which considers them partly as distinct and co-equal societies; partly as unequal members of the same society. The eventual election, again is to be made by that branch of the Legislature which consists of the national representatives; but in this particular act, they are to be thrown into the form of individual delegations from so many distinct and co-equal bodies politic. From this aspect of the Government, it appears to be of a mixed character presenting at least as many *federal* as *national* features.

The difference between a federal and national Government as it relates to the *operation of the Government* is supposed to consist in this, that in the former, the powers operate on the political bodies composing the confederacy, in their political capacities: In the latter, on the individual citizens, composing the nation, in their individual capacities. On trying the Constitution by this criterion, it falls under the *national*, not the *federal* character; though perhaps not so compleatly, as has been understood. In several cases and particularly in the trial of controversies to which States may be parties, they must be viewed and proceeded against in their collective and political capacities only. So far the national countenance of the Government on this side seems to be disfigured by a few federal features. But this blemish is perhaps unavoidable in any plan; and the operation of the Government on the people in their individual capacities, in its ordinary and most essential proceedings, may on the whole designate it in this relation a *national* Government.

But if the Government be national with regard to the *operation* of its powers, it changes its aspect when we contemplate it in relation to the *extent* of its powers. The idea of a national Government involves in it, not only an authority over the individual citizens; but an indefinite supremacy over all persons and things, so far as they are objects of lawful Government. Among a people consolidated into one nation, this supremacy is compleatly vested in the national Legislature. Among communities united for particular purposes, it is vested partly in the general, and partly in the municipal Legislatures. In the former case, all local authorities are subordinate to the supreme; and may be controuled, directed or abolished by it at pleasure. In the latter the local or municipal authorities form distinct and independent portions of the supremacy, no more subject within their respective spheres to the general authority, than the general authority is subject to them, within its own sphere. In this relation then the proposed Government cannot be deemed a *national* one; since its jurisdiction extends to certain enumerated objects only, and leaves to the several States a residuary and inviolable sovereignty over all other objects. It is true that in controversies relating to the boundary between the two jurisdictions, the tribunal which is ultimately to decide, is to be established under the general Government. But this does not change the principle of the case. The decision is to be impartially made, according to the rules of the Constitution; and all the usual and most effectual precautions are taken to secure this impartiality. Some such tribunal is clearly essential to prevent an appeal to the sword, and a dissolution of the compact; and that it ought to be established under the general, rather than under the local Governments; or to speak more properly, that it could be safely established under the first alone, is a position not likely to be combated.

If we try the Constitution by its last relation, to the authority by which amendments are to be made, we find it neither wholly *national*, nor wholly *federal*. Were it wholly national, the supreme and ultimate authority would reside in the *majority* of the people of the Union; and this authority would be competent at all times, like that of a majority of every national society, to alter or abolish its established Government. Were it wholly federal on the other hand, the concurrence of each State in the Union would be essential to every alteration that would be binding on all. The mode provided by the plan of the Convention is not founded on either of these principles. In requiring more than a majority, and particularly, in computing the proportion by *States*, not by *citizens*, it departs from the *national*, and advances towards the *federal* character: In rendering the concurrence of less than the whole number of States sufficient, it loses again the *federal*, and partakes of the *national* character.

The proposed Constitution therefore is in strictness neither a national nor a federal constitution; but a composition of both. In its foundation, it is federal, not national; in the sources from which the ordinary powers of the Government are drawn, it is partly federal, and partly national: in the operation of these powers, it is national, not federal: In the extent of them again, it is federal, not national: And finally, in the authoritative mode of introducing amendments, it is neither wholly federal, nor wholly national.

The Federalist No. 51
[Madison]

February 6, 1788

To what expedient then shall we finally resort for maintaining in practice the necessary partition of power among the several departments, as laid down in the constitution? The only answer that can be given is, that as all these exterior provisions are found to be inadequate, the defect must be supplied, by so contriving the interior structure of the government, as that its several constituent parts may, by their mutual relations, be the means of keeping each other in their proper places. Without presuming to undertake a full developement of this important idea, I will hazard a few general observations, which may perhaps place it in a clearer light, and enable us to form a more correct judgment of the principles and structure of the government planned by the convention.

In order to lay a due foundation for that separate and distinct exercise of the different powers of government, which to a certain extent, is admitted on all hands to be essential to the preservation of liberty, it is evident that each department should have a will of its own; and consequently should be so constituted, that the members of each should have as little agency as possible in the appointment of the members of the others. Were this principle rigorously adhered to, it would require that all the appointments for the supreme executive, legislative, and judiciary magistracies, should be drawn from the same fountain of authority, the people, through channels, having no communication whatever with one another. Perhaps such a plan of constructing the several departments would be less difficult in practice than it may in contemplation appear. Some difficulties however, and some additional expence, would attend the execution of it. Some deviations therefore from the principle must be admitted. In the constitution of the judiciary department in particular, it might be inexpedient to insist rigorously on the principle; first, because peculiar qualifications being essential in the members, the primary consideration ought to be to select that mode of choice, which best secures these qualifications; secondly, because the permanent tenure by which the appointments are held in that department, must soon destroy all sense of dependence on the authority conferring them.

It is equally evident that the members of each department should be as little dependent as possible on those of the others, for the emoluments annexed to their offices. Were the executive magistrate, or the judges, not independent of the legislature in this particular, their independence in every other would be merely nominal.

But the great security against a gradual concentration of the several powers in the same department, consists in giving to those who administer each department, the necessary constitutional means, and personal motives, to resist encroachments of the others. The provision for defence must in this, as in all other cases, be made commensurate to the danger of attack. Ambition must be made to counteract ambition. The interest of the man must be connected with the constitutional rights of the place. It may be a reflection on human nature, that such devices should be necessary to controul the abuses of government. But what is government itself but the greatest of all reflections on human nature? If men were angels, no government would be necessary. If angels were to govern men, neither external nor internal controuls on government would be necessary. In framing a government which is to be administered by men over men, the great difficulty lies in this: You must first enable the government to controul the governed; and in the next place, oblige it to controul itself. A dependence on the people is no doubt the primary controul on the government; but experience has taught mankind the necessity of auxiliary precautions.

This policy of supplying by opposite and rival interests, the defect of better motives, might be traced through the whole system of human affairs, private as well as public. We see it particularly displayed in all the subordinate distributions of power; where the constant aim is to divide and arrange the several offices in such a manner as that each may be a check on the other; that the private interest of every individual, may be a centinel over the public rights. These inventions of prudence cannot be less requisite in the distribution of the supreme powers of the state.

But it is not possible to give to each department an equal power of self defence. In republican government the legislative authority, necessarily, predominates. The remedy for this inconveniency is, to divide the legislature into different branches; and to render them by different modes of election, and different principles of action, as little connected with each other, as the nature of their common functions, and their common dependence on the society, will admit. It may even be necessary to guard against dangerous encroachments by still further precautions. As the weight of the legislative authority requires that it should be thus divided, the weakness of the executive may require, on the other hand, that it should be fortified. An absolute negative, on the legislature, appears at first view to be the natural defence with which the executive magistrate should be armed. But perhaps it would be neither altogether safe, nor alone sufficient. On ordinary occasions, it might not be exerted with the requisite firmness; and on extraordinary occasions, it might be perfidiously abused. May not this defect of an absolute negative be supplied, by some qualified connection between this weaker department, and the weaker branch of the stronger department, by which the latter may be led to support the constitutional rights of the former, without being too much detached from the rights of its own department?

If the principles on which these observations are founded be just, as I persuade myself they are, and they be applied as a criterion, to the several state constitutions, and to the federal constitution, it will be found, that if the latter does not perfectly correspond with them, the former are infinitely less able to bear such a test.

There are moreover two considerations particularly applicable to the federal system of America, which place that system in a very interesting point of view.

First. In a single republic, all the power surrender by the people, is submitted to the administration of a single government; and usurpations are guarded against by a division of the government into distinct and separate departments. In the compound republic of America, the power surrendered by the people, is first divided between two distinct governments, and then the portion allotted to each, subdivided among distinct and separate departments. Hence a double security arises to the rights of the people. The different governments will controul each other; at the same time that each will be controuled by itself.

Second. It is of great importance in a republic, not only to guard the society against the oppression of its rulers; but to guard one part of the society against the injustice of the other part. Different interests necessarily exist in different classes of citizens. If a majority be united by a common interest, the rights of the minority will be insecure. There are but two methods of providing against this evil: The one by creating a will in the community independent of the majority, that is, of the society itself; the other by comprehending in the society so many separate descriptions of citizens, as will render an unjust combination of a majority of the whole, very improbable, if not impracticable. The first method prevails in all governments possessing an hereditary or self appointed authority. This at best is but a precarious security; because a power independent of the society may as well espouse the unjust views of the major, as the rightful interests, of the minor party, and may possibly be turned against both parties. The second method will be exemplified in the federal republic of the United States, Whilst all authority in it will be derived from and dependent on the society, the society itself will be broken into so many parts, interests and classes of citizens, that the rights of individuals or of the minority, will be in little danger from interested combinations of the majority. In a free government, the security for civil rights must be the same as for the religious rights. It consists in the one case in the multiplicity of interests, and in the other, in the multiplicity of sects. The degree of security in both cases will depend on the number of interests and sects; and this may be presumed to depend on the extent of country and number of people comprehended under the same government. This view of the subject must particularly recommend a proper federal system to all the sincere and considerate friends of republican government: Since it shews that in exact proportion as the territory of the union may be formed into more circumscribed confederacies or states, oppressive combinations of a majority will be facilitated, the best security under the republican form, for the rights of every class of citizens, will be diminished; and consequently, the stability and independence of some member of the government, the only other security, must be proportionally increased. Justice is the end of government. It is the end of civil society. It ever has been, and ever will be pursued, until it be obtained, or until liberty be lost in the pursuit. In a society under the forms of which the stronger faction can readily unite and oppress the weaker, anarchy may as truly be said to reign, as in a state of nature where the weaker individual is not secured against the violence of the stronger: And as in the latter state even the stronger individuals are prompted by the uncertainty of their condition, to submit to a government which may protect the weak as well as themselves: So in the former state, will the more powerful factions or parties be gradually induced by a like motive, to wish for a government which will protect all parties, the weaker as well as the more powerful. It can be little doubted, that if the state of Rhode Island was separated from the confederacy, and left to itself, the insecurity of rights under the popular form of government within such narrow limits, would be displayed by such reiterated oppressions of factious majorities, that some power altogether independent of the people would soon be called for by the voice of the very factions whose misrule had proved the necessity of it. In the extended republic of the United States, and among the great variety of interests, parties and sects which it embraces, a coalition of a majority of the whole society could seldom take place on any other principles than those of justice and the general good; and there being thus less danger to a minor from the will of the major party, there must be less pretext also, to provide for the security of the former, by introducing into the government a will not dependent on the latter; or in other words, a will independent of the society itself. It is no less certain than it is important, notwithstanding the contrary opinions which have been entertained, that the larger the society, provided it lie within a practicable sphere, the more duly capable it will be of self government. And happily, for the *republican cause*, the practicable sphere may be carried to a very great extent, by a judicious modification and mixture of the *federal principle*.

The Federalist No. 78
[Hamilton]

May 28, 1788

We proceed now to an examination of the judiciary department of the proposed government.

In unfolding the defects of the existing confederation, the utility and necessity of a federal judicature have been clearly pointed out. It is the less necessary to recapitulate the considerations there urged; as the propriety of the institution in the abstract is not disputed: The only questions which have been raised being relative to the manner of constituting it, and to its extent. To these points therefore our observations shall be confined.

The manner of constituting it seems to embrace these several objects—1st. The mode of appointing the judges. 2d. The tenure by which they are to hold their places. 3d. The partition of the judiciary authority between different courts, and their relations to each other.

First. As to the mode of appointing the judges: This is the same with that of appointing the officers of the union in general, and has been so fully discussed in the two last numbers, that nothing can be said here which would not be useless repetition.

Second. As to the tenure by which the judges are to hold their places: This chiefly concerns their duration in office; the provisions for their support; and the precautions for their responsibility.

According to the plan of the convention, all the judges who may be appointed by the United States are to hold their offices *during good behaviour,* which is conformable to the most approved of the state constitutions; and among the rest, to that of this state. Its propriety having been drawn into question by the adversaries of that plan, is no light symptom of the rage for objection which disorders their imaginations and judgments. The standard of good behaviour for the continuance in office of the judicial magistracy is certainly one of the most valuable of the modern improvements in the practice of government. In a monarchy it is an excellent barrier to the despotism of the prince: In a republic it is a no less excellent barrier to the encroachments and oppressions of the representative body. And it is the best expedient which can be devised in any government, to secure a steady, upright and impartial administration of the laws.

Whoever attentively considers the different departments of power must perceive, that in a government in which they are separated from each other, the judiciary, from the nature of its functions, will always be the least dangerous to the political rights of the constitution; because it will be least in a capacity to annoy or injure them. The executive not only dispenses the honors, but holds the sword of the community. The legislature not only commands the purse, but prescribes the rules by which the duties and rights of every citizen are to be regulated. The judiciary on the contrary has no influence over either the sword or the purse, no direction either of the strength or of the wealth of the society, and can take no active resolution whatever. It may truly be said to have neither Force nor Will, but merely judgment; and must ultimately depend upon the aid of the executive arm even for the efficacy of its judgments.

This simple view of the matter suggests several important consequences. It proves incontestibly that the judiciary is beyond comparison the weakest of the three departments of power;* that it can never attack with success either of the other two; and that all possible care is requisite to enable it to defend itself against their attacks. It equally proves, that though individual oppression may now and then proceed from the courts of justice, the general liberty of the people can never be endangered from that quarter: I mean, so long as the judiciary remains truly distinct from both the legislative and executive. For I agree that "there is no liberty, if the power of judging be not separated from the legislative and executive powers."† And it proves, in the last place, that as liberty can have nothing to fear from the judiciary alone, but would have everything to fear from its union with either of the other departments; that as all the effects of such an union must ensue from a dependence of the former on the latter, notwithstanding a nominal and apparent separation; that as from the natural feebleness of the judiciary, it is in continual jeopardy of being overpowered, awed or influenced by its coordinate branches; and that as nothing can contribute so much to its firmness and independence, as permanency in office, this quality may therefore be justly regarded as an indispensable ingredient in its constitution; and in a great measure as the citadel of the public justice and the public security.

The complete independence of the courts of justice is peculiarly essential in a limited constitution. By a limited constitution I understand one which contains certain specified exceptions to the legislative authority; such for instance as that it shall pass no bills of attainder, no *ex post facto* laws, and the like. Limitations of this kind can be preserved in practice no other way than through the medium of the courts of justice; whose duty it must be to declare all acts contrary to the manifest tenor of the constitution void. Without this, all the reservations of particular rights or privileges would amount to nothing.

Some perplexity respecting the right of the courts to pronounce legislative acts void, because contrary to the constitution, has arisen from an imagination that the doctrine would imply a superiority of the judiciary to the legislative power. It is urged that the authority which can declare the acts of another void, must necessarily be superior to the one whose acts may be declared void. As this doctrine is of great importance in all the American constitutions, a brief discussion of the grounds on which it rests cannot be unacceptable.

There is no position which depends on clearer principles, than that every act of a delegated authority, contrary to the tenor of the commission under which it is exercised, is void. No legislative act therefore contrary to the constitution can be valid. To deny this would be to affirm that the deputy is greater than his principal; that the servant is above his master; that the representatives of the people are superior to the people themselves; that men acting by virtue of powers may do not only what their powers do not authorise, but what they forbid.

If it be said that the legislative body are themselves the constitutional judges of their own powers, and that the construction they put upon them is conclusive upon the other

---

*The celebrated Montesquieu speaking of them says, "of the three powers above mentioned, the JUDICIARY is next to nothing," *Spirit of Laws*, vol. 1, page 186.
†Idem. page 181.

departments, it may be answered, that this cannot be the natural presumption, where it is not to be collected from any particular provisions in the constitution. It is not otherwise to be supposed that the constitution could intend to enable the representatives of the people to substitute their *will* to that of their constituents. It is far more rational to suppose that the courts were designed to be an intermediate body between the people and the legislature, in order, among other things, to keep the latter within the limits assigned to their authority. The interpretation of the laws is the proper and peculiar province of the courts. A constitution is in fact, and must be, regarded by the judges as a fundamental law. It therefore belongs to them to ascertain its meaning as well as the meaning of any particular act proceeding from the legislative body. If there should happen to be an irreconcileable variance between the two, that which has the superior obligation and validity ought of course to be preferred; or in other words, the constitution ought to be preferred to the statute, the intention of the people to the intention of their agents.

Nor does this conclusion by any means suppose a superiority of the judicial to the legislative power. It only supposes that the power of the people is superior to both; and that where the will of the legislature declared in its statutes, stands in opposition to that of the people declared in the constitution, the judges ought to be governed by the latter, rather than the former. They ought to regulate their decisions by the fundamental laws, rather than by those which are not fundamental.

This exercise of judicial discretion in determining between two contradictory laws, is exemplified in a familiar instance. It not uncommonly happens, that there are two statutes existing at one time, clashing in whole or in part with each other, and neither of them containing any repealing clause or expression. In such a case, it is the province of the courts to liquidate and fix their meaning and operation: So far as they can by any fair construction be reconciled to each other; reason and law conspire to dictate that this should be done. Where this is impracticable, it becomes a matter of necessity to give effect to one, in exclusion of the other. The rule which has obtained in the courts for determining their relative validity is that the last in order of time shall be preferred to the first. But this is mere rule of construction, not derived from any positive law, but from the nature and reason of the thing. It is a rule not enjoined upon the courts by legislative provision, but adopted by themselves, as consonant to truth and propriety, for the direction of their conduct as interpreters of the law. They thought it reasonable, that between the interfering acts of an *equal* authority, that which was the last indication of its will, should have the preference.

But in regard to the interfering acts of a superior and subordinate authority, of an original and derivative power, the nature and reason of the thing indicate the converse of that rule as proper to be followed. They teach us that the prior act of a superior ought to be preferred to the subsequent act of an inferior and subordinate authority; and that, accordingly, whenever a particular statute contravenes the constitution, it will be the duty of the judicial tribunals to adhere to the latter, and disregard the former.

It can be of no weight to say, that the courts on the pretence of a repugnancy, may substitute their own pleasure to the constitutional intentions of the legislature. This might as well happen in the case of two contradictory statutes; or it might as well happen in every adjudication upon any single statute. The courts must declare the sense of the law; and if they should be disposed to exercise WILL instead of JUDGMENT, the consequence would equally be the substitution of their pleasure to that of the legislative body. The observation, if it proved any thing, would prove that there ought to be no judges distinct from that body.

If then the courts of justice are to be considered as the bulwarks of a limited constitution against legislative encroachments, this consideration will afford a strong argument for the permanent tenure of judicial offices, since nothing will contribute so much as this to that independent spirit in the judges, which must be essential to the faithful performance of so arduous a duty.

This independence of the judges is equally requisite to guard the constitution and the rights of individuals from the effects of those ill humours which the arts of designing men, or the influence of particular conjunctures, sometimes disseminate among the people themselves, and which, though they speedily give place to better information and more deliberate reflection, have a tendency in the mean time to occasion dangerous innovations in the government, and serious oppressions of the minor party in the community. Though I trust the friends of the proposed constitution will never concur with its enemies* in questioning that fundamental principle of republican government, which admits the right of the people to alter or abolish the established constitution whenever they find it inconsistent with their happiness; yet it is not to be inferred from this principle, that the representatives of the people, whenever a momentary inclination happens to lay hold of a majority of their constituents incompatible with the provisions in the existing constitution, would on that account be justifiable in a violation of those provisions; or that the courts would be under a greater obligation to connive at infractions in this shape, than when they had proceeded wholly from the cabals of the representative body. Until the people have by some solemn and authoritative act annulled or changed the established form, it is binding upon themselves collectively, as well as individually; and no presumption, or even knowledge of their sentiments, can warrant their representatives in a departure from it, prior to such an act. But it is easy to see that it would require an uncommon portion of fortitude in the judges to do their duty as faithful guardians of the constitution, where legislative invasions of it had been instigated by the major voice of the community.

But it is not with a view to infractions of the constitution only that the independence of the judges may be an essential safeguard against the effects of occasional ill humours in the society. These sometimes extend no farther than to the injury of the private rights of particular classes of citizens, by unjust and partial laws. Here also the firmness of the judicial magistracy is of vast importance in mitigating the severity, and confining the operation of such laws. It not only serves to moderate the immediate mischiefs of those which may have been passed, but it operates as a check upon the legislative body in passing them; who, perceiving that obstacles to the success of an iniquitous intention are to be expected from the scruples of the courts, are in a manner compelled by the very motives of the injustice they meditate, to qualify their attempts. This is a circumstance calculated to have more influence upon the character of our governments, than but few may be aware of. The benefits of the integrity and moderation of the judiciary have already been felt in more states than one; and though they may have displeased those whose sinister expectations they may have disappointed, they must have commanded the esteem and applause of all the virtuous and disinterested. Considerate men of every description ought to prize whatever will tend to beget or fortify that temper in the courts; as no man can be sure that he may not be tomorrow the victim of a spirit of injustice, by which he may be a gainer to-day. And every man must now feel that the inevitable tendency of such a spirit is to sap the foundations of public and private confidence, and to introduce in its stead, universal distrust and distress.

* Vide Protest of the minority of the convention of Pennsylvania, Martin's speech &c. (Publius) Hamilton referred to "The Address and Reasons of Dissent of the Minority of the Convention of the State of Pennsylvania to their Constituents." Signed by twenty-one members of the Pennsylvania Convention, the "Address" appeared in *The Pennsylvania Packet and Daily Advertiser* on December 18, 1787, six days after Pennsylvania had ratified the Constitution. "Martin's speech" presumably referred to an address by Luther Martin, member of the Constitutional Convention but bitter foe of the proposed Constitution, before the Maryland House of Delegates on January 7, 1788. (Editor)

That inflexible and uniform adherence to the rights of the constitution and of individuals, which we perceive to be indispensable in the courts of justice, can certainly not be expected from judges who hold their offices by a temporary commission. Periodical appointments, however regulated, or by whomsoever made, would in some way or other be fatal to their necessary independence. If the power of making them was committed either to the executive or legislature, there would be danger of an improper complaisance to the branch which possessed it; if to both, there would be an unwillingness to hazard the displeasure of either; if to the people, or to persons chosen by them for the special purpose, there would be too great a disposition to consult popularity, to justify a reliance that nothing would be consulted but the constitution and the laws.

There is yet a further and a weighty reason for the permanency of the judicial offices; which is deducible from the nature of the qualifications they require. It has been frequently remarked with great propriety, that a voluminous code of laws is one of the inconveniences necessarily connected with the advantages of a free government. To avoid an arbitrary discretion in the courts, it is indispensable that they should be bound down by strict rules and precedents, which serve to define and point out their duty in every particular case that comes before them; and it will readily be conceived from the variety of controversies which grow out of the folly and wickedness of mankind, that the records of those precedents must unavoidably swell to a very considerable bulk, and must demand long and laborious study to acquire a competent knowledge of them. Hence it is that there can be but few men in the society, who will have sufficient skill in the laws to qualify them for the stations of judges. And making the proper deductions for the ordinary depravity of human nature, the number must be still smaller of those who unite the requisite integrity with the requisite knowledge. These considerations apprise us, that the government can have no great option between fit characters; and that a temporary duration in office, which would naturally discourage such characters from quitting a lucrative line of practice to accept a seat on the bench, would have a tendency to throw the administration of justice into hands less able, and less well qualified to conduct it with utility and dignity. In the present circumstances of this country, and in those in which it is likely to be for a long time to come, the disadvantages on this score would be greater than they may at first sight appear; but it must be confessed that they are far inferior to those which present themselves under the other aspects of the subject.

Upon the whole there can be no room to doubt that the convention acted wisely in copying from the models of those constitutions which have established *good behaviour* as the tenure of their judicial offices in point of duration; and that so far from being blameable on this account, their plan would have been inexcuseably defective if it had wanted this important feature of good government. The experience of Great Britain affords an illustrious comment on the excellence of the institution.

The Federalist No. 84
[Hamilton]

May 28, 1788

In the course of the foregoing review of the constitution I have taken notice of, and endeavoured to answer, most of the objections which have appeared against it. There however remain a few which either did not fall naturally under any particular head, or were forgotten in their proper places. These shall now be discussed; but as the subject has been drawn into great length, I shall so far consult brevity as to comprise all my observations on these miscellaneous points in a single paper.

The most considerable of these remaining objections is, that the plan of the convention contains no bill of rights. Among other answers given to this, it has been upon different occasions remarked, that the constitutions of several of the states are in a similar predicament. I add, that New-York is of this number. And yet the opposers of the new system in this state, who profess an unlimited admiration for its constitution, are among the most intemperate partizans of a bill of rights. To justify their zeal in this matter, they alledge two things; one is, that though the constitution of New-York has no bill of rights prefixed to it, yet it contains in the body of it various provisions in favour of particular privileges and rights, which in substance amount to the same thing; the other is, that the constitution adopts in their full extent the common and statute law of Great-Britain, by which many other rights not expressed in it are equally secured.

To the first I answer, that the constitution proposed by the convention contains, as well as the constitution of this state, a number of such provisions.

Independent of those, which relate to the structure of the government, we find the following: Article I. section 3. clause 7. "Judgment in cases of impeachment shall not extend further than to removal from office, and disqualification to hold and enjoy any office of honour, trust or profit under the United States; but the party convicted shall nevertheless be liable and subject to indictment, trial, judgment and punishment, according to law." Section 9. of the same article, clause 2. "The privilege of the writ of *habeas corpus* shall not be suspended, unless when in cases of rebellion or invasion the public safety may require it." Clause 3. "No bill of attainder or *ex post facto* law shall be passed." Clause 7.* "No title of nobility shall be granted by the United States: And no person holding any office of profit or trust under them, shall, without the consent of the congress, accept of any present, emolument, office or title, of any kind whatever, from any king, prince or foreign state." Article III. section 2. clause 3. "The trial of all crimes, except in cases of impeachment, shall be by jury; and such trial shall be held in the state where the said crimes shall have been committed; but when not committed within any state, the trial shall be at such place or places as the congress may by law have directed." Section 3, of the same article, "Treason against the United States shall consist only in levying war against them, or in adhering to their enemies, giving them aid and comfort. No person shall be convicted of treason unless on the testimony of two witnesses to the same overt act, or on confession in open court." And clause 3,† of the same section. "The congress shall have power to declare the punishment of treason, but no attainder of treason shall work corruption of blood, or forfeiture, except during the life of the person attainted."

It may well be a question whether these are not upon the whole, of equal importance with any which are to be found in the constitution of this state. The establishment of the writ of *habeas corpus*, the prohibition of *ex post facto* laws, and of TITLES OF NOBILITY, *to which we have no corresponding provisions in our constitution*, are perhaps greater securities to liberty and republicanism than any it contains. The creation of crimes after the commission of the fact, or in other words, the subjecting of men to punishment for things which, when they were done, were breaches of no law, and the practice of arbitrary imprisonments have been in all ages the favourite and most formidable instruments of tyranny. The observations of the judicious Blackstone‡ in reference to the latter, are well worthy of recital. "To bereave a man of life (says he) or by violence to confiscate his estate, without accusation or trial, would be so gross and notorious an act of despotism, as must at once convey the alarm of tyranny throughout the whole nation; but confinement of the person by secretly hurrying him to gaol, where

---

*This is Clause 8 in the present-day Constitution. (Editor)

†This is Clause 2 in the present-day Constitution. (Editor)

‡Vide Blackstone's Commentaries, vol. 1, page 136. (The reference is, of course, to Sir William Blackstone's *Commentaries on the Laws of England*, ten editions of which had appeared by 1787.—Editor)

his sufferings are unknown or forgotten, is a less public, a less striking, and therefore a *more dangerous engine* of arbitrary government." And as a remedy for this fatal evil, he is every where peculiarly emphatical in his encomiums on the *habeas corpus* act, which in one place he calls "the BULWARK of the British constitution."*

Nothing need be said to illustrate the importance of the prohibition of titles of nobility. This may truly be denominated the corner stone of republican government; for so long as they are excluded, there can never be serious danger that the government will be any other than that of the people.

To this second, that is, to the pretended establishment of the common and statute law by the constitution, I answer, that they are expressly made subject "to such alterations and provisions as the legislature shall from time to time make concerning the same." They are therefore at any moment liable to repeal by the ordinary legislative power, and of course have no constitutional sanction. The only use of the declaration was to recognize the ancient law, and to remove doubts which might have been occasioned by the revolution. This consequently can be considered as no part of a declaration of rights, which under our constitutions must be intended as limitations of the power of government itself.

It has been several times truly remarked, that bills of rights are in their origin, stipulations between kings and their subjects, abridgments of prerogative in favor of privilege, reservations of rights not surrendered to the prince. Such was MAGNA CHARTA, obtained by the Barons, sword in hand, from king John. Such were the subsequent confirmations of that charter by subsequent princes. Such was the *petition of right* assented to by Charles the First, in the beginning of his reign. Such also was the declaration of right presented by the lords and commons to the prince of Orange in 1688, and afterwards thrown into the form of an act of parliament, called the bill of rights. It is evident, therefore, that according to their primitive signification, they have no application to constitutions professedly founded upon the power of the people, and executed by their immediate representatives and servants. Here, in strictness, the people surrender nothing, and as they retain every thing, they have no need of particular reservations. "WE THE PEOPLE of the United States, to secure the blessings of liberty to ourselves and our posterity, do *ordain* and *establish* this constitution for the United States of America." Here is a better recognition of popular rights than volumes of those aphorisms which make the principal figure in several of our state bills of rights, and which would sound much better in a treatise of ethics than in a constitution of government.

But a minute detail of particular rights is certainly far less applicable to a constitution like that under consideration, which is merely intended to regulate the general political interests of the nation, than to a constitution which has the regulation of every species of personal and private concerns. If therefore the loud clamours against the plan of the convention on this score, are well founded, no epithets of reprobation will be too strong for the constitution of this state. But the truth is, that both of them contain all, which in relation to their objects, is reasonably to be desired.

I go further, and affirm that bills of rights, in the sense and in the extent in which they are contended for, are not only unnecessary in the proposed constitution, but would even be dangerous. They would contain various exceptions to powers which are not granted; and on this very account, would afford a colourable pretext to claim more than were granted. For why declare that things shall not be done which there is no power to do? Why for instance, should it be said, that the liberty of the press shall not be restrained, when no power is given by which restrictions may be imposed? I will not contend that such a provision would confer a regulating power; but it is evident that it would furnish, to men disposed to usurp, a plausible pretence for claiming that power. They might urge with a semblance of reason, that the

---

* Idem, vol. 4, page 438. (The correct page reference is 421 instead of 438.—Editor)

constitution ought not to be charged with the absurdity of providing against the abuse of an authority, which was not given, and that the provision against restraining the liberty of the press afforded a clear implication, that a power to prescribe proper regulations concerning it, was intended to be vested in the national government. This may serve as a specimen of the numerous handles which would be given to the doctrine of constructive powers, by the indulgence of an injudicious zeal for bills of rights.

On the subject of the liberty of the press, as much has been said, I cannot forbear adding a remark or two: In the first place, I observe that there is not a syllable concerning it in the constitution of this state, and in the next, I contend that whatever has been said about it in that of any other state, amounts to nothing. What signifies a declaration that "the liberty of the press shall be inviolably preserved?" What is the liberty of the press? Who can give it any definition which would not leave the utmost latitude for evasion? I hold it to be impracticable; and from this, I infer, that its security, whatever fine declarations may be inserted in any constitution respecting it, must altogether depend on public opinion, and on the general spirit of the people and of the government.* And here, after all, as intimated upon another occasion, must we seek for the only solid basis of all our rights.

There remains but one other view of this matter to conclude the point. The truth is, after all the declamation we have heard, that the constitution is itself in every rational sense, and to every useful purpose, A BILL OF RIGHTS. The several bills of rights, in Great-Britain, form its constitution, and conversely the constitution of each state is its bill of rights. And the proposed constitution, if adopted, will be the bill of rights of the union. Is it one object of a bill of rights to declare and specify the political privileges of the citizens in the structure and administration of the government? This is done in the most ample and precise manner in the plan of the convention, comprehending various precautions for the public security, which are not to be found in any of the state constitutions. Is another object of a bill of rights to define certain immunities and modes of proceeding, which are relative to personal and private concerns? This we have seen has also been attended to, in a variety of cases, in the same plan. Advertising therefore to the substantial meaning of a bill of rights, it is absurd to allege that it is not to be found in the work of the convention. It may be said that it does not go far enough, though it will not be easy to make this appear; but it can with no propriety be contended that there is no such thing. It certainly must be immaterial what mode is observed as to the order of declaring the rights of the citizens, if they are to be found in any part of the instrument which establishes the government. And hence it must be apparent that much of what has been said on this subject rests merely on verbal and nominal distinctions, which are entirely foreign from the substance of the thing.

Another objection, which has been made, and which from the frequency of its repetition it is to be presumed is relied on, is of this nature:—It is improper (say the objectors) to confer

---

* To show that there is a power in the constitution by which the liberty of the press may be affected, recourse has been had to the power of taxation. It is said that duties may be laid upon publications so high as to amount to a prohibition. I know not by what logic it could be maintained that the declarations in the state constitutions, in favour of the freedom of the press, would be a constitutional impediment to the imposition of duties upon publications by the state legislatures. It cannot certainly be pretended that any degree of duties, however low, would be an abrigement of the liberty of the press. We know that newspapers are taxed in Great-Britain, and yet it is notorious that the press no where enjoys greater liberty than in that country. And if duties of any kind may be laid without a violation of that liberty, it is evident that the extent must depend on legislative discretion, regulated by public opinion; so that after all, general declarations respecting the liberty of the press will give it no greater security than it will have without them. The same invasions of it may be effected under the state constitutions which contain those declarations through the means of taxation, as under the proposed constitution which has nothing of the kind. It would be quite as significant to declare the government ought to be free, that taxes ought not to be excessive, &c., as that the liberty of the press ought not to be restrained.

such large powers, as are proposed, upon the national government; because the seat of that government must of necessity be too remote from many of the states to admit of a proper knowledge on the part of the constituent, of the conduct of the representative body. This argument, if it proves any thing, proves that there ought to be no general government whatever. For the powers which it seems to be agreed on all hands, ought to be vested in the union, cannot be safely intrusted to a body which is not under every requisite controul. But there are satisfactory reasons to shew that the objection is in reality not well founded. There is in most of the arguments which relate to distance a palpable illusion of the imagination. What are the sources of information by which the people in Montgomery county must regulate their judgment of the conduct of their representatives in the state legislature? Of personal observation they can have no benefit. This is confined to the citizens on the spot. They must therefore depend on the information of intelligent men, in whom they confide—and how must these men obtain their information? Evidently from the complection of public measures, from the public prints, from correspondences with their representatives, and with other persons who reside at the place of their deliberation. This does not apply to Montgomery county only, but to all the counties, at any considerable distance from the seat of government.

It is equally evident that the same sources of information would be open to the people, in relation to the conduct of their representatives in the general government; and the impediments to a prompt communication which distance may be supposed to create, will be overballanced by the effects of the vigilance of the state governments. The executive and legislative bodies of each state will be so many centinels over the persons employed in every department of the national administration; and as it will be in their power to adopt and pursue a regular and effectual system of intelligence, they can never be at a loss to know the behaviour of those who represent their constituents in the national councils, and can readily communicate the same knowledge to the people. Their disposition to apprise the community of whatever may prejudice its interests from another quarter, may be relied upon, if it were only from the rivalship of power. And we may conclude with the fullest assurance, that the people, through that channel, will be better informed of the conduct of their national representatives, then they can be by any means they now possess of that of their state representatives.

It ought also to be remembered, that the citizens who inhabit the country at and near the seat of government, will in all questions that affect the general liberty and prosperity, have the same interest with those who are at a distance; and that they will stand ready to sound the alarm when necessary, and to point out the actors in any pernicious project. The public papers will be expeditious messengers of intelligence to the most remote inhabitants of the union.

Among the many extraordinary objections which have appeared against the proposed constitution, the most extraordinary and the least colourable one, is derived from the want of some provision respecting the debts due *to* the United States. This has been represented as a tacit relinquishment of those debts, and as a wicked contrivance to screen public defaulters. The newspapers have teemed with the most inflammatory railings on this head; and yet there is nothing clearer than that the suggestion is entirely void of foundation, and is the offspring of extreme ignorance or extreme dishonesty. In addition to the remarks I have made upon the subject in another place, I shall only observe, that as it is a plain dictate of common sense, so it is also an established doctrine of political law, that *"States neither lose any of their rights, nor are discharged from any of their obligations by a change in the form of their civil government."**

The last objection of any consequence which I at present recollect, turns upon the article of expence. If it were even true that the adoption of the proposed government would occa-

---

* Vide Rutherford's Institutes, vol. 2. book II, chap. x. sect. xiv, and xv.—Vide also Grotius, book II, chap. ix, sect. viii, and ix.

sion a considerable increase of expence, it would be an objection that ought to have no weight against the plan. The great bulk of the citizens of America, are with reason convinced that union is the basis of their political happiness. Men of sense of all parties now, with few exceptions, agree that it cannot be preserved under the present system, nor without radical alterations; that new and extensive powers ought to be granted to the national head, and that these require a different organization of the federal government, a single body being an unsafe depository of such ample authorities. In conceding all this, the question of expence must be given up, for it is impossible, with any degree of safety, to narrow the foundation upon which the system is to stand. The two branches of the legislature are in the first instance, to consist of only sixty-five persons, which is the same number of which congress, under the existing confederation, may be composed. It is true that this number is intended to be increased; but this is to keep pace with the increase of the population and resources of the country. It is evident, that a less number would, even in the first instance, have been unsafe; and that a continuance of the present number would, in a more advanced stage of population, be a very inadequate representation of the people.

Whence is the dreaded argumentation of expence to spring? One source pointed out, is the multiplication of offices under the new government. Let us examine this a little.

It is evident that the principal departments of the administration under the present government, are the same which will be required under the new. There are now a secretary of war, a secretary for foreign affairs, a secretary for domestic affairs, a board of treasury consisting of three persons, a treasurer, assistant, clerks, &c. These offices are indispensable under any system, and will suffice under the new as well as under the old. As to ambassadors and other ministers and agents in foreign countries, the proposed constitution can make no other difference, than to render their characters, where they reside, more respectable, and their services more useful. As to persons to be employed in the collection of the revenues, it is unquestionably true that these will form a very considerable addition to the number of federal officers; but it will not follow, that this will occasion an increase of public expence. It will be in most cases nothing more than an exchange of state officers for national officers. In the collection of all duties, for instance, the persons employed will be wholly of the latter description. The states individually will stand in no need of any for this purpose. What difference can it make in point of expence, to pay officers of the customs appointed by the state, or those appointed by the United States? There is no good reason to suppose, that either the number or the salaries of the latter, will be greater than those of the former.

Where then are we to seek for those additional articles of expence which are to swell the account to the enormous size that has been represented to us? The chief item which occurs to me, respects the support of the judges of the United States. I do not add the president, because there is now a president of congress, whose expences may not be far, if any thing, short of those which will be incurred on account of the president of the United States. The support of the judges will clearly be an extra expence, but to what extent will depend on the particular plan which may be adopted in practice in regard to this matter. But it can upon no reasonable plan amount to a sum which will be an object of material consequence.

Let us now see what there is to counterballance any extra expences that may attend the establishment of the proposed government. The first thing that presents itself is, that a great part of the business, which now keeps congress sitting through the year, will be transacted by the president. Even the management of foreign negociations will naturally devolve upon him according to general principles concerted with the senate, and subject to their final concurrence. Hence it is evident, that a portion of the year will suffice for the session of both the senate and the house of representatives: We may suppose about a fourth for the latter, and a third or perhaps a half for the former. The extra business of treaties and appointments may give this extra occupation to the senate. From this circumstance we may infer, that until the house of representatives shall be increased greatly beyond its present number, there will be a considerable saving of expence from the difference between the constant session of the present, and the temporary session of the future congress.

But there is another circumstance, of great importance in the view of economy. The business of the United States has hitherto occupied the state legislatures as well as congress. The latter has made requisitions which the former have had to provide for. Hence it has happened that the sessions of the state legislatures have been protracted greatly beyond what was necessary for the execution of the mere local business of the states. More than half their time has been frequently employed in matters which related to the United States. Now the members who compose the legislatures of the several states amount to two thousand and upwards; which number has hitherto performed what under the new system will be done in the first instance by sixty-five persons, and probably at no future period by above a fourth or a fifth of that number. The congress under the proposed government will do all the business of the United States themselves, without the intervention of the state legislatures, who thenceforth will have only to attend to the affairs of their particular states, and will not have to sit in any proportion as long as they have heretofore done. This difference, in the time of the sessions of the state legislatures, will be all clear gain, and will alone form an article of saving, which may be regarded as an equivalent for any additional objects of expence that may be occasioned by the adoption of the new system.

The result from these observations is, that the sources of additional expence from the establishment of the proposed constitution are much fewer than may have been imagined, that they are counterbalanced by considerable objects of saving, and that while it is questionable on which side the scale will preponderate, it is certain that a government less expensive would be incompetent to the purposes of the union.

Elbridge Gerry to the Massachusetts General Court, October 18, 1787.

I have the honour to inclose, pursuant to my commission, the constitution proposed by the federal Convention.

To this system I gave my dissent, and shall submit my objections to the honourable Legislature.

It was painful for me, on a subject of such national importance, to differ from the respectable members who signed the constitution: But conceiving as I did, that the liberties of America were not secured by the system, it was my duty to oppose it.—

My principal objections to the plan, are, that there is no adequate provision for a representation of the people—that they have no security for the right of election—that some of the powers of the Legislature are ambiguous, and others indefinite and dangerous—that the Executive is blended with and will have an undue influence over the Legislature—that the judicial department will be oppressive—that treaties of the highest importance may be formed by the President with the advice of two thirds of a *quorum* of the Senate—and that the system is without the security of a bill of rights. These are objections which are not local, but apply equally to all the States.

As the Convention was called for "the *sole* and *express* purpose of revising the Articles of Confederation, and reporting to Congress and the several Legislatures such alterations and provisions as shall render the Federal Constitution adequate to the exigencies of government and the preservation of the union," I did not conceive that these powers extended to the formation of a plan proposed, but the Convention being of a different *opinion*, I acquiesced in *it*, being fully convinced that to preserve the union, an efficient government was indispensibly necessary; and that it would be difficult to make proper amendments to the articles of Confederation.

The Constitution proposed has few, if any *federal* features, but is rather a system of *national* government: Nevertheless, in many respects I think it has great merit, and by proper amendments, may be adapted to the "exigencies of government," and preservation of liberty.

The question on this plan involves others of the highest importance—1st. Whether there shall be a dissolution of the *federal* government? 2dly. Whether the several State Governments shall be so altered, as in effect to be dissolved? and 3dly, Whether in lieu of the *federal* and *State* Governments, the *national* Constitution now proposed shall be substituted without amendment? Never perhaps were a people called on to decide a question of greater magnitude—Should the citizens of America adopt the plan as it now stands, their liberties may be lost: Or should they reject it altogether Anarchy may ensue. It is evident therefore, that they should not be precipitate in their decisions; that the subject should be well understood, lest they should refuse to *support* the government, after having *hastily* accepted it.

If those who are in favour of the Constitution, as well as those who are against it, should preserve moderation, their discussions may afford much information and finally direct to an happy issue.

It may be urged by some, that an *implicit* confidence should be placed in the Convention: But, however respectable the members may be who signed the Constitution, it must be admitted, that a free people are the proper guardians of their rights and liberties—that the greatest men may err—and that their errours are sometimes, of the greatest magnitude.

Others may suppose, that the Constitution may be safely adopted, because therein provision is made to *amend* it: But cannot *this object* be better attained before a ratification, than after it? And should a *free* people adopt a form of Government, under conviction that it wants amendment?

And some may conceive, that if the plan is not accepted by the people, they will not unite in another: but surely whilst they have the power to amend, they are not under the necessity of rejecting it. . . .

I shall only add, that as the welfare of the union requires a better Constitution than the Confederation, I shall think it my duty as a citizen of Massachusetts, to support that which shall be finally adopted, sincerely hoping it will secure the liberty and happiness of America.

George Mason, "Objections to the Constitution of Government Formed by the Convention," November 1787.

There is no Declaration of Rights; and the Laws of the general Government being paramount to the Laws and Constitutions of the several States, the Declaration of Rights in the separate States are no Security. Nor are the people secured even in the Enjoyment of the Benefits of the common-Law: which stands here upon no other Foundation than its having been adopted by the respective Acts forming the Constitutions of the several States.

In the House of Representatives there is not the Substance, but the Shadow only of Representation; which can never produce proper Information in the Legislature, or inspire Confidence in the People: the Laws will therefore be generally made by Men little concern'd in, and unacquainted with their Effects and Consequences.

The Senate have the Power of altering all Money-Bills, and of originating Appropriations of Money and the Sallerys of the Officers of their own Appointment in Conjunction with the President of the United States; altho' they are not the Representatives of the People, or amenable to them.

These with their other great Powers (vizt. their Power in the Appointment of Ambassadors and all public Officers, in making Treaties, and in trying all Impeachments) their Influence upon and Connection with the supreme Executive from these Causes, their Duration of Office, and their being a constant existing Body almost continually sitting, joined with their being one compleat Branch of the Legislature, will destroy any Balance in the Government, and enable them to accomplish what Usurpations they please upon the Rights and Libertys of the People.

The Judiciary of the United States is so constructed and extended, as to absorb and destroy the Judiciarys of the several States; thereby rendering Law as tedious[,] intricate and expensive, and Justice as unattainable, by a great part of the Community, as in England, and enabling the Rich to oppress and ruin the Poor.

The President of the United States has no constitutional Council (a thing unknown in any safe and regular Government) he will therefore be unsupported by proper Information and Advice; and will generally be directed by Minions and Favourites—or He will become a Tool to the Senate—or a Council of State will grow out of the principal Officers of the great Departments; the worst and most dangerous of all Ingredients for such a Council, in a free Country; for they may be induced to join in any dangerous or oppressive Measures, to shelter themselves, and prevent an Inquiry into their own Misconduct in Office; whereas had a constitutional Council been formed (as was proposed) of six Members; vizt. two from the Eastern, two from the Middle, and two from the Southern States, to be appointed by Vote of the States in the House of Representatives, with the same Duration and Rotation of Office as the Senate, the Executive wou'd always have had safe and proper Information and Advice, the President of such a Council might have acted as Vice President of the United States, pro tempore, upon any Vacancy or Disability of the chief Magistrate; and long continued Sessions of the Senate wou'd in a great Measure have been prevented.

From this fatal Defect of a constitutional Council has arisen the improper Power of the Senate, in the Appointment of public Officers, and the alarming Dependence and Connection between that Branch of the Legislature, and the supreme Executive.

Hence also sprung that unnecessary and dangerous Officer, the Vice President; who for want of other Employment, is made President of the Senate; thereby dangerously blending the executive and legislative Powers; besides always giving to some one of the States an unnecessary and unjust Pre-eminence over the others.

The President of the United States has the unrestrained Power of granting Pardon for Treason; which may be sometimes exercised to screen from Punishment those whom he had secretly instigated to commit the Crime, and thereby prevent a Discovery of his own Guilt.

By declaring all Treaties supreme Laws of the Land, the Executive and the Senate have in many Cases, an exclusive Power of Legislation; which might have been avoided by proper Distinctions with Respect to Treaties, and requiring the Assent of the House of Representatives, where it cou'd be done with Safety.

By requiring only a Majority to make all commercial and navigation Laws, the five Southern States (whose Produce and Circumstances are totally different from that of the eight Northern and Eastern States) will be ruined; for such rigid and premature Regulations may be made, as will enable the Merchants of the Northern and Eastern States not only to demand an exorbitant Freight, but to monopolize the Purchase of the Commodities at their own Price, for many years: to the great Injury of the landed Interest, and Impoverishment of the People: and the Danger is the greater, as the Gain on one Side will be in Proportion to the Loss on the other. Whereas requiring two thirds of the members present in both Houses wou'd have produced mutual moderation, promoted the general Interest, and removed an insuperable Objection to the Adoption of the Government.

Under their own Construction of the general Clause at the End of the enumerated powers the Congress may grant Monopolies in Trade and Commerce, constitute new Crimes, inflict unusual and severe Punishments, and extend their Power as far as they shall think proper; so that the State Legislatures have no Security for the Powers now presumed to remain to them; or the People for their Rights.

There is no Declaration of any kind for preserving the Liberty of the Press, the Tryal by Jury in civil Causes; nor against the Danger of standing Armys in time of Peace.

The State Legislatures are restrained from laying Export Duties on their own Produce.

The general Legislature is restrained from prohibiting the further Importation of Slaves for twenty odd Years; tho' such Importations render the United States weaker, more vulnerable, and less capable of Defence.

Both the general Legislature and the State Legislatures are expressly prohibited making ex post facto Laws; tho' there never was, or can be a Legislature but must and will make such Laws, when necessity and the public Safety require them; which will hereafter be a Breach of all the Constitutions in the Union, and afford precedents for other Innovations.

This Government will commence in a moderate Aristocracy; it is at present impossible to foresee whether it will, in its Operation, produce a Monarchy, or a corrupt oppressive Aristocracy; it will most probably vibrate some Years between the two, and then terminate in the one or the other.

Robert Yates and John Lansing to Governor George Clinton, "Reasons of Dissent," December 21, 1787.

We do ourselves the honor to advise your excellency, that in pursuance of concurrent resolutions of the honorable senate and assembly, we have, together with Mr. Hamilton, attended the convention, appointed for revising the articles of confederation, and reporting amendments to the same.

It is with the sincerest concern we observe, that in the prosecution of the important objects of our mission, we have been reduced to the disagreeable alternative, of either exceeding the powers delegated to us, and giving our assent to measures which we conceived distructive of the political happiness of the citizens of the United States, or opposing our opinion to that of a body of respectable men, to whom those citizens had given the most unequivocal proofs of confidence.—Thus circumstanced, under these impressions, to have hesitated, would have been to be culpable: we therefore, gave the principles of the constitution, which has received the sanction of a majority of the convention, our decided and unreserved dissent: but we must candidly confess, that we should have been equally opposed to any system, however modified, which had in object the consolidation of the United States into one government.

We beg leave briefly to state some cogent reasons, which, among others, influenced us to decide against a consolidation of the states. These are reducible into two heads.

1st. The limited and well-defined powers under which we acted, and which could not, on any possible construction, embrace an idea of such magnitude, as to assent to a general constitution, in subversion of that of the state.

2dly. A conviction of the impracticability of establishing a general government, pervading every part of the United States, and extending essential benefits to all.

Our powers were explicit, and confined to the *sole and express purpose of revising the articles of confederation*, and reporting such alterations and provisions therein, as should render the federal constitution adequate to the exigencies of government, and the preservation of the Union.

From these expressions we were led to believe, that a system of consolidated government could not, in the remotest degree, have been in contemplation of the legislature of this state; for that so important a trust as the adopting measures which tended to deprive the state government of its most essential rights of sovereignty, and to place it in a dependent situation, could not have been confided by implication; and the circumstance, that the acts of the convention were to receive a state approbation in the last resort, forcibly corroborated the opinion, that our powers could not involve the subversion of a constitution, which being immediately derived from the people, could only be abolished by their express consent, and not by a legislature, possessing authority vested in them for its preservation. Nor could we suppose, that if it had been the intention of the legislature, to abrogate the existing confederation, they would, in such pointed terms, have directed the attention of their delegates to the revision and amendment of it, in total exclusion of every other idea.

Reasoning in this manner, we were of opinion, that the leading feature of every amendment, ought to be the preservation of the individual states, in their uncontrouled constitutional rights, and that in reserving these, a mode might have been devised of granting to the confederacy, the monies arising from a general system of revenue; the power of regulating commerce, and enforcing the observance of foreign treaties, and other necessary matters of less moment.

Exclusive of our objections, originating from the want of power, we entertained an opinion, that a general government, however guarded by declarations of rights, or cautionary provisions, must unavoidably, in a short time, be productive of the destruction of the civil liberty of such citizens who could be effectually coerced by it; by reason of the extensive territory of the United States, the dispersed situation of its inhabitants, and the insuperable difficulty of controuling or counteracting the views of a set of men (however unconstitutional and oppressive their acts might be) possessed of all the powers of government; and who, from their remoteness from their constituents, and necessary permanency of office, could not be supposed to be uniformly actuated by an attention to their welfare and happiness; that however wise and energetic, the principles of the general government might be, the extremities of the United States could not be kept in due submission and obedience to its laws, at the distance of many hundred miles from the seat of government; that if the general legislature was composed of so numerous a body of men, as to represent the interests of all the inhabitants of the United States, in the usual and true ideas of representation, the expence of supporting it would become intolerably burthensome; and that, if a few only were vested with a power of legislation, the interests of a great majority of the inhabitants of the United States, must necessarily be unknown; or if known, even in the first stages of the operations of the new government, unattended to.

These reasons were, in our opinion, conclusive against any system of consolidated government: To that recommended by the convention, we suppose most of them very forcibly apply.

It is not our intention to pursue this subject farther than merely to explain our conduct in the discharge of the trust which the honorable the legislature reposed in us—Interested, however, as we are, in common with our fellow citizens, in the result, we cannot forbear to declare, that we have the strongest apprehensions, that a government so organized, as that recommended by the convention, cannot afford that security to equal and permanent liberty which we wished to make an invariable object of our pursuit.

We were not present at the completion of the new constitution; but before we left the convention, its principles were so well established as to convince us, that no alteration was to be expected to conform it to our ideas of expediency and safety. A persuasion, that our further attendance would be fruitless, and unavailing, rendered us less solicitous to return.

We have thus explained our motives for opposing the adoption of the national constitution, which we conceived it our duty to communicate to your Excellency, to be submitted to the consideration of the honorable legislature.

Letters from the "Federal Farmer."
[Richard Henry Lee?]

I

October 8, 1787

My letters to you last winter, on the subject of a well balanced national government for the United States, were the result of free enquiry; when I passed from that subject to enquiries relative to our commerce, revenues, past administration, etc. I anticipated the anxieties I feel, on carefully examining the plan of government proposed by the convention. It appears to be a plan retaining some federal features; but to be the first important step, and to aim strongly to one consolidated government of the United States. It leaves the powers of government, and the representation of the people, so unnaturally divided between the general and state governments, that the operations of our system must be very uncertain. My uniform federal attachments, and the interest I have in the protection of property, and a steady execution of the laws, will convince you, that, if I am under any biass at all, it is in favor of any general system which shall promise those advantages. The instability of our laws increases my wishes for firm and steady government; but then, I can consent to no government, which, in my opinion, is not calculated equally to preserve the rights of all orders of men in the community. My object has been to join with those who have endeavoured to supply the defects in the forms of our governments by a steady and proper administration of them. Though I have long apprehended that fraudalent debtors, and embarrassed men, on the one hand, and men, on the other, unfriendly to republican equality, would produce an uneasiness among the people, and prepare the way, not for cool and deliberate reforms in the governments, but for changes calculated to promote the interests of particular orders of men. Acquit me, sir, of any agency in the formation of the new system; I shall be satisfied with seeing, if it shall be adopted, a prudent administration. Indeed I am so much convinced of the truth of Pope's maxim, that "That which is best administered is best," that I am much inclined to subscribe to it from experience. I am not disposed to unreasonably contend about forms. I know our situation is critical, and it behoves us to make the best of it. A federal government of some sort is necessary. We have suffered the present to languish; and whether the confederation was capable or not originally of answering any valuable purposes, it is now but of little importance. I will pass by the men, and states, who have been particularly instrumental in preparing the way for a change, and, perhaps, for governments not very favourable to the people at large. A constitution is now presented which we may reject, or which we may accept, with or without amendments; and to which point we ought to direct our exertions, is the question. To determine this question, with propriety, we must attentively examine the system itself, and the probable consequences of either step. This I shall endeavour to do, so far as I am able, with candor and fairness; and leave you to decide upon the propriety of my opinions, the weight of my reasons, and how far my conclusions are well drawn. Whatever may be the conduct of others, on the present occasion, I do not mean, hastily and positively to decide on the merits of the constitution proposed. I shall be open to conviction, and always disposed to adopt that which, all things considered, shall appear to me to be most for the happiness of the community. It must be granted, that if men hastily and blindly adopt a system of government, they will as hastily and as blindly be led to alter or abolish it; and changes must ensue, one after another, till the peaceable and better part of the community will grow weary with changes, tumults and disorders, and be disposed to accept any government, however despotic, that shall promise stability and firmness.

The first principal question that occurs, is, Whether, considering our situation, we ought to precipitate the adoption of the proposed constitution? If we remain cool and temperate, we are in no immediate danger of any commotions; we are in a state of perfect peace, and in no danger of invasions; the state governments are in the full exercise of their powers; and our governments answer all present exigencies, except the regulation of trade, securing credit, in some cases, and providing for the interest, in some instances, of the public debts; and whether we adopt a change, three or nine months hence, can make but little odds with the private circumstances of individuals; their happiness and prosperity, after all, depend principally upon their own exertions. We are hardly recovered from a long and distressing war: The farmers, fishmen, &c. have not yet fully repaired the waste made by it. Industry and frugality are again assuming their proper station. Private debts are lessened, and public debts incurred by the war have been, by various ways, diminished; and the public lands have now become a productive source for diminishing them much more. I know uneasy men, who wish very much to precipitate, do not admit all these facts; but they are facts well known to all men who are thoroughly informed in the affairs of this country. It must, however, be admitted, that our federal system is defective, and that some of the state governments are not well administered; but, then, we impute to the defects in our governments many evils and embarrassments which are most clearly the result of the late war. We must allow men to conduct on the present occasion, as on all similar ones. They will urge a thousand pretences to answer their purposes on both sides. When we want a man to change his condition, we describe it as miserable, wretched, and despised; and draw a pleasing picture of that which we would have him assume. And when we wish the contrary, we reverse our descriptions. Whenever a clamor is raised, and idle men get to work, it is highly necessary to examine facts carefully, and without unreasonably suspecting men of falshood, to examine, and enquire attentively, under what impressions they act. It is too often the case in political concerns, that men state facts not as they are, but as they wish them to be; and almost every man, by calling to mind past scenes, will find this to be true.

Nothing but the passions of ambitious, impatient, or disorderly men, I conceive, will plunge us into commotions, if time should be taken fully to examine and consider the system proposed. Men who feel easy in their circumstances, and such as are not sanguine in their expectations relative to the consequences of the proposed change, will remain quiet under the existing governments. Many commercial and monied men, who are uneasy, not without just cause, ought to be respected; and, by no means, unreasonably disappointed in their expectations and hopes; but as to those who expect employments under the new constitution; as to those weak and ardent men who always expect to be gainers by revolutions, and whose lot it generally is to get out of one difficulty into another, they are very little to be regarded: and as to those who designedly avail themselves of this weakness and ardor, they are to be despised. It is natural for men, who wish to hasten the adoption of a measure, to tell us, now is the crisis—now is the critical moment which must be seized, or all will be lost: and to shut the door against free enquiry, whenever conscious the thing presented has defects in it, which time and investigation will probably discover. This has been the custom of tyrants and their dependants in all ages. If it is true, what has been so often said, that the people of this country cannot change their condition for the worse, I presume it still behoves them to endeavour deliberately to change it for the better. The fickle and ardent, in any community, are the proper tools for establishing despotic government. But it is deliberate and thinking men, who must establish and secure governments on free principles. Before they decide on the plan proposed, they will enquire whether it will probably be a blessing or a curse to this people.

The present moment discovers a new face in our affairs. Our object has been all along, to reform our federal system, and to strengthen our governments—to establish peace, order and justice in the community—but a new object now presents. The plan of government now proposed is evidently calculated totally to change, in time, our condition as a people. Instead of being thirteen republics, under a federal head, it is clearly designed to make us one consolidated government. Of this, I think, I shall fully convince you, in my following letters on this subject. This consolidation of the states has been the object of several men in this country for some time past. Whether such a change can ever be effected in any manner; whether it can be effected without convulsions and civil wars; whether such a change will not totally destroy the liberties of this country—time only can determine.

To have a just idea of the government before us, and to shew that a consolidated one is the object in view, it is necessary not only to examine the plan, but also its history, and the politics of its particular friends.

The confederation was formed when great confidence was placed in the voluntary exertions of individuals, and of the respective states; and the framers of it, to guard against usurpation, so limited and checked the powers, that, in many respects, they are inadequate to the exigencies of the union. We find, therefore, members of congress urging alterations in the federal system almost as soon as it was adopted. It was early proposed to vest congress with powers to levy an impost, to regulate trade, etc. but such was known to be the caution of the states in parting with power, that the vestment, even of these, was proposed to be under several checks and limitations. During the war, the general confusion, and the introduction of paper money, infused in the minds of people vague ideas respecting government and credit. We expected too much from the return of peace, and of course we have been disappointed. Our governments have been new and unsettled; and several legislatures, by making tender, suspension, and paper money laws, have given just cause of uneasiness to creditors. By these and other causes, several orders of men in the community have been prepared, by degrees, for a change in government; and this very abuse of power in the legislatures, which, in some cases, has been charged upon the democratic part of the community, has furnished aristocratical men with those very weapons, and those very means, with which, in great measure, they are rapidly effecting their favourite object. And should an oppressive government be the consequence of the proposed change, posterity may reproach not only a few overbearing unprincipled men, but those parties in the states which have misused their powers.

The conduct of several legislatures, touching paper money, and tender laws, has prepared many honest men for changes in government, which otherwise they would not have thought of—when by the evils, on the one hand, and by the secret instigations of artful men, on the other, the minds of men were become sufficiently uneasy, a bold step was taken, which is usually followed by a revolution, or a civil war. A general convention for mere commercial purposes was moved for—the authors of this measure saw that the people's attention was turned solely to the amendment of the federal system; and that, had the idea of a total change been started, probably no state would have appointed members to the convention. The idea of destroying, ultimately, the state government, and forming one consolidated system, could not have been admitted—a convention, therefore, merely for vesting in congress power to regulate trade was proposed. This was pleasing to the commercial towns; and the landed people had little or no concern about it. September, 1786, a few men from the middle states met at Annapolis, and hastily proposed a convention to be held in May, 1787, for the purpose, generally, of amending the confederation—this was done before the delegates of Massachusetts, and of the other states arrived—still not a word was said about destroying the old constitution, and making a new one—The states still unsuspecting, and not aware that they were passing the Rubicon, appointed members to the new convention, for the sole and express purpose of revising and amending the confederation—and, probably, not one man in ten thousand in the United States, till within these ten or twelve days, had an idea that the old ship was to be destroyed, and be put to the alternative of embarking in the new ship presented, or of being left in danger of sinking—The States, I believe, universally supposed the convention would report alterations in the confederation, which would pass an examination in congress, and after being agreed to there, would be confirmed by all the legislatures, or be rejected. Virginia made a very respectable appointment, and placed at the head of it the first man in America: In this appointment there was a mixture of political characters; but Pennsylvania appointed principally those men who are esteemed aristocratical. Here the favourite moment for changing the government was evidently discerned by a few men, who seized it with address. Ten other states appointed, and tho' they chose men principally connected with commerce and the judicial department yet they appointed many good republican characters—had they all attended we should now see, I am persuaded a better system presented. The non-attendance of eight or nine men, who were appointed members of the convention, I shall ever consider as a very unfortunate event to the United States.—Had they attended, I am pretty clear, that the result of the convention would not have had that strong tendency to aristocracy now discernable in every part of the plan. There would not have been so great an accumulation of powers, especially as to the internal police of the country, in a few hands, as the constitution reported proposes to vest in them—the young visionary men, and the consolidating aristocracy, would have been more restrained than they have been. Eleven states met in the convention, and after four months close attention presented the new constitution, to be adopted or rejected by the people. The uneasy and fickle part of the community may be prepared to receive any form of government; but, I presume, the enlightened and substantial part will give any constitution presented for their adoption, a candid and thorough examination; and silence those designing or empty men, who weakly and rashly attempt to precipitate the adoption of a system of so much importance—We shall view the convention with proper respect—and, at the same time, that we reflect there were men of abilities and integrity in it, we must recollect how disproportionably the democractic and aristocratic parts of the community were represented—Perhaps the judicious friends and opposers of the new constitution will agree, that it is best to let it rest solely on its own merits, or be condemned for its own defects.

In the first place, I shall premise, that the plan proposed is a plan of accommodation—and that it is in this way only, and by giving up a part of our opinions, that we can ever expect to obtain a government founded in freedom and compact. This circumstance candid men will always keep in view, in the discussion of this subject.

The plan proposed appears to be partly federal, but principally however, calculated ultimately to make the states one consolidated government.

The first interesting question, therefore suggested, is, how far the states can be consolidated into one entire government on free principles. In considering this question extensive objects are to be taken into view, and important changes in the forms of government to be carefully attended to in all their consequences. The happiness of the people at large must be the great object with every honest statesman, and he will direct every movement to this point. If we are so situated as a people, as not to be able to enjoy equal happiness and advantages under one government, the consolidation of the states cannot be admitted.

There are three different forms of free government under which the United States may exist as one nation; and now is, perhaps, the time to determine to which we will direct our views. 1. Distinct republics connected under a federal head. In this case the respective state governments must be the principal guardians of the peoples rights, and exclusively regulate their internal police; in them must rest the balance of government. The congress of the states, or federal head, must consist of delegates amenable to, and removeable by the respective states: This congress must have general directing powers; powers to require men and monies of the states; to make treaties, peace and war; to direct the operations of armies, etc. Under this federal modification of government, the powers of congress would be rather advisory or recommendatory than coercive. 2. We may do away the several state governments, and form or consolidate all the states into one entire government, with one executive, one judiciary, and one legislature, consisting of senators and representatives collected from all parts of the union: In this case there would be a compleat consolidation of the states. 3. We may consolidate the states as to certain national objects, and leave them severally distinct independent republics, as to internal police generally. Let the general government consist of an executive, a judiciary, and balanced legislature, and its powers extend exclusively to all foreign concerns, causes arising on the seas to commerce, imports, armies, navies, Indian affairs, peace and war, and to a few internal concerns of the community; to the coin, post-offices, weights and measures, a general plan for the militia, to naturalization, *and, perhaps to bankruptcies,* leaving the internal police of the community, in other respects, exclusively to the state governments; as the administration of justice in all causes arising internally, the laying and collecting of internal taxes, and the forming of the militia according to a general plan prescribed. In this case there would be a compleat consolidation, *quoad* certain objects only.

Touching the first, or federal plan, I do not think much can be said in its favor: The sovereignty of the nation, without coercive and efficient powers to collect the strength of it, cannot always be depended on to answer the purposes of government; and in a congress of representatives of sovereign states, there must necessarily be an unreasonable mixture of powers in the same hands.

As to the second, or compleat consolidating plan, it deserves to be carefully considered at this time, by every American: If it be impracticable, it is a fatal error to model our governments, directing our views ultimately to it.

The third plan, or partial consolidation, is, in my opinion, the only one that can secure the freedom and happiness of this people. I once had some general ideas that the second plan was practicable, but from long attention, and the proceedings of the convention, I am fully satisfied, that this third plan is the only one we can with safety and propriety proceed upon. Making this the standard to point out, with candor and fairness, the parts of the new constitution which appear to be improper, is my object. The convention appears to have proposed the partial consolidation evidently with a view to collect all powers ultimately, in the United States into one entire government; and from its views in this respect, and from the tenacity of the small states to have an equal vote in the senate, probably originated the greatest defects in the proposed plan.

Independant of the opinions of many great authors, that a free elective government cannot be extended over large territories, a few reflections must evince, that one government and general legislation alone, never can extend equal benefits to all parts of the United States: Different laws, customs, and opinions exist in the different states, which by a uniform system of laws would be unreasonably invaded. The United States contain about a million of square miles, and in half a century will, probably, contain ten millions of people; and from the center to the extremes is about 800 miles.

Before we do away the state governments, or adopt measures that will tend to abolish them, and to consolidate the states into one entire government, several principles should be considered and facts ascertained:—These, and my examination into the essential parts of the proposed plan, I shall pursue in my next.

II

October 9, 1787

The essential parts of a free and good government are a full and equal representation of the people in the legislature, and the jury trial of the vicinage in the administration of justice—a full and equal representation, is that which possesses the same interests, feelings, opinions, and views the people themselves would were they all assembled—a fair representation, therefore, should be so regulated, that every order of men in the community, according to the common course of elections, can have a share in it—in order to allow professional men, merchants, traders, farmers, mechanics, etc. to bring a just proportion of their best informed men respectively into the legislature, the representation must be considerably numerous—We have about 200 state senators in the United States, and a less number than that of federal representatives cannot, clearly, be a full representation of this people, in the affairs of internal taxation and police, were there but one legislature for the whole union. The representation cannot be equal, or the situation of the people proper for one government only—if the extreme parts of the society cannot be represented as fully as the central—It is apparently impracticable that this should be the case in this extensive country—it would be impossible to collect a representation of the parts of the country five, six, and seven hundred miles from the seat of government.

Under one general government alone, there could be but one judiciary, one supreme and a proper number of inferior courts. I thnk it would be totally impracticable in this case to preserve a due administration of justice, and the real benefits of the jury trial of the vicinage,—there are now supreme courts in each state in the union; and a great number of county and other courts subordinate to each supreme court—most of these supreme and inferior courts are itinerant, and hold their sessions in different parts every year of their respective states, counties and districts—with all these moving courts, our citizens, from the vast extent of the country must travel very considerable distances from home to find the place where justice is administered. I am not for bringing justice so near to individuals as to afford them any temptation to engage in law suits; though I think it one of the greatest benefits in a good government, that each citizen should find a court of justice within a reasonable distance, perhaps, within a day's travel of his home; so that, without great inconveniences and enormous expences, he may have the advantages of his witnesses and jury—it would be impracticable to derive these advantages from one judiciary—the one supreme court at most could only set in the centre of the union, and move once a year into the centre of the eastern and southern extremes of it—and, in this case, each citizen, on an average, would travel 150 or 200 miles to find this court—that, however, inferior courts might be properly placed in the different counties, and districts of the union, the appellate jurisdiction would be intolerable and expensive.

If it were possible to consolidate the states, and preserve the features of a free government, still it is evident that the middle states, the parts of the union, about the seat of government, would enjoy great advantages, while the remote states would experience the many inconveniences of remote provinces. Wealth, offices, and the benefits of government would collect in the centre: and the extreme states and their principal towns, become much less important.

There are other considerations which tend to prove that the idea of one consolidated whole, on free principles, is ill-founded—the laws of a free government rest on the confidence of the people, and operate gently—and never can extend their influence very far—if they are executed on free principles, about the centre, where the benefits of the government induce the people to support it voluntarily; yet they must be executed on the principles of fear and force in the extremes—This has been the case with every extensive republic of which we have any accurate account.

There are certain unalienable and fundamental rights, which in forming the social compact, ought to be explicitly ascertained and fixed—a free and enlightened people, in forming this compact, will not resign all their rights to those who govern, and they will fix limits to their legislators and rulers, which will soon be plainly seen by those who are governed, as well as by those who govern: and the latter will know they cannot be passed unperceived by the former, and without giving a general alarm—These rights should be made the basis of every constitution: and if a people be so situated, or have such different opinions that they cannot agree in ascertaining and fixing them, it is a very strong argument against their attempting to form one entire society, to live under one system of laws only.—I confess, I never thought the people of these states differed essentially in these respects; they having derived all these rights from one common source, the British systems; and having in the formation of their state constitutions, discovered that their ideas relative to these rights are very similar. However, it is now said that the states differ so essentially in these respects, and even in the important article of the trial by jury, that when assembled in convention, they can agree to no words by which to establish that trial, or by which to ascertain and establish many other of these rights, as fundamental articles in the social compact. If so, we proceed to consolidate the states on no solid basis whatever.

But I do not pay much regard to the reasons given for not bottoming the new constitution on a better bill of rights. I still believe a complete federal bill of rights to be very practicable. Nevertheless I acknowledge the proceedings of the convention furnish my mind with many new and strong reasons, against a complete consolidation of the states. They tend to convince me, that it cannot be carried with propriety very far—that the convention have gone much farther in one respect than they found it practicable to go in another; that is, they propose to lodge in the general government very extensive powers—*powers* nearly, if not altogether, complete and unlimited, over the purse and the sword. But, in its organization, they furnish the strongest proof that the proper limbs, or parts of a government, to support and execute those powers on proper principles (or in which they can be safely lodged) cannot be formed. These powers must be lodged somewhere in every society; but then they should be lodged where the strength and guardians of the people are collected. They can be wielded, or safely used, in a free country only by an able executive and judiciary, a respectable senate, and a secure, full, and equal representation of the people. I think the principles I have premised or brought into view, are well founded—I think they will not be denied by any fair reasoner. It is in connection with these, and other solid principles, we are to examine the constitution. It is not a few democratic phrases, or a few well formed features, that will prove its merits; or a few small omissions that will produce its rejection among men of sense; they will enquire what are the essential powers in a community, and what are nominal ones; where and how the essential powers shall be lodged to secure government, and to secure true liberty.

In examining the proposed constitution carefully, we must clearly perceive an unnatural separation of these powers from the substantial representation of the people. The state governments will exist, with all their governors, senators, representatives, officers and expences; in these will be nineteen-twentieths of the representatives of the people; they will have a near connection, and their members an immediate intercourse with the people; and the probability is, that the state governments will possess the confidence of the people, and be considered generally as their immediate guardians.

The general government will consist of a new species of executive, a small senate, and a very small house of representatives. As many citizens will be more than three hundred miles from the seat of this government as will be nearer to it, its judges and officers cannot be very numerous, without making our governments very expensive. Thus will stand the state and the general governments, should the constitution be adopted without any alterations in their organization; but as to powers, the general government will possess all essential ones, at least on paper, and those of the states a mere shadow of power. And therefore, unless the people shall make some great exertions to restore to the state governments their powers in matters of internal police; as the powers to lay and collect, exclusively, internal taxes, to govern the militia, and to hold the decisions of their own judicial courts upon their own laws final, the balance cannot possibly continue long; but the state governments must be annihilated, or continue to exist for no purpose.

It is however to be observed, that many of the essential powers given the national government are not exclusively given; and the general government may have prudence enough to forbear the exercise of those which may still be exercised by the respective states. But this cannot justify the impropriety of giving powers, the exercise of which prudent men will not attempt, and imprudent men will, or probably can, exercise only in a manner destructive of free government. The general government, organized as it is, may be adequate to many valuable objects, and be able to carry its laws into execution on proper principles in several cases; but I think its warmest friends will not contend, that it can carry all the powers proposed to be lodged in it into effect, without calling to its aid a military force, which must very soon destroy all elective governments in the country, produce anarchy, or establish despotism. Though we cannot have now a complete idea of what will be the operations of the proposed system, we may, allowing things to have their common course, have a very tolerable one. The powers lodged in the general government, if exercised by it, must intimately effect the internal police of the states, as well as external concerns; and there is no reason to expect the numerous state governments, and their connections, will be very friendly to the execution of federal laws in those internal affairs, which hitherto have been under their own immediate management. There is more reason to believe, that the general government, far removed from the people, and none of its members elected oftener than once in two years, will be forgot or neglected, and its laws in many cases disregarded, unless a multitude of officers and military force be continually kept in view, and employed to enforce the execution of the laws, and to make the government feared and respected. No position can be truer than this, that in this country either neglected laws, or a military execution of them, must lead to a revolution, and to the destruction of freedom. Neglected laws must first lead to anarchy and confusion; and a military execution of laws is only a shorter way to the same point—despotic government.

The Bill of Rights, 1789–1791

ART. I. Congress shall make no law respecting an establishment of religion, or prohibiting the free exercise thereof; or abridging the freedom of speech, or of the press; or the right of the people peaceably to assemble, and to petition the government for a redress of grievances.

ART. II. A well regulated militia being necessary to the security of a free State, the right of the people to keep and bear arms shall not be infringed.

ART. III. No soldier shall, in time of peace, be quartered in any house without the consent of the owner; nor in time of war, but in a manner to be prescribed by law.

ART. IV. The right of the people to be secure in their persons, houses, papers, and effects, against unreasonable searches and seizures, shall not be violated; and no warrants shall issue, but upon probable cause, supported by oath or affirmation, and particularly describing the place to be searched, and the persons or things to be seized.

ART. V. No person shall be held to answer for a capital or otherwise infamous crime, unless on a presentment or indictment of a grand jury, except in cases arising in the land or naval forces, or in the militia, when in actual service, in time of war or public danger; nor shall any person be subject for the same offence to be twice put in jeopardy of life or limb; nor shall be compelled, in any criminal case, to be witness against himself; nor be deprived of life, liberty, or property, without due process of law; nor shall private property be taken for public use without just compensation.

ART. VI. In all criminal prosecutions the accused shall enjoy the right to a speedy and public trial, by an impartial jury of the State and district wherein the crime shall have been committed, which district shall have been previously ascertained by law, and to be informed of the nature and cause of the accusation; to be confronted with the witnesses against him; to have compulsory process for obtaining witnesses in his favour; and to have the assistance of counsel for his defence.

ART. VII. In suits at common law, where the value in controversy shall exceed twenty dollars, the right of trial by jury shall be preserved; and no fact tried by a jury shall be otherwise re-examined in any court of the United States than according to the rules of the common law.

ART. VIII. Excessive bail shall not be required, nor excessive fines imposed, nor cruel and unusual punishments inflicted.

ART. IX. The enumeration in the Constitution of certain rights, shall not be construed to deny or disparage others retained by the people.

ART. X. The powers not delegated to the United States by the Constitution, nor prohibited by it to the States, are reserved to the States respectively or to the people.

16

Civil Disobedience

Henry David Thoreau

Civil Disobedience

Henry David Thoreau

I heartily accept the motto,—"That government is best which governs least"; and I should like to see it acted up to more rapidly and systematically. Carried out, it finally amounts to this, which I also believe,—"That government is best which governs not at all"; and when men are prepared for it, that will be the kind of government which they will have. Government is at best but an expedient; but most governments are usually, and all governments are sometimes, inexpedient. The objections which have been brought against a standing army, and they are many and weighty, and deserve to prevail, may also at last be brought against a standing government. The standing army is only an arm of the standing government. The government itself, which is only the mode which the people have chosen to execute their will, is equally liable to be abused and perverted before the people can act through it. Witness the present Mexican war, the work of comparatively a few individuals using the standing government as their tool; for, in the outset, the people would not have consented to this measure.

This American government,—what is it but a tradition, though a recent one, endeavoring to transmit itself unimpaired to posterity, but each instant losing some of its integrity? It has not the vitality and force of a single living man; for a single man can bend it to his will. It is a sort of wooden gun to the people themselves. But it is not the less necessary for this; for the people must have some complicated machinery or other, and hear its din, to satisfy that idea of government which they have. Governments show thus how successfully men can be imposed on, even impose on themselves, for their own advantage. It is excellent, we must all allow. Yet this government never of itself furthered any enterprise, but by the alacrity with which it got out of its way. *It* does not keep the country free. *It* does not settle the West. *It* does not educate. The character inherent in the American people has done all that has been accomplished; and it would have done somewhat more, if the government had not sometimes got in its way. For government is an expedient by which men would fain succeed in letting one another alone; and, as has been said, when it is most expedient, the governed are most let alone by it. Trade and commerce, if they were not made of India-rubber, would never manage to bounce over the obstacles which legislators are continually putting in their way; and, if one were to judge these men wholly by the effects of their actions and not partly by their intentions, they would deserve to be classed and punished with those mischievous persons who put obstructions on railroads.

But, to speak practically and as a citizen, unlike those who call themselves no-government men, I ask for, not at once no government, but *at once* a better government. Let every man make known what kind of government would command his respect, and that will be one step toward obtaining it.

After all, the practical reason why, when the power is once in the hands of the people, a majority are permitted, and for a long period continue, to rule, is not because they are most likely to be in the right, nor because this seems fairest to the minority, but because they are physically the strongest. But a government in which the majority rule in all cases cannot be based on justice, even as far as men understand it. Can there not be a government in which majorities do not virtually decide right and wrong, but conscience?—in which majorities decide only those questions to which the rule of expediency is applicable? Must the citizen ever for a moment, or in the least degree, resign his conscience to the legislator? Why has every man a conscience, then? I think that we should be men first, and subjects afterward. It is not desirable to cultivate a respect for the law, so much as for the right. The only obligation which I have the right to assume, is to do at any time what I think right. It is truly enough said, that a corporation has no conscience; but a corporation of conscientious men is a corporation *with* a conscience. Law never made men a whit more just; and, by means of their respect for it, even the well-disposed are daily made the agents of injustice. A common and natural result of an undue respect for law is, that you may see a file of soldiers, colonel, captain, corporal, privates, powder-monkeys, and all, marching in admirable order over hill and dale to the wars, against their wills, ay, against their common sense and consciences, which makes it very steep marching indeed, and produces a palpitation of the heart. They have no doubt that it is a damnable business in which they are concerned; they are all peaceably inclined. Now, what are they? Men at all? or small movable forts and magazines, at the service of some unscrupulous man in power? Visit the Navy-Yard, and behold a marine, such a man as an American government can make, or such as it can make a man with its black arts,—a mere shadow and reminiscence of humanity, a man laid out alive and standing, and already, as one may say, buried under arms with funeral accompaniments, though it may be,—

> "Not a drum was heard, not a funeral note,
>   As his corse to the rampart we hurried;
> Not a soldier discharged his farewell shot
>   O'er the grave where our hero we buried."

The mass of men serve the state thus, not as men mainly, but as machines, with their bodies. They are the standing army, and the militia, jailers, constables, posse comitatus, &c. In most cases there is no free exercise whatever of the judgment or of the moral sense; but they put themselves on a level with wood and earth and stones; and wooden men can perhaps be manufactured that will serve the purpose as well. Such command no more respect than men of straw or a lump of dirt. They have the same sort of worth only as horses and dogs. Yet such as these even are commonly esteemed good citizens. Others,—as most legislators, politicians, lawyers, ministers, and officeholders,—serve the state chiefly with their heads; and, as they rarely make any moral distinctions, they are as likely to serve the Devil, without *intending* it, as God. A very few, as heroes, patriots, martyrs, reformers in the great sense, and *men*, serve the state with their consciences also, and so necessarily resist it for the most part; and they are commonly treated as enemies by it. A wise man will only be useful as a man, and will not submit to be "clay," and "stop a hole to keep the wind away," but leave that office to his dust at least:—

> "I am too high-born to be propertied,
> To be a secondary at control,
> Or useful serving-man and instrument
> To any sovereign state throughout the world."

He who gives himself entirely to his fellow-men appears to them useless and selfish; but he who gives himself partially to them is pronounced a benefactor and philanthropist.

How does it become a man to behave toward this American government to-day? I answer, that he cannot without disgrace be associated with it. I cannot for an instant recognize that political organization as *my* government which is the *slave's* government also.

All men recognize the right of revolution; that is, the right to refuse allegiance to, and to resist, the government, when its tyranny or its inefficiency are great and unendurable. But almost all say that such is not the case now. But such was the case, they think, in the Revolution of '75. If one were to tell me that this was a bad government because it taxed certain foreign commodities brought to its ports, it is most probable that I should not make an ado about it, for I can do without them. All machines have their friction; and possibly this does enough good to counterbalance the evil. At any rate, it is a great evil to make a stir about it. But when the friction comes to have its machine, and oppression and robbery are organized, I say, let us not have such a machine any longer. In other words, when a sixth of the population of a nation which has undertaken to be the refuge of liberty are slaves, and a whole country is unjustly overrun and conquered by a foreign army, and subjected to military law, I think that it is not too soon for honest men to rebel and revolutionize. What makes this duty the more urgent is the fact, that the country so overrun is not our own, but ours is the invading army.

Paley, a common authority with many on moral questions, in his chapter on the "Duty of Submission to Civil Government," resolves all civil obligation into expediency; and he proceeds to say, "that so long as the interest of the whole society requires it, that is, so long as the established government cannot be resisted or changed without public inconveniency, it is the will of God that the established government be obeyed, and no longer. . . . . This principle being admitted, the justice of every particular case of resistance is reduced to a computation of the quantity of the danger and grievance on the one side, and of the probability and expense of redressing it on the other." Of this, he says, every man shall judge for himself. But Paley appears never to have contemplated those cases to which the rule of expediency does not apply, in which a people, as well as an individual, must do justice, cost what it may. If I have unjustly wrested a plank from a drowning man, I must restore it to him though I drown myself. This, according to Paley, would be inconvenient. But he that would save his life, in such a case, shall lose it. This people must cease to hold slaves, and to make war on Mexico, though it cost them their existence as a people.

In their practice, nations agree with Paley; but does any one think that Massachusetts does exactly what is right at the present crisis?

> "A drab of state, a cloth-o'-silver slut,
> To have her train borne up, and her soul trail in the dirt."

Practically speaking, the opponents to a reform in Massachusetts are not a hundred thousand politicians at the South, but a hundred thousand merchants and farmers here, who are more interested in commerce and agriculture than they are in humanity, and are not prepared to do justice to the slave and to Mexico, *cost what it may*. I quarrel not with far-off foes, but with those who, near at home, co-operate with, and do the bidding of, those far away, and without whom the latter would be harmless. We are accustomed to say, that the mass of men are unprepared; but improvement is slow, because the few are not materially wiser or better than the many. It is not so important that many should be as good as you, as that there be some absolute goodness somewhere; for that will leaven the whole lump. There are thousands who are *in opinion* opposed to slavery and to the war, who yet in effect do nothing to put an end to them; who, esteeming themselves children of Washington and Franklin, sit down with their hands in their pockets, and say that they know not what to do, and do nothing; who even postpone the question of freedom to the question of free-trade, and quietly read the prices-current along with the latest advices from Mexico, after dinner, and, it may be, fall asleep over them both. What is the price-current of an honest man and a patriot to-day? They hesitate, and they regret, and sometimes they petition; but they do nothing in earnest and with effect. They will wait, well disposed, for others to remedy the evil, that they may no longer have it to regret. At most, they give only a cheap vote, and a feeble countenance and God-speed, to the right, as it goes by them. There are nine hundred and ninety-nine patrons of virtue to one virtuous man. But it is easier to deal with the real possessor of a thing than with the temporary guardian of it.

All voting is a sort of gaming, like checkers or backgammon, with a slight moral tinge to it, a playing with right and wrong, with moral questions; and betting naturally accompanies it. The character of the voters is not staked. I cast my vote, perchance, as I think right; but I am not vitally concerned that that right should prevail. I am willing to leave it to the majority. Its obligation, therefore, never exceeds that of expediency. Even voting *for the right* is *doing* nothing for it. It is only expressing to men feebly your desire that it should prevail. A wise man will not leave the right to the mercy of chance, nor wish it to prevail through the power of the majority. There is but little virtue in the action of masses of men. When the majority shall at length vote for the abolition of slavery, it will be because they are indifferent to slavery, or because there is but little slavery left to be abolished by their vote. *They* will then be the only slaves. Only *his* vote can hasten the abolition of slavery who asserts his own freedom by his vote.

I hear of a convention to be held at Baltimore, or elsewhere, for the selection of a candidate for the Presidency, made up chiefly of editors, and men who are politicians by profession; but I think, what is it to any independent, intelligent, and respectable man what decision they may come to? Shall we not have the advantage of his wisdom and honesty, nevertheless? Can we not count upon some independent votes? Are there not many individuals in the country who do not attend conventions? But no: I find that the respectable man, so called, has immediately drifted from his position, and despairs of his country, when his country has more reason to despair of him. He forthwith adopts one of the candidates thus selected as the only *available* one, thus proving that he is himself *available* for any purposes of the demagogue. His vote is of no more worth than that of any unprincipled foreigner or hireling native, who may have been bought. O for a man who is a *man*, and, as my neighbor says, has a bone in his back which you cannot pass your hand through! Our statistics are at fault: the population has been returned too large. How many *men* are there to a square thousand miles in this country? Hardly one. Does not America offer any inducement for men to settle here? The American has dwindled into an Odd Fellow,—one who may be known by the development of his organ of gregariousness, and a manifest lack of intellect and cheerful self-reliance; whose first and chief concern, on coming into the world, is to see that the Almshouses are in good repair; and, before yet he has lawfully donned the virile garb, to collect a fund for the support of the widows and orphans that may be; who, in short, ventures to live only by the aid of the Mutual Insurance company, which has promised to bury him decently.

It is not a man's duty, as a matter of course, to devote himself to the eradication of any, even the most enormous wrong; he may still properly have other concerns to engage him; but it is his duty, at least, to wash his hands of it, and, if he gives it no thought longer, not to give it practically his support. If I devote myself to other pursuits and contemplations, I must first see, at least, that I do not pursue them sitting upon another man's shoulders. I must get off him first, that he may pursue his contemplations too. See what gross inconsistency is tolerated. I have heard some of my townsmen say, "I should like to have them order me out to help put down an insurrection of the slaves, or to march to Mexico;—see if I would go"; and yet these very men have each, directly by their allegiance, and so indirectly, at least, by their money, furnished a substitute. The soldier is applauded who refuses to serve in an unjust war by those who do not refuse to sustain the unjust government which makes the war; is applauded by those whose own act and authority he disregards and sets at naught; as if the State were penitent to that degree that it hired one to scourge it while it sinned, but not to that degree that it left off sinning for a moment. Thus, under the name of Order and Civil Government, we are all made at last to pay homage to and support our own meanness. After the first blush of sin comes its indifference; and from immoral it becomes, as it were, *un*moral, and not quite unnecessary to that life which we have made.

The broadest and most prevalent error requires the most disinterested virtue to sustain it. The slight reproach to which the virtue of patriotism is commonly liable, the noble are most likely to incur. Those who, while they disapprove of the character and measures of a government, yield to it their allegiance and support, are undoubtedly its most conscientious supporters, and so frequently the most serious obstacles to reform. Some are petitioning the State to dissolve the Union, to disregard the requisitions of the President. Why do they not dissolve it themselves,—the union between themselves and the State,—and refuse to pay their quota into its treasury? Do not they stand in the same relation to the State, that the State does to the Union? And have not the same reasons prevented the State from resisting the Union, which have prevented them from resisting the State?

How can a man be satisfied to entertain an opinion merely, and enjoy *it*? Is there any enjoyment in it, if his opinion is that he is aggrieved? If you are cheated out of a single dollar by your neighbor, you do not rest satisfied with knowing that you are cheated, or with saying that you are cheated, or even with petitioning him to pay you your due; but you take effectual steps at once to obtain the full amount, and see that you are never cheated again. Action from principle, the perception and the performance of right, changes things and relations; it is essentially revolutionary, and does not consist wholly with anything which was. It not only divides states and churches, it divides families; ay, it divides the *individual*, separating the diabolical in him from the divine.

Unjust laws exist: shall we be content to obey them, or shall we endeavor to amend them, and obey them until we have succeeded, or shall we transgress them at once? Men generally, under such a government as this, think that they ought to wait until they have persuaded the majority to alter them. They think that, if they should resist, the remedy would be worse than the evil. But it is the fault of the government itself that the remedy *is* worse than the evil. *It* makes it worse. Why is it not more apt to anticipate and provide for reform? Why does it not cherish its wise minority? Why does it cry and resist before it is hurt? Why does it not encourage its citizens to be on the alert to point out its faults, and *do* better than it would have them? Why does it always crucify Christ, and excommunicate Copernicus and Luther, and pronounce Washington and Franklin rebels?

One would think, that a deliberate and practical denial of its authority was the only offence never contemplated by government; else, why has it not assigned its definite, its suitable and proportionate penalty? If a man who has no property refuses but once to earn nine shillings for the State, he is put in prison for a period unlimited by any law that I know, and determined only by the discretion of those who placed him there; but if he should steal ninety times nine shillings from the State, he is soon permitted to go at large again.

If the injustice is part of the necessary friction of the machine of government, let it go, let it go: perchance it will wear smooth,—certainly the machine will wear out. If the injustice has a spring, or a pulley, or a rope, or a crank, exclusively for itself, then perhaps you may consider whether the remedy will not be worse than the evil; but if it is of such a nature that it requires you to be the agent of injustice to another, then, I say, break the law. Let your life be a counter friction to stop the machine. What I have to do is to see, at any rate, that I do not lend myself to the wrong which I condemn.

As for adopting the ways which the State has provided for remedying the evil, I know not of such ways. They take too much time, and a man's life will be gone. I have other affairs to attend to. I came into this world, not chiefly to make this a good place to live in, but to live in it, be it good or bad. A man has not everything to do, but something; and because he cannot do *everything*, it is not necessary that he should do *something* wrong. It is not my business to be petitioning the Governor or the Legislature any more than it is theirs to petition me; and, if they should not hear my petition, what should I do then? But in this case the State has provided no way: its very Constitution is the evil. This may seem to be harsh and stubborn and unconciliatory; but it is to treat with the utmost kindness and consideration the only spirit that can appreciate or deserves it. So is all change for the better, like birth and death, which convulse the body.

I do not hesitate to say, that those who call themselves Abolitionists should at once effectually withdraw their support, both in person and property, from the government of Massachusetts, and not wait till they constitute a majority of one, before they suffer the right to prevail through them. I think that it is enough if they have God on their side, without waiting for that other one. Moreover, any man more right than his neighbors constitutes a majority of one already.

I meet this American government, or its representative, the State government, directly, and face to face, once a year—no more—in the person of its tax-gatherer; this is the only mode in which a man situated as I am necessarily meets it; and it then says distinctly, Recognize me; and the simplest, the most effectual, and, in the present posture of affairs, the indispensablest mode of treating with it on this head, of expressing your little satisfaction with and love for it, is to deny it then. My civil neighbor, the tax-gatherer, is the very man I have to deal with,—for it is, after all, with men and not with parchment that I quarrel,—and he has voluntarily chosen to be an agent of the government. How shall he ever know well what he is and does as an officer of the government, or as a man, until he is obliged to consider whether he shall treat me, his neighbor, for whom he has respect, as a neighbor and well-disposed man, or as a maniac and disturber of the peace, and see if he can get over this obstruction to his neighborliness without a ruder and more impetuous thought or speech corresponding with his action. I know this well, that if one thousand, if one hundred, if ten men whom I could name,—if ten *honest* men only,—ay, if *one* HONEST man, in this State of Massachusetts, *ceasing to hold slaves*, were actually to withdraw from this copartnership, and be locked up in the county jail therefor, it would be the abolition of slavery in America. For it matters not how small the beginning may seem to be: what is once well done is done forever. But we love better to talk about it: that we say is our mission. Reform keeps many scores of newspapers in its service, but not one man. If my esteemed neighbor, the State's ambassador, who will devote his days to the settlement of the question of human rights in the Council Chamber, instead of being threatened with the prisons of Carolina, were to sit down the prisoner of Massachusetts, that State which is so anxious to foist the sin of slavery upon her sister,—though at present she can discover only an act of inhospitality to be the ground of a quarrel with her,—the Legislature would not wholly waive the subject the following winter.

Under a government which imprisons any unjustly, the true place for a just man is also a prison. The proper place to-day, the only place which Massachusetts has provided for her freer and less desponding spirits, is in her prisons, to be put out and locked out of the State by her own act, as they have already put themselves out by their principles. It is there that the fugitive slave, and the Mexican prisoner on parole, and the Indian come to plead the wrongs of his race, should find them; on that separate, but more free and honorable ground, where the State places those who are not *with* her, but *against* her,—the only house in a slave State in which a free man can abide with honor. If any think that their influence would be lost there, and their voices no longer afflict the ear of the State, that they would not be as an enemy within its walls, they do not know by how much truth is stronger than error, nor how much more eloquently and effectively he can combat injustice who has experienced a little in his own person. Cast your whole vote, not a strip of paper merely, but your whole influence. A minority is powerless while it conforms to the majority; it is not even a minority then; but it is irresistible when it clogs by its whole weight. If the alternative is to keep all just men in prison, or give up war and slavery, the State will not hesitate which to choose. If a thousand men were not to pay their tax-bills this year, that would not be a violent and bloody measure, as it would be to pay them, and enable the State to commit violence and shed innocent blood. This is, in fact, the definition of a peaceable revolution, if any such is possible. If the tax-gatherer, or any other public officer, asks me, as one has done, "But what shall I do?" my answer is, "If you really wish to do anything, resign your office." When the subject has refused allegiance, and the officer has resigned his office, then the revolution is accomplished. But even suppose blood should flow. Is there not a sort of blood shed when the conscience is wounded? Through this wound a man's real manhood and immortality flow out, and he bleeds to an everlasting death. I see this blood flowing now.

I have contemplated the imprisonment of the offender, rather than the seizure of his goods,—though both will serve the same purpose,—because they who assert the purest right, and consequently are most dangerous to a corrupt State, commonly have not spent much time in accumulating property. To such the State renders comparatively small service, and a slight tax is wont to appear exorbitant, particularly if they are obliged to earn it by special labor with their hands. If there were one who lived wholly without the use of money, the State itself would hesitate to demand it of him. But the rich man,—not to make any invidious comparison,—is always sold to the institution which makes him rich. Absolutely speaking, the more money, the less virtue; for money comes between a man and his objects, and obtains them for him; and it was certainly no great virtue to obtain it. It puts to rest many questions which he would otherwise be taxed to answer; while the only new question which it puts is the hard but superfluous one, how to spend it. Thus his moral ground is taken from under his feet. The opportunities of living are diminished in proportion as what are called the "means" are increased. The best thing a man can do for his culture when he is rich is to endeavor to carry out those schemes which he entertained when he was poor. Christ answered the Herodians according to their condition. "Show me the tribute-money," said he;—and one took a penny out of his pocket;—if you use money which has the image of Cæsar on it, and which he has made current and valuable, that is, *if you are men of the State*, and gladly enjoy the advantages of Cæsar's government, then pay him back some of his own when he demands it; "Render therefore to Cæsar that which is Cæsar's, and to God those things which are God's,"—leaving them no wiser than before as to which was which; for they did not wish to know.

When I converse with the freest of my neighbors, I perceive that, whatever they may say about the magnitude and seriousness of the question, and their regard for the public tranquillity, the long and the short of the matter is, that they cannot spare the protection of the existing government, and they dread the consequences to their property and families of disobedience to it. For my own part, I should not like to think that I ever rely on the protection of the State. But, if I deny the authority of the State when it presents its tax-bill, it will soon take and waste all my property, and so harass me and my children without end. This is hard. This makes it impossible for a man to live honestly, and at the same time comfortably, in outward respects. It will not be worth the while to accumulate property; that would be sure to go again. You must hire or squat somewhere, and raise but a small crop, and eat that soon. You must live within yourself, and depend upon yourself always tucked up and ready for a start, and not have many affairs. A man may grow rich in Turkey even, if he will be in all respects a good subject of the Turkish government. Confucius said: "If a state is governed by the principles of reason, poverty and misery are subjects of shame; if a state is not governed by the principles of reason, riches and honors are the subjects of shame." No: until I want the protection of Massachusetts to be extended to me in some distant Southern port, where my liberty is endangered, or until I am bent solely on building up an estate at home by peaceful enterprise, I can afford to refuse allegiance to Massachusetts, and her right to my property and life. It costs me less in every sense to incur the penalty of disobedience to the State, than it would to obey. I should feel as if I were worth less in that case.

Some years ago, the State met me in behalf of the Church, and commanded me to pay a certain sum toward the support of a clergyman whose preaching my father attended, but never I myself. "Pay," it said, "or be locked up in the jail." I declined to pay. But, unfortunately, another man saw fit to pay it. I did not see why the schoolmaster should be taxed to support the priest, and not the priest the schoolmaster; for I was not the State's schoolmaster, but I supported myself by voluntary subscription. I did not see why the lyceum should not present its tax-bill, and have the State to back its demand, as well as the Church. However, at the request of the selectmen, I condescended to make some such statement as this in writing:—"Know all men by these presents, that I, Henry Thoreau, do not wish to be regarded as a member of any incorporated society which I have not joined." This I gave to the town clerk; and he has it. The State, having thus learned that I did not wish to be regarded as a member of that church, has never made a like demand on me since; though it said that it must adhere to its original presumption that time. If I had known how to name them, I should then have signed off in detail from all the societies which I never signed on to; but I did not know where to find a complete list.

I have paid no poll-tax for six years. I was put into a jail once on this account, for one night; and, as I stood considering the walls of solid stone, two or three feet thick, the door of wood and iron, a foot thick, and the iron grating which strained the light, I could not help being struck with the foolishness of that institution which treated me as if I were mere flesh and blood and bones, to be locked up. I wondered that it should have concluded at length that this was the best use it could put me to, and had never thought to avail itself of my services in some way. I saw that, if there was a wall of stone between me and my townsmen, there was a still more difficult one to climb or break through, before they could get to be as free as I was. I did not for a moment feel confined, and the walls seemed a great waste of stone and mortar. I felt as if I alone of all my townsmen had paid my tax. They plainly did not know how to treat me, but behaved like persons who are underbred. In every threat and in every compliment there was a blunder; for they thought that my chief desire was to stand the other side of that stone wall. I could not but smile to see how industriously they locked the door on my meditations, which followed them out again without let or hindrance, and *they* were really all that was dangerous. As they could not reach me, they had resolved to punish my body; just as boys, if they cannot come at some person against whom they have a spite, will abuse his dog. I saw that the State was half-witted, that it was timid as a lone woman with her silver spoons, and that it did not know its friends from its foes, and I lost all my remaining respect for it, and pitied it.

Thus the State never intentionally confronts a man's sense, intellectual or moral, but only his body, his senses. It is not armed with superior wit or honesty, but with superior physical strength. I was not born to be forced. I will breathe after my own fashion. Let us see who is the strongest. What force has a multitude? They only can force me who obey a higher law than I. They force me to become like themselves. I do not hear of *men* being *forced* to live this way or that by masses of men. What sort of life were that to live? When I meet a government which says to me, "Your money or your life," why should I be in haste to give it my money? It may be in a great strait, and not know what to do: I cannot help that. It must help itself; do as I do. It is not worth the while to snivel about it. I am not responsible for the successful working of the machinery of society. I am not the son of the engineer. I perceive that, when an acorn and a chestnut fall side by side, the one does not remain inert to make way for the other, but both obey their own laws, and spring and grow and flourish as best they can, till one, perchance, overshadows and destroys the other. If a plant cannot live according to its nature, it dies; and so a man.

The night in prison was novel and interesting enough. The prisoners in their shirt-sleeves were enjoying a chat and the evening air in the doorway, when I entered. But the jailer said, "Come, boys, it is time to lock up"; and so they dispersed, and I heard the sound of their steps returning into the hollow apartments. My roommate was introduced to me by the jailer, as "a first-rate fellow and a clever man." When the door was locked, he showed me where to hang my hat, and how he managed matters there. The rooms were white-washed once a month; and this one, at least, was the whitest, most simply furnished, and probably the neatest apartment in the town. He naturally wanted to know where I came from, and what brought me there; and, when I had told him, I asked him in my turn how he came there, presuming him to be an honest man, of course; and, as the world goes, I believe he was. "Why," said he, "they accuse me of burning a barn; but I never did it." As near as I could discover, he had probably gone to bed in a barn when drunk, and smoked his pipe there; and so a barn was burnt. He had the reputation of being a clever man, had been there some three months waiting for his trial to come on, and would have to wait as much longer; but he was quite domesticated and contented, since he got his board for nothing, and thought that he was well treated.

He occupied one window, and I the other; and I saw, that, if one stayed there long, his principal business would be to look out the window. I had soon read all the tracts that were left there, and examined where former prisoners had broken out, and where a grate had been sawed off, and heard the history of the various occupants of that room; for I found that even here there was a history and a gossip which never circulated beyond the walls of the jail. Probably this is the only house in the town where verses are composed, which are afterward printed in a circular form, but not published. I was shown quite a long list of verses which were composed by some young men who had been detected in an attempt to escape, who avenged themselves by singing them.

I pumped my fellow-prisoner as dry as I could, for fear I should never see him again; but at length he showed me which was my bed, and left me to blow out the lamp.

It was like travelling into a far country, such as I had never expected to behold, to lie there for one night. It seemed to me that I never had heard the town-clock strike before, nor the evening sounds of the village; for we slept with the windows open, which were inside the grating. It was to see my native village in the light of the Middle Ages, and our Concord was turned into a Rhine stream, and visions of knights and castles passed before me. They were the voices of old burghers that I heard in the streets. I was an involuntary spectator and auditor of whatever was done and said in the kitchen of the adjacent village-inn,—a wholly new and rare experience to me. It was a closer view of my native town. I was fairly inside of it. I never had seen its institutions before. This is one of its peculiar institutions; for it is a shire town. I began to comprehend what its inhabitants were about.

In the morning, our breakfasts were put through the hole in the door, in small oblong-square tin pans, made to fit, and holding a pint of chocolate, with brown bread, and an iron spoon. When they called for the vessels again, I was green enough to return what bread I had left; but my comrade seized it, and said that I should lay that up for lunch or dinner. Soon after he was let out to work at haying in a neighboring field whither he went every day, and would not be back till noon; so he bade me good-day, saying that he doubted if he should see me again.

When I came out of prison,—for some one interfered, and paid that tax,—I did not perceive that great changes had taken place on the common, such as he observed who went in a youth, and emerged a tottering and gray-headed man; and yet a change had to my eyes come over the scene,—the town, and State, and country,—greater than any that mere time could effect. I saw yet more distinctly the State in which I lived. I saw to what extent the people among whom I lived could be trusted as good neighbors and friends; that their friendship was for summer weather only; that they did not greatly propose to do right; that they were a distinct race from me by their prejudices and superstitions, as the Chinamen and Malays are; that, in their sacrifices to humanity, they ran no risks, not even to their property; that, after all, they were not so noble but they treated the thief as he had treated them, and hoped, by a certain outward observance and a few prayers, and by walking in a particular straight though useless path from time to time, to save their souls. This may be to judge my neighbors harshly; for I believe that many of them are not aware that they have such an institution as the jail in their village.

It was formerly the custom in our village, when a poor debtor came out of jail, for his acquaintances to salute him, looking through their fingers, which were crossed to represent the grating of a jail window, "How do ye do?" My neighbors did not thus salute me, but first looked at me, and then at one another, as if I had returned from a long journey. I was put into jail as I was going to the shoemaker's to get a shoe which was mended. When I was let out the next morning, I proceeded to finish my errand, and having put on my mended shoe, joined a huckleberry party, who were impatient to put themselves under my conduct; and in half an hour,—for the horse was soon tackled,—was in the midst of a huckleberry field, on one of our highest hills, two miles off, and then the State was nowhere to be seen.

This is the whole history of "My Prisons."

I have never declined paying the highway tax, because I am as desirous of being a good neighbor as I am of being a bad subject; and, as for supporting schools, I am doing my part to educate my fellow-countrymen now. It is for no particular item in the tax-bill that I refuse to pay it. I simply wish to refuse allegiance to the State, to withdraw and stand aloof from it effectually. I do not care to trace the course of my dollar, if I could, till it buys a man or a musket to shoot one with,—the dollar is innocent,—but I am concerned to trace the effects of my allegiance. In fact, I quietly declare war with the State, after my fashion, though I will still make what use and get what advantage of her I can, as is usual in such cases.

If others pay the tax which is demanded of me, from a sympathy with the State, they do but what they have already done in their own case, or rather they abet injustice to a greater extent than the State requires. If they pay the tax from a mistaken interest in the individual taxed, to save his property, or prevent his going to jail, it is because they have not considered wisely how far they let their private feelings interfere with the public good.

This, then, is my position at present. But one cannot be too much on his guard in such a case, lest his action be biassed by obstinacy, or an undue regard for the opinions of men. Let him see that he does only what belongs to himself and to the hour.

I think sometimes, Why, this people mean well; they are only ignorant; they would do better if they knew how: why give your neighbors this pain to treat you as they are not inclined to? But I think again, this is no reason why I should do as they do, or permit others to suffer much greater pain of a different kind. Again, I sometimes say to myself, When many millions of men, without heat, without ill will, without personal feeling of any kind, demand of you a few shillings only, without the possibility, such is their constitution, of retracting or altering their present demand, and without the possibility, on your side, of appeal to any other millions, why expose yourself to this overwhelming brute force? You do not resist cold and hunger, the winds and the waves, thus obstinately; you quietly submit to a thousand similar necessities. You do not put your head into the fire. But just in proportion as I regard this as not wholly a brute force, partly a human force, and consider that I have relations to those millions as to so many millions of men, and not of mere brute or inanimate things, I see that appeal is possible, first and instantaneously, from them to the Maker of them, and, secondly, from them to themselves. But, if I put my head deliberately into the fire, there is no appeal to fire or to the Maker of fire, and I have only myself to blame. If I could convince myself that I have any right to be satisfied with men as they are, and to treat them accordingly, and not according, in some respects, to my requisitions and expectations of what they and I ought to be, then, like a good Mussulman and fatalist, I should endeavor to be satisfied with things as they are, and say it is the will of God. And, above all, there is this difference between resisting this and a purely brute or natural force, that I can resist this with some effect; but I cannot expect, like Orpheus, to change the nature of the rocks and trees and beasts.

I do not wish to quarrel with any man or nation. I do not wish to split hairs, to make fine distinctions, or set myself up as better than my neighbors. I seek rather, I may say, even an excuse for conforming to the laws of the land. I am but too ready to conform to them. Indeed, I have reason to suspect myself on this head; and each year, as the tax-gatherer comes round, I find myself disposed to review the acts and position of the general and State governments, and the spirit of the people, to discover a pretext for conformity.

> "We must affect our country as our parents;
> And if at any time we alienate
> Our love or industry from doing it honor,
> We must respect effects and teach the soul
> Matter of conscience and religion,
> And not desire of rule or benefit."

I believe that the State will soon be able to take all my work of this sort out of my hands, and then I shall be no better a patriot than my fellow-countrymen. Seen from a lower point of view, the Constitution, with all its faults, is very good; the law and the courts are very respectable; even this State and this American government are, in many respects, very admirable and rare things, to be thankful for, such as a great many have described them; but seen from a point of view a little higher, they are what I have described them; seen from a higher still, and the highest, who shall say what they are, or that they are worth looking at or thinking of at all?

However, the government does not concern me much, and I shall bestow the fewest possible thoughts on it. It is not many moments that I live under a government, even in this world. If a man is thought-free, fancy-free, imagination-free, that which *is not* never for a long time appearing *to be* to him, unwise rulers or reformers cannot fatally interrupt him.

I know that most men think differently from myself; but those whose lives are by profession devoted to the study of these or kindred subjects, content me as little as any. Statesmen and legislators, standing so completely within the institution, never distinctly and nakedly behold it. They speak of moving society, but have no resting-place without it. They may be men of a certain experience and discrimination, and have no doubt invented ingenious and even useful systems, for which we sincerely thank them; but all their wit and usefulness lie within certain not very wide limits. They are wont to forget that the world is not governed by policy and expediency. Webster never goes behind government, and so cannot speak with authority about it. His words are wisdom to those legislators who contemplate no essential reform in the existing government; but for thinkers, and those who legislate for all time, he never once glances at the subject. I know of those whose serene and wise speculations on this theme would soon reveal the limits of his mind's range and hospitality. Yet, compared with the cheap professions of most reformers, and the still cheaper wisdom and eloquence of politicians in general, his are almost the only sensible and valuable words, and we thank Heaven for him. Comparatively, he is always strong, original, and, above all, practical. Still his quality is not wisdom, but prudence. The lawyer's truth is not Truth, but consistency, or a consistent expediency. Truth is always in harmony with herself, and is not concerned chiefly to reveal the justice that may consist with wrong-doing. He well deserves to be called, as he has been called, the Defender of the Constitution. There are really no blows to be given by him but defensive ones. He is not a leader, but a follower. His leaders are the men of '87. "I have never made an effort," he says, "and never propose to make an effort; I have never countenanced an effort, and never mean to countenance an effort, to disturb the arrangement as originally made, by which the various States came into the Union." Still thinking of the sanction which the Constitution gives to slavery, he says, "Because it was a part of the original compact,—let it stand." Notwithstanding his special acuteness and ability, he is unable to take a fact out of its merely political relations, and behold it as it lies absolutely to be disposed of by the intellect,—what, for instance, it behooves a man to do here in America to-day with regard to slavery, but ventures, or is driven, to make some such desperate answer as the following, while professing to speak absolutely, and as a private man,—from which what new and singular code of social duties might be inferred? "The manner," says he, "in which the governments of those States where slavery exists are to regulate it, is for their own consideration, under their responsibility to their constituents, to the general laws of propriety, humanity, and justice, and God. Associations formed elsewhere, springing from a feeling of humanity, or any other cause, have nothing whatever to do with it. They have never received any encouragement from me, and they never will."*

They who know of no purer sources of truth, who have traced up its stream no higher, stand, and wisely stand, by the Bible and the Constitution, and drink at it there with reverence and humility; but they who behold where it comes trickling into this lake or that pool, gird up their loins once more, and continue their pilgrimage toward its fountain-head.

No man with a genius for legislation has appeared in America. They are rare in the history of the world. There are orators, politicians, and eloquent men, by the thousand; but the speaker has not yet opened his mouth to speak, who is capable of settling the much-vexed questions of the day. We love eloquence for its own sake, and not for any truth which it may utter, or any heroism it may inspire. Our legislators have not yet learned the comparative value of free-trade and of freedom, of union, and of rectitude, to a nation. They have no genius or talent for comparatively humble questions of taxation and finance, commerce and manufactures and agriculture. If we were left solely to the wordy wit of legislators in Congress for our guidance, uncorrected by the seasonable experience and the effectual complaints of the people, America would not long retain her rank among the nations. For eighteen hundred years, though perchance I have no right to say it, the New Testament has been written; yet where is the legislator who has wisdom and practical talent enough to avail himself of the light which it sheds on the science of legislation?

The authority of government, even such as I am willing to submit to,—for I will cheerfully obey those who know and can do better than I, and in many things even those who neither know nor can do so well,—is still an impure one: to be strictly just, it must have the

---

* These extracts have been inserted since the Lecture was read.

sanction and consent of the governed. It can have no pure right over my person and property but what I concede to it. The progress from an absolute to a limited monarchy, from a limited monarchy to a democracy, is a progress toward a true respect for the individual. Even the Chinese philosopher was wise enough to regard the individual as the basis of the empire. Is a democracy, such as we know it, the last improvement possible in government? Is it not possible to take a step further towards recognizing and organizing the rights of man? There will never be a really free and enlightened State, until the State comes to recognize the individual as a higher and independent power, from which all its own power and authority are derived, and treats him accordingly. I please myself with imagining a State at last which can afford to be just to all men, and to treat the individual with respect as a neighbor; which even would not think it inconsistent with its own repose, if a few were to live aloof from it, not meddling with it, nor embraced by it, who fulfilled all the duties of neighbors and fellowmen. A State which bore this kind of fruit, and suffered it to drop off as fast as it ripened, would prepare the way for a still more perfect and glorious State, which also I have imagined, but not yet anywhere seen.

17

Selection from Life and Times of Frederick Douglass

Frederick Douglass

I. Escape from Slavery
III. Introduced to the Abolitionists
IV. Recollections of Old Friends
V. One Hundred Conventions

Life and Times of Frederick Douglass

Frederick Douglass

<hr/>

Second Part
Chapter I.
Escape from Slavery.

Reasons for not having revealed the manner of escape—Nothing of romance in the method—Danger—Free Papers—Unjust tax—Protection papers—"Free trade and sailors' rights"—American eagle—Railroad train—Unobserving conductor—Capt. McGowan—Honest German—Fears—Safe arrival in Philadelphia—Ditto in New York.

In the first narrative of my experience in slavery, written nearly forty years ago, and in various writings since, I have given the public what I considered very good reasons for withholding the manner of my escape. In substance these reasons were, first, that such publication at any time during the existence of slavery might be used by the master against the slave, and prevent the future escape of any who might adopt the same means that I did. The second reason was, if possible, still more binding to silence—for publication of details would certainly have put in peril the persons and property of those who assisted. Murder itself was not more sternly and certainly punished in the State of Maryland, than that of aiding and abetting the escape of a slave. Many colored men, for no other crime than that of giving aid to a fugitive slave, have, like Charles T. Torrey, perished in prison. The abolition of slavery in my native State and throughout the country, and the lapse of time, render the caution hitherto observed no longer necessary. But even since the abolition of slavery, I have sometimes thought it well enough to baffle curiosity by saying that while slavery existed there were good reasons for not telling the manner of my escape, and since slavery had ceased to exist there was no reason for telling it. I shall now, however, cease to avail myself of this formula, and, as far as I can, endeavor to satisfy this very natural curiosity. I should perhaps have yielded to that feeling sooner, had there been anything very heroic or thrilling in the incidents connected with my escape, for I am sorry to say I have nothing of that sort to tell; and yet the courage that could risk betrayal and the bravery which was ready to encounter death if need be, in pursuit of freedom, were essential features in the undertaking. My success was due to address rather than courage; to good luck rather than bravery. My means of escape were provided for me by the very men who were making laws to hold and bind me more securely in slavery. It was the custom in the State of Maryland to require of the free colored people to have what were called free papers. This instrument they were required to renew very often, and by charging a fee for this writing, considerable sums from time to time were collected by the State. In these papers the name, age, color, height, and form of the free man were described, together with any scars or other marks upon his person, which could assist in his identification. This device of slaveholding ingenuity, like other devices of wickedness, in some measures defeated itself—since more than one man could be found to answer the same general description. Hence many slaves could escape by personating the owner of one set of papers; and this was often done as follows: A slave nearly or sufficiently answering the description set forth in the papers, would borrow or hire them till he could by their means escape to a free State, and then, by mail or otherwise, return them to the owner. The operation was a hazardous one for the lender as well as the borrower. A failure on the part of the fugitive to send back the papers would imperil his benefactor, and the discovery of the papers in possession of the wrong man would imperil both the fugitive and his friend. It was therefore an act of supreme trust on the part of a freeman of color thus to put in jeopardy his own liberty that another might be free. It was, however, not unfrequently bravely done, and was seldom discovered. I was not so fortunate as to sufficiently resemble any of my free acquaintances as to answer the description of their papers. But I had one friend—a sailor—who owned a sailor's protection, which answered somewhat the purpose of free papers—describing his person, and certifying to the fact that he was a free American sailor. The instrument had at its head the American eagle, which gave it the appearance at once of an authorized document. This protection did not, when in my hands, describe its bearer very accurately. Indeed, it called for a man much darker than myself, and close examination of it would have caused my arrest at the start. In order to avoid this fatal scrutiny on the part of the railroad official, I had arranged with Isaac Rolls, a hackman, to bring my baggage to the train just on the moment of its starting, and jumped upon the car myself when the train was already in motion. Had I gone into the station and offered to purchase a ticket, I should have been instantly and carefully examined, and undoubtedly arrested. In choosing this plan upon which to act, I considered the jostle of the train, and the natural haste of the conductor, in a train crowded with passengers, and relied upon my skill and address in playing the sailor as described in my protection, to do the rest. One element in my favor was the kind feeling which prevailed in Baltimore and other seaports at the time, towards "those who go down to the sea in ships." "Free trade and sailors' rights" expressed the sentiment of the country just then. In my clothing I was rigged out in sailor style. I had on a red shirt and a tarpaulin hat and black cravat, tied in sailor fashion, carelessly and loosely about my neck. My knowledge of ships and sailor's talk came much to my assistance, for I knew a ship from stem to stern, and from keelson to cross-trees, and could talk sailor like an "old salt." On sped the train, and I was well on the way to Havre de Grace before the conductor came into the negro car to collect tickets and examine the papers of his black passengers. This was a critical moment in the drama. My whole future depended upon the decision of this conductor. Agitated I was while this ceremony was proceeding, but still externally, at least, I was apparently calm and self-possessed. He went on with his duty—examining several colored passengers before reaching me. He was somewhat harsh in tone, and peremptory in manner until he reached me, when, strangely enough, and to my surprise and relief, his whole manner changed. Seeing that I did not readily produce my free papers, as the other colored persons in the car had done, he said to me in a friendly contrast with that observed towards the others: "I suppose you have your free papers?" To which I answered: "No, sir; I never carry my free papers to sea with me." "But you have something to show that you are a free man, have you not?" "Yes, sir," I answered; "I have a paper with the American eagle on it, and that will carry me round the world." With this I drew from my deep sailor's pocket my seaman's protection, as before described. The merest glance at the paper satisfied him, and he took my fare and went on about his business. This moment of time was one of the most anxious I ever experienced. Had the conductor looked closely at the paper, he could not have failed to discover that it called for a very different looking person from myself, and in that case it would have been his duty to arrest me on the instant, and send me back to Baltimore from the first station. When he left me with the assurance that I was all right, though much relieved, I realized that I was still in great danger: I was still in Maryland, and subject to arrest at any moment. I saw on the train several persons who would have known me in any other clothes, and I feared they might recognize me, even in my sailor "rig," and report me to the conductor, who would then subject me to a closer examination, which I knew well would be fatal to me.

Though I was not a murderer fleeing from justice I felt perhaps quite as miserable as such a criminal. The train was moving at a very high rate of speed for that time of railroad travel, but to my anxious mind, it was moving far too slowly. Minutes were hours, and hours were days during this part of my flight. After Maryland I was to pass through Delaware—another slave State, where slave catchers generally awaited their prey, for it was not in the interior of the State, but on its borders, that the human hounds were most vigilant and active. The border lines between slavery and freedom were the dangerous ones, for the fugitives. The heart of no fox or deer, with hungry hounds on his trail, in full chase, could have beaten more anxiously or noisily than did mine, from the time I left Baltimore till I reached Philadelphia. The passage of the Susquehanna river at Havre de Grace was made by ferry boat at that time, on board of which I met a young colored man by the name of Nichols, who came very near betraying me. He was a "hand" on the boat, but instead of minding his business, he insisted upon knowing me, and asking me dangerous questions as to where I was going, and when I was coming back, etc. I got away from my old and inconvenient acquaintance as soon as I could decently do so, and went to another part of the boat. Once across the river I encountered a new danger. Only a few days before I had been at work on a revenue cutter, in Mr. Price's ship-yard, under the care of Captain McGowan. On the meeting at this point of the two trains, the one going south stopped on the track just opposite to the one going north, and it so happened that this Captain McGowan sat at a window where he could see me very distinctly, and would certainly have recognized me had he looked at me but for a second. Fortunately, in the hurry of the moment, he did not see me; and the trains soon passed each other on their respective ways. But this was not my only hair-breadth escape. A German blacksmith whom I knew well, was on the train with me, and looked at me very intently as if he thought he had seen me somewhere before in his travels. I really believe he knew me, but had no heart to betray me. At any rate he saw me escaping and held his peace.

The last point of imminent danger, and the one I dreaded most, was Wilmington. Here we left the train and took the steamboat for Philadelphia. In making the changes here I again apprehended arrest, but no one disturbed me, and I was soon on the broad and beautiful Delaware, speeding away to the Quaker City. On reaching Philadelphia in the afternoon I inquired of a colored man how I could get on to New York? He directed me to the William street depot, and thither I went, taking the train that night. I reached New York Tuesday morning, having completed the journey in less than twenty-four hours. Such is briefly the manner of my escape from slavery—and the end of my experience as a slave. Other chapters will tell the story of my life as a freeman.

Chapter III.
Introduced to the Abolitionists.

Anti-Slavery Convention at Nantucket—First Speech—Much Sensation—Extraordinary Speech of Mr. Garrison—Anti-Slavery Agency—Youthful Enthusiasm—Fugitive Slaveship Doubted—Experience in Slavery Written—Danger of Recapture.

In the summer of 1841 a grand anti-slavery convention was held in Nantucket, under the auspices of Mr. Garrison and his friends. I had taken no holiday since establishing myself in New Bedford, and feeling the need of a little rest, I determined on attending the meeting, though I had no thought of taking part in any of its proceedings. Indeed, I was not aware that any one connected with the convention so much as knew my name. Mr. William C. Coffin, a prominent abolitionist in those days of trial, had heard me speaking to my colored friends in the little school house on Second street, where we worshiped. He sought me out in the crowd and invited me to say a few words to the convention. Thus sought out, and thus invited, I was induced to express the feelings inspired by the occasion, and the fresh recollection of the scenes through which I had passed as a slave. It was with the utmost difficulty that I could stand erect, or that I could command and articulate two words without hesitation and stammering. I trembled in every limb. I am not sure that my embarrassment was not the most effective part of my speech, if speech it could be called. At any rate, this is about the only part of my performance that I now distinctly remember. The audience sympathized with me at once, and from having been remarkably quiet, became much excited. Mr. Garrison followed me, taking me as his text, and now, whether *I* had made an eloquent plea in behalf of freedom, or not, his was one, never to be forgotten. Those who had heard him oftenest, and had known him longest, were astonished at his masterly effort. For the time he possessed that almost fabulous inspiration, often referred to but seldom attained, in which a public meeting is transformed, as it were, into a single individuality, the orator swaying a thousand heads and hearts at once, and by the simple majesty of his all-controlling thought, converting his hearers into the express image of his own soul. That night there were at least a thousand Garrisonians in Nantucket!

At the close of this great meeting I was duly waited on by Mr. John A. Collins, then the general agent of the Massachusetts Anti-Slavery Society, and urgently solicited by him to become an agent of that society, and publicly advocate its principles. I was reluctant to take the proffered position. I had not been quite three years from slavery and was honestly distrustful of my ability, and I wished to be excused. Besides, publicity might discover me to my master, and many other objections presented themselves. But Mr. Collins was not to be refused, and I finally consented to go out for three months, supposing I should in that length of time come to the end of my story and my consequent usefulness.

Here opened for me a new life—a life for which I had had no preparation. Mr. Collins used to say when introducing me to an audience, I was a "graduate from the peculiar institution, with my diploma *written on my back.*" The three years of my freedom had been spent in the hard school of adversity. My hands seemed to be furnished with something like a leather coating, and I had marked out for myself a life of rough labor, suited to the hardness of my hands, as a means of supporting my family and rearing my children.

Young, ardent, and hopeful, I entered upon this new life in the full gush of unsuspecting enthusiasm. The cause was good, the men engaged in it were good, the means to attain its triumph, good. Heaven's blessing must attend all, and freedom must soon be given to the millions pining under a ruthless bondage. My whole heart went with the holy cause, and my most fervent prayer to the Almighty Disposer of the hearts of men, was continually offered for its early triumph. In this enthusiastic spirit I dropped into the ranks of freedom's friends and went forth to the battle. For a time I was made to forget that my skin was dark and my hair crisped. For a time I regretted that I could not have shared the hardships and dangers endured by the earlier workers for the slave's release. I found, however, full soon that my enthusiasm had been extravagant, that hardships and dangers were not all over, and that the life now before me had its shadows also, as well as its sunbeams.

Among the first duties assigned me on entering the ranks was to travel in company with Mr. George Foster to secure subscribers to the *Anti-Slavery Standard* and the *Liberator.* With him I traveled and lectured through the eastern counties of Massachusetts. Much interest was awakened—large meetings assembled. Many came, no doubt from curiosity to hear what a negro could say in his own cause. I was generally introduced as a "chattel,"—a "thing"—a piece of southern property—the chairman assuring the audience that *it* could speak. *Fugitive slaves* were rare then, and as a fugitive slave lecturer, I had the advantage of being a "bran new fact"—the first one out. Up to that time, a colored man was deemed a fool who confessed himself a runaway slave, not only because of the danger to which he exposed himself of being retaken, but because it was a confession of a very low origin. Some of my colored friends in New Bedford thought very badly of my wisdom in thus exposing and degrading myself. The only precaution I took at the beginning, to prevent Master Thomas from knowing where I was and what I was about, was the withholding my former name, my master's name, and the name of the State and county from which I came. During the first three or four months my speeches were almost exclusively made up of narrations of my own personal experience as a slave. "Let us have the facts," said the people. So also said Friend George Foster, who always wished to pin me down to my simple narrative. "Give us the facts," said Collins, "we will take care of the philosophy." Just here arose some embarrassment. It was impossible for me to repeat the same old story, month after month, and to keep up my interest in it. It was new to the people, it is true, but it was an old story to me; and to go through with it night after night, was a task altogether too mechanical for my nature. "Tell your story, Frederick," would whisper my revered friend, Mr. Garrison, as I stepped upon the platform. I could not always follow the injunction, for I was now reading and thinking. New views of the subject were being presented to my mind. It did not entirely satisfy me to *narrate* wrongs; I felt like *denouncing* them. I could not always curb my moral indignation for the perpetrators of slaveholding villainy, long enough for a circumstantial statement of the facts which I felt almost sure everybody must know. Besides, I was growing, and needed room. "People won't believe you ever was a slave, Frederick, if you keep on this way," said friend Foster. "Be yourself," said Collins, "and tell your story." "Better have a little of the plantation speech than not," it was said to me;

"it is not best that you seem too learned." These excellent friends were actuated by the best of motives, and were not altogether wrong in their advice; and still I must speak, just the word that seemed to *me* the word to be spoken *by* me.

At last the apprehended trouble came. People doubted if I had ever been a slave. They said I did not talk like a slave, look like a slave, nor act like a slave, and that they believed I had never been south of Mason and Dixon's line. "He don't tell us where he came from—what his master's name was, nor how he got away; besides he is educated, and is, in this, a contradiction of all the facts we have concerning the ignorance of the slaves." Thus I was in a pretty fair way to be denounced as an impostor. The committee of the Massachusetts Anti-Slavery Society knew all the facts in my case, and agreed with me thus far in the prudence of keeping them private; but going down the aisles of the churches in which my meetings were held, and hearing the out-spoken Yankees repeatedly saying, "He's never been a slave, I'll warrant you," I resolved to dispel all doubt at no distant day, by such a revelation of facts as could not be made by any other than a genuine fugitive. In a little less than four years, therefore, after becoming a public lecturer, I was induced to write out the leading facts connected with my experience in slavery, giving names of persons, places, and dates—thus putting it in the power of any who doubted to ascertain the truth or falsehood of my story. This statement soon became known in Maryland, and I had reason to believe that an effort would be made to recapture me.

It is not probable that any open attempt to secure me as a slave could have succeeded, further than the obtainment, by my master, of the money value of my bones and sinews. Fortunately for me, in the four years of my labors in the abolition cause, I had gained many friends who would have suffered themselves to be taxed to almost any extent to save me from slavery. It was felt that I had committed the double offense of running away and exposing the secrets and crimes of slavery and slaveholders. There was a double motive for seeking my re-enslavement—avarice and vengeance; and while, as I have said, there was little probability of successful recapture, if attempted openly, I was constantly in danger of being spirited away at a moment when my friends could render me no assistance. In traveling about from place to place, often alone, I was much exposed to this sort of attack. Any one cherishing the design to betray me, could easily do so by simply tracing my whereabouts through the anti-slavery journals, for my movements and meetings were made through these in advance. My friends, Mr. Garrison and Mr. Phillips, had no faith in the power of Massachusetts to protect me in my right to liberty. Public sentiment and the law, in their opinion, would hand me over to the tormentors. Mr. Phillips especially considered me in danger, and said when I showed him the manuscript of my story, if in my place, he would "throw it into the fire." Thus the reader will observe that the overcoming one difficulty only opened the way for another; and that though I had reached a free State, and had attained a position for public usefulness, I was still under the liability of losing all I had gained.

Chapter IV.
Recollections of Old Friends.

———— • ————

Work in Rhode Island—Dorr War—Recollections of old friends—Further labors in Rhode Island and elsewhere in New England.

In the State of Rhode Island, under the leadership of Thomas W. Dorr, an effort was made in 1841 to set aside the old colonial charter, under which that State had lived and flourished since the Revolution, and to replace it with a new constitution having such improvements as it was thought that time and experience had shown to be wise and necessary. This new constitution was especially framed to enlarge the bases of representation so far as the white people of the State were concerned—to abolish an odious property qualification, and to confine the right of suffrage to white male citizens only. Mr. Dorr was himself a well-meaning man, and, after his fashion, a man of broad and progressive views, quite in advance of the party with which he acted. To gain their support, he consented to this restriction to a class, a right which ought to be enjoyed by all citizens. In this he consulted policy rather than right, and at last shared the fate of all compromisers and trimmers, for he was disastrously defeated. The proscriptive features of his constitution shocked the sense of right and roused the moral indignation of the abolitionists of the State, a class which would otherwise have gladly cooperated with him, at the same time that it did nothing to win support from the conservative class which clung to the old charter. Anti-slavery men wanted a new constitution, but they did not want a defective instrument which required reform at the start. The result was that such men as William M. Chase, Thomas Davis, George L. Clark, Asa Fairbanks, Alphonso Janes, and others of Providence, the Perry brothers of Westerly, John Brown and C. C. Eldridge of East Greenwich, Daniel Mitchell, William Adams, and Robert Shove of Pawtucket, Peleg Clark, Caleb Kelton, G. J. Adams, and the Anthonys and Goulds of Coventry and vicinity, Edward Norris of Woonsocket, and other abolitionists of the State, decided that the time had come when the people of Rhode Island might be taught a more comprehensive gospel of human rights than had gotten itself into this Dorr constitution. The public mind was awake, and one class of its people at least was ready to work with us to the extent of seeking to defeat the proposed constitution, though their reasons for such work were far different from ours. Stephen S. Foster, Parker Pillsbury, Abby Kelley, James Monroe, and myself, were called into the State to advocate equal rights as against this narrow and proscriptive constitution. The work to which we were invited was not free from difficulty. The majority of the people were evidently with the new constitution; even the word *white* in it chimed well with the popular prejudice against the colored race, and at the first helped to make the movement popular. On the other hand, all the arguments which the Dorr men could urge against a property qualification for suffrage were equally cogent against a color qualification, and this was our advantage. But the contest was intensely bitter and exciting. We were as usual denounced as intermeddlers (carpet-bagger had not come into use at that time) and were told to mind our own business, and the like, a mode of defense common to men when called to account for mean and discreditable conduct. Stephen S. Foster, Parker Pillsbury, and the rest of us were not the kind of men to be ordered off by that sort of opposition. We cared nothing for the Dorr party on the one hand, nor the "law and order party" on the other. What we wanted, and what we labored to obtain, was a constitution free from the narrow, selfish, and senseless limitation of the word *white*. Naturally enough when we said a strong and striking word against the Dorr Constitution the conservatives were pleased and applauded, while the Dorr men were disgusted and indignant. Foster and Pillsbury were like the rest of us, young, strong, and at their best in this contest. The splendid vehemence of the one, and the weird and terrible denunciations of the other, never failed to stir up mobocratic wrath wherever they spoke. Foster especially, was effective in this line. His theory was that he must make converts or mobs. If neither came he charged it either to his want of skill or his unfaithfulness. I was much with Mr. Foster during the tour in Rhode Island, and though at times he seemed to me extravagant and needlessly offensive in his manner of presenting his ideas, yet take him for all in all, he was one of the most impressive advocates the cause of the American slave ever had. No white man ever made the black man's cause more completely his own. Abby Kelley, since Abby Kelley Foster, was perhaps the most successful of any of us. Her youth and simple Quaker beauty combined with her wonderful earnestness, her large knowledge and great logical power, bore down all opposition in the end, wherever she spoke, though she was before pelted with foul eggs, and no less foul words from the noisy mobs which attended us.

Monroe and I were less aggressive than either of our coworkers, and of course did not provoke the same resistance. He at least, had the eloquence that charms, and the skill that disarms. I think that our labors in Rhode Island during this Dorr excitement did more to abolitionize the State, than any previous, or subsequent work. It was the "tide," "taken at the flood." One effect of those labors was to induce the old "Law and Order" party, when it set about making its new constitution, to avoid the narrow folly of the Dorrites, and make a constitution which should not abridge any man's rights on account of race or color. Such a constitution was finally adopted.

Owing perhaps to my efficiency in this campaign I was for a while employed in farther labors in Rhode Island by the State Anti-Slavery Society, and made there many friends to my cause as well as to myself. As a class the abolitionists of this State partook of the spirit of its founder. They had their own opinions, were independent, and called no man master. I have reason to remember them most gratefully. They received me as a man and a brother, when I was new from the house of bondage, and had few of the graces derived from free and refined society. They took me with earnest hand to their homes and hearths, and made me feel that though I wore the burnished livery of the sun I was still a countryman and kinsman of whom they were never ashamed. I can never forget the Clarks, Keltons, Chaces, Browns, Adams, Greenes, Sissons, Eldredges, Mitchells, Shoves, Anthonys, Applins, Janes, Goulds, and Fairbanks, and many others.

While thus remembering the noble anti-slavery men and women of Rhode Island, I do not forget that I suffered much rough usage within her borders. It was like all the northern States at that time, under the influence of slave power, and often showed a proscription and persecuting spirit, especially upon its railways, steamboats, and public houses. The Stonington route was a "hard road" for a colored man "to travel" in that day. I was several times dragged from the cars for the *crime* of being colored. On the Sound between New York and Stonington, there were the same proscriptions which I have before named as enforced on the steamboats running between New York and Newport. No colored man was allowed abaft the wheel, and in all seasons of the year, in heat or cold, wet or dry, the deck was his only place. If I would lie down at night I must do so upon the freight on deck, and this in cold weather was not a very comfortable bed. When traveling in company with my white friends I always urged them to leave me and go into the cabin and take their comfortable berths. I saw no reason why they should be miserable because I was. Some of them took my advice very readily. I confess, however, that while I was entirely honest in urging them to go, and saw no principle that should bind them to stay and suffer with me, I always felt a little nearer to those who did not take my advice and persisted in sharing my hardships with me.

There is something in the world above fixed rules and the logic of right and wrong, and there is some foundation for recognizing works, which may be called works of supererogation. Wendell Phillips, James Monroe, and William White, were always dear to me for their nice feeling at this point. I have known James Monroe to pull his coat about him and crawl upon the cotton bales between decks and pass the night with me, without a murmur. Wendell Phillips would never go into a first-class car while I was forced into what was called the Jim Crow car. True men they were, who could accept welcome at no man's table where I was refused. I speak of these gentlemen, not as singular or exceptional cases, but as representatives of a large class of the early workers for the abolition of slavery. As a general rule there was little difficulty in obtaining suitable places in New England after 1840, where I could plead the cause of my people. The abolitionists had passed the Red Sea of mobs, and had conquered the right to a respectful hearing. I, however, found several towns in which the people closed their doors and refused to entertain the subject. Notably among these was Hartford, Conn., and Grafton, Mass. In the former place Messrs. Garrison, Hudson, Foster, Abby Kelley, and myself determined to hold our meetings under the open sky, which we did in a little court under the eaves of the "sanctuary" ministered unto by the Rev. Dr. Hawes, with much satisfaction to ourselves, and I think with advantage to our cause. In Grafton I was alone, and there was neither house, hall, church, nor market-place in which I could speak to the people, but *determined to speak* I went to the hotel and borrowed a dinner bell with which in hand I passed through the principal streets, ringing the bell and crying out, "*Notice!* Frederick Douglass, recently a slave, will lecture on American Slavery, on Grafton Common, this evening at 7 o'clock. Those who would like to hear of the workings of slavery by one of the slaves are respectfully invited to attend." This notice brought out a large audience, after which the largest church in town was open to me. Only in one instance was I compelled to pursue this course thereafter, and that was in Manchester, N. H., and my labors there were followed by similar results. When people found that I would be heard, they saw it was the part of wisdom to open the way for me.

My treatment in the use of public conveyances about these times was extremely rough, especially on the "Eastern Railroad, from Boston to Portland." On that road, as on many others, there was a mean, dirty, and uncomfortable car set apart for colored travelers, called the "Jim Crow" car. Regarding this as the fruit of slaveholding prejudice, and being determined to fight the spirit of slavery wherever I might find it, I resolved to avoid this car, though it sometimes required some courage to do so. The colored people generally accepted the situation, and complained of me as making matters worse rather than better by refusing to submit to this proscription. I, however, persisted, and sometimes was soundly beaten by conductor and brakeman. On one occasion six of these "fellows of the baser sort," under the direction of the conductor, set out to eject me from my seat. As usual, I had purchased a first-class ticket, and paid the required sum for it, and on the requirement of the conductor to leave refused to do so, when he called on these men "to snake me out." They attempted to obey with an air which plainly told me they relished the job. They, however, found me *much attached* to my seat, and in removing me I tore away two or three of the surrounding ones, on which I held with a firm grasp, and did the car no service in some other respects. I was strong and muscular, and the seats were not then so firmly attached or of as solid make as now. The result was that Stephen A. Chase, superintendent of the road, ordered all passenger trains to pass through Lynn (where I then lived) without stopping. This was a great inconvenience to the people, large numbers of whom did business in Boston, and at other points of the road. Led on, however, by James N. Buffum, Jonathan Buffum, Christopher Robinson, William Bassett, and others, the people of Lynn stood bravely by me, and denounced the railroad management in emphatic terms. Mr. Chase made reply that a railroad corporation was neither a religious nor reformatory body; that the road was run for the accommodation of the public, and that *it* required the exclusion of colored people from its cars. With an air of triumph he told us that we ought not to expect a railroad company to be better than the evangelical church, and that until the churches abolished the "negro pew," we ought not to expect the railroad company to abolish the negro car. This argument was certainly good enough as against the church, but good for nothing as against the demands of justice and equality. My old and dear friend, J. N. Buffum, made a point against the company that they "often allowed dogs and monkeys to ride in first-class cars, and yet excluded a man like Frederick Douglass!" In a very few years this barbarous practice was put away, and I think there have been no instances of such exclusion during the past thirty years; and colored people now, everywhere in New England, ride upon equal terms with other passengers.

Chapter V.
One Hundred Conventions.

Anti-slavery conventions held in parts of New England, and in some of the Middle and Western States—Mobs—Incidents, etc.

The year 1843 was one of remarkable anti-slavery activity. The New England Anti-Slavery Society at its annual meeting, held in the spring of that year, resolved, under the auspices of Mr. Garrison and his friends, to hold a series of one hundred conventions. The territory embraced in this plan for creating anti-slavery sentiment included New Hampshire, Vermont, New York, Ohio, Indiana, and Pennsylvania. I had the honor to be chosen one of the agents to assist in these proposed conventions, and I never entered upon any work with more heart and hope. All that the American people needed, I thought, was light. Could they know slavery as I knew it, they would hasten to the work of its extinction. The corps of speakers who were to be associated with me in carrying on these conventions were Messrs. George Bradburn, John A. Collins, James Monroe, William A. White, Charles L. Remond, and Sydney Howard Gay. They were all masters of the subject, and some of them able and eloquent orators. It was a piece of great good fortune to me, only a few years from slavery as I was, to be brought into contact with such men. It was a real campaign, and required nearly six months for its accomplishment.

Those who only know the State of Vermont as it is to-day, can hardly understand, and must wonder that there was need for anti-slavery effort within its borders forty years ago. Our first convention was held in Middlebury, its chief seat of learning, and the home of William Slade, who was for years the co-worker with John Quincy Adams in Congress; and yet in this town the opposition to our anti-slavery convention was intensely bitter and violent. The only man of note in the town whom I now remember as giving us sympathy or welcome was Mr. Edward Barber, who was a man of courage as well as ability, and did his best to make our convention a success. In advance of our arrival, the college students had very industriously and mischievously placarded the town with violent aspersions of our characters, and the grossest misrepresentations of our principles, measures, and objects. I was described as an escaped convict from the State Prison, and the other speakers were assailed not less slanderously. Few people attended our meeting, and apparently little was accomplished by it. In the neighboring town of Ferrisburgh the case was different and more favorable. The way had been prepared for us by such stalwart anti-slavery workers as Orson S. Murray, Charles C.

Burleigh, Rowland T. Robinson, and others. Upon the whole, however, the several towns visited showed that Vermont was surprisingly under the influence of the slave power. Her proud boast that no slave had ever been delivered up to his master within her borders did not hinder her hatred to *anti*-slavery. What was true of the Green Mountain State in this respect, was most discouragingly true of New York, the State next visited. All along the Erie canal, from Albany to Buffalo, there was apathy, indifference, aversion, and sometimes mobocratic spirit evinced. Even Syracuse, afterwards the home of the humane Samuel J. May, and the scene of the "Jerry rescue," where Gerrit Smith, Beriah Greene, William Goodell, Alvin Stewart, and other able men since taught their noblest lessons, would not at that time furnish us with church, market, house, or hall in which to hold our meetings. Discovering this state of things, some of our number were disposed to turn our backs upon the town, and shake its dust from our feet, but of these, I am glad to say, I was not one. I had somewhere read of a command to go into the hedges and highways and compel men to come in. Mr. Stephen Smith, under whose hospitable roof we were made at home, thought as I did. It would be easy to silence anti-slavery agitation if refusing its agents the use of halls and churches could effect that result. The house of our friend Smith stood on the southwest corner of the park, which was well covered with young trees, too small to furnish shade or shelter, but better than none. Taking my stand under a small tree, in the southeast corner of this park, I began to speak in the morning to an audience of five persons, and before the close of my afternoon meeting I had before me not less than five hundred. In the evening I was waited upon by officers of the Congregational church, and tendered the use of an old wooden building, which they had deserted for a better, but still owned; and here our convention was continued during three days. I believe there has been no trouble to find places in Syracuse in which to hold anti-slavery meetings since. I never go there without endeavoring to see that tree, which, like the cause it sheltered, has grown large and strong and imposing.

I believe my first offence against our Anti-Slavery Israel was committed during these Syracuse meetings. It was on this wise: Our general agent, John A. Collins, had recently returned from England full of communistic ideas, which ideas would do away with individual property, and have all things in common. He had arranged a corps of speakers of his communistic persuasion, consisting of John O. Wattles, Nathaniel Whiting, and John Orvis, to follow our anti-slavery conventions, and while our meeting was in progress in Syracuse, a meeting, as the reader will observe, obtained under much difficulty, Mr. Collins came in with his new friends and doctrines, and proposed to adjourn our anti-slavery discussions and take up the subject of communism. To this I ventured to object. I held that it was imposing an additional burden of unpopularity on our cause, and an act of bad faith with the people, who paid the salary of Mr. Collins, and were responsible for these hundred conventions. Strange to say, my course in this matter did not meet the approval of Mrs. M. W. Chapman, an influential member of the board of managers of the Massachusetts Anti-Slavery Society, and called out a sharp reprimand from her, for my insubordination to my superiors. This was a strange and distressing revelation to me, and one of which I was not soon relieved. I thought I had only done my duty, and I think so still. The chief reason for the reprimand was the use which the liberty party papers would make of my seeming rebellion against the commanders of our Anti-Slavery Army.

In the growing city of Rochester we had in every way a better reception. Abolitionists of all shades of opinion were broad enough to give the Garrisonians (for such we were) a hearing. Samuel D. Porter and the Avery family, though they belonged to the Gerrit Smith, Myron Holly, and William Goodell school, were not so narrow as to refuse us the use of their church for the convention. They heard our moral suasion arguments, and in a manly way met us in debate. We were opposed to carrying the anti-slavery cause to the ballot-box, and they believed in carrying it there. They looked at slavery as a creature of *law;* we regarded it as a creature of public opinion. It is surprising how small the difference appears as I look back to it, over the space of forty years; yet at the time of it this difference was immense.

During our stay at Rochester we were hospitably entertained by Isaac and Amy Post, two people of all-abounding benevolence, the truest and best of Long Island and Elias Hicks Quakers. They were not more amiable than brave, for they never seemed to ask, What will the world say? but walked straight forward in what seemed to them the line of duty, please or offend whomsoever it might. Many a poor fugitive slave found shelter under their roof when such shelter was hard to find elsewhere, and I mention them here in the warmth and fullness of earnest gratitude.

Pleased with our success in Rochester, we—that is Mr. Bradburn and myself—made our way to Buffalo, then a rising city of steamboats, bustle, and business. Buffalo was too busy to attend to such matters as we had in hand. Our friend, Mr. Marsh, had been able to secure for our convention only an old delapidated and deserted room, formerly used as a post-office. We went at the time appointed, and found seated a few cabmen in their coarse, every-day clothes, whips in hand, while their teams were standing on the street waiting for a job. Friend Bradburn looked around upon this unpromising audience, and turned upon his heel, saying he would not speak to "such a set of ragamuffins," and took the first steamer to Cleveland, the home of his brother Charles, and left me to "do" Buffalo alone. For nearly a week I spoke every day in this old post-office to audiences constantly increasing in numbers and respectability, till the Baptist church was thrown open to me; and when this became too small I went on Sunday into the open Park and addressed an assembly of four or five thousand persons. After this my colored friends, Charles L. Remond, Henry Highland Garnett, Theodore S. Wright, Amos G. Beaman, Charles M. Ray, and other well-known colored men, held a convention here, and then Remond and myself left for our next meeting in Chester county, Ohio. This was held under a great shed, built by the abolitionists, of whom Dr. Abram Brook and Valentine Nicholson were the most noted, for this special purpose. Thousands gathered here and were addressed by Bradburn, White, Monroe, Remond, Gay, and myself. The influence of this meeting was deep and wide-spread. It would be tedious to tell of all, or a small part of all that was interesting and illustrative of the difficulties encountered by the early advocates of anti-slavery in connection with this campaign, and hence I leave this part of it at once.

From Ohio we divided our forces and went into Indiana. At our first meeting we were mobbed, and some of us got our good clothes spoiled by evil-smelling eggs. This was at Richmond, where Henry Clay had been recently invited to the high seat of the Quaker meeting-house just after his gross abuse of Mr. Mendenhall, because of his presenting him a respectful petition, asking him to emancipate his slaves. At Pendleton this mobocratic spirit was even more pronounced. It was found impossible to obtain a building in which to hold our convention, and our friends, Dr. Fussell and others, erected a platform in the woods, where quite a large audience assembled. Mr. Bradburn, Mr. White, and myself were in attendance. As soon as we began to speak a mob of about sixty of the roughest characters I ever looked upon ordered us, through its leaders, to "be silent," threatening us, if we were not, with violence. We attempted to dissuade them, but they had not come to parley but to fight, and were well armed. They tore down the platform on which we stood, assaulted Mr. White and knocking out several of his teeth, dealt a heavy blow on William A. White, striking him on the back part of the head, badly cutting his scalp and felling him to the ground. Undertaking to fight my way through the crowd with a stick which I caught up in the mêlée, I attracted the fury of the mob, which laid me prostrate on the ground under a torrent of blows. Leaving me thus, with my right hand broken, and in a state of unconsciousness, the mobocrats hastily mounted their horses and rode to Andersonville, where most of them resided. I was soon raised up and revived by Neal Hardy, a kind-hearted member of the Society of Friends, and carried by him in his wagon about three miles in the country to his home, where I was tenderly nursed and bandaged by good Mrs. Hardy till I was again on my feet, but as the bones broken were not properly set my hand has never recovered its natural strength and dexterity. We lingered long in Indiana, and the good effects of our labors there are felt at this day. I have lately visited Pendleton, now one of the best republican towns in the State, and looked again upon the spot where I was beaten down, and have again taken by the hand some of the witnesses of that scene, amongst whom was the kind, good lady—Mrs. Hardy—who, so like the good Samaritan of old, bound up my wounds, and cared for me so kindly. A complete history of these hundred conventions would fill a volume far larger than the one in which this simple reference is to find a place. It would be a grateful duty to speak of the noble young men, who forsook ease and pleasure, as did White, Gay, and Monroe, and endured all manner of privations in the cause of the enslaved and down-trodden of my race. Gay, Monroe, and myself are the only ones who participated as agents in the one hundred conventions who now survive. Mr. Monroe was for many years consul to Brazil, and has since been a faithful member of Congress from the Oberlin District, Ohio, and has filled other important positions in his State. Mr. Gay was managing editor of the *National Anti-Slavery Standard,* and afterwards of the New York *Tribune,* and still later of the New York *Evening Post.*

18

Selection from
Uncle Tom's Cabin

Harriet Beecher Stowe

Uncle Tom's Cabin

Harriet Beecher Stowe

Chapter I.
In Which the Reader is Introduced
to a Man of Humanity.

LATE in the afternoon of a chilly day in February, two gentlemen were sitting alone over their wine, in a well-furnished dining parlor, in the town of P——, in Kentucky. There were no servants present, and the gentlemen, with chairs closely approaching, seemed to be discussing some subject with great earnestness.

For convenience' sake, we have said, hitherto, two *gentlemen*. One of the parties, however, when critically examined, did not seem, strictly speaking, to come under the species. He was a short thick-set man, with coarse commonplace features, and that swaggering air of pretension which marks a low man who is trying to elbow his way upward in the world. He was much overdressed, in a gaudy vest of many colors, a blue neckerchief, be-dropped gayly with yellow sports, and arranged with a flaunting tie, quite in keeping with the general air of the man. His hands, large and coarse, were plentifully bedecked with rings; and he wore a heavy gold watch chain, with a bundle of seals of portentous size, and a great variety of colors, attached to it,—which, in the ardor of conversation, he was in the habit of flourishing and jingling with evident satisfaction. His conversation was in free and easy defiance of Murray's Grammar, and was garnished at convenient intervals with various profane expressions, which not even the desire to be graphic in our account shall induce us to transcribe.

His companion, Mr. Shelby, had the appearance of a gentleman; and the arrangements of the house, and the general air of the housekeeping, indicated easy, and even opulent, circumstances. As we before stated, the two were in the midst of an earnest conversation.

"That is the way I should arrange the matter," said Mr. Shelby.

"I can't make trade that way,—I positively can't, Mr. Shelby," said the other, holding up a glass of wine between his eye and the light.

"Why, the fact is, Haley, Tom is an uncommon fellow; he is certainly worth that sum anywhere,—steady, honest, capable, manages my whole farm like a clock."

"You mean honest, as niggers go," said Haley, helping himself to a glass of brandy.

"No; I mean, really, Tom is a good, steady, sensible, pious fellow. He got religion at a camp-meeting, four years ago; and I believe he really *did* get it. I've trusted him, since then, with everything I have,—money, house, horses,—and let him come and go round the country; and I always found him true and square in everything."

"Same folks don't believe there is pious niggers, Shelby," said Haley, with a candid flourish of his hand, "but *I do*. I had a fellow, now, in this yer last lot I took to Orleans,—'t was as good as a meetin', now, really, to hear that critter pray; and he was quite gentle and quiet like. He fetched me a good sum, too, for I bought him cheap of a man that was 'bliged to sell out; so I realized six hundred on him. Yes, I consider religion a valeyable thing in a nigger, when it's the genuine article, and no mistake."

"Well, Tom's got the real article, if ever a fellow had," rejoined the other. "Why, last fall, I let him go to Cincinnati alone, to do business for me, and bring home five hundred dollars. 'Tom,' says I to him, 'I trust you, because I think you're a Christian,—I know you wouldn't cheat.' Tom comes back, sure enough; I knew he would. Some low fellows, they say, said to him, 'Tom, why don't you make tracks for Canada?' 'Ah, master trusted me and I couldn't,'— they told me about it. I am sorry to part with Tom, I must say. You ought to let him cover the whole balance of the debt; and you would, Haley, if you had any conscience."

"Well, I've got just as much conscience as any man in business can afford to keep,—just a little, you know, to swear by, as 'twere," said the trader, jocularly; "and, then, I'm ready to do anything in reason to 'blige friends; but this yer, you see, is a leetle too hard on a fellow,—a leetle too hard." The trader sighed contemplatively, and poured out some more brandy.

"Well then, Haley, how will you trade?" said Mr. Shelby, after an uneasy interval of silence.

"Well, haven't you a boy or gal that you could throw in with Tom?"

"Hum!—none that I could well spare; to tell the truth, it's only hard necessity makes me willing to sell at all. I don't like parting with any of my hands, that's a fact."

Here the door opened, and a small quadroon boy, between four and five years of age, entered the room. There was something in his appearance remarkably beautiful and engaging. His black hair, fine as floss silk, hung in glossy curls about his round dimpled face, while a pair of large dark eyes, full of fire and softness, looked out from beneath the rich, long lashes, as he peered curiously into the apartment. A gay robe of scarlet and yellow plaid, carefully made and neatly fitted, set off to advantage the dark and rich style of his beauty; and a certain comic air of assurance, blended with bashfulness, showed that he had been not unused to being petted and noticed by his master.

"Hulloa, Jim Crow!" said Mr. Shelby, whistling, and snapping a bunch of raisins towards him, "pick that up, now!"

The child scampered, with all his little strength, after the prize, while his master laughed.

"Come here, Jim Crow," said he. The child came up and the master patted the curly head, and chucked him under the chin.

"Now, Jim, show this gentleman how you can dance and sing." The boy commenced one of those wild, grotesque songs common among the Negroes, in a rich, clear voice, accompanying his singing with many evolutions of the hands, feet, and whole body, all in perfect time to the music.

"Bravo!" said Haley, throwing him a quarter of an orange.

"Now, Jim, walk like old Uncle Cudjoe when he has the rheumatism," said his master.

Instantly the flexible limbs of the child assumed the appearance of deformity and distortion, as, with his back humped up, and his master's stick in his hand, he hobbled about the room, his childish face drawn into a doleful pucker, and spitting from right to left, in imitation of an old man.

Both gentlemen laughed uproariously.

"Now, Jim," said his master, "show us how old Elder Robbins leads the psalm." The boy drew his chubby face down to a formidable length, and commenced toning a psalm tune through his nose with imperturbable gravity.

"Hurrah! bravo! what a young un!" said Haley; "that chap's a case, I'll promise. Tell you what," said he, suddenly clapping his hand on Mr. Shelby's shoulder, "fling in that chap and I'll settle the business,—I will. Come, now, if that an't doing the thing up about the rightest!"

At this moment, the door was pushed gently open, and a young quadroon woman, apparently about twenty-five, entered the room.

There needed only a glance from the child to her, to identify her as its mother. There was the same rich, full, dark eye, with its long lashes; the same ripples of silky black hair. The brown of her complexion gave way on the cheek to a perceptible flush, which deepened as she saw the gaze of the strange man fixed upon her in bold and undisguised admiration. Her dress was of the neatest possible fit, and set off to advantage her finely moulded shape; a delicately formed hand and a trim foot and ankle were items of appearance that did not escape the quick eye of the trader, well used to run up at a glance the points of a fine female article.

"Well, Eliza?" said her master, as she stopped and looked hesitatingly at him.

"I was looking for Harry, please, sir;" and the boy bounded toward her, showing his spoils, which he had gathered in the skirt of his robe.

"Well, take him away, then," said Mr. Shelby; and hastily she withdrew, carrying the child on her arm.

"By Jupiter," said the trader, turning to him in admiration, "there's an article, now! You might make your fortune on that ar gal in Orleans, any day. I've seen over a thousand, in my day, paid down for gals not a bit handsomer."

"I don't want to make my fortune on her," said Mr. Shelby, dryly; and, seeking to turn the conversation, he uncorked a bottle of fresh wine, and asked his companion's opinion of it.

"Capital, sir,—first chop!" said the trader; then turning, and slapping his hand familiarly on Shelby's shoulder, he added,—

"Come, how will you trade about the gal?—what shall I say for her,—what'll you take?"

"Mr. Haley, she is not to be sold," said Shelby. "My wife would not part with her for her weight in gold."

"Ay, ay! women always say such things, cause they han't no sort of calculation. Just show 'em how many watches, feathers, and trinkets one's weight in gold would buy, and that alters the case, *I* reckon."

"I tell you, Haley, this must not be spoken of; I say no, and I mean no," said Shelby, decidedly.

"Well, you'll let me have the boy, though," said the trader; "you must own I've come down pretty handsomely for him."

"What on earth can you want with the child?" said Shelby.

"Why, I've got a friend that's going into this yer branch of the business,—wants to buy up handsome boys to raise for the market. Fancy articles entirely,—sell for waiters, and so on, to rich 'uns, that can pay for handsome 'uns. It sets off one of yer great places,—a real handsome boy to open door, wait, and tend. They fetch a good sum; and this little devil is such a comical, musical concern, he's just the article."

"I would rather not sell him," said Mr. Shelby, thoughtfully; "the fact is, sir, I'm a humane man, and I hate to take the boy from his mother, sir."

"Oh, you do?—La! yes,—something of that ar natur. I understand, perfectly. It is mighty onpleasant getting on with women, sometimes. I al'ays hates these yer screechin' screamin' times. They are *mighty* onpleasant; but, as I manages business, I generally avoids 'em, sir. Now, what if you get the girl off for a day, or a week, or so; then the thing's done quietly,—all over before she comes home. Your wife might get her some ear-rings, or a new gown or some such truck, to make up with her."

"I'm afraid not."

"Lor bless ye, yes! These critters an't like white folks, you know; they gets over things, only manage right. Now, they say," said Haley, assuming a candid and confidential air, "that this kind o' trade is hardening to the feelings; but I never found it so. Fact is, I never could do things up the way some fellers manage the business. I've seen 'em as would pull a woman's child out of her arms, and set him up to sell, and she screechin' like mad all the time;—very bad policy,—damages the article,—makes 'em quite unfit for service sometimes. I knew a real handsome gal once, in Orleans, as was entirely ruined by this sort o' handling. The fellow that was trading for her didn't want her baby; and she was one of your real high sort, when her blood was up. I tell you, she squeezed up her child in her arms, and talked, and went on real awful. It kinder makes my blood run cold to think on't; and when they carried off the child, and locked her up, she jest went ravin' mad, and died in a week. Clear waste, sir, of a thousand dollars, jest for want of management,—there's where 'tis. It's always best to do the humane thing, sir; that's been *my* experience." And the trader leaned back in his chair, and folded his arms, with an air of virtuous decision, apparently considering himself a second Wilberforce.

The subject appeared to interest the gentleman deeply; for while Mr. Shelby was thoughtfully peeling an orange, Haley broke out afresh, with becoming diffidence, but as if actually driven by the force of truth to say a few words more.

"It don't look well, now, for a feller to be praisin' himself; but I say it jest because it's the truth. I believe I'm reckoned to bring in about the finest droves of niggers that is brought in,—at least, I've been told so; if I have once, I reckon I have a hundred times, all in good case,—fat and likely, and I lose as few as any man in the business. And I lays it all to my management, sir; and humanity, sir, I may say, is the great pillar of *my* management."

Mr. Shelby did not know what to say, and so he said, "Indeed!"

"Now, I've been laughed at for my notions, sir, and I've been talked to. They an't pop'lar, and they an't common; but I stuck to 'em, sir; I've stuck to 'em, and realized well on 'em; yes, sir, they have paid their passage, I may say," and the trader laughed at his joke.

There was something so piquant and original in these elucidations of humanity, that Mr. Shelby could not help laughing in company. Perhaps you laugh too, dear reader; but you know humanity comes out in a variety of strange forms nowadays, and there is no end to the odd things that humane people will say and do.

Mr. Shelby's laugh encouraged the trader to proceed.

"It's strange now, but I never could beat this into people's heads. Now, there was Tom Loker, my old partner, down in Natchez; he was a clever fellow, Tom was, only the very devil with niggers,—on principle 'twas, you see, for a better-hearted feller never broke bread; 'twas his *system*, sir. I used to talk to Tom. 'Why, Tom,' I used to say, 'when your gals takes on and cry, what's the use o' crackin' on 'em over the head, and knockin' on 'em round? It's ridiculous,' says I, 'and don't do no sort o' good. Why, I don't see no harm in their cryin',' says I; 'it's natur,' says I, 'and if natur can't blow off one way, it will another. Besides Tom,' says I, 'it jest spiles your gals; they get sickly and down in the mouth; and sometimes they gets ugly,—particular yellow gals do,—and it's the devil and all gettin' on 'em broke in. Now,' says I, 'why can't you kinder coax 'em up, and speak 'em fair? Depend on it, Tom, a little humanity, thrown in along, goes a heap further than all your jawin' and crackin'; and it pays better,' says I, 'depend on 't.' But Tom couldn't get the hang on 't; and he spiled so many for me, that I had to break off with him, though he was a good-hearted fellow, and as fair a business hand as is goin'."

"And do you find your ways of managing do the business better than Tom's?" said Mr. Shelby.

"Why, yes, sir, I may say so. You see, when I any ways can, I takes a leetle care about the onpleasant parts, like selling young uns and that,—get the gals out of the way,—out of sight, out of mind, you know,—and when it's clean done, and can't be helped, they naturally gets used to it. 'Tan't, you know, as if it was white folks, that's brought up in the way of 'spectin' to keep their children and wives, and all that. Niggers, you know, that's fetched up properly han't no kind of 'spectations of no kind; so all these things comes easier."

"I'm afraid mine are not properly brought up, then," said Mr. Shelby.

"S'pose not; you Kentucky folks spile your niggers. You mean well by 'em, but 'tan't no real kindness, arter all. Now, a nigger, you see, what's got to be hacked and tumbled round the world, and sold to Tom, and Dick, and the Lord knows who, 'tan't no kindness to be givin' on him notions and expectations, and bringin' on him up too well, for the rough and tumble comes all the harder on him arter. Now, I venture to say, your niggers would be quite chop-fallen in a place where some of your plantation niggers would be sunging and whooping like all possessed. Every man, you know, Mr. Shelby, naturally thinks well of his own ways; and I think I treat niggers just about as well as it's ever worth while to treat 'em."

"It's a happy thing to be satisfied," said Mr. Shelby, with a slight shrug, and some perceptible feelings of a disagreeable nature.

"Well," said Haley, after they had both silently picked their nuts for a season, "what do you say?"

"I'll think the matter over, and talk with my wife," said Mr. Shelby. "Meantime, Haley, if you want the matter carried on in the quiet way you speak of, you'd best not let your business in this neighborhood be known. It will get out among my boys, and it will not be a particularly quiet business getting away any of my fellows, if they know it, I'll promise you."

"Oh, certainly, by all means, mum! of course. But I'll tell you, I'm in a devil of a hurry, and shall want to know, as soon as possible, what I may depend on," said he, rising and putting on his overcoat.

"Well, call up this evening, between six and seven, and you shall have my answer," said Mr. Shelby, and the trader bowed himself out of the apartment.

"I'd like to have been able to kick the fellow down the steps," said he to himself, as he saw the door fairly closed, "with his impudent assurance; but he knows how much he has me at advantage. If anybody had ever said to me that I should sell Tom down south to one of those rascally traders, I should have said, 'Is thy servant a dog, that he should do this thing?' And now it must come, for aught I see. And Eliza's child, too! I know that I shall have some fuss with wife about that; and, for that matter about Tom, too. So much for being in debt,—heigh-ho! The fellow sees his advantage, and means to push it."

Perhaps the mildest form of the system of slavery is to be seen in the State of Kentucky. The general prevalence of agricultural pursuits of a quiet and gradual nature, not requiring those periodic seasons of hurry and pressure that are called for in the business of more southern districts, makes the task of the Negro a more healthful and reasonable one; while the master, content with a more gradual style of acquisition, has not those temptations to hardheartedness which always overcome frail human nature when the prospect of sudden and rapid gain is weighed in the balance, with no heavier counterpoise than the interests of the helpless and unprotected.

Whoever visits some estates there, and witnesses the good-humored indulgence of some masters and mistresses, and the affectionate loyalty of some slaves, might be tempted to dream the oft-fabled poetic legend of a patriarchal institution, and all that; but over and above the scene there broods a portentous shadow,—the shadow of *law*. So long as the law considers all these human beings, with beating hearts and living affections only as so many *things* belonging to a master,—so long as the failure, or misfortune, or imprudence, or death of the kindest owner may cause them any day to exchange a life of kind protection and indulgence for one of hopeless misery and toil,—so long it is impossible to make anything beautiful or desirable in the best-regulated administration of slavery.

Mr. Shelby was a fair average kind of man, good natured and kindly, and disposed to easy indulgence of those around him, and there had never been a lack of anything which might contribute to the physical comfort of the Negroes on his estate. He had, however, speculated largely and quite loosely; had involved himself deeply, and his notes to a large amount had come into the hands of Haley; and this small piece of information is the key to the preceding conversation.

Now, it had so happened that, in approaching the door, Eliza had caught enough of the conversation to know that a trader was making offers to her master for somebody.

She would gladly have stopped at the door to listen, as she came out; but her mistress just then calling, she was obliged to hasten away.

Still she thought she heard the trader make an offer for her boy,—could she be mistaken? Her heart swelled and throbbed, and she involuntarily strained him so tight that the little fellow looked up into her face in astonishment.

"Eliza, girl, what ails you to-day?" said her mistress, when Eliza had upset the washpitcher, knocked down the work-stand, and finally was abstractedly offering her mistress a long nightgown in place of the silk dress she had ordered her to bring from the wardrobe.

Eliza started. "Oh, missis!" she said, raising her eyes; then, bursting into tears, she sat down in a chair, and began sobbing.

"Why, Eliza, child! what ails you?" said her mistress.

"Oh, Missis," said Eliza, "there's been a trader talking with Master in the parlor! I heard him."

"Well, silly child, suppose there has."

"Oh, Missis, *do* you suppose Mas'r would sell my Harry?" And the poor creature threw herself into a chair, and sobbed convulsively.

"Sell him! No, you foolish girl! you know your master never deals with those southern traders, and never means to sell any of his servants, as long as they behave well. Why, you silly child, who do you think would want to buy your Harry? Do you think all the world are set on him as you are, you goosie! Come, cheer up, and hook my dress. There now, put my back hair up in that pretty braid you learnt the other day, and don't go listening at doors any more."

"Well, but, missis, *you* never would give your consent—to—to"—

"Nonsense, child! to be sure I shouldn't. What do you talk so for? I would as soon have one of my own children sold. But really, Eliza, you are getting altogether too proud of that little fellow. A man can't put his nose into the door, but you think he must be coming to buy him."

Reassured by her mistress's confident tone, Eliza proceeded nimbly and adroitly with her toilet, laughing at her own fears, as she proceeded.

Mrs. Shelby was a woman of a high class, both intellectually and morally. To that natural magnanimity and generosity of mind which one often marks as characteristic of the women of Kentucky, she added high moral and religious sensibility and principle, carried out with great energy and ability into practical results. Her husband, who made no professions to any particular religious character, nevertheless, reverenced and respected the consistency of hers, and stood, perhaps, a little in awe of her opinion. Certain it was that he gave her unlimited scope in all her benevolent efforts for the comfort, instruction, and improvement of her servants, though he never took any decided part in them himself. In fact, if not exactly a believer in the doctrine of the efficacy of the extra good works of saints, he really seemed somehow or other to fancy that his wife had piety and benevolence enough for two,—to indulge a shadowy expectation of getting into heaven through her superabundance of qualities to which he made no particular pretension.

The heaviest load on his mind, after his conversation with the trader, lay in the foreseen necessity of breaking to his wife the arrangement contemplated,—meeting the importunities and opposition which he knew he should have reason to encounter.

Mrs. Shelby, being entirely ignorant of her husband's embarrassments, and knowing only the general kindliness of his temper, had been quite sincere in the entire incredulity with which she had met Eliza's suspicions. In fact, she dismissed the matter from her mind, without a second thought; and being occupied in preparations for an evening visit, it passed out of her thoughts entirely.

Chapter II.
The Mother.

ELIZA had been brought up by her mistress, from girlhood, as a petted and indulged favorite.

The traveller in the south must often have remarked that peculiar air of refinement, that softness of voice and manner, which seems in many cases to be a particular gift to the quadroon and mulatto women. These natural graces in the quadroon are often united with beauty of the most dazzling kind, and in almost every case with a personal appearance prepossessing and agreeable. Eliza, such as we have described her, is not a fancy sketch, but taken from remembrance, as we saw her, years ago, in Kentucky. Safe under the protecting care of her mistress, Eliza had reached maturity without those temptations which make beauty so fatal an inheritance to a slave. She had been married to a bright and talented young mulatto man, who was a slave on a neighboring estate, and bore the name of George Harris.

This young man had been hired out by his master to work in a bagging factory, where his adroitness and ingenuity caused him to be considered the first hand in the place. He had invented a machine for the cleaning of the hemp, which, considering the education and circumstances of the inventor, displayed quite as much mechanical genius as Whitney's cotton-gin.[1]

He was possessed of a handsome person and pleasing manners, and was a general favorite in the factory. Nevertheless, as this young man was in the eye of the law not a man, but a thing, all these superior qualifications were subject to the control of a vulgar, narrow-minded, tyrannical master. This same gentleman, having heard of the fame of George's invention, took a ride over to the factory, to see what this intelligent chattel had been about. He was received with great enthusiasm by the employer, who congratulated him on possessing so valuable a slave.

He was waited upon over the factory, shown the machinery by George, who, in high spirits, talked so fluently, held himself so erect, looked so handsome and manly, that his master began to feel an uneasy consciousness of inferiority. What business had his slave to be marching round the country, inventing machines, and holding up his head among gentlemen? He'd soon put a stop to it. He'd take him back, and put him to hoeing and digging, and "see if he'd step about so smart." Accordingly, the manufacturer and all hands concerned were astounded when he suddenly demanded George's wages, and announced his intention of taking him home.

"But, Mr. Harris," remonstrated the manufacturer, "isn't this rather sudden?"

"What if it is?—isn't the man *mine*?"

"We would be willing, sir, to increase the rate of compensation."

"No object at all, sir. I don't need to hire any of my hands out, unless I've a mind to."

"But, sir, he seems peculiarly adapted to this business."

"Dare say he may be; never was much adapted to anything that I set him about, I'll be bound."

"But only think of his inventing this machine," interposed one of the workmen, rather unluckily.

"Oh, yes!—a machine for saving work, is it? He'd invent that, I'll be bound; let a nigger alone for that, any time. They are all labor-saving machines themselves, every one of 'em. No, he shall tramp!"

George had stood like one transfixed, at hearing his doom thus suddenly pronounced by a power that he knew was irresistible. He folded his arms, tightly pressed in his lips, but a whole volcano of bitter feelings burned in his bosom, and sent streams of fire through his veins. He breathed short, and his large dark eyes flashed like live coals; and he might have broken out into some dangerous ebullition, had not the kindly manufacturer touched him on the arm, and said, in a low tone,—

"Give way, George; go with him for the present. We'll try to help you, yet."

The tyrant observed the whisper, and conjectured its import though he could not hear what was said; and he inwardly strengthened himself in his determination to keep the power he possessed over his victim.

George was taken home, and put to the meanest drudgery of the farm. He had been able to repress every disrespectful word; but the flashing eye, the gloomy and troubled brow, were part of a natural language that could not be repressed,—indubitable signs, which showed too plainly that the man could not become a thing.

It was during the happy period of his employment in the factory that George had seen and married his wife. During that period,—being much trusted and favored by his employer,—he had free liberty to come and go at discretion. The marriage was highly approved of by Mrs. Shelby, who, with a little womanly complacency in match-making, felt pleased to unite her handsome favorite with one of her own class who seemed in every way suited to her; and so they were married in her mistress's great parlor, and her mistress herself adorned the bride's beautiful hair with orange-blossoms, and threw over it the bridal veil, which certainly could scarce have rested on a fairer head; and there was no lack of white gloves, and cake and wine,—of admiring guests to praise the bride's beauty, and her mistress's indulgence and liberality. For a year or two Eliza saw her husband frequently, and there was nothing to interrupt their happiness, except the loss of two infant children, to whom she was passionately attached, and whom she mourned with a grief so intense as to call for gentle remonstrance from her mistress, who sought with maternal anxiety, to direct her naturally passionate feelings within the bounds of reason and religion.

After the birth of little Harry, however, she had gradually become tranquillized and settled; and every bleeding tie and throbbing nerve, once more entwined with that little life, seemed to become sound and healthful, and Eliza was a happy woman up to the time that her husband was rudely torn from his kind employer, and brought under the iron sway of his legal owner.

The manufacturer, true to his word, visited Mr. Harris a week or two after George had been taken away, when, as he hoped, the heat of the occasion had passed away, and tried every possible inducement to lead him to restore him to his former employment.

"You needn't trouble yourself to talk any longer," said he, doggedly; "I know my own business, sir."

"I did not presume to interfere with it, sir. I only thought that you might think it for your interest to let your man to us on the terms proposed."

"Oh, I understand the matter well enough. I saw your winking and whispering, the day I took him out of the factory; but you don't come it over me that way. It's a free country, sir; the man's *mine*, and I do what I please with him,—that's it!"

And so fell George's last hope;——nothing before him but a life of toil and drudgery, rendered more bitter by every little smarting vexation and indignity which tyrannical ingenuity could devise.

A very humane jurist once said, The worst use you can put a man to is to hang him. No; there is another use that a man can be put to that is WORSE!

Chapter III.
The Husband and Father.

MRS. SHELBY had gone on her visit, and Eliza stood in the veranda, rather dejectedly looking after the retreating carriage when a hand was laid on her shoulder. She turned, and a bright smile lighted up her fine eyes.

"George, is it you? How you frightened me! Well! I am so glad you's come! Missis is gone to spend the afternoon; so come into my little room, and we'll have the time all to our selves."

Saying this, she drew him into a neat little apartment opening on the veranda, where she generally sat at her sewing, within call of her mistress.

"How glad I am!—why don't you smile?—and look at Harry,—how he grows." The boy stood shyly regarding his father through his curls, holding close to the skirts of his mother's dress. "Isn't he beautiful?" said Eliza, lifting his long curls and kissing him.

"I wish he'd never been born!" said George, bitterly. "I wish I'd never been born myself!"

Surprised and frightened, Eliza sat down, leaned her head on her husband's shoulder, and burst into tears.

"There now, Eliza, it's too bad for me to make you feel so, poor girl!" said he, fondly; "it's too bad. Oh, how I wish you never had seen me,—you might have been happy!"

"George! George! how can you talk so? What dreadful thing has happened, or is going to happen? I'm sure we've been very happy, till lately."

"So we have, dear," said George. Then drawing his child on his knee, he gazed intently on his glorious dark eyes, and passed his hands through his long curls.

"Just like you, Eliza; and you are the handsomest woman I ever saw, and the best one I ever wish to see but, oh, I wish I'd never seen you, nor you me!"

"Oh, George, how can you!"

"Yes, Eliza, it's all misery, misery, misery! My life is bitter as wormwood; the very life is burning out of me. I'm a poor, miserable, forlorn drudge; I shall only drag you down with me, that's all. What's the use of our trying to do anything, trying to know anything, trying to be anything? What's the use of living? I wish I was dead!"

"Oh, now, dear George, that is really wicked! I know how you feel about losing your place in the factory, and you have a hard master; but pray be patient, and perhaps something—"

"Patient!" said he, interrupting her; "haven't I been patient? Did I say a word when he came and took me away, for no earthly reason, from the place where everybody was kind to me? I'd paid him truly every cent of my earnings,—and they all say I worked well,"

"Well, it *is* dreadful," said Eliza; "but, after all, he is your master, you know."

"My master! and who made him my master? That's what I think of,—what right has he to me? I'm a man as much as he is. I'm a better man than he is. I know more about business than he does; I am a better manager than he is; I can read better than he can; I can write a better hand,—and I've learned it all myself, and no thanks to him,—I've learned it in spite of him; and now what right has he to make a drayhorse of me?—to take me from things I can do, and do better than he can, and put me to work that any horse can do? He tries to do it; he says he'll bring me down and humble me, and he puts me to just the hardest, meanest, and dirtiest work, on purpose!"

"Oh, George! George! you frighten me! Why, I never heard you talk so; I'm afraid you'll do something dreadful. I don't wonder at your feelings at all; but oh, do be careful—do, do—for my sake,—for Harry's!"

"I have been careful, and I have been patient, but it's growing worse and worse; flesh and blood can't bear it any longer;—every chance he can get to insult and torment me, he takes. I thought I could do my work well, and keep on quiet, and have some time to read and learn out of work hours; but the more he sees I can do, the more he loads on. He says that though I don't say anything, he sees I've got the devil in me, and he means to bring it out; and one of these days it will come out in a way that he won't like, or I'm mistaken!"

"Oh, dear! what shall we do?" said Eliza, mournfully.

"It was only yesterday," said George, "as I was busy loading stones into a cart, that young Mas'r Tom stood there, slashing his whip so near the horse that the creature was frightened. I asked him to stop, as pleasant as I could,—he just kept right on. I begged him again, and then he turned on me, and began striking me. I held his hand, and then he screamed and kicked and ran to his father, and told him that I was fighting him. He came in a rage, and said he'd teach me who was my master; and he tied me to a tree, and cut switches for young master and told him that he might whip me till he was tired;—and he did do it! If I don't make him remember it, some time!" and the brow of the young man grew dark, and his eyes burned with an expression that made his young wife tremble. "Who made this man my master? That's what I want to know!" he said.

"Well," said Eliza mournfully, "I always thought that I must obey my master and mistress, or I couldn't be a Christian."

"There is some sense in it, in your case; they have brought you up like a child, fed you, clothed you, indulged you, and taught you, so that you have a good education; that is some reason why they should claim you. But I have been kicked and cuffed and sworn at, and at the best only let alone; and what do I owe? I've paid for all my keeping a hundred times over. I *won't* bear it. No, I *won't*!" he said, clenching his hand with a fierce frown.

Eliza trembled, and was silent. She had never seen her husband in this mood before; and her gentle system of ethics seemed to bend like a reed in the surges of such passions.

"You know poor little Carlo, that you gave me," added George; "the creature has been about all the comfort that I've had. He has slept with me nights, and followed me round days, and kind o' looked at me as if he understood how I felt. Well, the other day I was just feeding him with a few old scraps I picked up by the kitchen door, and Mas'r came along, and said I was feeding him up at his expense, and that he couldn't afford to have every nigger keeping his dog, and ordered me to tie a stone to his neck and throw him in the pond."

"Oh, George, you didn't do it!"

"Do it? not I!—but he did. Mas'r Tom pelted the poor drowning creature with stones. Poor thing! he looked at me so mournful, as if he wondered why I didn't save him. I had to take a flogging because I wouldn't do it myself. I don't care. Mas'r will find out that I'm one that whipping won't tame. My day will come yet, if he don't look out."

"What are you going to do? Oh, George, don't do anything wicked; if you only trust in God, and try to do right, he'll deliver you."

"I an't Christian like you, Eliza; my heart's full of bitterness; I can't trust in God. Why does he let things be so?"

"Oh, George, we must have faith. Mistress says that when all things go wrong to us, we must believe that God is doing the very best."

"That's easy to say for people that are sitting on their sofas and riding in their carriages; but let 'em be where I am, I guess it would come some harder. I wish I could be good; but my heart burns, and can't be reconciled, anyhow. You couldn't, in my place,—you can't now, if I tell you all I've got to say. You don't know the whole yet."

"What can be coming now?"

"Well, lately Mas'r has been saying that he was a fool to let me marry off the place; that he hates Mr. Shelby and all his tribe, because they are proud, and hold their heads up above him, and that I've got proud notions from you; and he says he won't let me come here any more, and that I shall take a wife and settle down on his place. At first he only scolded and grumbled these things; but yesterday he told me that I should take Mina for a wife, and settle down in a cabin with her, or he would sell me down river."

"Why—but you were married to *me*, by the minister, as much as if you'd been a white man!" said Eliza, simply.

"Don't you know a slave can't be married? There is no law in this country for that; I can't hold you for my wife if he chooses to part us. That's why I wish I'd never seen you,— why I wish I'd never been born; it would have been better for us both,—it would have been better for this poor child if he had never been born. All this may happen to him yet!"

"Oh, but master is so kind!"

"Yes, but who knows?—he may die,—and then he may be sold to nobody knows who. What pleasure is it that he is handsome, and smart, and bright? I tell you, Eliza, that a sword will pierce through your soul for every good and pleasant thing your child is or has; it will make him worth too much for you to keep!"

The words smote heavily on Eliza's heart; the vision of the trader came before her eyes, and, as if some one had struck her a deadly blow, she turned pale and gasped for breath. She looked nervously out on the veranda, where the boy, tired of the grave conversation, had retired, and where he was riding triumphantly up and down on Mr. Shelby's walking-stick. She would have spoken to tell her husband her fears, but checked herself.

"No, no,—he has enough to bear, poor fellow!" she thought. "No, I won't tell him; besides, it an't true. Missis never deceives us."

"So, Eliza, my girl," said the husband, mournfully, "bear up, now; and good-by, for I'm going."

"Going, George! Going where?"

"To Canada," said he, straightening himself up; "and when I'm there, I'll buy you; that's all the hope that's left us. You have a kind master, that won't refuse to sell you. I'll buy you and the boy;—God helping me, I will!"

"Oh, dreadful! if you should be taken?"

"I won't be taken, Eliza; I'll *die* first! I'll be free, or I'll die!"

"You won't kill yourself!"

"No need of that. They will kill me, fast enough; they never will get me down the river alive!"

"Oh, George, for my sake, do be careful! Don't do anything wicked; don't lay hands on yourself, or anybody else. You are tempted too much—too much; but don't—go you must—but go carefully, prudently; pray God to help you."

"Well, then, Eliza, hear my plan. Mas'r took it into his head to send me right by here, with a note to Mr. Symmes, that lives a mile past. I believe he expected I should come here to tell you what I have. It would please him if he thought it would aggravate 'Shelby's folks,' as he calls 'em. I'm going home quite resigned you understand, as if all was over. I've got some preparations made,—and there are those that will help me; and, in the course of a week or so, I shall be among the missing; some day. Pray for me, Eliza; perhaps the good Lord will hear *you*."

"Oh, pray yourself, George, and go trusting in him; then you won't do anything wicked."

"Well, now, *good-by*," said George, holding Eliza's hands, and gazing into her eyes, without moving. They stood silent; then there were last words, and sobs, and bitter weeping,—such parting as those may make whose hope to meet again is as the spider's web,—and the husband and wife were parted.

Chapter IV.
An Evening in Uncle Tom's Cabin.

THE cabin of Uncle Tom was a small log building close adjoining to "the house," as the Negro *par excellence* designates his master's dwelling. In front it had a neat garden-patch, where, every summer, strawberries, raspberries, and a variety of fruits and vegetables flourished under careful tending. The whole front of it was covered by a large scarlet bignonia and a native multiflora rose, which, entwisting and interlacing, left scarce a vestige of the rough logs to be seen. Here, also, in summer, various brilliant annuals, such as marigolds, petunias, four-o'clocks, found an indulgent corner in which to unfold their splendors, and were the delight and pride of Aunt Chloe's heart.

Let us enter the dwelling. The evening meal at the house is over, and Aunt Chloe, who presided over its preparation as head cook, has left to inferior officers in the kitchen the business of clearing away and washing dishes, and come out into her own snug territories, to "get her ole man's supper"; therefore, doubt not that it is she you see by the fire, presiding with anxious interest over certain frizzling items in a stewpan, and anon with grave consideration lifting the cover of a bake-kettle from whence steam forth indubitable intimations of "something good." A round, black, shining face is hers, so glossy as to suggest the idea that she might have been washed over with white of eggs, like one of her own tea rusks. Her whole plump countenance beams with satisfaction and contentment from under her well-starched checked turban, bearing on it, however, if we must confess it, a little of that tinge of self-consciousness which becomes the first cook of the neighborhood, as Aunt Chloe was universally held and acknowledged to be.

A cook she certainly was, in the very bone and centre of her soul. Not a chicken or turkey or duck in the barnyard but looked grave when they saw her approaching, and seemed evidently to be reflecting on their latter end; and certain it was that she was always meditating on trussing, stuffing, and roasting, to a degree that was calculated to inspire terror in any reflecting fowl living. Her corn-cake, in all its varieties of hoe-cake, dodgers, muffins, and other species too numerous to mention, was a sublime mystery to all less practised compounders; and she would shake her fat sides with honest pride and merriment, as she would narrate the fruitless efforts that one and another of her compeers had made to attain to her elevation.

The arrival of company at the house, the arranging of dinners and suppers "in style," awoke all the energies of her soul; and no sight was more welcome to her than a pile of travelling trunks launched on the veranda, for then she foresaw fresh efforts and fresh triumphs.

Just at present, however, Aunt Chloe is looking into the bakepan; in which congenial operation we shall leave her till we finish our picture of the cottage.

In one corner of it stood a bed, covered neatly with a snowy spread; and by the side of it was a piece of carpeting, of some considerable size. On this piece of carpeting Aunt Chloe took her stand, as being decidedly in the upper walks of life; and it and the bed by which it lay, and the whole corner, in fact, were treated with distinguished consideration, and made, so far as possible, sacred from the marauding inroads and desecrations of little folks. In fact, that corner was the *drawing-room* of the establishment. In the other corner was a bed of much humbler pretensions, and evidently designed for *use*. The wall over the fireplace was adorned with some very brilliant scriptural prints, and a portrait of General Washington, drawn and colored in a manner which would certainly have astonished that hero, if ever he had happened to meet with its like.

On a rough bench in the corner, a couple of woolly-headed boys, with glistening black eyes and fat shining cheeks, were busy in superintending the first walking operations of the baby, which, as is usually the case, consisted in getting up on its feet, balancing a moment, and then tumbling down,—each successive failure being violently cheered, as something decidedly clever.

A table, somewhat rheumatic in its limbs, was drawn out in front of the fire, and covered with a cloth, displaying cups and saucers of a decidedly brilliant pattern, with other symptoms of an approaching meal. At this table was seated Uncle Tom, Mr. Shelby's best hand, who, as he is to be the hero of our story, we must daguerreotype for our readers. He was a large, broad-chested, powerfully made man, of a full glossy black, and a face whose truly African features were characterized by an expression of grave and steady good sense, united with much kindliness and benevolence. There was something about his whole air self-respecting and dignified, yet united with a confiding and humble simplicity.

He was very busily intent at this moment on a slate lying before him, on which he was carefully and slowly endeavoring to accomplish a copy of some letters, in which operation he was overlooked by young Mas'r George, a smart, bright boy of thirteen, who appeared fully to realize the dignity of his position as instructor.

"Not that way, Uncle Tom,—not that way," said he briskly, as Uncle Tom laboriously brought up the tail of his *g* the wrong side out; "that makes a *q*, you see."

"La sakes, now, does it?" said Uncle Tom, looking with a respectful, admiring air, as his young teacher flourishingly scrawled *q*'s and *g*'s innumerable for his edification; and then, taking the pencil in his big, heavy fingers, he patiently recommenced.

"How easy white folks al'us does things!" said Aunt Chloe, pausing while she was greasing a griddle with a scrap of bacon on her fork, and regarding young Master George with pride. "The way he can write, now! and read, too! and then to come out here evenings and read his lessons to us,—it's mighty interestin'!"

"But, Aunt Chloe, I'm getting mighty hungry," said George. "Isn't that cake in the skillet almost done?"

"Mose done, Mas'r George," said Aunt Chloe, lifting the lid and peeping in,—"browning beautiful,—a real lovely brown. Ah! let me alone for dat. Missis let Sally try to make some cake, t' other day, jes to *larn* her she said. 'Oh, go way Missis,' says I; 'it really hurts my feelin's, now, to see good vittles spiled dat ar way! Cake ris all to one side,—no shape at all; no more than my shoe;—go way!'"

And with this final expression of contempt for Sally's greenness, Aunt Chloe whipped the cover off the bake-kettle, and disclosed to view a neatly baked pound-cake of which no city confectioner need to have been ashamed. This being evidently the central point of the entertainment, Aunt Chloe began now to bustle about earnestly in the supper department.

"Here you, Mose and Pete! get out de way, you niggers! Get away, Polly honey,—mammy'll give her baby somefin, by and by. Now, Mas'r George, you jest take off dem books, and set down now with my old man, and I'll take up de sausages, and have de first griddle full of cakes on your plates in less dan no time."

"They wanted me to come to supper in the house," said George; "but I knew what was what too well for that, Aunt Chloe."

"So you did,—so you did, honey," said Aunt Chloe, heaping the smoking batter-cakes on his plate, "you know'd your old aunty'd keep the best for you. Oh, let you alone for dat! Go way!" and, with that, aunty gave George a nudge with her finger, designed to be immensely facetious, and turned again to her griddle with great briskness.

"Now for the cake," said Mas'r George, when the activity of the griddle department had somewhat subsided; and, with that, the youngster flourished a large knife over the article in question.

"La bless you, Mas'r George!" said Aunt Chloe, with earnestness, catching his arm, "you wouldn't be for cuttin' it wid dat ar great heavy knife! Smash all down,—spile all de pretty rise of it. Here, I've got a thin old knife, I keeps sharp a purpose. Dar now, see! comes apart light as a feather! Now eat away,—you won't get anything to beat dat ar."

"Tom Lincon says," said George, speaking with his mouth full, "that their Jinny is a better cook than you."

"Dem Lincons an't much 'count, no way!" said Aunt Chloe, contemptuously: "I mean, set alongside *our* folks. They's 'spectable folks enough in a kinder plain way; but, as to gettin' up anything in style, they don't begin to have a notion on 't. Set Mas'r Lincon, now, alongside Mas'r Shelby! Good Lor! and Missis Lincon,—can she kinder sweep it into a room like my missis,—so kinder splendid, yer know! Oh, go way! don't tell me nothin' of dem Lincons!"—and Aunt Chloe tossed her head as one who hoped she did know something of the world.

"Well, though, I've heard you say," said George, "that Jinny was a pretty fair cook."

"So I did," said Aunt Chloe,—"I may say dat. Good, plain, common cookin' Jinny'll do;—make a good pone o' bread,—bile her taters *far*;—her corn cakes isn't extra, not extra now, Jinny's corn cakes isn't, but then they's *far*,—but, Lor, come to de higher branches, and what *can* she do? Why, she makes pies,—sartin she does; but what kinder crust? Can she make your real flecky paste, as melts in your mouth, and flies all up like a puff? Now I went over thar when Miss Mary was gwine to be married, and Jinny she jest showed me de weddin' pies. Jinny and I is good friends, ye know. I never said nothin'; but go long, Mas'r George! Why, I shouldn't sleep a wink for a week, if I had a batch of pies like dem ar. Why, dey warn't no 'count 't all."

"I suppose Jinny thought they were ever so nice," said George.

"Thought so!—didn't she? Thar she was, showing 'em as innocent,—ye see, it's jest here, Jinny *don't know*. Lor, the family an't nothing! She can't be spected to know! 'Tan't no fault o' hern. Ah, Mas'r George, you doesn't know half your privileges in yer family and bringin' up!" Here Aunt Chloe sighed, and rolled up her eyes with emotion.

"I'm sure, Aunt Chloe, I understand all my pie and pudding privileges," said George. "Ask Tom Lincon if I don't crow over him, every time I meet him."

Aunt Chloe sat back in her chair, and indulged in a hearty guffaw of laughter, at this witticism of young Mas'r's, laughing till the tears rolled down her black, shining cheeks, and varying the exercise with playfully slapping and poking Mas'r Georgey, and telling him to go way, and that he was a case,—that he was fit to kill her, and that he sartin would kill her, one of these days; and, between each of these sanguinary predictions, going off into a laugh, each longer and stronger than the other, till George really began to think that he was a very dangerously witty fellow, and that it became him to be careful how he talked "as funny as he could."

"And so ye telled Tom, did ye? Oh, Lor! what young uns will be up ter! Ye crowed over Tom? Oh, Lor! Mas'r George, if ye wouldn't make a hornbug laugh!"

"Yes," said George, "I says to him, 'Tom, you ought to see some of Aunt Chloe's pies; they're the right sort,' says I."

"Pity now, Tom couldn't," said Aunt Chloe, on whose benevolent heart the idea of Tom's benighted condition seemed to make a strong impression. "Ye oughter just ask him here to dinner, some o' these times, Mas'r George," she added; "it would look quite pretty of ye. Ye know, Mas'r George, ye oughtenter feel 'bove nobody, on 'count yer privileges, 'cause all our privileges is gi'n to us; we ought al'ays to 'member that," said Aunt Chloe, looking quite serious.

"Well, I mean to ask Tom here, some day next week," said George; "and you do your prettiest, Aunt Chloe and we'll make him stare. Won't we make him eat so he won't get over it for a fortnight?"

"Yes, yes,—sartin," said Aunt Chloe, delighted; "you'll see. Lor! to think of some of our dinners! Yer mind dat ar great chicken-pie I made when we guv de dinner to Giner al Knox? I and Missis, we come pretty near quarrelling about dat ar crust. What does get into ladies sometimes; I don't know; but, sometimes, when a body has de heaviest kind o' 'sponsibility on 'em, as ye may say, and is all kinder '*seris*' and taken up dey takes dat ar time to be hangin' round and kinder interferin'! Now, Missis, she wanted me to do dis way, and she wanted me to do dat way; and, finally, I got kinder sarcy, and, says I, 'Now, Missis, do jist look at dem beautiful white hands o' yourn, with long fingers, and all a sparkling with rings, like my white lilies when de dew's on 'em; and look at my great black stumpin' hands. Now, don't ye think dat de Lord must have meant *me* to make de pie-crust, and you to stay in de parlor?' Dar! I was jist so sarcy, Mas'r George."

"And what did mother say?" said George.

"Say?—why, she kinder larfed in her eyes,—dem great handsome eyes o' hern; and, says she, 'Well, Aunt Chloe, I think you are about in the right on 't,' says she; and she went off in de parlor. She oughter cracked me over de head for bein' so sarcy; but dar's whar 'tis,—I can't do nothin' with ladies in de kitchen!"

"Well, you made out well with that dinner,—I remember everybody said so," said George.

"Didn't I? And wan't I behind de dinin'-room door dat bery day? and didn't I see de Gineral pass his plate three times for some more dat bery pie?—and, says he, 'You must have an uncommon cook, Mrs. Shelby.' Lor! I was fit to split myself.

"And de Gineral, he knows what cookin' is," said Aunt Chloe, drawing herself up with an air. "Bery nice man, de Gineral! He comes of one of de bery *fustest* families in Old Virginny! He knows what's what, now, as well as I do,—de Gineral. Ye see, there's *pints* in all pies, Mas'r George; but 'tan't everybody knows what they is, or orter be. But the Gineral, he knows; I knew by his 'marks he made. Yes, he knows what de pints is!"

By this time, Master George had arrived at that pass to which even a boy can come (under uncommon circumstances), when he really could not eat another morsel, and, therefore he was at leisure to notice the pile of woolly heads and glistening eyes which were regarding their operations hungrily from the opposite corner.

"Here, you Mose, Pete," he said, breaking off liberal bits and throwing it at them; "you want some, don't you? Come Aunt Chloe, bake them some cakes."

And George and Tom moved to a comfortable seat in the chimney-corner, while Aunt Chloe, after baking a goodly pile of cakes, took her baby on her lap, and began alternately filling its mouth and her own, and distributing to Mose and Pete, who seemed rather to prefer eating theirs as they rolled about on the floor under the table, tickling each other, and occasionally pulling the baby's toes.

"Oh, go long, will ye?" said the mother, giving now and then a kick, in a kind of general way, under the table, when the movement became too obstreperous. "Can't ye be decent when white folks comes to see ye? Stop dat ar, now, will ye? Better mind yerselves, or I'll take ye down a button-hole lower, when Mas'r George is gone!"

What meaning was couched under this terrible threat, it is difficult to say; but certain it is that its awful indistinctness seemed to produce very little impression on the young sinners addressed.

"La, now!" said Uncle Tom, "they are so full of tickle all the while, they can't behave theirselves."

Here the boys emerged from under the table, and, with hands and faces well plastered with molasses, began a vigorous kissing of the baby.

"Get along wid ye!" said the mother, pushing away their woolly heads. "Ye'll all stick together, and never get clar, if ye do dat fashion. Go long to de spring and wash yerselves!" she said, seconding her exhortations by a slap, which resounded very formidably, but which seemed only to knock out so much more laugh from the young ones, as they tumbled precipitately over each other out of doors, where they fairly screamed with merriment.

"Did ye ever see such aggravating young uns?" said Aunt Chloe, rather complacently, as, producing an old towel, kept for such emergencies, she poured a little water out of the cracked teapot on it, and began rubbing off the molasses from the baby's face and hands; and, having polished her till she shone, she set her down in Tom's lap, while she busied herself in clearing away supper. The baby employed the intervals in pulling Tom's nose, scratching his face, and burying her fat hands in his woolly hair, which last operation seemed to afford her special content.

"An't she a peart young un?" said Tom, holding her from him to take a full-length view; then, getting up, he set her on his broad shoulder and began capering and dancing with her while Mas'r George snapped at her with his pocket-handkerchief, and Mose and Pete, now returned again, roared after her like bears, till Aunt Chloe declared that they "fairly took her head off" with their noise. As, according to her own statement, this surgical operation was a matter of daily occurrence in the cabin, the declaration no whit abated the merriment, till every one had roared and tumbled and danced themselves down to a state of composure.

"Well, now, I hopes you're done," said Aunt Chloe, who had been busy in pulling out a rude box of a trundle-bed; "and now, you Mose and you Pete, get into thar; for we's goin' to have the meetin'."

"Oh, mother, we don't wanter. We wants to sit up to meetin',—meetin's is so curis. We likes 'em."

"La, Aunt Chloe, shove it under, and let 'em sit up," said Mas'r George, decisively, giving a push to the rude machine.

Aunt Chloe, having thus saved appearances, seemed highly delighted to push the thing under, saying, as she did so, "Well, mebbe 't will do 'em some good."

The house now resolved itself into a committee of the whole, to consider the accommodations and arrangements for the meeting.

"What we's to do for cheers, now, *I* declar I don't know," said Aunt Chloe. As the meeting had been held at Uncle Tom's, weekly, for an indefinite length of time without any more "cheers," there seemed some encouragement to hope that a way would be discovered at present.

"Old Uncle Peter sung both de legs out of dat oldest cheer, last week," suggested Mose.

"You go long! I'll boun' you pulled 'em out; some o' your shines," said Aunt Chloe.

"Well, it'll stand, if it only keeps jam up agin de wall!" said Mose.

"Den Uncle Peter mus'n't sit in it, cause he al'ays hitches when he gets a singing. He hitched pretty nigh across de room, t' other night," said Pete.

"Good Lor! get him in it, then," said Mose, "and den he'd begin, 'Come saints and sinners, hear me tell,' and den down he'd go,"—and Mose imitated precisely the nasal tones of the old man, tumbling on the floor, to illustrate the supposed catastrophe.

"Come now, be decent, can't ye?" said Aunt Chloe: "an't yer shamed?"

Mas'r George, however, joined the offender in the laugh, and declared decidedly that Mose was a "buster." So the maternal admonition seemed rather to fail of effect.

"Well, ole man," said Aunt Chloe, "you'll have to tote in them ar bar'ls."

"Mother's bar'ls is like dat ar widder's, Mas'r George was reading 'bout, in de good book,—dey never fails," said Mose, aside to Pete.

"I'm sure one of 'em caved in last week," said Pete, "and let 'em all down in de middle of de singin'; that ar was failin', warn't it?"

During this aside between Mose and Pete two empty casks had been rolled into the cabin, and being secured from rolling, by stones on each side, boards were laid across them, which arrangement, together with the turning down of certain tubs and pails, and the disposing of the rickety chairs, at last completed the preparation.

"Mas'r George is such a beautiful reader, now, I know he'll stay to read for us," said Aunt Chloe; "'pears like 't will be so much more interestin'."

George very readily consented, for your boy is always ready for anything that makes him of importance.

The room was soon filled with a motley assemblage, from the old gray-headed patriarch of eighty, to the young girl and lad of fifteen. A little harmless gossip ensued on various themes, such as where old Aunt Sally got her new red head-kerchief, and how "Missis was a going to give Lizzy that spotted muslin gown, when she'd got her new berage made up"; and how Mas'r Shelby was thinking of buying a new sorrel colt, that was going to prove an addition to the glories of the place. A few of the worshippers belonged to families hard by, who had got permission to attend, and who brought in various choice scraps of information, about the sayings and doings at the house and on the place, which circulated as freely as the same sort of small change does in higher circles.

After a while the singing commenced, to the evident delight of all present. Not even all the disadvantages of nasal intonation could prevent the effect of the naturally fine voices, in airs at once wild and spirited. The words were sometimes the well-known and common hymns sung in the churches about; and sometimes of a wilder, more indefinite character, picked up at camp-meetings.

The chorus of one of them, which ran as follows, was sung with great energy and unction:—

> "Die on the field of battle,
> Die on the field of battle,
> Glory in my soul."

Another special favorite had oft repeated the words,—

"Oh, I'm going to glory,—won't you come along with me?
Don't you see the angels beck'ning, and a calling me away?
Don't you see the golden city and the everlasting day?"

There were others, which made incessant mention of "Jordan's banks," and "Canaan's fields," and the "New Jerusalem"; for the Negro mind, impassioned and imaginative, always attaches itself to hymns and expressions of a vivid and pictorial nature; and, as they sung, some laughed, and some cried, and some clapped hands, or shook hands rejoicingly with each other, as if they had fairly gained the other side of the river.

Various exhortations, or relations of experience, followed, and intermingled with the singing. One old grayheaded woman, long past work, but much revered as a sort of chronicle of the past, rose, and leaning on her staff, said,—

"Well, chil'en! Well, I'm mighty glad to hear ye all and see ye all once more, 'cause I don't know when I'll be gone to glory; but I've done got ready, chil'en; 'pears like I'd got my little bundle all tied up, and my bonnet on, jest a waitin' for the stage to come along to take me home; sometimes, in the night, I think I hear the wheels a rattlin', and I'm lookin' out all the time; now, you jest be ready too, for I tell ye all, chil'en," she said, striking her staff hard on the floor, "dat ar *glory* is a mighty thing! It's a mighty thing, chil'en,—you don'no nothing about it,—it's *wonderful*." And the old creature sat down, with streaming tears, as wholly overcome, while the whole circle struck up,—

"O Canaan, bright Canaan,
I'm bound for the land of Canaan."

Mas'r George, by request, read the last chapters of Revelation, often interrupted by such exclamations as "The *sakes* now!" "Only hear that!" "Jest think on 't!" "Is all that a comin' sure enough?"

George, who was a bright boy, and well trained in religious things by his mother, finding himself an object of general admiration, threw in expositions of his own from time to time, with a commendable seriousness and gravity, for which he was admired by the young and blessed by the old; and it was agreed, on all hands, that "a minister couldn't lay it off better than he did", that "'twas reely 'mazin'!"

Uncle Tom was a sort of patriarch in religious matters, in the neighborhood. Having, naturally, an organization in which the *morale* was strongly predominant together with a greater breadth and cultivation of mind than obtained among his companions, he was looked up to with great respect, as a sort of minister among them; and the simple hearty, sincere style of his exhortations might have edified even better educated persons. But it was in prayer that he especially excelled. Nothing could exceed the touching simplicity, the childlike earnestness of his prayer, enriched with the language of Scripture, which seemed so entirely to have wrought itself into his being as to have become a part of himself, and to drop from his lips unconsciously; in the language of a pious old Negro, he "prayed right up." And so much did his prayer always work on the devotional feelings of his audiences, that there seemed often a danger that it would be lost altogether in the abundance of the responses which broke out everywhere around him.

While this scene was passing in the cabin of the man, one quite otherwise passed in the halls of the master.

The trader and Mr. Shelby were seated together in the dining-room aforenamed, at a table covered with papers and writing utensils.

Mr. Shelby was busy in counting some bundles of bills, which, as they were counted, he pushed over to the trader, who counted them likewise.

"All fair," said the trader; "and now for signing these yer."

Mr. Shelby hastily drew the bills of sale towards him and signed them, like a man that hurries over some disagreeable business, and then pushed them over with the money. Haley produced, from a well-worn valise, a parchment, which, after looking over it a moment, he handed to Mr. Shelby, who took it with a gesture of suppressed eagerness.

"Wal, now, the thing's *done*!" said the trader, getting up.

"It's *done!*" said Mr. Shelby, in a musing tone; and, fetching a long breath, he repeated, "*It's done!*"

"Yer don't seem to feel much pleased with it, 'pears to me," said the trader.

"Haley," said Mr. Shelby, "I hope you'll remember that you promised, on your honor, you wouldn't sell Tom, without knowing what sort of hands he's going into."

"Why, you've just done it, sir," said the trader.

"Circumstances, you well know, *obliged* me," said Shelby, haughtily.

"Wal, you know, they may 'bilge *me*, too," said the trader. "Howsomever, I'll do the very best I can in gettin' Tom a good berth; as to my treatin' on him bad, you needn't be a grain afeard. If there's anything that I thank the Lord for, it is that I'm never noways cruel."

After the expositions which the trader had previously given of his humane principles, Mr. Shelby did not feel particularly reassured by these declarations; but, as they were the best comfort the case admitted of, he allowed the trader to depart in silence, and betook himself to a solitary cigar.

Chapter V.
Showing the Feelings of Living Property on Changing Owners.

———————•—•——•——•———————

MR. and Mrs. Shelby had retired to their apartment for the night. He was lounging in a large easy chair, looking over some letters that had come in the afternoon mail, and she was standing before her mirror, brushing out the complicated braids and curls in which Eliza had arranged her hair; for, noticing her pale cheeks and haggard eyes, she had excused her attendance that night and ordered her to bed. The employment, naturally enough, suggested her conversation with the girl in the morning; and, turning to her husband, she said, carelessly,—

"By the by, Arthur, who was that low-bred fellow that you lugged in to our dinner-table to-day?"

"Haley is his name," said Shelby, turning himself rather uneasily in his chair, and continuing with his eyes fixed on a letter.

"Haley! Who is he, and what may be his business here, pray?"

"Well, he's a man that I transacted some business with, last time I was at Natchez," said Mr. Shelby.

"And he presumed on it to make himself quite at home, and call and dine here, ay?"

"Why, I invited him; I had some accounts with him," said Shelby.

"Is he a Negro-trader?" said Mrs. Shelby, noticing a certain embarrassment in her husband's manner.

"Why, my dear, what put that into your head?" said Shelby, looking up.

"Nothing,—only Eliza came in here, after dinner, in a great worry, crying and taking on, and said you were talking with a trader, and that she heard him make an offer for her boy,—the ridiculous little goose!"

"She did, hey?" said Mr. Shelby, returning to his paper, which he seemed for a few moments quite intent upon, not perceiving that he was holding it bottom upwards.

"It will have to come out," said he, mentally; "as well now as ever."

"I told Eliza," said Mrs. Shelby, as she continued brushing her hair, "that she was a little fool for her pains, and that you never had anything to do with that sort of persons. Of course, I knew you never meant to sell any of our people,—least of all, to such a fellow."

"Well, Emily," said her husband, "so have I always felt and said; but the fact is that my business lies so that I cannot get on without. I shall have to sell some of my hands."

"To that creature? Impossible! Mr. Shelby, you cannot be serious."

"I'm sorry to say that I am," said Mr. Shelby. "I've agreed to sell Tom."

"What! our Tom?—that good, faithful creature!—been your faithful servant from a boy! Oh, Mr. Shelby!—and you have promised him his freedom too,—you and I have spoken to him a hundred times of it. Well, I can believe anything now,—I can believe *now* that you could sell little Harry, poor Eliza's only child!" said Mrs. Shelby, in a tone between grief and indignation.

"Well, since you must know all, it is so. I have agreed to sell Tom and Harry both; and I don't know why I am to be rated, as if I were a monster, for doing what every one does every day."

"But why, of all others, choose these?" said Mrs. Shelby. "Why sell them, of all on the place, if you must sell at all?"

"Because they will bring the highest sum of any,—that's why. I could choose another, if you say so. The fellow made me a high bid on Eliza, if that would suit you any better," said Mr. Shelby.

"The wretch!" said Mrs. Shelby, vehemently.

"Well, I didn't listen to it, a moment,—out of regard to your feelings, I wouldn't;—so give me some credit."

"My dear," said Mrs. Shelby, recollecting herself, "forgive me. I have been hasty. I was surprised, and entirely unprepared for this;—but surely you will allow me to intercede for these poor creatures. Tom is a noble-hearted, faithful fellow, if he is black. I do believe, Mr. Shelby, that if he were put to it, he would lay down his life for you."

"I know it,—I dare say;—but what's the use of all this?—I can't help myself."

"Why not make a pecuniary sacrifice? I'm willing to bear my part of the inconvenience. Oh, Mr. Shelby, I have tried—tried most faithfully, as a Christian woman should—to do my duty to these poor, simple, dependent creatures. I have cared for them, instructed them, watched over them, and known all their little cares and joys, for years; and how can I ever hold up my head again among them, if, for the sake of a little paltry gain, we sell such a faithful, excellent, confiding creature as poor Tom, and tear from him in a moment all we have taught him to love and value? I have taught them the duties of the family, of parent and child, and husband and wife; and how can I bear to have this open acknowledgment that we care for no tie, no duty, no relation, however sacred, compared with money? I have talked with Eliza about her boy,—her duty to him as a Christian mother, to watch over him, pray for him, and bring him up in a Christian way; and now what can I say, if you tear him away, and sell him, soul and body, to a profane, unprincipled man, just to save a little money? I have told her that one soul is worth more than all the money in the world; and how will she believe me when she sees us turn round and sell her child?—sell him perhaps, to certain ruin of body and soul!"

"I'm sorry you feel so about it, Emily,—indeed I am," said Mr. Shelby; "and I respect your feelings, too, though I don't pretend to share them to their full extent; but I tell you now, solemnly, it's of no use,—I can't help myself. I didn't mean to tell you this, Emily; but in plain words, there is no choice between selling these two and selling everything. Either they must go, or *all* must. Haley has come into possession of a mortgage, which, if I don't clear off with him directly, will take everything before it. I've raked, and scraped, and borrowed, and all but begged,—and the price of these two was needed to make up the balance, and I had to give them up. Haley fancied the child; he agreed to settle the matter that way and no other. I was in his power, and *had* to do it. If you feel so to have them sold, would it be any better to have *all* sold?"

Mrs. Shelby stood like one stricken. Finally, turning to her toilet, she rested her face in her hands, and gave a sort of groan.

"This is God's curse on slavery!—a bitter, bitter, most accursed thing!—a curse to the master and a curse to the slave! I was a fool to think I could make anything good out of such a deadly evil. It is a sin to hold a slave under laws like ours,—I always felt it was,—I always thought so when I was a girl,—I thought so still more after I joined the church; but I thought I could gild it over,—I thought, by kindness, and care, and instruction, I could make the condition of mine better than freedom,—fool that I was!"

"Why, wife, you are getting to be an abolitionist, quite."

"Abolitionist! if they knew all I know about slavery they *might* talk! We don't need them to tell us; you know I never thought that slavery was right,—never felt willing to own slaves."

"Well, therein you differ from many wise and pious men," said Mr. Shelby. "You remember Mr. B.'s sermon, the other Sunday?"

"I don't want to hear such sermons; I never wish to hear Mr. B. in our church again. Ministers can't help the evil, perhaps,—can't cure it, any more than we can,—but defend it!—it always went against my common sense. And I think you didn't think much of that sermon, either."

"Well," said Shelby, "I must say these ministers sometimes carry matters further than we poor sinners would exactly dare to do. We men of the world must wink pretty hard at various things, and get used to a deal that isn't the exact thing. But we don't quite fancy, when women and ministers come out broad and square, and go beyond us in matters of either modesty or morals, that's a fact. But now, my dear, I trust you see the necessity of the thing, and you see that I have done the very best that circumstances would allow."

"Oh yes, yes!" said Mrs. Shelby, hurriedly and abstractedly fingering her gold watch,—"I haven't any jewelry of any amount," she added, thoughtfully; "but would not this watch do something?—it was an expensive one when it was bought. If I could only at least save Eliza's child, I would sacrifice anything I have."

"I'm sorry, very sorry, Emily," said Mr. Shelby, "I'm sorry that this takes hold of you so, but it will do no good. The fact is, Emily, the thing's done; the bills of sale are already signed, and in Haley's hands; and you must be thankful it is no worse. That man has had it in his power to ruin us all,—and now he is fairly off. If you knew the man as I do, you'd think that we had had a narrow escape."

"Is he so hard, then?"

"Why, not a cruel man, exactly, but a man of leather,—a man alive to nothing but trade and profit,—cool, and unhesitating, and unrelenting, as death and the grave. He'd sell his own mother at a good percentage,—not wishing the old woman any harm, either."

"And this wretch owns that good, faithful Tom, and Eliza's child!"

"Well, my dear, the fact is that this goes rather hard with me; it's a thing I hate to think of. Haley wants to drive matters, and take possession to-morrow. I'm going to get out my horse bright and early, and be off. I can't see Tom, that's a fact; and you had better arrange to drive somewhere, and carry Eliza off. Let the thing be done when she is out of sight."

"No, no," said Mrs. Shelby; "I'll be in no sense accomplice or help in this cruel business. I'll go and see poor old Tom, God help him, in his distress! They shall see, at any rate, that their mistress can feel for and with them. As to Eliza, I dare not think about it. The Lord forgive us! What have we done, that this cruel necessity should come on us?"

There was one listener to this conversation whom Mr. and Mrs. Shelby little suspected.

Communicating with their apartment was a large closet, opening by a door into the outer passage. When Mrs. Shelby had dismissed Eliza for the night her feverish and excited mind had suggested the idea of this closet; and she had hidden herself there, and with her ear pressed close against the crack of the door, had lost not a word of the conversation.

When the voices died into silence, she rose and crept stealthily away. Pale, shivering, with rigid features and compressed lips, she looked an entirely altered being from the soft and timid creature she had been hitherto. She moved cautiously along the entry, paused one moment at her mistress's door and raised her hands in mute appeal to Heaven, and then turned and glided into her own room. It was a quiet, neat apartment, on the same floor with her mistress. There was the pleasant sunny window, where she had often sat singing at her sewing; there, a little case of books, and various little fancy articles, ranged by them, the gifts of Christmas holidays; there was her simple wardrobe in the closet and in the drawers:—here was, in short, her home; and, on the whole, a happy one it had been to her. But there, on the bed, lay her slumbering boy, his long curls falling negligently around his unconscious face, his rosy mouth half open, his little fat hands thrown out over the bedclothes, and a smile spread like a sunbeam over his whole face.

"Poor boy! poor fellow!" said Eliza; "they have sold you! but your mother will save you yet!"

No tear dropped over that pillow; in such straits as these the heart has no tears to give,—it drops only blood, bleeding itself away in silence. She took a piece of paper and a pencil; and wrote hastily,—

"Oh, Missis! dear Missis! don't think me ungrateful,—don't think hard of me, any way,—I heard all you and master said to-night. I am going to try to save my boy,—you will not blame me! God bless and reward you for all your kindness!"

Hastily folding and directing this, she went to a drawer and made up a little package of clothing for her boy, which she tied with a handkerchief firmly round her waist; and, so fond is a mother's remembrance, that, even in the terrors of that hour, she did not forget to put in the little package one or two of his favorite toys, reserving a gayly painted parrot to amuse him when she should be called on to awaken him. It was some trouble to arouse the little sleeper; but, after some effort, he sat up, and was playing with his bird, while his mother was putting on her bonnet and shawl.

"Where are you going, mother?" said he, as she drew near the bed, with his little coat and cap.

His mother drew near, and looked so earnestly into his eyes, that he at once divined that something unusual was the matter.

"Hush, Harry," she said; "mustn't speak loud, or they will hear us. A wicked man was coming to take little Harry away from his mother, and carry him 'way off in the dark; but mother won't let him,—she's going to put on her little boy's cap and coat, and run off with him, so the ugly man can't catch him."

Saying these words, she had tied and buttoned on the child's simple outfit, and, taking him in her arms, she whispered to him to be very still; and, opening a door in her room which led into the outer veranda, she glided noiselessly out.

It was a sparkling, frosty, starlight night, and the mother wrapped the shawl close round her child, as, perfectly quiet with vague terror, he clung round her neck.

Old Bruno, a great Newfoundland, who slept at the end of the porch, rose, with a low growl, as she came near. She gently spoke his name, and the animal, an old pet and playmate of hers, instantly, wagging his tail, prepared to follow her, though apparently revolving much, in his simple dog's head, what such an indiscreet midnight promenade might mean. Some dim ideas of imprudence or impropriety in the measure seemed to embarrass him considerably; for he often stopped, as Eliza glided forward, and looked wistfully, first at her and then at the house, and then, as if reassured by reflection, he pattered along after her again. A few minutes brought them to the window of Uncle Tom's cottage, and Eliza, stopping, tapped lightly on the window-pane.

The prayer-meeting at Uncle Tom's had, in the order of hymn-singing, been protracted to a very late hour; and, as Uncle Tom had indulged himself in a few lengthy solos afterwards, the consequence was, that, although it was now between twelve and one o'clock, he and his worthy helpmeet were not yet asleep.

"Good Lord! what's that?" said Aunt Chloe, starting up and hastily drawing the curtain. "My sakes alive, if it an't Lizy! Get on your clothes, old man, quick!—there's old Bruno, too, a pawin' round; what on airth! I'm gwine to open the door."

And, suiting the action to the word, the door flew open, and the light of the tallow candle, which Tom had hastily lighted, fell on the haggard face and dark, wild eyes of the fugitive.

"Lord bless you!—I'm skeered to look at ye, Lizy! Are ye tuck sick, or what's come over ye?"

"I'm running away,—Uncle Tom and Aunt Chloe,—carrying off my child,—Master sold him!"

"Sold him?" echoed both, lifting up their hands in dismay.

"Yes, sold him!" said Eliza, firmly; "I crept into the closet by Mistress's door to-night, and I heard Master tell Missis that he had sold my Harry, and you, Uncle Tom, both, to a trader; and that he was going off this morning on his horse, and that the man was to take possession to-day."

Tom had stood, during this speech, with his hands raised, and his eyes dilated, like a man in a dream. Slowly and gradually, as its meaning came over him, he collapsed, rather than seated himself, on his old chair and sunk his head down upon his knees.

"The good Lord have pity on us!" said Aunt Chloe. "Oh, it don't seem as if it was true! What has he done, that Mas'r should sell *him*?"

"He hasn't done anything,—it isn't for that. Master don't want to sell; and Missis,—she's always good. I heard her plead and beg for us; but he told her 'twas no use; that he was in this man's debt, and that this man had got the power over him; and that if he didn't pay him off clear, it would end in his having to sell the place and all the people, and move off. Yes, I heard him say there was no choice between selling these two and selling all, the man was driving him so hard. Master said he was sorry; but oh, Missis,—you ought to have heard her talk! If she an't a Christian and an angel, there never was one. I'm a wicked girl to leave her so; but, then, I can't help it. She said, herself, one soul was worth more than the world; and this boy has a soul, and if I let him be carried off, who knows what'll become of it? It must be right; but, if it an't right, the Lord forgive me, for I can't help doing it!"

"Well, old man!" said Aunt Chloe, "why don't you go, too? Will you wait to be toted down river, where they kill niggers with hard work and starving? I'd a heap rather die than go there, any day! There's time for ye,—be off with Lizy,—you've got a pass to come and go any time. Come, bustle up, and I'll get your things together."

Tom slowly raised his head, and looked sorrowfully but quietly around, and said,—

"No, no,—I an't going. Let Eliza go,—it's her right! I wouldn't be the one to say no,— 'tan't in *natur* for her to stay; but you heard what she said! If I must be sold, or all the people on the place, and everything go to rack, why, let me be sold. I s'pose I can b'ar it as well as any on 'em," he added, while something like a sob and a sigh shook his broad, rough chest convulsively. "Mas'r always found me on the spot,—he always will. I never have broke trust, nor used my pass no ways contrary to my word, and I never will. It's better for me alone to go, than to break up the place and sell all. Mas'r an't to blame, Chloe, and he'll take care of you and the poor"—

Here he turned to the rough trundle-bed full of little woolly heads, and broke fairly down. He leaned over the back of the chair, and covered his face with his large hands. Sobs, heavy, hoarse, and loud, shook the chair, and great tears fell through his fingers on the floor: just such tears, sir, as you dropped into the coffin where lay your first-born son; such tears, woman, as you shed when you heard the cries of your dying babe. For, sir, he was a man,— and you are but another man. And, woman, though dressed in silk and jewels, you are but a woman, and, in life's great straits and mighty griefs, ye feel but one sorrow!

"And now," said Eliza, as she stood in the door, "I saw my husband only this afternoon, and I little knew then what was to come. They have pushed him to the very last standing-place, and he told me, to-day, that he was going to run away. Do try, if you can, to get word to him. Tell him how I went, and why I went; and tell him I'm going to try and find Canada. You must give my love to him, and tell him, if I never see him again,"—she turned away, and stood with her back to them for a moment, and then added, in a husky voice, "tell him to be as good as he can, and try and meet me in the kingdom of heaven."

"Call Bruno in there," she added. "Shut the door on him, poor beast! He mustn't go with me!"

A few last words and tears, a few simple adieus and blessings, and, clasping her wondering and affrighted child in her arms, she glided noiselessly away.

Chapter IX.
In Which It Appears That
a Senator is But a Man.

THE light of the cheerful fire shone on the rug and carpet of a cosey parlor, and glittered on the sides of the teacups and well brightened teapot, as Senator Bird was drawing off his boots, preparatory to inserting his feet in a pair of new, handsome slippers, which his wife had been working for him while away on his senatorial tour. Mrs. Bird, looking the very picture of delight, was superintending the arrangements of the table, ever and anon mingling admonitory remarks to a number of frolicsome juveniles, who were effervescing in all those modes of untold gambol and mischief that have astonished mothers ever since the flood.

"Tom, let the door-knob alone,—there's a man! Mary! Mary! don't pull the cat's tail,—poor pussy! Jim, you mustn't climb on that table,—no, no!—You don't know, my dear, what a surprise it is to us all, to see you here to-night!" said she, at last, when she found a space to say something to her husband.

"Yes, yes, I thought I'd just make a run down, spend the night, and have a little comfort at home. I'm tired to death, and my head aches!"

Mrs. Bird cast a glance at a camphor-bottle, which stood in the half-open closet, and appeared to meditate an approach to it, but her husband interposed.

"No, no, Mary, no doctoring! a cup of your good, hot tea, and some of our good home living, is what I want. It's a tiresome business, this legislating!"

And the senator smiled, as if he rather liked the idea of considering himself a sacrifice to his country.

"Well," said his wife, after the business of the tea-table was getting rather slack, "and what have they been doing in the Senate?"

Now, it was a very unusual thing for gentle little Mrs. Bird ever to trouble her head with what was going on in the house of the state, very wisely considering that she had enough to do to mind her own. Mr. Bird, therefore, opened his eyes in surprise, and said,—

"Not very much of importance."

"Well; but is it true that they have been passing a law forbidding people to give meat and drink to those poor colored folks that come along? I heard they were talking of some such law, but I didn't think any Christian legislature would pass it!"

"Why, Mary, you are getting to be a politician, all at once."

"No, nonsense! I wouldn't give a fig for all your politics, generally, but I think this is something downright cruel and unchristian. I hope, my dear, no such law has been passed."

"There has been a law passed forbidding people to help off the slaves that come over from Kentucky, my dear; so much of that thing has been done by these reckless Abolitionists, that our brethren in Kentucky are very strongly excited, and it seems necessary, and no more than Christian and kind, that something should be done by our state to quiet the excitement."

"And what is the law? It don't forbid us to shelter these poor creatures a night, does it, and to give 'em something comfortable to eat, and a few old clothes, and to send them quietly about their business?"

"Why, yes, my dear; that would be aiding and abetting, you know."

Mrs. Bird was a timid, blushing little woman, about four feet in height, and with mild blue eyes, and a peach-blow complexion, and the gentlest, sweetest voice in the world; as for courage, a moderate-sized cock-turkey had been known to put her to rout at the very first gobble, and a stout housedog, of moderate capacity, would bring her into subjection merely by a show of his teeth. Her husband and children were her entire world, and in these she ruled more by entreaty and persuasion than by command or argument. There was only one thing that was capable of arousing her, and that provocation came in on the side of her unusually gentle and sympathetic nature;—anything in the shape of cruelty would throw her into a passion, which was the more alarming and inexplicable in proportion to the general softness of her nature. Generally the most indulgent and easy to be entreated of all mothers, still her boys had a very reverent remembrance of a most vehement chastisement she once bestowed on them, because she found them leagued with several graceless boys of the neighborhood, stoning a defenceless kitten.

"I'll tell you what," Master Bill used to say, "I was scared that time. Mother came at me so that I thought she was crazy, and I was whipped and tumbled off to bed, without any supper, before I could get over wondering what had come about; and, after that, I heard mother crying outside the door, which made me feel worse than all the rest. I'll tell you what," he'd say, "we boys never stoned another kitten!"

On the present occasion, Mrs. Bird rose quickly, with very red cheeks, which quite improved her general appearance, and walked up to her husband, with quite a resolute air, and said, in a determined tone,—

"Now, John, I want to know if you think such a law as that is right and Christian?"

"You won't shoot me, now, Mary, if I say I do!"

"I never could have thought it of you, John; you didn't vote for it?"

"Even so, my fair politician."

"You ought to be ashamed, John! Poor, homeless, houseless creatures! It's a shameful, wicked, abominable law, and I'll break it, for one, the first time I get a chance; and I hope I *shall* have a chance, I do! Things have got to a pretty pass, if a woman can't give a warm supper and a bed to poor, starving creatures, just because they are slaves, and have been abused and oppressed all their lives, poor things!"

"But, Mary, just listen to me. Your feelings are all quite right, dear, and interesting, and I love you for them; but, then, dear, we mustn't suffer our feelings to run away with our judgment; you must consider it's not a matter of private feeling,—there are great public interests involved,—there is such a state of public agitation rising, that we must put aside our private feelings."

"Now, John, I don't know anything about politics, but I can read my Bible; and there I see that I must feed the hungry, clothe the naked, and comfort the desolate; and that Bible I mean to follow."

"But in cases where your doing so would involve a great public evil"—

"Obeying God never brings on public evils. I know it can't. It's always safest, all round, to *do as he* bids us."

"Now, listen to me, Mary, and I can state to you a very clear argument, to show"—

"Oh, nonsense, John! you can talk all night, but you wouldn't do it. I put it to you, John,—would *you*, now, turn away a poor, shivering, hungry creature from your door, because he was a runaway? *Would* you, now?"

Now, if the truth must be told, our senator had the misfortune to be a man who had a particularly humane and accessible nature, and turning away anybody that was in trouble never had been his forte; and what was worse for him in this particular pinch of the argument was, that his wife knew it, and, of course, was making an assault on rather an indefensible point. So he had recourse to the usual means of gaining time for such cases made and provided; he said "ahem," and coughed several times, took out his pocket-handkerchief, and began to wipe his glasses. Mrs. Bird, seeing the defenceless condition of the enemy's territory, had no more conscience than to push her advantage.

"I should like to see you doing that, John,—I really should! Turning a woman out of doors in a snow-storm, for instance; or, may be you'd take her up and put her in jail, wouldn't you? You would make a great hand at that!"

"Of course, it would be a very painful duty," began Mr. Bird, in a moderate tone.

"Duty, John! don't use that word! You know it isn't a duty,—it can't be a duty! If folks want to keep their slaves from running away, let 'em treat 'em well,—that's my doctrine. If I had slaves (as I hope I never shall have), I'd risk their wanting to run away from me, or you either, John. I tell you folks don't run away when they are happy; and when they do run, poor creatures! they suffer enough with cold and hunger and fear, without everybody's turning against them; and, law or no law, I never will, so help me God!"

"Mary! Mary! My dear, let me reason with you."

"I hate reasoning, John,—especially reasoning on such subjects. There's a way you political folks have of coming round and round a plain right thing; and you don't believe in it yourselves, when it comes to practice. I know *you* well enough, John. You don't believe it's right any more than I do; and you wouldn't do it any sooner than I."

At this critical juncture, old Cudjoe, the black man-of-all-work, put his head in at the door, and wished "Missis woud come into the kitchen," and our senator, tolerably relieved, looked after his little wife with a whimsical mixture of amusement and vexation, and, seating himself in the arm-chair, began to read the papers.

After a moment, his wife's voice was heard at the door, in a quick, earnest tone,—"John! John! I do wish you'd come here, a moment."

He laid down his paper, and went into the kitchen, and started, quite amazed at the sight that presented itself:—A young and slender woman, with garments torn and frozen, with one shoe gone, and the stocking torn away from the cut and bleeding foot, was laid back in a deadly swoon upon two chairs. There was the impress of the despised race on her face, yet none could help feeling its mournful and pathetic beauty, while its stony sharpness, its cold, fixed, deathly aspect, struck a solemn chill over him. He drew his breath short, and stood in silence. His wife, and their only colored domestic, old Aunt Dinah, were busily engaged in restorative measures; while old Cudjoe had got the boy on his knee, and was busy pulling off his shoes and stockings, and chafing his little cold feet.

"Sure, now, if she an't a sight to behold!" said old Dinah, compassionately; "'pears like 'twas the heat that made her faint. She was tol'able peart when she cum in, and asked if she couldn't warm herself here a spell; and I was just a askin' her where she cum from, and she fainted right down. Never done much hard work, guess, by the looks of her hands."

"Poor creature!" said Mrs. Bird, compassionately, as the woman slowly unclosed her large, dark eyes, and looked vacantly at her. Suddenly an expression of agony crossed her face, and she sprang up, saying, "Oh, my Harry! Have they got him?"

The boy, at this, jumped from Cudjoe's knee, and, running to her side, put up his arms. "Oh, he's here! he's here!" she exclaimed.

"Oh, ma'am!" said she, wildly, to Mrs. Bird, "do protect us! don't let them get him!"

"Nobody shall hurt you here, poor woman," said Mrs. Bird, encouragingly. "You are safe; don't be afraid."

"God bless you!" said the woman, covering her face and sobbing; while the little boy, seeing her crying, tried to get into her lap.

With many gentle and womanly offices which none knew better how to render than Mrs. Bird, the poor woman was, in time, rendered more calm. A temporary bed was provided for her on the settle, near the fire; and, after a short time, she fell into a heavy slumber, with the child, who seemed no less weary, soundly sleeping on her arm; for the mother resisted, with nervous anxiety, the kindest attempts to take him from her; and, even in sleep, her arm encircled him with an unrelaxing clasp, as if she could not even then be beguiled of her vigilant hold.

Mr. and Mrs. Bird had gone back to the parlor, where, strange as it may appear, no reference was made, on either side, to the preceding conversation; but Mrs. Bird busied herself with her knitting work, and Mr. Bird pretended to be reading the paper.

"I wonder who and what she is!" said Mr. Bird, at last, as he laid it down.

"When she wakes up and feels a little rested we will see," said Mrs. Bird.

"I say, wife!" said Mr. Bird, after musing in silence over his newspaper.

"Well, dear!"

"She couldn't wear one of your gowns, could she, by any letting down, or such matter? She seems to be rather larger than you are."

A quite perceptible smile glimmered on Mrs. Bird's face as she answered, "We'll see."

Another pause, and Mr. Bird again broke out,—

"I say, wife!"

"Well! what now?"

"Why, there's that old bombazine cloak, that you keep on purpose to put over me when I take my afternoon's nap; you might as well give her that,—she needs clothes."

At this instant, Dinah looked in to say that the woman was awake, and wanted to see Missis.

Mr. and Mrs. Bird went into the kitchen, followed by the two eldest boys, the smaller fry having, by this time, been safely disposed of in bed.

The woman was now sitting up on the settle, by the fire. She was looking steadily into the blaze, with a calm heartbroken expression, very different from her former agitated wildness.

"Did you want me?" said Mrs. Bird, in gentle tones. "I hope you feel better now, poor woman!"

A long-drawn, shivering sigh was the only answer; but she lifted her dark eyes, and fixed them on her with such a forlorn and imploring expression, that the tears came into the little woman's eyes.

"You needn't be afraid of anything; we are friends here, poor woman! Tell me where you came from, and what you want," said she.

"I came from Kentucky," said the woman.

"When?" said Mr. Bird, taking up the interrogatory.

"To-night."

"How did you come?"

"I crossed on the ice."

"Crossed on the ice!" said every one present.

"Yes," said the woman, slowly, "I did. God helping me, I crossed on the ice; for they were behind me,—right behind,—and there was no other way!"

"Law, Missis," said Cudjoe, "the ice is all in broken-up blocks, a swinging and a teetering up and down in the water."

"I know it was,—I know it!" said she wildly; "but I did it! I wouldn't have thought I could,—I didn't think I should get over, but I didn't care! I could but die if I didn't. The Lord helped me; nobody knows how much the Lord can help 'em, till they try," said the woman, with a flashing eye.

"Were you a slave?" said Mr. Bird.

"Yes, sir; I belonged to a man in Kentucky."

"Was he unkind to you?"

"No, sir; he was a good master."

"And was your mistress unkind to you?"

"No, sir,—no! my mistress was always good to me."

"What could induce you to leave a good home, then, and run away, and go through such dangers?"

The woman looked up at Mrs. Bird with a keen, scrutinizing glance, and it did not escape her that she was dressed in deep mourning.

"Ma'am," she said, suddenly, "have you ever lost a child?"

The question was unexpected, and it was a thrust on a new wound; for it was only a month since a darling child of the family had been laid in the grave.

Mr. Bird turned around and walked to the window, and Mrs. Bird burst into tears; but, recovering her voice, she said,—

"Why do you ask that? I have lost a little one."

"Then you will feel for me. I have lost two, one after another,—left 'em buried there when I came away; and I had only this one left. I never slept a night without him; he was all I had. He was my comfort and pride day and night; and, ma'am, they were going to take him away from me,—to *sell* him,—sell him down south, ma'am, to go all alone,—a baby that had never been away from his mother in his life! I couldn't stand it ma'am, I knew I never should be good for anything, if they did; and when I knew the papers were signed, and he was sold, I took him and came off in the night; and they chased me,—the man that bought him, and some of Mas'r's folks,—and they were coming down right behind me, and I heard 'em. I jumped right on to the ice; and how I got across, I don't know,—but, first I knew, a man was helping me up the bank."

The woman did not sob nor weep. She had gone to a place where tears are dry; but every one around her was, in some way characteristic of themselves, showing signs of hearty sympathy.

The two little boys, after a desperate rummaging in their pockets, in search of those pocket-handkerchiefs which mothers know are never to be found there, had thrown themselves disconsolately into the skirts of their mother's gown, where they were sobbing, and wiping their eyes and noses, to their hearts' content;—Mrs. Bird had her face fairly hidden in her pocket-handkerchief; and old Dinah, with tears streaming down her black, honest face, was ejaculating, "Lord have mercy on us!" with all the fervor of a camp-meeting,—while old Cudjoe, rubbing his eyes very hard with his cuffs, and making a most uncommon variety of wry faces, occasionally responded in the same key, with great fervor. Our senator was a statesman, and of course could not be expected to cry, like other mortals; and so he turned his back to the company, and looked out of the window, and seemed particularly busy in clearing his throat and wiping his spectacle-glasses, occasionally blowing his nose in a manner that was calculated to excite suspicion, had any one been in a state to observe critically.

"How came you to tell me you had a kind master?" he suddenly exclaimed, gulping down very resolutely some kind of rising in his throat, and turning suddenly round upon the woman.

"Because he *was* a kind master; I'll say that of him, any way;—and my mistress was kind; but they couldn't help themselves. They were owing money; and there was some way, I can't tell how, that a man had a hold on them, and they were obliged to give him his will. I listened, and heard him telling mistress that, and she begging and pleading for me,—and he told her he couldn't help himself, and that the papers were all drawn;—and then it was I took him and left my home, and came away. I knew 'twas no use of my trying to live, if they did it; for 't 'pears like this child is all I have."

"Have you no husband?"

"Yes, but he belongs to another man. His master is real hard to him, and won't let him come to see me hardly ever; and he's grown harder and harder upon us, and he threatens to sell him down south;—it's like I'll never see *him* again!"

The quiet tone in which the woman pronounced these words might have led a superficial observer to think that she was entirely apathetic; but there was a calm, settled depth of anguish in her large, dark eye, that spoke of something far otherwise.

"And where do you mean to go, my poor woman?" said Mrs. Bird.

"To Canada, if I only knew where that was. Is it very far off, is Canada?" said she, looking up, with a simple, confiding air, to Mrs. Bird's face.

"Poor thing!" said Mrs. Bird, involuntarily.

"Is 't a very great way off, think?" said the woman, earnestly.

"Much further than you think, poor child!" said Mrs. Bird; "but we will try to think what can be done for you. Here, Dinah, make her up a bed in your own room, close by the kitchen, and I'll think what to do for her in the morning. Meanwhile, never fear, poor woman; put your trust in God; he will protect you."

Mrs. Bird and her husband reëntered the parlor. She sat down in her little rocking-chair before the fire, swaying thoughtfully to and fro. Mr. Bird strode up and down the room, grumbling to himself "Pish! pshaw! confounded awkward business!" At length, striding up to his wife, he said,—

"I say, wife, she'll have to get away from here, this very night. That fellow will be down on the scent bright and early to-morrow morning; if 'twas only the woman, she could lie quiet till it was over; but that little chap can't be kept still by a troop of horse and foot, I'll warrant me; he'll bring it all out, popping his head out of some window or door. A pretty kettle of fish it would be for me, too, to be caught with them both here, just now! No; they'll have to be got off to-night."

"To-night! How is it possible?—where to?"

"Well, I know pretty well where to," said the senator, beginning to put on his boots, with a reflective air; and, stopping when his leg was half in, he embraced his knee with both hands, and seemed to go off in deep meditation.

"It's a confounded awkward, ugly business," said he, at last, beginning to tug at his boot-straps again, "and that's a fact!" After one boot was fairly on, the senator sat with the other in his hand, profoundly studying the figure of the carpet. "It will have to be done, though, for aught I see,—hang it all!" and he drew the other boot anxiously on, and looked out of the window.

Now, little Mrs. Bird was a discreet woman,—a woman who never in her life said, "I told you so!" and, on the present occasion, though pretty well aware of the shape her husband's meditations were taking, she very prudently forbore to meddle with them, only sat very quietly in her chair, and looked quite ready to hear her liege lord's intentions, when he should think proper to utter them.

"You see," he said, "there's my old client, Van Trompe, has come over from Kentucky, and set all his slaves free; and he has bought a place seven miles up the creek, here, back in the woods, where nobody goes, unless they go on purpose; and it's a place that isn't found in a hurry. There she'd be safe enough; but the plague of the thing is, nobody could drive a carriage there to-night, but *me.*"

"Why not? Cudjoe is an excellent driver."

"Ay, ay, but here it is. The creek has to be crossed twice; and the second crossing is quite dangerous, unless one knows it as I do. I have crossed it a hundred times on horseback and know exactly the turns to take. And so, you see, there's no help for it. Cudjoe must put in the horses, as quietly as may be, about twelve o'clock, and I'll take her over; and then, to give color to the matter, he must carry me on to the next tavern, to take the stage for Columbus, that comes by about three or four, and so it will look as if I had had the carriage only for that. I shall get into business bright and early in the morning. But I'm thinking I shall feel rather cheap there, after all that's been said and done; but, hang it, I can't help it!"

"Your heart is better than your head, in this case, John," said the wife, laying her little white hand on his. "Could I ever have loved you, had I not known you better than you know yourself?" And the little woman looked so handsome, with the tears sparkling in her eyes, that the senator thought he must be a decidedly clever fellow, to get such a pretty creature into such a passionate admiration of him; and so, what could he do but walk off soberly, to see about the carriage. At the door, however, he stopped a moment, and then coming back, he said, with some hesitation,—

"Mary, I don't know how you'd feel about it, but there's that drawer full of things—of—of—poor little Henry's." So saying, he turned quickly on his heel, and shut the door after him.

His wife opened the little bedroom door adjoining her room, and, taking the candle, set it down on the top of a bureau there then from a small recess she took a key, and put it thoughtfully in the lock of a drawer, and made a sudden pause, while two boys, who, boy-like, had followed close on her heels, stood looking, with silent, significant glances, at their mother, And oh, mother that reads this, has there never been in your house a drawer, or a closet, the opening of which has been to you like the opening again of a little grave? Ah! happy mother that you are, if it has not been so.

Mrs. Bird slowly opened the drawer. There were little coats of many a form and pattern, piles of aprons, and rows of small stockings; and even a pair of little shoes, worn and rubbed at the toes, were peeping from the folds of a paper. There was a toy horse and wagon, a top, a ball,—memorials gathered with many a tear and many a heart-break? She sat down by the drawer, and, leaning her head on her hands over it, wept till the tears fell through her fingers into the drawer; then suddenly raising her head, she began, with nervous haste, selecting the plainest and most substantial articles, and gathering them into a bundle.

"Mamma," said one of the boys, gently touching her arm, "are you going to give away *those* things?"

"My dear boys," she said, softly and earnestly, "if our dear, loving little Henry looks down from heaven he would be glad to have us do this. I could not find it in my heart to give them away to any common person,—to anybody that was happy; but I give them to a mother more heartbroken and sorrowful than I am; and I hope God will send his blessings with them!"

There are in this world blessed souls, whose sorrows all spring up into joys for others; whose earthly hopes, laid in the grave with many tears, are the seed from which spring healing flowers and balm for the desolate and the distressed. Among such was the delicate woman who sits there by the lamp, dropping slow tears, while she prepares the memorials of her own lost one for the outcast wanderer.

After a while, Mrs. Bird opened a wardrobe, and, taking from thence a plain, serviceable dress or two, she sat down busily to her work-table, and, with needle, scissors, and thimble, at hand, quietly commenced the "letting down" process which her husband had recommended, and continued busily at it till the old clock in the corner struck twelve, and she heard the low rattling of wheels at the door.

"Mary," said her husband, coming in, with his overcoat in his hand, "you must wake her up now; we must be off."

Mrs. Bird hastily deposited the various articles she had collected in a small plain trunk, and locking it, desired her husband to see it in the carriage, and then proceeded to call the woman. Soon, arrayed in a cloak, bonnet and shawl, that had belonged to her benefactress, she appeared at the door with her child in her arms. Mr. Bird hurried her into the carriage, and Mrs. Bird pressed on after her to the carriage steps. Eliza leaned out of the carriage, and put out her hand,—a hand as soft and beautiful as was given in return. She fixed her large, dark eyes, full of earnest meaning, on Mrs. Bird's face, and seemed going to speak. Her lips moved,—she tried once or twice, but there was no sound,—and pointing upward, with a look never to be forgotten, she fell back in the seat, and covered her face. The door was shut, and the carriage drove on.

What a situation, now, for a patriotic senator, that had been all the week before spurring up the legislature of his native state to pass more stringent resolutions against escaping fugitives, their harborers and abettors!

Our good senator in his native state had not been exceeded by any of his brethren at Washington, in the sort of eloquence which has won for them immortal renown! How sublimely he had sat with his hands in his pockets, and scouted all sentimental weakness of those who would put the welfare of a few miserable fugitives before great state interests!

He was as bold as a lion about it, and "mightily convinced" not only himself, but everybody that heard him;—but then his idea of a fugitive was only an idea of the letters that spell the word,—or, at the most, the image of a little newspaper picture of a man with a stick and bundle, with "Ran away from the subscriber" under it. The magic of the real presence of distress,—the imploring human eye, the frail, trembling human hand, the despairing appeal of helpless agony,—these he had never tried. He had never thought that a fugitive might be a hapless mother, a defenceless child,—like that one which was now wearing his lost boy's little well-known cap; and so, as our poor senator was not stone or steel,—as he was a man, and a down-right noble-hearted one, too,—he was, as everybody must see, in a sad case for his patriotism. And you need not exult over him, good brother of the Southern States; for we have some inklings that many of you, under similar circumstances, would not do much better. We have reason to know, in Kentucky, as in Mississippi, are noble and generous hearts, to whom never was tale of suffering told in vain. Ah, good brother! is it fair for you to expect of us services which your own brave, honorable heart would not allow you to render, were you in our place?

Be that as it may, if our good senator was a political sinner, he was in a fair way to expiate it by his night's penance. There had been a long continuous period of rainy weather, and the soft, rich earth of Ohio, as every one knows, is admirably suited to the manufacture of mud,— and the road was an Ohio railroad of the good old times.

"And pray, what sort of a road may that be?" says some eastern traveller, who has been accustomed to connect no ideas with a railroad but those of smoothness or speed.

Know, then, innocent eastern friend, that in benighted regions of the west, where the mud is of unfathomable and sublime depth, roads are made of round rough logs arranged transversely side by side, and coated over in their pristine freshness with earth, turf, and whatsoever may come to hand, and then the rejoicing native calleth it a road, and straightway essayeth to ride thereupon. In process of time, the rains wash off all the turf and grass aforesaid, move the logs hither and thither in picturesque positions, up, down, and crosswise, with divers chasms and ruts of black mud intervening.

Over such a road as this our senator went stumbling along, making moral reflections as continuously as under the circumstances could be expected,—the carriage proceeding along much as follows,—bump! bump! bump! slush! down in the mud!—the senator, woman, and child reversing their positions so suddenly as to come, without any very accurate adjustment, against the windows of the down-hill side. Carriage sticks fast, while Cudjoe on the outside is heard making a great muster among the horses. After various ineffectual pullings and twitchings, just as the senator is losing all patience, the carriage suddenly rights itself with a bounce,—two front wheels go down into another abyss, and senator, woman, and child all tumble promiscuously on to the front seat,—senator's hat is jammed over his eyes and nose quite unceremoniously, and he considers himself fairly extinguished;—child cries, and Cudjoe on the outside delivers animated addresses to the horses, who are kicking, and floundering, and straining, under repeated cracks of the whip. Carriage springs up, with another bounce,—down go the hind wheels,—senator, woman, and child fly over on to the back seat, his elbows encountering her bonnet, and both her feet being jammed into his hat, which flies off in the concussion. After a few moments the "slough" is passed, and the horses stop, panting;—the senator finds his hat, the woman straightens her bonnet and hushes her child, and they brace themselves firmly for what is yet to come.

For a while only the continuous bump! bump! intermingled, just by way of variety, with divers side plunges and compound shakes; and they begin to flatter themselves that they are not so badly off, after all. At last, with a square plunge, which puts all on to their feet and then down into their seats with incredible quickness, the carriage stops,—and, after much outside commotion, Cudjoe appears at the door.

"Please, sir, it's powerful bad spot, this yer. I don't know how we's to get clar out. I'm a thinkin' we'll have to be a gettin' rails."

The senator despairingly steps out, picking gingerly for some firm foothold; down goes one foot an immeasurable depth,—he tries to pull it up, loses his balance, and tumbles over into the mud, and is fished out, in a very despairing condition, by Cudjoe.

But we forbear, out of sympathy to our readers' bones. Western travellers, who have beguiled the midnight hour in the interesting process of pulling down rail fences, to pry their carriages out of mud-holes, will have a respectful and mournful sympathy with our unfortunate hero. We beg them to drop a silent tear, and pass on.

It was full late in the night when the carriage emerged, dripping and bespattered, out of the creek, and stood at the door of a large farm-house.

It took no inconsiderable perseverance to arouse the inmates; but at last the respectable proprietor appeared, and undid the door. He was a great, tall, bristling Orson of a fellow, full six feet and some inches in his stockings, and arrayed in a red flannel hunting-shirt. A very heavy *mat* of sandy hair, in a decidedly tousled condition, and a beard of some days' growth, gave the worthy man an appearance, to say the least, not particularly prepossessing. He stood for a few minutes holding the candle aloft, and blinking on our travellers with a dismal and mystified expression that was truly ludicrous. It cost some effort of our senator to induce him to comprehend the case fully; and while he is doing his best at that, we shall give him a little introduction to our readers.

Honest old John Van Trompe was once quite a considerable land-holder and slave-owner in the State of Kentucky. Having "nothing of the bear about him but the skin," and being gifted by nature with a great, honest, just heart, quite equal to his gigantic frame, he had been for some years witnessing with repressed uneasiness the workings of a system equally bad for oppressor and oppressed. At last, one day, John's great heart had swelled altogether too big to wear his bonds any longer; so he just took his pocket-book out of his desk, and went over into Ohio, and bought a quarter of a township of good, rich land, made out free papers for all his people,—men, women, and children,—packed them up in wagons, and sent them off to settle down; and then honest John turned his face up the creek, and sat quietly down on a snug, retired farm, to enjoy his conscience and his reflections.

"Are you the man that will shelter a poor woman and child from slave-catchers?" said the senator, explicitly.

"I rather think I am," said honest John, with some considerable emphasis.

"I thought so," said the senator.

"If there's anybody comes," said the good man, stretching his tall muscular form upward, "why here I'm ready for him, and I've got seven sons, each six foot high, and they'll be ready for 'em. Give our respects to 'em," said John; "tell 'em it's no matter how soon they call,—make no kinder difference to us," said John, running his fingers through the shock of hair that thatched his head, and bursting out into a great laugh.

Weary, jaded, and spiritless, Eliza dragged herself up to the door, with her child lying in a heavy sleep on her arm. The rough man held the candle to her face, and uttering a kind of compassionate grunt, opened the door of a small bedroom adjoining to the large kitchen where they were standing, and motioned her to go in. He took down a candle, and lighting it, set it upon the table, and then addressed himself to Eliza.

"Now, I say, gal, you needn't be a bit afeard, let who will come here. I'm up to all that sort o' thing," said he, pointing to two or three goodly rifles over the mantelpiece; "and most people that know me know that 't wouldn't be healthy to try to get anybody out o' my house when I'm agin it. So *now* you jist go to sleep now, as quiet as if yer mother was a rockin' ye," said he, as he shut the door.

"Why, this is an uncommon handsome un," he said to the senator. "Ah, well; handsome uns has the greatest cause to run, sometimes, if they has any kind o' feelin', such as decent women should. I know all about that."

The senator, in a few words, briefly explained Eliza's history.

"Oh! ou! aw! now, I want to know?" said the good man, pitifully; "sho! now sho! That's natur now, poor crittur! hunted down now like a deer,—hunted down, jest for havin' natural feelin's, and doin' what no kind o' mother could help a doin'! I tell ye what, these yer things make me come the nighest to swearin', now, o' most anything," said honest John, as he wiped his eyes with the back of a great, freckled, yellow hand. "I tell yer what, stranger, it was years and years before I'd jine the church, 'cause the ministers round in our parts used to preach that the Bible went in for these ere cuttings up,—and I couldn't be up to 'em with their Greek and Hebrew, and so I took up agin 'em, Bible and all. I never jined the church till I found a minister that was up to 'em all in Greek and all that, and he said right the contrary; and then I took right hold, and jined the church,—I did now, fact," said John, who had been all this time uncorking some very frisky bottled cider, which at this juncture he presented.

"Ye'd better jest put up here, now, till daylight," said he, heartily, "and I'll call up the old woman, and have a bed got ready for you in no time."

"Thank you, my good friend," said the senator. "I must be along, to take the night stage for Columbus."

"Ah! well, then, if you must, I'll go a piece with you, and show you a cross road that will take you there better than the road you came on. That road's mighty bad."

John equipped himself, and, with a lantern in hand, was soon seen guiding the senator's carriage towards a road that ran down in a hollow, back of his dwelling. When they parted, the senator put into his hand a ten-dollar bill.

"It's for her," he said, briefly.

"Ay, ay," said John, with equal conciseness.

They shook hands, and parted.

Chapter XXX.
The Slave Warehouse.

A SLAVE warehouse! Perhaps some of my readers conjure up horrible visions of such a place. They fancy some foul, obscure den, some horrible *Tartarus "informis, ingens, cui lumen ademptum."* But no, innocent friend; in these days men have learned the art of sinning expertly and genteelly, so as not to shock the eyes and senses of respectable society. Human property is high in the market; and is, therefore, well fed, well cleaned, tended, and looked after, that it may come to sale sleek, and strong, and shining. A slave warehouse in New Orleans is a house externally not much unlike many others, kept with neatness; and where every day you may see arranged, under a sort of shed along the outside, rows of men and women, who stand there as a sign of the property sold within.

Then you shall be courteously entreated to call and examine, and shall find an abundance of husbands, wives, brothers, sisters, fathers, mothers, and young children, to be "sold separately, or in lots, to suit the convenience of the purchaser;" and that soul immortal, once bought with blood and anguish by the Son of God, when the earth shook, and the rocks were rent, and the graves were opened, can be sold, leased, mortgaged, exchanged for groceries or dry goods, to suit the phases of trade, or the fancy of the purchaser.

It was a day or two after the conversation between Marie and Miss Ophelia, that Tom, Adolph, and about half a dozen others of the St. Clare estate, were turned over to the loving kindness of Mr. Skeggs, the keeper of a depot on — street, to await the auction next day.

Tom had with him quite a sizable trunk full of clothing, as had most others of them. They were ushered, for the night, into a long room, where many other men, of all ages, sizes, and shades of complexion, were assembled, and from which roars of laughter and unthinking merriment were proceeding.

"Ah, ha! that's right. Go it, boys,—go it!" said Mr. Skeggs, the keeper. "My people are always so merry! Sambo, I see!" he said, speaking approvingly to a burly Negro who was performing tricks of low buffoonery, which occasioned the shouts which Tom had heard.

As might be imagined, Tom was in no humor to join these proceedings; and, therefore, setting his trunk as far as possible from the noisy group, he sat down on it, and leaned his face against the wall.

The dealers in the human article make scrupulous and systematic efforts to promote noisy mirth among them, as a means of drowning reflection, and rendering them insensible to their condition. The whole object of the training to which the Negro is put, from the time he is sold in the northern market till he arrives south, is systematically directed towards making him callous, unthinking, and brutal. The slave-dealer collects his gang in Virginia or Kentucky, and drives them to some convenient, healthy place,—often a watering-place,—to be fattened. Here they are fed full daily; and, because some incline to pine, a fiddle is kept commonly going among them, and they are made to dance daily; and he who refuses to be merry—in whose soul thoughts of wife, or child, or home, are too strong for him to be gay— is marked as sullen and dangerous, and subjected to all the evils which the ill-will of an utterly irresponsible and hardened man can inflict upon him. Briskness, alertness, and cheerfulness of appearance, especially before observers, are constantly enforced upon them, both by the hope of thereby getting a good master, and the fear of all that the driver may bring upon them, if they prove unsalable.

"What dat ar nigger doin' here?" said Sambo, coming up to Tom, after Mr. Skeggs had left the room. Sambo was a full black, of great size, very lively, voluble, and full of trick and grimace.

"What you doin' here?" said Sambo, coming up to Tom, and poking him facetiously in the side. "Meditatin', eh?"

"I am to be sold at the auction, to-morrow!" said Tom, quietly.

"Sold at auction,—haw! haw! boys, an't this yer fun? I wish 't I was gwin that ar way!— tell ye, wouldn't I make 'em laugh? but how is it,—dis yer whole lot gwine to-morrow?" said Sambo, laying his hand freely on Adolph's shoulder.

"Please to let me alone!" said Adolph, fiercely, straightening himself up, with extreme disgust.

"Law, now, boys! dis yer's one o' yer white niggers,—kind o' cream-color, ye know, scented!" said he, coming up to Adolph and snuffing. "O Lor! he'd do for a tobaccer-shop; they could keep him to scent snuff! Lor, he'd keep a whole shop agwine,—he would!"

"I say, keep off, can't you?" said Adolph, enraged.

"Lor, now, how touchy we is,—we white niggers! Look at us, now!" and Sambo gave a ludicrous imitation of Adolph's manner; "here's de airs and graces. We's been in a good family, I specs."

"Yes," said Adolph; "I had a master that could have bought you all for old truck!"

"Laws, now, only think," said Sambo, "the gentlemens that we is!"

"I belonged to the St. Clare family," said Adolph, proudly.

"Lor, you did! Be hanged if they aren't lucky to get shet of ye. Spects they's gwine to trade ye off with a lot o' cracked teapots and sich like!" said Sambo, with a provoking grin.

Adolph, enraged at this taunt, flew furiously at his adversary, swearing and striking on every side of him. The rest laughed and shouted, and the uproar brought the keeper to the door.

"What now, boys? Order,—order!" he said, coming in and flourishing a large whip.

All fled in different directions, except Sambo, who, presuming on the favor which the keeper had to him as a licensed wag, stood his ground, ducking his head with a facetious grin, whenever the master made a dive at him.

"Lor, Mas'r, 't an't us,—we's reg'lar stiddy,—it's these yer new hands; they's real aggra-vatin',—kinder pickin' at us, all time!"

The keeper, at this, turned upon Tom and Adolph, and distributing a few kicks and cuffs without much inquiry, and leaving general orders for all to be good boys and go to sleep, left the apartment.

While this scene was going on in the men's sleeping-room, the reader may be curious to take a peep at the corresponding apartment allotted to the women. Stretched out in various attitudes over the floor, he may see numberless sleeping forms of every shade of complexion from the purest ebony to white, and of all years, from childhood to old age, lying now asleep. Here is a fine bright girl, of ten years, whose mother was sold out yesterday, and who to-night cried herself to sleep when nobody was looking at her. Here, a worn old Negress, whose thin arms and callous fingers tell of hard toil, waiting to be sold to-morrow, as a cast-off article, for what can be got for her; and some forty or fifty others, with heads variously enveloped in blankets or articles of clothing, lie stretched around them. But, in a corner, sitting apart from the rest, are two females of a more interesting appearance than common. One of these is a respectably dressed mulatto woman between forty and fifty, with soft eyes and a gentle and pleasing physiognomy. She has on her head a high-raised turban, made of a gay red Madras handkerchief, of the first quality, and her dress is neatly fitted, and of good material, showing that she has been provided for with a careful hand. By her side, and nestling closely to her, is a young girl of fifteen,—her daughter. She is a quadroon, as may be seen from her fairer complexion, though her likeness to her mother is quite discernible. She has the same soft, dark eye, with longer lashes, and her curling hair is of a luxuriant brown. She also is dressed with great neatness, and her white, delicate hands betray very little acquaintance with servile toil. These two are to be sold to-morrow, in the same lot with the St. Clare servants; and the gentleman to whom they belong, and to whom the money for their sale is to be transmitted, is a member of a Christian church in New York, who will receive the money, and go thereafter to the sacrament of his Lord and theirs, and think no more of it.

These two, whom we shall call Susan and Emmeline, had been the personal attendants of an amiable and pious lady of New Orleans, by whom they had been carefully and piously instructed and trained. They had been taught to read and write, diligently instructed in the truths of religion, and their lot had been as happy an one as in their condition it was possible to be. But the only son of their protectress had the management of her property; and, by carelessness and extravagance, involved it to a large amount, and at last failed. One of the largest creditors was the respectable firm of B. & Co., in New York. B. & Co. wrote to their lawyer in New Orleans, who attached the real estate (these two articles and a lot of plantation hands formed the most valuable part of it), and wrote word to that effect to New York. Brother B., being, as we have said, a Christian man, and a resident in a free state, felt some uneasiness on the subject. He didn't like trading in slaves and souls of men,—of course, he didn't; but, then, there were thirty thousand dollars in the case, and that was rather too much money to be lost for a principle; and so, after much considering, and asking advice from those that he knew would advise to suit him, Brother B. wrote to his lawyer to dispose of the business in the way that seemed to him the most suitable, and remit the proceeds.

The day after the letter arrived in New Orleans, Susan and Emmeline were attached, and sent to the depot to await a general auction on the following morning; and as they glimmer faintly upon us in the moonlight which steals through the grated window, we may listen to their conversation. Both are weeping, but each quietly, that the other may not hear.

"Mother, just lay your head on my lap, and see if you can't sleep a little," says the girl, trying to appear calm.

"I haven't any heart to sleep, Em; I can't; it's the last night we may be together!"

"Oh, mother, don't say so! perhaps we shall get sold together,—who knows?"

"If 't was anybody's else case, I should say so, too, Em," said the woman; "but I'm so 'feard of losin' you that I don't see anything but the danger."

"Why, mother, the man said we were both likely, and would sell well."

Susan remembered the man's looks and words. With a deadly sickness at her heart, she remembered how he had looked at Emmeline's hands, and lifted up her curly hair, and pronounced her a first-rate article. Susan had been trained as a Christian, brought up in the daily reading of the Bible, and had the same horror of her child's being sold to a life of shame that any other Christian mother might have; but she had no hope,—no protection.

"Mother, I think we might do first-rate, if you could get a place as cook, and I as chambermaid or seamstress, in some family. I dare say we shall. Let's both look as bright and lively as we can, and tell all we can do, and perhaps we shall," said Emmeline.

"I want you to brush your hair all back straight, to-morrow," said Susan.

"What for, mother? I don't look near so well, that way."

"Yes, but you'll sell better so."

"I don't see why!" said the child.

"Respectable families would be more apt to buy you, if they saw you looked plain and decent, as if you wasn't trying to look handsome. I know their ways better 'n you do," said Susan.

"Well, mother then I will."

"And, Emmeline, if we shouldn't ever see each other again, after to-morrow,—if I'm sold way up on a plantation somewhere, and you somewhere else,—always remember how you've been brought up, and all Missis has told you; take your Bible with you, and your hymn-book; and if you're faithful to the Lord, he'll be faithful to you."

So speaks the poor soul, in sore discouragement; for she knows that to-morrow any man, however vile and brutal, however godless and merciless, if he only has money to pay for her, may become owner of her daughter, body and soul; and then, how is the child to be faithful? She thinks of all this, as she holds her daughter in her arms, and wishes that she were not handsome and attractive. It seems almost an aggravation to her to remember how purely and piously, how much above the ordinary lot, she has been brought up. But she has no resort but to *pray*; and many such prayers to God have gone up from those same trim, neatly arranged, respectable slave-prisons,—prayers which God has not forgotten, as a coming day shall show; for it is written, "Whoso causeth one of these little ones to offend, it were better for him that a mill-stone were hanged about his neck, and that he were drowned in the depths of the sea."

The soft, earnest, quiet moonbeam looks in fixedly, marking the bars of the grated windows on the prostrate, sleeping forms. The mother and daughter are singing together a wild and melancholy dirge, common as a funeral hymn among the slaves:—

> "Oh, where is weeping Mary?
> Oh, where is weeping Mary?
>   'Rived in the goodly land.
> She is dead and gone to heaven;
> She is dead and gone to heaven;
>   'Rived in the goodly land."

These words, sung by voices of a peculiar and melancholy sweetness, in an air which seemed like the sighing of earthly despair after heavenly hope, floated through the dark prison-rooms with a pathetic cadence, as verse after verse was breathed out,—

> "Oh, where are Paul and Silas?
> Oh, where are Paul and Silas?
>   Gone to the goodly land.
> They are dead and gone to heaven;
> They are dead and gone to heaven;
>   'Rived in the goodly land."

Sing on, poor souls! The night is short, and the morning will part you forever!

But now it is morning, and everybody is astir; and the worthy Mr. Skeggs is busy and bright, for a lot of goods is to be fitted out for auction. There is a brisk lookout on the toilet; injunctions passed around to every one to put on their best face and be spry; and now all are arranged in a circle for a last review, before they are marched up to the Bourse.

Mr. Skeggs, with his palmetto on and his cigar in his mouth, walks around to put farewell touches on his wares.

"How's this?" he said, stepping in front of Susan and Emmeline. "Where's your curls, gal?"

The girl looked timidly at her mother who, with the smooth adroitness common among her class, answers,—

"I was telling her, last night, to put up her hair smooth and neat, and not havin' it flying about in curls; looks more respectable so."

"Bother!" said the man, peremptorily, turning to the girl; "you go right along, and curl yourself real smart!" He added, giving a crack to a rattan he held in his hand, "And be back in quick time, too!"

"You go and help her," he added, to the mother. "Them curls may make a hundred dollars difference in the sale of her."

Beneath a splendid dome were men of all nations, moving to and fro, over the marble pave. On every side of the circular area were little tribunes, or stations, for the use of speakers and auctioneers. Two of these, on opposite sides of the area, were now occupied by brilliant and talented gentlemen, enthusiastically forcing up, in English and French commingled, the bids of connoisseurs in their various wares. A third one, on the other side, still unoccupied, was surrounded by a group, waiting the moment of sale to begin. And here we may recognize the St. Clare servants,—Tom, Adolph, and others; and there, too, Susan and Emmeline, awaiting their turn with anxious and dejected faces. Various spectators, intending to purchase, or not intending, as the case might be, gathered around the group, handling, examining, and commenting on their various points and faces with the same freedom that a set of jockeys discuss the merits of a horse.

"Hulloa, Alf! what brings you here?" said a young exquisite, slapping the shoulder of a sprucely dressed young man, who was examining Adolph through an eye-glass.

"Well, I was wanting a valet, and I heard that St. Clare's lot was going. I thought I'd just look at his"—

"Catch me ever buying any of St. Clare's people! Spoilt niggers, every one. Impudent as the devil!" said the other.

"Never fear that!" said the first. "If I get 'em, I'll soon have their airs out of them; they'll soon find that they've another kind of master to deal with than Monsieur St. Clare. 'Pon my word, I'll buy that fellow. I like the shape of him."

"You'll find it'll take all you've got to keep him. He's deucedly extravagant!"

"Yes, but my lord will find that he *can't* be extravagant with *me*. Just let him be sent to the calaboose a few times, and thoroughly dressed down! I'll tell you if it don't bring him to a sense of his ways! Oh, I'll reform him, up hill and down,—you'll see. I buy him, that's flat!"

Tom had been standing wistfully examining the multitude of faces thronging around him, for one whom he would wish to call master. And if you should ever be under the necessity, sir, of selecting, out of two hundred men, one who was to become your absolute owner and disposer, you would, perhaps, realize, just as Tom did, how few there were that you would feel at all comfortable in being made over to. Tom saw abundance of men, great, burly, gruff men; little, chirping, dried men; long-favored, lank, hard men; and every variety of stubbed-looking, commonplace men, who pick up their fellow-men as one picks up chips, putting them into the fire or a basket with equal unconcern, according to their convenience; but he saw no St. Clare.

A little before the sale commenced, a short, broad, muscular man, in a checked shirt considerably open at the bosom, and pantaloons much the worse for dirt and wear, elbowed his way through the crowd, like one who is going actively into a business; and, coming up to the group, began to examine them systematically. From the moment that Tom saw him approaching, he felt an immediate and revolting horror at him, that increased as he came near. He was evidently, though short, of gigantic strength. His round, bullet-head, large, light-gray eyes, with their shaggy, sandy eyebrows, and stiff, wiry, sunburned hair, were rather unprepossessing items, it is to be confessed; his large, coarse mouth was distended with tobacco, the juice of which, from time to time, he ejected from him with great decision and explosive force; his hands were immensely large, hairy, sunburned, freckled, and very dirty, and garnished with long nails, in a very foul condition. This man proceeded to a very free personal examination of the lot. He seized Tom by the jaw, and pulled open his mouth to inspect his teeth; made him strip up his sleeve, to show his muscle; turned him round, made him jump and spring, to show his paces.

"Where was you raised?" he added, briefly, to these investigations.

"In Kintuck, Mas'r," said Tom, looking about, as if for deliverance.

"What have you done?"

"Had care of Mas'r's farm," said Tom.

"Likely story!" said the other, shortly, as he passed on. He paused a moment before Dolph; then spitting a discharge of tobacco-juice on his well-blacked boots, and giving a contemptuous umph, he walked on. Again he stopped before Susan and Emmeline. He put out his heavy, dirty hand, and drew the girl towards him; passed it over her neck and bust, felt her arms, looked at her teeth, and then pushed her back against her mother, whose patient face showed the suffering she had been going through at every motion of the hideous stranger.

The girl was frightened, and began to cry.

"Stop that, you minx!" said the salesman; "no whimpering here,—the sale is going to begin." And accordingly the sale began.

Adolph was knocked off, at a good sum, to the young gentleman who had previously stated his intention of buying him; and the other servants of the St. Clare lot went to various bidders.

"Now, up with you, boy! d'ye hear?" said the auctioneer to Tom.

Tom stepped upon the block, gave a few anxious looks round; all seemed mingled in a common, indistinct noise,—the clatter of the salesman crying off his qualifications in French and English, the quick fire of French and English bids; and almost in a moment came the final thump of the hammer, and the clear ring on the last syllable of the word "*dollars*," as the auctioneer announced his price, and Tom was made over.—He had a master.

He was pushed from the block; the short, bullet-headed man, seizing him roughly by the shoulder, pushed him to one side, saying, in a harsh voice, "Stand there, *you!*"

Tom hardly realized anything; but still the bidding went on,—rattling, clattering, now French, now English. Down goes the hammer again,—Susan is sold! She goes down from the block, stops, looks wistfully back,—her daughter stretches her hands towards her. She looks with agony in the face of the man who has bought her,—a respectable, middle-aged man, of benevolent countenance.

"Oh, Mas'r, please do buy my daughter!"

"I'd like to, but I'm afraid I can't afford it!" said the gentleman, looking, with painful interest, as the young girl mounted the block, and looked around her with a frightened and timid glance.

The blood flushes painfully in her otherwise colorless cheek, her eye has a feverish fire, and her mother groans to see that she looks more beautiful than she ever saw her before. The auctioneer sees his advantage, and expatiates volubly in mingled French and English, and bids rise in rapid succession.

"I'll do anything in reason," said the benevolent-looking gentleman, pressing in and joining with the bids. In a few moments they have run beyond his purse. He is silent; the auctioneer grows warmer; but bids gradually drop off. It lies now between an aristocratic old citizen and our bullet-headed acquaintance. The citizen bids for a few turns, contemptuously measuring his opponent; but the bullet-head has the advantage over him, both in obstinacy and concealed length of purse, and the controversy lasts but a moment; the hammer falls,—he has got the girl, body and soul, unless God help her.

Her master is Mr. Legree, who owns a cotton plantation on the Red River. She is pushed along into the same lot with Tom and two other men, and goes off, weeping as she goes.

The benevolent gentleman is sorry; but, then, the thing happens every day! One sees girls and mothers crying, at these sales, *always*! it can't be helped, etc.; and he walks off, with his acquisition, in another direction.

Two days after, the lawyer of the Christian firm of B. & Co., New York, sent on their money to them. On the reverse of that draft, so obtained, let them write these words of the great Paymaster, to whom they shall make up their account in a future day: *"When he maketh inquisition for blood, he forgetteth not the cry of the humble!"*

Chapter XXXIII.
Cassy.

"And behold, the tears of such as were oppressed, and they had no comforter, and on the side of their oppressors there was *power*, but they had no comforter."—
Eccl. iv. 1.

IT took but a short time to familiarize Tom with all that was to be hoped or feared in his new way of life. He was an expert and efficient workman in whatever he undertook, and was, both from habit and principle, prompt and faithful. Quiet and peaceable in his disposition, he hoped, by unremitting diligence, to avert from himself at least a portion of the evils of his condition. He saw enough of abuse and misery to make him sick and weary; but he determined to toil on, with religious patience, committing himself to Him that judgeth righteously, not without hope that some way of escape might yet be opened to him.

Legree took silent note of Tom's availability. He rated him as a first-class hand; and yet he felt a secret dislike to him,—the native antipathy of bad to good. He saw plainly, that when, as was often the case, his violence and brutality fell on the helpless, Tom took notice of it; for so subtle is the atmosphere of opinion, that it will make itself felt, without words; and the opinion even of a slave may annoy a master. Tom in various ways manifested a tenderness of feeling, a commiseration for his fellow-sufferers, strange and new to them, which was watched with a jealous eye by Legree. He had purchased Tom with a view of eventually making him a sort of overseer, with whom he might, at times, intrust his affairs, in short absences; and, in his view, the first, second, and third requisite for that place was *hardness*. Legree made up his mind, that, as Tom was not hard to his hand, he would harden him forthwith; and some few weeks after Tom had been on the place, he determined to commence the process.

One morning, when the hands were mustered for the field, Tom noticed, with surprise, a new-comer among them, whose appearance excited his attention. It was a woman, tall and slenderly formed, with remarkably delicate hands and feet, and dressed in neat and respectable garments. By the appearance of her face, she might have been between thirty-five and forty; and it was a face that, once seen, could never be forgotten,—one of those that, at a glance, seem to convey to us an idea of a wild, painful, and romantic history. Her forehead was high, and her eyebrows marked with beautiful clearness. Her straight, well-formed nose, her finely cut mouth, and the graceful contour of her head and neck, showed that she must once have been beautiful; but her face was deeply wrinkled with lines of pain, and of proud and bitter endurance. Her complexion was sallow and unhealthy, her cheeks thin, her features sharp, and her whole form emaciated. But her eye was the most remarkable feature,—so large, so heavily black, overshadowed by long lashes of equal darkness, and so wildly, mournfully despairing. There was a fierce pride and defiance in every line of her face, in every curve of the flexible lip, in every motion of her body; but in her eye was a deep, settled night of anguish,—an expression so hopeless and unchanging as to contrast fearfully with the scorn and pride expressed by her whole demeanor.

Where she came from, or who she was, Tom did not know. The first he did know, she was walking by his side, erect and proud, in the dim gray of the dawn. To the gang, however, she was known; for there was much looking and turning of heads, and a smothered yet apparent exultation among the miserable, ragged, half-starved creatures by whom she was surrounded.

"Got to come to it, at last,—glad of it!" said one.

"He! he! he!" said another, "you'll know how good it is, Misse!"

"We'll see her work!"

"Wonder if she'll get a cutting up, at night, like the rest of us!"

"I'd be glad to see her down for a flogging, I'll bound!" said another.

The woman took no notice of these taunts, but walked on, with the same expression of angry scorn, as if she heard nothing. Tom had always lived among refined and cultivated people, and he felt intuitively, from her air and bearing, that she belonged to that class; but how or why she could be fallen to those degrading circumstances, he could not tell. The woman neither looked at him nor spoke to him, though, all the way to the field, she kept close at his side.

Tom was soon busy at his work; but, as the woman was at no great distance from him, he often glanced an eye to her, at her work. He saw, at a glance, that a native adroitness and handiness made the task to her an easier one than it proved to many. She picked very fast and very clean, and with an air of scorn, as if she despised both the work and the disgrace and humiliation of the circumstances in which she was placed.

In the course of the day, Tom was working near the mulatto woman who had been bought in the same lot with himself. She was evidently in a condition of great suffering, and Tom often heard her praying, as she wavered and trembled, and seemed about to fall down. Tom silently, as he came near to her, transferred several handfuls of cotton from his own sack to hers.

"Oh, don't, don't!" said the woman, looking surprised; "it'll get you into trouble."

Just then Sambo came up. He seemed to have a special spite against this woman; and, flourishing his whip, said, in brutal, guttural tones, "What dis yer, Luce,—foolin' a'?" and, with the word, kicking the woman with his heavy cowhide shoe, he struck Tom across the face with his whip.

Tom silently resumed his task; but the woman, before at the last point of exhaustion, fainted.

"I'll bring her to!" said the driver, with a brutal grin. "I'll give her something better than camphire!" and, taking a pin from his coat-sleeve, he buried it to the head in her flesh. The woman groaned, and half rose. "Get up, you beast, and work, will yer, or I'll show yer a trick more!"

The woman seemed stimulated, for a few moments, to an unnatural strength, and worked with desperate eagerness.

"See that you keep to dat ar," said the man, "or yer'll wish yer's dead to-night, I reckin!"

"That I do now!" Tom heard her say; and again he heard her say, "O Lord, how long! O Lord, why don't you help us?"

At the risk of all that he might suffer, Tom came forward again, and put all the cotton in his sack into the woman's.

"Oh, you mustn't! you donno what they'll do to ye!" said the woman.

"I can bar it!" said Tom, "better'n you;" and he was at his place again. It passed in a moment.

Suddenly, the stranger woman whom we have described, and who had, in the course of her work, come near enough to hear Tom's last words, raised her heavy black eyes, and fixed them, for a second, on him; then, taking a quantity of cotton from her basket, she placed it in his.

"You know nothing about this place," she said, "or you wouldn't have done that. When you've been here a month, you'll be done helping anybody; you'll find it hard enough to take care of your own skin!"

"The Lord forbid, Missis!" said Tom, using instinctively to his field companion the respectful form proper to the high bred with whom he had lived.

"The Lord never visits these parts," said the woman bitterly, as she went nimbly forward with her work; and again the scornful smile curled her lips.

But the action of the woman had been seen by the driver, across the field; and flourishing his whip, he came up to her.

"What! what!" he said to the woman, with an air of triumph, "YOU a foolin'? Go along! yer under me now,—mind yourself or yer'll cotch it!"

A glance like sheet-lightning suddenly flashed from those black eyes; and, facing about, with quivering lip and dilated nostrils, she drew herself up, and fixed a glance, blazing with rage and scorn, on the driver.

"Dog!" she said, "touch *me*, if you dare! I've power enough, yet, to have you torn by the dogs, burnt alive, cut to inches! I've only to say the word!"

"What de devil you here for, den!" said the man, evidently cowed, and sullenly retreating a step or two. "Didn't mean no harm, Misse Cassy!"

"Keep your distance, then!" said the woman. And, in truth, the man seemed greatly inclined to attend to something at the other end of the field, and started off in quick time.

The woman suddenly turned to her work, and labored with a dispatch that was perfectly astonishing to Tom. She seemed to work by magic. Before the day was through, her basket was filled, crowded down, and piled, and she had several times put largely into Tom's. Long after dusk, the whole weary train, with their baskets on their heads, defiled up to the building appropriated to the storing and weighing the cotton. Legree was there, busily conversing with the two drivers.

"Dat ar Tom's gwine to make a powerful deal o' trouble; kept a puttin' into Lucy's basket.—One o' these yer dat will get all der niggers to feelin' 'bused, if Mas'r don't watch him!" said Sambo.

"Hey-dey! The black cuss!" said Legree. "He'll have to get a breakin' in, won't he, boys?"

Both Negroes grinned a horrid grin at this intimation.

"Ay, ay! let Mas'r Legree alone, for breakin' in! De debil heself couldn't beat Mas'r at dat!" said Quimbo.

"Wal, boys, the best way is to give him the flogging to do, till he gets over his notions. Break him in!"

"Lord, Mas'r'll have hard work to get dat out o' him!"

"It'll have to come out of him, though!" said Legree, as he rolled his tobacco in his mouth.

"Now, dar's Lucy,—de aggravatinest, ugliest wench on de place!" pursued Sambo.

"Take care, Sam; I shall begin to think what's the reason for your spite agin Lucy."

"Well, Mas'r knows she sot herself up agin Mas'r, and wouldn't have me, when he telled her to."

"I'd a flogged her into 't," said Legree, spitting, "only there's such a press o' work, it don't seem wuth a while to upset her jist now. She's slender; but these yer slender gals will bear half killin' to get their own way!"

"Wal, Lucy was real aggravatin' and lazy, sulkin' round; wouldn't do nothin',—and Tom he tuck up for her."

"He did, eh! Wal, then, Tom shall have the pleasure of flogging her. It'll be a good practice for him, and he won't put it on to the gal like you devils, neither."

"Ho, ho! haw! haw! haw!" laughed both the sooty wretches; and the diabolical sounds seemed, in truth, a not unapt expression of the fiendish character which Legree gave them.

"Wal, but, Mas'r, Tom and Misse Cassy, and dey among 'em, filled Lucy's basket. I ruther guess der weight's in it, Mas'r!"

"*I do the weighing!*" said Legree, emphatically.

Both the drivers laughed again their diabolical laugh.

"So!" he added, "Misse Cassy did her day's work."

"She picks like de debil and all his angels!"

"She's got 'em all in her, I believe!" said Legree; and growling a brutal oath, he proceeded to the weighing-room.

Slowly the weary, dispirited creatures wound their way into the room, and, with crouching reluctance, presented their baskets to be weighed.

Legree noted on a slate, on the side of which was pasted a list of names, the amount.

Tom's basket was weighed and approved; and he looked, with an anxious glance, for the success of the woman he had befriended.

Tottering with weakness, she came forward, and delivered her basket. It was of full weight, as Legree well perceived; but, affecting anger, he said,—

"What, you lazy beast! short again! stand aside, you'll catch it, pretty soon!"

The woman gave a groan of utter despair, and sat down on a board.

The person who had been called Misse Cassy now came forward, and, with a haughty, negligent air, delivered her basket. As she delivered it, Legree looked in her eyes with a sneering yet inquiring glance.

She fixed her black eyes steadily on him, her lips moved slightly, and she said something in French. What it was, no one knew, but Legree's face became perfectly demoniacal in its expression, as she spoke; he half raised his hand as if to strike,—a gesture which she regarded with fierce disdain as she turned and walked away.

"And now," said Legree, "come here, you Tom. You see, I told ye I didn't buy ye jest for the common work; I mean to promote ye, and make a driver of ye; and to-night ye may jest as well begin to get yer hand in. Now, ye jest take this yer gal and flog her; ye've seen enough on 't to know how."

"I beg Mas'r's pardon," said Tom; "hopes Mas'r won't set me at that. It's what I an't used to,—never did,—and can't do, no way possible."

"Ye'll larn a pretty smart chance of things ye never did know, before I've done with ye!" said Legree, taking up a cowhide, and striking Tom a heavy blow across the cheek, and following up the infliction by a shower of blows.

"There!" he said, as he stopped to rest; "now will ye tell me ye can't do it?"

"Yes, Mas'r," said Tom, putting up his hand, to wipe the blood that trickled down his face. "I'm willin' to work night and day, and work while there's life and breath in me; but this yer thing I can't feel it right to do; and, Mas'r, I *never* shall do it,—*never!*"

Tom had a remarkably smooth, soft voice, and a habitually respectful manner, that had given Legree an idea that he would be cowardly, and easily subdued. When he spoke these last words, a thrill of amazement went through every one; the poor woman clasped her hands and said, "O Lord!" and every one involuntarily looked at each other, and drew in their breath, as if to prepare for the storm that was about to burst.

Legree looked stupefied and confounded; but at last burst forth,—

"What! ye blasted black beast! tell *me* ye don't think it *right* to do what I tell ye! What have any of you cussed cattle to do with thinking what's right? I'll put a stop to it! Why, what do ye think ye are? May be ye think ye're a gentleman, master Tom, to be a telling your master what's right, and what an't! So you pretend it's wrong to flog the gal!"

"I think so, Mas'r," said Tom; "the poor crittur's sick and feeble; 't would be downright cruel, and it's what I never will do, nor begin to. Mas'r, if you mean to kill me, kill me; but, as to my raising my hand agin any one here, I never shall,—I'll die first!"

Tom spoke in a mild voice, but with a decision that could not be mistaken. Legree shook with anger; his greenish eyes glared fiercely, and his very whiskers seemed to curl with passion; but, like some ferocious beast, that plays with its victim before he devours it, he kept back his strong impulse to proceed to immediate violence, and broke out into bitter raillery.

"Well, here's a pious dog, at last, let down among us sinners!—a saint, a gentleman, and no less, to talk to us sinners about our sins! Powerful holy crittur, he must be! Here, you rascal, you make believe to be so pious,—didn't you never hear, out of yer Bible, 'Servants, obey yer masters'? An't I yer, master? Didn't I pay down twelve hundred dollars, cash, for all there is inside yer old cussed black shell? An't yer mine, now, body and soul?" he said, giving Tom a violent kick with his heavy boot; "tell me!"

In the very depth of physical suffering, bowed by brutal oppression, this question shot a gleam of joy and triumph through Tom's soul. He suddenly stretched himself up, and, looking earnestly to heaven, while the tears and blood that flowed down his face mingled, he exclaimed,—

"No! no! no! my soul an't yours, Mas'r! You haven't bought it,—ye can't buy it! It's been bought and paid for, by one that is able to keep it;—no matter, no matter, you can't harm me!"

"I can't!" said Legree, with a sneer, "we'll see,—we'll see! Here, Sambo, Quimbo, give this dog such a breakin' in as he won't get over, this month!"

The two gigantic Negroes that now laid hold of Tom, with fiendish exultation in their faces, might have formed no unapt personification of the powers of darkness. The poor woman screamed with apprehension, and all rose, as by a general impulse, while they dragged him unresisting from the place.

Chapter XL.
The Martyr.

"Deem not the just by Heaven forgot!
Though life its common gifts deny,—
Though, with a crushed and bleeding heart,
And spurned of man, he goes to die!
For God hath marked each sorrowing day,
And numbered every bitter tear;
And heaven's long years of bliss shall pay
For all his children suffer here."
                                    —*Bryant.*

THE longest way must have its close,—the gloomiest night will wear on to a morning. An eternal, inexorable lapse of moments is ever hurrying the day of the evil to an eternal night, and the night of the just to an eternal day. We have walked with our humble friend thus far in the valley of slavery; first through flowery fields of ease and indulgence, then through heart-breaking separations from all that man holds dear. Again, we have waited with him in a sunny island, where generous hands concealed his chains with flowers; and, lastly, we have followed him when the last ray of earthly hope went out in night, and seen how, in the blackness of earthly darkness, the firmament of the unseen has blazed with stars of new and significant lustre.

The morning star now stands over the tops of the mountains, and gales and breezes, not of earth, show that the gates of day are unclosing.

The escape of Cassy and Emmeline irritated the before surly temper of Legree to the last degree; and his fury, as was to be expected, fell upon the defenceless head of Tom. When he hurriedly announced the tidings among his hands, there was a sudden light in Tom's eye, a sudden upraising of his hands, that did not escape him. He saw that he did not join the muster of the pursuers. He thought of forcing him to do it; but having had, of old, experience of his inflexibility when commanded to take part in any deed of inhumanity, he would not, in his hurry, stop to enter into any conflict with him.

Tom, therefore, remained behind, with a few who had learned of him to pray, and offered up prayers for the escape of the fugitives.

When Legree returned, baffled and disappointed, all the long-working hatred of his soul towards his slave began to gather in a deadly and desperate form. Had not this man braved him,—steadily, powerfully, resistlessly,—ever since he bought him? Was there not a spirit in him which, silent as it was, burned on him like the fires of perdition?

"I *hate* him!" said Legree, that night as he sat up in his bed; "I *hate* him! And isn't he MINE? Can't I do what I like with him? Who's to hinder, I wonder?" And Legree clenched his fist, and shook it, as if he had something in his hands that he could rend in pieces.

But, then, Tom was a faithful, valuable servant; and, although Legree hated him the more for that, yet the consideration was still somewhat of a restraint to him.

The next morning, he determined to say nothing, as yet; to assemble a party, from some neighboring plantations, with dogs and guns; to surround the swamp, and go about the hunt systematically. If it succeeded, well and good; if not he would summon Tom before him, and—his teeth clenched and his blood boiled—*then* he would break that fellow down, or— there was a dire inward whisper, to which his soul assented.

Ye say that the *interest* of the master is a sufficient safeguard for the slave. In the fury of man's mad will, he will wittingly, and with open eye, sell his own soul to the devil to gain his ends; and will he be more careful of his neighbor's body?

"Well," said Cassy, the next day, from the garret, as she reconnoitred through the knothole, "the hunt's going to begin again, to-day!"

Three or four mounted horsemen were curvetting about, on the space front of the house; and one or two leashes of strange dogs were struggling with the Negroes who held them, baying and barking at each other.

The men are, two of them, overseers of plantations in the vicinity; and others were some of Legree's associates at the tavern-bar of a neighboring city, who had come for the interest of the sport. A more hard-favored set, perhaps, could not be imagined. Legree was serving brandy, profusely, round among them, as also among the Negroes, who had been detailed from the various plantations for this service; for it was an object to make every service of this kind, among the Negroes, as much of a holiday as possible.

Cassy placed her ear at the knot-hole; and, as the morning air blew directly towards the house, she could overhear a good deal of the conversation. A grave sneer overcast the dark, severe gravity of her face, as she listened, and heard them divide out the gound, discuss the rival merits of the dogs, give orders about firing, and the treatment of each, in case of capture.

Cassy drew back; and, clasping her hands, looked upward, and said, "Oh great Almighty God! we are *all* sinners, but what have *we* done, more than all the rest of the world, that we should be treated so?"

There was a terrible earnestness in her face and voice, as she spoke.

"If it wasn't for *you*, child," she said, looking at Emmeline, "I'd *go* out to them; and I'd thank any one of them that *would* shoot me down; for what use will freedom be to me? Can it give me back my children, or make me what I used to be?"

Emmeline, in her childlike simplicity, was half afraid of the dark moods of Cassy. She looked perplexed, but made no answer. She only took her hand, with a gentle, caressing movement.

"Don't!" said Cassy, trying to draw it away; "you'll get me to loving you; and I never mean to love anything, again!"

"Poor Cassy!" said Emmeline, "don't feel so! If the Lord gives us liberty, perhaps he'll give you back your daughter; at any rate, I'll be like a daughter to you. I know I'll never see my poor old mother again! I shall love you, Cassy, whether you love me or not!"

The gentle, childlike spirit conquered. Cassy sat down by her, put her arm around her neck, stroked her soft, brown hair and Emmeline then wondered at the beauty of her magnificent eyes, now soft with tears.

"Oh, Em!" said Cassy, "I've hungered for my children, and thirsted for them, and my eyes fail with longing for them! Here! here!" she said, striking her breast, "it's all desolate, all empty! If God would give me back my children, then I could pray."

"You must trust him, Cassy," said Emmeline; "he is our Father!"

"His wrath is upon us," said Cassy; "he has turned away in anger."

"No, Cassy! He will be good to us! Let us hope in him," said Emmeline,—"I always have had hope."

The hunt was long, animated, and thorough, but unsuccessful; and with grave, ironic exultation, Cassy looked down on Legree, as, weary and dispirited, he alighted from his horse.

"Now, Quimbo," said Legree, as he stretched himself down in the sitting-room, "you jest go and walk that Tom up here, right away! The old cuss is at the bottom of this yer whole matter; and I'll have it out of his old black hide, or I'll know the reason why."

Sambo and Quimbo, both, though hating each other, were joined in one mind by a no less cordial hatred of Tom. Legree had told them, at first, that he had bought him for a general overseer, in his absence; and this had begun an ill will on their part, which had increased, in their debased and servile natures, as they saw him becoming obnoxious to their master's displeasure. Quimbo, therefore, departed, with a will, to execute his orders.

Tom heard the message with a forewarning heart; for he knew all the plan of the fugitives' escape, and the place of their present concealment; he knew the deadly character of the man he had to deal with, and his despotic power. But he felt strong in God to meet death, rather than betray the helpless.

He set his basket down by the row, and, looking up, said, "Into thy hands I commend my spirit! Thou hast redeemed me, O Lord God of truth!" and then quietly yielded himself to the rough, brutal grasp with which Quimbo seized him.

"Ay, ay!" said the giant, as he dragged him along; "ye'll cotch it, now! I'll boun' Mas'r's back's up *high*! No sneaking out, now! Tell ye, ye'll get it, and no mistake! See how ye'll look, now, helpin' Mas'r's niggers to run away! See what ye'll get!"

The savage words none of them reached that ear!—a higher voice there was saying, "Fear not them that kill the body, and, after that, have no more that they can do." Nerve and bone of that poor man's body vibrated to those words, as if touched by the finger of God; and he felt the strength of a thousand souls in one. As he passed along, the trees and bushes, the huts of his servitude, the whole scene of his degradation, seemed to whirl by him as the landscape by the rushing car. His soul throbbed,—his home was in sight,—and the hour of release seemed at hand.

"Well, Tom!" said Legree, walking up, and seizing him grimly by the collar of his coat, and speaking through his teeth, in a paroxysm of determined rage "do you know I've made up my mind to KILL you?"

"It's very likely, Mas'r," said Tom, calmly.

"I *have*," said Legree, with grim, terrible calmness, "*done—just—that—thing*, Tom, unless you'll tell me what you know about these yer gals!"

Tom stood silent.

"D'ye hear?" said Legree, stamping, with a roar like that of an incensed lion. "Speak!"

"*I han't got nothing to tell, Mas'r*," said Tom, with a slow, firm, deliberate utterance.

"Do you dare to tell me, ye old black Christian, ye don't *know*?" said Legree.

Tom was silent.

"Speak!" thundered Legree, striking him furiously. "Do you know anything?"

"I know, Mas'r; but I can't tell anything. *I can die!*"

Legree drew in a long breath; and, suppressing his rage, took Tom by the arm, and, approaching his face almost to his, said in a terrible voice, "Hark 'e Tom!—ye think, 'cause

I've let you off before, I don't mean what I say; but, this time, I've *made up my mind,* and counted the cost. You've always stood it out agin me: now, I'll *conquer ye or kill ye!*—one or t' other. I'll count every drop of blood there is in you, and take 'em, one by one, till ye give up!"

Tom looked up to his master, and answered, "Mas'r, if you was sick, or in trouble, or dying, and I could save ye, I'd *give* ye my heart's blood; and, if taking every drop of blood in this poor old body would save your precious soul. I'd give 'em freely, as the Lord gave his for me. Oh, Mas'r! don't bring this great sin on your soul! It will hurt you more than 't will me! Do the worst you can, my troubles'll be over soon; but, if ye don't repent, yours won't *never* end!"

Like a strange snatch of heavenly music, heard in the lull of a tempest, this burst of feeling made a moment's blank pause. Legree stood aghast, and looked at Tom; and there was such a silence that the tick of the old clock could be heard, measuring, with silent touch, the last moments of mercy and probation to that hardened heart.

It was but a moment. There was one hesitating pause,—one, irresolute, relenting thrill,— and the spirit of evil came back, with sevenfold vehemence; and Legree, foaming with rage, smote his victim to the ground.

Scenes of blood and cruelty are shocking to our ear and heart. What man has nerve to do, man has not nerve to hear. What brother-man and brother-Christian must suffer, cannot be told us, even in our secret chamber, it so harrows up the soul! And yet, oh, my country! these things are done under the shadow of thy laws! O Christ! thy church sees them, almost in silence!

But, of old, there was One whose suffering changed an instrument of torture, degradation, and shame, into a symbol of glory, honor, and immortal life; and, where his spirit is, neither degrading stripes, nor blood, nor insults, can make the Christian's last struggle less than glorious.

Was he alone, that long night, whose brave, loving spirit was bearing up, in that old shed, against buffeting and brutal stripes?

Nay! There stood by him ONE,—seen by him alone,—"like unto the Son of God."

The tempter stood by him, too,—blinded by furious, despotic will,—every moment pressing him to shun that agony by the betrayal of the innocent. But the brave, true heart was firm on the Eternal Rock. Like his Master, he knew that, if he saved others, himself he could not save; nor could utmost extremity wring from him words, save of prayer and holy trust.

"He's most gone, Mas'r," said Sambo, touched, in spite of himself, by the patience of his victim.

"Pay away, till he gives up! Give it to him!—give it to him!" shouted Legree. "I'll take every drop of blood he has, unless he confesses!"

Tom opened his eyes, and looked upon his master. "Ye poor miserable crittur!" he said, "there an't no more ye can do! I forgive ye, with all my soul!" and he fainted entirely away.

"I b'lieve, my soul, he's done for, finally," said Legree, stepping forward, to look at him "Yes, he is! Well, his mouth's shut up, at last,—that's one comfort!"

Yes, Legree; but who shall shut up that voice in thy soul? that soul, past repentance, past prayer, past hope, in whom the fire that never shall be quenched is already burning!

Yet Tom was not quite gone. His wondrous words and pious prayers had struck upon the hearts of the imbruted blacks, who had been the instruments of cruelty upon him; and, the instant Legree withdrew, they took him down, and, in their ignorance, sought to call him back to life,—as if *that* were any favor to him.

"Sartin, we's been doin' a drefful wicked thing!" said Sambo; "hopes Mas'r'll have to 'count for it, and not we."

They washed his wounds,—they provided a rude bed, of some refuse cotton, for him to lie down on; and one of them, stealing up to the house, begged a drink of brandy of Legree, pretending that he was tired, and wanted it for himself. He brought it back and poured it down Tom's throat.

"Oh, Tom!" said Quimbo, "we's been awful wicked to ye!"

"I forgive ye, with all my heart!" said Tom, faintly.

"Oh, Tom! do tell us who is *Jesus*, anyhow?" said Sambo,—"Jesus, that's been a standin' by you so, all this night?—Who is he?"

The word roused the failing, fainting spirit. He poured forth a few energetic sentences of that wondrous One,—his life, his death, his everlasting presence, and power to save.

They wept,—both the two savage men.

"Why didn't I never hear this before?" said Sambo; "but I do believe!—I can't help it! Lord Jesus, have mercy on us!"

"Poor critturs!" said Tom, "I'd be willin' to bar all I have, if it'll only bring ye to Christ! O Lord! give me these two more souls, I pray!"

That prayer was answered.

Chapter XLI.
The Young Master.

TWO days after, a young man drove a light wagon up through the avenue of China-trees, and, throwing the reins hastily on the horses' necks, sprang out and inquired for the owner of the place.

It was George Shelby; and, to show how he came to be there, we must go back in our story.

The letter of Miss Ophelia to Mrs. Shelby had, by some unfortunate accident, been detained, for a month or two, at some remote post-office, before it reached its destination; and, of course, before it was received, Tom was already lost to view among the distant swamps of the Red River.

Mrs. Shelby read the intelligence with the deepest concern; but any immediate action upon it was an impossibility. She was then in attendance on the sick-bed of her husband, who lay delirious in the crisis of a fever. Master George Shelby, who, in the interval, had changed from a boy to a tall young man, was her constant and faithful assistant, and her only reliance in superintending his father's affairs. Miss Ophelia had taken the precaution to send them the name of the lawyer who did business for the St. Clares; and the most that, in the emergency, could be done, was to address a letter of inquiry to him. The sudden death of Mr. Shelby, a few days after, brought, of course, an absorbing pressure of other interests for a season.

Mr. Shelby showed his confidence in his wife's ability, by appointing her sole executrix upon his estates; and thus immediately a large and complicated amount of business was brought upon her hands.

Mrs. Shelby, with characteristic energy, applied herself to the work of straightening the entangled web of affairs; and she and George were for some time occupied with collecting and examining accounts, selling property, and settling debts; for Mrs. Shelby was determined that everything should be brought into tangible and recognizable shape, let the consequences to her prove what they might. In the mean time, they received a letter from the lawyer to whom Miss Ophelia had referred them, saying that he knew nothing of the matter: that the man was sold at a public auction, and that, beyond receiving the money, he knew nothing of the affair.

Neither George nor Mrs. Shelby could be easy at this result; and accordingly some six months after, the latter, having business for his mother, down the river, resolved to visit New Orleans, in person, and push his inquiries, in hopes of discovering Tom's whereabouts, and restoring him.

After some months of unsuccessful search, by the merest accident, George fell in with a man, in New Orleans, who happened to be possessed of the desired information; and with his money in his pocket, our hero took steamboat for Red River, resolving to find out and repurchase his old friend.

He was soon introduced into the house, where he found Legree in the sitting-room.

Legree received the stranger with a kind of surly hospitality.

"I understand," said the young man, "that you bought, in New Orleans, a boy, named Tom. He used to be on my father's place, and I came to see if I couldn't buy him back."

Legree's brow grew dark, and he broke out, passionately: "Yes, I did buy such a fellow,—and a h—l of a bargain I had of it, too! The most rebellious, saucy, impudent dog! Set up my niggers to run away; got off two gals, worth eight hundred or a thousand dollars apiece. He owned to that, and, when I bid him tell me where they was, he up and said he knew, but he wouldn't tell; and stood to it, though I gave him the cussedest flogging I ever gave nigger yet. I b'lieve he's trying to die; but I don't know as he'll make it out."

"Where is he?" said George, impetuously. "Let me see him." The cheeks of the young man were crimson, and his eyes flashed fire; but he prudently said nothing, as yet.

"He's in dat ar shed," said a little fellow, who stood holding George's horse.

Legree kicked the boy, and swore at him; but George, without saying another word, turned and strode to the spot.

Tom had been lying two days since the fatal night; not suffering, for every nerve of suffering was blunted and destroyed. He lay, for the most part, in a quiet stupor; for the laws of a powerful and well-knit frame would not at once release the imprisoned spirit. By stealth, there had been there, in the darkness of the night, poor desolated creatures, who stole from their scanty hours' rest, that they might repay to him some of those ministrations of love in which he had always been so abundant. Truly, those poor disciples had little to give,—only the cup of cold water; but it was given with full hearts.

Tears had fallen on that honest, insensible face,—tears of late repentance in the poor, ignorant heathen, whom his dying love and patience had awakened to repentance, and bitter prayers, breathed over him to a late-found Saviour, of whom they scarce knew more than the name, but whom the yearning ignorant heart of man never implores in vain.

Cassy, who had glided out of her place of concealment, and, by overhearing, learned the sacrifice that had been made for her and Emmeline, had been there, the night before, defying the danger of detection; and, moved by the few last words which the affectionate soul had yet strength to breathe, the long winter of despair, the ice of years, had given way, and the dark, despairing woman had wept and prayed.

When George entered the shed, he felt his head giddy and his heart sick.

"Is it possible,—is it possible?" said he, kneeling down by him. "Uncle Tom, my poor, poor old friend!"

Something in the voice penetrated to the ear of the dying. He moved his head gently, smiled, and said,—

> "Jesus can make a dying bed
> Feel soft as downy pillows are."

Tears which did honor to his manly heart fell from the young man's eyes, as he bent over his poor friend.

"Oh, dear Uncle Tom! do wake,—do speak once more! Look up! Here's Mas'r George—your own little Mas'r George. Don't you know me?"

"Mas'r George!" said Tom, opening his eyes, and speaking in a feeble voice. "Mas'r George!" He looked bewildered.

Slowly the idea seemed to fill his soul; and the vacant eye became fixed and brightened, the whole face lighted up, the hard hands clasped, and tears ran down the cheeks.

"Bless the Lord! it is,—it is,—it's all I wanted! They haven't forgot me. It warms my soul; it does my old heart good! Now I shall die content! Bless the Lord, oh, my soul!"

"You shan't die! you *mustn't* die, nor think of it. I've come to buy you, and take you home," said George, with impetuous vehemence.

"Oh, Mas'r George, ye're too late. The Lord's bought me, and is going to take me home,—and I long to go. Heaven is better than Kintuck."

"Oh don't die! It'll kill me!—it'll break my heart to think what you've suffered,—and lying in this old shed, here! Poor, poor fellow!"

"Don't call me poor fellow!" said Tom, solemnly. "I *have* been poor fellow; but that's all past and gone, now. I'm right in the door, going into glory! Oh, Mas'r George! *Heaven has come!* I've got the victory!—the Lord Jesus has given it to me! Glory be to his name!"

George was awe-struck at the force, the vehemence, the power, with which these broken sentences were uttered. He sat gazing in silence.

Tom grasped his hand, and continued,—"Ye mustn't, now, tell Chloe, poor soul! how ye found me;—'t would be so drefful to her. Only tell her ye found me going into glory; and that I couldn't stay for no one. And tell her the Lord's stood by me everywhere and al'ays, and made everything light and easy. And oh, the poor chil'en, and the baby!—my old heart's been most broke for 'em, time and agin! Tell 'em all to follow me—follow me! Give my love to Mas'r, and dear good Missis, and everybody in the place! Ye don't know! 'Pears like I loves 'em all! I loves every creatur' everywhar!—it's nothing *but* love! Oh, Mas'r George, what a thing 't is to be a Christian!"

At this moment, Legree sauntered up to the door of the shed, looked in, with a dogged air of affected carelessness, and turned away.

"The old Satan!" said George, in his indignation. "It's a comfort to think the devil will pay *him* for this, some of these days!"

"Oh, don't!—Oh, ye mustn't!" said Tom, grasping his hand; "he's a poor mis'able crittur! it's awful to think on 't! Oh, if he only could repent, the Lord would forgive him now; but I'm 'feard he never will!"

"I hope he won't!" said George; "I never want to see *him* in heaven!"

"Hush, Mas'r George!—it worries me! Don't feel so! He an't done me no real harm,—only opened the gate of the kingdom for me; that's all!"

At this moment, the sudden flush of strength which the joy of meeting his young master had infused into the dying man gave way. A sudden sinking fell upon him; he closed his eyes; and that mysterious and sublime change passed over his face, that told the approach of other worlds.

He began to draw his breath with long, deep inspirations, and his broad chest rose and fell, heavily. The expression of his face was that of a conqueror.

"Who—who—who shall separate us from the love of Christ?" he said, in a voice that contended with mortal weakness; and, with a smile, he fell asleep.

George sat fixed with solemn awe. It seemed to him that the place was holy; and, as he closed the lifeless eyes, and rose up from the dead, only one thought possessed him,—that expressed by his simple old friend,—"What a thing it is to be a Christian!"

He turned; Legree was standing, sullenly, behind him.

Something in that dying scene had checked the natural fierceness of youthful passion. The presence of the man was simply loathsome to George; and he felt only an impulse to get away from him, with as few words as possible.

Fixing his keen dark eyes on Legree, he simply said, pointing to the dead, "You have got all you ever can of him. What shall I pay you for the body? I will take it away, and bury it decently."

"I don't sell dead niggers," said Legree, doggedly. "You are welcome to bury him where and when you like."

"Boys," said George, in an authoritative tone, to two or three Negroes, who were looking at the body, "help me lift him up, and carry him to my wagon; and get me a spade."

One of them ran for a spade; the other two assisted George to carry the body to the wagon.

George neither spoke to nor looked at Legree, who did not countermand his orders, but stood, whistling, with an air of forced unconcern. He sulkily followed them to where the wagon stood at the door.

George spread his cloak in the wagon, and had the body carefully disposed of in it,—moving the seat, so as to give it room. Then he turned, fixed his eyes on Legree, and said, with forced composure,—

"I have not, as yet, said to you what I think of this most atrocious affair;—this is not the time and place. But, sir, this innocent blood shall have justice. I will proclaim this murder. I will go to the very first magistrate and expose you."

"Do!" said Legree, snapping his fingers, scornfully. "I'd like to see you doing it. Where you going to get witnesses?—how you going to prove it?—Come, now!"

George saw, at once, the force of this defiance. There was not a white person on the place; and, in all southern courts, the testimony of colored blood is nothing. He felt, at that moment, as if he could have rent the heavens with his heart's indignant cry for justice; but in vain.

"After all, what a fuss, for a dead nigger!" said Legree.

The word was as a spark to a powder-magazine. Prudence was never a cardinal virtue of the Kentucky boy. George turned, and, with one indignant blow, knocked Legree flat upon his face; and, as he stood over him, blazing with wrath and defiance, he would have formed no bad personification of his great namesake triumphing over the dragon.

Some men, however, are decidedly bettered by being knocked down. If a man lays them fairly flat in the dust, they seem immediately to conceive a respect for him; and Legree was one of this sort. As he rose, therefore, and brushed the dust from his clothes, he eyed the slowly retreating wagon with some evident consideration; nor did he open his mouth till it was out of sight.

Beyond the boundaries of the plantation, George had noticed a dry, sandy knoll, shaded by a few trees; there they made the grave.

"Shall we take off the cloak, Mas'r?" said the Negroes, when the grave was ready.

"No, no,—bury it with him! It's all I can give you, now, poor Tom, and you shall have it."

They laid him in; and the men shovelled away, silently. They banked it up, and laid green turf over it.

"You may go, boys," said George, slipping a quarter into the hand of each. They lingered about, however.

"If young Mas'r would please buy us"—said one.

"We'd serve him so faithful!" said the other.

"Hard times here, Mas'r!" said the first. "Do, Mas'r, buy us, please!"

"I can't,—I can't!" said George, with difficulty, motioning them off; "it's impossible!"

The poor fellows looked dejected, and walked off in silence.

"Witness eternal God!" said George, kneeling on the grave of his poor friend; "Oh, witness that, from this hour, I will do *what one man can* to drive out this curse of slavery from my land!"

There is no monument to mark the last resting-place of our friend. He needs none! His Lord knows where he lies, and will raise him up, immortal, to appear with him when he shall appear in his glory.

Pity him not! Such a life and death is not for pity! Not in the riches of omnipotence is the chief glory of God; but in self-denying, suffering love! And blessed are the men whom he calls to fellowship with him, bearing their cross after him with patience. Of such it is written, "Blessed are they that mourn, for they shall be comforted."

Chapter XLIII.
Results.

THE rest of our story is soon told. George Shelby, interested, as any other young man might be, by the romance of the incident, no less than by feelings of humanity, was at the pains to send to Cassy the bill of sale of Eliza, whose date and name all corresponded with her own knowledge of facts, and left no doubt upon her mind as to the identity of her child. It remained now only for her to trace out the path of the fugitives.

Madame de Thoux and she, thus drawn together by the singular coincidence of their fortunes, proceeded immediately to Canada, and began a tour of inquiry among the stations, where the numerous fugitives from slavery are located. At Amherstburg they found the missionary with whom George and Eliza had taken shelter, on their first arrival in Canada; and through him were enabled to trace the family to Montreal.

George and Eliza had now been five years free. George had found constant occupation in the shop of a worthy machinist, where he had been earning a competent support for his family, which, in the mean time, had been increased by the addition of another daughter.

Little Harry—a fine bright boy—had been put to a good school, and was making rapid proficiency in knowledge.

The worthy pastor of the station, in Amherstburg, where George had first landed, was so much interested in the statements of Madame de Thoux and Cassy, that he yielded to the solicitations of the former, to accompany them to Montreal, in their search,—she bearing all the expense of the expedition.

The scene now changes to a small, neat tenement, in the outskirts of Montreal; the time, evening. A cheerful fire blazes on the hearth; a tea-table, covered with a snowy cloth, stands prepared for the evening meal. In one corner of the room was a table covered with a green cloth, where was an open writing-desk, pens, paper, and over it a shelf of well-selected books.

This was George's study. The same zeal for self-improvement, which led him to steal the much coveted arts of reading and writing, amid all the toils and discouragements of his early life, still led him to devote all his leisure time to self-cultivation.

At this present time, he is seated at the table, making notes from a volume of the family library he has been reading.

"Come George," says Eliza, "you've been gone all day. Do put down that book, and let's talk, while I'm getting tea,—do."

And little Eliza seconds the effort, by toddling up to her father, and trying to pull the book out of his hand and install herself on his knee as a substitute.

"Oh, you little witch!" says George, yielding, as, in such circumstances, man always must.

"That's right," says Eliza, as she begins to cut a loaf of bread. A little older she looks; her form a little fuller; her air more matronly than of yore; but evidently contented and happy as woman need be.

"Harry, my boy, how did you come on in that sum, today?" says George, as he laid his hand on his son's head.

Harry has lost his long curls; but he can never lose those eyes and eyelashes, and that fine, bold brow, that flushes with triumph, as he answers, "I did it, every bit of it, *myself*, father; and *nobody* helped me!"

"That's right," says his father; "depend on yourself, my son. You have a better chance than ever your poor father had."

At this moment, there is a rap at the door; and Eliza goes and opens it. The delighted— "Why!—this you?"—calls up her husband, and the good pastor of Amherstburg is welcomed. There are two women with him and Eliza asks them to sit down.

Now, if the truth must be told, the honest pastor had arranged a little programme, according to which this affair was to develop itself; and, on the way up, all had very cautiously and prudently exhorted each other not to let things out, except according to previous arrangement.

What was the good man's consternation, therefore, just as he had motioned to the ladies to be seated, and was taking out his pocket-handkerchief to wipe his mouth, so as to proceed to his introductory speech in good order, when Madame de Thoux upset the whole plan, by throwing her arms around George's neck, and letting all out at once, by saying, "Oh, George! don't you know me? I'm your sister Emily."

Cassy had seated herself more composedly, and would have carried on her part very well, had not little Eliza suddenly appeared before her in exact shape and form, every outline and curl, just as her daughter was when she saw her last. The little thing peered up in her face; and Cassy caught her up in her arms, pressed her to her bosom, saying, what at the moment she really believed, "Darling, I'm your mother!"

In fact, it was a troublesome matter to do up exactly in proper order; but the good pastor, at last, succeeded in getting everybody quiet, and delivering the speech with which he had intended to open the exercises; and in which, at last, he succeeded so well, that his whole audience were sobbing about him in a manner that ought to satisfy any orator, ancient or modern.

They knelt together, and the good man prayed,—for there are some feelings so agitated and tumultuous, that they can find rest only by being poured into the bosom of Almighty love,—and then, rising up, the new-found family embraced each other, with a holy trust in Him who from such peril and dangers, and by such unknown ways, had brought them together.

The note-book of a missionary, among the Canadian fugitives, contains truth stranger than fiction. How can it be otherwise, when a system prevails which whirls families and scatters their members, as the wind whirls and scatters the leaves of autumn? These shores of refuge, like the eternal shore, often unite again, in glad communion, hearts that for long years have mourned each other as lost. And affecting beyond expression is the earnestness with which every new arrival among them is met, if, perchance, it may bring tidings of mother, sister, child, or wife, still lost to view in the shadows of slavery.

Deeds of heroism are wrought here more than those of romance, when, defying torture, and braving death itself, the fugitive voluntarily threads his way back to the terrors and perils of that dark land, that he may bring out his sister, or mother, or wife.

One young man, of whom a missionary has told us, twice recaptured, and suffering shameful stripes for his heroism, had escaped again; and, in a letter which we heard read, tells his friends that he is going back a third time, that he may, at last, bring away his sister. My good sir, is this man a hero, or a criminal? Would not you do as much for your sister? And can you blame him?

But, to return to our friends, whom we left wiping their eyes, and recovering themselves from too great and sudden a joy. They are now seated around the social board, and are getting decidedly companionable; only that Cassy, who keeps little Eliza on her lap, occasionally squeezes the little thing, in a manner that rather astonishes her, and obstinately refuses to have her mouth stuffed with cake to the extent the little one desires,—alleging, what the child rather wonders at, that she has got something better than cake, and doesn't want it.

And, indeed, in two or three days, such a change has passed over Cassy, that our readers would scarcely know her. The despairing, haggard expression of her face had given way to one of gentle trust. She seemed to sink, at once, into the bosom of the family, and take the little ones into her heart, as something for which it long had waited. Indeed, her love seemed to flow more naturally to the little Eliza than to her own daughter; for she was the exact image and body of the child whom she had lost. The little one was a flowery bond between mother and daughter, through whom grew up acquaintanceship and affection. Eliza's steady, consistent piety, regulated by the constant reading of the sacred word, made her a proper guide for the shattered and wearied mind of her mother. Cassy yielded at once, and with her whole soul, to every good influence, and became a devout and tender Christian.

After a day or two, Madame de Thoux told her brother more particularly of her affairs. The death of her husband had left her an ample fortune, which she generously offered to share with the family. When she asked George what way she could best apply it for him, he answered, "Give me an education, Emily; that has always been my heart's desire. Then, I can do all the rest."

On mature deliberation, it was decided that the whole family should go, for some years, to France; whither they sailed, carrying Emmeline with them.

The good looks of the latter won the affection of the first mate of the vessel; and, shortly after entering the port, she became his wife.

George remained four years at a French university, and, applying himself with an unintermitted zeal, obtained a very thorough education.

Political troubles in France, at last, led the family again to seek an asylum in this country.

George's feelings and views, as an educated man, may be best expressed in a letter to one of his friends.

"I feel somewhat at a loss, as to my future course. True, as you have said to me, I might mingle in the circles of the whites, in this country, my shade of color is so slight, and that of my wife and family scarce perceptible. Well, perhaps, on sufferance, I might. But, to tell you the truth, I have no wish to.

"My sympathies are not for my father's race, but for my mother's. To him I was no more than a fine dog or horse; to my poor heart-broken mother I was a *child*; and, though I never saw her, after the cruel sale that separated us, till she died, yet I *know* she always loved me dearly. I know it by my own heart. When I think of all she suffered, of my own early sufferings, of the distresses and struggles of my heroic wife, of my sister, sold in the New Orleans slavemarket,—though I hope to have no unchristian sentiments, yet I may be excused for saying, I have no wish to pass for an American, or to identify myself with them.

It is with the oppressed, enslaved African race that I cast in my lot; and, if I wished anything, I would wish myself two shades darker, rather than one lighter.

"The desire and yearning of my soul is for an African *nationality*. I want a people that shall have a tangible, separate existence of its own; and where am I to look for it? Not in Hayti; for in Hayti they had nothing to start with. A stream cannot rise above its fountain. The race that formed the character of the Haytiens was a worn-out, effeminate one; and, of course, the subject race will be centuries in rising to anything.

"Where, then, shall I look? On the shores of Africa I see a republic,—a republic formed of picked men, who, by energy and self-educating force, have, in many cases, individually, raised themselves above a condition of slavery. Having gone through a preparatory stage of feebleness, this republic has, at last, become an acknowledged nation on the face of the earth,—acknowledged by both France and England. There it is my wish to go, and find myself a people.

"I am aware, now, that I shall have you all against me; but, before you strike, hear me. During my stay in France, I have followed up, with intense interest, the history of my people in America. I have noted the struggle between abolitionist and colonizationist, and have received some impressions, as a distant spectator, which could never have occurred to me as a participator.

"I grant that this Liberia may have subserved all sorts of purposes, by being played off, in the hands of our oppressors, against us. Doubtless the scheme may have been used, in unjustifiable ways, as a means of retarding our emancipation. But the question to me is, Is there not a God above all man's schemes? May he not have overruled their designs, and founded for us a nation by them?

"In these days, a nation is born in a day. A nation starts, now, with all the great problems of republican life and civilization wrought out to its hand;—it has not to discover, but only to apply. Let us, then, all take hold together, with all our might, and see what we can do with this new enterprise, and the whole splendid continent of Africa opens before us and our children. *Our nation* shall roll the tide of civilization and Christianity along its shores, and plant there mighty republics, that, growing with the rapidity of tropical vegetation, shall be for all coming ages.

"Do you say that I am deserting my enslaved brethren? I think not. If I forget them one hour, one moment of my life, so may God forget me! But, what can I do for them here? Can I break their chains? No, not as an individual; but, let me go and form part of a nation, which shall have a voice in the councils of nations, and then we can speak. A nation has a right to argue, remonstrate, implore, and present the cause of its race,—which an individual has not.

"If Europe ever becomes a grand council of free nations,—as I trust in God it will,—if, there, serfdom, and all unjust and oppressive social inequalities, are done away; and if they, as France and England have done, acknowledge our position,—then, in the great congress of nations, we will make our appeal, and present the cause of our enslaved and suffering race: and it cannot be that free enlightened America will not then desire to wipe from her escutcheon that bar sinister which disgraces her among nations, and is as truly a curse to her as to the enslaved.

"But, you will tell me, our race have equal rights to mingle in the American republic as the Irishman, the German, and the Swede. Granted, they have. We *ought* to be free to meet and mingle,—to rise by our individual worth, without any consideration of caste or color; and they who deny us this right are false to their own professed principles of human equality. We ought, in particular, to be allowed *here*. We have *more* than the rights of common men;—we have the claim of an injured race for reparation. But, then, *I do not want it*; I want a country, a nation, of my own. I think that the African race has peculiarities, yet to be unfolded in the light of civilization and Christianity, which, if not the same with those of the Anglo-Saxon, may prove to be, morally, of even a higher type.

"To the Anglo-Saxon race has been intrusted the destinies of the world, during its pioneer period of struggle and conflict. To that mission its stern, inflexible, energetic elements were well adapted; but, as a Christian, I look for another era to arise. On its borders I trust we stand; and the throes that now convulse the nations are, to my hope, but the birth-pangs of an hour of universal peace and brotherhood.

"I trust that the development of Africa is to be essentially a Christian one. If not a dominant and commanding race, they are, at least, an affectionate, magnanimous, and forgiving one. Having been called in the furnace of injustice and oppression, they have need to bind closer to their hearts that sublime doctrine of love and forgiveness, through which alone they are to conquer, which it is to be their mission to spread over the continent of Africa.

"In myself, I confess, I am feeble for this,—full half the blood in my veins is the hot and hasty Saxon; but I have an eloquent preacher of the Gospel ever by my side, in the person of my beautiful wife. When I wander, her gentler spirit ever restores me, and keeps before my eyes the Christian calling and mission of our race. As a Christian patriot, as a teacher of Christianity, I go to *my country,*—my chosen, my glorious Africa!—and to her, in my heart, I sometimes apply those splendid words of prophecy: 'Whereas thou hast been forsaken and hated, so that no man went through thee; *I* will make thee an eternal excellence, a joy of many generations!'

"You will call me an enthusiast: you will tell me that I have not well considered what I am undertaking. But I have considered, and counted the cost. I go to *Liberia,* not as to an Elysium of romance, but as to a *field of work.* I expect to work with both hands,—to work *hard;* to work against all sorts of difficulties and discouragements; and to work till I die. This is what I go for; and in this I am quite sure I shall not be disappointed.

"Whatever you may think of my determination, do not divorce me from your confidence; and think that, in whatever I do, I act with a heart wholly given to my people.

"GEORGE HARRIS."

George, with his wife, children, sister, and mother, embarked for Africa, some few weeks after. If we are not mistaken, the world will yet hear from him there.

Of our other characters we have nothing very particular to write, except a word relating to Miss Ophelia and Topsy, and a farewell chapter, which we shall dedicate to George Shelby.

Miss Ophelia took Topsy home to Vermont with her, much to the surprise of that grave deliberative body whom a New Englander recognizes under the term *"Our folks."* "Our folks," at first, thought it an odd and unnecessary addition to their well-trained domestic establishment; but, so thoroughly efficient was Miss Ophelia in her conscientious endeavor to do her duty by her èlève, that the child rapidly grew in grace and in favor with the family and neighborhood. At the age of womanhood, she was, by her own request, baptized, and became a member of the Christian church in the place; and showed so much intelligence, activity, and zeal, and desire to do good in the world, that she was at last recommended, and approved, as a missionary to one of the stations in Africa; and we have heard that the same activity and ingenuity which, when a child, made her so multiform and restless in her developments, is now employed, in a safer and wholesomer manner, in teaching the children of her own country.

P. S.—It will be a satisfaction to some mother, also, to state, that some inquiries, which were set on foot by Madame de Thoux, have resulted recently in the discovery of Cassy's son. Being a young man of energy, he had escaped, some years before his mother, and been received and educated by friends of the oppressed in the north. He will soon follow his family to Africa.

Chapter XLIV.
The Liberator.

GEORGE SHELBY had written to his mother merely a line, stating the day that she might expect him home. Of the death scene of his old friend he had not the heart to write. He had tried several times, and only succeeded in half choking himself; and invariably finished by tearing up the paper, wiping his eyes, and rushing somewhere to get quiet.

There was a pleased bustle all through the Shelby mansion, that day, in expectation of the arrival of young Mas'r George.

Mrs. Shelby was seated in her comfortable parlor, where a cheerful hickory fire was dispelling the chill of the late autumn evening. A supper-table, glittering with plate and cut glass, was set out, on whose arrangements our former friend, old Chloe, was presiding.

Arrayed in a new calico dress, with clean, white apron, and high, well-starched turban, her black polished face glowing with satisfaction, she lingered, with needless punctiliousness, around the arrangements of the table, merely as an excuse for talking a little to her mistress.

"Laws, now! won't it look natural to him?" she said. "Thar,—I set his plate just whar he likes it,—round by the fire. Mas'r George allers wants de warm seat. Oh, go way!—why didn't Sally get out de *best* teapot,—de little new one, Mas'r George got for Missis, Christmas? I'll have it out! And Missis has heard from Mas'r George?" she said, inquiringly.

"Yes, Chloe; but only a line, just to say he would be home to-night, if he could,—that's all."

"Didn't say nothin' 'bout my old man, s'pose?" said Chloe, still fidgeting with the teacups.

"No, he didn't. He did not speak of anything, Chloe. He said he would tell all when he got home."

"Jes like Mas'r George,—he's allers so ferce for tellin' everything hisself. I allers minded dat ar in Mas'r George. Don't see, for my part, how white people gen'lly can bar to hev to write things much as they do, writin's such slow, oneasy kind o' work."

Mrs. Shelby smiled.

"I'm a thinkin' my old man won't know de boys and de baby. Lor'! she's de biggest gal, now,—good she is, too, and peart, Polly is. She's out to the house, now, watchin' de hoecake. I's got jist de very pattern my old man liked so much, a bakin'. Jist sich as I gin him the mornin' he was took off. Lord bless us! how I felt dat ar morning!"

Mrs. Shelby sighed, and felt a heavy weight on her heart, at this allusion. She had felt uneasy, ever since she received her son's letter, lest something should prove to be hidden behind the veil of silence which he had drawn.

"Missis has got dem bills?" said Chloe, anxiously.

"Yes, Chloe."

"'Cause I wants to show my old man dem very bills de *perfectioner* gave me. 'And,' says he, 'Chloe, I wish you'd stay longer.' 'Thank you, Mas'r,' says I, 'I would, only my old man's coming home, and Missis,—she can't do without me no longer.' There's jist what I telled him. Berry nice man, dat Mas'r Jones was."

Chloe had pertinaciously insisted that the very bills in which her wages had been paid should be preserved, to show to her husband, in memorial of her capability. And Mrs. Shelby had readily consented to humor her in the request.

"He won't know Polly,—my old man won't. Laws, it's five year since they tuck him! She was a baby den,—couldn't but jist stand. Remember how tickled he used to be, 'cause she would keep a fallin' over, when she sot out to walk. Laws a me!"

The rattling of wheels now was heard.

"Mas'r George!" said Aunt Chloe, starting to the window.

Mrs. Shelby ran to the entry door, and was folded in the arms of her son. Aunt Chloe stood anxiously straining her eyes out into the darkness.

"Oh, *poor* Aunt Chloe!" said George, stopping compassionately, and taking her hard, black hand between both his; "I'd have given all my fortune to have brought him with me, but he's gone to a better country."

There was a passionate exclamation from Mrs. Shelby, but Aunt Chloe said nothing.

The party entered the supper-room. The money, of which Chloe was so proud, was still lying on the table.

"Thar," said she, gathering it up, and holding it, with a trembling hand, to her mistress, "don't never want to see nor hear on 't again. Jist as I knew 't would be,—sold, and murdered on dem ar old plantations!"

Chloe turned, and was walking proudly out of the room. Mrs. Shelby followed her softly and took one of her hands, drew her down into a chair, and sat down by her.

"My poor, good Chloe!" said she.

Chloe leaned her head on her mistress's shoulder, and sobbed out, "Oh, Missis! 'scuse me, my heart's broke,—dat's all!"

"I know it is," said Mrs. Shelby, as her tears fell fast; "and *I* cannot heal it, but Jesus can. He healeth the broken-hearted, and bindeth up their wounds."

There was a silence for some time, and all wept together. At last, George, sitting down beside the mourner, took her hand, and, with simple pathos, repeated the triumphant scene of her husband's death, and his last messages of love.

About a month after this, one morning, all the servants of the Shelby estate were convened together in the great hall that ran through the house, to hear a few words from their young master.

To the surprise of all, he appeared among them with a bundle of papers in his hand, containing a certificate of freedom to every one on the place, which he read successively, and presented, amid the sobs and tears and shouts of all present.

Many, however, pressed around him, earnestly begging him not to send them away; and, with anxious faces, tendering back their free papers.

"We don't want to be no freer than we are. We's allers had all we wanted. We don't want to leave de ole place, and Mas'r and Missis, and de rest!"

"My good friends," said George, as soon as he could get a silence, "there'll be no need for you to leave me. The place wants as many hands to work it as it did before. We need the same about the house that we did before. But, you are now free men and free women. I shall pay you wages for your work, such as we shall agree on. The advantage is, that in case of my getting in debt, or dying,—things that might happen,—you cannot now be taken up and sold.

I expect to carry on the estate, and to teach you what, perhaps, it will take you some time to learn,—how to use the rights I give you as free men and women. I expect you to be good, and willing to learn; and I trust in God that I shall be faithful, and willing to teach. And now, my friends, look up, and thank God for the blessing of freedom."

An aged, patriarchal Negro, who had grown gray and blind on the estate, now rose, and, lifting his trembling hand, said, "Let us give thanks unto the Lord!" As all kneeled by one consent, a more touching and hearty Te Deum never ascended to heaven, though borne on the peal of organ, bell, and cannon, than came from that honest old heart.

On rising, another struck up a Methodist hymn, of which the burden was,—

> "The year of Jubilee is come,—
> Return, ye ransomed sinners, home."

"One thing more," said George, as he stopped the congratulations of the throng; "you all remember our good old Uncle Tom?"

George here gave a short narration of the scene of his death and of his loving farewell to all on the place, and added,—

"It was on his grave, my friends, that I resolved, before God, that I would never own another slave, while it was possible to free him; that nobody, through me, should ever run the risk of being parted from home and friends and dying on a lonely plantation, as he died. So, when you rejoice in your freedom, think that you owe it to that good old soul, and pay it back in kindness to his wife and children. Think of your freedom every time you see UNCLE TOM'S CABIN; and let it be a memorial to put you all in mind to follow in his steps, and be as honest and faithful and Christian as he was."

Note

[1] A machine of this description was really the invention of a young colored man in Kentucky.

19

Lecture Outlines

Professor Kornfeld

Lecture One
<u>The European Invasion of America</u>

I.   Captain John Smith's "Virgin Land"

II. America Before the Europeans Came
     A. Comparison with Europe
     B. Peopling the Americas
     C. Emergence of Civilizations
     D. America North of the Rio Grande

III. Backward Europe Expands
     A. Significance
     B. Portuguese Expansion Eastward
     C. Spanish Expansion Westward
     D. "The Jackals of Europe"

IV. Consequences: Progress or Disaster?

Lecture Outlines

Powhatan
Speech to Captain John Smith
1609

Captaine Smith, you may understand that I having seene the death of all my people thrice, and not anyone living of these three generations but my selfe; I know the difference of Peace and Warre better than any in my Country. But now I am old and ere long must die, my brethren, namely Opitchapam, Opechancanough, and Kekataugh, my two sisters, and their two daughters, are distinctly each others successors. I wish their experience no lesse then mine, and your love to them no lesse then mine to you. But this bruit from Nandsamund, that you are come to destroy my Country, so much affrighteth all my people as they dare not visit you. What will it availe you to take that by force you may quickly have by love, or to destroy them that provide you food. What can you get by warre, when we can hide our provisions and fly to the woods? whereby you must famish by wronging us your friends. And why are you thus jealous of our loves seeing us unarmed, and both doe, and are willing still to feede you, with that you cannot get but by our labours? Thinke you I am so simple, not to know it is better to eate good meate, lye well, and sleepe quietly with my women and children, laugh and be merry with you, have copper, hatchets, or what I want being your friend: then be forced to flie from all, to lie cold in the woods, feede upon Acornes, rootes, and such trash, and be so hunted by you, that I can neither rest, eate, nor sleepe; but my tyred men must watch, and if a twig but breake, every one cryeh there commeth Captaine Smith: then must I fly I know not whether: and thus with miserable feare, end my miserable life, leaving my pleasures to such youths as you, which through your rash unadvisednesse may quickly as miserably end, for want of that, you never know where to finde. Let this therefore assure you of our loves, and every yeare our friendly trade shall furnish you with Corne; and now also, if you would come in friendly manner to see us, and not thus with your guns and swords as to invade your foes.

Philip L. Barbour, ed., *The Complete Works of Captain John Smith* (Chapel Hill: University of North Carolina Press, 1986), 1:247.

Professor Kornfeld

Lecture Two
Chesapeake Society: From Opportunity to Caste

I. Two Views of Early Virginia: John Pory
   (1619) and Richard Frethorne (1623)

II. Establishing a New Society, 1607–1675
   A. Motives for Settlement
   B. Demographic Realities
   C. Tobacco and Opportunity

III. From Crisis to Stability, 1676–1720
   A. Bacon's Rebellion, 1676
   B. Toward Stability
   C. Components of Stability

IV. Conclusion: From Opportunity to Caste

Lecture Outlines

Professor Kornfeld

Lecture Three
<u>Puritan New England:</u>
<u>From Radical Vision to Conservative Community</u>

I.   A City Upon a Hill

II. Puritanism
     A. What Puritanism Was Not
     B. What Puritanism Was
     C. Persistent Tensions

III. Migration and Settlement

IV. The Shape of Puritan New England
     A. Economy
     B. Demography
     C. Components of Seventeenth-
         century Stability
     D. Sources of Conflict

V.   Conclusion: From Radical Vision to
     Conservative Community

Lecture Outlines

Professor Kornfeld

Puritan New England

A. Covenant Theology:

	Personal	*Social*
Human Affairs	Covenant of Works	National Covenant
Salvation	Covenant of Grace	Church Covenant

B. Persistent Tensions:

Individual conscience	v.	Orthodoxy
Sinner	v.	Saint
Autonomous person	v.	Covenanted community
Work ethic (wealth)	v.	Asceticism (charity)
Calling (mobility)	v.	Social order (traditional hierarchy)
Freedom	v.	Authority

What U.S. became?   What Puritans sought?

Professor Kornfeld

Lecture Four
Completing the Spectrum of Settlement

I. The Atlantic Prism and the Spectrum of English Settlement

II. Completing the Spectrum
- A. Patterns of Pluralism: the Middle Colonies
- B. Violent Societies: the English West Indies and Carolina

III. The Spectrum
- A. Immigration and Survival
- B. Demography
- C. Culture and Politics

IV. Counter-trends

V. Conclusion: the Search for "America"

Lecture Outlines

Spectrum of Settlement in English America to c. 1700

Category	English West Indies	South Carolina	Chesapeake	Middle Atlantic	New England
Immigrants to c. 1700	535,000 (61% black) (74% of total)	Most from other colonies; 2–3000 from Europe/Africa (0.4% of total)	140,000 (20,000 slave) (19% of total)	Over 20,000 (3% of total)	Under 20,000 (3% of total)
Population c. 1700	148,000 (37% of total)	5700 (1.5%)	100,000 (25%)	54,000 (13%)	93,000 (23%)
Ethnic Mix by c. 1700	3/4 African; many Irish	Toward African majority (by c. 1710)	English majority; African minority	NW European mix; English minority?	Overwhelmingly English
Male Life Expectancy at Age 20	Under 20 years	c. 22 years	c. 25 years rising slowly	40–45 years	45+ years falling slowly
Sex Ratio	From overwhelmingly male toward balance among whites	From c. 3:1 male toward 1.5:1	From 5 or 6:1 male toward balance	From 2:1 male toward balance	From 3:2 male toward slight female edge
Family Size	Few children; population not self-sustaining	Unknown; probably similar to Islands	Population becoming self-sustaining after 1680	Large families, rapid natural growth, and high immigration	Large families, rapid natural growth; few immigrants after 1640
Religion	Formally Anglican (Old World establishment—New World establishment)	Toward Anglican establishment	Anglican establishment in VA (and in MD after 1692)	No established church Toleration & lay piety	Puritan (Old World dissent becomes New World establishment)
Economy	Staple crop: sugar & slaves	Toward staple crop: rice & slaves	Staple crop: tobacco; from servants to slaves	Cereal crops; family labor & slaves (NY) or servants (PA)	Mixed economy & family labor
Mentalité	Future-oriented and optimistic ———————————————————→			NY ←———— PA ———→	Past-oriented and pessimistic
Provincial Government	Royal of 1660; model for elsewhere	Proprietary to 1720s	VA–royal MID–proprietary (except 1689–1716)	Proprietary into 1680s / Royal intrusions c. 1686 ff.	Autonomous corporations into 1680s
Who Rules	Young, rich, male slaveholders	Similar to Islands by c. 1700	Young to middle-aged well-to-do male owners of servants/slaves	Middle-aged, male, moderate to well-to-do	Elderly male saints to 1686; thereafter respectable well-to-do

Professor Kornfeld

Lecture Five
<u>Provincial Culture:</u>
<u>Enlightenment and Awakening in America</u>

I.   Two Eighteenth-century Creeds:
     Benjamin Franklin and Jonathan
     Edwards

II. Enlightenment Thought
     A.   European Models
     B.   Enlightened Virtue
     C.   The Enlightened

III. The Great Awakening
     A.   British Models
     B.   Awakened Virtue
     C.   The Awakened

IV. Conclusion: Provincial Culture

Professor Kornfeld

Lecture Six
<u>The Origins of the American Revolution</u>

I.   Why Revolution?

II.   Cycles of War and the First British Empire
- A. Anglo-Dutch Wars, 1652–1674
- B. Anglo-French Wars I, 1689–1713
- C. Anglo-French Wars II, 1739–1763
- D. Revolutionary Wars, 1775–1815

III.   Empire and Political Culture
- A. Anglo-Dutch Wars: England Discovers Its Colonies
- B. Anglo-French Wars I: Creation of British Political Culture

IV.   Imperial Reform and Crisis
- A. Anglo-French Wars II: Origins of Imperial Reform
- B. Definition: Stamp Act Crisis, 1764–1766
- C. Escalation: Townshend Crisis, 1767–1770
- D. Polarization: Tea and Intolerable Acts, 1773–1776

V.   Conclusion: American Independence

Lecture Outlines

Paul Revere, *The Boston Massacre.*

Professor Kornfeld

Lecture Eight
<u>The Precarious Republic: Liberty and Order</u>

I.   Liberty and Order: An Exchange of John and Abigail Adams

II.   The Trauma of Revolutionary War
    A.   The Role of the Militia
    B.   Civil War
    C.   "To Starve the Army at Will"

III. The People Transform the Government
    A.   Revolutionary Equality
    B.   Revolutionary Constitutionalism
    C.   Anti-colonialism

IV.   America's Revolutionary Settlement
    A.   Federal Constitution as Revolutionary Conservatism
    B.   Court vs. Country in America

V.   Conclusion: The Precarious Republic

Lecture Outlines

Professor Kornfeld

Political Alignments, c. 1787–1800

	Federalists	Antifederalists
North	Merchants	
	Professionals	
	◄————— Speculators	
	Continental Army officers	
	Militia officers with	Ordinary militia officers
	long service	
	Urban artisans ————————————►	
		Rural artisans
	Commercial farmers	
		Subsistence farmers
	Frontier areas	
	Ethnic minorities ————————►	
South	Planters ————►	
		Small farmers

Key: As listed, groups are placed according to their stand on the Constitution. Arrows indicate direction of movement by 1800, when Jefferson defeated Adams for the presidency.

There is an 80% correlation between these blocs and reaction to the Federal Constitution. Variables seem to include residence (urban or rural), age (Federalists are younger), and, most important, life experience ("cosmopolitan" types—including Continental Army officers, those involved in commercial markets, and those who were better educated and travelled—tended toward Federalism, while "localists" tended toward Antifederalism).

A Dialogue on the Rights of Women in the Revolutionary Era

Abigail and John Adams

I long to hear that you have declared an independancy—and by the way in the New Code of Laws which I suppose it will be necessary for you to make I desire you would Remember the Ladies, and be more generous and favourable to them than your ancestors. Do not put such unlimited power into the hands of the Husbands. Remember all Men would be tyrants if they could. If perticuliar care and attention is not paid to the Laidies we are determined to foment a Rebelion, and will not hold ourselves bound by any laws in which we have no voice, or Representation.

That your Sex are Naturally Tyrannical is a Truth so thoroughly established as to admit of no dispute, but such of you as wish to be happy willingly give up the harsh title of Master for the more tender and endearing one of Friend. Why, then, not put it out of the power of the vicious and the Lawless to use us with cruelty and indignity with impunity. Men of Sense in all Ages abhor those customs which treat us only as the vassals of your Sex. Regard us then as Beings placed by providence under your protection and in immitation of the Supreme Being make use of that power only for our happiness.

Your ever faithful friend.

—Abigail Adams to John Adams, March 31, 1776

As to your extraordinary Code of Laws, I cannot but laugh. We have been told that our Struggle has loosened the bands of Government every where. That Children and Apprentices were disobedient—that schools and Colledges were grown turbulent—that Indians slighted their Guardians and Negroes grew insolent to their Masters. But your Letter was the first Intimation that another Tribe more numerous and powerfull than all the rest were grown discontented.—This is rather too coarse a Compliment but you are so saucy, I wont blot it out.

Depend upon it, We know better than to repeal our Masculine systems. Altho they are in full Force, you know they are little more than Theory. We dare not exert our Power in its full Latitude. We are obliged to go fair, and softly, and in practice you know We are the subjects. We have only the Name of Masters, and rather than give up this, which would compleatly subject Us to the Despotism of the Peticoat, I hope General Washington, and all our brave Heroes would fight. I am sure every good Politician would plot, as long as he would against Despotism. Empire, Monarchy, Aristocracy, Oligarchy, or Ochlocracy.—A fine Story indeed. I begin to think the Ministry as deep as they are wicked. After stirring up Tories, Landjobbers, Trimmers, Bigots, Canadians, Indians, Negroes, Hanoverians, Hessians, Russians, Irish Roman Catholicks, Scotch Renegadoes, at last they have stimulated the ladies to demand new Priviledges and threaten to rebell.

—John Adams to Abigail Adams, April 14, 1776

Professor Kornfeld

Lecture Nine
The Unsettling of American Society

I. Two Journeys through America: George Washington (1789) and Charles Dickens (1840)

II. Areas of "Deep Change"
   A. Expansion and Growth
   B. Political Culture: Democracy and Liberalism
   C. Economics: Commercialization and Urbanization
   D. Demography and Culture

III. The Web of Market Relations
   A. The Making of a Working Class
   B. The Making of a Middle Class
   C. The Cult of Domesticity

IV. Conclusion: The Unsettling of American Society

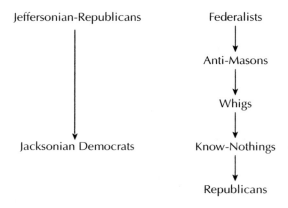

American Political Parties of the Early Republic

Jeffersonian-Republicans

Federalists

Anti-Masons

Whigs

Jacksonian Democrats

Know-Nothings

Republicans

Professor Kornfeld

Political Culture of the Early Republic

I. The Dominance of Political Parties in the 1830s:

A. Observations of a Whig Congressman:

"The spirit of party [is] a more deadly foe to free institutions than the spirit of despotism. There is a spirit of devotion to party that seems willing to surrender to it the Constitution, the laws, and the happiness of the country; and this is not surprising since the object of party devotion is party itself."

B. Observations of a Democratic Congressman:

"The public man is taught in his official character to look not to the welfare or the judgment of the people as a whole, but . . . to the success and approbation of his party. Thus means usurp the place of ends. . . . He has sold his manhood for a little pelf; he must revile, and he must glorify; he must shout huzzas, or whisper calumnies, just as he is bidden. His time is not his own. His thoughts are not his own. His soul is not his own."

II. Classical Liberalism (from Andrew Jackson's Bank-Veto Message):

"It is to be regretted that the rich and the powerful too often bend the acts of government to their selfish purposes. Distinctions in society will always exist under every just government. Equality of talents, of education, or of wealth can not be produced by human institutions. In the full enjoyment of the gifts of Heaven and the fruits of superior industry, economy, and virtue, every man is equally entitled to protection by law; but when the laws undertake to add to these natural and just advantages artificial distinctions, to grant titles, gratuities, and exclusive privileges, to make the rich richer and the potent more powerful, the humble members of society—the farmers, mechanics, and laborers—who have neither the time nor the means of securing like favors to themselves, have a right to complain of the injustice of their Government. There are no necessary evils in government. Its evils exist only in its abuses. If it would confine itself to equal protection and, as Heaven does its rain, shower its favors alike on the high and low, the rich and the poor, it would be an unqualified blessing."

Professor Kornfeld

Lecture Ten
<u>Visions of Reform</u>

I.   Anna Mowat's <u>Fashion</u> (1845)

II. "The Benevolent Empire"
   A.   From Temperance to Perfection
   B.   Schools and Asylums
   C.   Abolitionism and Women's Rights

III. Dreams of Liberation
   A.   Utopian Communities: New Harmony and Brook Farm
   B.   Transcendentalism

IV. Conclusion: The Dangers of Reform

Professor Kornfeld

Lecture Twelve
<u>One Nation, One Culture?</u>

I.   America's Centennial Fair, 1876

II.   Outsiders in America
    A.   African-Americans and the Failure of Reconstruction
    B.   Women and the Fifteenth Amendment
    C.   Workers and the Great Railroad Strike
    D.   The "New Immigrants" and Their Ghettoes

III.   Conclusion: American Diversity

Lecture Outlines

A Black Code

All freedmen, free Negroes and mulattoes in this State, over the age of eighteen years, found on the second Monday in January, 1866, or thereafter, with no lawful employment or business, or found unlawfully assembling themselves together, either in the day or night time, and all white persons so assembling with freedmen, free Negroes or mulattoes, on terms of equality, or living in adultery or fornication with a freedwoman, free Negro, or mulatto, shall be deemed vagrants, and on conviction thereof shall be fined in the sum of not exceeding, in the case of a freedman, free Negro or mulatto, fifty dollars, and a white man two hundred dollars, and imprisoned at the discretion of the court, the free Negro not exceeding ten days, and the white man not exceeding six months. . . .

And in case any freedman, free Negro or mulatto shall fail for five days after the imposition of any fine or forfeiture upon him or her for violation of any of the provisions of this act to pay the same, that it shall be . . . the duty of the sheriff of the proper county to hire out said freedman, free Negro or mulatto, to any person who will, for the shortest period of service, pay said fine and forfeiture and all costs. . . .

—*Laws of Mississippi, 1865*

Lecture Outlines

Lecture Outlines